Baldwin Pap

A CONSERVATIVE STAT

1908–1947

The significance of Stanley Baldwin (1867–1947) is self-evident. As Conservative party leader and three times Prime Minister, he was at the heart of most of the great political debates and national events of interwar Britain. Yet understanding the positions he adopted and his contribution to public life has not been easy, in part because of his unusual political character and in part because private evidence on him was neither conveniently assembled nor readily interpreted.

This edition contains a selection of Baldwin's letters, reports of his conversations and related documents and illustrations, with an extensive commentary. It has two main purposes. The first is to publish important documents on Conservative and ministerial politics, as perceived and practised by their leader. These deal with major issues and episodes from the destruction of the Lloyd George Coalition to the Abdication, and with relationships among leading politicians and other public figures, notably Churchill, the Chamberlains, press controllers, and three kings. Less explicit but of equal importance is considerable evidence on the environments, routines, courtesies and culture of high political society.

Baldwin's colleagues found him difficult to understand, and during a severe relapse in his reputation after his retirement the criticisms turned on supposed deficiencies in his character. The second purpose of this edition is to provide a documentary account of Baldwin himself, revealing in his own words his circumstances, personality, beliefs, friendships and enmities. Beginning with his election to Parliament in 1908, the volume contains testimony to his early values, and by continuing beyond his retirement it includes his own reflections on his career. These sources on national politics and the Prime Minister will make this edition indispensable for studies of public life in interwar Britain.

PHILIP WILLIAMSON is Professor of History at the University of Durham. He is the author of *National Crisis and National Government 1926–1932* (1992) and *Stanley Baldwin. Conservative Leadership and National Values* (1999), and has edited the papers of Baldwin's Conservative colleague William Bridgeman (1988).

EDWARD BALDWIN is the Prime Minister's grandson, and after a career in education he has since 1988 sat as 4th Earl Baldwin of Bewdley in the House of Lords, speaking on educational, medical and environmental matters.

Baldwin Papers

A CONSERVATIVE STATESMAN
1908–1947

EDITED BY

Philip Williamson

AND

Edward Baldwin

CAMBRIDGE
UNIVERSITY PRESS

CAMBRIDGE UNIVERSITY PRESS
Cambridge, New York, Melbourne, Madrid, Cape Town, Singapore, São Paulo, Delhi

Cambridge University Press
The Edinburgh Building, Cambridge CB2 8RU, UK

Published in the United States of America by Cambridge University Press, New York

www.cambridge.org
Information on this title: www.cambridge.org/9780521118477

First published 2004
This digitally printed version 2009

A catalogue record for this publication is available from the British Library

Library of Congress Cataloguing in Publication data

A conservative prime minister : Baldwin papers, 1908–1947 / edited by Philip Williamson
and Edward Baldwin
p.   cm.
Includes bibliographical references and index.
ISBN 0 521 58080 3 (hardback)
1. Baldwin, Stanley Baldwin, Earl, 1867–1947.   2. Great Britain – Politics and government –
20th century – Sources.   3. Conservatism – Great Britain – History – 20th century – Sources.
4. Conservative Party (Great Britain) – Biography – Sources.   5. Prime ministers –
Great Britain – Biography – Sources.   I. Williamson, Philip, 1953–   II. Baldwin, Edward, 1938–
DA566.9.B15C65   2004
941.083′092–dc22   2003065441

ISBN 978-0-521-58080-9 hardback
ISBN 978-0-521-11847-7 paperback

IN MEMORY OF

Windham Baldwin

(1904–1976)

CONTENTS

ILLUSTRATIONS

Between pp. 268 and 269

1 Lucy and Stanley Baldwin, in the 1920s
2 Baldwin's homes
  (a) Lower Park House, Bewdley, 1867–1870
  (b) Wilden House, 1870–1892
  (c) Dunley Hall, 1892–1902
  (d) Astley Hall, 1902–1947
  (e) 27 Queen's Gate, South Kensington, 1908–1913 (courtesy of Mrs Jill Lumsden)
  (f) 93 Eaton Square, Belgravia, 1913–1925 (in the 1990s)
  (g) 69 Eaton Square, Belgravia, 1937–1947 (in the 1990s)
3 Wilden works (from T. E. Elias (ed.), *British Commerce and Industry 1919–1934* (1934))
4 Baldwin the father, 1906
5 Oliver Baldwin, *c.* 1929 (courtesy of Christopher Walker)
6 Windham Baldwin, *c.* 1954
7 Baldwin's study at Astley Hall
8 Baldwin's library at 10 Downing Street, *c.* 1937 (courtesy of Mrs Jill Lumsden)
9 The Baldwins and the Davidsons, 1923
10 Baldwin and his letters
  (a) reading, at Chequers in 1923
  (b) writing, at the Cabinet table, 10 Downing Street, *c.* 1935

All plates are from Stanley Baldwin additional papers, unless otherwise stated.

FIGURES

PREFACE

❧

Edward Baldwin

The only written communication I have from Stanley Baldwin is a picture postcard of the interior of the church at Bourg en Bresse. It is dated 21 August 1938, addressed in mauve ink to 'Monsieur Edouard Baudouin, Astley Hall, Stourport-on-Severn, Angleterre', and reads 'Please give our love to your Parents. G. F.' Nothing remarkable: just a gently humorous message via a seven-month-old grandson from the ex-Prime Minister and his wife as they made their way to their usual summer destination of Aix-les-Bains.

He was not 'S. B.' to my generation of the family. He was 'G. F.', standing for Grandfather. Curiously our Grandmother was not 'G. M.' but 'G.' I was the youngest of the grandchildren, and was not quite ten when he died in December 1947. Although I could not have known him as well as my older cousins did, I probably absorbed as much or more of his ethos and personality by virtue of my father's unremitting efforts, as I was growing up, to counter the distortions of fact, motivation and character which attached to Baldwin's reputation soon after he retired. I grew up to hear many hurtful things said about my grandfather; and I clearly remember the climate of the 1950s in which my father found it difficult to persuade a publisher to touch his book *My Father. The True Story* (1955), involving as it did some necessary criticisms of Churchill, who had been responsible for some of the more damaging imputations, and who was still in office with the status almost of a demigod.

This edition, which owes its existence almost entirely to the efforts of my co-editor, will present new perspectives on a man who for so long puzzled his contemporaries and later commentators. The reasons for this puzzlement should be clearer in the wake of more recent historical writings. In the words of an old neighbour, writing at the time of a Baldwin centenary event in 1967:

'There was never anyone like Stan . . . He was always <u>so</u> different from all other politicians!'

Families, except of course where there are feuds and factions, can be expected to support their own. But I have reached retirement age without, from an extended family, ever once hearing a hostile comment about SB; and that must be unusual. From family near and distant, and from Worcestershire neighbours, the sentiments have been those of love, admiration, devotion, or all three. From a son-in-law, to my father: 'As I think you realize, I revered and loved your father, who was in many ways a second father to me.' From a grandson: 'He <u>always</u> had time to see me, with or without my friends, when I called in at Astley Hall. He loved the young.' The same can be heard from residents of Stourport, Bewdley, Kidderminster, some of whom still remember him from the 1930s and have a fund of stories of his kindness, humanity and humour. Not long ago, from a wider context, the son of one of his parliamentary private secretaries remarked to me 'My father *adored* your grandfather.' It was said with real intensity. This devotion to SB from those who knew him well was exceptional.

Readers will form their own impressions from these letters and recorded conversations. There is a light-heartedness that lay not far below the surface of a man who found, early in his tenure of the top job, that public humour carried too high a risk of misunderstanding. The minister who told the House of Commons when introducing a finance bill 'The next clause is incomprehensible. I can't understand it and you won't either, but it's all right', became more careful when speaking as Prime Minister. But the Baldwin who appeared calm and phlegmatic at the centre of affairs could be high-spirited, vehement, incautious, and surprisingly critical when he felt it safe or appropriate to unbutton his feelings. There was never malice, however, and always the desire to see good in his fellow man.

I wish I had truly known him. The humour does not surprise me, nor the sharp and often striking use of language, nor the engaging whimsicality which sometimes shows through; these can be seen in other generations of the family as well. Perhaps the passion does, when I watch videos of old newsreels and see the energy which Baldwin put into big speeches, giving the lie to epithets such as 'bovine' which were coined by commentators in later times. But it should not, for how else could he have held audiences and commanded a following in a way that few others were able to do? You do not achieve that simply by being the 'nicest' Prime Minister of the twentieth century, as he has sometimes been called. And if the nervous output often left him spent, how essential to ensure that he had the rest and the holidays which he knew his constitution demanded, acknowledging the strains of an unbroken twenty-year period in office when his leadership of the opposition is included. If he was right in his stated belief during his premiership that half the bad decisions since the war had been taken by tired men, he would have been irresponsible to do otherwise.

His family and friends could experience his quickness of mind and his breadth of reading and knowledge, which unusually for one of his calling he did not parade much in public. ('S. B. went through his correspondence at an incredible speed' wrote a manager who worked under him in business, while adding how 'My chief's sly humour was always peeping out.') 'Avoid logic' is an injunction of his that many find difficult. Did he really believe that 'no one was ever persuaded by argument'? It may, as *My Father* has suggested, have been a way of bringing calm when his children were fractious. It was also, without doubt, a denial of the *primacy* of the intellect, which caused obvious problems for his later reputation with certain articulate sections of society. Baldwin, while intensely practical, operated much in the realms of the heart and the spirit, which was why so few colleagues talked 'the same language' as he did, or grasped what (in his own words) he was 'driving at'. It was a form of realism in his public life, not to say wisdom, to recognise that most people make up their minds on grounds deeper than logic, and that this was the level on which, with perfect integrity, any discourse must be directed.

'Be yourself always' was the advice he gave Sir John Reith when the latter entered the House of Commons in 1940. It was largely because Baldwin was so obviously himself, and this self was more concerned with service than power, that he was trusted and respected by an unusually wide spectrum of British society. If oratory to him was the harlot of the arts, it was because of what he saw as its falsity. Many of Baldwin's speeches were humdrum: others, on big themes such as peace in industry, India and the Abdication, drew extravagant praise from old political hands for their eloquence, sincerity, emotional force and lofty vision. *Ars est celare artem*, perhaps: the art that conceals art. If Baldwin was an artist, however, there was not much artifice in him, in the sense of a wish to dissemble. An exception might be made for his tendency to portray himself as slower and less intelligent or informed than he really was, another curious trait in a politician. Part of this was due to a genuine modesty, and part perhaps to his ever-present desire to break down barriers, to be the 'one of you' which he so strongly felt himself to be, even if it was one who was 'called to special service'. It led to him being consistently underestimated by those who did not know him well, an advantage of which he was surely aware.

He had a broader awareness, too, that probably ran deeper than most. As Prime Minister his days as a managing director in industry and as an efficient departmental minister were behind him. It was his task now to think out strategic directions: the restoring of high standards to public life in the early 1920s; then the 'binding together of all classes' into a healthier and more united society; then the emphasis on the spiritual foundations of democracy when faced with the rise of totalitarianism, leading to practical measures of rearmament in the early to mid 1930s as the electorate were weaned away from a near-pacifist mentality which had outlived its time. These were not the product of chance, or political tactics, or justification after the event. They sprang from a thoughtful and wide-ranging intelligence, as his contemporary speeches make clear. Baldwin's combination of the reflective and the practical, and his sense of duty and honour, were familiar to those who knew him of old, and they can be seen in many of the letters in this collection. And he made little attempt to disguise his blunders, of which he certainly had his share in public life. Indeed he could be over-quick to apologise, which endeared him to the public if not always to the more combative elements of his party.

All this made for a character uncommon in its breadth and depth and, as his Worcestershire neighbour remarked, in significant ways different from other politicians. It is hard to get the true essence of a personality after sixty years of conflicting interpretations and confused psychology. Those who were closest during his lifetime knew best what he was made of. One who started working for him as an office boy wrote on his death: 'The name of Lord Baldwin was a household word with the . . . family, and my late Father held him before his family and before all comers a great ideal [*sic*], and as one who had few equals and no superior.' Another workman wrote: 'He was a grand man, and I feel too big for this little world of intrigues and selfishness.' A Downing Street private secretary, recalling that 'It is 26 years since I came within his influence', went on 'It is a wonderful thing to work with someone one loves – quite different from working with someone one just likes . . . I never met any-one who possessed so much essential sweetness and sanity or carried so much "of the herb Hearts Ease in his bosom" or, at any rate, could give so much of it away to other people.' 'God rest his dear heart & soul', wrote another parliamentary private secretary who had recalled 'his genuine affection and concern for close colleagues in the Govt', as well as 'the kind of impish chuckle with which he used to greet the foibles of correspondents or minor errors in service on the part of his staff'.

Two who did not know him well shall have the last word in describing the man. The writers Hesketh Pearson and Hugh Kingsmill decided to visit Baldwin at Astley in the year before he died, and recorded in *Talking of Dick Whittington* (1947) the conversation of a long May evening in which the three of them looked back over people and events in Baldwin's life. Their account ends with the words; 'As they drove off, Pearson murmured "Very, very lovable", and Kingsmill gave an assenting nod.' If this edition leaves something of that impression, whatever else it may show of Baldwin's motives and actions in a long public career, then those who knew and admired him as family, friends or neighbours will be content.

ACKNOWLEDGEMENTS

This edition has been made possible only by the assistance of many individuals and institutions. It consists of a selection from a considerably larger number of letters and other documents dispersed across Britain, the former British Dominions and the USA, in public, institutional and private collections of papers. We are much indebted to the staff in the many record offices, libraries, manuscripts and special collections rooms listed in the Sources, for advice, arranging access to collections, locating fugitive letters and memoranda, and supplying copies. We are particularly obliged to Godfrey Waller, Peter Meadows and the staff of the manuscripts room of Cambridge University Library; Colin Harris, Helen Langley, and Elizabeth Turner at the Bodleian Library, Oxford; Lady de Bellaigue and Pamela Clark at the Royal Archives; Philippa Bassett, Christine Penney and their staff at the University of Birmingham Library; Katherine Bligh at the Parliamentary Archives; John Graham Jones at the National Library of Wales; Alan Kucia and Allen Packwood at the Churchill Archives Centre, Cambridge; A. M. Wherry and R. Whittacker and their staff at the Worcestershire County Record Office; Lawrence Aspden at the University of Sheffield Library; Miss S. J. Acton of the Shropshire Records and Research Centre; Anne Craig at the Public Record Office of Northern Ireland; Naomi Evetts at Liverpool Record Office; Aline Faunce of the Oxford Group archives; Mary Flagg and Patti Spencer at the Harriet Irving Library, University of New Brunswick; John Hodgson of the John Rylands University Library of Manchester; Mrs S. M. Laithwaite at Devon Record Office; Kate O'Brien at the Liddell Hart Centre for Military Archives, King's College, London; Mrs L. Richardson at the Centre for Kentish Studies; Jonathan Smith of Trinity College Library, Cambridge; Jeff Walden of the

BBC Written Archives Centre; and Dr C. M. Woolgar at the Hartley Library, University of Southampton.

Much important material remains in private collections. For documents from papers of members of the Baldwin, Macdonald and Ridsdale families, we are grateful to Charles Yorke, Mrs Meryl Macdonald Bendle, and Sir Julian Ridsdale for the supply of copies; and to Mrs Jill Lumsden, Miles Huntington-Whiteley and Christopher Walker for their hospitality, access to papers, and assistance with illustrations. We are also indebted to Lord and Lady Crathorne and to Richard Oldfield and Lord Davidson for access to their family papers; to Victoria Zinovieff and Simon Craven for the loan of papers; and to Robin Harcourt Williams at Hatfield House Archives. Copies from further collections were kindly supplied by Jane Anderson at Blair Castle; Viscount Brentford; Peter Day at the Devonshire Collections, Chatsworth House; Sister Philippa Edwards at Stanbrook Abbey; Martin Farr; the Earl of Sandwich; and Peter Stansky.

For advice and for assistance in obtaining material, we are indebted to Stuart Ball, John Barnes, Michael Brock, Kathleen Burk, Anne Chisholm, Maurice Cowling, Jeremy Dobson, David Dutton, Judith Flanders, Peter Ghosh, Cameron Hazlehurst, Alan Heesom, James Hollis, Mira Luethje, Andrew Lycett, Ian McBride, Michael Meznar, Thomas Pinney, Mark Pottle, David Rollason, Patrick Salmon, the Hon. Jean Strutt, and John Vincent. Pauline Annis and Melvyn Thompson have supplied useful material on Stourport and Worcestershire, and we also thank those who responded to a request for information placed in the Worcestershire local newspapers. For answering enquiries about the Lord Baldwin Fund, we are grateful to Bill Rubinstein, Joanna Newman, and especially Chana Kotzin. Susan Williams has given invaluable advice about Lucy Baldwin; and special thanks are due to her and to Gervase Hood for greatly easing the collection of material at the National Archives.

For permission to print or cite documents, we thank Lady Avon, Lady Warner and Mrs Jane Anderson; the Earl of Balfour; the Master and Fellows of Balliol College, Oxford; University of Birmingham Library; BBC Written Archives Centre; Viscount Brentford; the Trustees of the Broadlands Archives; the National Archives of Canada; Carmarthen Record Office; the Trustees of the Chequers Estate; the Sir Winston Churchill Archive Trust, the Churchill Archives Centre, and the Master and Fellows of Churchill College, Cambridge; Mr Ron Citrine; Lord Cobbold; Lord Crathorne; the Earl of Crawford and Balcarres; Mr Stanley Clement Davies and Mr John Graham Jones; the Earl of

Derby; the Elgar Foundation; Lord Elibank; Vice-Admiral Sir Ian Hogg; Mrs P. D. Howard; the Clerk of the Records, House of Lords Record Office, acting on behalf of the Beaverbrook Trust; Lord Kennet; the Trustees of Lambeth Palace Library; the Trustees of the Liddell Hart Centre for Military Archives; Lady Lloyd; Mr Alan Maclean; the Director and University Librarian, John Rylands University Library of Manchester; Dr Alexander Murray; the Deputy Keeper of the Records, Public Record Office of Northern Ireland; the Marquess of Salisbury; the Earl of Sandwich; the Keeper of the Records of Scotland; Mrs Anne Stacey and the Trustees of the Bridgeman family archive; the Master and Fellows of Trinity College, Cambridge; the National Library of Wales. Material from the Royal Archives is used with the gracious permission of Her Majesty the Queen. Extracts from Cabinet and government department records are Crown copyright.

Philip Williamson was assisted by research funds from the University of Durham and its Department of History. Wendy Shoulder and her staff in the History Department office helped considerably to convert copies of documents into a word-processed text. Peter Ghosh made helpful suggestions on the introduction; Christine Woodhead and Duncan Bythell read and commented on the whole text. We thank them all.

ABBREVIATIONS AND CONVENTIONS

AC	Austen Chamberlain papers, University of Birmingham Library
AC Letters	*The Austen Chamberlain Diary Letters*, ed. Robert Self (Cambridge, 1995)
Amery Diaries	*The Leo Amery Diaries*, ed. John Barnes and David Nicholson (2 vols., 1980, 1988)
My Father	A. W. Baldwin, *My Father: The True Story* (1955)
Bridgeman Diaries	*The Modernisation of Conservative Politics. The Diaries and Letters of William Bridgeman 1904–1935*, ed. Philip Williamson (1988)
Cabinet	(with number and year) Cabinet conclusions, i.e. minutes
CAB	Cabinet records, in the National Archives
CP	(with number) Cabinet paper
Crawford Papers	*The Crawford Papers*, ed. John Vincent (Manchester, 1984)
CUL MS Add.	Cambridge University Library, additional manuscripts
Davidson Memoirs	*Memoirs of a Conservative. J. C. C. Davidson's Memoirs and Papers*, ed. R. Rhodes James (1969)
DBFP	*Documents on British Foreign Policy*
FO	Foreign Office papers, in the National Archives
HC Debs	*House of Commons Debates*, 5th series
Jones *DL*	Thomas Jones, *Diary with Letters 1931–1950* (1954)
Jones *WD*	Thomas Jones, *Whitehall Diary*, ed. Keith Middlemas (3 vols., Oxford, 1969)
M&B	Keith Middlemas and John Barnes, *Baldwin* (1969)
NC	Neville Chamberlain papers, University of Birmingham Library

NC Letters	*The Neville Chamberlain Diary Letters*, ed. Robert Self (4 vols., Aldershot, 2000–4)
PREM	Prime Minister's office papers, in the National Archives
PRO	Public Record Office class of files, in the National Archives
RA	The Royal Archives, Windsor Castle
SB papers, SB add. papers	Stanley Baldwin political papers and additional papers, Cambridge University Library
T	Treasury papers, in the National Archives
WCRO	Worcestershire County Record Office
WSC	*Winston S. Churchill. Companion Volumes IV–VI* (each in several part-volumes), ed. Martin Gilbert (1976–94)

Unless otherwise stated, letters are handwritten.

Letters indicated just by 'to', without being preceded by the writer's name, were written by Baldwin.

Ellipses indicate omission of material with no reference to Baldwin, or of no historical or biographical interest. Otherwise the main texts are as close to the original as possible, retaining the original punctuation, abbreviations, ampersands and spellings (including, for instance, Baldwin's use of 'shew' and 'develope'). Exceptions are the expansion of initials or other forms of names in order to assist identification, where this is not obvious; and, in a handful of cases, the supply of a word evidently omitted during composition. The symbol '[ ]' indicates such editorial insertions, unless otherwise explained. Very occasional slips of the pen have been silently corrected. The sign '/' indicates a line break.

Addresses are given in full on the first mention, and thereafter abbreviated. Where Baldwin is writing from an address different from that of his notepaper (e.g from Astley Hall but using 10 Downing Street paper), the address is given in square brackets.

All letters to Louisa Baldwin are in SB add. papers.

Original diaries – e.g. Tom Jones diary, Mackenzie King diary – are easily located among the papers of the diarists, as listed in the Sources: accordingly no precise source reference for these is given.

Unless stated otherwise, the place of publication for cited books is London.

Contemporary money sums are also expressed in approximate modern (i.e. about the year 2000) values, using the Economic History Services program on EH.NET.

Introduction

As Conservative party leader from 1923 to 1937 and three times Prime Minister, Stanley Baldwin was one of the pre-eminent public figures of interwar Britain. This volume of his selected letters, records of his private statements, and related documents and illustrations has two purposes. It makes important evidence on political leadership and national events readily available. It also provides a documentary life and portrait of an intriguing, much-liked, but controversial statesman.

For much of his career Baldwin was unusually well respected – personally admired even by opponents of his party, and credited with a larger command over the House of Commons and public feelings and with a wider electoral appeal than any other contemporary politician. Nevertheless on occasion he suffered harsh criticism, facing rebellions within his own party as well as attacks from Labour and Liberal opponents. After the outbreak of the Second World War his reputation collapsed, under accusations that he had 'failed to rearm' the nation against the threat from Nazi Germany. In the early 1950s his first historical biographer attributed his supposed political shortcomings to deficiencies in his character and personal life.

In understanding Britain in the 1920s and 1930s, much turns on how Baldwin and his place in public life are assessed – interpretations not only of party politics and government but more broadly of public values, revealed most dramatically during the Abdication crisis. A difficulty in making such assessments has been that Baldwin published no memoirs, kept no diary and, compared to some other leading politicians, wrote few political letters or memoranda. Although he bequeathed a large collection of political papers to the University of Cambridge, these consist overwhelmingly of material he received, the letters and memoranda sent to him by ministerial colleagues,

politicians, officials, diplomats and members of the public. While these papers are certainly important for historians, they reveal little directly about
Baldwin himself.[1] Biographers and historians have achieved much by exploit-
ing other sources. A 1955 biography by his second son, Windham Baldwin,
used family papers and Baldwin's speeches to defend his character and record
on rearmament. The 1969 political biography by Keith Middlemas and John
Barnes – an essential reference work – and numerous later party and policy
histories found substantial evidence about him in government records and in
the papers of ministerial colleagues and officials. It has also been argued that
the special qualities of Baldwin's leadership mean that his public speeches,
addresses and broadcasts should be regarded as the primary evidence about
his political purposes and impact.[2]

Even so, the private sources for Baldwin are more extensive and richer than
is generally appreciated, and searches by the present editors in a large number
of archives and private collections have added further documents to those
available to his biographers. This edition prints almost all Baldwin's surviving
political letters and memoranda, material of public importance from his family
papers, and the more significant or characteristic of his many personal letters.
These are supplemented by records of his private conversations and statements
in Cabinet. A number of documents already printed but scattered in various
books and journals have been gathered but, with just a few exceptions, items
published in other editions of interwar diaries and letters are not reprinted.

Although the assembled material is diverse, this has the strength of showing
Baldwin in different capacities and contexts, and in discussion with individuals
other than the familiar diarists of the period. The result is a collection of
sources which provides considerable evidence on interwar public life and a
fuller understanding of Baldwin's personality and politics, to be set alongside –
and perhaps, in some cases, to counterbalance – the published papers of
Winston Churchill, Austen Chamberlain, Neville Chamberlain, Leo Amery,
Thomas Jones and others.

§

Why did Baldwin commit less of his politics to paper than some other senior
politicians? What is the value of the material collected here?

---

[1] These political papers are not entirely complete: see Appendix E.
[2] Philip Williamson, *Stanley Baldwin. Conservative Leadership and National Values* (Cambridge,
1999). For details of other historical studies see Sources, below pp. 517–18. Philip Williamson,
'Baldwin's reputation: politics and history 1937–1967', *Historical Journal*, 47 (2004), pp. 127–68,
examines the wartime and postwar criticisms, including the peculiarities of G. M. Young's 1952
biography.

The comparison with other politicians must not be overstated, nor should misleading conclusions be drawn. As will be seen, Baldwin was far from averse to letter-writing as such. Where he differed was in his style of politics, and his purposes in writing. Voluminous and detailed letters on policy, tactics and management exchanged between ministers, party organisers, MPs, officials, and media controllers have become the staple evidence for historical studies of political leadership, to such an extent that they may appear to have been the primary medium for political business and to provide a measure of political activity or commitment. Such impressions have not been to the advantage of Baldwin's reputation; the relative scarcity of his political letters seemed to indicate a lack of application.[3] Yet Churchill, the Chamberlains, and the other assiduous political letter-writers were the exception, not the norm. In any Cabinet or shadow cabinet a large proportion of its members similarly wrote few political letters, because there was no necessity to do so. Plainly enough, most ministerial and party transactions were conducted by interview and meetings. Baldwin was among those who worked chiefly by word of mouth. In his own description, he was 'in constant conference' and 'at the beck and call of everyone for 14 hours a day'.[4] Colleagues learned to accept that the letters and memoranda they sent to him on policy or strategy would normally receive a verbal reply, or be treated as briefs for Cabinet or committee discussions. Alternatively they might sometimes receive a letter drafted by a secretary from brief instructions, because Baldwin made full use of the private office staffs at 10 Downing Street and Conservative Central Office which had been formed under his predecessors precisely in order to assist them with much of their business and correspondence. Certain letters despatched over the Prime Minister's or party leader's signature had for some time been handled entirely by private secretaries, most notably, since Lloyd George's wartime tenure, the traditional letter to the King on each day's proceedings in the House of Commons.[5] Such secretarial letters have not been included in this volume.

Moreover, Baldwin deliberately conducted his politics at a different level from that of other ministers and senior party politicians. In the threatening circumstances of the 1920s and 1930s he considered the greatest task of the

---

[3] A. J. P. Taylor, *English History 1914–1945* (revised 1975 edn), p. 603: 'The reputation of a statesman who leaves a rich store of papers goes up. That of a statesman not given to writing letters or memoranda goes down.'

[4] Below pp. 125, 96. For Baldwin's working methods and the style and purposes of his leadership, see M&B, ch. 18, and Williamson, *Baldwin*, chs. 2, 5.

[5] See Appendix D for the Prime Minister's staff and their responsibilities in 1927 and also, for the 'King's letters', Jones *DL*, p. 262, and Lord Vansittart, *The Mist Procession* (1958), p. 349.

Conservative leader was that of general strategy, shaping opinions and gathering the widest possible support: hence the importance of his speeches. If the principal aim of the Conservative party was to conserve, there was no special advantage in activity for its own sake. Within government and party, his further task was the work of co-ordination, trouble-shooting, and seeking to restrain the sort of partisan excesses which might repel less committed voters and provoke socialist 'extremism'. He did not regard it as his job to help run departments nor, after his unsuccessful initiative on protection in 1923, to create programmes or policies. These were properly the responsibilities of departmental ministers or shadow cabinet specialists and of collective Cabinet or committee decision, so after his own period as a departmental minister in 1921–3 he felt no inclination to write policy or administrative memoranda and letters. Nor did Baldwin write documents for the record, any more than he considered writing memoirs. He had a detached attitude towards his historical reputation, believing that 'no man can write the truth about himself' and that 'whether our work has been good or not will not appear until long after we have passed away, and no worrying on our part will affect the verdict'.[6]

All this emphasises the importance of those of Baldwin's political letters and notes that have survived, while indicating something of their character. They tended to be occasional and short, responding to letters in special circumstances or reporting general political news rather than bringing forward new issues, but often giving sharp insights on his perspectives on public affairs and his estimations of his colleagues and opponents. It also explains why much and often the best private evidence about Baldwin is not in his letters, but in his reported conversations.

Here another of his characteristics should be considered, which is also pertinent to his correspondence but is especially important for weighing the value of records written by his interlocutors. On some issues and at certain times Baldwin would take particular colleagues into his confidence. Generally, however, he was very cautious when speaking with his senior colleagues, on occasion to the point of becoming reticent or evasive. This was perhaps their most frequent complaint against him, and contributed to charges that he was indecisive, inert or complacent. It is striking that only after working with Neville Chamberlain for twelve years, and then only because Chamberlain had become his inevitable successor, did Baldwin feel he should speak freely with him. There were several reasons for such restraint. He thought that few

---

[6] To Salisbury, 1 July 1943, Hatfield House archives 4M/188/1, and below p. 475.

of his colleagues shared his deeper views: in 1935 he gave just two, Bridgeman and Halifax, as having talked 'the same language as I do'.[7] As leader and manager of powerful and often prickly individuals, having to maintain their co-operation and to reconcile competing opinions and ambitions, he was alert to the risks of provoking unnecessary disagreements and jealousies. As he said in 1924, 'fourteen hours a day seeing people and having to be at your best and guarding every word . . . is a fearful strain . . . every smallest word is liable to burst into flame'.[8] His trait of sometimes 'closing up like an oyster' might be a reaction variously to aggrieved colleagues, tactical disagreements, unwanted suggestions, inconvenient questions, or unreasonable demands.[9] He knew that he could give the impression of being slow-witted, but this was part of his technique for 'making the other fellow talk' and divulge more than they perhaps intended. 'I am a very quick thinker but I do not like people knowing it': he wanted to listen, to learn and to give himself ample time for reflection on the often delicate issues.[10]

Consequently the most revealing of Baldwin's reported conversations – many printed in this edition – were often with trusted individuals other than his close official colleagues, because it was with those making no claims of departmental, sectional or personal interest that he felt most able to be open and forthcoming. These included King George V and the private secretaries at Buckingham Palace; a fellow Commonwealth Prime Minister, Mackenzie King of Canada, and the Swedish ambassador, who prompted him to extended comments on his career and beliefs.[11] Some individuals he valued because they could offer informed but (relatively) disinterested opinions, on anything from high policy to Cabinet appointments. This was true of Geoffrey Dawson, editor of *The Times*, but especially of Tom Jones, assistant Cabinet secretary until 1930 and a friend, confidant and speech-writer. In four published volumes of diaries and letters Jones comes nearest to being Baldwin's Boswell; valuable material which Jones omitted from his volume for the years after 1930 is printed here. In a different category are records of occasions when Baldwin thought

[7] Jones *DL*, p. 207 and see below p. 249. For Chamberlain, see below p. 478, and see p. 170 for Baldwin reported as saying that 'he told nobody his political ambitions & trend, but he knew them well enough'.
[8] *The Diary of A. C. Benson*, ed. P. Lubbock (1926), pp. 302–3 (2 Feb. 1924).
[9] Consequently some of the familiar evidence about him from his colleagues (notably the Chamberlains and Amery) almost certainly gives a misleading impression. This is especially so for periods when he felt beleaguered by some or most of them, as after the election defeat of 1923 or during the challenges to his leadership in 1929–31: see Williamson, *Baldwin*, pp. 70–3.
[10] Davidson to W. Baldwin, 29 Oct. 1952, W. Baldwin papers, and below p. 385.
[11] See Appendix C.

candour would be effective in disarming deputations of critics, as over rearmament in July 1936,[12] or discontented individuals, as with Austen Chamberlain in May 1923 and December 1935 – two striking examples of how frankness could be counter-productive.[13] Like other political leaders he also found it easy to confide in sympathetic women who lacked complicating political concerns, even when, as in the case of Kathleen Hilton Young, they were married to a member of another party. In such reported conversations Baldwin made observations about issues and personalities which have considerable historical interest, and in these too the real personal and political character of the man becomes apparent. The unbuttoned Baldwin was sometimes solemn and reflective, but often vivid, frank, mordant and funny.

*

Although those who confine their researches to political and government papers alone may conclude that Baldwin 'was always reluctant to put pen to paper', he was actually a prolific letter-writer with a very large and varied range of correspondents, probably broader than that of any contemporary politician except Churchill.[14] Although most of these letters were personal or social they often contain striking or moving phrases, and even apparently trivial notes were valued and kept by their recipients. One Cabinet minister hoped that 'someone would edit a volume of [his] private letters' because they 'would reveal a wise, sympathetic, humorous and subtle man'.[15]

Many of the Baldwin letters that survive in the papers of politicians and others associated with political life are, by strict definition, personal. Although they might contain a political comment or two, they were prompted by other purposes. These might, for example, be encouragement: 'My dear Anthony,/ Just a line to express my delight./ You are doing admirably./ Yours always S.B.'[16] Or they might be arrangements for a public or social engagement, advice on some private matter, or to mark birthdays, congratulation, illness, or condolence. Or they might be thanks, for letters, information, gifts, acts

---

[12] Below pp. 374–9.   [13] Below pp. 86–92, 359–6.
[14] S. Roskill, *Hankey. Man of Secrets*, 3 vols. (1970–4), III, p. 47; and compare G. M. Young, *Stanley Baldwin* (1952), p. 11, on the paucity of political letters, with p. 19: 'few men can ever have written more [letters]'.
[15] Ernest Brown foreword to D. C. Somervell, *Stanley Baldwin* (1953), p. 14, and see similarly A. Bryant, *Stanley Baldwin. A Tribute* (1937), p. 158, and Vansittart, *Mist Procession*, p. 353. Brown's papers have become dispersed; the only known collection, in the Parliamentary Archives, does not contain his letters from Baldwin.
[16] To Eden, 9 Dec. 1934, Avon papers 14/1/259.

of kindness, or a weekend visit, like this to an MP and political hostess: 'My dear,/ Bless you and thank you for a most happy little visit./ No worst fears materialized and one's best hopes realized./ Our love and grateful thanks,/ Your affectionate/ S.B.'[17] Yet however mundane the purpose, such attentions from the Prime Minister or party leader carried special weight – and Baldwin's letters, though usually brief, had an attractive spontaneity, wit and humanity. 'No one', he wrote, 'writes a letter to be a literary essay: one just likes to hear a friend talk to one naturally and without constraint.'[18] The letters were an aspect or extension of what made him so likeable and difficult to cross or, when political differences did arise, impossible to hate. There could be a winning or indiscreet sentence, or a barbed observation on some mutual irritant. He could play up amusingly to his own or his correspondent's traits or ailments. He might evoke shared associations, in his own love of books and the countryside, or else contrasting interests, in his colleagues' love of sport or gardening. He would subordinate public disagreement to private friendship or, with trade unionists and socialists, bridge social or ideological distances by expressions of fellow feeling. In these ways – spreading goodwill, recognising the importance of matters other than the political, applying the light touch to troublesome tensions, ever so gently offering warning – Baldwin lubricated political relationships and assisted his management of the government, the House of Commons, and the party. Such letters were an instrument for what his cousin Rudyard Kipling early recognised as his 'quiet faculty for bossing men and things'.[19] In this sense, any sharp distinction between his 'political' and 'personal' correspondence would be misleading, and so a selection of the best of these personal letters is included in this edition.

Even in his more obviously personal and social correspondence there could be a public aspect. 'Writing charming, if brief, epistles to sweeten the existence of his friends and acquaintances' was for Baldwin a form of relaxation from the burdens of office.[20] The substance of most of these letters is too historically inconsequential to deserve publication, though a few containing characteristic comments or displaying his manner of addressing public figures outside politics are printed. It is, rather, the range of this correspondence that is significant and deserves reflection. Addressees included novelists, poets, historians, classical scholars, literary critics, teachers, clergymen and free

[17] To Lady Astor, 2 June 1935, Thomas Jones 'diary', Jones papers.
[18] To Joan Davidson, 24 Jan. 1921.
[19] Kipling to Louisa Baldwin, undated but early 1900s, Kipling papers 11/2.
[20] *The Times* [Thomas Jones], *Lord Baldwin. A Memoir* (1947), p. 21.

church ministers, artists, musicians, and scientists. Together with his speeches on 'non-political' subjects to a great variety of organisations, these letters attest to his contact with many aspects of national life and to the breadth of admiration he could attract on grounds other than the party-political.[21] Another type of correspondence was with friends in 'Society'. Although he sometimes attended Grillions, The Club and other all-male dining clubs where he could meet leading figures from other parties and other professions, he did not much enjoy social dinners, parties and balls (and he took his lunches in the unpolitical seclusion of the Travellers' Club). But he enjoyed visits to country houses – Hatfield, Blair Atholl, Chevening, Longleat, Wynyard – whether as the base for speaking engagements or for relaxation, even though he had no interest in the typical landed pursuits of hunting, riding, shooting or fishing. The flavour of these visits is given in an account of a weekend at an Essex house in July 1935.[22] On such occasions, and at small private dinners in London, at his own preferred social meal of breakfast, or less commonly over a weekend at Chequers, he met some of the leading men and women of Conservative and Liberal society. The former provincial manufacturing employer and wealthy City director had friends and acquaintances in numerous ranks and occupations, but it is striking that these also came to include great hostesses such as Lady Desborough, the Countess of Stanhope, and the Marchionesses of Salisbury and Londonderry. The social milieu of interwar Conservative leadership has been little studied, but it is plain that for all the structural shifts in the distribution of political power since the Victorian period, much remained that would have been familiar to the senior politicians of that era.

※

Two further sets of letters – to his family, and to his chief personal correspondent – require special comment, not least because these contradict the claim that 'a certain discomfort in his nearer relationships' was a key to Baldwin's public career.[23] His mother Louisa seems to have kept every letter she received from him, from early childhood onwards. From 1908, after she was widowed and after Baldwin became an MP and moved to London, until her death in 1925, over four hundred letters survive. Many naturally consist of family news,

---

[21] Examples of such letters not published here are those to Helen Waddell, the writer on medieval subjects, in Monica Blackett, *The Mark of the Maker. A Portrait of Helen Waddell* (1973).
[22] Below, pp. 335–43.
[23] This was the main theme of Young, *Baldwin* (see esp. p. 23), which left its mark on numerous later accounts.

as Baldwin wrote to 'cheer her in her lonely life'; nor was she greatly interested in politics. Even so a good number from the period of the First World War and its aftermath contain important indications of his early political attitudes and moral values. Baldwin himself re-read the letters in 1940–1, and thought that a selection might be published together with other family papers.[24] Those which deal most fully with public affairs are printed, while significant sentences or phrases from others are included in the commentaries. Baldwin's letters to his father do not survive, which is almost certainly a serious loss. Alfred Baldwin was a Conservative political organiser and MP as well as a considerable businessman, and their correspondence presumably contained much on public matters. What Alfred's journals and both parents' few surviving letters to Baldwin ('My very dear Stan . . . Your loving father') do show is their secure pride and love for their only child: 'You have been a joy & a comfort to me all your life, as you were to your dear Father.'[25]

Nor have Baldwin's letters to his wife Lucy ('Cissie') been preserved.[26] Probably few were written, because they were so rarely apart; but there are indications that whenever separated they wrote to each other every day. Windham Baldwin considered the letters that still survived at their deaths to be so private that he burnt them, after transcribing extracts relating to the August 1931 political crisis: these are printed here in full. Lucy Baldwin was a substantial public figure in her own right, involved in the Young Women's Christian Association and other charitable bodies for women, most notably in those concerned to improve maternity care, after having herself suffered difficult pregnancies.[27] As vice-chairman from 1928 of the newly established National Birthday Trust Fund, she was an active member of its policy committee, and in

---

[24] Arthur Baker, *The House is Sitting* (1958), p. 43. A number of these letters were quoted in *My Father*, esp. ch. 5.

[25] Louisa to Stanley Baldwin, 2 Aug. 1924, SB add. papers; and for Alfred see *My Father*, pp. 53–4, for a twenty-first birthday letter, and p. 61 for a 1891 journal comment: 'a satisfactory son in every way'.

[26] It should be added that little has survived from Baldwin to his large extended family of uncles, aunts and cousins – both the Baldwins and, on his mother's side, the much-studied Macdonald clan: see the family trees in Appendix A. Of his closest early companions, Harold Baldwin's letters from Baldwin were destroyed by his widow (Baldwin to Constance Marshall, a Baldwin cousin, 26 Dec. 1927, Baldwin WCRO collection 9229/12ii); Ambrose Poynter and Philip Burne-Jones left no papers; and – the chief disappointment – although there are Rudyard Kipling collections, the frequent meetings between the two men and, perhaps, their tendency to reinforce each other's brevity of style, meant that Baldwin's letters to him are very short and contain nothing on public matters.

[27] A. Susan Williams, *Ladies of Influence. Women of the Elite in Interwar Britain* (2000), ch. 2, is a pioneering study of Mrs Baldwin, whose independent public work has largely escaped authors writing on her husband.

1929 founded the Anaesthetics Fund, which she assisted by speeches, broadcasts and fund-raising. This too developed into a national campaign. One of her supporters and donors built a Lucy Baldwin Maternity Hospital in the Baldwin home town of Stourport-on-Severn, and her lobbying contributed to the 1936 Midwives Act, which created a national midwifery service. Although she and her husband had differing temperaments and interests, and her own political views were so artlessly moralistic as to bemuse the sophisticated, Baldwin plainly relied upon her support and discussed important political matters with her, most clearly when his own career was at stake, in October 1922 and March 1931. She also wrote valuable notes of two major episodes, the fall of the Lloyd George Coalition and the Abdication crisis, which draw on her husband's verbal reports and which are printed here. As her occasional surviving letters to Baldwin also suggest – 'Darling heart . . . Fondest Love my precious/ Always thine own most loving Cissie' – there is no reason to doubt the closeness and warmth of their marriage.

The Baldwins had six surviving children (their first was stillborn).[28] Within a world of servants and boarding schools, and with Lucy taking the leading part in the household, Baldwin seems to have been a loving father but one who in the Edwardian style was not closely involved in his children's lives. It was Lucy who created a small theatre at Astley Hall where for many years the children, with their cousins and neighbours, performed their own reviews and plays. All of them developed strong and free-spirited characters, to the extent that both parents joked that 'having a child is like letting loose a bomb on the world. You never know when it will explode or how, nor why it does.' Of the daughters, only the youngest, Betty, had serious political interests (she spoke on some Conservative platforms in the 1930s), while the second son, Windham, early settled on a business career. With Lucy keeping up the family correspondence once they left home, Baldwin himself only wrote to his children occasionally – typically on birthdays or anniversaries – in letters which hardly ever alluded to public matters. But they were good, and certainly sincere, father's letters. Consider this extract to his third daughter: 'Darling Margot,/ Blessings on the day that brought you into this very odd world, for you do it a lot of good./ . . . Thank you for being my daughter and not somebody else's/ Your own loving/ Father.' Or again 'you are a very dear daughter and there is nothing better on earth'. His correspondence with the young Windham included exchanges of schoolboy jokes, and this from

---

[28] See Appendix A.

1922: 'Dearest Little/ It is impossible to believe that you are eighteen to-morrow, but as with other profound truths, I believe it because it is impossible, and this brings much love of the finest quality./ You are one of the happinesses of my life: . . . blessings on you and seventy or eighty many happy returns!/ Your ever loving Father.'

With his elder son, Baldwin's relations were more difficult. Service in the First World War and traumatic experiences during wars in the Near East disrupted Oliver Baldwin's life and aggravated a rebellious temperament. Shortly after Baldwin became Prime Minister in 1923 Oliver publicly declared himself a socialist and broke with his parents. He spoke on socialist platforms, stood as a Labour candidate at the 1924 general election, and was Labour MP for Dudley in 1929–31. The Baldwins were certainly hurt. Stanley told one of his daughters that he 'nearly died' when he first saw Oliver sitting on the opposite benches to himself in the House of Commons. He, though perhaps not Lucy, almost certainly understood that Oliver was homosexual. Yet contrary to a common assumption, neither parents nor son allowed the difference in politics and lifestyle to cause a permanent breach. Oliver never attacked his father in public and, assisted by tacit agreement to avoid political discussion, good personal relations were restored after a short period, with the parents occasionally travelling from Chequers to visit Oliver and his partner, John Boyle, at their Oxfordshire farmhouse. Boyle was accepted, winning over Lucy with, in effect, the attentions of a dutiful son-in-law. Baldwin came to write to him as 'My dear Johnny', and during the Second World War used government contacts to help him send letters and parcels to Oliver, serving overseas.[29] Baldwin's letters to Oliver, the best of which are published here, are among his most humane: tolerant, open-hearted, merry and affectionate.

Baldwin's immediate family did not, however, share all his interests nor exhaust his liking for affectionate companionship and unrestrained, amusing, or even frivolous, conversation. None would accompany him on his strenuous country walks (or in London, brisk walks around the parks before breakfast). In pre-war Worcestershire a neighbour, Phyllis Broome, would join him on these walks ('Dearest Phillippina . . . your loving Stan'),[30] but from 1916 his closest female friend and chief walking companion was Joan ('Mimi')

---

[29] See Christopher Walker, *Oliver Baldwin. A Life of Dissent* (2003), and Oliver's early autobiography, *The Questing Beast* (1932). Baldwin's letters to Oliver are in CUL MS Add. 8795 and 9569: the latter bundle also has his letters to Boyle.
[30] Miss Broome gave some of Baldwin's letters to her to his daughter, Lorna Howard.

Dickinson, daughter of the Liberal MP Sir Willoughby Dickinson. She was some twenty-five years younger than him, and originally became acquainted with the Baldwins as a friend of one of their daughters. A correspondence began, which lasted to the end of his life and from Baldwin's side eventually ran to many hundreds of letters. These soon became fond: 'Mimi my dear . . . Much love, S.B.', then 'Dear Maid' or 'Very dear Maid', before settling into 'Little Maid' – an endearment used even after she became a mother and, in the 1940s, a grandmother. Such endearments and repeated references to his love belong to an idiom which might mislead later generations. Although her letters to Baldwin do not survive – he destroyed them all in the 1940s, along with other purely personal correspondence[31] – it seems that she herself initially came close to some misunderstanding, prompting a delicate warning:

> dear child, don't idealize me. You think far too much of me. Don't. The reaction will only be the stronger when it comes. Friendship between those of different generations may be a beautiful thing – and it may not. We will keep ours on the heights, please God./ Your loving S.B.[32]

This indicates the nature of the enduring relationship, that of an affection in which Joan was placed as a 'child', a status which sometimes warmed to 'beloved Dream Daughter' or ideal 'daughter-in-law'.[33] The friendship was strengthened when in 1919 she married Baldwin's friend, protégé, and later, as MP, junior minister and party chairman, his political lieutenant, John ('David') Davidson. Baldwin now referred to them both as being like 'dearest children, or brother and sister', and as their home was close to the House of Commons it provided him with a further social base. Together they became an extension or adjunct to his family, as close to Lucy as to himself. They usually shared part of the Baldwins' holidays in France, and acted as confidants with whom he could switch easily from serious political discussion to light

---

[31] He also asked Joan to destroy all his letters to her (3 May 1944). However, as he suggested the alternative of keeping them in a bank or other safe place, his main worry was evidently that expressed earlier in the 1940s, that wartime conditions increased the risks of an embarrassing dispersal of personal effects: 'life is mighty uncertain. I have got rid of a quantity of old letters that I shouldn't like to be scattered about' (22 June 1940).

[32] 10 Nov. 1916. *Davidson Memoirs*, esp. pp. 76–84, was the first to describe the relationship and print extracts from the letters, which were also used by M&B; but neither book indicates the full quantity or affectionate tone of the letters. Windham Baldwin prepared a typescript and annotated edition of many of these letters; this draft is now in SB add. papers.

[33] 27 May 1918, 20 March 1919.

social conversation. From them he could receive candid opinions, advice and criticism:

> Little Maid/I like to tell you, if only once a year, and in case you don't know or forget it, how much your unfailing loving friendship means to me. You and David give me a second home where I can hide from the world: you give up countless mornings to me to make me take exercise that never would be taken without you: you alone tell me things I ought to hear which no one else will tell me: and together you sacrifice a large part of your holiday together to make mine a happier one.[34]

Baldwin's letters now sometimes went to both of them ('dearest couple'), or began as letters to her and ended as letters to him. He sometimes referred Davidson to matters written in a letter to Joan, or – when she was unexpectedly absent – asked him to open his letters to her. Letters to the wife were plainly available for reading by the husband too. A few of the letters reported political events or his reflections on them, but mostly they were summary reports of social meetings, concerts, recitals, meals and travels. In another strain, they consisted of humorous stories or comments on individuals or newspaper items, or flights of fancy (such as pretended letters from a dog, Towser) – what he himself described as his 'lighter news', 'my gossip', or 'all my nonsense'. The letters to Joan Davidson and many of those to her husband were, in sum, a magnified version of much of his personal correspondence, a relaxation or escape. Aside from political extracts, just a small sample of these (mostly from the earlier years) is included below.

❧

Baldwin was punctilious about the forms of address in his letters. He used several different salutations and valedictions, in order to indicate precisely the relationship he had with, or wished to suggest towards, his correspondent. An individual he gradually came to know, or wanted to draw closer, might pass beyond the formal 'Dear [surname] . . . Yours sincerely, Stanley Baldwin' to 'My Dear [surname] . . . Yours ever, S.B.', and then on to the closer 'Dear [forename] . . . Yours S.B.' – and Baldwin may well have been the first Prime Minister to address all his Cabinet colleagues by their Christian names. Alternatively correspondents might retreat from his regard or seem less desirable as

---

[34] 24 Dec. 1925.

allies, slipping back towards the formal. The variation in his forms of address in letters to Beaverbrook in 1929–31 is particularly telling. He was equally sensitive to such forms in the letters he received. In an indicative comedy of misunderstanding, during a difference over Indian policy an exasperated friend, the Duchess of Atholl, addressed him as 'Mr'. Thinking this marked the beginning of a breach, Baldwin duly replied to 'Dear Duchess', only for her to take umbrage – so he immediately reverted to his usual 'My dear Kitty . . . Affectionately yours S.B.'[35]

For this reason, both the salutations and the valedictions of letters are normally included in the texts printed here. Similarly, any classification of the letters – 'Private', 'Confidential' and so on – has been retained. The place from which the letter was written (not always the same as the address on the notepaper) is also given, to indicate something of Baldwin's movements. More broadly, such details draw attention to other subjects and layers in these documents, beyond overt political action and aspects of Baldwin's personality. There is evidence on political courtesies and social conventions; on the personal burdens of disappointing office-seeking friends, or dismissing ministers; on public relationships beyond the political and ministerial; and on the environments and routines of political leadership.

The commentaries and the footnote apparatus are directed towards elucidating the documents rather than providing a consistent narrative of Baldwin's career or comment on every important political episode. Certain supplementary material – including family trees, a history of his papers, a notorious newspaper interview, and a rare account of a Prime Minister's daily routine – is included in appendices. Facsimiles in the text give a few more documents, and illustrations of Baldwin's handwriting and speech notes. The plates have been chosen to supplement the text, notably by showing Baldwin's successive private homes.[36]

Baldwin's letters and other documents have been selected chiefly from the original papers of many other individuals. All the collections that have been searched are listed in the first section of the Sources. Footnote references are given to the most significant reports of conversations published elsewhere, though it is taken for granted that specialists in the study of interwar politics

---

[35] 8 Dec. 1933, Duchess of Atholl papers 72; S.J. Hetherington, *Katherine Atholl 1874–1960* (Aberdeen, 1989), pp. 160–1.
[36] The one exception is 10 Upper Brook Street, Mayfair: no contemporary photograph has been found, and the present building has changed considerably from when the Baldwins occupied it in 1929–31.

will refer to other printed editions of political papers: these are listed in the second section of Sources. Space has not permitted frequent citation of the relevant biographical and historical literature, but these works, which have been as invaluable in preparing this edition as they are for all serious study of Baldwin, are listed in the last three sections of the Sources.

ONE

❧

Businessman-MP and junior minister

1908 – MARCH 1921

Stanley Baldwin was born on 3 August 1867 at Lower Park House, Bewdley, in Worcestershire, the son of a partner in several family iron-manufacturing, worsted-spinning and carpet-making firms. In 1870, on his father Alfred becoming sole proprietor of the sheet-metal firm of E. P. & W. Baldwin, the family moved to the master's house alongside its main works in the small village of Wilden, just outside the home town of the extended Baldwin family, Stourport-on-Severn. An unusual combination of influences from Stanley's family and early life – in religion, culture, business, public service and politics – shaped his distinctive form of political leadership.[1] Both his parents came from earnestly Methodist families, whose forebears included Wesleyan ministers; one of his maternal uncles was a president of the Wesleyan Conference and secretary of its missionary society. After his parents joined the Church of England in the 1860s, they remained devoutly religious and were influenced by ideals of Christian social concern, building a church and church school in Wilden and becoming active in lay churchmanship. Stanley taught in the village Sunday school, and as a Cambridge undergraduate considered ordination and became interested in church politics and church 'missions' to help slum-dwellers. His mother Louisa and her sisters had when young been part of the artistic and literary circles of D. G. Rossetti and William Morris, and Baldwin's uncles included the artists and designers Sir Edward Burne-Jones, Sir Edward Poynter and Lockwood Kipling. Louisa Baldwin and his closest aunt, Edith Macdonald, were themselves published authors, and in early manhood his cousins Philip Burne-Jones, Ambrose Poynter and Rudyard Kipling gave him continuing links with the worlds of art and literature.[2] For an only son neither these

---

[1] Williamson, *Baldwin*, chs. 3–4, has a fuller discussion.
[2] For these family connections see especially A. W. Baldwin, *The Macdonald Sisters* (1960), and more recently Judith Flanders, *A Circle of Sisters. Alice Kipling, Georgiana Burne-Jones, Agnes Poynter and Louisa Baldwin* (2001).

nor the church offered serious career choices, but their perspectives extended his political sensibilities and enriched his public language.

Like his father, Stanley Baldwin had two careers, and like him too he initially regarded them as complementary rather than exclusive. The first was in manufacturing and commerce. In 1888 he entered E. P. & W. Baldwin, already a major producer of tinned and corrugated iron sheets with international markets. During 1890 he spent seven weeks in North America, visiting Quebec, Montreal, Toronto, New York, Philadelphia, Chicago, New Orleans, Washington and Boston. He was partly an avid tourist, meeting artists and academics through introductions from his uncles and aunts;[3] but the chief purpose was to visit customers of the firm. On his return to Wilden, the firm's letterbooks show him handling their requests and problems: 'Dear Sirs,/ On receipt of your samples, the writer at once took up the matter of the "Taylor Roofing Tin", and now places before you his opinion on the different finish between the sample lot and subsequent lots.'[4] He was now a partner, given oversight at the firm's second works at Swindon near Dudley, and as his father became increasingly busy in London later in the 1890s, he took effective charge of the whole firm. The Baldwins were leaders and modernisers in their trade. Stanley became chairman of the Tinned Sheet Association, representing the main manufacturers, subscribed to the industrial and investment press, and joined the British Economic Association (later the Royal Economic Society).[5] During downturns in trade, the firm's correspondence shows him seeking new markets, appointing new commercial agents, and making personal tours to stimulate fresh business, including a long trip in 1897–8 through Copenhagen, Lübeck, Hamburg, Berlin (where he visited the Reichstag), Dresden, Prague, Brno, Vienna and Cologne. Over the next three years, he managed the conversion of the firm into a limited company – recruiting Rudyard Kipling among the shareholders – and its purchase of two further works. Together, the firm's four works – linked by canals and rivers to the international export outlets at Bristol and Liverpool – employed several hundred men. Alfred Baldwin was now a considerable industrial and City figure, a director of numerous companies and chairman from 1901 of the Metropolitan Bank and from 1905 of the Great Western Railway (GWR). When in

---

[3] The papers of Charles Norton, Emeritus Professor of Art, in the Houghton Library, Harvard, contain letters of recommendation from Lockwood Kipling – 'a nice boy and sincere and unaffected . . . promising in all ways' – and Georgiana Burne-Jones: 'a plain young man, but a good one, and the heart's delight of his parents . . . [he] had to take his place in his father's business . . . because there is no other son to do it. I bet it was a hard thing for him at first, for he likes books, but he saw the justice of it, and applied himself to office work with all his might, and is already so helpful to his father that he will soon be admitted into full partnership': ibid., p. 236.
[4] To Messrs N. & G. Taylor Co, Philadelphia, 10 Dec. 1890, E. P. & W. Baldwin letterbook, Baldwin WCRO collection 8229/17.
[5] See letter to the BEA secretary, 11 Feb. 1896, RES/1/3/12, British Library of Political and Economic Science.

Swindon Stock   June 30. 1900.

Pig Iron in Yard.

				£	s	d
18 ton	Clowsuolls	73/-		65	14	0
17 „	Stanton	82/6 77/-		65	9	0
5½ „	Lilleshall	82/6		22	13	9
6½ „	Madeley Wood	6/1/-		39	6	6
9½ „	Swedish	5/2/1		48	9	9
6 „	mixed pig at furnace	80/-		24	0	0
				265	13	—
Slack.	25½ tons in boats	9/-		11	9	6
25 cwr. coke 10/.	18 sack breeze 9d 5 T. charcoal 2/6 cwr			12	11	0
B.J. cinder 14 tons	17/6	tap 125 tons 3/-		31	0	0
roll scale 6 tons	2/-	Char. cinder 35 Ton 17/6 2/wt		31	4	6
10 tons gas lime nil		1½ ton basic slag £1 .		87	15— 10—	0 —
Puddled iron bar	34 cwt. 70/-			5	19	0
Scrap „ „	70 „ 60/-			10	10	0
Puddled staff	81 cwt. 21 lbs. £5.			20	5	11
Charcoal lumps from scrap 61 cwr. £6				18	6	0
Scrap faggots , puddl. iron t.d 6. 57 cwr. 80/-				11	8	0
„ all scrap 18¾ tons 70/-				76	10	0
Best char. lumps from pig + scrap 22¾ cwr £7				7	15	9
				5"14	2	8
Bars. Brymbo 2.17.2.0	6.15.0			19	8	1
				523	10	9

Figure 1 Baldwin as an industrialist: notes in the stock-taking book for
Swindon works

1902 he combined his iron, steel, coal and manufacturing interests in the Midlands, Monmouthshire, South Wales and London in a great integrated firm – Baldwins Ltd – Stanley became managing director of its Midlands division. He also began to obtain further company directorships, and as the Baldwins Ltd main office was in the City of London he too began a career there, marked by admission into its traditional form of commercial and social association, a livery company, Goldsmiths.

His second career was in public service and politics. From 1887 to 1892 he was an officer in the Volunteer Force, with a gunnery certificate from Woolwich Arsenal. Later he became a parish councillor, justice of the peace, county councillor and governor of local schools and hospitals. His father had been a local Liberal party organiser but in 1877, committed to a 'national', integrative form of constitutional politics, which he now contrasted to Liberal 'sectionalism', he joined the Conservative party. During the 1880s Alfred became one of the leaders of Worcestershire Conservatism, and in 1892 MP for the West (Bewdley) division of the county. At Cambridge Stanley absorbed the constitutional doctrines of ordered liberty and unionism, and as one of his father's political lieutenants and from 1896 a member of the West Worcestershire Conservative Association's executive, he served a long apprenticeship in local politics. As a Primrose League organiser and patron of friendly societies and workmen's clubs, his familiarity as an industrial employer with the lives of working men and their families was extended. At the 1906 general election he stood as Conservative candidate for the nearby town of Kidderminster. He fought as an opponent of Irish home rule, church disestablishment and secularisation of schools. As his 'positive creed' he offered tariff reform, presented as the means to secure 'more employment for the people' and to protect their wages: 'I have always been interested in whatever tends to the bettering of life for those who have to earn their daily bread.'[6] He was defeated by the Liberal candidate, and in the following year the family ambition that he would join his father in the Commons was further disappointed when a protégé of Joseph Chamberlain was preferred over him for the nomination as Conservative candidate for Worcester.[7]

In February 1908 Alfred Baldwin died suddenly. A month later Stanley replaced him as MP and became vice-chairman of Baldwins Ltd. He also succeeded his father on several boards of directors, including those of the GWR and Metropolitan Bank. By 1916 he had acquired further directorships – a total of eleven – which with his growing portfolio of shares added substantially to the sum left by his father, £198,346 (almost £12 million in modern prices). Baldwin was a wealthy man. Already, on his marriage in 1892 he had leased a large house near Stourport, Dunley Hall. In 1902 he moved to a Jacobean mansion, Astley Hall, buying the property in 1912 and extending it with a new wing. From 1908 he also rented a substantial London townhouse, 27 Queen's Gate, South Kensington, before buying a still larger and more fashionable house, 93 Eaton Square, Belgravia, in 1912. He was well travelled, in addition to his business trips. From his youth onwards he had long holidays in France, Belgium, Germany, Switzerland and Italy. Building on

---

[6] Election address, in SB papers 35/2–3. [7] See below, p. 313.

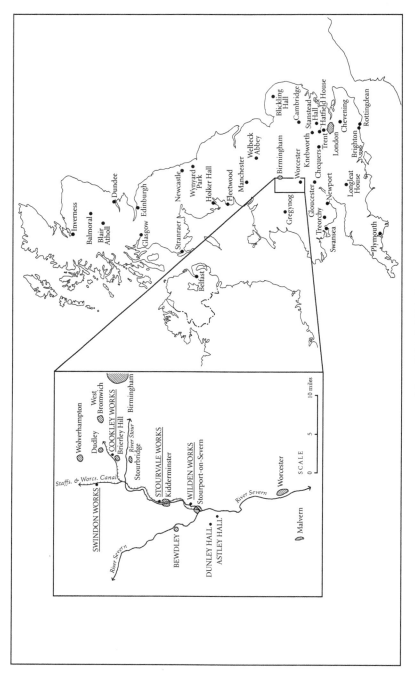

Map 1 Baldwin's Britain

his education in the classical languages, he became fluent in French, knew Italian, and during a long 1888 visit to Dresden began to learn German, continuing with a tutor at home. During the Edwardian period he also developed a love of winter holidays in Switzerland, writing to his mother from St Moritz of going 'up in the mountains, ski-ing up the Val Suvretta and down the Beversthal to the mouth of the Albula tunnel. I don't know of any environment on this earth that brings me more into tune with unseen things.'[8]

Baldwin's election as MP for West Worcestershire in March 1908 was unopposed, and he had stood simply as his father's son, with no reference to policies: 'I will content myself... with saying that my political views are those that were held by my father, and that I stand on the same platform to fight for the cause that was dear to him./ Should you do me the honour of electing me, I shall feel it a great privilege to continue his work to the best of my ability for the welfare of all classes in the Division he loved so well.'[9] For him, as for his father, entry into Parliament was not the beginning of a political career but an expression of service, status and leadership within county society and the business community. They were natural backbenchers, the businessman equivalent of the old country-gentleman MP. Stanley's engagement diaries before 1914 record a routine of board and committee meetings at Paddington (for GWR),[10] in the City, in Birmingham and Gloucester; visits to Newport and Wilden (for Baldwins Ltd) and to his constituency; and only occasional attendance in the House of Commons. He participated in the parliamentary lobbying of the British Iron Trade Association and the Railway Companies Association, but made only a few Commons speeches, chiefly on industrial relations or commercial and financial issues. When in March 1909 he won first place in the ballot for private members' motions, his chosen subject was 'the question of the investment of British capital in foreign countries' – a characteristic tariff-reform businessman's charge that the Liberal government's increases in direct taxation were driving investment overseas. In May 1909, such was his position in the business world that he was asked to join the petition from City of London bankers and merchants protesting against the tax increases in Lloyd George's 'people's budget', alongside such leading City names as Rothschild, Baring, Hambro, Goschen and

---

[8] 11 February 1914. For glimpses of the Baldwins on holiday with the Kiplings at Engelberg in January 1910, and Stanley's enthusiasm for skating and skiing, see *'O Beloved Kids', Rudyard Kipling's Letters to his Children*, ed. E. L. Gilbert (1983), pp. 98–101.
[9] Election address, 20 Feb. 1908, Bewdley Museum.
[10] A note in GWR records in RAIL 258/248, the National Archives, lists his membership of three subsidiary boards and four committees as well as the main board: he was evidently an executive director.

Schuster.[11] Another aspect of his politics was his membership and financial support for the Unionist Social Reform Committee. Nevertheless, before the crises of the First World War Baldwin was not an aspirant minister. His experience of another career (and his knowledge that he had the contacts to return to business), his criticism of 'professional politicians', and his sense that politics was about service rather than personal ambition, help to explain the detached attitudes he often brought to party leadership.

*

A few documents from Baldwin's backbench period indicate his perspectives, and contain occasional comments on leading politicians.[12] The first was written during the fierce second general election of 1910.

6 DECEMBER 1910: TO EDITH MACDONALD

SB add. papers

Queen's Hotel, Birmingham

My dear Edith

I am glad the spirit moved you to send a long line across the void just at this time. Until these infernal elections are over, I shall hardly have a moment to sit down and think.

But it would all be unbearable if it wasn't one's rather obvious duty and if one hadn't the love of friends all around.

And when one of the generation in front of me drops out of the ranks, it acts as a stimulus to me to push on for the time is short so that I may not be ashamed when I meet once more those who fought a good fight while they were with us.

That's my view.

Always your loving/ Nephew

During 1912 a national miners' strike forced a stoppage in industries dependent on coal supplies. Baldwin issued the following notice to the employees of the four Midland works of Baldwins Ltd.

---

[11] *The Times*, 15 May 1909; see D. Kynaston, *The City of London*, vol. II: *1890–1914* (1995), pp. 494–6.
[12] Further material is quoted in M&B, ch. 3.

PRIVATE NOTICE
TO EMPLOYEES.

ASTLEY HALL,

March 20th, 1912.

I do not like to see men who have worked for E. P. & W. BALDWIN thrown out of employment through no fault of their own. I therefore hope to make an allowance to every one working for Weekly Wages at the following rates, such allowance to be paid on March 23rd to those who have been without any wages coming on for at least a week.

MEN	10s. 0d.
BOYS under 18 years .	5s. 0d.
WOMEN	5s. 0d.
GIRLS under 18 years .	2s. 6d.

It is my hope to be able to continue these payments, if necessary, for some weeks.

STANLEY BALDWIN.

Figure 2

By such means Baldwin carried the paternalistic work relations of the earlier family firm into his division of the new large company. After the stoppage ended, the workmen for all four works presented him with an illuminated address of gratitude for his 'thoughtfulness and generosity', and in endorsement of the 'good feeling that exists between you and your men'.

At the end of the 'Marconi scandal' in 1913 he thought Lloyd George's 'prestige is dimmed for many a day to come.' He looked very vicious when brought to bay and while making his apology.'[13] During the constitutional troubles of 1913–14 Baldwin was all for conciliation. His Commons speech on the Welsh Church disestablishment bill was described by Lloyd George as 'very fair, temperate and able'; but as Baldwin commented during the Irish 'Curragh crisis', he considered Lloyd George and Churchill among the sources of discord.

31 MARCH 1914: TO LOUISA BALDWIN

House of Commons Library

Dearest Mother,

I wonder what you in peaceful Wilden think of this mad world?

Certain it is that never in our lives have we been standing on such a perilous brink.

There is a move among moderate men on both sides to get together on the Irish question and try to arrange some compromise that will make for peace, the one idea being at any cost to save the country either from civil war or from a wild campaign against the army.

Grey is in charge to-day and neither George nor Winston is in the House, with the result that the debate is proceeding in a calmer air, and Grey has said in effect that the Government will consider almost any suggestion from our side.

Ordinarily it would not be for us to suggest. But I hope we may now: things are much too serious for us to fold our hands and wait . . .

Much love from thy/ loving Son

At the outbreak of the First World War, Baldwin extended a patriotic act of his father's during the Boer War, of paying the friendly society subscriptions of all working men in his constituency and Worcester city who volunteered for the armed services. This commitment eventually amounted to a large sum, but it became the first of numerous philanthropic gifts. As the war effort increased, during 1915 he was drawn into increased parliamentary and departmental work. This included membership of committees on trade relations after the war, War Office expenditure, and war loans for small investors (the origin of the National Savings scheme). He was one of four MPs appointed in May 1915 to sit with two High Court judges on the Home Office Aliens Advisory Committee, interviewing individuals seeking exemption from internment and repatriation as 'alien enemies' under the Defence of the Realm Act. By late July they had dealt with

---

[13] To Louisa Baldwin, 20 June 1913.

1,200 cases, and the work continued into the following year. 'I had some difficult cases this afternoon . . . one miserable specimen, a bit of rotten human driftwood blown ashore by the gale of the great war. The other cases were redeemed by the witnesses who one after another were straight out of Dickens: Dickensy men who led Dickensy lives.'[14] After the 1916 Easter Rising the committee was given the further task of interrogating Sinn Fein prisoners, meeting regularly in Wormwood Scrubs prison. Baldwin called the tribunal his 'spy committee', and it almost certainly gave him contacts in the secret services. In January 1915 he was a founder member of the Unionist Business Committee, a backbench group formed to scrutinise commercial aspects of the war effort. On behalf of the committee he initiated a debate on 'national organisation', and with other executive committee members participated in deputations to ministers.[15] In September he signed a cross-party open letter calling for conscription, and by mid 1916 had become critical of the Asquith coalition government. His correspondence with Joan Dickinson began in the autumn. She was working as an official with the Red Cross, tracing wounded and missing troops.

17 OCTOBER 1916: TO JOAN DICKINSON

Lady Davidson papers

93 Eaton Square, S.W.

Dear Maid

. . . I had a curious confirmation the other day of an old theory of my own. I have always felt, knowing the Working Man pretty intimately as I ought to, that a good deal of shall we say misunderstanding between classes arises from the fact that they don't speak the same language. That is, words convey different meanings to different classes. A shade of meaning is a thing not understood by Working Men . . . Here is an illustration.

I was talking to one Wardle the other day in the smoking room. He is the present leader of the Labour party.[16] Sitting apart was an unpleasant trio, often seen together, Pringle, Dalziel and Houston.[17] I called Wardle's attention to the group and observed partly to draw him, 'Houston isn't a type that appeals to me' or words to that effect. To which Wardle, edging near to me and lowering his voice 'No: I want to use a word about him

---

[14] To Joan Dickinson, 25 Oct. 1916.
[15] Minute books in Hewins papers 26, and material in Bull papers 4/11, 12.
[16] George Wardle, acting chairman of the parliamentary Labour party in 1916.
[17] W. M. R. Pringle, a Liberal critic of conscription; Sir Henry Dalziel, a newspaper owner and Liberal supporter of Lloyd George; Robert Houston, a millionaire shipowner and Conservative.

that I don't like to use'. Every word of abuse current in the circles in which Wardle had been brought up rushed through my brain. I held on to the table near, and prepared for the worst. It soon came. 'He has a <u>sinister</u> look.' With great emphasis on the evil word. I told him he had employed the mot juste . . . Wonderful how everything in the heights or the depths can be reached by the English language.

I had the misfortune lately to allude to Prigg and Hongle (meaning Pringle and Hogge[18]) before some of my friends. The metathesis was evidently considered a 'succès' for I had the pleasure of hearing it retailed the same evening and attributed to some one else! Such is fame. I kept silence. . .

Much love,/ S.B.

16 NOVEMBER 1916: TO JOAN DICKINSON

Lady Davidson papers

House of Commons Library

Dear Maid,

. . . Poets are always right. I was highly pleased to find that Kipling had come to the same conclusion about the government that I had, and by the same road, after almost as long and anxious a cogitation. We have common puritan blood in us and he said a thing I have so often said and acted on. 'When you have two courses open to you and you thoroughly dislike one of them, that is the one you must choose for it is sure to be the right one'.

How much happier not to be made like that! . . .

Who is to be Food Controller? I think he ought to be anonymous and referred to as Mr X. for he will certainly swing on a lamp post before the war is over . . .

Your father has just entered the room: I shall shew him this letter . . .

Your loving/ S.B.

In early December Lloyd George replaced Asquith as Prime Minister, and began constructing a new coalition government.

---

[18] J. M. Hogge, a Liberal who worked closely with Pringle on radical causes.

8 DECEMBER 1916: TO JOAN DICKINSON

Lady Davidson papers

Carlton Club, Pall Mall, S.W.

Very dear Maid

. . . I was at Paddington till half past one at our Board: many of my excellent colleagues were afflicted with a futile loquacity and we wasted such a lot of time. Then I had to bolt to the City for another meeting . . .

I wonder what I shall have to do if Lloyd George mobilises the nation. You will of course be left where you are, but I daresay I shall be put to drive the Chelsea refuse carts, and you will see me attired in a wideawake hat leading my charge down Egerton Terrace. What price a General Election within three months? A hideous but very possible event. I used to enjoy an election in the heyday of an ebullient youth: I hate 'em now . . .

Much love/ S.B.

11 DECEMBER 1916: TO JOAN DICKINSON

Lady Davidson papers

93 Eaton Square, S.W.

Very dear Maid

. . . you feel you would like to chuck it and something tells you you oughtn't to and that it wouldn't be a very brave thing to do. Isn't that so? My dear, you are going through, probably for the first time, what is a common experience with anyone who has tried to do anything in common with other people since the world began! There are two paths in life: one to cuddle up sheltered (Browning has some remarks on this – as on many other things)[19] the other to go out and help in the melee of life. And the light isn't very good and there is a lot of dust about and we get banged on the head by friend as well as foe. You have chosen the better part, but you have just had your first bad bang on the head, and you wonder if the game is worth the candle. It is, a thousand times. Face it and go on, with the same cheerful courage that took you back to work in the middle of your holiday. I always have a double prayer about my work – ability to do it, whatever and wherever it is, and to do it with cheerfulness. Every day for eight years have I asked for those two things. Try it . . .

[19] Browning was one of Baldwin's favourite poets, especially admired for his religious verse.

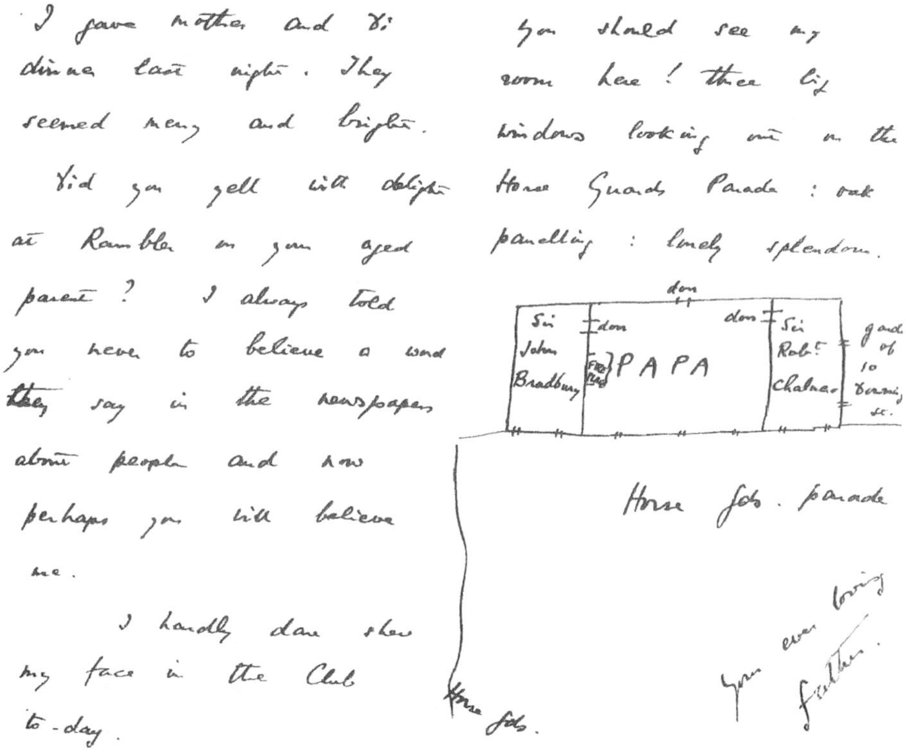

I gave mother and Di dinner last night. They seemed merry and bright.

Did you yell with delight at Rambler on your aged parent? I always told you never to believe a word ~~they~~ say in the newspapers about people and now perhaps you will believe me.

I hardly dare show my face in the Club to-day.

You should see my room here! three big windows looking out on the Horse Guards Parade: oak panelling: lonely splendour.

Your ever loving Father.

Figure 3 From a Baldwin letter to his daughter Lorna, 31 January 1917, indicating the location of his Treasury office: Sir John Bradbury and Sir Robert Chalmers were the department's joint permanent secretaries.

On 21 December 1916 Baldwin was appointed parliamentary private secretary to Bonar Law, the Unionist party leader and now Chancellor of the Exchequer and Leader of the House of Commons. Given wartime pressures on ministerial man-power Baldwin's duties quickly expanded to departmental work. On 29 January 1917 he was made an unpaid Junior Lord of the Treasury in order to deputise for the Financial Secretary, Lever, sent to Washington to manage British war purchases in North America. Baldwin now had a full-time ministerial job, 'in the very centre of the spider's web'.[20] Baldwin participated in intensive Treasury work to overcome domestic aspects of the financial crisis, notably organisation of an immense new war loan – to which both he and his mother committed large sums of their own money.

11 FEBRUARY 1917: TO LOUISA BALDWIN

partly in *My Father*, p. 81

Treasury Chambers, Whitehall, S.W.

Dearest Mother,

... I have a big block of new shares to take up, and shall sell most of them as I conveniently can, as I have borrowed £50,000 to put into War Loan. I reckon to clear most of this during the year if I can peddle out my new Baldwins.[21]

You will get this on the morning of the 13th,[22] and I shall feel peculiarly conscious of father's presence that day because I shall be making my first appearance on the front bench in charge of a small group of supplementary estimates. He would have been so pleased, and if there be any knowledge with him of what we do, the knowledge that in our several ways we try to do our duty must be a joy to him. I wish I could look in on you on Tuesday, and indeed often, but I am sure I am doing right in undertaking this work here. We both believe there is guidance in these things. I never sought a place, never expected it, and suddenly a way opened and an offer of wider service was made. If one tackles public life in the right spirit, it is unselfish service. (And don't bother about other work – I have none. I am attending no boards at all so long as this government lasts.) If we are returned again, and I am offered a post, then I shall have to decide finally between commerce

---

[20] To Louisa Baldwin, 29 Jan. 1917.
[21] With the wartime boom in iron and steel production, Baldwins Ltd expanded their capital and Baldwin received a new issue of shares ('Baldwins'). In modern terms this £50,000 would be equivalent to around £1.5 million.
[22] The anniversary of Alfred Baldwin's death.

and public life. And if I live, the experience of the next six months should enable me to choose.

My best love to you, particularly on this day . . . / Ever thy loving/ Son

As acting Financial Secretary, Baldwin took charge of financial business affecting not just the Treasury itself but also its dealings with spending departments and Parliament. 'My peaceful life is a thing of the past: it is all alarums and excursions, and in the House when I am not the butt of that assembly, I am cornered and button-holed by all and sundry'; 'There is no job which brings you in such close and constant touch with the House as mine.'[23]

30 MARCH 1917: TO LOUISA BALDWIN

House of Commons

Dearest Mother

. . . I had my first experience one evening of having to reply to a portion of the debate and got through it all right. There is nothing calculated to keep you awake more than being on the front bench when you have to reply to a succession of foolish speeches! . . .

I have had to give up all my directorships while I am in office: Ld. Churchill has been most kind and assures me that it is the unanimous wish that as soon as I am kicked out I should come back to the Board,[24] and . . . he says he won't fill up my place . . .

Submarines and payments in America are still the two outstanding danger points but otherwise I think all goes well. The next three months are bound to be a particularly anxious time all over Europe on account of the food shortage. After that, the situation should be easier.

Best love & much from thy/ Ever loving/ Son

After the United States' entry into the war he noted that 'all London is beflagged in somewhat hysterical fashion with the Stars and Stripes. They tell me that the great service in St. Pauls was very impressive, and the emotional Americans were quite overcome, weeping with a facility denied to us English. Anyway, it will make them very happy over the water./ I can't say it gives me any pleasure to see American

[23] To Joan Dickinson, 16 Feb. 1917; to Louisa Baldwin, 15 May 1917.
[24] Victor, 1st Viscount Churchill, Alfred Baldwin's successor as chairman of the Great Western Railway. He repeated this offer in January 1918.

flags alongside ours on the Government buildings. The Admiralty will have none of it and preserves its ancient dignity by flying as always its own flag.' He recurred to the point twelve months later: 'There is a Mansion House luncheon to-day to celebrate the entry of America into the war but I declined with thanks because (A) I hate luncheons and (B) I don't feel like celebrating the entry of an ally nearly three years too late.' In May 1917 he commented that 'Russia so far as we can tell will be of no military use this year. If she had only held together and been organised (two impossibilities, I fear) the war would have been over this summer. But you can't have a revolution without loosening discipline through the whole life of the country.'[25]

On 18 June Baldwin's position was regularised by appointment as Joint Financial Secretary to the Treasury. During the long committee stages of the Finance Bill he worked days of thirteen or fourteen hours, starting with briefings from Treasury, Inland Revenue and Customs officials, followed by discussion with the Commons chairman of committees, then six or seven hours on the front bench handling the debate on the Bill's clauses, and ending with an hour's preparation of the next day's work.[26]

15 AUGUST 1917: TO LOUISA BALDWIN

House of Commons

Dearest Mother

. . . I am very fully occupied all the week and feel as fit as a fiddle.

. . . It will be a great relief when the House is up. I find I am gradually being put on committees of ministers e.g. I am on a small committee of which Carson is chairman to consider the question of soldiers' & sailors' pay; I sit daily except Saturdays on the Exchange committee. That deals with the Foreign exchanges and consists of the governor and deputy governor of the Bank of England, Felix Schuster, chairman of the Union Bank, Gaspard Farrar of Barings and so on.[27] Then I represent the Treasury with one other English representative and two Frenchmen on a committee which watches the financial situation constantly between France and ourselves . . .

[25] To Louisa Baldwin, 20 April 1917, 6 April 1918, 15 May 1917.
[26] Ibid., 4 July 1917.
[27] The London Exchange Committee, a key body in monetary policy established in November 1915, originally consisted solely of bankers. Baldwin was added to its membership after the Governor, Lord Cunliffe, lost a famous row with Law over ultimate control of the national gold reserve.

Henderson made an ass of himself. He is a stupid, conceited man who has bumped into events too big for him[28] . . .

Much love from thy/ loving/ Son

Baldwin's correspondence with Joan Dickinson was now in full spate. The following letter indicates their normal length, content and tone, and introduces Davidson, who as Law's private secretary since 1915 had with Baldwin become part of a tightly knit group of friends at the Treasury and 11 Downing Street.[29] Joan had visited Astley Hall during the parliamentary recess, and stayed on with Baldwin's family after he returned to London.

28 SEPTEMBER 1917, 10 P.M.: TO JOAN DICKINSON

Lady Davidson papers

The Athenaeum, Pall Mall, S.W. 1

Dear Little Maid,

The sweet briar scented the Treasury this morning and brought before me the Broad Walk [at Astley Hall] with that wonderful valley and line of hills till I could have rushed off to Paddington and leaped into the first train I saw! I loved to hear your adventures since I left and rejoice that you were rewarded with such an evening walk.

Skies like that stand out in one's memory as dinners do in some peoples'.

Do you remember the ten minutes in the stubble field the evening after you arrived when the ends of the world caught fire, blazed and died? It was a real kind thought to write as you did, for I found it hard work buckling to again and Astley was tugging very hard. Yet, bless me, how much of it should I see if I were in France? Shame on me! I rejoice too to think of you there, and your more than deserved holiday, and that Astley is giving you what you need . . .

I am contemplating a walk on Sunday in Buckinghamshire. I think I can combine a dozen miles with a call on an old friend whom I haven't seen for years . . .

I wonder what the two important questions are that you want to discuss? I am always ready with advice as you know! Or perhaps it's not advice you

---

[28] Arthur Henderson, the Labour party leader, had been forced to resign from the War Cabinet for advocating British participation in an international socialist conference, which would include representatives from enemy countries.

[29] *Davidson Memoirs*, pp. 78–80, prints short extracts from this period (though on p. 80 the extract from the following letter and an earlier reference to Davidson are incorrectly dated as 1918).

want but only discussion. Davidson and I have been having a talk. He is a remarkably sensible man, because he worries over the same things that I do and we agree wonderfully in the things we should like to do. I think I may say "he has an interesting mind".

Charles Bathurst[30] has been doing his best to get me down to Lydney for a long week end but I couldn't just after such a splendid holiday. It tempted me though. But as I often yield to temptations, it's just as well to be firm occasionally, or one will never be able to say no. Can you say no easily? I wish I could. It is a most useful thing.

My poor old Chief rushed off to France yesterday morning to try and get news of his eldest son but he is back already having failed to learn anything.[31] He is passing through a very terrible time and I am quite powerless to help him which I don't like. I don't really know the inner man of him.

This is a poor return for your delightful letters. But my only quiet time to write is after dinner, and after a long day's work I get so stupid. You shall have a brighter one before you come back. I understand all you say about friendship, but you think far too much of me. That's not fishing. I've told you so often. You say you thank God for our friendship. I want you to be able to say so from your heart when the time comes that you are looking back over your life and long after I shall have passed on.

I am going to walk home now: it is bright moonlight and wild beasts are trooping out of Battersea Park to drink in the river before going to bed . . .

Your loving/ S.B.

4 OCTOBER 1917: TO JOAN DICKINSON

Lady Davidson papers

Treasury Chambers

Dear Maid

. . . No words can describe the peace and beauty of the nights and no words can describe the beastliness of the raids.[32] On Monday, the day my wife came up, we spent two hours in our own basement with the servants, and had the full benefit of a bomb dropped just out of the square in South Eaton Place . . .

---

[30] Conservative MP for South Wiltshire 1910–18, when created Lord Bledisloe.
[31] James Law, serving with the Royal Flying Corps in France, had been reported missing in action; Charles Law, serving in Palestine, had similarly been lost in April.
[32] German aircraft had started a series of bombing raids on London.

Sunday evening I spent in the Mackails'[33] lower regions with them, two servants, a cat and a refugee policeman.

To-day I made my first appearance at the War Cabinet, which was amusing. But we have been much cheered by the news from the War Office: 'All objectives secured: 2000 prisoners counted by mid-day': so we have had a really successful push. The only fly in the ointment is labour and if we get through without trouble at home – !

. . . One seems to be all amongst the depressing things here. Never a politician out for his own hand, or a profiteer for his own pocket, or the anarchist workman for chaos and topsy-turvydom, but we know all about it in this office. I can tell you some strange stories some day . . .

I wish you had been here and free last Sunday. I had a solitary tramp in Epping Forest and came back on a 'bus from Chingford. It was very beautiful . . .

During the autumn Baldwin was appointed to further Cabinet committees, on the economic offensive against Germany, trade relations within the Empire, and the Dutch exchange. He himself chaired a conference on Rumanian financial questions, and participated in discussions with the American financial mission. The pressure of work was relentless. 'Here is the close of one of the most tiring, worrying, exhausting weeks I have ever had! . . . from when I have finished breakfast to eleven at night I am hunted like a hart on the mountains. Every hand is against this noble but unhappy office.' He was told that a Liberal MP had said of him '"That's the hardest worked man in the House of Commons!" meaning me!! It ain't true, but I preened myself and did the goose-step to the smoking room.'[34] He also noted the peculiar course of the war: 'If anyone had told us three or four years ago that we should take Bagdad and Jerusalem, but not Ostend, what should we have said?' During early 1918, he attended several political breakfasts hosted by Lord Derby to bring Lloyd George into contact with his junior ministers. These were 'very agreeable meetings and give one a good opportunity of studying that strange little genius who presides over us. He is an extraordinary compound.'[35]

30 JANUARY 1918: TO LOUISA BALDWIN

House of Commons

Dearest Mother,

. . . I was at a very interesting breakfast at Ld. Derby's a week ago to meet the P.M. and we sat around the table till nearly eleven. The talk was on Ireland.

---

[33] Margaret Mackail, a cousin, and her husband, the classical scholar J. W. Mackail.
[34] To Joan Dickinson, 3, 14 Nov. 1917.   [35] To Louisa Baldwin, 14 Dec. 1917, 4 March 1918.

Events in this war are bringing home to some of us an understanding of the attitude of our rude forefathers to the Church of Rome.

If the hopes of an Irish settlement are broken it will be owing to the Roman bishops i.e. the Vatican. They swing round against Redmond without a word of warning to him just when agreement was in sight, confirming the belief one had had for years that the official church would keep the country disturbed but would never help a settlement by Home Rule for fear of an anti-clerical government. The Vatican influence has been against us in Europe all the time, and in Quebec and Australia it has thrown its' weight against conscription by working in one case on the Catholic French and in the other on the Irish. A plausible theory is that the Vatican hopes by busting the Irish Convention to bring Lloyd George down, thus paving (as they think) the way to an early and German peace.

We have had two raids the last two nights . . . Last night's was the noisiest yet though thank God they were kept out of London. Every gun near us was in full blast and our bedroom windows rattled and one could imagine one felt the walls shaking . . .

I expect the news about German strikes is exaggerated, but there is no doubt they are in a queer state and no man can prophesy from day to day what may happen – anywhere in the world . . .

Division bell ringing so I must be off.

Much love from thy ever loving/ Son

Baldwin's elder son had become unhappy at Eton, and helped by the Kiplings he persuaded his father during 1915 to allow him to leave school and join a cadet battalion. In August 1917 Oliver joined the Irish Guards and prepared for active service. The dangers were all too obvious: Kipling's son and Bonar Law's two eldest sons were now presumed dead.

1 MARCH 1918: TO OLIVER BALDWIN

CUL MS Add. 8795/2

Treasury Chambers

Dearest Son,

I little thought, all those long years ago in St. Ermin's Mansions,[36] what your nineteenth birthday would mean.

---

[36] The London home of Baldwin's parents, where Oliver was born.

But now that it is come, and we know that it means that soon you will be carrying a high heart to France with all our hopes and prayers, and it is a very special message of love I send you to-day and say in no conventional sense 'Many many happy returns of the day!'

... I understand you are to choose your present and it is to be of bag-like nature.

Be sure and get just what you want.

                           Always your loving/ Father

In May the government was threatened with a political crisis when the former director of military operations, General Maurice, claimed in *The Times* that Lloyd George had misled the House of Commons about British military strength before the great German offensive in March. On 9 May Lloyd George successfully defended himself in the Commons.

15 MAY 1918: TO LOUISA BALDWIN

                                                   Treasury Chambers
Dearest Mother,

... You may be amused to hear of a brief conversation which took place last Thursday morning between your son and the Prime Minister as they walked up Whitehall together. It was the morning of the debate on Gen. Maurice's letter and I told him that doubtless the humour of the situation had not escaped him. We proceeded thus:

S.B.: 'You know, Prime Minister, that for ten years we have been trying to catch you deviating by an inch from the strict path of veracity and pin you down. We never succeeded. But now others think they have got you and they will find out this afternoon that they have caught you speaking the truth. They will have the shock of their lives.'

The little man roared with laughter and it evidently pleased him for he went about afterwards telling members of the Cabinet that he had been caught telling the truth![37]

He continued: 'Poor old Bonar: he feels it very much. He doesn't like being called a liar. I don't mind it. I have been called a liar all my life. I've had more of the rough and tumble of life than he has!'

---

[37] For a report of Lloyd George repeating the phrase almost immediately, see *Crawford Papers*, p. 389 (9 May 1918).

I lunched with him to-day to meet the Belgian Prime Minister and Finance Minister, but I hate lunches, they take up too much time and it is difficult to avoid overeating.

We have utilised the west wind the last few days in giving the Hun an awful dose of gas: you may have seen he is urging through the Geneva Red Cross that both sides should give up gas. He is a strange creature . . .

Much love from your ever loving/ Son

25 MAY 1918: TO LOUISA BALDWIN

Treasury Chambers

Dearest Mother,

. . . That bombing of the hospital at Etaples was perhaps the wickedest thing they have done yet. More and more one feels that Kaiserdom has got to be rolled in the dust if it takes a generation to do it, if the world is ever to progress to something better. The Bosche seems to have gone off the rails onto the main line to Hell . . .

Much love from yr ever loving/ Son

On 31 May Oliver Baldwin left to join his regiment in France. On the previous evening his father asked him 'what I should like done in my memory should I not come back. I was much surprised at this, and suggested alms-houses or a working-men's club. He promised it should be done.'[38]

During this year Baldwin first became involved in an issue which would be an important feature of his leadership – distaste towards the so-called 'press lords', given peerages and government appointments by Lloyd George. Baldwin was especially sensitive about Lord Beaverbrook, made Minister of Information in February, because he had a dubious reputation yet also a well-known friendship with Bonar Law. The appointment provoked criticism in the House of Commons on 19 February 1918 from Austen Chamberlain. Afterwards Baldwin wrote to Chamberlain: 'Thank you for your speech yesterday. You have given expression to what every decent man has been feeling for months.'[39] Following later criticism of the Ministry of Information, it fell to Baldwin to defend the department and minister, and Beaverbrook supplied briefing materials for his speech. Immediately

[38] Oliver Baldwin, *Questing Beast*, p. 62. In 1921 Baldwin had a club-house built at Stourport, but now in thanksgiving for Oliver's safe return. Oliver donated it to the local ex-servicemen.
[39] 20 Feb. 1918, AC 15/7/2.

after the debate on 5 August, Beaverbrook thanked him 'most warmly'.[40] But two days later Baldwin discovered a further transgression.

7 AUGUST 1918: TO BEAVERBROOK

Beaverbrook papers E/3/42

Treasury, S.W.

My dear Beaverbrook,

Your department wants to send out to Venezuela and Colombia a man who is or has been connected with the Marconi Co. and they describe him as indispensable.

I know the House of Commons pretty well, and it would be a fatal error to employ anyone connected however remotely with that Co.

The House has for the time being swallowed your business men, but they would throw this particular appointment up. I know the feelings of the silent men as well as of the vocal.

My chief concern is that any error of judgement you make reacts on Bonar pretty quickly, and I am sure that any result of that kind would be as unwelcome to you as it would be to me.[41]

Yours sincerely/ Stanley Baldwin

Baldwin had now sensed a decline from the earlier wartime spirit of unity and sacrifice, as when he was 'depressed' by the railway union's attitude during an industrial dispute: 'I get an obsession that everybody is out for what they can get during the war and it makes me sick.'[42] Baldwin's own wealth and income had risen considerably, as war production increased the value and dividends on his various industrial shares. He now increased his donations to good causes, including substantial sums for Wilden Church, Worcestershire hospitals and, sometimes using the pseudonym of 'Mr Dingle', to various charities with which Joan Dickinson and her family were associated.[43] His reaction to the armistice had a similar ethical quality.

---

[40] *HC Debs* 109, cc. 991–1002; correspondence, 1–5 Aug. 1918, Beaverbrook papers E/3/38; Beaverbrook to Baldwin, 6 Aug. 1918, SB papers 175/7–8.
[41] Beaverbrook accepted Baldwin's advice on the individual mentioned, but replied robustly on the point about Law – an early expression of a Baldwin–Beaverbrook tussle over Law's reputation which continued long after his death.
[42] To Joan Dickinson, 28 Nov. 1917.
[43] Williamson, *Baldwin*, pp. 138–9; *Davidson Memoirs*, pp. 94–5, and to Joan Dickinson, 14 Nov. 1917, 6 April, 30 Sept. 1918.

2 OCTOBER 1918: TO AN UNKNOWN CORRESPONDENT

printed in Baldwin's obituary, *Berrow's Worcester Journal*, 20 Dec. 1947

My dear – ,

I am slowly getting rid of my war profits and I want you to be good enough to convey £5,000 to the Worcestershire Prisoner of War Fund in such a way as will effectually conceal my identity.[44] You can give it in a lump sum from ANONYMOUS or split it up. But I rely on your discretion.

These new issues of Baldwins have brought in a wicked amount of money which could never have come to me except for the war, and I know you at any rate will sympathise with my point of view.

Yours ever,/ S.B.

11 NOVEMBER 1918: TO LOUISA BALDWIN

House of Commons

Dearest Mother,

The strain of the last few days has been great and I think a good many people are nearer tears than shouting to-day. Old Bill Crooks[45] came up to me and taking both of my hands in his big paws said tremulously 'This is a great day'. To which I replied 'Yes, but I feel very like crying myself' to which he replied 'I've 'ad my cry this morning!'

It is getting dark now and drizzling which is not a bad thing. There has been no horseplay yet in the streets: plenty of flags and shouting and bugles blowing the 'All Clear' . . .

It is curious to hear Big Ben strike again. The clocks were stopped striking years ago: and after lunch I heard bells pealing over Southwark way as I walked on the terrace.

St. Margaret's was very full for a short service we had. Two hymns, lesson, a few prayers, Te Deum, God Save the King.

My brain is reeling at it all. I find three impressions strongest: thankfulness that the slaughter is stopped, the thought of the millions of dead, and the vision of Europe in ruins. And now to work! pick up the bits.

Much love from your/ most loving/ Son

---

[44] £5,000 is about £122,000 in modern terms.
[45] William Crooks, Labour MP for Woolwich 1903–21, with whom Baldwin had become friendly before the war.

Baldwin was returned unopposed at the December 1918 general election. During the January 1919 government reconstruction he knew he had insufficient ministerial experience to be promoted, and was content to remain in his current post, with Austen Chamberlain as Chancellor.[46] He did, however, become sole Financial Secretary in May.

One of Baldwin's wartime Treasury colleagues had been Keynes, then an acting principal clerk. Writing to him ('My dear Keynes') on a Treasury matter in the following year, Baldwin observed that 'I believe you have conferred anonymous fame on me for if I am not the "Conservative friend" alluded to . . . [in] your immortal work, I should like to know who he is!' The reference was indeed to Baldwin's own phrase, itself immortal. As Keynes later described the circumstances: 'I was sitting in Chalmers' room in the Treasury having tea on the first day of the new Parliament after the Coupon Election. Baldwin, who . . . had the adjoining room, poked his nose through the door, as I can see him now, to us at tea. I asked him – "What do they look like?"' Baldwin then gave the celebrated reply published by Keynes in *The Economic Consequences of the Peace*: 'They are a lot of hard-faced men', he said, 'who look as if they had done very well out of the war.'[47]

In January 1919 Joan Dickinson and Davidson became engaged to be married, giving Baldwin great pleasure. Davidson was offered a place on the Prince of Wales' staff, and was uncertain whether to accept. Baldwin unsuccessfully tried to persuade him to accept, in a note which reveals much about his own attitudes to public service. The Davidson marriage was in April 1919.

28 JANUARY 1919: TO DAVIDSON

Lady Davidson papers[48]

A few Comforting Thoughts in Times of Difficulty

It takes me out of the dust of conflict   Yes, but I can choke just as well in a Court.

---

[46] To Louisa Baldwin, 9 Jan. 1919, in *My Father*, p. 82.

[47] To Keynes, 31 Dec. 1920, Keynes papers L/20/149; J.M. Keynes, *The Economic Consequences of the Peace* (1919), p. 91, same pagination in *The Collected Writings of J. M. Keynes* (1971–89), vol. II, with circumstances described in vol. XXVII, p. 163. Baldwin had found the reference, belatedly, in a popular 1920 edition. He wrote similarly to Louisa Baldwin, 12 Feb. 1919 (*My Father*, p. 82): 'The prevailing type is a rather successful-looking business kind which is not very attractive.'

[48] See also *Davidson Memoirs*, p. 95, and M&B, p. 71, though both mistakenly take this note to refer to possibilities in Baldwin's own career. Davidson remained Austen Chamberlain's private secretary, until elected Unionist MP for Hemel Hempstead in November 1920. He then became parliamentary private secretary to Law 1920–1, Baldwin 1921–2, and again Law, as Prime Minister, 1922–3.

What about my Soul?	That's all right. The essence of such service is unselfishness. My first thought has to be of others, of the relationship of Crown and people: there will be no room to think of money or of my own career. For this relief much thanks. That's all to the good.
What good shall I do?	A d–d sight more than I should do as a member of Parliament or fifty Parliaments. That is self-evident.
I shall lose the 'common touch'	Not if I see SB. Anything commoner than him I have yet to meet.
I shall probably lose some friends	Yes, but I shall make others.
I am not sure that I want it . . .	'When in doubt, choose the path you like least.' I shall make a Lady of my wife – in time.

9 APRIL 1919: TO JOAN DICKINSON

Lady Davidson papers

Just a year ago we were sitting together on a hill beyond Tring, looking out over a vast landscape and listening to a solitary lark who was near bursting his little throat as he was singing into the face of the sun. May the lark be singing to-morrow[49] to welcome you and your man as you step out hand in hand into your new life – and may this song in your hearts never cease! A little invisible cloud of my love and prayers will accompany you but it won't get in the way and you will be quite unconscious of it and it will be near you both.

. . . God bless you everywhere and always, and give you long life with your John and bring you nearer as the years pass. Love each other with all your hearts.

---

[49] I.e. her wedding day. *Davidson Memoirs*, p. 82, has Baldwin's equivalent letter to Davidson.

Baldwin's 1919 letters give only glancing references to his work during the difficult post-war reconstruction. He helped prepare budgets and conduct the Finance Bill, and received many deputations. He was a member of the Cabinet's home affairs and finance committees. He played a leading part in reimposing Treasury control and retrenchment on other departments. In the autumn he chaired a committee of chief finance officers of the spending ministries, whose report established a new system of financial accountability. His letters contain occasional nervous comments on industrial relations: 'I am thankful the P.M. is in Paris and is leaving all these strike questions to those at home. The new minister of Labour is a capital man and a friend of mine ... His name is Robert Horne ... and [he] is full of sanity and courage'; 'The labour element so far is quiet and decorous. But these are very early days'; 'We are all very thankful at having avoided a police strike so far but it is a very rough road we are driving on at present.'[50] In May he summarised his fears and hopes: 'I still feel we are all dancing on a pie-crust, but every day is a day to the good and if we can pull through the first year after peace we shall get along.'[51]

The circumstances of the famous next letter, published as the Versailles peace treaties were about to be signed, were recalled in 1930 by Brumwell of *The Times* editorial staff: 'Baldwin imparted his decision and entrusted his letter to J. C. C. Davidson ... and asked him to secure publication in *The Times*. Davidson being a friend of mine put the letter into my own hands with a full explanation of the circumstances and with a request that the name of the writer should go no further. I explained that it would be necessary for me to let the Editor into the secret, but promised that it should not be revealed to anyone else. My promise was faithfully kept in Printing House Square, and disclosure came ultimately after many months from another source.' The letter, which Baldwin signed with the initials of his ministerial office, was accompanied by a favourable leading article from the editor, Wickham Steed. Later, in May 1925, Steed publicised its authorship by republishing the letter, 'with Baldwin's knowledge and consent', in an article about him.[52] The printed *Times* version made small changes to Baldwin's text, which is the one printed here.

---

[50] To Louisa Baldwin, 31 Jan., 12 Feb., 3 June 1919.
[51] Ibid., 21 May 1919.
[52] Brumwell reported in Dawson to Steed, 21 Oct. 1930, and see Steed (whose recollection was slightly different) to Dawson, 17, 22 Oct. 1930, W. Steed papers 74120/224–9; W. Steed, 'Mr Stanley Baldwin', *Review of Reviews*, May–June 1925. The first widely publicised identification of the author was in an 'appreciation' of Baldwin by 'a close personal friend' in *The Morning Post*, 23 May 1923, later reprinted as a Conservative party pamphlet. Davidson seems the most likely source: Williamson, *Baldwin*, p. 140.

JUNE 1919: AS 'F.S.T.' TO THE EDITOR OF *THE TIMES*,
PUBLISHED 24 JUNE

handwritten original, SB add. papers

Sir, It is now a truism to say that in August 1914 the nation was face to face with the greatest crisis in her history. She was saved by the free will offerings of her people. The best of her men rushed to the colours: the best of her women left their homes to spend and be spent: the best of her older men worked as they had never worked before, to a common end and with a sense of unity and fellowship as new as it was exhilarating. It may be that in four and a half years the ideals of many became dim, but the spiritual impetus of those early days carried the country through to the end.

To-day on the eve of peace we are faced with another crisis, less obvious but not less searching. The whole country is exhausted. By a natural reaction not unlike that which led to the excesses of the Restoration after the reign of the Puritans, all classes are in danger of being submerged by a wave of extravagance and materialism. It is so easy to live on borrowed money: so difficult to realise that you are doing so. It is so easy to play: so hard to learn that you cannot play for long without work. A fool's paradise is only the ante-room to a fool's hell.

How can the nation be made to understand the gravity of the financial situation? that love of country is better than love of money?

This can only be done by example, and the wealthy classes have to-day an opportunity of service which can never recur.

They know the danger of the present debt: they know the weight of it in the years to come. They know the practical difficulties of a universal statutory capital levy. Let them impose upon themselves, each as he is able, a voluntary levy. It should be possible to pay to the Exchequer within 12 months such a sum as would save the taxpayers 50 millions a year.

I have been considering this matter for nearly two years but my mind moves slowly; I dislike publicity, and I hoped that some one else might lead the way. I have made as accurate an estimate as I am able of the value of my own estate and have arrived at a total of about £580,000. I have decided to realise twenty percent of that amount or say £120,000 which will purchase £150,000 of the new war loan,[53] and present it to the government for cancellation.

[53] £580,000 in modern prices is over £15 million, and £120,000 over £3 million.

I give this portion of my estate as a thankoffering, in the firm conviction that never again shall we have such a chance of giving our country that form of help which is so vital at the present time.

Yours etc./ F.S.T.

24 JUNE 1919: TO DAVIDSON

Lady Davidson papers; *Davidson Memoirs*, p. 94

Treasury Chambers

My dear old David,

You and I and Miss Watson[54] have done it with a vengeance! I don't know what you said to the <u>Times</u> man, but when I opened the paper in bed (ut mea mos est[55]) wondering whether my letter would find a place at all – well, I dived under the bed clothes and went pink all over – as pink as you!

I feel like a criminal in momentary fear of detection. BUT – remember this, mon chou. Next time you get a letter from me and feel inclined to belittle my style, remember that the leading journal of the world calls it NOBLE. Put that in your pipe and smoke it!

To-morrow night I hope to dine with the Child[56] and I will be a delightful mixture of grandfather and step-brother and bless you for all your kindness to me.

F.S.T. (Ferdinando Smike-Thompson)

31 AUGUST 1919: TO JOAN DAVIDSON

Lady Davidson papers

Astley Hall

Little Maid

. . . Yesterday was a day from Heaven. A light N.W. wind, that had swept the atmosphere into a translucent clarity: that bright pale blue sky you know, with horizontal layers of woolly cloud lying one behind the other like a

---

[54] Edith Watson, private secretary to Bonar Law 1916–21, later to Austen Chamberlain 1921–2, then to each Prime Minister from Law to Churchill, retiring in 1945.
[55] 'As is my custom'.
[56] Joan Davidson.

succession of drop scenes in a theatre lying all around but some distance above the horizon: the heavy dew of earliest autumn on everything. So I got up betimes and was out on the Broad Walk by half past eight. It was so clear that even at that time in the morning I could see the Cotswolds from the Old Hill. Wherefore, in the afternoon, what did I do but take myself to my beloved Woodbury! Not a soul about, and I sat for half an hour at the top on one of the most perfect evenings I have ever seen. The city of Worcester seemed at my feet: every cranny on the Malverns shewed up. Bredon you could pat on the head, and behind it the very fields on the Cotswolds were visible, and that glorious rampart stood out like the Alps from Lombardy until they were cut off abruptly by the intervening Malverns. . . .

The peace of God is on the landscape and in my heart . . .

Now for a little music!

Your loving/ S.B.

From 26 September to 5 October there was a railwaymen's strike.

7 OCTOBER 1919: TO LOUISA BALDWIN

Treasury

Dearest Mother,

And how have you kept during this last thrilling week? The strike caught us all scattered: you at Wilden, wife and Betty at Astley, Di in Sussex, Little at Eton, Lorna in Hertfordshire and Olly in Paris!

I think it has been a great victory over the wild men, and in one feature at least no other country could compete. You have had in some ways the biggest strike we have ever had, with masses of other men thrown out of work, and there has been practically no violence or sabotage. Nothing beyond what the blackguard part of the community would do any time it had the chance and the spare time.

On Saturday it looked pretty black.

All Europe was watching, and if we had had any kind of an upset here, you would have had Italy alight and perhaps France as well. I hope it will have a steadying effect in both those countries . . .

Ever thy loving/ Son

As a young child Baldwin had been given a clockwork pig, inscribed 'For a good boy, love from Mummy and Daddy', a toy that long remained in the family and was probably the source of Baldwin's humorous liking for pigs, and indeed for pork pies and hams (comic letters of thanks to friends, colleagues and ambassadors for the gift of these survive). The joke was not just shared within his family and among friends. After commenting publicly just before he became Prime Minister in May 1923 of looking forward to a retirement in which to read books and keep pigs, it became part of the imagery associated with him.

30 DECEMBER 1919: TO JOAN DAVIDSON

Lady Davidson papers

Astley Hall

Your pig smiles at me as I write, and by him a primitive pig of wood, given me by Mr Kipling,[57] and bearing an autograph poem on his side:

> Some to Women, some to Wine –
> Some to Wealth or Power incline,
> Proper people cherish Swine.

> Cattle from the Argentine –
> Poultry tough as office twine –
> Give no pleasure when we dine:

> But, from nose-tip unto Chine,
> Via every intesTINE
> Nothing is amiss in swine

> Roast, or smoked or soaked in brine
> (We have proved it, Cousin mine)
> Every part of him is fine.

> So, till Income Tax decline,
> Or Truth exists across the Rhine,
> Or GEORGE[58] can speak it, praise we Swine
> Common, honest, decent SWINE.

[57] Evidently both items were jocular Christmas gifts. The Kipling family had spent Christmas at Astley Hall. The text and a facsimile of part of this letter were printed in *The Kipling Journal*, March 1986, pp. 42–4.
[58] I. e. Lloyd George.

Isn't that sweet? he went into Harrods, and said 'I want a Pig'. And they: 'We have one at four guineas'. 'That' said the Poet 'is no good to me. My limit is half-a-crown'. So he bought one made by a wounded warrior . . .

21 MARCH 1920: TO WINDHAM BALDWIN

SB add. papers

Travellers' Club, Pall Mall, S.W.1[59]

Very dearest Little,

Many many happy returns to you and a happy year before you!

I wish we could spend your birthday together, but I shall be stuck in the House of Commons all day and you stuck at school, and there we are.

Never mind, I hope to be at Astley to welcome you and have a few days then with you and we will have some wonderful games of chess and I will give you a birthday present.

I like to hear of all your ante finals: what fun if you win something. But never mind if you don't: do your best and it'll be all right.

I went on a lovely walk to-day near Guildford . . . I saw one or two jolly little sulphur coloured butterflies, and the birds were shouting with joy. Lots of plum blossom, and the hedges on the low ground coming out gallantly.

I had a cheery postcard from Olly a day or two ago from a place called Bari Saada on the edge of the [Algerian] desert. But in this weather I don't feel I care to change England for anything. I am so looking forward to having a week at home and hope to be there in a fortnight.

Do you feel mortal old being sixteen? it seems a great age. I am sure you are much nicer than I was at sixteen.

Always God bless you./ Much fine love from/ Your loving old/ Father

The Davidsons went to Argentina for two months on family business. As most of Baldwin's family and servants were at Astley, he briefly stayed in the Davidsons' convenient Westminster house.

---

[59] Baldwin had just been elected to what became his favourite club. He described it as 'a really peaceful club where no one talks to you unless you want it', reputedly where a member lay dead for three days before anyone noticed: to Phyllis Broome, 20 March 1920, Lorna Howard papers. A qualification for membership was to have travelled 500 or more miles by direct line out of Britain.

18 APRIL 1920: TO THE DAVIDSONS

Lady Davidson papers

10 Barton Street, Westminster

Dearest couple

I think this must be to both of you, for I am writing late at night alone in the little drawing room . . . by candlelight with a rather smoky wood fire slowly burning. The quiet can be felt, and except for an occasional hurrying footfall and the quarterly chiming of the clocks there is silence . . .

. . . Bonar is at Windsor with Isabel.[60] He tried to get out of it though he cheered up when I told him I would try and get Barnett to go as his valet to play chess with him in the evenings. He has had a horrid week in the Goat's absence[61] owing to the hunger strikers in Mountjoy prison. He took even my breath away at Questions. Tuesday he announced that in no circumstances would they be released: on Wednesday they were released: on Thursday he was asked 'What led to the change of policy?' To which he, looking like an inspired infant with round surprised eyes 'There is no change of policy!', and he believed it. The only possible explanation is that there was no policy and ∴ there could be no change.

. . . Mond has bought five short horn cows and has gone into the country to look at them. There seems to be something almost indecent in subjecting an English cow to inspection by Mond. All this at lunch on Friday to which George Stanley listened in silence but when the olive coloured oriental said that he was a farmer, George guffawed (I am sorry no other word will do) till he nearly choked.[62]

. . . George Gibbs has lost his wife and Jack Gilmour has married his deceased wife's sister.[63] Some people call such a marriage a cosy arrangement: it always seems to me to border on the stuffy. Besides the sister is so very patently a second string. Moreover – no, enough . . .

---

[60] Isabel Law, accompanying her father in fulfilling the King's summons to stay at Windsor Castle.

[61] Lloyd George, now at the San Remo Conference. The sobriquet 'the Goat', a comment on his nimbleness, was coined by the Treasury permament secretary (and prolific inventor of *mots*), Sir Robert Chalmers.

[62] Sir Alfred Mond, industrialist of German-Jewish extraction and Coalition Liberal First Commissioner of Works 1916–21; George Stanley, Unionist whip 1919–21.

[63] Both were Unionist MPs and whips. After being made illegal in 1835, the issue of marriage to a deceased wife's sister had been a perennial Victorian controversy. The practice was allowed by legislation in 1907.

27 MAY 1920: TO DAVIDSON

Lady Davidson papers

North End House, Rottingdean

... By the time you get this you will be nearing home and I think you ought to have a line to put you in touch with affairs again. The Coalition has taken new life and is in a much stronger position than when you left.

That is partly owing to the fact that we have won every bye-election easily, Runciman being badly beaten in Clyde's old seat when Clyde was made Lord Justice General.[64]

Then Asquith has been a great disappointment to the Wee Frees:[65] his few speeches have really been in support of our front bench except an ineffective speech on Home Rule and his attack has no bite. Bonar has done excellently, the Goat having been away all the time. He has been resting ever since he returned from San Remo on imperative orders from his doctor ...

Austen did well too in his Budget on which so far we have spent six days. Horne is doing well at the Board of Trade: Addison still muddles on:[66] no particular mark has been made by any new men, nor have any of the older hands done anything out of the common.

The split between the Coalition Liberals and the Wee Frees is widened, owing to a conference at Leamington where the Coalition ministers, including Macnamara, Hewart, Addison and Kellaway were howled down. This has made them exceedingly bitter.

The advent of an Honours List is bringing many urgent callers to no.11 and I could not help connecting a forty minutes visit from Inverforth with that event![67] The P.M. advised Niemeyer not to take a C.B. till next list on account of his name but he spoke of him warmly and said he was the best

[64] Walter Runciman, Liberal Cabinet minister 1908–16, defeated as an Asquithian Liberal in 1918 and again in the North Edinburgh by-election, April 1920; James Clyde, Unionist MP, Lord Advocate 1916–20, thereafter as Lord Clyde a senior Scottish judge.
[65] Asquith, defeated at the 1918 election, had won the Paisley by-election in February 1920 and resumed the parliamentary leadership of the Independent Liberals ('Wee Frees').
[66] Christopher Addison, Liberal MP and first Minister of Health 1919–21, suffered prolonged criticism because he was responsible for a high-spending department, particularly for housing.
[67] Lord Inverforth, shipowner and Minister of Munitions 1919–21.

of the lot sent up. This was told to our good little Hun who was pleased and he is content to wait.[68]

By the way, you nearly lost me! Between ourselves, Bonar took my breath away the other day by saying to me 'Would you like to go to S. Africa?' To which I 'No, I don't think so. In what capacity?' 'To succeed Buxton'. 'Are you joking?' quoth I. 'No' said he. 'Well' said I 'there are plenty of men would do that job as well as or better than I: I think I am more use at home'. 'Would you like Australia?' said he. 'Not a bit', said I. 'Well' quoth he 'I thought you wouldn't look at it!'[69] And some further and rather amusing conversation brought the matter to a close. It's an odd world. You would have been surprised, though, wouldn't you?

I saw Ld. Churchill the other day and he told me two sweet little stories of F.E.[70] Victor Churchill you know is not extraordinarily happy in his domestic relationships, and speaking to F.E. during the passage of the Divorce Bill he asked him how he would be affected, 'for' said he to F.E., 'I don't want to appear in the Divorce Court. It isn't as if my name were Smith!' To which the Ld. Chancellor: 'May I suggest that for the purpose of illustration you should use the name of Brown or Robinson?'

Then Churchill went on to say how he admired F.E.'s replies on committee stage, to which F.E. 'Oh, that's nothing: I never have had any difficulty in finding a reply to anything. But yesterday my small daughter said something to me to which I had no answer. I had been in court all day and got home tired at seven o'clock and threw myself into an armchair and had a cigar and a big whiskey. She put her head in at the door and looked at me solemnly and said 'Drinking again, daddy?'

. . . I . . . am alone in this beautiful house that I have known and loved so well since I was a boy of fourteen. Nothing has been disturbed, and I am writing at my aunt's table in the old studio which she used as her living and

---

[68] Otto Niemeyer, a senior Treasury official, English-born but of German extraction; he obtained his CB in 1921 and a knighthood in 1924.

[69] Lord Athlone, brother of Queen Mary, became High Commissioner in South Africa. A Conservative MP and junior minister, H. W. Forster (made Lord Forster) replaced Munro-Ferguson (Lord Novar, 1920) as Governor-General of Australia. Baldwin, telling his mother (20 May) that he had 'refused being considered' for the posts, commented: 'Not in my line but it is a compliment.'

[70] Lord Birkenhead, the Lord Chancellor, as amusing as he was sensitive about his plebeian family name of Smith. He was a notoriously hard drinker.

working room since my uncle's death. It is extraordinarily peaceful and full of lovely memories[71] . . .

There was occasional newspaper speculation that Baldwin might be made Speaker of the House of Commons. 'It is funny how that odd rumour of the Speakership keeps cropping up . . . / I don't know whether there is anything in it, and if I were offered it, I haven't an idea what I should do./ Sufficient unto the day. It would postpone for years those days of cultured leisure (with pigs) to which we both look forward in our dreams.'[72] Few letters of interest survive for the next twelve months. Those to the Davidsons contain numerous descriptions of country walks, and one notable comment: 'Countryfolk are my own folk: in London I am a stranger: in the country at home.'[73]

31 AUGUST 1920: TO DAVIDSON

Astley Hall

Dear old David,

. . . I am alone, writing letters with one eye, and the other on the hills which look miles away with the afternoon sun streaming on them through an easterly haze . . . Contact with my native soil for a week is making a new and I trust more agreeable man of me.

I am going out beyond Witley on Thursday to preside at some Country Sports, and on Saturday and Saturday week I am to receive deputations from Friendly Societies who are making me a presentation: goodness knows what for, but it pleases their kind hearts.[74] At any rate a sight of their ugly faces and the sound of my ancestral tongue will do me good.

. . . The country is alive with the sound of reaping machines by day and owls by night. And over all a mellow September sun. The amazing beauty of it all fills me with fresh wonder every year . . .

For many months the Baldwins suffered anxiety about their elder son. After being demobilised in 1919 Oliver became increasingly restless. During 1920 he announced

---

[71] Philip Burne-Jones had offered Baldwin the use of his parents' home, following the death of his mother and pending the sale of the house.
[72] To Geoffrey Fry, 29 Aug. 1920, Fry papers.   [73] To Joan Dickinson, Michaelmas Day 1920.
[74] In fact, a series of presentations to thank him for his payment of the membership subscriptions of volunteers for the armed forces during the war.

that he was going to Armenia, the scene of a war with both Turkey and Russian Bolsheviks. The Baldwins heard nothing for four months, until in February 1921 a message came from Erivan, saying he had been imprisoned but was now paroled.[75] While serving as a colonel in the Armenian army he had been captured by the invading Bolsheviks. Later, while trying to leave the country, he was imprisoned by the Turks. He returned to London in July 1921.

1 MARCH 1921: TO JOAN DAVIDSON

Lady Davidson papers

House of Commons

Little Maid,

. . . Those primroses last night made my heart ache and started again that dreary string of useless questions. 'What good do you think you are doing in London? Why don't you live among your own people? Why be called a Waster[76] when you might be making daisy chains?'

And to these there is no answer.

The wood smoke in the early morning, the corncrake on the hot afternoons of early summer, the owl in the twilight, the flight of rooks towards the setting sun in a December afternoon: the alder buds before the spring, the ash buds in March, the bluebell in May, poppies in the chalkland in July, the cloud shadows racing over the ripe corn in the downs, beechwoods in the autumn –

all these things go on, and we dodge taxis, and read the Daily Mail, and chat with Bottomley,[77] and answer silly questions.

Idiot! Some one has to help to clear up the mess? very well then, get to work and don't chatter. I won't . . .

---

[75] See Walker, *Oliver Baldwin*, chs. 4–5.

[76] The government was being accused of excessive public spending, particularly by an 'Anti-Waste League'.

[77] Horatio Bottomley, Independent MP until expelled in August 1922 for fraud; owner of the populist magazine *John Bull* and, like *The Daily Mail*, a generator of vulgarity and critic of government 'waste'.

TWO

٭

The Coalition Cabinet

APRIL 1921 – OCTOBER 1922

On 1 April Baldwin entered the Cabinet. His promotion was part of a reshuffle associated with Law's retirement due to ill-health. Austen Chamberlain replaced Law as Unionist party leader, Horne became Chancellor of the Exchequer, and Baldwin took Horne's place as President of the Board of Trade. Politically Baldwin had one of the most difficult positions, because he inherited Horne's Safeguarding of Industries Bill. This 'anti-dumping' measure, by raising the issue of import duties, had the potential to create division between the free-trade Liberal and protectionist Unionist members of the Coalition. In securing the bill's smooth parliamentary passage in August, Baldwin had a marked success.

After announcing his retirement, Law had written to Baldwin that 'No one ever had a better or more loyal friend than I have had in you & though neither you nor I are great talkers about these things I always relied on you & knew that you would have helped me in every need to the limit, & our friendship will always remain.'[1]

2 APRIL 1921: TO BONAR LAW

Bonar Law papers 107/1/10; *Davidson Memoirs*, p. 104

Board of Trade, Great George Street, S.W.1

My dear Bonar,

I cannot tell you what pleasure your letter gave me: my whole heart was in my work with you, and I don't mind confessing to you that I nearly took advantage of the shuffle to go back to private life and to business.

---

[1] 21 March 1921, SB papers 175/15–16.

But it came over me that were I to do that I should have fallen far from the standard that you have set for so long, and I should have felt later as ashamed of myself as you would have been of me.

I owe you a great deal and I still marvel at your patience with me on the Bench at the beginning of 1917 when I was all at sea.

Our friendship indeed remains, for it was welded and tested in stern years.

Take great care of yourself and don't try and do too much. You must now be realising how tired you were.

But we shall be very glad to see you back...

Ever yours,/ Stanley Baldwin

6 MAY 1921: TO LOUISA BALDWIN

Board of Trade

Dearest Mother,

Silence does not mean forgetfulness.

Naturally I have been busy. The business of a Minister is different from that of a Financial Secretary: far less detail work, more time in conferences, cabinets, and giving decisions. Less work in the House except when I have a Bill as I have next Monday and Tuesday. So I am off to Surrey to the little house[2] I have taken to put in two days hard preparing a difficult speech, for my Bill which I have inherited is THE controversial bill of the Session. But the job is interesting and I like my staff so far as I have seen them...

Much love as ever/ from your loving/ Son

Lloyd George, on summer holiday at Gairloch on the far north-west coast of Scotland, but deep in negotiations with de Valera on ending the Irish troubles, summoned a special Cabinet to meet in the town hall of the nearest substantial town, Inverness. This rare instance of a meeting outside London caused much inconvenience, especially because of the great distances involved. Some ministers travelled up by night-sleeper train on 6–7 September.

---

[2] A farmhouse he had rented for three months, in order to take weekend breaks out of London to keep up with ministerial paperwork and to take walks. He did the same in 1922.

8 SEPTEMBER 1921: TO JOAN DAVIDSON

Lady Davidson papers

In the train, near Oxford

... At Euston I got some dinner ... Macnamara, looking very cross was at another table, and we were joined by [Griffith-]Boscawen who had been torn from a protracted honeymoon.[3]

It is always amusing starting on a long journey. I made my way to the platform in good time and seeing a crowd some way along guessed that my friends were there. There were photographs and pressmen: Tom Jones[4] was master of the ceremonies ... Looking into the train the first familiar figure to greet my eyes was the Lord High Chancellor, seated not on a woolsack but on a cane bottomed chair, with a cigar a foot long in his mouth and a case of cider at his feet and looking sunk in profound melancholy. Austen in a very light suit, in a melancholy more articulate and eruptive: then Mond, resigned, with a tiny soft hat nesting in his curls, and at last but not least the Home Secretary[5] with a dinner basket, a bottle of Irish Whiskey under his arm and six bottles of soda water. But I have forgotten the secretary of state from India,[6] saturnine and feline.

A pretty crew! the Ld. Chancellor, voluble as he became later was at first peculiarly costive in his speech and his vocabulary singularly limited. 'This bloody journey': those were for an hour the only words I could clearly distinguish ... At Crewe I went to bed. I suppose I am unused to travelling but I didn't get to sleep till Motherwell: dozing with an active brain, if you know that condition. At Blair Atholl, I got up and was back in our compartment at seven o'clock, revelling in the beauty of everything. But what a surprise awaited us!

At Kingussie, the very prince of breakfast baskets! so needed and so good that we finished up the journey in beautiful tempers and emerged at Inverness, each a separate ray of sunshine. There we found Macready, Edmund, Hamar (who according to F.E. started life selling tin watches for silver ones at a fair in Toronto!), Munro[7] and others.

---

[3] Respectively the Liberal Minister of Labour 1920–2 and Unionist Minister of Agriculture 1921–2.
[4] The deputy, and on this occasion acting, Cabinet secretary.   [5] Edward Shortt, Liberal.
[6] Edwin Montagu, Liberal.
[7] Respectively the commander of British forces in Ireland; Viscount Fitzalan, Viceroy of Ireland; Sir Hamar Greenwood (born in Canada), the Liberal Chief Secretary for Ireland; and Munro, Liberal Secretary for Scotland.

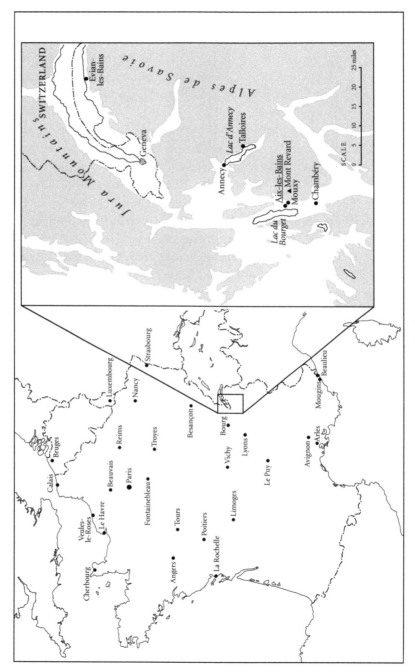

Map 2 Baldwin's France

There was a crowd round the Town Hall and we all got there by eleven but it was twenty minutes later when a burst of cheering heralded the arrival of our one and only Goat. Heather in his buttonhole and a light in his eye! We sat till just on four with an interval for lunch. Have you seen the picture of the Goat on a pony? (front page Tatler)

When Edmund saw it he said with a sniff 'Back to the riding school'. No pleasing these old cavalry officers!

We caught the 4.2 and again had an exquisite journey so long as daylight held which it did nearly to Perth. We were delayed by fog as I feared we should be and we were three quarters of an hour late . . . Breakfast at Euston, and I caught the 9.45 and here I am . . .

On 18 September the Baldwins went for the first time to Aix-les-Bains in south-east France for their holiday. This became their regular late summer holiday destination, as Lucy enjoyed the spa baths and Stanley the countryside and strenuous hill walks. As Baldwin later wrote, a further consideration was that 'it is difficult to travel like a private person so I have formed the habit of going to the same place where everyone knows one and they leave one alone and respect our desire for peace and quiet'.[8]

24 SEPTEMBER 1921: TO JOAN DAVIDSON

Lady Davidson papers

on a heap of stones, under Mouxy church at the foot of Mt Revard

Little Maid

Here I am, after a long climb and wandering among Alpine meadows drenched in dew, and covered with autumn crocuses and harebells, and look! I found a gentian! I shouted aloud with joy . . .

I am writing on my knee so forgive it. I went to Geneva on Tuesday and had lunch with Fisher and Bob Cecil. I saw A.J.B.[9] for a few minutes and a heap of officials . . .

I am walking a great deal, sometimes with Oliver, sometimes alone. My wife is doing the baths and they are no joke. But I think they will make a job of the arthritis which is all that matters.

---

[8] To Evelyn Gwynn Brown (a cousin), 28 Dec. 1929, CUL MS Add. 8770.
[9] Respectively the Liberal President of the Board of Education; Lord Robert Cecil, Unionist MP; and Balfour, Lord President of the Council. All were attending the League of Nations Assembly.

I keep stopping just to look at the mountains and to thank God that I am alive and have eyes. And the sun is pouring down, and I hear a trickle of water, and now and again an ox-wagon passes, or a child with goats. I like these Savoyards: they are a good-looking race . . .

Baldwin was recalled in early October for Cabinet meetings on Ireland and on plans Lloyd George had developed at Gairloch for dealing with a growing unemployment problem, caused by a severe trade depression.

12 OCTOBER 1921: TO LLOYD GEORGE

Lloyd George papers F/3/1/14

Travellers' Club

My dear Prime Minister,

If there is a Cabinet on Friday I beg you will excuse my attendance, as I propose being away for three days to see my wife who is just arrived in Paris after doing a somewhat severe treatment for arthritis. I am very anxious to see how she has stood it and hear for myself what the doctor says, and to impress on her the need to go easy for a time. I have left everything in train at the office and shall be back Sunday night.

I am feeling hopeful about the Gairloch plans, and everything must be done to get the Indian R[ailwa]y. orders placed here. The mere placing of big orders of that nature converts the men employed into consumers as well as producers, and <u>may</u> give confidence. The trouble is not only that some people <u>can't</u> buy, but that nobody <u>will</u>: when they once start, they will be like sheep running through a gate.

Yours sincerely, / Stanley Baldwin

8 NOVEMBER 1921: TO JOAN DAVIDSON

Lady Davidson papers

Board of Trade

Little Maid

. . . Yesterday morning in the cold words of the Court Circular, the President of the Board of Trade had an audience of His Majesty after the Council. How little does that give the outside world any idea of the scintillating dialogue that actually took place! You would never guess from that that H.M. said 'I could tell the most extraordinary things that have been said, if I chose' and that the President replied 'I hope, sir, that you will not write autobiographical articles in the Press?' and that H.M. laughingly rejoined 'Not till I'm broke!'

Moreover, when we spoke of the possibility of an enquiry being held into the circumstances of Gen. Byrne's leaving Dublin,[10] I observed 'I never like washing dirty linen in public: but when the linen has been two years in the basket it is much worse': a point H.M. took at once and worried as a terrier would worry a rat.

We parted with mutual protestations of regret and a very suitable wish expressed on His Majesty's part that I should take a holiday!

...We have...had [an] apology from...a labour member, Mr John by name,[11] who had accused his opponents in the House of drinking. It is curious how a conscience which prevents you fighting for your country permits you to slander those with whom you work...

Lloyd George's negotiations with Sinn Fein leaders finally produced a treaty on 6 December, in the face of considerable Unionist backbench criticism. On the advice of Unionist whips, Chamberlain asked Baldwin to speak during the parliamentary debate on 14 December, because he was believed to be well respected among Unionist backbenchers. His defence of the treaty caused strain in some of his personal relations. Baldwin had already noted the delicate condition of Unionist feeling about Lloyd George: 'our party has a hair-trigger tummy and can't digest all the dishes prepared by the P.M.'[12] From late 1921 his letters indicate his own unease about the Prime Minister, especially during January 1922 when Lloyd George tried to manoeuvre Unionist leaders into perpetuating the Coalition at an early general election which most did not want.

5 DECEMBER 1921: TO JOAN DAVIDSON

Lady Davidson papers

Board of Trade

Little Maid

...We had a Cabinet on Ireland at noon, sitting till half-past one: at half past two Collins and Griffiths were to be interviewed again, and a second

---

[10] Byrne, head of the Royal Irish Constabulary, regarded as a force for moderation in dealing with Sinn Fein, but dismissed in December 1919.
[11] William John, Labour MP for West Rhondda 1920–50.   [12] To Fry, 5 Nov. 1921, Fry papers.

Cabinet is expected about six. It is now a quarter past four and no news yet. Saturday's Times had the proposals pretty accurately.

. . . Stinnes met the Goat at dinner and of course a denial ran all through the press! He is going to see Krassin next. The Marquess[13] has been confiding his annoyance about these clandestine meetings to the President of the Bd. of Trade who concurs.

Your loving/ S.B.

22 DECEMBER 1921: TO JOAN DAVIDSON

Lady Davidson papers

Astley Hall

Little Maid

. . . the Westminster play I enjoyed thoroughly and saw several friends . . . I had a seat reserved in the front row, so I discovered, but I didn't sit in it. It always seems odd to me to be put in the seats of the mighty.

. . . I met Carson in Downing St. from whom I got a very chilly nod, the sort of greeting a corpse would give to an undertaker. There was some restraint about cousin Kipling too whom I saw at the Carlton in earnest converse with Rupert Gwynne.[14]

I hope it will wear off by tomorrow when he is due here!

The P.M. is off to the Riviera next week, but I have brought the Geddes Report[15] with me to study so as to be ready for the worst . . .

It seems so stupid to say 'thank you, both', but what can I say. It is most dear of you to take me again into your happy little home and treat me as you always do. You have been so good to me, so patient and understanding: is it any wonder that I turn up again like a cat who gets her feet buttered every time she calls? . . .

Your loving/ S.B.

---

[13] Curzon, the Foreign Secretary. Lloyd George was bypassing both the Foreign Office and Board of Trade in negotiations with, respectively, the German finance minister and the head of the Soviet Russian trade delegation.

[14] Unionist MP and like Kipling and Edward Carson, the Ulster Unionist leader, an opponent of the Irish settlement.

[15] The first of three reports from the Committee on National Expenditure 1921–2, chaired by Sir Eric Geddes and consisting of leading businessmen. For Baldwin's distaste for the composition of this 'millionaires' committee, and his opposition to an election, see Davidson to Law, 13 Jan. 1922, in Hyde, Baldwin, p. 94.

16 JANUARY 1922: TO JOAN DAVIDSON

Lady Davidson papers; partly in *Davidson Memoirs*, p. 112

Brighton

Little Maid

... We have got nice rooms looking out on the sea[16] and I took a jolly mixed lot of books with me: Keynes' new book on the Peace, Bertrand Russell on Anarchy etc., a lot of Wordsworth (Prelude and Excursion), and a new book about the Greeks (not these modern *bastards) and a novel of Tourgenev ...

... How they are all intriguing: I am so sick of it all sometimes. I want a cleaner atmosphere. Cowardice. Does the pig make the sty or 'tother way on? That's all rather elliptical, but you understand.

Your loving/ S.B

* I think this is quite a seemly word in this context: ask David.

17 JANUARY 1922: TO LOUISA BALDWIN

Carlton Club

Dearest mother,

... The little P.M. is very busy and I don't know what he is up to. I think he was trying to get the old Liberal party united under his leadership and then throw us over. But he has failed in that enterprise and I have no idea where he will break out next!!

Ever thy loving/ Son

17 JANUARY 1922: TO GEOFFREY FRY[17]

Fry papers

Board of Trade

My dear Geoffrey,

... Here we are in dirtier waters than usual and the Goat and his gang (of which Beaverbrook is now the most intimate member) rooting about to find

---

[16] Baldwin and his wife had taken rooms in Brighton for a few weeks, from where he took work trips to London as well as walks on the South Downs.
[17] Private secretary to Law, and from 1923 until the 1940s to Baldwin.

the tide of opportunity and a party to lead to victory. I don't think there will be an election. One possibility is that the Goat may follow Briand's example & resign, under the impression that he would be recalled and might effect changes in the gov<u>mt</u>. If he does, I hope our party will have the guts to say 'Very well: we have a majority and will carry on'. However all these things are on the knees of the devil.

I am with Winston and Montagu, par nobile fratrum,[18] to vet the Geddes committee report on the fighting services. It is a lengthy job and will be troublesome. I went before that august body the other day when they treated me with a charming old world courtesy.

It will be pleasant to see your healthy country face again. You bring with you an air of enthusiasm which is as welcome to me as it is rare. I sometimes get so sick with politics that I could go into the desert. The incredible folly with which the world is governed!

I shall return to the book of the prophet Jeremiah which I last read in the VI<u>th</u> at Harrow. He had a good many pertinent things to say of his period.

I am going to the Treasury now to hear Horne explain the latest ramp – the 20 million international syndicate – to the Bankers![19]

All good wishes / Yrs ever / S.B.

11 FEBRUARY 1922: TO FRY

Fry papers

Travellers' Club

My dear Geoffrey,

... The Coalition is in a queasy condition: everybody disgruntled. I think really we are all stale.

... The Lord Chancellor has taken to the bottle again. There are many stories about as to his behaviour at St Moritz and I think he has done for himself so far as his chances of the leadership go, if he doesn't pull up once for all. Our men simply will not have it. It is a thousand pities.

Geddes fills all the picture just now ... There will be a royal row on the naval suggestions. I was on Winston's committee which examined the

---

[18] 'A noble pair of brothers' (Horace). Churchill was Colonial Secretary, Edwin Montagu Secretary of State for India: both were Coalition Liberals.
[19] A new issue of government securities, to assist management of the national debt.

fighting services: we sat many hours for many days and we are recommending a good deal less to the Cabinet than our stout friend . . .

Ever yours / S.B.

Lady Davidson papers

In the train

Little Maid

. . . A day with me is so often an epitome of life. I start very young, full of spirits, innocent and cheerful. By lunch time I am middle-aged with a calm, almost autumnal view of life. And evening comes and with it age, and I am worn out, garrulous and taciturn at intervals, senile.

That by the way. We started in a car and we made for the moors. Up and up, soon leaving Plymouth behind: the air became thin and intoxicating: and the roads wound up and down and round and round through hills and over little mountain streams into a land of heath and gorse, and rock, a land where I wanted to leap out and plunge into its' heart and walk to the horizon! Three heavenly hours did I have before I left it and was deposited at the station for the long journey back . . .

It is such ages since we met, I haven't told you of the party at Buckingham Palace.[20] We arrived very early and walked miles in solemn state, up staircases, along passages, through staterooms, with rows of silent beefeaters watching us. I felt as if I were in a fairy tale, and if a dwarf had stepped out of a door, or Cinderella, or a dragon, I shouldn't have been the least bit surprised.

We had a thorough look at the presents and I enjoyed it. But the chief joy was to come. Everyone (men) was in black knee-breeches, black stockings, white waistcoat and evening tail coat. We looked like a flight of swallows, only differing among ourselves in that some had fuller crops than others. When lo! enter Sir Alfred Mond in full dress Privy Council uniform, plastered with gold lace, white breaks and all. And he never turned a hair. I could not take my eyes from him. The Prime Minister was very cheery: what calves he had! I talked to his wife for I noticed she seemed lonely. We were standing by a case full of beautifully worked household linen presented by ladies of Ulster.

---

[20] For Cabinet ministers and their wives, to present the Cabinet's gift to Princess Mary on her wedding to Viscount Lascelles, later 6th Earl of Harewood.

The linen had lace-like borders and there were splashes of ribbon about so that at a casual glance you would have thought the case was full of intimate articles for the bride, and a gentleman would have just glanced and passed swiftly but unostentatiously on. Not so our Goat. He gazed on them with a light in his eye which my quick wife observing she looked firmly at him and said 'They are not what you think they are'. The Goat regarded her for one second as [if] she had been a thought reader and then laughed and laughed and laughed.

Horne was very funny. Greeting ladies with effusion with an eye roving the while in search of kindred eyes and catching one he would dart through the crowd and fall on a friendly neck.

The Cabinet gave their present in due course. Our wives were permitted to enter the room where they stood discreetly behind us, and the P.M. said a few kind words to the Princess who replied and shook each of us warmly by the hand . . .

Your loving/ S.B.

In March, with no sign of economic recovery, Baldwin was charged by the Cabinet with 'a special trade investigation'. His report is an important statement of his economic views: the comments on wage reductions, 'over-industrialisation', the permanently unemployed, and emigration, are especially noteworthy. Its pessimism and emphasis on the commercial damage caused by reparations payments generated sharp ministerial discussions during the preparations for the Genoa Conference, at which Lloyd George hoped to achieve a general European settlement that would restore trade.[21]

25 MARCH 1922: CABINET MEMORANDUM

CP 3890, CAB 24/134

Trade Prospects

1 . . . submitted in compliance of Cabinet decision of 8 March. I have seen a number of leading businessmen in the principal industries as well as the ablest managers of the big banks and I have studied all the relevant memoranda prepared in my own department and in that of Overseas Trade.

---

[21] See e.g. *WSC IV/3*, pp. 1828, 1862.

2. I anticipate a slight expansion in business as a whole; possibly continuous and in some directions more marked in the Autumn, but I do not believe that it will be of such dimensions as to reduce unemployment to any considerable extent during the present year.

To look further ahead is hazardous, but I can see nothing to warrant us looking for much better conditions next year; the most I hope for is a slowly improving trade.

3. It is true that the world needs goods, and certainly in normal times that need would soon be translated into demand. But there is a new factor which disturbs the equation and that is the poverty of the consumer.

It remains to be seen to what extent people will do without goods in themselves desirable and content themselves with purchasing absolute necessities. If this purchase of things in themselves desirable be still deferred, there will only be a flicker here and there, a demand from this country or that for this or that class of goods, and the flame will burn low again for want of fuel to feed it.

4. The situation might be altered by a still further fall in prices, brought about as a result of lower wages and a reduction of railway rates. It is not possible to say positively that a substantial demand would spring up immediately but one illustration forces itself on my notice.

After much tribulation the Coal Trade is once more on an economic basis and the export trade has revived to an extent that no one engaged in it could have dreamed of a few months ago.

It may be that a similar revival awaits the next great trade that makes an equal sacrifice to face the realities of the position.

Until there is a closer relation between the wages of skilled and unskilled men in and around the pits, and the wages of skilled and unskilled men in other trades, I fear that the volume of business will show but little improvement. Of course a steady rise in world gold prices, which is anticipated in some quarters, would be a great factor in our favour.

5. Our Export Market is necessary to our existence: no other country in the world is in this position. We need it because we are over-industrialised. Now while it is true to say that Europe is not our chief market for manufactured goods, Europe is essential to us to help in providing credits with which countries overseas can purchase our manufactured goods.

6. The vast and complicated machine of international trade and credit has grown up almost unperceived through three generations. It had become

so beautifully adjusted in all its parts, there was such absence of friction in its working, that few were aware of its existence.

The war threw it out of gear. For three years we have been trying to start the machine: with difficulty the cog wheels are being fitted and some are revolving, but in Europe the damage is almost irreparable, and the whole refuses to function because a part will not work.

I am convinced that there will be little progress in Europe until the question of Reparations is out of the way, and reductions are effected in the expenditure of the various countries comparable to those we are proposing in England. By that means alone can the purchasing power of the nations be increased. Until Europe can purchase freely, the conditions are wanting in which a lasting improvement of trade is possible.

7. I have purposely avoided discussing markets in detail lest we should not see the wood for the trees but I cannot refrain from alluding to the political unrest in India and to a lesser degree in China which is causing traders the greatest anxiety.

8. There is one point upon which I have myself considerable apprehension and I think it is worth investigation. Having regard to our increasing population and the ever increasing productive power of modern machinery and methods I feel that we have reached the point or perhaps have been passed it where we are able to find continuous employment under satisfactory conditions for our people. My fear is that we may find even after an expansion of trade that we shall have with us a pool of unemployed who will quickly degenerate into unemployable and become a perpetual danger to the social and political life of the country. A great effort should be made to move our surplus labour into the Dominions to relieve conditions at home and to increase our most valuable markets. Of the political importance to Australasia of a large population I need say nothing.

The Safeguarding of Industries measure continued to cause political difficulties, because reports of committees assessing applications for duties from particular industries were subject to Cabinet confirmation, and so to divisions between Liberal and Unionist ministers. The test case became fabric gloves, not least because other sections of the Lancashire cotton industry remained committed to free trade and feared that duties on gloves would provoke foreign retaliation against their own exports. A resulting split within Lancashire Conservatism was a further complication. At a depleted meeting chaired by Chamberlain, the Cabinet rejected the application.

AC 24/4/2

Private   House of Commons

My dear Austen,

I have just been round to your room (10.20 p.m) and found it in darkness and Gower's[22] room too.

I wanted to tell you that I cannot defend in the House the decision come to in to-day's Cabinet on the Safeguarding of Industries Act Reports.

If the Cabinet is willing to defer a final decision until the return of our colleagues from Genoa (seeing that barely half our number was present to-day) I will do my best to hold the fort on Wednesday and to argue that in view of the complexity of the cases further consideration is necessary.

I will of course be at your disposal any time you may want to see me to-morrow.

I wish it were anyone in the world but you that I have to worry in this way!

Yours sincerely/ Stanley Baldwin

As Baldwin requested, the decision was suspended. The disagreement soon became public knowledge. Backbench Unionist MPs supported him as a standard bearer of Unionist causes against Coalition Liberal obstruction. The Cabinet twisted and turned over the issue for three months, with Churchill becoming Baldwin's main opponent. Even after Baldwin's case was generally accepted, further Lancashire objections gave Liberal ministers opportunities to seek postponement. At some point Baldwin seems to have threatened resignation.

Lloyd George papers F/3/1/16

Private   Board of Trade

My dear Prime Minister,

I have given very careful consideration to Churchill's suggestion made at yesterday's Cabinet and regret that I cannot fall in with it.

I have myself seen three separate deputations from Bolton and heard their case.

---

[22] Patrick Gower, private secretary to Chamberlain 1919–22, then to successive prime ministers 1922–8, becoming a friend of Baldwin's; Conservative party chief publicity officer 1929–39.

Sir Henry Rea's committee[23] took evidence from four representatives from the Bolton district and I would call your attention to the paragraph in their Report dealing with that evidence.

The same interests placed their case before the Lancashire members yesterday and you are to hear them to-day. Every opportunity is thus being afforded them.

The Government after a protracted delay decided to make the order.

Are we now to say that we didn't really know our own minds and are prepared to delay an ultimate decision for as long again or longer? For it would be November before the Order could be ratified.

Some of the Lancashire Conservative members would be annoyed at what they would call a surrender and I think you underestimate the feelings in our wing of the Coalition. If I am right, what many of our loyal rank & file would say, would be something like this 'Our ministers give unqualified loyal support to the P.M. in his liberal policy, but when something is decided on which the liberals in the Cabinet don't like, they won't play the game.'

Yours sincerely/ Stanley Baldwin

Baldwin's persistence and pressure succeeded, and the safeguarding order was approved in late July. In September, he and his wife made their second visit to Aix-les-Bains. Stanley's enthusiasm for the area is noteworthy, belying a common view that he was an insular Englishman, attached to the beauties of the English countryside and disliking foreigners.

22 SEPTEMBER 1922: TO WINDHAM BALDWIN

SB add. papers

Grand Hotel D'Albion, Aix-les-Bains

Dearest Little,

Since you slowly disappeared into the gloom and left me alone on that dismal platform, I often wondered how you fared and it was a great joy to get your letter[24] . . . [You should] see me . . . with my coat slung over my back

---

[23] The committee that had investigated the fabric glove manufacturers' application.
[24] Windham was about to start at Trinity College, Cambridge; this letter and a further one on 4 October continues with detailed advice on managing the financial allowance Baldwin was giving him.

and the sweat raining off my nose as I toil up mountains in the vain search of a beautiful figure. This is a lovely place and I wish you were here . . .

The country all round is very hilly, sub-mountainous really, vines, Indian corn, walnuts, chestnuts . . . The meadows are covered with autumn crocuses. The lake has all the colours of Italy, varying its shades of blue from pale turquoise to aquamarine, while away to the South there stands the line of Alps with their everlasting snows catching and reflecting all the lights of heaven. My walks are a daily joy and I am rapidly getting into some sort of condition. I find I can now do six hours, climbing to a couple of thousand feet, with ease, and though I am very happy by myself I often feel I want some one for a minute to enjoy the beauty of it all and to shout 'Thank God!' . . .

And much love to yourself, bless you/ Ever your loving old/ Father

While Baldwin was in France, the Chanak crisis developed. Turkish nationalist armies marched on the neutral zone along the Dardanelles and confronted a British-led allied force, and Lloyd George, encouraged by Churchill and Birkenhead, threatened war.

29 SEPTEMBER 1922: TO JOAN DAVIDSON

Lady Davidson papers; partly in *Davidson Memoirs*, p. 114

[Aix-les-Bains]

Little Maid

. . . I have got into training again and yesterday I did a 5000 ft. little mountain to the top and back on my own legs in about seven hours and fit as a fiddle after it. I couldn't have done it three weeks ago to save my life. My agility in the descent surprised me and I can only conclude that living with goats has made me sure-footed among rocks.

. . . If I am not summoned back earlier, I intend crossing on Sunday week, the 8th, and if I might dine with you that evening, it would be delightful. I want to see you: I want all the political news and I want to talk with David . . .

For a fortnight I never looked at a newspaper and then I got so apprehensive about Turkey from the headlines in the French papers that last Sunday [25th] I bought a Times, Observer and Sunday Express. Such a surfeit on a clean stomach made me quite ill. We seem to have messed up everything in the near East, from the years preceding the war till to-day.

I walked last week to a little inn, perched on a rock looking 2000 ft. down into the lake. It was divine. During the fine weather I was out hours a day, and when I had walked myself into a lather, I lay like a lizard in the sun. You should see me on the march! no hat, waistcoat open, coat carried over my back . . . Lord! how I have loved it all . . .

UNDATED [BUT LATE 1922] LUCY BALDWIN MEMORANDUM[25]

handwritten, SB add. papers; typescript copy, SB papers 42/3–10; partly printed in *My Father*, pp. 114–17.

September 30th, and October 12th to October 22nd 1922
THE RECOLLECTIONS OF A CABINET BREAKER'S WIFE ON THE GOVERNMENT CRISIS, OCTOBER 1922

S. [Stanley] and I were off abroad, I to take the baths at Aix and he to enjoy a month's repose which he had been ordered by the doctor. It was agreed that he shouldn't read any papers so that his mind should have as much rest from Public affairs as possible. We had been at Aix just over a fortnight when his eye caught a French poster telling of trouble in the East with the Turks and the likelihood of England going to war. I tried to persuade him that things couldn't be so bad as the French paper made out or he would have been wired for. The next day he went for a long walk, about 20 miles, during which time he did a good deal of clear thinking in the mountains. The next day[26] he and I went for a shorter walk and returned about 6. I was a little tired and went to my room to rest before dressing for dinner and he sat down to a game of Patience. During our walk we had discussed the situation and on our way back had purchased our first English newspaper and there we saw that things were looking very black, though apparently there had been a sort of lull the previous two days, and now things seemed getting worse instead of better. Suddenly S. entered my room with a telegram in his

[25] Jones *DL*, p. 60 (18 Sept. 1932), records Lucy saying that she wrote the story of the Coalition's fall 'at the time and got Miss Watson to type a few copies for record'. She and Baldwin then gave Jones a verbal account of the episode, pp. 60–2. For Baldwin's own later comments, see below pp. 97–8, 104, 119–20, 204–5, 315, 370, 445, 454, 492, 496. There is no evidence to support an account in Mabel, Countess of Airlie, *Thatched With Gold* (1962), p. 173, that Baldwin kept a diary of this period.
[26] 29 September. There is a discrepancy in dating between Lucy's following reference to an English newspaper, and Baldwin's own statement in the previous letter.

hand saying, 'It has come. I have been expecting it. There is some devilment afoot and I must get back to back up poor dear old Austen'. We planned and revised plans and it was decided that he should leave next day for London and that I should stop on and finish my baths and meet him at Paris. Next morning, Saturday, September 30th, he left for England.[27]

I got to Paris on October 4th. There was a letter which I got next morning saying that everything was very difficult but that he hoped to get out from Saturday to Monday. Then the same tale came in each letter, – he couldn't leave. On Monday, the 9th, the tune changed – he was very worried – he was faced with difficult problems, etc. Next day, Tuesday, October 10th, his letter said, 'I wish I had you to consult but I don't want to cut short your holiday; do you like to finish it at Folkestone?' From that I gathered I was wanted and wired that I was coming straight back on Thursday; that left me a day to finish up in Paris. On Thursday, October 12th, I arrived at Victoria with my maid and was met by S. Sending the maid back with the luggage, I elected to walk home – it being quite near and a lovely evening. S. began, 'I have done something dreadful without consulting you – I do hope you won't mind. I have been fearfully worried, but I felt that it had to come. I am resigning from the Cabinet – I shall never get a job again. I do hope you won't mind fearfully, but I've said I cannot continue to serve under the G[oat] any longer. Do tell me what you think'. Then he proceeded to tell me how he had found out that W[inston Churchill] and L.G. had been all for war and had schemed to make this country go to war with Turkey so that they should have a 'Christian' (save the mark) war v. the Mahomedan and turn the Turks out of Europe. On the strength of that, they would call a General Election at once and go to the country which, they calculated, would return them to office for another period of years. I had hardly time to say 'You did right, quite right; I am absolutely with you,' when he continued, 'And then at a Cabinet meeting of Unionist Ministers it was decided to have the General Election and go to the country at once (without consulting any of the party) under the L.G. banner as Coalitionists. I arose and spoke and told them that I for one could not and would not do it. I must be free and stand as a Conservative; I could not serve under L.G. again.'[28] The rest

---

[27] He attended two emergency Cabinet meetings on Sunday, 1 October.

[28] *Crawford Papers*, pp. 449–50 (10 Oct. 1922), records Baldwin saying that 'Ll.G. was the albatross round our neck and we ought to get rid of him.'

of the Unionist Ministers were aghast and they were all apparently against me. The next meeting of the Unionist Cabinet Ministers Boscawen threw in his lot with me. Curzon was sympathetic, but that was all.[29] So there it is. They will follow the G. and I can't, so it means that I shall drop out of politics altogether'. Then we planned what we would do – how we would go abroad for the winter and probably not stand at the next General Election, or, if there was nobody else to carry on, stand at the next and then bid goodbye to politics and try and work for humanity instead. S. didn't seem depressed but merely as though a great weight had been lifted. He told me that Sir G.Y.[30] had called together a meeting of the National Unionist Council and that the Leader of the Party had called one for the following Thursday at the Carlton Club. Also how much S. had felt it breaking with his friends and Leader. S. also told me that W. had been to the B.o.T. to see him on business and had proceeded to harangue him upon the disloyalty of anyone daring to leave the P.M., all of which S. received without reply until W. said, 'There'll be some pretty mud slinging'; to which S. replied, 'That would be a pity, because some pretty big chunks could come from the other side'. I think that was about all that I heard on my way from the station and during the evening we planned about our holiday abroad that we thought was coming.

The next day S. was to see B.L.[31] and see if he would come out and lead the party. The result was not encouraging but B.L. agreed to see his doctor and see what he said and was to come and see S. on Tuesday with the verdict. Saturday S. worked with me at the Albemarle[32] ... and he told me that things were beginning to move and that the Under Secretaries thought of joining him and we were to give some of them tea that afternoon at 93 [Eaton Square]. We walked back buying cakes on the way as the household wasn't yet up and we were only camping there until they came. To tea there

---

[29] Lucy appears to have confused the sequence of events. Other sources have the next Unionist Cabinet ministers' meeting on 16 October, after her arrival in London. *Crawford Papers*, p. 451, records that 'Baldwin indicated pretty clearly that as Chamberlain won't abandon Lloyd George, he, Baldwin must abandon Chamberlain.'

[30] George Younger, the Unionist party chairman, a critic of his leader's decision to perpetuate the Coalition.

[31] Bonar Law, despite his retirement and ill-health, was the only senior Unionist apart from Chamberlain and other Coalition Cabinet ministers who was considered to have sufficient authority to form an alternative, Unionist, government.

[32] The Albemarle Club in Dover Street, used by Lucy because her own club was temporarily closed. Saturday was 14 October.

arrived Sir P.L-G., Colonel L. A.;[33] the latter's first words were 'Johnny[34] is lost – I can't find Johnny' which made us all laugh. I gave them all tea and left them to their talk. We went to the theatre that night to distract S.

Next day being Sunday we went to Brighton – S. very worried and he thought a walk on the downs would help him. On our return E.W. from 88[35] came in and talked. My Lord C[urzon] was getting very active on the telephone and kept ringing S. up. Once he was in his bath when Lord C. wished to speak to him, such an early bird was his lordship.

Monday, October 16th, Sir J.B[aird] arrived and was found at last; he had travelled all night from Scotland. S. was due at the Roumanian reception with me, but was too busy to come and so I went alone. S. hardly slept he was so worried. The telephone is getting active.

Tuesday, October 17th. A good deal of excitement seemed in the air and S. was rather depressed. Afternoon B.L. came to report on his visit to the doctor. After his departure S. came in to me and said, 'It's no go; B[onar] can't join us; he says that the doctor's verdict is bad but won't tell me what it is'. S. still depressed but cheered up when Sir J.B. came to dinner whose one anxiety seemed to be that S. shouldn't send in his resignation five minutes before he did. David[son] came in in the evening and put quite a different complexion on affairs. His report was that he had seen Aunt M.[36] who had seen B.'s doctor and said that the report was good and that he can work again and that was what depressed B. so much. He doesn't want to come and feels that duty calls. S. again had hardly any sleep, but was cheered next morning by hearing that B. and A. C[hamberlain] also had hardly slept. My Lord C. appears to be playing a sort of puss in the corner, to our amusement.

Wednesday, October 18th. Most agitating time. S. went off early with Sir J.B. and E.W. and later he and David were to see B[onar].S. told me that he and D. talked to him for three hours without moving him and that B. had

---

[33] Philip Lloyd-Greame (adopted surname Cunliffe-Lister 1924; Viscount Swinton 1935), secretary of the Overseas Trade Department, Board of Trade; President of the Board of Trade 1922–4, 1924–9; and Leo Amery, parliamentary secretary, Admiralty; First Lord 1922–4; Colonial Secretary 1924–9, also Dominions 1925–9.

[34] Sir John Baird (Lord Stonehaven, 1925), under-secretary, Home Office.

[35] Edward Wood (Lord Irwin 1925, 3rd Viscount Halifax 1934), Colonial under-secretary; President of the Board of Education 1922–4; Minister of Agriculture 1924–5. His London house was 88 Eaton Square.

[36] Mary Law, Bonar Law's sister.

written his letter of resignation to his chairman in Glasgow and was going
to retire from politics. S. left him with these words: 'Well, you are leaving all
the white men on the beach. They can't get on without you to lead and it
means we shall just all sink out of politics and we shall leave it to those who
are not as honest'. In the evening after dinner to which Sir J.B. came there
was a great gathering of Under Secretaries in the dining-room.[37] Some of
them had prepared a formula which they hoped would meet the case, but S.
didn't approve; he didn't think it quite straight and would have nothing of
it. Just before the assembly met David blew in very pleased and excited. He
had gone back to B. and tackled him again and said that S.'s parting words
had moved him somewhat about the white men on the beach and he had
got B. to promise to come to the Carlton meeting on the morrow.[38] Several
of us all talked together and then they moved off to the next room leaving
David and me and the telephone; we all did our share of conversation. Soon
after 11 I went to bed and S. came up about 12.30. He seemed happier and
David's optimism about our winning to-morrow had cheered him.

Thursday, October 19th. I had arranged with M[imi] D[avidson] to go
and sit outside the Carlton Club so that we should hear the verdict as soon
as possible. I did not tell S. as I thought that it would fuss him knowing
that I was outside; so I arranged that he was to ring me up as to the result.
Betty was too nervous and declined to come with me but stayed at home.
The morning was very long, and I walked and I walked and I walked to pass
the time and at 12.30 started to call for M.D., picked her up, and then we
waited with other cars in the side street by the Carlton which leads to Carlton
Gardens. Such a crowd outside the Carlton, – photographers, cinema men,
policemen among others. We were the only occupants of a car; all the others
were empty waiting for their owners. It was a most exciting time. We caught
sight of G[eoffrey] F[ry] and he came out and sat with us a little and then,
excitement needing action, he walked about, reporting to us every now and

---

[37] Other sources show that Younger, Wilson (the chief whip) and a backbench MP, Hoare, were
also present. Baldwin and Davidson played a large part in bringing together various dissentient
groups – junior ministers, party officials, Cabinet members and a gathering of 'typical' Conservative MPs, organised by Hoare: see *Amery Diaries*, I, pp. 294–5, 297, 299; Lord Templewood
[Hoare], *Empire of the Air* (1957), pp. 23–5, 28–30; Griffith-Boscawen memo. 'The break-up of
the Coalition'. Baldwin appears not to have had contact with other groups assembled by Lords
Long and Salisbury.
[38] Numerous Unionist politicians and some newspaper editors had urged Law to speak out
against the Coalition, and probably no one individual was decisive: see R. J. Q. Adams, *Bonar
Law* (1999), pp. 317–26.

again. Then Sy. – B.'s son-in-law,[39] joined us and the excitement grew more and more tense. It was now 1.30 and G.F. acknowledged to us that he had got people to luncheon, but he couldn't go so he telephoned his guests to begin without him. Opposite our car was stationed a rather unwholesome-looking Rolls Royce car with a smart but 'booky'[40] looking chauffeur and with a snake about to strike as its mascot. Suddenly there burst through the crowd a yellowish-white drawn face and the slight figure of a man appeared who jumped into his car and was off in a flash. 'P.S.[41] going to the P.M.', said M.D. clutching me, and at the same moment Sy. brought us news that the figures were 187–186. M.D. and I said in one breath, 'What's the good of that?' Then I saw Sir A. G-B[oscawen] hurrying away (afterwards I heard, to report to Lord C.) and I called to him and asked the figures. '186–187', he replied, and hurried off. Still we didn't know which was which. Then we saw David emerging with G.F. on one side and Sy. on the other, looking as though he was emerging from a football scrimmage, and he told us that our side had won by 99, and that B.L. had come down plump on our side and carried the room with him. A.C. spoke just announcing his action and S. replied, followed by those who proposed and seconded the motion, which was to stand as independent Tories, apart from the Coalition. Then B.L. spoke and A.J.B. = L.G.[42] but this latter seemed quite off the rails and made no impression, they said. Some, too, nailed their colours firmly to the fence and did not vote. I heard afterwards that the day before Sir L.W.[43] had approached A.C. with a deputation of 40 Members from different parts of the party, a representative gathering, and that they could not get him to listen and at one time threatened that he wouldn't come to the meeting. Luckily wiser counsels prevailed. But I hear that they expected to win and that the P.M. said he would win with A.J.B.! M.D. and I were nearly off our heads with excitement. I took her home to luncheon at 2 p.m. and heard that S. had already rung me up and that Betty had got the result. Next followed the resignations. S. sent in his at once,[44] followed by all the Under Secretaries

---

[39] Major-General Frederick Sykes, Controller General of Civil Aviation 1919–22; married Isabel Law 1920; Conservative MP 1922–8.

[40] I.e. 'bookie', a bookmaker, in a shifty, suspicious-looking, sense.

[41] Sir Philip Sassoon, Unionist MP but parliamentary private secretary to Lloyd George.

[42] I.e. Balfour spoke in favour of continued coalition with Lloyd George.

[43] Sir Laming Worthington-Evans, Secretary of State for War 1921–2; Postmaster-General 1923–4; War Secretary 1924–9.

[44] Lloyd George papers F/3/1/17: 'Dear Prime Minister,/ In the present circumstances I have no alternative but to place my resignation in your hands and to beg that you will communicate this

who had thrown in their lot with S. Later in the afternoon, according to the evening papers, all the rest of the Cabinet resigned and the P.M. went to see the King who had come up unexpectedly. Then B.L. was sent for, and asked to form a Government which he said he'd do. B.L. had to be appointed leader in place of A.C. resigned and so there was a big meeting at the Hotel Cecil [on 23 October] of all the Conservative party and B.L. was appointed leader. Lord C. proposed him for the Lords and S. for the Commons. The P.M. = B.L. set to work to form his Cabinet and offered the Exchequer to S., but S. had a feeling that he didn't want to make anything out of the bouleversement and said he thought McK.,[45] if he'd take it, would be the stronger and more experienced for the country, and so S. was empowered to ask McK. This latter was perfectly overpowered and asked for three days to think it over, but promising that if he didn't take it he would do all in his power to help S. Three days passed; evenings passed with visits from David and his wife, Sir J.B., all of us suggesting names for the future Cabinet. I was fortunate enough to name Lord C[ave] for the Woolsack; doubtless B.L. had thought of him before but I was pleased at the appointment being made and accepted.

On the third evening after the McK. invitation, he and B.L. met at 93, S. waiting until he was sent for and Betty and I in a fever upstairs. By and by S. walked into my room and said, 'Treat me with respect, I am the Chancellor of the Exchequer'. Then he told us what had happened. McK. had declined and had told S. he would give him all the help that he could in the City and he left. B.L. and S. talked for a little; then B.L. said, 'I must get home'. 'But,' said S., 'how about the Exchequer, am I to go there?' 'Why, of course' replied B.L., and that is how S. was asked to take that important post!

After the Carlton Club meeting Chamberlain, Balfour, Birkenhead, Horne, Worthington-Evans and eight other ministers expressed continued loyalty to Lloyd George, and declined to associate with a purely Unionist government. On 30 November, two weeks after Law's government had won the general election,

---

to His Majesty./ I should like to thank you for the personal consideration that you have always shown me.'
[45] Reginald McKenna, Liberal MP to 1918, Chancellor of the Exchequer 1915–16, Chairman of the Midland Bank from 1919. With both Treasury and City experience, he would command authority in dealing with the pressing issues of German reparations and inter-allied debts. He was *persona grata* with Unionist anti-coalitionists as originator of the 1915 'McKenna' protective duties, and as an opponent of Lloyd George.

a dinner of Chamberlain's 'friends' was attended by forty-nine Unionist MPs and seven peers. This 'Chamberlainite' or 'Coalition Unionist' separation from the government and official party leadership not only elevated Baldwin to senior Cabinet rank, but also had considerable effects on his political position over the next fifteen months.

On 23 October Baldwin commented to his mother that 'a fortnight ago I thought I was out of politics for good.[46] Such is the amazing whirligig./ It is a tremendous job but we shall have a loyal team and I am told that my appointment will be welcome in the City and the business world. All of which leaves me gasping.' Later he wrote that congratulation was 'the last thing to be offered to anyone who takes on this job at the present time. Still it is something to start with so much goodwill and I shall need it all. I am going to be very unpopular before I've done!/ . . . If I survive this Parliament I think I shall get out of it all and keep pigs and read the classics in my old age.'[47]

---

[46] See, similarly, to Buckmaster (Liberal Lord Chancellor, 1915–16), 26 Oct. 1923, in R. F. V. Heuston, *Lives of the Lord Chancellors 1885–1940* (Oxford, 1964), p. 294.
[47] To Constance Marshall, 11 Dec. 1923, Baldwin WCRO collection 8229/12(ii).

THREE

*

Chancellor and Prime Minister

OCTOBER 1922 – SEPTEMBER 1923

Baldwin was appointed Chancellor of the Exchequer on 24 October. His main tasks were to enforce further retrenchment on spending departments, to reduce the burden of taxation and to seek a re-scheduling of inter-government debts, which were contributing to an international economic recession. A crisis over German reparations produced a conference of allied Prime Ministers in London, at which Baldwin met the 'extraordinary Mussolini . . . I wonder how long he will last!',[1] and would lead in January 1923, after a default in German payments, to a French and Belgian occupation of the Ruhr. On 27 December Baldwin sailed for New York and Washington to negotiate a funding of the British government's war debts to the United States.

20 NOVEMBER 1922: CABINET MEMORANDUM

CP 4314, CAB 24/140

The Necessity for National Economy
Note by the Chancellor of the Exchequer

My colleagues, on taking office, will no doubt receive pressing applications for expenditure, in many cases on objects with which we should all sympathise.

I desire therefore to take the earliest opportunity to make clear that, without any new expenditure whatsoever and without any reduction in existing taxation, the problem of making next year's Budget balance will be one of supreme difficulty. So far from increased expenditure being incurred,

---

[1] To Beatrix Warrack (a cousin), 22 Dec. 1922, CUL MS Add. 8770.

very considerable reductions in existing expenditure over and above the reductions made last year and at present contemplated for 1923/24 will be necessary if we are to avoid increased taxation next year. Any appreciable addition to our expenditure will certainly mean a proportionate increase in the Income Tax.[2]

I only wished to add that, if the present tendency to improved trade continues, State borrowing e.g. to meet maturing short term debt will be increasingly difficult. Money taken for Government purposes is money taken away from trade and borrowing will thus tend to depress trade and increase unemployment.

S.B.

3 JANUARY 1923: TO JOAN DAVIDSON

Lady Davidson papers

S. S. Majestic

Little Maid,

... We are completing a record passage, the longest ever taken by this ship. On six days out of seven we have logged gales, from moderate gales to strong gales and whole gales, and all the time with head seas . . .

But with all that, it has been a wonderful rest and I feel as fit as a whole orchestra of fiddles.

. . . We have about half our complement of passengers: no one of note except Backhaus the pianist[3] who played gloriously for us on New Year's night. He gave us five Chopins, a wonderfully beautiful Schumann and two Liszts . . . I like him, he is entirely unaffected and free from pose . . .

Our party is very happy. The Griggs disappeared for three days or so: Betty ditto[4] . . . The Governor[5] like me has enjoyed the rest so much and looks pounds better already.

---

[2] In CP 4330, 1 Dec. 1922, Baldwin and his Treasury officials increased the pressure by stating their current estimate to be a budget deficit equivalent to an extra shilling on income tax.
[3] Wilhelm Backhaus, German-born, Professor at the Royal College of Music, Manchester.
[4] P. J. Grigg, Baldwin's Treasury private secretary, his wife, and Baldwin's youngest daughter Betty, all prostrated with sea-sickness.
[5] Montagu Norman, Governor of the Bank of England 1920–44, who became a close friend of Baldwin.

I haven't worried a bit: in fact I successfully dismissed all thoughts of work, but I am beginning to wonder now whether we shall have any luck. It would give such a fillip all round if we could bring off a decent deal.

I am anxious to get news of Paris[6] which I suppose I shall find waiting for me at Washington . . .

The debt negotiations were difficult, because the US Debt Commission proposed terms higher than Baldwin and the Cabinet had expected. Baldwin obtained some concessions and argued for the long-term benefits of financial stabilisation and Anglo-American co-operation. As he later wrote, 'If the English speaking peoples don't pull together now, western civilization will slide into the abyss.'[7] But Law, supported by McKenna, Keynes and a depleted Cabinet, wanted to reject the terms as too onerous, and asked Baldwin to return to London for consultation. After his return on 27 January, Baldwin persuaded most of the full Cabinet to accept his recommendation, even though Law threatened to resign as Prime Minister. Law was persuaded to stay, and Baldwin and his officials continued the negotiations from London, completing the debt settlement in July.

14 JANUARY 1923: TO LAW, TELEGRAM

CP 18(23), CAB 24/150 (extract); Jones *WD*, I. pp. 225–7[8]

. . . We feel very strongly that a settlement is well nigh essential and that without it we cannot expect improvement in general financial conditions. Any such improvement will presumably be preceded by a general economic conference and at this it is vital that we should not have to take a place amongst the ranks of defaulters.

Issue then is whether settlement now proposed is so burdensome as to outweigh all [the] disadvantages. In my opinion it is not. I have little doubt that Great Britain would not regard 33 million sterling yearly as being too high a price to escape appearing as a defaulter. This is annual payment for first ten years and it ought to be within our powers. The increase of 5 millions in ten years time is comparatively small and we have time to provide against

---

[6] Discussions on the Ruhr crisis.
[7] To Lord Midleton, 11 March 1923, Midleton papers PRO 30/67/26/1370, and see Baldwin's verdict in A. Fitzroy, *Memoirs* (2 vols., 1923), II, p. 794.
[8] The Jones volume has the full text, much of it technical and on US opinion; the extract here gives Baldwin's more general grounds for acceptance.

it.[9] Further, much may happen in ten years. What is quite certain is that if we fail to settle now not only American opinion but world opinion will question our willingness to pay with serious damage to our prestige.

All of us who are working here are convinced of necessity of settlement and I urge Cabinet to accept.

It appears to me in all the circumstances that honesty and expediency for once go hand in hand and I gravely fear lest trying for shadow we lose the bone.

16 MARCH 1923: CABINET MEMORANDUM

CP150(23), CAB 24/159

Note by the Chancellor of the Exchequer

After consultation with the Prime Minister, I circulate the draft of a letter which I propose should be sent from the Treasury to every Department of the Public Service on the question of financial procedure.[10] Those of my colleagues who have at any time been concerned with the management of a business will recognise that the proposed letter does no more than set out the A B C of business procedure; and my colleagues generally – whether they have been connected with private business or not – will, I am sure, agree with me that as trustees for the taxpayer a Cabinet has at all events no less a degree of responsibility than the Board of a Company has for its shareholders, and that at the present time there is no issue so vital to the strength and well-being of this country as the reduction of expenditure to a point which will enable its citizens to rebuild the financial reserves which proved the decisive factor in the winning of the European War.

S.B.

Baldwin announced his budget on 16 April. His warnings to colleagues on the need for retrenchment amply served their unstated purpose, of maximising an already substantial surplus. With expenditure considerably less than estimated, this £101.5 million surplus was applied to debt redemption. In order to assist further

---

[9] The terms were 3 per cent for ten years, 3½ per cent for a further forty-two years. £33 million is around £1,165 million in modern prices.

[10] The accompanying letter, drafted by officials, stated that no departmental proposal involving taxpayers' money would be submitted to the Cabinet until the Treasury had assessed its value for money, and ensured that the funds were available.

debt redemption and tax reduction, he also established a statutory sinking fund. Estimating a future surplus of £36 million, he reduced income tax, corporation tax, postal charges and beer, table water and cider duties. This combination of financial probity with tax reduction was widely praised, as much by Liberals as Unionists, and in much of the press.

*

Law's health had declined and in late April he took a long holiday in France, leaving Curzon as acting Prime Minister and Baldwin as acting leader of the House of Commons. By mid May Law had become so ill that he decided to resign. With the Chamberlainite leaders still outside the government, this left Curzon and Baldwin as the obvious alternatives to succeed him as Prime Minister – but Curzon was in the House of Lords. Law, reluctant to express any preference between them, wished to avoid being asked to offer formal advice on his successor. Instead, on Sunday 20 May he sent Waterhouse, his private secretary, and Sykes, his son-in-law, to deliver his letter of resignation to the King, who was at Aldershot with his own private secretary, Lord Stamfordham. The King's responsibility for choosing the Prime Minister raised constitutional issues, and his selection of Baldwin caused some surprise, given his short ministerial experience as compared to Curzon's. The controversy was revived in 1955 when Robert Blake revealed documents from the Royal Archives showing that Waterhouse had submitted an unsigned memorandum in Baldwin's favour, which he claimed expressed Law's views.[11] It has been established that the memorandum was written by Davidson, who as Law's parliamentary private secretary had accompanied him on his return from France.

Further details concerning Baldwin can be added from Joan Davidson's brief diary of the episode. Arriving in London on the evening of the 19th, Baldwin went to the Davidsons' club at 9.30, found Joan Davidson[12] (who thought him 'despondent') with Waterhouse and Fry. Baldwin left at 10.15 p.m. to join Davidson at 10 Downing Street, and Amery arrived soon after. Discussion continued until the early hours. On the 20th Baldwin went for breakfast at the Davidsons' house 'in excellent form. Very cheery & amusing.' At 10 a.m. Davidson 'dashed to No. 10 to prepare a memorandum for H.M.[His Majesty]',[13] while Baldwin saw Law at

---

[11] The memorandum is printed in R. Blake, *The Unknown Prime Minister* (1955), pp. 520–1; M&B, pp. 163–4; and *Davidson Memoirs*, pp. 154–5.

[12] Not Davidson himself, as stated in *Davidson Memoirs*, p. 152.

[13] A. J. Sylvester, another Downing Street private secretary who shared a room with Davidson and Waterhouse, recalled in 1971 that he had witnessed Waterhouse being consulted as Davidson wrote the memorandum, and that he himself typed it in their presence, keeping his own copy: memo, Sylvester papers B15. Neither Joan Davidson's account nor Sylvester's gives credence to suggestions that Amery was a co-author.

10.30 before catching the noon train to Chequers.[14] In the evening, after Sykes and Waterhouse had returned from Aldershot, Waterhouse reported to Davidson and his wife: 'results excellent'. After Sykes had handed Law's resignation to the King, Waterhouse 'had long interview. Memorandum of great use & King agreed to SB.'[15]

At the very least, this evidence suggests that Baldwin was aware that a memorandum was being composed in his interest. There is, however, no indication that Davidson (or Baldwin) knew that Waterhouse would, or had, presented it as a statement of Law's views. Nor is it certain that the memorandum or Waterhouse's comments were decisive. The King and Stamfordham had their own views, and collected further advice. Joan Davidson noted that Waterhouse's report had included a caveat, that the King 'first wished to see Lord Salisbury', a senior Unionist peer and Lord President of the Council. Salisbury, actually interviewed by Stamfordham on Monday 21st, recommended Curzon; but the King himself consulted Balfour as a former Unionist Prime Minister, and he recommended Baldwin. It appears that the King did not make his decision until late that Monday afternoon.[16] The grounds of his choice were probably those stated or, most likely, reinforced by Balfour: that a Prime Minister in the House of Lords, where the Labour party had no representative, would provoke constitutional and political controversy; and that Curzon's egotism and arrogance had made him unpopular even among his Cabinet colleagues.[17]

Baldwin had 'heard nothing' on Monday afternoon, when the Davidsons arrived at Chequers. But he was summoned back to London for a meeting with Stamfordham on Tuesday, 22 May.

22 MAY 1923 STAMFORDHAM MEMORANDUM

RA PS/GV/K.1853/17 (extract)[18]

. . . at about 10.30 a.m., I saw Mr Baldwin by appointment.

We agreed to be perfectly frank with each other. I told him of the King's difficulties and asked him, if His Majesty were to entrust him with the

---

[14] Baldwin had the use of Chequers, because Law as Prime Minister declined to occupy it.
[15] The last three words were later deleted, and replaced with the words 'while expressing no opinion left no doubt that PM must be in Commons'.
[16] Dawson diary, 21 May 1923, in J. E. Wrench, *Geoffrey Dawson and Our Times* (1953), p. 217, reports Stamfordham receiving a telephone call from the King announcing his decision.
[17] Stamfordham to Balfour, 25 May 1923, Balfour Whittingehame papers GD 433/2/1/48, reported the King's 'satisfaction' that Balfour had 'confirmed his opinion that, at all events in the present circumstances, the Prime Minister . . . should be in the House of Commons'.
[18] The first part of the memo, an interview with Waterhouse about Law's views, is printed in Blake, *Unknown Prime Minister*, p. 523.

carrying on of the Government, whether he would be prepared to retain Lord Curzon as Foreign Minister. His reply was – that he would welcome such an arrangement, but that he had been told that Lord Curzon had declared that he would not be able to serve under him, Mr Baldwin. We discussed various possibilities, always, of course, subject to his being sent for by the King. Mr Baldwin said he could not continue to be Chancellor of the Exchequer as well as Prime Minister and would try to secure the return of Sir Robert Horne for that office. If Lord Curzon resigned he should then hope to induce Mr Austen Chamberlain to return to the Party to fill that office, failing him perhaps Lord Robert Cecil. He also, in strict confidence, said that he thought it would be necessary to have the Secretary of State for the Colonies in the House of Commons as the work in that office would this year not only include the Dominions but the Dominion conference, in addition to South Ireland and Mesopotamia.[19] But this was all contingent upon events.

The only colleagues he had seen were Mr Bridgeman[20] and Mr Amery, both of whom said they should like the offer of the Premiership to be made to Lord Curzon, if they felt certain he would refuse it! Speaking for himself, Mr Baldwin said that I did not know him intimately, but asked me to believe that he had no ambition to be Prime Minister: he would, of course, have gladly served under Lord Curzon, he loved his present job and would have liked to continue it under a Prime Minister in the Commons.

Our interview was most pleasant and reassuring.

Later that day, the King appointed Baldwin Prime Minister. On the 28th a meeting of Unionist MPs and peers elected him as party leader. He was fifty-six years old.

22 MAY 1923: TO LOUISA BALDWIN

10, Downing Street, Whitehall

Dearest Mother,

My first letter shall be to you.

Prayers and not congratulations for anyone called to this particular post.[21]

---

[19] In the event the Duke of Devonshire remained at the Colonial Office.
[20] Home Secretary 1922–4; First Lord of the Admiralty 1924–9.
[21] He had just said to journalists as he returned from the Palace that 'I need your prayers more than your congratulations', a phrase which received much newspaper comment.

The King was very friendly but worried by Curzon's grief at being passed over. I don't think he'll serve with me. Anyway, I shall have a couple of busy days trying to form a government, and I hope to get it completed by Friday.

Much love from your devoted/ Son

I am not a bit excited and don't realise it in the least.

22 MAY 1923: TO LORD CURZON

Curzon papers F112/320

<u>Private & Confidential</u>   11, Downing Street, Whitehall, S. W.

My dear Curzon,

I hope, both on personal and public grounds, that you will feel able to continue your great work at the Foreign Office in the new administration.

There never was a time when foreign affairs caused more anxiety than they do at present, and your unrivalled experience is to-day one of the greatest assets of the Empire.

Yours very sincerely,/ Stanley Baldwin

Curzon decided to remain, but Horne refused the Chancellorship of the Exchequer. Baldwin again offered the post to McKenna, who reported his doctor's verdict that he needed three months to convalesce from a recent illness. Baldwin decided to wait, in the meantime remaining Chancellor as well as Prime Minister. A personal complication arose when Joan Davidson became 'distressed & furious' and spoke angrily to Baldwin, because she mistakenly thought he was not going to appoint her husband to a ministerial post. After Davidson was appointed Chancellor of the Duchy of Lancaster on the 25th,[22] she wrote an apology.

25 MAY 1923: TO JOAN DAVIDSON

Lady Davidson papers

10, Downing Street

Little Maid, always beloved,

Don't worry. I did wish you hadn't said one or two things you did because I love you so much that I can't bear to see you slip even for a moment from the high pinnacle on which I always keep you.

---

[22] Joan Davidson diary, May 1923, suggesting this was the office he had wanted. He was not given Cabinet rank (and never received this status).

But, foolish though I am in many things, in public things NO ONE could move me if I thought the course desired was wrong. And I felt you might have known it!

But never for a shadow of a second did it make my affection waver.

And it is all forgotten except your dear letter.

Your loving/ S.B.

One purpose in appointing Horne would have been to advance reunion with the Chamberlainites, but they had agreed not to take office individually. Baldwin did not want them returning as a group and he was embarrassed about Chamberlain himself. He was owed respect, yet so soon after the leadership split he would have been an awkward colleague and he was unwanted by other Cabinet ministers. Baldwin decided that the best tactic was to speak candidly with him, and to offer him something in consolation. The outcome was an excruciating interview between a deposed and resentful party leader and his former junior minister, whose rebellion had now brought him to the premiership.

27 MAY 1923 AUSTEN CHAMBERLAIN MEMORANDUM

AC 35/2/11b; partly in C. Petrie, *The Life and Letters of Sir Austen Chamberlain* (1940), II, pp. 220–3

I reached Chequers at 4 o'clock [on 26 May] and was met at the door by Baldwin who was on the look out for me. He welcomed me cordially and I at once said that he and I were old friends and were friends even when we differed. He interjected, 'Yes, and are friends still.' I replied, 'Yes, and are friends still. And it is therefore easy for me to offer you personal congratulations on your appointment as Prime Minister and leader.' He then took me into his room and almost at once turned to business. He said he wished to tell me exactly what had happened. He had no idea how serious Bonar Law's illness was until summoned to town on Saturday, the 19th, to meet Davidson and Waterhouse on their return with Bonar Law. They told him the situation late that night. He saw Bonar Law the next morning. Bonar Law told him that he was resigning at once by letter and that he should make no recommendation as to his successor. It was not till Tuesday that Stanley knew for certain that the King would send for him. He could then do nothing until he had ascertained Curzon's intentions. He knew that the choice of himself had been a very severe blow to Curzon and that Curzon took it very hard. He did not therefore like to go and see him, but he wrote him a short note asking him to continue in office and giving reasons why he should do so. If Curzon declined it had been his intention to offer me the Foreign Secretaryship which he thought was an office that it might have been agreeable to me to accept. He heard nothing from Curzon till lunch-time on Wednesday, when Curzon's acceptance reached him and thus put that particular proposal in regard to me out of the question. He still wished to offer me a suitable position, but on consulting some of his colleagues he found that two or three would resign if I were admitted at the present time. He had done his best at repeated interviews to change their opinion but he had found it impossible to do so and he had felt that he could not quarrel with men who had 'joined the boat when it was a very ricketty thing.' He had therefore sent for Horne on Thursday morning and had seen him again that afternoon. It being, for the reasons which he had explained, impossible to make me any offer, Horne had refused[23] and he had then approached McKenna at 9.30 o'clock on Thursday evening. He was anxious to make it clear that he had not thought of McKenna until after Horne had refused. That was the history of the week as given to me by Baldwin and exactly agreed with what I had learned from other sources.

Baldwin then with considerable hesitation and, I think, choosing his words rather carefully, said he wanted to ask me a question – he did not want an immediate answer but he wanted me 'to have it in my mind'. If the position changed and he was able – say in three months' time – to offer me office would I then be willing to accept? And there was another question which he wished to put, to which again he did not want an immediate answer, but he would like me to think it over and perhaps at some future date we might discuss it again. The Washington Embassy was shortly to be vacant. There was no position of greater consequence to the British Empire and it was a very difficult one to fill, because not only must the man have the necessary qualifications but the qualifications of the wife were equally important. He thought that I was admirably suited for the post: that my appointment would be most acceptable to the Americans and Mrs Chamberlain would be a perfect Ambassadress.

---

[23] Horne to Baldwin, 25 May 1923, Baldwin papers 42/29-30, gave his new business commitments as the ostensible reason.

He repeated that he did not ask for any answer now but would like me to think this over.

I asked him if he had mentioned this idea to Curzon. He replied in the affirmative. I said that I supposed Curzon had told him that I had already refused it. He replied that Curzon had not done so. I said I thought that Curzon ought not to have left him in ignorance of what had passed and I should like to tell him. After resignation of the Secretaryship for India I had been offered the Paris Embassy which I believed was considered the best diplomatic appointment and had declined it because I was unwilling to abandon a parliamentary career. When Chancellor of the Exchequer I had been urgently pressed to accept the Viceroyalty of India. That tempted me because of the special interest I had felt in India since serving at the India Office – but I had refused it because of my children. And then later whilst still holding office as Chancellor of the Exchequer, when there was no idea in the minds of any of us that Bonar's active life would not be at least as long as mine, I had been offered the Embassy at Washington – not in terms, because, as Curzon explained to me, he did not wish it to be said that it had been offered to and refused by anyone, and that he would therefore put the enquiry in this form – if you are asked to accept it would you do so, and he had urged the same reasons for acceptance as Baldwin had just given. You will see, therefore, I said that when I was holding office, when I could have accepted with perfect honour without any reflection upon the Government which made the offer to me or on myself for accepting, I declined. I am not very easily made angry, but when I heard, as I did from my colleagues that you intended to make me this offer, I frankly say that I lost my temper. You have made it, however, with such consideration and with such evident good-will and sincerity that I cannot be angry with you now. But of course I refuse absolutely, and that not only because having given the best years of my life to Parliament I am not prepared to take up an appointment abroad, but because it would neither be to your credit nor to mine that the offer should be made or accepted. You would have the appearance of trying to buy off possible opposition and I of accepting a fat salary as compensation for the discourtesy shown to me.

Baldwin repeated that he had known nothing of my previous refusal of the Embassies, but he would at once withdraw the proposal – let us treat it as not having been made. But he rather naively went on to explain that whether he could carry on and make a success of the job or not, he was now Prime Minister: that he was a younger man than I: that if he succeeded, then he blocked my path and he had thought perhaps that under those circumstances I should like a diplomatic appointment! It is perhaps to my credit that I did not lose my temper again.

I then turned to his question about my contingent willingness to accept office in the future. I said I was sorry that he had put that question. It was not a question that I could answer, and, indeed it was not a suggestion that [he] ought to have made. What assurance could he have that the obstacles which he had been unable to overcome at the present time would not be equally strong three months hence? He interjected that he would tell me why he thought the position would be changed, but I said that I did not wish to know, for, as I had already said, I was sorry that he had even put the question to me. I was not prepared to be treated as a boy on probation who was told that if he behaved well he might get a remove next term or to have a bundle of carrots dangled before my nose to induce me to gallop. I intimated that any approach on those lines was offensive. It could only alienate me and drive me into opposition. He at once disclaimed any such idea, to which I replied that this was exactly what was being said by a section of his supporters and by some of his colleagues. He said not by his colleagues, who were the only people for whom he cared. I replied that I thought it represented the views of some of his colleagues – say the three who had vetoed his intention to offer me office. He again demurred and insisted on giving his reason for thinking that the situation would be changed. Their objection to me had been that at the present moment difficult questions in connection with the Irish settlement were just coming up and that I had been too closely associated with that settlement to permit of my admission to the Government at this moment in view of the strong feelings of Irish loyalists. I replied that it was not for me to measure my services or claims or qualifications against those of the colleagues whose veto he had felt unable to disregard, but that the situation being what it was, it was impossible that I should give any sort of answer as to what my position might be three months hence in circumstances which neither he nor I could at present foresee. I could however tell him that as far as I was concerned my position and attitude were at present unchanged. I had deliberately gone away in order that I might not be a source of embarrassment to Bonar Law or to the Government in their early days. I had always intended when I returned to resume my place in Parliament and to take my part in their discussions as an independent member of the party. There was a new Prime Minister and Leader of the party – that was the only change and it did not affect my attitude or intentions.

I then turned to the general question. I said to him, My dear Stanley, why didn't you send for me? If you wanted to offer me office with some of my colleagues in order to restore the unity of the party, why didn't you ask me to come and see you? I had gone to Paris in order to be readily available. I should have come at once at any moment if you had sent for me, and I think agreement might have been secured. He said that, as he had explained to me, this was what he wanted to do but had been prevented from doing by the resistance of colleagues. I continued, But even so, Stanley, why didn't you send for me – we are old friends. You could have talked to me with the same frankness that you have shown to-day. You could have explained your difficulty and made your appeal to me to help you with my colleagues. I can tell you that there would have been no insistence by any of them on personal claims – as it was, I had set them free as far as lay in my power from any sense of obligation to myself; but Horne had refused without consultation with me before I knew anything of what was passing. Suppose, I said, the position had been reversed and I had tried to secure your services whilst excluding Bonar Law and without communicating with him. You know you would not have accepted. No man of honour could. How could you think that Horne would do differently? Why, my dear Stanley, why didn't you send for me?

The Prime Minister twice repeated slowly and, as I thought, sadly, 'I am very sorry. I never thought of it'.

It was then that he said that he would like to make clear to me that he had not thought of McKenna till after Horne had refused: that I perhaps knew that McKenna had been offered the position last November at his (Baldwin's) request, he being of opinion that McKenna's combination of Treasury and City experience was exactly what was required in the post when they came to the question of Reparations and Debts: that the idea had therefore recurred to him upon receiving Horne's refusal to serve. I said that I should not have mentioned this matter at all if he had not done so, but that I could not help feeling there was a certain humour in the attitude of his Government who were so jealous for the purity of the Conservative faith that they proscribed me and accepted McKenna. Might I ask him, however, what McKenna's attitude on fiscal questions now was? For instance, Amery had been indicating publicly and privately that he hoped as a result of the Imperial Economic Conference in the autumn for a great advance in Imperial Preference. Was McKenna prepared for that? The Prime Minister said that anything of the kind was precluded by Bonar Law's election address.[24] I said I was sorry to hear it, but if that was so, what was McKenna's attitude on the existing Preference? Was he prepared to maintain it? What was his attitude on the Safeguarding of Industries Bill – did he accept it? And though the question might seem an absurd one, what was his attitude on the 'McKenna duties'? The Prime Minister replied that he really had not thought about any of these matters and he did not know what view McKenna would take. There were obviously a great number of questions which he would have to go into with McKenna before he finally accepted the Chancellorship.[25] I said that I understood that he had already definitely accepted (subject to the restoration of his health) and that his acceptance had been officially announced from Downing Street. Baldwin seemed surprised, asked 'Is that so'? and gave me the impression that he had not seen the terms of the announcement.

The Prime Minister then asked whether I thought that if the offer of the Chancellorship were repeated to Horne in three months' time he would then accept. I replied that that was a question that I was absolutely unable to answer. Nobody could answer except Horne, and I doubted whether Horne himself could answer it in advance. But, I said, I will tell you my attitude in regard to your offer to Worthy.[26] He has not answered you and I don't know what his answer is going to be. I have made it clear to Worthington that I do not wish him to refuse on my account if he thinks it right to accept, but I say to you, Stanley, what I have not said to Worthington – that if I could eliminate myself from the question and give my advice to Worthington as a friend, I should tell him not to accept; for, if he now goes in alone after all that has passed you will have no respect for him and he will lose all credit

[24] Actually statements made in election speeches, most clearly on 7 Nov. 1922: 'this Parliament will not make any fundamental change in the fiscal system of this country'.
[25] McKenna to Reading, 30 May 1923, Reading papers F118/97, does indicate some understanding with Baldwin: 'If and when the arrangement is completed I shall think of myself as no more than a technical man called in to do a job of work. Happily Free Trade cannot become an issue, as Bonar Law's pledge put it out of the question during the present Parliament.'
[26] Worthington-Evans, who became Postmaster-General with a Cabinet seat on 28 May.

with others. I cannot answer your question about Horne but I have told you that as an indication of the way my mind works. To this he made no reply.

Before leaving I told him that there was one charge which was being made against me in certain quarters against which I was entitled to protect myself, namely, the charge that I had declined to co-operate in endeavouring to restore unity. There was a second charge against which I was entitled to protest and must protect both myself and my friends. It was that we had adopted the attitude of 'all or none' and declined any participation unless we were all restored to our old posts. He knew that both these statements were unfounded and I proposed to make an early statement on the subject, probably in the form of a letter to my Association.

The interview had lasted about an hour and a half. It had been conducted throughout, as any such talk between old friends should be, with the utmost candour and good temper and we parted most cordially. I was left with the impression that Baldwin sincerely regretted that he had not communicated with me at once, even if he had felt unable to invite me to join his Ministry.

Baldwin began his premiership with evident determination to establish a new tone in Unionist politics, and to address what he considered to be the outstanding policy problem – the Ruhr crisis, which from being a dispute about reparations had caused a general disruption of European trade and finance. The Cabinet was divided over whether the French or the German government was more to blame, but most ministers agreed in preferring a more conciliatory manner towards the French than that adopted by Curzon.

30 MAY 1923 C. P. TREVELYAN TO ARTHUR PONSONBY[27]

Ponsonby papers, Ms Eng.Hist.*c*.668/119–20 (extract)

... I think Baldwin is an improvement upon Bonar Law. I had a talk with him yesterday, when he was surprisingly frank. Of course he knows my views well. The things he said were as follows.

---

[27] Both former Liberal MPs, now Labour MPs. Trevelyan, as another old Harrovian, had become friendly with Baldwin while a prewar junior minister.

That he was going to try and settle Europe, though he failed and failed
   again.[28]

That he had hopes of avoiding the breach with Russia.

That he regarded the stabilizing of the German mark as of the first importance, though it might lead to an irresistible protectionist outcry
   here.

That the French papers were receiving him well, but that he didn't know
   how long that would go on.

That he was trying to get McKenna to help him for the sake of dealing
   with Europe.

That it wasn't worth being P.M. except to do something of the kind.

Very frank and well-intentioned! He shall have his due from us where he
does well.

17 JUNE 1923 GEOFFREY DAWSON[29] MEMORANDUM

Dawson papers 70/16–23; partly in Wrench, *Dawson*, pp. 218–19

An afternoon with the Prime Minister at Chequers, motoring over on my
way from Oxford, where I'd seen him the night before & suggested a talk.
No other man there – John Baird was out golfing – so I had him to myself
4–6, & sat & walked about the garden discussing all sorts of things & people.
I set down some of them –

The Ruhr. No news from France & no hurry for it. B. was obviously not
very hopeful & was thinking of the next stage in case of a breakdown. He was
inclined for a public statement of British policy & a subsequent attempt to
get other adherents to it. He was prepared to speak plainly to Poincaré,[30] but
saw no real settlement without France. Curzon was with him over this, but
was difficult generally – scrapping with R. Cecil & exchanging long letters w.
him.[31] Would he go? C. had talked of just seeing Lausanne[32] through, but he
doubted this limit. It might come to a row between C. & himself. What then?

[28] 'Europe' in the sense of Franco-German relations. See also Jones *WD*, I, pp. 237–8 (28 May 1923); *NC Letters*, II, pp. 167, 168 (16, 24 June 1923).
[29] Editor of *The Times* 1912–19, 1923–41, who became a confidant of Baldwin.
[30] French Prime Minister and foreign minister 1922–4.
[31] As a founder of the League of Nations, Cecil on being made Lord Privy Seal in May 1923 considered he had ministerial interests in foreign policy. He was president of the British League of Nations Union 1923–45.
[32] The Lausanne Treaty of 24 July settled the Near East problem.

He was disposed to try for Grey, whom he'd seen twice lately.[33] How would the public take that? McKenna too. A seat must be found for him. He could still get a peerage for Banbury, whose reluctance to budge was probably not final.[34]

Wanted also to do something for Austen – on general grounds of reconciliation. He agreed with me that it was of no importance from the personal point of view & recent events had convinced him of A.'s essential stupidity & narrowness. Would he do as Viceroy? He would have none of Washington – who should go to W, where there was likely to be a vacancy? It was exceedingly important to find a good man – & a lady. I asked if he'd thought of Eustace Percy,[35] who'd shown himself popular there & a 'mixer' & had a charming wife.

Birkenhead must be kept at a distance. A good platform man, said Garvin.[36] Yes, but his speeches from the platform swelled the Labour Party every time. He wouldn't do for India – nor Winston (this à propos my suggestion that the Viceroy needed a spark of imagination). Nothing had ever impressed him so much as Winston's reckless determination last autumn to plunge into war with Turkey. We discussed George Lloyd. I said Egypt for him, & he agreed that Allenby was now the wrong man.[37]

This led to S. Africa, which he hadn't considered. I gave him an account of Smuts. He admitted that he knew little of the Dominions & was sorry the autumn Conference was inevitable. What he'd heard of Bruce of Australia had impressed him (a man who'd rowed in the Cambridge boat!).

Of the younger men in Parl[t] he thought well of Billy Gore & very highly of Edward Wood. Joynson-Hicks was doing well, but he hankered after

---

[33] Viscount Grey, like other Asquithian Liberal leaders, had been publicly friendly towards Baldwin's appointment: see his speech in *The Times*, 1 June 1923.

[34] See Baldwin's later recollection: 'McKenna naturally didn't want to be hunting for a seat all over the country and wanted the City. Banbury, the senior member, wouldn't give up his seat on any terms. Nor would the other member [Grenfell] . . . I, of course, had not the authority that I acquired with time, and my efforts proved fruitless . . . I have no recollection of "party feeling" playing any part. Old Banbury, who was always a good friend of mine, was the last man who would make room for anybody else!': to Jones, 13 Sept. 1943, Jones papers A6/202. Banbury did accept a peerage in January 1924.

[35] Parliamentary secretary, Ministry of Health, but with earlier diplomatic service in the USA. Sir Esme Howard became ambassador in the USA in February 1924.

[36] Editor of *The Observer* 1908–42.

[37] Lloyd replaced Allenby as High Commissioner for Egypt and the Sudan in 1925.

Jack Hills.[38] Of the Lloyd Georgians he was watching Hilton Young & Ned Grigg.[39] L.G. himself he regarded as a real corrupter of public life & couldn't understand the spell. Like me he could no longer see him coming back quickly, as Bonar apparently predicted.

He was anxious about Cave's illness. If it led to his withdrawal he meant to take Sterndale, Master of the Rolls – a good man and old, which was an advantage.

We discussed oratory & 'first-class brains', for both of which he expressed great contempt. Altogether an interesting & extremely frank talk. I left him puddling off over the fields with Mrs B. to Ellesborough Church . . .

24 JUNE 1923: TO SIR BASIL BLACKETT[40]

Blackett papers E397/20

[Chequers]

My dear Blackett,

. . . I think that it was the best Budget we could manage in the circumstances: risky for next year, perhaps. But we should have had great difficulty in getting our Sinking Fund in if we had done less.

. . . I will go into the India Office question myself before long. I realise what a devil of a time you have had but you must carry on as I am trying to do, and you will win through. And if we are broken, we'll get broken in a good cause.

McKenna has had a very satisfactory talk with [Montagu] Norman: I don't anticipate any difficulty there. I wanted him for Reparations and Economy, the two things that matter in the immediate future . . .

Forgive such a scribble. I have had over a thousand letters, and I can't help trying to answer a number of them myself, but I haven't much time and I feel the result is a scrappy kind of note of little interest except to shew that I cling to all my old friends.

---

[38] William Ormsby-Gore, colonial under-secretary; Wood, now President of the Board of Education; William Joynson-Hicks, Financial Secretary of the Treasury, the post which Hills had earlier held under Baldwin.
[39] Liberal MPs who both became Conservatives, Hilton Young in 1926, Edward Grigg in 1933.
[40] Controller of Finance in the Treasury 1919–22, now Finance Member of the Viceroy of India's Council.

All good be with you and don't hesitate to write to me directly or through Fisher[41] if troubles seem to be meeting over your head.

Yours very sincerely/ Stanley Baldwin

9 JULY 1923: TO LOUISA BALDWIN

Dearest Mother,

. . . The work goes on, one week like another, and pretty incessant till Friday night, and then the break which gives one time to get one's breath again. So far, I am thankful to say, it is not too heavy. Of course there are things that cause anxiety, but I don't worry. The French settlement is the most difficult and that worried Bonar frightfully.

. . . There are only four more parliamentary weeks, which is good to think of. I shall want a few days of complete rest and shall try and get them at home. But I am never sanguine of being left alone there. When you are at the beck and call of everyone for 14 hours a day for four days and for eight hours on the fifth day each week, you want a short space in which you relax and do just what you like . . .

Much love from thy ever loving/ Son

25 JULY 1923 SIR DONALD MACLEAN MEMORANDUM

Maclean papers, MS Dep c.467/52–4

On June 28th I went to the Prime Minister's room at the House of Commons to have a chat in accordance with a previous arrangement made at the dinner of the Aliens Internment Committee.[42] After a few interchanges of reminiscences, S.B. said that he would like to give me an account of the more important steps which led to his being Prime Minister.

He reminded me of a conversation we had in July of last year when he offered the then Prime Minister his resignation. The chief reason was

---

[41] Sir Warren Fisher, permanent secretary at the Treasury, 1919–39.

[42] Maclean had served with Baldwin on this committee, and was among the Asquithian Liberal MPs who publicly welcomed his appointment as Prime Minister. See to Maclean, 16 June 1923, Maclean papers c.467/50, replying to his congratulations: 'You and I sit on opposite sides but there are many of the fundamental things we hold in common, and the day I forfeit your respect I know I should lose my own'.

S.B.'s insistence on the putting into force of the Safeguarding of Industries Act in opposition to the desire of L.G. to sidetrack an unpopular measure. S.B. went to the continent with his wife for a prolonged holiday and was summoned back by a telegram from A.C[hamberlain] in September. He returned to London thinking that some domestic difficulty had arisen with L.G. but found that the summons was in connection with the acute situation at Chanak. S.B. at once joined the Peace Party in the Cabinet. It also became clear that a substantial if not a dominant motive in connection with the endeavour to secure a declaration of War against Turkey was the opportunity it gave for a Khaki election in October. This, he added, decided him never to be again associated in Government with L.G., W.C[hurchill]., and Birkenhead who were the trio responsible for the project.

After the danger of War had subsided he, S.B., heard that that it was proposed to go to the country as a Coalition in October. On this he decided, although, in his own words, 'Not in the Inner Ring, but only a minor member of the Cabinet', to insist that this step should not be taken without the full consent of the Conservative Party. He spoke to A.C. and informed him that in his opinion a meeting of the Conservative members of the Cabinet should be called forthwith. After some difficulty this was agreed to. The meeting was accordingly held at which S.B. at the outset stood alone in the view he took. The first member of the Cabinet to adopt this position was G. B[oscawen]. and the numbers were soon added to, so much so that A.C. offered a meeting at the Carlton Club but would not consent to a meeting of the National Conservative Union. This meeting at the Carlton was regarded as a 'soft' option, as many Members were away; many of the most powerful of the restive section of the Party would be excluded and it was thought that the great majority of those likely to attend would stand by the existing order. The most that S.B. hoped for was that there would be a substantial minority against going to the country as a Coalition and when he entered the Club he had not the slightest idea of the ultimate result.

Bonar Law was undecided up to the last moment as to whether he would intervene or not. It was only after S.B. had been speaking for a few minutes that he realised the strength of opinion which was behind the line, which with much reluctance, he had decided to take.

He told me that during the discussions between himself and A.C. he had asked his wife to come from Aix to Paris to meet him in order to tell her that in his view his career in office was about to terminate and that there was no course open to him but to go to the back benches again. Indeed, he then contemplated a retirement altogether from political life, but thought that loyalty to the Party for the present was an obstacle to this.

We had some more conversation, in which I expressed the view that circumstances showed clearly that he had been led to his present position by single-minded devotion to honour and to duty, and men and women of good will throughout the country, irrespective of Party, wished him well in his difficult task.

A deterioration in Anglo-French relations brought criticism from Chamberlainites and some of the conservative press, as well as the opposition parties. The hostility of the Beaverbrook and Rothermere newspapers was sharpened by their owners' resentment at Baldwin's refusal to acknowledge their personal political influence. 'We are having a great attack on us from the gutter press (Daily Mail and Express) but I don't mind it one little bit./ All in a day's work.'[43] In mid August he decided to attempt to break the deadlock over the Ruhr by seeking a meeting with Poincaré.

10 AUGUST 1923: TO LORD DERBY[44]

typescript copy, SB papers 127/124

My dear Derby,

The draft note[45] of which you have a copy was toned down in many places, and finally agreed to at the Cabinet. Various reasons made it necessary to get it published quickly. I will not go into them in case this letter is opened, but L.G. and his friends are displaying considerable activity in conjunction with some of our old Unionist friends, not forgetting Rothermere, Hulton[46] and the Beaver. They are like submarines eager to discharge their torpedoes, but unknown to them their wash is apparent!

---

[43] To Louisa Baldwin, 8 Aug. 1923.
[44] Secretary of State for War, as a former ambassador to Paris a critic of Curzon's combative attitude towards the French government.
[45] A stern Curzon reply to French and Belgian government notes insisting on maintaining their occupation of the Ruhr.
[46] Owner of a newspaper chain including *The Daily Sketch* and *Evening Standard*.

Our note makes the financial position very clear: and though anger may be the first experience in Paris, I cling to a faint hope that common sense may follow.

At any rate the English position is set out clear for all to read, and if the English people don't like it —[47]

I hope you are enjoying yourself.

Yours ever/ S.B.

19 AUGUST 1923: TO JOAN DAVIDSON

Lady Davidson papers

Astley Hall

Little Maid,

It seems months since we parted, and the House of Commons seems to belong to a former stage of existence. I have been up and down [to London] three times, and on Friday night . . . I had H. A. Gwynne[48] to dinner at the old University [Club].

I've had a quietly happy time and not worried, though I have the Ruhr on my mind. That is, whenever my mind is vacant, it pops in. It has a way of joining me last thing at night, and being with me first thing in the morning. I brought Tyrrell down here last Tuesday evening for our Flower Show which he enjoyed immensely.[49] So did my policemen. The big man, whose name is Ashley, pulled in a tug-of-war and was on the winning side . . .

Tell David I had a good letter from McKenna, to be published with the new appointments. I have offered N.C. [Neville Chamberlain] the Exchequer but haven't yet had his reply.[50]

. . . I shall go to town probably Wednesday. I had a long talk with Barlow on Friday about unemployment and I have asked Worthy to call his committee together next week.[51]

---

[47] *Sic:* just a dash.
[48] Editor of *The Morning Post* 1911–37, with whom Baldwin had been acquainted before the war. He was a severe critic of Curzon's policy towards France.
[49] Assistant under-secretary, Foreign Office, actually brought to Astley to discuss the Ruhr crisis.
[50] McKenna had finally withdrawn. Chamberlain at first declined the offer, but Baldwin successfully persisted: *NC Letters*, II, pp. 177–9 (26 Aug. 1924) is a good example of his persuasive powers.
[51] Montague-Barlow, Minister of Labour; Worthington-Evans chaired an unemployment policy committee.

... If I get to Aix next Saturday I want to stay till after the 12th and then come back, by which time I think it possible that Poincaré will want to see me . . .

The Baldwins were again troubled about Oliver. He had seemed to be settling down, becoming engaged to be married and starting a career in journalism. But he soon rebelled against his parents' values. He broke off his engagement, and influenced by the Macdonald family connection became interested in the socialism of William Morris. He also became enraged at the Unionist government's willingness to abandon Armenia to Soviet control. Three days after Baldwin became Prime Minister, a newspaper published an interview with Oliver in 11 Downing Street, in which he announced his socialist beliefs. He had now also met his future partner, John Boyle. For both reasons he felt that he should no longer remain in his parents' houses.

25 AUGUST 1923: TO OLIVER BALDWIN

CUL MS Add. 9569/1

10, Downing Street

Dearest Son,

You have vanished into thin air and I don't know where you are or what you are doing, but my love is with you and I follow in spirit! I am just at the end of my tether and am off to Aix to try and get a short rest. Don't even try try my job: it doesn't stop night or day.

I don't even know for certain if you are going to Kenya,[52] but if you are I will tell my banker to send a contribution towards the ticket for these steamer journeys are pretty expensive. I can't send as much as I would because I am rather heavily overdrawn.

I can't help thinking you are wise, if you are going. I believe for a time you will be far happier in a new country.

There is so much to trouble, so much to discourage, in the old world at present that unless you have the stomach of an ostrich, life becomes indigestible.

So as I said this brings much love and remember you are never far from my thoughts.

Your loving old/ Father

---

[52] Oliver had visited East Africa during 1922, as a special correspondent for the *Morning Post.*

25 AUGUST 1923: TO CURZON

typescript copy, SB papers 114/171

10, Downing Street

My dear Curzon,

My plans are – Aix to-day for 2/3 weeks. I haven't had a holiday yet and I need one.

I have seen Derby, Bob [Cecil], Sam Hoare,[53] N. Chamberlain, Barlow, Joynson-Hicks and Worthington-Evans. We all agree that no immediate Cabinet is necessary and that a pause for reflection is advisable.

I have intimated to the F.O. that if Poincaré wishes to see me privately I will meet him. The time for a personal interview is rapidly approaching. If that happens I would report immediately to the Cabinet.

I have been in close touch with Tyrrell who will tell you of our conversations.

I shall do a lot of quiet thinking at Aix. I wouldn't put the amount of daylight at more than a ray. I will write to you at Aix.

Neville accepted the Chancellorship yesterday and Hicks goes to Health.

Derby came to tender his resignation yesterday! but withdrew it on learning that I was willing to meet P.! It is an odd world!

I do hope you have had a rest.

Yours very sincerely,/ S.B.

While at Aix-les-Bains, the Baldwins were joined by the Davidsons. Joan accompanied Baldwin on his long hill walks, and Baldwin and Davidson prepared for the meeting with Poincaré. During his holidays in Aix, he remained in touch with ministers and officials on important matters by cypher telegrams, as well as by post.

14 SEPTEMBER 1923: TO CURZON

Curzon papers F112/229/40–2; M&B, p. 196

[Aix-les-Bains]

My dear Curzon,

Let me thank you for your kind telegram about my return. I have had a splendid holiday and am now feeling ready for anything.

[53] Secretary of State for Air.

If you get Mussolini out of Corfu this month, you will have done a great thing.

I saw Bob last Sunday – we lunched together at Talloires – and from all I have seen and heard I think he has done admirably in Geneva.[54]

I am delighted with your general direction of affairs in a most difficult situation and I hope the country will realise what an awkward corner you have got them round.

Now, as to Poincaré. If you can spare Tyrrell for a night – and I know it is asking a good deal – I should like to see him in Paris on my arrival, about half past ten on Tuesday evening, at the Crillon. I want to get into touch with the events of the last three weeks and to know in what direction your mind has been moving. My chief desire in seeing this singularly difficult President of the Council is to get into his head that our government speaks the truth and can be trusted and that the Prime Minister and the F.O. speak with one voice. I am convinced that profound distrust of Lloyd George was the primary cause of the lessened confidence between Paris and London: the feeling grew in France until it became an obsession. If I can make him believe I speak the truth I propose to tell him of the various currents of feeling in England: how failure to settle or attempt to settle promptly with Germany and to provide other sanctions than the military occupation of the Ruhr will infallibly alienate English sentiment and this sentiment once alienated will be difficult to recapture. I shall point out how we have done everything in our power to help him in our financial proposals and if I can think of anything more we can do, I shall suggest it.

Further, how little he has done to help, and if it is seen that I fail to agree with him as did my two predecessors, the coincidence will be so remarkable that every country in the world except France will know where to lay the blame for the disagreement. I shall tell him how proud the French were of the Entente when they felt they needed support, and remind him of his letter at the end of July 1914 when he called to us for help, contrasting his attitude to-day when we make considered requests of him.

In short, my object is to work for the Entente and for a prompt settlement, by every means that may occur to me. If I cannot move him, we shall have

---

[54] After telegraphic exchanges with Baldwin and Curzon, Cecil had taken a firm stand at the League of Nations against the Italian government's occupation of Corfu.

a difficult course to steer: but we can discuss that on my return. I am going very carefully into the financial questions on Sunday,

Yours very sincerely/ Stanley Baldwin

Although Baldwin could speak French, when he and Poincaré met at the British Embassy they chose to speak through an interpreter. The following extracts, giving Baldwin's side of the two-hour discussion, are taken from the original French verbatim record.[55] As well as the conversation being a unique instance of Baldwin attempting personal diplomacy, it is another example of his faith in the efficacy of candour. As such, it produced a rare report of his reflections on foreign relations, and astonishingly frank comments on British politics.

19 SEPTEMBER 1923 TRANSCRIPT OF POINCARÉ–BALDWIN
CONVERSATION

SB papers 108/41–60 (extracts)

. . . M. Baldwin began by saying he was delighted to meet M. Poincaré, and how very grateful he was for all the courtesy and kindness shown to him during his stay in Savoy. Everybody there from the Préfet downwards had done everything to make his visit pleasant, he had met several of the authorities, deputies, and all had been extremely kind to him. This was his third visit to Savoy, and the happiest one. He also wished to express his thanks to those who were responsible for bringing him to Paris in such conditions of comfort.

M. Poincaré (s'exprimant en français) . . .[56]

M. Baldwin then said he believed M. Poincaré was a lawyer; he himself was not. But, if he might use a lawyer's phrase, he hoped they would talk together with 'no prejudice'.

. . .

M. Baldwin declared that, as they were alone he would express him-self with the utmost frankness. The first thing that struck him when he became Prime Minister was that there seemed to be an absence of the

[55] Baldwin and his secretaries edited this document for the British official record, deleting his most personal comments and observations on individuals (notably Curzon): for the editing process see SB papers 108/2–38. The 'expurgated' version is printed in M&B, pp. 197–201, and *DBFP* (1s.), xxi. 529–34 (but see these for Poincaré's statements). Baldwin considered even this version to be so secret that the circulation of copies was strictly controlled: CAB 21/271.
[56] The ellipses below indicate the omissions of Poincaré's statements.

confidence and close harmony that ought to exist between the two countries if the Entente was to be preserved.

He would like to point out some of the dangers that he saw in England at the present time and with which M. Poincaré might not be acquainted. It was better to tell him, as perhaps nobody else would, so as to avoid any misunderstanding at the start. A great deal of the difficulties that had arisen between the two countries were due to two reasons: first, the unhappy break-down of the agreement which President Wilson came to about a tripartite Alliance; and next, if he might say so, the peculiar nature of his last predecessor but one, Mr Lloyd George. Mr. Baldwin had the feeling that most of the trouble came from the fact that France had lost confidence in Mr Lloyd George and did not trust him. Mr. Baldwin now asked M. Poincaré, whether they agreed or not, to trust him entirely as France implicitly trusted England in the times of Sir Edward Grey. He spoke the truth and hoped he would be believed, otherwise it would be no use to go on.

. . .

M. Baldwin thanked M. Poincaré . . . and agreed that the strength of the Entente depended entirely on the confidence existing between the two governments.

After all, when the War began, France staked her all on Sir Edward Grey's word, and not in vain. That was the feeling that he wanted to be restored. Mr Baldwin said he would not again mention Mr Lloyd George's name – or once only – but he would like to remind M. Poincaré that a year ago, when he was having a quiet holiday at Aix, he had made up his mind never to serve under Mr Lloyd George in any capacity whatever; witness to this was what he had said last October at the Carlton Club, when the Coalition Ministry fell. If it had not been for the serious crisis which threatened the peace of Europe in the last week of September and beginning of October, and nearly brought about a war with Turkey, he would have resigned; but he could not then leave the Cabinet, and only did so in October, as soon as he could. He would say no more on that head.

Mr. Baldwin then went on assuring M. Poincaré that for every reason the maintenance of the Entente appeared to him extremely desirable, and he knew they agreed as to this. He would not say anything about the bonds which had closely united France and Great Britain during the last few years. As was known, he was a cousin of Mr Kipling, rightly considered as one of the best friends of France in England; and they held the same views in common.

There was hardly a spot in the North East of France where their sons and brothers did not lie buried – and that they could never forget. Every village in Great Britain had its memorial – as in France – dedicated to the men who lay in French soil. In fact, they never spoke about the 'English war'; they always said 'the Great War', remembering how they all fought in it side by side. It would indeed be a lamentable thing if, with those sacred memories in common, the statesmen of the two countries allowed the Entente to perish in their hands. It must not be. (M. Poincaré fait un signe d'assentiment; M. Baldwin, après un instant, poursuit ainsi:) The best thing then was to look at the difficulties they had encountered, and find out where they originated. First he would say they were probably due to the fact that the English and the French nations were temperamentally different.

Then a reason why before the war it was easy to maintain the Entente was to be found in the common fear inspired by the attitude of Germany and also another Power in Central Europe. That fear had largely been removed and sometimes people in England had the impression, at least by reading the French press, that France no longer felt she wanted England to be with her. This puzzled English people. What struck him most was that if M. Poincaré and he did not ultimately agree, bad results would surely follow. There were impelling forces that ought to make them agree, and not only the duty to the dead: their duty to mankind and to the civilization of Europe. If they disagreed, there would be no hope left for the world; while, by mutual help and understanding they had perhaps, in the course of the last fortnight, saved Europe from another war. They had in this respect a tremendous responsibility.

At this point, Mr. Baldwin said he wished to speak on a matter of great privacy, concerning Lord Curzon. He sometimes had the impression that in France people did closely associate the name of Lord Curzon with that of Lloyd George; and there seemed to be a feeling that Lord Curzon somehow or other was not animated by perfectly friendly intentions towards France.

Now it should be realized that Lord Curzon was in a very difficult position in Mr Lloyd George's ministry. The latter, owing to the circumstances arising from the war, had found himself in 1918 almost in the position of a dictator – and the idea of dictatorship was simply abhorrent to the English mind. Well, not only did Mr L.G. act then as Prime Minister, but he also usurped the functions of Foreign Minister, and often went behind the back of his own Minister, to discuss matters with other countries in a contrary sense to that

followed by his colleagues of the Cabinet. He (Mr Baldwin) was only thinking of certain Greek affairs, about which the truth would be known later,
and that he would leave for the present. The fact remained that L.C.'s [Lord
Curzon's] position had been very difficult at times, and he might have been
saddled with responsibilities that really belonged to Mr L.G. Last October,
when the Coalition Government fell, he had an opportunity of discussing
that point with L.C. 'Why not resign?' was the question that naturally arose.
L.C. answered him, and he could quite understand, that he had been in
two minds all the time about that. One side would say 'retire from this
Government!'; and the other side would reply that he, Lord Curzon, being
Foreign Secretary, was in a truly difficult position, because he naturally had
considerable knowledge of Foreign affairs; he was afraid that if he retired,
Mr Winston Churchill or Lord Birkenhead would be put in his place, and
then 'God help the foreign policy of England!'. So Lord Curzon had felt
strongly that in spite of all the difficulties, and though he might have the
appearance of clinging to office for the sake of office, the most patriotic and
self-denying action was for him to remain at his post. Of course it was a matter for him alone to decide, and he stayed, thus no doubt assuming responsibility for many things which were the Prime Minister's doing, and not his.

Mr Baldwin, both in Mr Bonar Law's Ministry and his own, had found
in L.C. a most loyal and trustworthy colleague – in spite, he might say,
of the great disappointment naturally felt by L.C. at not becoming Prime
Minister himself. He had proved loyal to him (Mr Baldwin) a younger and
less experienced man; and they worked so well together that on one or two
occasions, when Mr Baldwin desired to follow a certain course which L.C.
did not like, the latter acted throughout as a loyal colleague. If there was any
feeling in Mr Poincaré's mind or in the French Government that L.C. tried
to create difficulties or act contrary to the interests of France, he earnestly
begged them to dismiss that thought.

. . .

M. Baldwin thanked Mr Poincaré . . . and passed to another subject.
He wished to put before him a sketch of the present state of public feeling
in England; it was important he should know. If M. Paul Cambon[57]
had still been in London, with his long knowledge and experience of
England, he would have admirably informed M. Poincaré of the situation;

[57] French ambassador in London 1898–1920, and an architect of the 1904 Anglo-French entente.

the present Ambassador of course had not yet been long in England. So Mr Baldwin would like to state himself to Mr. Poincaré the difficulties with which he had to contend. He would speak with some diffidence about public opinion in France which he did not know so well, and was no doubt different, but he could say that in England public opinion counted for a great deal. In spite of what was sometimes said, it was not possible to manufacture English opinion by the means of newspapers. He had been told that the French press had more influence, but he did not know if it was the case or not. In England, when the people had made up their minds, for instance about a general election, no matter what the Press would say, they had their own way. The French Government must not be misled by what may appear in Lord Rothermere's Press. When it was Lord Northcliffe,[58] it threw its whole weight in 1906 on Mr Chamberlain's side, and yet this strong personality was beaten – smashed to pieces.

Another case in point was when last autumn, Mr Bonar Law, who received very little support from the newspapers and was not considered as likely to win, did actually win. At present the English Press was entirely independent from the Government. The Prime Minister could not tell the journalists to say 'this' or 'that'. Some of the last governments had perhaps more power in this respect and used to reward the Press liberally – but they were not doing that now.

Mr Baldwin then went on saying there were several currents in English public opinion to-day, some against the French and he would try to show why, thus explaining some of the difficulties he had to deal with, and in which M. Poincaré could help him. As to political parties, it might be said that practically the whole of the Labour party and Liberal party were taking a line which was not necessarily called pro-Boche but at any rate was an anti-French line. This existed even in his own party. And there were two or three reasons. The first was (he wished to say little about the Ruhr to-day, and only brought it in in connection with his argument) the feeling prevailing in England that while great willingness had been expressed to make large concessions in the matter of interallied debts in order to secure a settlement, no account seemed to have been taken of those offers in France and they had even been completely ignored in some quarters – so there was no recognition of the sacrifices Great Britain was ready to make. He was not

---

[58] I.e. when the Harmsworth newspapers had been under the control of Rothermere's elder brother, who died in 1922.

expressing his own views, but stating the currents of English feeling which it was necessary to bear in mind.

There was another feeling, and very wide-spread, that every day of delay in effecting a settlement of the reparations question made an ultimate settlement more difficult and more precarious. There was no desire to let the Boche off – far from it – in fact the general desire went the other way; but many people in England thought, contrary to the belief prevalent in France, that the events of the last months had postponed the possibility of a settlement and tended to fritter away the German assets still existing for all of them (the Allies).

Lastly, English temperament was of course very peculiar in certain respects, and it might be difficult for the French to understand it, but it was indispensable that M. Poincaré should be apprized of the situation as it was in England. The ordinary Englishman disliked more than anything a military occupation of a civilian district – nothing could antagonize or rouse him (especially among the working classes) more than the idea that appeared to him to savour of militarism.

It might appear stupid, but it was a feeling and a fact one had to reckon with, and there would be the greatest difficulties in making a settlement with the Germans as long as the military character of the occupation of the Ruhr was not changed. Unless it was, no British Government could give its hearty co-operation in order to make the Entente what it ought to be. Those were facts he begged to submit for reflection. No other Government in Great Britain could be formed as willing and desirous as the present one to work together with France. That close union was the only means of salvation, not only in the big question in hand, but for all. If they failed to agree, the civilization of Europe would be thrown back for many years.

One of the reasons why he was so anxious this conversation might be the prelude to a better understanding was that, after the disagreement with Mr Lloyd George and the one in January last, if there was again a breakdown, he was sure all his people would feel that the responsibilities did not rest with them, but with the other side. It might not be fair, but it would be so, and thus a settlement of future problems would be rendered still more difficult. Mr Lloyd George said it was absolutely impossible to agree with M. Poincaré. He (Mr Baldwin) had not that impression, and he had never met a man yet with whom he could not come to terms. That was why he was so anxious to return to the position that obtained in the times of Sir Edward

Grey. Unless difficulties were realized on both sides, no progress could be made. It was no good devising formulas – as they were hatched every day at the Hotel Crillon some years ago; they wanted something more solid than formulas upon which to build up things that would last.

Mr Baldwin wished to repeat that the differences between them were largely about methods; practically the whole of England desired a settlement and to make the Boche pay. About the principles, there could be no doubt. But, rightly or wrongly, the people doubted very largely the wisdom of the methods that had been employed. Now things looked as though there was a prospect of some agreement being arrived at with the Germans. He would like to recall the fact that only last Saturday, in London, at the Foreign Office, they were pressing upon Germany (as they had done before) to abandon passive resistance, and to try and come to terms.

Now what Mr Baldwin wanted to ask M. Poincaré was if he could tell him what he proposed to do when Germany did abandon passive resistance – whether he had any plans, already discussed or in his head, so that he would have time to study them and see with his colleagues in London how closely they could come together in any arrangement that was made. It would be a great thing if they could substantially be agreed before they came out before the public. They did not want any more of those conferences ending in clouds or in disagreement. What they wanted was to get so closely together that, when they did confer, they could settle something definite. So he would be glad to hear any views that M. Poincaré had in mind, for instance about the stabilisation of German currency, moratorium, or rate of payment, etc. This would give time to consider the matter, and be ready for the re-opening of the British Parliament, in about seven weeks time. There would probably be some fierce debates on this subject, and it was very desirable to be able to have something definite to say. And for the sake of the Entente, the sooner this vexing question was put out of the way, the better. If it was allowed to drag on indefinitely, with no new prospect of a settlement, he doubted if his government would be able to hold it, and the results might be very grave for the future.

He had only one more thing to add, while he was there. He had been told that in some French quarters there was an idea that a quick settlement was desired in England because it might be to the advantage of various speculators and people in the City of London. Now, that was all rubbish. People in England wanted a settlement for two reasons:

The first was they attributed, rightly or wrongly, the greater part of unemployment to the present disorganisation in the world's trade.

The second was that they thought, rightly or wrongly again, that until the great question was settled, there was the more probability of disorder and fighting in a Europe that had already suffered far too much. What the people wanted was ordered peace. There was no question of financial speculation in this. For himself, since he had been in office, he had acted like most honest men in politics would, and had neither bought nor sold shares of any kind, never speculated in marks or francs – nor had any of his friends, for the matter of that.

He trusted that M. Poincaré would turn over in his mind all he had said, and he hoped and believed they would be able by mutual confidence, and close friendship to accomplish their common desire for the good of France and England. He had carefully refrained from saying in his speeches anything that could militate against a friendly understanding. He felt sure that, once the question of the Ruhr [was] out of the way, the two countries could pull together as closely as ever. If M. Poincaré would give him his confidence as his own was given, (and he was faithfully interpreting the conviction of English people), he would not let him down. Together they could do a work of vital importance, render the greatest services to their countries and thus deserve well of posterity.

In concluding his words, Mr Baldwin apologized for speaking so long, again thanked M. Poincaré for his kindness, and express[ed] the hope that from this meeting and from this room would come forth good fruit in days to come . . .

Because Poincaré offered no immediate concessions on the French occupation of the Ruhr, only a bland press communiqué could be issued. This attracted criticism in Britain, even among Unionists. After German passive resistance ended on 26 September, the French government became no more conciliatory, and on 8 October Poincaré renewed his criticism of Curzon and British policy.[59] It was now clear that no early settlement of 'Europe' was possible.

[59] For Baldwin speaking further on foreign affairs in a private interview with a Liberal newspaper editor, see *The Political Diaries of C. P. Scott 1911–1928*, ed. T. Wilson (1970), pp. 444–6 (26–7 Oct. 1923).

❧

Protection and its aftermath

OCTOBER 1923 – JANUARY 1924

On 25 October Baldwin was to address the Unionist party's annual conference for the first time as party leader. After prior discussion with only a few ministers and without notification on the agenda Baldwin persuaded a doubtful Cabinet on 23 October to accept his announcement of a major policy change – adoption of a general tariff, or protection. Although most Unionists were protectionists, ever since the party's Edwardian splits and defeats on the issue it had been regarded as too full of risks to be re-adopted as official policy. On 12 November, just twelve months after the Unionist government had won a general election, Baldwin asked the King for an immediate dissolution.

Baldwin set out the *policy* grounds for his adoption of protection, turning on international trade and monetary dislocations and on unemployment, in a rare handwritten note of 7 October as well as in his Cabinet statement. His *political* thinking, and the link with his further decision to call an early election, was more complicated and altered as the situation developed. Here the evidence consists wholly of reported conversations, with the difficulty that he laid stress on different aspects to interlocutors with different information and attitudes.[1] Also, the considerations as recorded in the chronological order of the surviving reports do not necessarily represent their order of priority in Baldwin's mind. The strategic concern, largely taken for granted, was that at the 1922 election the Unionists had won less than three-fifths of the votes and Labour had become the second largest parliamentary party. With no prospect of early success over the Ruhr and European recovery and with unemployment certain to rise again during the winter, unless the government could produce an alternative economic initiative the Labour party might achieve a permanent and decisive advance among

---

[1] Further published conversations before the protectionist announcement are in *Amery Diaries*, I, pp. 344, 348, 349, 351; *NC Letters*, II, pp. 186–7, 188; *Bridgeman Diaries*, pp. 168–9. For an important Baldwin retrospective account of this episode, see below p. 476.

'working-class' voters. There were also tactical concerns, which received more prominence in discussion because they affected timing: mounting criticism from Unionist backbench groups, conservative newspapers, and Chamberlainites; the possibility of attaching the Chamberlainites to the government, and the fear that if this were not done Lloyd George might re-establish the coalitionists' alliance. From 1 October to 8 November an Imperial Conference was meeting in London, with economic issues among its main business; but as shown in the diary of Mackenzie King, the Canadian Prime Minister, this had little part in Baldwin's decisions.

1 OCTOBER 1923 MACKENZIE KING DIARY

Mackenzie King papers G3889/34–38 (extracts)

... Baldwin ... spoke first of the situation in Europe and said that it was really a very serious one; that there was a bad spirit abroad; that France had really become a great militarist power, in fact was a stronger power to-day than Great Britain. Britain had cut down armaments and gone very far in reducing her military and naval strength, perhaps too far. France had an unarmed neighbour on one side and with the airship equipment which she had, Britain's position was really insecure.

Baldwin said he was much struck by what was signified in the attitude, which I had expressed at the morning session of the Imperial Conference, that with good-will difficulties could be solved. It was what he had noticed in the United States. Fortunately the North American continent, and they should thank Providence for it, was a long way distant from Europe and had a wholly different attitude towards existing conditions. The spirit on the Continent was that things were bad and could not get better any way; that it was not worth while trying to improve. It was not the spirit which was seeking to overcome difficulties and which had faith in better times. This was the hardest of all factors to cope with. In England, he said, conditions were also bad; there were 1,500,000 unemployed, some of whom were very difficult to deal with, especially those in cities like Glasgow.

England, he thought, must get rid of some of her population. He intimated that Lord Curzon would disclose many things which would be a surprise and really indicated a very serious situation[2] ...

---

[2] On 5 October Curzon was to speak on foreign affairs at the Imperial Conference.

As to the Conference itself, it was quite plain that he felt it was adding considerably to his own burdens at a time when he was heavily pressed. He agreed with me that it would be an advantage to all concerned if we could conclude in a month and that we should work toward that end . . .

During our conversation, I spoke to him of his own burdens and obligations; he said to me that he would never find retirement a privation; no sooner did the public bring a man into office than they were trying to make it impossible for him to proceed with his work; they made him a target for all the attacks possible; put on him strains which no one could long endure.

Premier Baldwin said the only way in which he managed at all was by keeping Sunday to himself; he resolutely refused to have visitors to Chequers on Sunday[3] and whenever he could get away for Saturday as well as Sunday he would have his secretaries come down on Saturday, but took Sunday for reflection; he mentioned that General Smuts had said to him only this morning that he found that the only way in which he could manage his affairs was keeping Sunday entirely to himself and seeing no one. He also told me that he ate very lightly and was abstemious; that he had drunk more champagne since becoming Prime Minister than for many months before; one reason being that it was always there and it had the effect of bucking one up a little; he said he tried to avoid using it as much as he could. He said he did not take rest during the day, but took three quarters of an hour in the morning walking in the Park . . .

W. A. S. Hewins, the tariff-reform economist and organiser, and former colonial under-secretary, had been a friend of Baldwin since the wartime backbench Business Committee. Now chairman of the Empire Development Union, he was in close touch with around a hundred protectionist MPs headed by John Gretton who in late July had sent Baldwin a memorial on imperial trade. In September Rothermere employed him to advise on a planned protectionist campaign in *The Daily Mail*, partly with the intention of forcing Baldwin's resignation. Hewins had heard rumours of an intrigue to 'bring back Ll.G.', and as the Gretton group also proposed to put further pressure on the government he decided to warn Baldwin.

---

[3] As the Baldwins' Chequers visitors' book shows, this rather overstates matters. There were frequent weekend visitors, though mostly family or friends, which perhaps explains his meaning.

[4 OCTOBER 1923] HEWINS DIARY, WRITTEN
12 OCTOBER

Hewins papers 182/59–60 (extract)

[Baldwin] told me he had arranged to give me the whole morning so that we could go into matters thoroughly. So we sat & talked over our pipes. He first asked me what I thought of the Beaverbrook-Rothermere newspaper purchase.[4] He supposed it wd. be for Ll.G. I said it was not necessarily so; so far as I knew Rothermere was not, at present, for Ll.G; he wanted a strong Conservative party. Naturally I did not tell him of Rothermere's proposed tariff campaign; I was not entitled to do so & it might never materialise. But I told him all I knew of the designs of the Lloyd-Georgians, & the definite attempt wh. was to be made to get him out. He said he had suspected that. I showed him how attractive a programme could be made for them & how easy it wd. be to exploit the Empire & unemployment. It was not necessary for them to act inconsistently with their known & genuine views on these subjects. He agreed that if Ll.G. came out on these lines he wd. take most of the Conservative party with him in present circumstances. The situation could only be met by a definite policy. I said he must understand my position on the matter. I was attached to him but I could not oppose people who were supporting my policy. That policy I thought wd. certainly be carried if not by this Govt. then by another. If he refused to act the Conservative party wd. be broken. We shd. certainly get the policy but many things Conservatives valued wd. disappear. I did not desire that. He said he was prepared to go all the way with preference. I said that I did not mind very much how it was done provided it was done but I thought he wd. be well advised not to raise the question of duties on essential foodstuffs. There wd. remain a wide agricultural area in wh. he could operate. He thought the atmosphere about protection had changed & he was prepared for it in view of the unemployment wh. prevailed. He asked me my view about the pledge about wh. he had been to see Bonar Law within the last day or two. I said the fiscal position was defined by our adherence to the Paris Economic Resolutions, the resolutions of the Imperial Conferences of 1917 & 1918, the McKenna Tariff, the established preferences & the Safeguarding of Industries Act. Bonar Law had accepted this position & the policy of holding an Imperial Conference to continue the work of 1917 & 1918. If he had not

---

[4] They had just co-operated in buying the Hulton newspaper chain and dividing its various titles between themselves, considerably increasing their potential influence over political opinion.

done so we should not have supported him. No pledge or interpretation of a pledge wh. was incompatible with this position could be considered valid & I knew of no fundamental principles of the fiscal system except the deliberate decisions of the Empire & the Acts in operation. Stanley Baldwin said his view was that he could do anything e.g. wh. fell within the principles of the Safeguarding of Industries Act & he mentioned the McKenna duties... He asked me how one wd. select the articles for the imposition of duties & we discussed that question for some time, & also the treaty position. Then as to the time of making the announcement of his policy. He suggested Plymouth on the 25th or Swansea on the 30th. I said both these were party meetings & he should follow the constitutional practice of communicating his policy to the Imperial Conference. He asked me what I thought of his visit to Poincaré. Did I think 'he was right in going to see him'. I said of course he was. He said that when he became Prime Minister he found that the word of an English statesman was nowhere trusted ... & he went to Poincaré to put this right ...

7 OCTOBER 1923: NOTE

handwritten, SB papers 182/40–1; M&B, p. 220[5]

Sunday 7.x.23　　　　　　　　　　　　　　　　　　　　　Chequers

Unemployment

Condition of Europe. Evidently its' economic restoration postponed indefinitely. Must therefore seek for other markets.

Tariffs increased everywhere: we have no bargaining counter.

If and when Germany exports as she must if she is to pay reparations what safeguard has our industry? While foreign currencies are as they are, what safeguard has our own industry against the currency bounty?

American debt. America with her high tariff makes our task doubly difficult especially having regard to our imports from her. We must therefore lessen our purchases by producing cotton, tobacco & sugar elsewhere.

Every attempt to relieve Unemployment is only applying palliatives: the only way to safeguard the future is to protect our own industries and develope our own Empire. But Bonar's pledge stands in the way. ∴ I appeal to the people: if any one has anything else to propose, let him, and the people shall judge.

---

[5] This note survives among material for Baldwin's 25 October speech. But as it was written over two weeks earlier, it seems more a note of clarification than a speech draft; nor is it among the numbered sheets he used when delivering the speech.

Figure 4 Signatures in the Chequers visitors' book, 1923:
13–15 October, Amery and his wife, and Lloyd-Greame;
20–2 October, Mackenzie King, Neville Chamberlain and his wife,
Bruce and his wife, the Davidsons, Meriel Talbot, Ormsby-Gore,
Herbert, and Rosemary Troubridge (a family friend).

Identification of those with whom Baldwin spoke during these weeks has been important for interpretations of his adoption of protection. A later entry in Jones' published diary, reporting his examination of the Chequers visitors' book, established a view that Baldwin and his most protectionist ministers held crucial conversations with the Australian and Canadian Prime Ministers during the weekend of 13–15 October. But as both original visitors' books show, Jones had run together signatures for two separate weekends. Baldwin's chief weekend visitors were 6–8 October, Neville Chamberlain and Auckland Geddes;[6] 13–15 October, Amery and Lloyd-Greame; then weekends to entertain, in two batches, the Dominion Prime Ministers: 20–2 October, Mackenzie King and Bruce of Australia, with Neville Chamberlain; and 27–9 October, Massey of New Zealand, Smuts of South Africa and Warren of Newfoundland, with Montagu Norman.[7]

[16–18 OCTOBER 1923] DAWSON MEMORANDUM,
WRITTEN 20 DECEMBER[8]

handwritten, Dawson papers 70/92–119 (extract); partly in Wrench, *Dawson*, p. 222

Baldwin first broached his ideas to me on Oct. 16, when I went to Downing Street on a rather mysterious request by telephone. He put them rather vaguely, but very much as they afterwards took shape in his speeches – the hopeless problem of unemployment & still more hopeless problem of Europe, the difficulties for him personally of Bonar Law's pledge, his own belief in more general protection, the development of the Empire & its markets. A General Election would no doubt be necessary sooner or later, but there was no hint of any intention to appeal at once. He thought of speaking on the subject at Plymouth where there was to be a Party Conference next week, & asked me what I thought of the plan. I asked him in turn how far he'd thought it out in detail, & how far his colleagues were with him. He seemed to think it too soon for detail & said that the few colleagues to whom he'd so far spoken agreed – mentioning Neville Chamberlain, Amery, Lloyd-Greame, Willie Bridgeman. Derby, he said, had appeared to approve, but was now hedging. What about the others e.g. the Cecils? I suggested. He didn't know. There had evidently been nothing but a few individual talks, mostly with those who were certain to be sympathisers. He would like me

---

[6] British ambassador in the United States 1920–4.   [7] Compare Jones *WD*, I, p. 305.
[8] This memorandum was based on his daily diary entries.

to turn the whole thing over in my mind, keeping it, of course, to myself meanwhile.

I came away a good deal worried by the impression of rather a 'half-baked' & amateur project, thought about it at intervals all night and next day, & eventually asked Baldwin to see me again on the morning of the 18th.

I told him exactly what I felt so far as I understood his plans, & said that, in the present state of the world, with the British Government the only fixed point in Europe, I thought the risk he was apparently contemplating far too great. He seemed depressed himself and said sadly that I hadn't made him any more cheerful. This was the last time I saw him until after the Election . . .

20 OCTOBER 1923 MACKENZIE KING DIARY

Mackenzie King papers G3889/140–5 (extracts)

. . . At four o'clock left for Chequers arriving there about 5.30 p.m . . .

After conversation for a few minutes in front of an open fire in the large central hall, the Prime Minister invited me into his library and talked with what he remarked was 'appalling frankness' with respect to many important matters. He began by speaking of being very anxious about the whole situation in Europe and England; that the unemployment problem here was frightful and he did not see how they could go on with winter ahead and the prospect of more unemployed; that in the Ruhr, for example, there were quantities of steel and other raw materials which could come into England and still further undermine some of their leading industries, throwing many thousands out of employment; the Government had come to the conclusion that they must take steps to prevent this, and do what they could to get some of the population overseas.

We talked a little more of tariff matters and Mr Baldwin said he hoped to find 'within the bridge which Bonar had laid', scope for the changes which should be made at once. He evidently meant that Bonar Law had indicated that nothing of far-reaching character should be done but had left the way open for minor changes.

He doubted if wheat or meat could be touched at present.

. . . I told him frankly I believed he was taking a big chance and was liable to be un-horsed in any effort to alter materially the traditional fiscal policy of England. He appreciated the risks but felt that one effect of a campaign would be to restore the old political parties and prevent Labour, as a class, from attaining power. He thought Labour would be in a particularly awkward position in a campaign of the kind. If, for example, in certain industries which were now threatened with further unemployment the policy were to restore employment, it would be very difficult for Labour to argue against such a course. On the other hand the cry of cheap food would, of course, incline many to fall in with the Free Traders.

Mr Baldwin thought the Liberal Party at present was entirely smashed, and one effect of a tariff fight would be to bring them together again – to unite them. As to what Lloyd George would do, he couldn't say; if he, Baldwin, came out for protection Lloyd George would probably come out for free trade, and if he came out for free trade, Lloyd George would almost certainly come out for protection; he did not think Lloyd George had any convictions whatever – he was a pure opportunist.

This led to our speaking of the Near East situation of a year ago. Mr Baldwin told me it was that situation which had caused him to take the stand he did and it was the real cause of the break-up of the coalition. Roughly what Mr Baldwin said was as follows:

England and the Empire were in the hands of three dangerous men, all intoxicated with their own cleverness and love of power, and prepared to sacrifice everything to it; foolish and blind even to the point of believing that they could win an election by bringing on another war. They were determined to have war with Turkey and were doing everything in their power to bring it about; they felt that if they could once launch war they could then appeal to the people and come back all powerful as a government triumvirate (Mr Baldwin did not use this expression but it was what was implied). It was pure madness and we were within an ace of a conflict.

The message which had been sent to the Dominions had never been shown to the Cabinet. Lloyd George pretended that he had not seen it, but there was no doubt he had. Churchill had drafted it, but Birkenhead and Lloyd George were equally responsible for it; it was part of the campaign of war and the election manoeuvre which they had planned.

I outlined to Mr Baldwin all that took place at the time the despatch came regarding the Near East crisis and the action of our Cabinet. Mr Baldwin told me that he thought we had taken the entirely proper course and that our attitude had helped to save the day.

Mr Baldwin said that he was going to resign from the Ministry when he learned of the message to the Dominions; it was only through the persuasion of Bonar Law and other of his colleagues that he determined to stay.

What Lloyd George had had in view was uniting the two old political parties, the Liberals and Conservatives, against Labour, letting Labour become the other Party in England. He, Baldwin, felt that that was a disastrous course and told several of his colleagues, including Austen Chamberlain, what a course of this kind meant; many of them who were soberminded Conservatives, unwilling to go in for rash and mad ventures, would be left out of the politics of England altogether, and these other men would come into control, with what disastrous consequences no one could foresee.

It was in this frame of mind that the Carlton Club meeting had been called and that he, Baldwin, had taken the stand he did. Bonar Law's part was that of a patriot; he had not wanted to take office, and it was only to keep together the elements that were fighting Lloyd George and his group that Bonar Law had agreed to do so.

He, Baldwin, had thought at the time of his breaking the coalition that to him personally it meant permanent retirement from politics. His wife had been away at the time; he had to make a quick decision and when he met her afterwards . . . he told her that he had burnt his bridges and was now out of politics altogether. Then Bonar Law's health gave out and he decided that he could no longer retain office, it was but three days before he became Prime Minister that he had even thought of the possibility.

I told Mr Baldwin how I felt toward Lord Curzon, and he said he was very glad to know that he had made that impression on me. I told him in very strict confidence of what His Highness the Maharajah of Alwar had said as to the situation in Europe being in part due to the antagonism between Britain's Foreign Minister and the Ministers in Europe. Baldwin said that he realised that to some extent, and his visit to Paris with Poincaré had been largely to explain to Poincaré that the stand which Curzon was taking was not because of his own personal views, but was dictated by the needs of the situation; that he had tried his best to persuade Poincaré that Curzon was not the kind of person some of them believed him to be.

Mr Baldwin then told me that Curzon had been very kind with him himself; that his great weakness was his power to write despatches and a temptation to score over other men rather than to let the other man think that he was the one who was achieving the result. This was his real limitation. He, Baldwin, had had to alter, at different times, some of the despatches which Curzon had sent; one of the most important he had cut in half and altered; Curzon had accepted the changes without a word. 'That', said Mr Baldwin 'was pretty fine for a Foreign Secretary'. He spoke of the difficulty of getting a Foreign Secretary who had knowledge of the situation . . .

In speaking of Birkenhead, Baldwin remarked that it was a disgrace that the Lord Chancellor should drink as he did and behave in the manner in which he had been accustomed to do in Europe; that he could not be depended upon in any way and should be out of public life.

He told me that he was really very worried about the present situation; that he had not slept well the last couple of nights and felt that a good deal hung on the present week; that if a favourable answer was not received from Poincaré to the last despatch of Lord Curzon he thought we would have to consider the whole situation at the Conference very carefully. It is quite clear that he feels anything may happen in Europe at any moment . . .

23 OCTOBER 1923 HEWINS DIARY

Hewins papers 182/63 (extract)

. . . this morning the P.M.'s private secretary rang me up and asked me to go round to Downing St at once. So I went & spent the morning with him. He is going to make his announcement of economic policy at Plymouth on Thursday – duties on manufactures, no duties on wheat or meat, but subsidies for wheat; this is a wider policy than he could do on the principles of existing legislation & must clearly be fought out as a domestic issue on the question of unemployment. He will remove the Empire issue from the party arena as far as possible. He had thought of an immediate appeal to the country but decided that propaganda was desirable & he will have the election probably in January.[9] He was to tell the Cabinet this afternoon. He did not know how they would take it. He said 'I am Prime Minister & it is my business to declare my policy; if they don't like it they must lump it'. Last Thursday Derby was with him but he did not know how he wd. be today. We discussed arrangements for propaganda, some technical questions (tariff

---

[9] For similar statements, see *NC Letters*, II, p. 188, and *Amery Diaries*, I, p. 351.

making &c) & some international questions arising. He said he & I 'wd. stand or fall together' . . .

23 OCTOBER 1923 CABINET 50(23), ITEM 4

Cabinet conclusions, CAB 23/45

In view of his forthcoming speech to the Unionist Associations at Plymouth, the Prime Minister gave his colleagues an outline of what he thought should be the policy of the Government towards the problem of Unemployment . . . :-

Unemployment is the outstanding problem in the political life of the country. Failure to deal with it might wreck the Government.

The root problems in unemployment are as follows:-

Population has increased and the pool of unemployed, which has always existed, is therefore larger. Since the War the environment in which industry is carried on has changed. The whole economic system of Europe, including exchange and currency, has broken down. The economic recovery of Germany is inevitably delayed, involving indefinite delay in the stabilisation of currency and exchange in Central Europe. Consequently new factors have entered into the problem of industry, including currency bounties and low wages abroad. This has already been experienced in regard to Germany, and the fall of the franc in the next few months, which competent judges anticipate, may give rise to a similar phenomena in France, where we are already experiencing a new competition in such manufactured articles as woollen goods and rubber tyres. Uncertainty as to the direction and extent of competition paralyses industry. Another danger is the possible exploitation of Germany by cosmopolitan financiers bringing competition to this country, which usually has to play the rôle of 'shock absorber'. To these difficulties and handicaps to trade must be added those of reparations, which may arise sooner or later. In order to pay for the increased imports which she requires owing to depletion of stocks and reduction in her own production, Germany must export more. Similarly, reparations can only be paid by increased exports. Except in the event of a boom, comparable to the discovery of gold in California – and no such boom is in sight – the world can only absorb such exports by a great dislocation of trade, which must be disastrous to this country.

All that the Government has done for unemployment will be deemed insufficient.

There is only one way, not to cure, but to fight unemployment, and that is to protect the home market against foreign manufactures.

Without machinery for this, we are impotent to meet any of the dangers described.

The alternatives, viz., to do nothing or to temporise by putting the McKenna duties on a few more articles, are of no value.

It was not practicable to give protection to corn in the form of a tariff, and the feasibility of doing this by means of a bounty should be examined by a Cabinet Committee.

After some remarks as to the political advantages of the course proposed,[10] the Prime Minister added that he would like to combine with a protective policy the following:-

> Development of Empire and measures to obtain cheap raw materials within the Empire by stimulating the production of cotton, tobacco and sugar, a policy which, in conjunction with protective duties, would tend to bring the dollar and pound to parity in New York.

The Prime Minister proposed, in order to avoid any breach of Mr Bonar Law's pledge, to confine action during the Autumn Session to an extension of the McKenna duties on articles in regard to which the Board of Trade had received reports, but to take the verdict of the country within six months.

After some discussion, the Cabinet agreed:-

(a) That in announcing this policy the Prime Minister should endeavour to avoid committing the Cabinet as a whole or embarrassing those of his colleagues who, owing to election pledges or other reasons, required time to consider their attitude;

(b) That this might be affected by the Prime Minister announcing at Plymouth that the Government realised the steps already decided on in relief of unemployment were only palliatives; that, owing to Mr Bonar Law's pledge, they were prevented from going further in the present Parliament; but that, speaking for himself, he thought they might have to go further and apply a tariff. The Government would watch the

---

[10] Hankey, the Cabinet secretary, customarily did not record discussions of party-political matters. No other source supplies Baldwin's statements here.

situation carefully, and, if there was no improvement, the Prime Minister would hold himself free to propose further steps, of course consulting the country. With some such introduction the Prime Minister could then develop his proposals in full;

(c) That the Prime Minister should confer further with his colleagues in the House of Commons in regard to the form in which his policy should be presented.

At the party conference in Plymouth on 25 October, Baldwin said to an enthusiastic audience that 'I have come to the conclusion myself that the only way of fighting [unemployment] is by protecting the home market.' Bull, a Unionist MP, recorded an exchange with Baldwin immediately after his speech: '"This means a General Election". "No, certainly not", he replied.' As Bull was to deliver a speech that evening, he pressed Baldwin further: '"Have I your permission to say it does not mean an Election?" and he replied "Certainly".'[11]

27 OCTOBER 1923: TO LOUISA BALDWIN

10, Downing Street

Dearest Mother,

I am now in Mid Channel with a vengeance!

Since the Imperial Conference began, the work has been pretty heavy and it makes it so difficult to prepare speeches. In the happy pre-War days our statesmen could lock themselves up for days before a big speech, and now you have to prepare at odd moments.

And a big speech means a lot of brain sweat. You can't expect to hold 5000 people for an hour unless you have something to say and arrange it in proper sequence, and give out the nervous force all the time that rivets them. However, we got through Plymouth all right. Next week I have Swansea and Manchester, after which I get a couple of days rest at Knowsley (with the Derbys) . . .

I am thankful to say I don't feel a bit over-done though the strain is heavy. And there is a gleam of light at last – only a gleam – in the foreign situation. Still it is something to hold on to, to mix the metaphor. And we have had nothing for fourteen months.

---

[11] Bull pocket diary, 25 Oct. 1923, and end-of-year summary for 1923, Bull papers 6/5, 5/12.

I have been brooding over my Swansea speech this morning and am now expecting my second house party for the [Dominion] Prime Ministers.

You are very good in your patience: you know it is not forgetfulness – never: but I find it difficult to put pen to paper these days. One is in constant conference from after breakfast to dinner and being PM is different from anything else. One is in the front and has to lead, guide and decide all the time!

Much fine love/ Yr ever loving/ Son

Several Cabinet members – Salisbury, Cecil, Devonshire, Novar and to a lesser extent Wood and Derby – had expressed doubts about the policy and objections to a precipitate election. On 29 October Baldwin assured the Cabinet that at Swansea he 'intended to make clear that he had no desire to rush the country into an Election, but wished to give the electorate time to examine the Government's economic policy before they were called on to vote on it'. However, the Plymouth speech had created an election atmosphere, party officials advised that the government would win an election, and the Chamberlainites broadly supported protection. By around 6 November he was thinking of striking early. This produced some remarkable manoeuvres among leading Unionists. The Salisburyites hinted that if he persisted they might resign. Baldwin countered by making it known that he would meet the Chamberlainite they most disliked, Birkenhead, just returned from the USA. Lloyd George also returned from there on 9 November and immediately attacked Baldwin's adoption of protection, opening the way for his reunion with the Asquithian Liberals.

[12 NOVEMBER 1923] AUSTEN CHAMBERLAIN

MEMORANDUM WRITTEN 13 NOVEMBER

AC 35/3/21b (extracts); partly in Petrie, *Austen Chamberlain*, II, pp. 233–5.

... [Birkenhead] spent some three quarters of an hour with the Prime Minister. The Prime Minister began with enquiries about his American visit and talked of the relative merits of different hotels and steam-ship companies like a man who was rather diffident about approaching the real object of the meeting. Some allusion, however, to American agriculture brought Baldwin to the point. He gave some account of the reasons which had led him to undertake this new departure, and finally said that now that our Liberal opponents were re-united he was wondering whether the time had not come when we could completely re-unite the Conservative Party. F.E.

replied that that was his wish also. He presently said that of course he and I had been acting in close intimacy – that I knew that he was seeing the Prime Minister, and that he would wish to consult with me before giving any answer on the larger questions which were now being opened up. He therefore suggested, in accordance with what had been previously agreed between us, that he and I should return together ...

We returned at 2.45, Baldwin explaining that he had been obliged to advance the hour as the King desired to see him at 3.45. Baldwin ... said that he wanted to see whether it was possible to re-unite the party in this fight and added 'perhaps you would like to know why I decided upon the course which I have taken?' He explained both his reasons for taking up the subject and for not including wheat and meat – the reasons for the latter decision being that he was advised that the country was not prepared for it and that he would undoubtedly have split the Cabinet by it. I then again asked him 'but what do you mean by re-uniting the party? Do you mean merely that we are to fight together, or that we are to join your Government?', and I added 'Let me say at once, whatever the result of our interview, I shall, as I have already publicly stated, fight on your side,' and F.E. interjected, 'So shall I.' But I added that I should, and must, take a greater measure of independence if I spoke as a free-lance than would be compatible with my position if I accepted the well-understood obligations and restrictions of Cabinet responsibility.

Baldwin then said that his hope was that if we fought together in the elections it might be found possible afterwards that we should become colleagues, but on my repeating that I still did not understand exactly what was on his mind, he said, 'I want to know what is in your minds'. I therefore said that I would speak to him with perfect frankness; that I could not yet profess to know exactly what his policy was, and must have further explanations of it before I could take the responsibility of joining the Government; but that under no circumstances would I come under any conditional engagement to join at a future date. I hoped I had made it clear to him in our Chequers conversation[12] that I was not prepared to be put on probation or to have it intimated to me that if I ran well in the race there would perhaps be a bunch of carrots at the other end. The Prime Minister said, 'Oh, do not put it that way!' I replied that that was how it inevitably appeared and it was in any case an impossible position. He was contemplating that we should take ministerial

<hr>

[12] The previous May, above p. 89.

responsibility for a policy about which we had not been consulted and which
I must frankly say I thought went either too far or not far enough. But there
were still questions about which no decision had been taken. He said that
was principally agriculture. I assented but added that there was also the
question whether within his Manchester pledge[13] something might not still
be done in favour of Dominion wheat and beef on the analogy of what he
contemplated doing for home agriculture. In any case if we were not members of the Cabinet they might be taking decisions in the interval on one
subject or another which would raise new differences between them and
us. It was therefore quite impossible to give any contingent undertakings.
If we were to join at all, we ought to join at once: that I did not suggest
that there should be any displacement of existing ministers at the moment,
but that if he wished it, F.E. and I could join temporarily as ministers without portfolio and without salary. But I must be quite frank with him – I
thought he would have understood from what passed at Chequers (though
I had tried to speak with great restraint) that I felt that I had at that time
been subjected to great and public indignity, and that I was not prepared to
join the Government myself, nor could I ask or advise F.E. to join, except in
positions which could show clearly that we returned to the counsels of the
party on the same footing of influence and authority as we had previously
held. I said that in my case this did not mean a claim to any particular office
such, for instance, as the Foreign Office. The resumption of the Privy Seal,
or, indeed, several other alternatives, would equally satisfy my view; but that
the case of a Lord Chancellor was different. There was no other office which
an ex-Lord Chancellor could accept without derogating. Baldwin at once
said that this raised the question of Cave's position, and I said that I was very
sorry that private and public interests should clash in this way – that I had
not a word to say against Cave and had nothing but the most friendly feelings
for him – but it was, I feared, inevitable. We added that there were one or
two men to whom we were bound in honour and whose ultimate inclusion
in the Government would be necessary to enable us to take part in it.

Baldwin enquired who these were, and we told him Leslie Scott, who
ought to have the Solicitor-Generalship (Inskip getting the promise of a
puisne judgeship), Crawford, who had rendered great services to the party
in the past and been a most loyal friend to us in recent difficulties, Jack
Gilmour, to whom since the Carlton meeting he was scarcely less indebted

---

[13] Speaking on 2 November, Baldwin had gone further than before on imperial policy, promising
'substantial preference to our Dominions'.

than we were, and Oliver Locker-Lampson. He made no comment on these names except to acknowledge his obligations to Gilmour.

F.E. himself said that he had never made personal conditions for himself, that it was distasteful to do so, and that whilst he desired no office except the Lord Chancellorship he would be willing to accept office without portfolio for the election, to do all he could for the Government, and to retire as a friend and with no ill-will when the election was over.

We had some discussion as to the date of the election which both of us held ought now to take place at the earliest possible moment, but I think this is the whole substance of the conversation which Baldwin concluded by saying that he must now go to the King, but that he was very glad to feel that he knew exactly my mind which even after the Chequers conversation he was not quite sure that he understood. Baldwin was evidently unwilling to commit himself and was anxious to find out exactly where we stood without committing himself except to the pious hope that we re-join the Government in unspecified capacities after the election. Whether I was wise under these circumstances to talk so frankly depends upon whether he is genuinely anxious for re-union or only manoeuvring for position.

About 5.30 Baldwin telephoned for us to join him and Derby at Downing Street, which we immediately did. Derby at once took the floor and explained his reasons for desiring to postpone the election. I am told, and believe, that Derby is the man who has pressed most strongly upon Baldwin the necessity of including Birkenhead and it was clear Birkenhead and I were sent for in order that we might persuade Derby – which we did. The Prime Minister took no part in the conversation except to say that he entirely agreed with what we had said.

12 NOVEMBER 1923 KING GEORGE V MEMORANDUM

RA PS/GV K.1894/2; H. Nicolson, *King George V* (1952), p. 380

This afternoon, the Prime Minister came to see me and asked for an immediate dissolution: he said that probably after a speech he was making on Tuesday he would dissolve Parliament.

He assured me that it was absolutely necessary for him to appeal to the Country as he had gone so far that it was not possible for him to change his mind. I then pointed out to him that I strongly deprecated a dissolution at this moment as I had implicit confidence in him and in the Conservative

Party now in power, and I considered that as most countries in Europe, if not the world, were in a chaotic and indeed dangerous state, it would be a pity if this Country were to be plunged into the turmoil of a General Election on a question of domestic policy which will arouse all the old traditional bitterness of the hard fought battles between Protection and Free Trade: also that it was quite possible that his majority might be reduced, or that he might not get a majority at all.

I was therefore prepared to take the responsibility of advising him to change his mind, and I was also prepared for him to tell his friends that I had done so.

He answered that he had gone too far now and that the Country expected a dissolution; he would appeal to the Country at once, and he hoped to get the General Election over by about the 6th December, and he was ready to stand or fall by the result.

I asked him whether all the Peers who were his colleagues were in favour of tariff reform, and he said that several of them were, perhaps, too Conservative and did not want a change.

He also said he had seen Mr Austen Chamberlain and Lord Birkenhead today, and they had both assured him that they would give him their whole and entire support in this election; and he asked me whether he might make these two additional Cabinet Ministers without salaries, and I gave my approval.

I also asked him if he did not think that this would unite the Liberal Party and he said yes, probably it would, and it would be a very good thing if it did.

At the Cabinet next morning, 13 November, Baldwin announced the decision to dissolve Parliament on the 16th. He was now receiving objections from his allies against Birkenhead's appointment, while some Salisburyite ministers were close to resignation. In the evening Wood, acting as conciliator, asked Baldwin 'point blank whether he wished to get rid of Salisbury and Co. He said he certainly did not.' On Wood arguing that he should see Salisbury and 'make it as easy' as possible for him to stay, Baldwin said 'the reason he had taken no action was that he thought when he saw people wrestling with their consciences it was indecent for a third party to intervene'.[14] He did, however, later write to Salisbury.

---

[14] Wood, 'Record of some events preceding the dissolution and general election, Nov.–Dec. 1923', SB papers 35/9-15.

[13 NOVEMBER 1923] AUSTEN CHAMBERLAIN
MEMORANDUM, WRITTEN 14 NOVEMBER

AC 35/3/21c (extract)

. . . About 6 o'clock Baldwin sent for F.E. alone to his room in the House of Commons. There Baldwin appears to have said that he did not know whether F.E. was aware that he had aroused very considerable hostility to himself in some sections of the party, and that in addition his rectorial address had offended ecclesiastical circles[15] and he enquired whether it really was not possible for F.E. to agree to fight the election with them on the understanding that he would join the Government in some suitable – but undefined – position after the election. F.E. replied that this was quite out of the question: that I had stated our views upon the subject yesterday, and that that statement was final: Baldwin had got to make his choice; if there was any question of resignation, whether the strength he would gain by our accession was greater or less than that which he would lose – this was entirely a question for the Prime Minister and not for us. He advised the Prime Minister to take his own line and act without consultation with anybody: he did not believe that any resignation would follow.

F.E. told me that he felt sure that Baldwin's idea was to ask me to take the Colonial Secretaryship immediately if he had assented; Baldwin had made no suggestion that I also should stand out till after the election . . .

13 NOVEMBER 1923: TO LORD SALISBURY

Hatfield House archives 4M/107/87

House of Commons

My dear Salisbury,

I have a sort of feeling that it is indecent to butt in where a man is wrestling with his conscience, but I cannot help writing to you to tell you that it would be a real grief to me if you were to resign. I have been so proud of my team, that I should blame myself horribly if we could not face the election a united family. Forgive me.

Yours very sincerely/ Stanley Baldwin[16]

---

[15] Birkenhead's address as Rector of Glasgow University on 7 November had shocked many supporters of peace and the League of Nations, in all parties. Attacking 'international idealism', he had reinterpreted the Sermon on the Mount and declared that 'the world continues to offer glittering prizes to those who have stout hearts and sharp swords'.
[16] Salisbury's annotation to this letter states that it 'induced me to try and come to terms'.

Next day, 14 November, the Salisburyites decided to remain in office after reaching an arrangement with Baldwin on the detailed presentation of the policy. Birkenhead and Chamberlain wrote to Baldwin that they were now unwilling to join the government, but would support it at the election. Baldwin's replies were very carefully drafted, and in Birkenhead's case re-drafted.

14 NOVEMBER 1923: TO BIRKENHEAD (DRAFT)

handwritten, with Baldwin amendments, SB papers 35/93-4; final version published in *The Times*, 16 November 1923, p. 14d

10, Downing Street

Dear Birkenhead,

I have given most careful thought to the subject of our recent conversation and I am convinced that the proposals you & Austen made to me are impossible at the present moment.

I feel sure however that you will give the party your full support at the Election in obtaining a complete victory for the policy for which you and I have striven so long. Above all I feel confident that you will help Derby to keep our flag flying in Lancashire.

What is not possible now ~~will~~ [may][17] be more easily accomplished ~~after the election~~ [later] & I ~~am quite certain~~ [have every hope] that we shall then be able to ~~consummate~~ [achieve] the complete union of the Party ~~in a very short space of time~~.

I ought to thank you for coming to see me & for the frankness with which you expressed yourself to me.

If you would like to discuss plans for the campaign with Derby and myself, I should be very pleased to do so at anytime. I need hardly say how much I should value your's and Austen's advice.

15 NOVEMBER 1923: TO AUSTEN CHAMBERLAIN

AC 35/3/4; *The Times*, 16 November 1923, p. 14d

10, Downing Street

My dear Chamberlain,

I am obliged to you for your letter and I regret equally with you that it was not possible for me to fall in with the proposals which you and Birkenhead

---

[17] Square brackets indicate words inserted by Baldwin.

made to me. To have made supernumerary appointments to the Cabinet on the eve of an Election would have been open to obvious objections and, in my view, extremely difficult to justify. The only alternative would have been to replace two of my existing colleagues who have served in the present Cabinet for the past year and this, as you would be the first to appreciate, is unthinkable. I only write to make my point perfectly clear . . .

Yours very sincerely/ Stanley Baldwin

21 NOVEMBER 1923: TO LOUISA BALDWIN

10, Downing Street

Dearest Mother

Your noble offer has taken my breath away![18]

It really has lifted a little load from my mind.

I had to borrow £1000 for my election a year ago, and I have just borrowed £1000 for this election.

My expenditure is bound to exceed my income until Baldwins resume dividends. Of course one has no time to look after one's private affairs and I can always get straight by selling capital.[19]

But if I dropped out of office, I should have to economise pretty strictly for a year or so.

So most gratefully and unhesitatingly I say Yes!

I am just off to Reading, and have a ghastly programme ahead for the next fortnight . . .

It is too early to make any forecast of the result but I feel fairly hopeful.

Always thy loving/ Son

The Unionists faced criticism from both the Rothermere and the Beaverbrook newspapers, and a further concern was revival by the Liberal party, reinvigorated by former Coalition government leaders. 'We have had a bad lot to beat, L.G. and Winston, Beaverbrook & Rothermere. The syndicated press hate me

---

[18] Louisa had sent her son £2,000 (in modern terms worth about £70,000) to help with his West Worcestershire election campaign.

[19] Baldwin's private income and wealth had been much reduced by the industrial depression. Baldwins Ltd paid no dividend between 1921 and 1934. Even in 1922 he had considered moving to a smaller London house, until occupation of 11 and then 10 Downing Street postponed the decision.

because they can get nothing out of me, and we will down them once and for all.'[20]

At the election on 6 December, the Unionists lost over eighty seats and their overall House of Commons majority. With 258 Unionists, 191 Labour and 158 Liberals, there was uncertainty among leading politicians on how to proceed and among other public figures on what to advise. As Baldwin's responsibility for the Unionist setback was so complete, he began by sharing a common view that he should resign immediately from both the premiership and party leadership. The parliamentary arithmetic stimulated thoughts of some new coalition; Birkenhead sought revenge by trying to re-create the old Coalition; and Baldwin had reason to suspect wider intrigues against him. However, his bitter comments against his newspaper and Coalitionist enemies were balanced by more philosophical observations: 'you understand what many never will – that there are better things than high office'.[21]

[7 DECEMBER 1923] DAWSON MEMORANDUM,
WRITTEN 20 DECEMBER

Dawson papers 70/92–119 (extract)

... down to Downing St to see the P.M. (my first sight of him since Oct 18) & find out what he thought of the situation.

Baldwin was in the Cabinet room alone, looking rather worn but with an air almost of jauntiness, as of one who'd done the obvious thing & had no regrets. He began by thanking me for the help 'The Times' had given him &

---

[20] To Long, 24 Nov. 1923, Long papers 62427/201. Although Baldwin was evidently anxious about Lloyd George, a sentence from Jones' published diary has been misleading. His valuable record of Baldwin at Astley Hall at this time refers to a defaced picture of Lloyd George, and the implication has been that this was Baldwin's own work and proof of an extraordinary personal hatred. The original text gives a quite different explanation. Jones found 'a number of scrap albums compiled by S.B.'s mother for the grandchildren ... There were I think eight of them filled with newspaper photographs of famous statesmen.' Then follows the published text 'I came across a picture of Lloyd George as Chancellor of the Exchequer defaced! How they do hate him' (Jones unpublished diary 25 Nov. 1923; Jones *WD*, I, p. 256). This was evidently a small child's destructiveness, committed years earlier: the youngest grandchild was born in 1902, and Lloyd George had been Chancellor 1908–15. Oddly, there is similar disparity between printed and original texts of Kathleen Hilton Young's diary, 4 Feb. 1928. *Self-Portrait of an Artist*, ed. Lord Kennet (1949), p. 258, says that at Chequers Baldwin 'won't sleep in Lloyd George's bedroom', but the manuscript original has only the factual statement that Baldwin's bedroom was different from that used by Lloyd George. In contrast Airlie, *Thatched with Gold*, p. 173, records that a Lloyd George photograph was prominent in Baldwin's room at Chequers.
[21] To Sir Willoughby Dickinson (Joan Davidson's father), 16 Dec. 1923, Dickinson papers D6/X5/3.

went on, after his manner, to 'think aloud' of possible permutations and combinations. No one party, he assumed, could carry on the Govt alone. Was the best course a Conservative-Liberal, or a Liberal-Labour arrangement? If the former, was it to be under Asquith or Grey or Balfour or Austen Chamberlain? He himself was clearly ruled out. At that moment indeed he seemed to contemplate his own immediate withdrawal, not only from the Govt, but from the leadership of the party. He asked me to turn over the various possibilities & I left him very soon for a whole ante-room of people – Sam Hoare, Monty Norman of the Bank of England, Stanley Jackson his new party manager[22] – were waiting to see him. I gave up dinner & wrote another leader on getting back to the office – not minimising the result of the election, but pointing out some consoling features in it & ending on the note that it was still Baldwin's business to see that the King's Govt was carried on . . .

8 DECEMBER 1923 STAMFORDHAM MEMORANDUM

RA PS/GV/K.1918/14; R. Churchill, *Lord Derby, King of Lancashire* (1959), p. 551

I saw the Prime Minister at 10 a.m.

He asked that the King would postpone seeing him until Monday next, the 10th. instant; he had only returned last night, had so far only seen a few of his colleagues and therefore had come to no decision as to his action. But his present view was, not to meet Parliament but to resign. He had asked the country for a mandate for Tariff Reform, this had been refused and the honourable thing would be for him to resign at once.

He then touched upon the question of his successor; and, though he was aware that the choice of the Prime Minister was entirely the prerogative of the Sovereign, if the King should seek his advice it seemed to him that there were only two alternatives:

(1) A Liberal-Conservative Government; or

(2) A Liberal-Labour Government.

The latter seemed to him almost impossible, as the Labour policy was primarily based upon the two principles of a Levy on Capital and Nationalisation. Also, he did not believe that Labour would coalesce with a

---

[22] Unionist party chairman March 1923 – October 1926.

Government of which Mr Lloyd George was a member. But he thought that Mr Asquith might form a Coalition with the Conservatives, although there again Mr Lloyd George might be a difficulty.

I asked him if it would not be possible for someone else to form a Coalition and I mentioned Mr Austen Chamberlain, but this did not seem to appeal to him much.

Anyhow he considered his first duty was to ensure that the King had a Ministry to carry on the Government of the country.

He talked for some time about the extraordinary and unexpected result of the Election, which had upset every calculation made by the experts both on the Conservative and Liberal sides.

10 DECEMBER 1923 STAMFORDHAM MEMORANDUM

RA, PS/GV/K.1918/34; Churchill, *Derby*, p. 552

The King saw the Prime Minister at 12 noon: and began by asking what his views were as to his course of action and His Majesty was glad to find that, on the whole, they coincided with his own.

After the result of the Elections, Mr Baldwin's first thought was to resign immediately: but he found on reflection that there was a strong feeling amongst his supporters that he should meet Parliament[23] and that former precedent did not apply in this instance, in which the question at issue was one concerning not two but three Parties, and that the House of Commons was the proper place for the choice of the electorate to be made known.

The Prime Minister was not quite certain whether his resignation necessitated that of his Cabinet, but the King held that the one involved the other.

His Majesty gave his reasons for holding that the Prime Minister and his Government should meet the House of Commons and added that, so far as His Majesty could ascertain, it looked as if neither of the Parties in Opposition were anxious to assume office.

The King also put forward that it had been suggested as a dangerous possibility that, in the event of his sending for Mr Ramsay MacDonald, the latter might introduce a Budget including a Levy on Capital, increased

---

[23] For Baldwin's weekend talks with supporters, see *Bridgeman Diaries*, pp. 172–4, and *Amery Diaries*, I, p. 361.

income and super-tax and death duties and, on its being thrown out, go to the country with the cry that this splendid and tempting proposal had been turned down, which would probably result in an overwhelming Labour victory throughout the country.

The Prime Minister expressed himself as absolutely opposed to any Coalition: he had killed one and would never join another. The King suggested that, if Mr Baldwin continued in office, he might be able to approach Mr Asquith with a view to ascertaining what, if any, cooperation the Government might receive from the Liberals. Possibly the latter might be glad to make some working arrangement to maintain the Conservatives in power for the present. The Prime Minister, whom the King found most pleasant and amenable, said he would lay the whole matter before his colleagues at a Cabinet Meeting tomorrow, and express to them the King's views in which His Majesty hoped his Government would concur.

On 11 December the Cabinet agreed to face Parliament, and afterwards Baldwin met Asquith in the Athenaeum, but only to tell him 'as a matter of courtesy' what had been decided. Asquith later reported that 'there had been no arrangements between them, nor any detailed discussion on the political situation'.[24] Archbishop Davidson had long experience as an intermediary in potential constitutional difficulties.

12 DECEMBER 1923 ARCHBISHOP DAVIDSON MEMORANDUM

Archbishop Davidson papers 14/263–6 (extract)

... to Stamfordham, where I found the Duke of Devonshire, and we three discussed the whole matter for some time ... They were both inclined to agree with me that Asquith would act fairly and rightly if he allowed Baldwin his chance, and did not oust him at the beginning of things ... Stamfordham felt that what I had told him about Asquith's opinion[25] ... was of extreme importance, and the Prime Minister, who had, he said, been behaving with the utmost simplicity, frankness, and desire to do what is right, ought to know, and he suggested that he should ring Downing Street and ask whether

---

[24] Dawson memo., 20 Dec. 1923, Dawson papers 70/92-119; Archbishop Randall Davidson memo., 12 Dec. 1923, Archbishop Davidson papers 14/263-6.
[25] The memo. reports an earlier conversation with Asquith, who had said that 'he must support the Labour resolution of want of confidence in the Government', i.e. securing its defeat: 'He spoke of this as though it had always been a matter of course.'

the Prime Minister would like to see me as I had been in touch with central folk about the situation. The Prime Minister rather eagerly accepted it, and said it would be of very real help . . . I went to Downing Street at five o'clock and . . . spent some forty minutes with the Prime Minister – he was most cheery, and friendly and altogether pleasant to talk with. He said 'nothing would please me better than to have your advice at a very difficult juncture. I am being pulled different ways by different people, and your view would be very important'.

I told him what had passed with Asquith . . . [Baldwin] replied that it was not by any means easy to say what would be best, but that he was rather coming to the conclusion, which had not been his 24 hours before, that it would be better to let matters take their course, and that complication rather than help might arise from any symptom of what might be called 'backstairs arrangements' between himself and Liberals:

'The danger is that we may make it easy and plausible for Labour to say we got our proper chance for turning Baldwin out and getting power, but the Liberals and Tories, being capitalists, determined to thwart us, and we must stiffen ourselves now into firm alliance against such scheming, and call the country to our aid. Obviously it is difficult to say whether this would be a wise course for MacDonald or not.'

Like Asquith, Baldwin had no doubt that Ramsay MacDonald would accept the Premiership if offered, and try to form a Government. Asquith had told him that he was sure MacDonald would do this, though he, Asquith, thought him rather ill-advised in so acting, considering the difficulties he would have to face. Baldwin did not think it ill-advised. I gathered that if he were in Ramsay MacDonald's place he would certainly try to form a Government. He was vigorously awake to the extraordinary position which would arise as regards the House of Lords . . . Even if Haldane accepted office, he could hardly run all the Government Departments in the House of Lords, yet, except Lord Russell, there is probably no other man who can be plausibly called a supporter of Labour, and the position would be almost ludicrous, for Ramsay MacDonald could hardly begin to request that Labour members be made Viscounts.[26] Baldwin, however, spoke most friendlily of the Labour folk, and showed me one or two interesting letters, notably one from Ramsay

---

[26] There were no official Labour party members in the Lords. Haldane, the former Liberal Lord Chancellor, did agree to join the 1924 Labour government, which helped MacDonald to recruit and create enough peers to form a scratch ministerial front bench there.

MacDonald, who wished him a good Christmas, and congratulated him upon the sense he, Baldwin, must have of having acted with straightness and a good conscience and high purpose.

In the end I left Baldwin promising to think over what he had said, and to tell him if anything more occurred to me. 'Something more must occur to you, for you must come and see me again'. I told him I was to be out of London, but he urged me that if I could come up one day next week he would greatly value a further talk. When I apologised for intervening, he took quite the other line, and urged me to give him any counsel which might occur to me. He expressed himself with great personal regard for Asquith, both as an honest man and as a public-spirited and capable thinker. Asquith had spoken friendlily of Baldwin, but rather contemptuously of his intellectual powers.

16 DECEMBER 1923: TO LORD CARSON

Carson papers D1507/B/43/9

House of Commons

My dear Carson,

I am most grateful to you for your kind letter.

I will never draw down the blinds until I am a political corpse, but if I do become one it will be by an honest blow delivered in open fight and not by a syphilitic dagger from the syndicated press.[27]

Yours ever/ Stanley Baldwin

16 DECEMBER 1923: TO LADY LONDONDERRY

Londonderry papers D3099/3/15/11

House of Commons

Dear Lady Londonderry,

Thank you so much for your kind letter.

I know all about the 'dirty and underhand work' you speak of, but it has got to be smashed and it will be. But it can't be done in a moment.

---

[27] Presumably derived from a rumour that Northcliffe had died from general paralysis of the insane.

This is a long fight, inevitable from the latter days of the Coalition. We will see it through.

Yours sincerely/ Stanley Baldwin

24 DECEMBER 1923: TO JOAN DAVIDSON

Lady Davidson papers; Davidson *Memoirs*, pp. 192–3

[Astley Hall]

Little Maid

... We are in for a green Christmas. We had snow from London to the Cotswolds and then it turned soft. Yesterday was a jewel for beauty. Transparently clear, all the country in a deep russet dress, long vividly bright horizontal sunshine casting long shadows in the morning: a dull midday, and then a divine evening. I wrote 62 letters of thanks yesterday! My Christmas letters this morning comprised an impudent demand for help, a long poem in which a criticism for publication was requested and a tax-demand notice! ...

This is a time for hanging out signals to our friends. How can I tell you what you have been to me for yet another year? Life has nothing more precious than your friendship and I bless you for it every day. You will never know how you help me and what I have done that I should have that amazing friendship that you and David give me, I know not. But I am thankful for it.

And this is true, that the love that binds us three together makes it easier to generate that wider love that alone makes it possible to carry on in public life. Everything else is dead sea fruit. The longing to help the bewildered multitude of common folk is the only motive power to make me face the hundred and one things I loathe so much. And the longing to help only comes from love and pity. As I have said before, God bless you for all you are.

Your loving/ S.B.

On 18 December Asquith had publicly declared that Liberal MPs would not support the Unionist government when Parliament re-assembled in January. Various groups continued to discuss Baldwin's removal and new political alignments, but Baldwin had the strength of being for most Unionists the obstacle to any renewed coalition. The Cabinet agreed to make no effort to avoid defeat, and after the Liberals voted for a Labour censure motion Baldwin resigned as Prime Minister on 22 January 1924. Later that day, MacDonald formed the first Labour government.

FIVE

Leader of the Opposition

JANUARY – OCTOBER 1924

Before the House of Commons defeat, the Unionist party leaders and senior officials had agreed to hold a party meeting in February. Two major issues were at stake: Baldwin's leadership of the party, and the party's main policy, given the election majority against protection. With a Labour government taking office and Liberal MPs, including Lloyd George, giving it conditional support, Baldwin considered that early Unionist party reunion was now both highly desirable and possible. This effort to bring together the Chamberlainites, Salisburyites and his protectionist allies involved some embarrassment, personal as well as political.

[25 JANUARY 1924] HEWINS DIARY, WRITTEN 8 FEBRUARY

I saw Stanley Baldwin . . . at 10, Downing St upstairs. His furniture was being removed. He was in good spirits though he said he had found recent events a 'nervous strain'. He agreed with me about the present govt. & thought there was no danger of revolutionary legislation. But he did not want them to come out yet. It was first necessary to secure the complete reunion of the Conservative party. This was the subject he wanted to talk about. He said of course he wished . . . to bring Austen & his friends back into the counsels of the party as ex-Cabinet Ministers but they insisted on the full inclusion of Birkenhead & that was the real difficulty because of the strong feeling against him within the party. He asked me what I thought about it. I said he shd. be brought back. Everyone knew the real cause of his vagaries.[1] I preserved an affection for him & was very sorry for him. I could not sit in

---

[1] This might refer to Birkenhead's drinking, or his financial problems.

judgment on him. Nor could the party. He had the right to be admitted to the counsels of the party. But F.E. seems to do his best to make himself impossible. The second subject on wh. Baldwin wanted to talk to me was the future of Protection in view of the pressure within the party to give up the policy. I said that he had come deliberately to the conclusion that he could not deal with the economic situation, could not in fact stay in office, unless he could use a tariff. If he believed as he did that this was a true conclusion he could not now abandon the policy since one did not give up what was true. Therefore whatever might be the issue of the next election he must make it clear that he wd. be free to put on a tariff . . .

25 JANUARY 1924: TO LOUISA BALDWIN

Travellers' Club

Dearest Mother,

This has been a strenuous time but to-morrow we are off for a few days of what I hope will be real rest. Geoffrey Fry has lent us his house in the Wiltshire Downs . . .

The final debate was a good one, and I think we were on top all through. The new government will provide much of interest. It may break from the sheer weight of the work of unskilled men. The King has been very good all through and we had a very friendly half hour together.

It seems so curious after seven years having no office to go down to, and even after eight months to have no police with me.

Every one is extraordinarily kind and I feel happy and care-free.

I hope to breakfast with the Kiplings before I leave in the morning . . .

Much best love/ Ever thy loving/ Son

25 JANUARY 1924: TO SALISBURY

Hatfield House archives 4M/108/83

Private   Travellers' Club

My dear Salisbury,

I think Neville Chamberlain spoke to you about Austen and his friends.

The House of Commons members of the late Cabinet are unanimous in their opinion that we must have Austen & Horne on the front bench in Opposition and that it would be foolish to lose this opportunity of healing the breach. Some of us hate the idea of receiving F.E. in full communion, but if it is Austen + F.E. or no Austen, we feel it must be Austen + F.E.

There is no bargain or guarantee of office in the case.

Cave & Curzon both agree with me. I hope you will feel the same.

I tried to get you this morning when I saw Curzon but you had left town . . . Send me a line . . . if you will. I want to write to Austen soon.

I had intended when I saw you to thank you for your unvarying support during the last 8 months.

It hasn't been an easy time and you have all of you been very good to me.

Ever yours/ Stanley Baldwin

In reply Salisbury accepted Austen Chamberlain but objected to Birkenhead as personally 'disreputable' and politically repellent to 'the leaders of thought in the democracy'.[2] Similar objections came from Cecil and some others, so Baldwin did not proceed with his proposed letter of invitation to Chamberlain. At the end of the month he wrote that 'I am really worried about Austen and F.E. I cannot see the way clearly yet.'[3]

4 FEBRUARY 1924 LORD BALFOUR MEMORANDUM

Balfour Whittingehame papers GD 433/2/19/32

Mr Baldwin asked to see me this afternoon, and we had a long conversation, much of which was devoted to Cambridge and other topics unconnected with politics, but the important part dealing with the existing situation . . .

He asked me what had happened after the defeat of my Government in the election of 1906. I told him that, so far as I could remember, the question of my Leadership never was raised, and that there was an important difference between my position in January 1906 and his position in January 1924. The election of 1906 was not my act in the sense that the Election of 1923 was his. Undoubtedly he was in a somewhat peculiar position, because he had committed himself to the two propositions that the great pressing problem for British statesmanship at the present moment was Unemployment, and that the only way to deal with Unemployment was by Tariff reform. If he thought fit, therefore, it seemed to me that he would be perfectly justified

---

[2] Salisbury to Baldwin, 26 Jan. 1924, partly printed in M. Cowling, *The Impact of Labour 1920–24* (Cambridge, 1971), p. ix.
[3] To Joan Davidson, 30 Jan. 1924.

in not merely putting himself in the hands of the Party as to whether he should continue to lead or not, but in going further and saying that under no circumstances would he retain his personal position. I added that from what I could learn I was convinced that if he merely resigned and put himself in the hands of the Party he would be unanimously re-elected. I gather that of these two alternatives he proposed to adopt the second.

We then discussed the position of the members of the late Coalition Government who were still out of office when the Election took place. He told me that, so far as the members of the out-going Cabinet were concerned, he was convinced that all, even Jim Salisbury, would welcome the collaboration of Austen. F.E. was a more difficult proposition; and I admitted that F.E.'s actions since the break-up of the Coalition had not been of the kind which conciliated doubtful suffrages. Baldwin went to the length of saying that he thought at the present moment F.E. would be a liability rather than an asset to any Party which adopted him; and that there were other difficulties of which we both knew. I said that this might be true; but that F.E.'s abilities were so great that I did not think he could be ignored; or that the Party union could be regarded as complete if he was not in the councils of the Party. I understood that this was also Baldwin's view; though he foresaw considerable difficulties in carrying it out.

Finally I gathered that the policy on which he was determined was to have an interview with Austen tomorrow, and, if all went well, to write a letter to him and to F.E. asking them to join in what in old days was called a 'Shadow' Cabinet to decide upon the policy of the Party. This, of course, would take place before the meeting next Monday. I expressed my own personal adhesion to this policy.

[5 FEBRUARY 1924] AUSTEN CHAMBERLAIN MEMORANDUM, WRITTEN 7 FEBRUARY

typescript, AC 35/4/35; partly in Petrie, *Austen Chamberlain*, II, p. 240

Neville asked me to dine with him on Tuesday, February 5th, to meet Stanley Baldwin . . . as soon as dinner was over Neville . . . invited Baldwin to say what he had to say.[4]

Baldwin then said, 'Well, I think that in present circumstances and in the position in which we are now it is time for all of us to get together'. He had

[4] See also *NC Letters*, II, p. 207.

asked the members of the late Cabinet to meet him at 3 o'clock on Thursday to consider our policy, and he wished to know whether I would join their meeting and sit with them on the front Opposition bench. If I accepted, he proposed to ask the other Unionist Ministers who left office with me, and Lord Balfour had already agreed to come if we came.

I replied, after a moment's hesitation, that to such a proposal so made I could only give one answer. I accepted, and I was in a position to say that Lord Birkenhead would do the same.

We then had a long conversation on policy. I told Baldwin that, whilst I would not separate myself from him if he decided to stand by his Plymouth policy, I could not advise that course. He and Neville appeared to agree that the proper course was to get back to the pre-election attitude on tariff questions. I also protested strongly against Baldwin resigning the leadership and submitting himself for re-election like a company auditor. Such procedure would be undignified and farcical. If he had come to the conclusion that he could not, or ought not, to carry on, there was only one course for him to take. It was to withdraw definitely and absolutely and leave the Party to choose another Leader. As this was not his view, his proper course was to come as Leader to the meeting to make to his followers a clear statement of the policy which he recommended to them. There might be some grumbling but he would certainly get his vote of confidence and very probably by acclamation. I told him that F.E. and I had discussed the situation before I had any reason to think that he meant to see me: that whilst we felt we could easily have organised an opposition which would make his position impossible, that would not have been in the interests of the Party, for the position of any successor would have been quite as difficult. We, therefore, had given no encouragement to any opposition and were confident that no-one would have allowed his name to be put forward in competition to Baldwin even though the present overture had not been made and accepted. He thought it probable that Bob Cecil would refuse to attend if F.E. were invited and Salisbury might take the same line. I observed that neither of them had given assistance during the election and that Bob Cecil had not only been, as Asquith phrased it to me, 'up to the eyes in negotiations for joining the Liberal Party' before Baldwin invited him to become a member of the late Cabinet but had according to my information been with difficulty restrained by Salisbury from joining the Labour Government. He in fact only had one idea at the present time, namely, the League of Nations and had ceased to be in any real sense of the word a member of our Party sharing its general aspirations and wishes. If Salisbury took the same line, I should be surprised & sorry, but I presumed that Baldwin had by this time made up his mind on which side the balance of advantage lay.

Next day Baldwin invited the Chamberlainite ex-Cabinet ministers to attend a 'shadow Cabinet' at his Eaton Square house on 7 February. Only just before this leaders' meeting did he inform Salisbury that they would be present; Salisbury nevertheless attended, and silently acquiesced in their presence. The meeting accepted Austen Chamberlain's tactical proposals. At the meeting of the parliamentary party and defeated candidates on 11 February, the question of leadership was not raised. Baldwin declared that, given the election result, 'I do not feel justified in advising the Party again to submit the proposal for a general tariff to the country, except upon clear evidence that on this matter public opinion was disposed to reconsider its judgment.' In its place he spoke of social reform as the focus of Unionism idealism and a 'live, progressive, united party'.

The reunion suffered early strains, the most serious relating to Churchill. Defeated as a Liberal at the 1922 and 1923 elections, he now criticised Asquith's and Lloyd George's decision to tolerate a Labour government, and spoke of creating a breakaway Liberal movement. In late February he proposed to stand as an Independent candidate with Unionist support at the Abbey, Westminster by-election. Baldwin at first encouraged him, alert to the advantage of winning over Churchill and other anti-socialist Liberals to the Unionist side. But then the local Unionist party insisted on having their own candidate, Nicholson. Despite advice from some former Unionist Coalition allies, Churchill refused to withdraw and sought support from Balfour. Baldwin's most protectionist colleagues suspected Churchill's free-trade views, and argued that the official party candidate had to be supported. The issue became 'a great worry to him': 'Leading a party is like driving pigs to market!'[5]

13 MARCH 1924: TO JOAN DAVIDSON

Lady Davidson papers

House of Commons

Little Maid

... And while you have been living in velvet and wrapped in cotton wool and the telephone is silent and you are where the voice of the Beaver cannot

---

[5] To Louisa Baldwin, 10 March 1924. Further documentation on Baldwin's part in this awkward episode is in *WSC* V/1, pp. 113–25; *Amery Diaries*, I, pp. 372–4.

penetrate,[6] do you care to hear news from the devil's kitchen where I still am? Saturday and Sunday I worked, and on Saturday I suffered from paralysis of all my faculties.

I just could not think. One gets like that at times. And when I tried to work, excursions and alarums from Westminster – Jacker, Bobby,[7] und so weiter. But I did succeed in preparing a powerful speech for Monday on the Unemployment Debate and it really wasn't a bad one. Anyway, we gave Tom Shaw[8] a horrible time and it has shaken them badly. In response to my reiterated invitation to the Minister to produce the 'only positive remedy for unemployment' (vide the Labour Manifesto at the Election) he could only say 'I can't produce rabbits out of a top 'at'. That saying, which has run round the Empire by now, has caused the most painful sensation in Labour circles throughout Great Britain . . .

I hate your being away and I miss my walks . . .

20 MARCH 1924: TO JOAN DAVIDSON

Lady Davidson papers; *Davidson Memoirs*, pp. 194–5

Little Maid

. . . I am still having a heavy time. I filled myself up too much and have had to speak at lunch or dinner daily. After Scotland[9] I have a lull and shall breathe more freely.

Last Saturday I had a really worrying day. I got back tired and longing for bed soon after eleven on Friday night: Speaker's party. I found a letter which mercifully I opened. It contained a letter from Balfour to Winston wishing him success and a note saying he wouldn't send it if I objected. To leap into the car again and drive off to Carlton Gardens was the work of a moment. I stayed with him till after midnight. He was leaving for Cannes in the morning. We had a long and intimate talk and he decided without demur not to send the letter which I kept in my pocket.[10] So back and to bed feeling more at peace than for several nights. Now, I thought, there is nothing else that can happen till the election is over. Next morning I opened

---

[6] I.e. Beaverbrook's newspapers. The Davidsons were en route to Argentina.
[7] Jackson, and Eyres-Monsell, the chief whip.   [8] Minister of Labour.
[9] Baldwin spoke in Edinburgh on 24 March, and Perth on the following day.
[10] Balfour to Churchill, 15 March 1924, Balfour Whittingehame papers GD 433/2/1/15: Baldwin 'told me in so many words that if my letter went it would break up the Party'.

my <u>Times</u> in bed as is my custom and to my horror set eyes on a letter from Amery to Nicholson. I saw in a moment what that meant.[11]

By ten o'clock a letter came round from A. J. B. saying Amery's letter had altered everything and that it wasn't fair, etc. and his letter ought to go to Winston, but he was leaving at once and left me to do as I thought right.

About eleven, first communication from Austen: of course he was all over the place & if Balfour's letter was bottled up he would let fly! I found by lunch time that it was common knowledge that Balfour had written this letter, and that I had it. I released it, as I was in honour bound to after Amery's letter, for which I was responsible technically though I never dreamed he would be such a fool. We had succeeded up to that moment in keeping our differences out of the papers, and now the enemy have had a glorious time. While I write the counting is proceeding and the issue is very open.

. . . I am very overworked: I have to speak for an hour at Birkbeck College and the preparation at odd moments has worried me. Then I have Edinburgh and Perth to finish . . .

Churchill narrowly lost to Nicholson, but over the next few months he continued to organise a 'constitutionalist' group of Liberals and to move towards the Unionists. On 27 March Hewins caught Baldwin in a particularly low mood: he 'said he was very worried, that it was more difficult to be leader than Prime Minister & that he did not know whom to trust'.[12] The Beaverbrook newspapers again joined the Rothermere press in attacking him, and St Loe Strachey, editor of *The Spectator*, wrote in May to express 'indignation and indeed humiliation' at finding the press 'prostituted . . . as the medium of a private vendetta'.[13]

9 MAY 1924: TO STRACHEY

Strachey papers 2/3/16

United University Club, Pall Mall East, S.W.1.

Dear Mr Strachey,

Your kind and generous letter gave me real pleasure.

You are right: I am indifferent to Beaverbrook's attacks, but I understand your feeling and that of all honourable members of your great profession.

[11] I.e. that as the tacit agreement among leading Unionists to remain silent on Churchill's candidature had been breached, his Coalitionist Unionist sympathisers would insist on replying, and Unionist differences would again be publicly exposed.
[12] Hewins diary, written 8 April 1924. [13] 7 May 1924, SB papers 159/264.

He lowers everything he touches.

It was intimated to me some time ago that it would be different if I would consult with him and generally take him into my confidence!

Non tali auxilio.[14] He was spoiled by my predecessors.

I have no personal feelings against him: I have known him slightly for years.

But his ways are not mine and I prefer things as they are, in spite of certain obvious disadvantages.

Thank you again for writing and for your article which I have just seen.

Yours sincerely/ Stanley Baldwin

On 18 May *The People* published an interview with Baldwin, in which he reflected on his party's strategy but also made observations about Lloyd George, Churchill, Birkenhead, Austen Chamberlain, Beaverbrook and Rothermere which were startlingly caustic, and as such potentially damaging to Baldwin himself (see Appendix B). The Unionist Central Office issued statements declaring that the reported comments were inaccurate, and Baldwin wrote or spoke to the individuals concerned (except, it appears, Lloyd George), denying that he had said these things. The draft letter for Rothermere is given, as an example of the difficulty and delicacy of the task.[15] All the recipients chose not to seek advantage from the article, and readily indicated their acceptance that Baldwin had been misrepresented.

[19 MAY 1924]: TO ROTHERMERE

pencilled and amended draft, SB papers 56/4

~~Strictly personal~~ Private & confidential

Dear Lord R.

You will, I hope, pardon me for referring to what I am alleged to have said in an interview published in yesterday's issue of the 'People'.

I accept your statement which has – I understand – appeared in several of your journals, that we have never met. In any event, I trust you will believe me when I say that I never gave expression to the personal reflections on yourself ~~and other public men which were reported~~ nor to the remarks on the Daily Mail.

---

[14] 'Not with this kind of help' (Virgil, *Aeneid*).
[15] The letter to Churchill is printed in *WSC V/1*, p. 161.

~~Whatever my personal opinions might be about individuals, I could never be capable of giving them to the world through the intermediary of a third party, and~~ I am deeply concerned that I should have been so gravely misrepresented.

21 MAY 1924 AUSTEN CHAMBERLAIN MEMORANDUM

AC 24/6/3 (extract)

On getting to the House of Commons on Monday, May 19th, Eyres-Monsell told me that Baldwin wished to see me about the 'People' interview. I accordingly went towards his room and, meeting him in the passage, said that I understood that he wished to speak to me but that I had not seen the 'People' and that, when my wife read the paragraph concerning it in the 'Daily Mail' as we came up in the train from Norfolk, I had at once said that Baldwin was not the kind of man to say such things of his colleagues.

Baldwin thanked me and I went back with him to his room. He said that he wished to tell me exactly what had happened. He then explained how the interview had been arranged by Blain of the Central Office at the suggestion of the Editor of the 'People', who had pointed out that a part of the Press had boycotted Baldwin's speeches and had suggested that through the 'People' he could get what he wished to say to a large body of electors. Baldwin had received the reporter, who was with him for about an hour and a quarter, during which time he did not take a single note of any kind whatever. Baldwin had talked to him about his policy, and then the reporter had talked to Baldwin about various people, so that – Baldwin said – for the last quarter of an hour he had been a listener rather than a talker. The reporter had now put into his mouth things which the reporter had said, mixing them up with occasional bits of Baldwin's own talk. He was going to consult Hogg[16] as to the possibility of taking action for libel or in any other way protecting himself.

I am told by people connected with Downing Street that the particular reporter is notoriously untrustworthy and had been warned off Downing Street as long ago as Bonar Law's time.

---

[16] Sir Douglas Hogg, Attorney-General 1922–4, 1924–8, made Lord Chancellor and Viscount Hailsham 1928.

I have no doubt that Baldwin was grossly misrepresented, but he said enough to show me that he had been indiscreet in listening to talk which he ought at once to have stopped and had himself said one or two foolish things. He seemed very much obsessed by what he called 'the conspiracy of the syndicated press' and with the idea that unexampled intrigues were going on against him. I therefore talked freely about my own position and F.E.'s. I told him that until we rejoined his counsels we were obviously under no obligations to him: that before the party meeting at the Hotel Cecil we had considered the situation: we thought that it was well within our power, with a little organization and some critical speeches, to make his position as leader impossible; but we were equally convinced that no-one else could follow him under such circumstances with any reasonable prospect of success: that we had therefore decided to discourage any kind of opposition: that as regards myself in particular . . . I was not . . . and as far as I could see – never should be – a rival to him as long as he cared to hold the position: but I would tell him frankly that if he gave it up and it were offered to me, I should probably accept it.

I spoke to him with this – almost brutal – frankness in the hope that it might remove the suspicion which appeared to beset his mind . . .[17]

30 JULY 1924: TO JOAN DAVIDSON

Lady Davidson papers; *Davidson Memoirs*, p. 196

House of Commons

Little Maid,

I am so glad you liked the Manchester speech: it did not please me, and we all hated speaking through the amplifier or whatever its proper name is. I had to ascend a scaffold, surrounded by an immense crowd, possibly 20,000, and I had to stand stock still and speak into a thing like a beehive.[18] You can't look up or down, right or left, and you establish no personal contact with your audience nor do you know if they are gripped. The crowd stood all the time, packed like sardines in a tin, no interruptions and no movement.

---

[17] To A. Chamberlain, 21 July 1924 in *WSC V/1*, p. 170, is a further example of Baldwin having to deal with Chamberlain's prickliness.
[18] At Belle Vue, Manchester, on 26 July, he experienced the early use of loudspeakers to hold genuinely mass meetings.

It cramped Joynson-Hicks' style more than mine and he was less audible because he didn't stand sufficiently still. But I didn't enjoy it.

I don't yet know what the business will be next week and there are rumours of possible legislation on the Irish Boundary question, but we shall do our utmost to stave that off . . . I must get home Friday evening. I have a fortnight of intensive cultivation of my division! . . .

The Irish boundary issue raised considerable political dangers. Unionists had been divided over the 1921 Irish Treaty; the treatment of Northern Ireland and the Irish 'loyalists' remained sensitive, and these issues might be inflamed by the Unionists' opponents. Before leaving office in January, Baldwin told James Craig, the Prime Minister of Northern Ireland that 'I do not want the Irish conflict revived in the House of Commons in any shape or form if it can justly be avoided.'[19] But in late July 1924 Baldwin was informed that as the Northern Ireland government refused to appoint a representative for the boundary commission created under the Treaty, the Labour Cabinet would introduce legislation giving the London government the power to make the appointment instead. This not only threatened to divide the Unionist party; if the bill were defeated by the Unionist majority in the House of Lords, the minority Labour government with Liberal support might call a general election on a constitutional issue unfavourable to the Unionists. As Lord Derby noted, a 'Lords v. the people' election cry 'would be fatal to us'.[20] The bill was introduced in early August, but with the recess imminent its further stages were postponed until a special re-assembly of Parliament on 30 September. While at Astley, Baldwin decided to try and persuade Craig to co-operate. His continued anxiety about the issue and the dispersal of leading Unionists during the recess led him to write an unusual number of political letters.

21–2 AUGUST 1924: TO JOAN DAVIDSON

Lady Davidson papers

Astley Hall

Little Maid

Since we last met I have paid a visit to what journalists call the Emerald Isle[21] . . . The forecast was rather rough for the Irish Channel but I have long

---

[19] 14 Jan. 1924, SB papers 101/197–8. [20] Derby to Baldwin, 24 Sept. 1924, SB papers 99/130–1.
[21] Baldwin's unpublicised trip was on 16–18 August. He had wanted to meet Craig in London: 'I don't want to come to you unless it is absolutely necessary as it would be bound to attract attention and cause talk that might do harm': to Craig, 9 Aug. 1924, SB add. papers.

ignored forecasts political or meteorological, and I stepped on to the boat at Fleetwood full of courage and somnolence. As a matter of fact I didn't sleep well. Ships creak and rattle even when it is calm . . .

At six we entered Belfast Lough and the rain began and it rained all day . . . We had an early breakfast and left for Stormont at eight.

Stormont is the Ulster Prime Minister's official residence: the Cabinet meets there and the office is there, and the Craigs inhabit the rest. You see signs of the times: the windows all covered with iron wire netting to prevent bombs being thrown into the living rooms: sentries with rifles everywhere, and in the city the specials in their black uniforms. Two years ago in their relief works Catholics and Protestants had to be set on works on different sides of the city, or they would have shot each other at work! Last year they worked together but for this winter they are going back to the old arrangements as a precaution.

. . . Monday was a bright morning with blue sky, fresh wind and jolly little white horses out to sea as far as the eye could follow them. But I stepped on board gallantly and took my stand on the Bridge by the skipper.

We saw the Atlantic cliffs behind us, the Mull of Kintyre (what a jolly title that would make) away on our left, Ailsa Craig (not a lady: look it out on the map) and all sorts of jolly things. Then thro' very pretty country, Galloway, from Stranraer to Dumfries, Carlisle and home . . .

I have had rather a strenuous time: 84 miles yesterday and out all day.[22] And so on. But it has done good and I am filled with the beauty of it. We leave for the station in half an hour, and to-morrow for our holiday.

. . . As to Ireland. It is impossible to say anything definite till – well, almost until the 30th of September. But I am inclined to think that the election will not be on Ireland. There are strong forces working to that end. But there is no certainty.

I can't explain in a letter, but we shan't know till towards the end of September whether the policy I am advocating will prevail.

There – this long dull letter, begun at Astley yesterday, continued there before breakfast this morning . . . was interrupted by the advent of Tyrrell with whom I have just lunched after a long talk . . . I have much thinking to do.

---

[22] I.e. travelling and meeting people around his constituency.

At Aix-les-Bains Baldwin went on his long walks, sometimes up to six hours a day. One letter begins 'Footsore but happy, I am writing in a working class café in a back street in Chambéry. Outside, the town is blinking sleepily in the vivid sunshine: a few cats and a dog or two represent the population which is asleep indoors or eating. In other words it is a quarter past one and I have been walking since half past nine.'[23] Meanwhile Salisbury, Horne, and Lord Londonderry, a Northern Ireland minister, while staying at the latter's County Durham house, Wynyard Park, proposed that as the Northern Ireland government did not wish the boundary issue to cause a political crisis and party struggle in England, it should state this publicly. The Unionist peers might then be persuaded to let the bill pass.[24]

2 SEPTEMBER 1924: TO SALISBURY

Hatfield House archives 4M/110/25

Aix-les-Bains

My dear Salisbury,

Of course you put your finger on the point. The last thing I said to Craig was 'You will have to think over this while you are away: whether in the circumstances the bill must not be let through. Because the Lords will never assent until they have your assurance of agreement'. He was going to write fully to Carson, so that they could take up the discussion on his return in a fortnight's time. I think your talk with Horne & Londonderry followed properly and naturally on my talk with Craig.

I told Walter Guinness[25] for his own information alone what was in the air, because some of those who speak for the southern loyalists were getting anxious and active, and Craig's only chance lies in the temporary silence of his friends. They had seen Walter who had been in Dublin, and he thought in the light of what I told him that he could keep them quiet.

Yours ever/ Stanley Baldwin

Kathleen Hilton Young, the sculptress, widow of Captain Scott of the Antarctic, and wife of the Lloyd-Georgite Liberal MP Edward Hilton Young, had agreed to make a bust of Baldwin. His periodic sittings in her studio over several months established a warm friendship during the rest of the 1920s.

---

[23] To Joan Davidson, 27 Aug. 1924.
[24] Salisbury to Baldwin, 25 Aug. 1924, SB papers 99/122–5.
[25] Financial Secretary to the Treasury, Oct. 1923–Jan. 1924, 1924–5, Minister of Agriculture 1925–9.

3 SEPTEMBER 1924: TO KATHLEEN HILTON YOUNG

Kennet papers 112/2

Hotel d'Albion, Aix-les-Bains

Dear Mrs Young,

It was an unexpected pleasure to find a letter from you in the dreary heap that usually follows me abroad. I have been in this divine country for ten days and hope to have a month of it . . .

The lake is as blue as if it had been born in Italy. Well, it was really; and Annecy! I was there on Monday and it lay below me in streaks of peacock and sparrow egg! Figure to yourself. Not the effect of cloud or any nonsense of that sort: just its own self determination . . . I walk and walk. I was meant for a tramp and Fate took me by the dusty seat of the breeches and dumped me in the seats of the mighty.[26]

But the seat I really want to occupy is the one in your studio whither I shall come one of the first days in October, and you shall tell me of the big world and what has happened in Wiltshire and in places that really matter.

My love to Hilton,/ Very sincerely yours/ Stanley Baldwin

6 SEPTEMBER 1924: TO EDWARD WOOD

Halifax papers A4.410.14.1

Confidential   Hotel d'Albion, Aix-les-Bains

My dear Edward,

Figure to yourself how I saw in my mind's eye the Wood family pulling out into the blue lake for their bathe, as once again I embarked on the little steamer at Talloires. We had a cheery luncheon at the Abbaye, Lady Brassey, the Willingdons and a Miss Brand with my cousin Phil Burne Jones. They all fell in love with the place and Ireland wasn't mentioned.

But you are harping on the subject and I will tell you how I see it. You may have seen Salisbury who knows all there is to know, but I will assume you haven't.

I spent last Sunday fortnight at Belfast and stayed the night.

---

[26] To Joan Davidson, 2 Sept. 1924: 'You know, heaven meant me to be a tramp. A book in my pocket, but a tramp.'

Craig is willing to accept 'under duresse' as he puts it, the new Act, relying on the interpretation of the Treaty as expounded by its signatories in Parliament. If the Com^m. should give away counties, then of course Ulster couldn't accept it & we should back her. But the gov^nt. will nominate a proper representative and we hope that he and Feetham will do what is right.

He has written fully to Carson whose support is essential in the Lords, and on his (Craig's) return from his holiday next week, he will see him and he will call together the Ulster Council and do his best to get his view accepted. If it is, we tide over the difficulty for a time: perhaps more. But the question to be decided is, what should be the action of Parl^t.? The Lords are the crux. They will never let the Bill through except on a definite assurance that Ulster will accept it. Craig's first idea was to fight the Bill all along the line: the Lords to let it through at the last, but I shewed him the snag, and I told him he would have to consider at his leisure [whether] some pronouncement should not be made by the 30th so that the Bill could be let through. If the Lords once reject it, we may be in a grave difficulty.

However, there we are: and nothing more can be done till nearer the time. If we get over this fence, it looks as though the Soviet Treaty would be the next big event: and on that we can join issue gaily.

I hope to be here for another fortnight, and then as many days in Paris as I can steal. I wish you were here. My respects to your lady.

              Ever yours/ Stanley Baldwin

The Dean of Ch[rist]. Ch[urch].[27] is here & singularly enough he has what can only be described as a veneration for you.

9 SEPTEMBER 1924: TO SALISBURY

pencil note, Hatfield House archives 4M/110/34

              Hotel D'Albion, Aix-les-Bains

My dear Salisbury,

    Many thanks for your letter.[28] I had a long talk with the governor of the Bank yesterday & he will spend Sat. afternoon with me on his way home.

---

[27] The Very Revd Henry White. Wood was a leading layman in the Anglo-Catholic movement.
[28] Salisbury to Baldwin, 5 Sept. 1924, SB papers 99/132–3, reporting that he had informed Londonderry and Horne of Baldwin's 'general approval' of their proposal.

The whole German Loan question is in a tangle and Ramsay, more celtico, has left all the snags to settle themselves later![29]

I go to Paris on the 22 or 23$^{\underline{rd}}$ and can run over any day then. I hope by that time Craig will see how far he can go.

I have just walked my hind legs off and am lunching at a country inn high above the lake of Bourget with the snow alps bounding the S. E. horizon.

I am working on my Rectorial address for Edinburgh[30] and so far as I have written it, it looks tripe, ullage, bilge.

Ever yours/ Stanley Baldwin

10 SEPTEMBER 1924: TO LORD DERBY

Derby papers 920 DER(17)33

Confidential   Hotel d'Albion, Aix-les-Bains
My dear Derby,
. . . I only got away on the 23$^{\underline{rd}}$ of August: first there was Ireland and I had to go to Belfast to see Craig and I put in a fortnight's intensive cultivation of my own constituency.

We had at least a couple of conferences after you had gone to Evian. There was a real danger of the Bill being forced through before the House rose. L.G. was urging the gov$^{\underline{nt}}$ to do this which would have been disastrous for all concerned. I urged delay, and at the last moment they decided to postpone action and we got six weeks breathing space. We all fully realise the importance of getting through this crisis when the fight will come on the Soviet treaty.

Ulster cannot appoint without going back on everything she has said.

But Craig and I had a long talk and he is willing to accept the Bill and yield to what he calls 'duresse'. When he returns from his holiday on Saturday he will see his Council and try and obtain their agreement. He was to write Carson fully before he went away and see him on his return.

The question to be decided is how to make his intention (if he can carry his own people) known to Parliament because if there is any doubt, the

---

[29] To Joan Davidson, 9 Sept. 1924: 'I drove to Brioles, sixty miles each way . . . to see Monty Norman and have a talk about the French agreement.' The Dawes Commission had proposed an international loan to Germany, to enable it to resume reparations payments.
[30] The general election caused this annual address to be postponed until November 1925.

Lords will throw out the Bill. Londonderry was present at our talk, or at a good deal of it, and he has seen Salisbury & Horne at Wynyard.

I go to Paris on Sunday week and shall very likely find things ripe for another meeting but nothing can move now till Craig is in a position to say something definite.

I can tell you that the last week of the Session was the devil but we came through all right!

Send me a line of acknowledgement. There was no real difference of opinion before the house rose amongst our colleagues: we got about a dozen together representing all shades.

I hope you are fit. I was dead when I left England but I shall be fit for anything when I return.

Yours ever/ Stanley Baldwin

Baldwin briefly visited London from Paris on 18–19 September for consultations on the Irish issue, but by the time he finally returned on the 23rd it was being overshadowed by the Labour government's proposed treaty with Soviet Russia. This transformed the political permutations. By agreement with Lloyd George, Hilton Young asked to speak with Baldwin; a meeting was arranged for the 24th.[31]

25 SEPTEMBER 1924 HILTON YOUNG TO LLOYD GEORGE

Lloyd George papers G/10/14/15

...I related to [Baldwin] the substance of what I had learned from you. All but a few of the Wee-est of the Wee-Frees could probably be relied on to vote against the Government, on the issue of the government loan. On the other hand, if the Conservatives forced the issue onto a motion damning the whole of this treaty, or any treaty with Russia, without qualification, that would enable many Liberals to avoid putting the government out (which they are not too anxious to do). Was it not advisable therefore, if, as I supposed, he wanted to put the government out on this question, that the motion on the questions should give prominence to the matter of the loan?

---

[31] Kathleen Hilton Young diary, 21, 24 Sept. 1924, Kennet papers.

S.B. did not expand much in reply, but he grasped the position, and was impressed. He told me what he intended to say at Newcastle.[32] It was this, 'our word should be as good as our bond. This is a dishonest treaty, because it holds out hopes of a loan, and everybody knows that the loan will never be forthcoming'. In fact, he said, fake is a good word: but Mr Ll.G. has used it already. He asked me whether I did not think that such a line as that would be alright, from the point of view of closing the ranks against the government? I said that undoubtedly it would...

I said that I supposed both Liberal and Conservative motions would be put down on the treaty; and that was where the possibility of dissension and division might come...He...said that he would be willing himself that the motion should be made from Liberal benches, but supposed his people would think it should come from the official opposition.

In short...he was receptive, but not expansive.

UNDATED [1 OCTOBER 1924]: TO STRACHEY

Strachey papers 2/3/19

93, Eaton Square

Dear Mr Strachey,

I can't write: the gift has been denied to me.

I am often asked to contribute articles and I always refuse.

I would rather do it for you than for anyone. But no.

I am just off to Newcastle...The Irish debate has been one of great difficulty but I am still hopeful of a solution.

Things are moving: it is the spirit of spring rather than of autumn and the worm is turning! The liberals are in the process of revolt against labour.

I don't know how far they will go but the movement has certainly begun.

Yours very sincerely,/ Stanley Baldwin

In early October the Unionists in the Lords allowed the Irish Boundary Bill to pass, but now the Russian treaty was itself superseded by the controversy over the Cabinet's apparent intervention to halt the prosecution of a communist journalist for alleged sedition, 'the Campbell case'.

---

[32] At the Unionist party annual conference on 2 October.

7 OCTOBER 1924 STAMFORDHAM MEMORANDUM
FOR THE KING

RA PS/GV/K.1958/13 (extract)

Humbly submitted

... 12.30. Saw Mr Baldwin who in reply to my question, 'Do you want to turn the Govt. out' said 'Yes: but not on the Campbell issue[33] – but on the Russian treaties which the country generally condemn. He sees no alternative to Dissolution: it has always been expected. Some wished for it before now though he has opposed hastening the Govts. fall. He considers the P.M. instead of smashing his extremists has allowed them to smash him. He likes and trusts the P.M. and has had from time to time interesting talks with him & always gathered that the P.M. would adopt a quiet yet determined opposition to Communism, believing that in 5 years or so it would die out: but apparently he has not carried out this policy.

As to a Baldwin-Asquith combination the former said this was not <u>now</u> feasible, <u>whatever it might be after a Genl. Election</u>. He hears that the Labour party are not so very sanguine as to electoral results. If the King sent for him he could <u>not</u> form a Government and speaking for himself he did not see how the King could refuse a Dissolution. He asked if I had seen Asquith whose great knowledge and experience would be of greater use to me than his own. I replied I had not seen him but would do so.

He (B) hoped the King would come as soon as possible to London: tho of course he did not know whether the P.M. would ask for a Dissolution on his defeat on Wednesday ...

Secret exchanges continued between Lloyd George and leading Unionists over parliamentary tactics,[34] but chaotic final manoeuvring by all three party leaderships produced an outcome damaging to the Liberals. On 8 October both the Unionist leaders and the Labour Cabinet decided to treat a Liberal motion on the Campbell case as the occasion for securing a government defeat, and on the following day MacDonald asked for a dissolution. Oliver Baldwin was now Labour party candidate at Dudley.

---

[33] Kathleen Hilton Young diary, 7 Oct. 1924, records Baldwin reading out a letter 'saying that the reason the Government climbed down about the Campbell sedition prosecution was because the Communists threatened to expose the members who were in the pay of Moscow'.
[34] Hoare to Lloyd George, 7 Oct. 1924, Lloyd George papers G/19/18/1, including the comment that Baldwin was prepared to discuss electoral deals with Mond, Lloyd George's ally.

12 OCTOBER 1924: TO LOUISA BALDWIN

93, Eaton Square

Dearest Mother

Your welcome letter was received with joy and gratitude.

. . . the £1000 will be invaluable, and even if not opposed an election runs into hundreds and the balance will clear off my by-election of 1921 of which I have a few hundreds outstanding and cover my travelling costs which may easily run to £70 or so. You can't think what a relief it is to have such help just now.[35]

I have a heavy three weeks ahead, and in addition to speeches I am as it were at the helm all the time, so I make my headquarters here . . .

Nor will I prophesy. But our party is in good heart and we have an excellent list of candidates. I hope you will worry as little as I do!

. . . If I had only stuck to business I should have been a really rich man! but I doubt if I should have been as happy.

Thy ever loving/ Son

21 OCTOBER 1924 STAMFORDHAM MEMORANDUM

RA PS/GV/K.1958/30

Mr Baldwin came to see me this morning with reference to a statement made by a Liberal candidate that it was Mr Baldwin who, in December of last year, advised the King to send for Mr Ramsay MacDonald and, consequently, it was not the Liberals but the Conservatives who put the Labour Party into Office.

Mr Baldwin reminded me that Your Majesty had never consulted him at all, nor did he expect to be consulted, and that, naturally, the Sovereign had the right to send for the person he considered best able to form an Administration. Obviously the King's name could not be brought into this matter: but Mr Baldwin asked me whether there would be any objection to

---

[35] The loss of Baldwin's ministerial salary during 1924 revived his financial worries, and his effort to sell his London house: M&B, p. 260. In August 1924 he raised £2,000 by the sale of a Wilden farm: Baldwin WCRO collection 8229/10(v), and in early 1925 finally sold 93 Eaton Square, for around £12,000 (about £400,000 in modern terms).

his announcing merely that there was no truth whatever in this statement. I told him I was certain that Your Majesty would have no objection to his doing so.

We discussed at some length the political situation. He says that all his people are in very good spirits and that everywhere far greater interest and activity is evinced among the electorate and that there will be a much larger number of votes recorded than at previous elections, in which people from lethargy and indifference abstained from voting: and it is the question in which direction this large increase will swing which no one can possibly foretell.

As to the elections where Liberals and Conservatives have stood down in order to fight the Labour single handed, he thinks that there will always be a strong left party among the Liberals who will give their votes to the Labour rather than to the Conservative candidate.

Mr Baldwin had been much struck with the enthusiastic reception given to him at Taunton, where a year or two ago the 'Red Flag' was sung in the Market Place. In 1906 Mr Arthur Ponsonby stood as a Liberal, but was defeated: but the police said they could not recall such a demonstration as was given in favour of the Conservatives on the occasion of Mr Baldwin's visit.

I called Mr Baldwin's attention to the leading article in the 'Manchester Guardian' of yesterday, openly advocating that the Liberals should support the Conservatives in the coming Parliament: but on a very strict understanding that the Conservatives would not attempt to make any change in the direction of protection, or to alter the existing agreement with the Irish Free State. Mr Baldwin had not seen this article: but said that no doubt this was Mr Lloyd George's policy: but Mr Baldwin is quite alive to the fact that Mr Lloyd George will never cordially work with him and that no doubt the solution which would most strongly appeal to Mr Lloyd George would be that he himself should be Prime Minister.

At the general election on 29 October, the Unionists with 412 MPs obtained a huge majority over the 151 Labour MPs and just 40 Liberals. The Liberal leader was among those defeated.

30 OCTOBER 1924: TO ASQUITH

Asquith papers 33/310; partly in J. A. Spender and C. Asquith, *Life of Asquith* (1932), II, p. 351

Travellers' Club

My dear Asquith,

I saw the result of the Paisley election with real regret.

It would be an impertinence on my part to say more, but I think you would have felt pleased if you could have heard the genuine expressions of regret and sympathy which were uttered spontaneously by typists and lift boys working in the Unionist Central Office.

It was a simple tribute well worth having.

May I send a special message of sympathy to Mrs Asquith and your daughter?

Believe me,

Yours very sincerely/ Stanley Baldwin

Baldwin's second government

NOVEMBER 1924 – JUNE 1929

4 NOVEMBER 1924 STAMFORDHAM MEMORANDUM

RA PS/GV/K.1958/44

At 7 p.m. the King saw Mr Baldwin and entrusted him with the formation of a new Government.

During their conversation His Majesty dwelt upon the great responsibility imposed upon him and his Government by the enormous electoral declaration in favour of the Conservative Party: and urged upon Mr Baldwin the importance of his collecting around him men of ability, character, zeal, experience and of administrative capacity, who will be prepared to tackle and deal with the many difficult and what have hitherto proved to be insoluble problems. The Prime Minister expressed most cordial agreement with all that the King said and, although his task of selection was by no means an easy one, he hoped that his efforts would be successful and meet with His Majesty's approval.

The King also dwelt upon the importance of combatting the idea of anything like class war, which the extremists in the Labour Party were inclined to make a sort of War Cry. The Opposition would come back to Westminster disappointed and embittered: and the King expressed an earnest hope that the Prime Minister would restrain his followers from doing anything in the House of Commons to irritate their opponents, and even refrain from replying or in any way taking notice of attacks and recriminations which may be initiated by the Opposition. Otherwise it is to be feared that there may be disagreeable incidents and unruly disorder in the House. Mr Baldwin promised His Majesty that he would do all in his power to prevent such unfortunate occurrences.

With regard to appointments, he had seen no one except Mr Austen Chamberlain, whose name he would submit to the King as Foreign Minister. He had decided to ask Mr Winston Churchill to join the Government at once: this would have to be done sooner or later and the Prime Minister thought it was better to give him office now, rather than run the chance of his having a grievance and being disgruntled at being omitted.

Having now won a general election, Baldwin had greater freedom than in May 1923 in his selection of ministers. He discussed the possibilities as much with Jones and Dawson, as informed individuals not seeking places for themselves, as with political colleagues.[1] Accommodating the Chamberlainites – on his own terms, as individuals rather than a group – and Churchill, now elected as a 'Constitutionalist' MP, and dealing with disappointed office-seekers, were not easy tasks: 'This personal business of choosing people for the various offices in the administration is the most hateful thing I have ever had to face. I have seen a great deal of human nature in the last few days, some of it very white, but not all.'[2]

5 NOVEMBER 1924: TO CURZON

Curzon papers F112/319

Palace Chambers, Bridge Street, London[3]

My dear Curzon,

I received the King's command last night to form a government.

In view of the number of our old colleagues whose services we all wish to secure, this is a task of exceptional difficulty.

I have every hope that you will serve as Lord President of the Council and preside over the C.I.D.[4]

---

[1] Jones WD, I, pp. 301–5; Wrench, Dawson, p. 233. Other discussions with Baldwin at this time are in Crawford Papers, p. 500 (misdated, but 5 Nov. 1924), Amery Diaries, I, p. 391.

[2] Leslie Scott memo., Scott papers MSS 119/3/P/BA/1/1, an account of Baldwin's efforts to soothe a Chamberlainite denied one of the ministerial law offices, by suggesting he should concentrate on a legal rather than political career. Scott became a Lord Justice of Appeal in 1935.

[3] The address of the Conservative Central Office.

[4] Committee of Imperial Defence. Earlier rumours that Baldwin would change his Foreign Secretary had prompted Curzon to write to Baldwin on 31 October that 'I cannot believe that you would propose to put a terrible slur on my administration of that office.' Baldwin replied neutrally and blandly that he was going away for the weekend: Curzon papers F112/319. At an interview with Baldwin later on the 5th Curzon was 'painfully lachrymose' (Crawford Papers, p. 500), but accepted the demotion. He died in March 1925.

There is no one with your lifelong experience better fitted for that task and much will depend on wise guidance at this critical time.

When you left the Foreign Office you had successfully overcome the great difficulties surrounding a number of unsettled questions of varying degrees of gravity.

A fresh start can now be made and in the present condition of public affairs I regard it as of first importance to have the Foreign Secretary in the Commons.

You would of course continue to lead in the House of Lords.

You will of course want to consider this but I should be glad of a reply at your earliest convenience as other appointments necessarily depend on your decision. But I have no anticipation that you will decline to serve in a capacity that would give pleasure and satisfaction to me and to all your colleagues and which would be gratifying to the country.

Yours very sincerely/ Stanley Baldwin

5 NOVEMBER 1924: TO LOUISA BALDWIN

Palace Chambers

Dearest Mother

My first letter as P.M. was a very unpleasant one to Curzon to tell him I couldn't give him the Foreign Office again! And my second is a most agreeable one to send you heaps of my very best love.

Cabinet making is a horrible job. But I am utilising a brief interval between interviews – here a pause of an hour and a half – while I have been seeing postulants for office. I hope to get my Cabinet approved to-morrow and get it in the press on Friday morning. Quick work!

I hope you kept comparatively calm during the election. We won't see another like it. . .

Ever thy loving/ Son

18 NOVEMBER 1924 KATHLEEN HILTON YOUNG DIARY

Kennet papers; partly in Lord Kennet (ed.), *Self-Portrait of an Artist* (1949), p. 229

Stanley Baldwin now Prime Minister again blew in at 10 am. . . He was full of talk. I think he came chiefly to ask Bill [Hilton Young] about Russia, but he told a good tale of Thomas' contempt for Sidney Webb's smooth tongue &

'bloody goatee'.[5] He said he thought Austen was happy; he'd done enough to make him so! Said that he had given him the post of deputy leader, to please him, but that he, Baldwin, meant to lead the house. Said Austen had written letters like a hysterical woman. 'I read them but I pay no attention, he should sleep on his troubles before he writes about them'. He seemed to be very glad to be without Horne, said he'd offered him the post for which he was fitted (Labour). I said yes, but of course he wouldn't accept that. 'Why not' 'Why because of the sacrifice'. 'What sacrifice?' 'Oh don't be tiresome, Directorships etc.' 'Oh well, if that's the greatest value —!!'[6] Said Neville was a 'real white man', had asked to be changed from Exchequer to Health.[7] Said he'd given Winston Exchequer[8] where he wouldn't be able to talk about Labour, nothing but finance. When I said he would have a difficult team especially when it came to enlarging the Safeguarding of Industries Act he said, 'Ah well, I've got the people's mandate & that makes me very independent'. That, I fear, may be his undoing; he may be too confident. He seemed very excited. He strode up & down the room, jumping the fat round stool every time. I couldn't decide whether to move it & give him a clear run, but feared I'd put him out of his stride. He sat on the side of the sofa swinging his legs; he seems as happy as a schoolboy.

The Kiplings again spent Christmas with the Baldwins at Astley Hall. Rudyard found a cameo of Pitt the Younger, and proposed to present it to his cousin with a

---

[5] J. H. Thomas and Webb had been colleagues in the Labour Cabinet.

[6] Austen Chamberlain was angry that Baldwin had ignored his recommendations for appointments of former Chamberlainites, and his advice to tell Horne that the Minister of Labour's status and salary would be raised. Horne, having hoped for the Exchequer, was 'cut to the quick' by the proposed demotion: A. Chamberlain to Baldwin, 6 Nov. 1924, AC 35/5/4, and see *AC Letters*, pp. 260–1. Horne had around five directorships, including briefly in 1923–4 a vice-chairmanship of Baldwins Ltd.

[7] To N. Chamberlain, 6 Nov. 1924, NC 7/11/17/1: 'My dear Neville,/ What you did yesterday was fine. I thank God for such a spirit and rejoice to think that it is to be found in many of those I am happy to call my friends./ I had not the least idea but that you would accept my offer to go back to the Treasury./ You are a man after my own heart./ Yours ever/ S.B.' Chamberlain's account of their conversation is in Iain Macleod, *Neville Chamberlain* (1961), pp. 110–11.

[8] Young, *Baldwin*, p. 88, repeated a rumour that Churchill first thought the offer of 'Chancellor' meant the Chancellorship of the Duchy of Lancaster. Churchill commented that this was 'a silly story ... without any foundation at all': Colville to Brook, 30 Sept. 1952, PREM 11/239/44–5. Churchill's own account of the conversation is in M. Gilbert, *Winston S. Churchill*, vol. V, 1922–1939 (1976), p. 59. Baldwin wrote more frequent and fuller letters to Churchill during this government than to any other Cabinet minister: these are published in *WSC V/1*.

'suitable set of verses'. Baldwin later recalled[9] that 'On Christmas morning I found this on my plate at breakfast written on a half sheet of Astley note paper:

> To him who lost and fell – who rose and won,
> Because his aim was other than men's praise,
> This for an omen that in all things done
> Strength shall be born of unselfseeking days.
>   R.K.'

27 DECEMBER 1924: TO LADY LONDONDERRY

Londonderry papers D3099/3/15/14

[Astley Hall]

Dear Lady Londonderry,

Thank you for your letter and drawing my attention to a man who seems to deserve an honour. I will try and tuck him in in June: I was already more than full up for the New Year's list.

I have taken immense pains this time, and I have got a small and I think thoroughly sound list.

Honours always worry me: they have been so flung about the last ten years that it takes a herculean effort to restore them to something like their old position.

I want to make them worth having . . .

Yours sincerely/ Stanley Baldwin

30 DECEMBER 1924: TO STRACHEY

Strachey papers 2/3/21

[Astley Hall]

My dear Strachey,

I delayed replying to your most kind letter until returned from your High Alps.[10]

It was truly kind of you to send me your book which I shall always value.

I had not had it five minutes before I fired off material from its pages in the House of Commons!

To what base uses —.

---

[9] To Bryant, 2 Jan. 1941, Bryant papers C62; with further explanation in Kipling to Elsie Bambridge, 17–19 Dec. 1924, extract courtesy of Thomas Pinney.
[10] Before leaving for an Alpine holiday, Strachey had sent a copy of his book, *The River of Life*.

I am enjoying a real rest at home, with grandchildren and the Kiplings, and am on the point of returning to what is called 'real life'.

What is there in one's native soil that renews strength and restores perspective and that sense of relation and proportion that so often seems lacking in the most brilliant men?

Every good wish for the New Year.

Yours very sincerely/ Stanley Baldwin

Lord Robert Cecil had been given a peerage in 1923 and was now Chancellor of the Duchy of Lancaster and leader of the British delegation at the League of Nations in Geneva. The Conservative government had doubts about the 'Geneva protocol' on European security, negotiated by the Labour government. Instead it promoted a more limited western security pact, the 1925 Locarno Treaty. Churchill, wanting to reduce income tax in his first budget, demanded a large cut in the Navy estimates.

21 JANUARY 1925: TO CURZON

Curzon papers F112/324

10, Downing Street

My dear Curzon

. . . We had a full Cabinet to-day except for one or two invalids and yourself and of course Bob Cecil who is in an opium den at Geneva.

But our travellers have returned looking amazingly well.

F.E.[11] and Amery the colour of walnut juice, Worthy red as fire, and Jix[12] carrying 200lb. of steam to the square inch till every rivet in him is strained to the uttermost.

Yours ever/ Stanley Baldwin

29 JANUARY 1925: TO LORD CECIL

Cecil of Chelwood papers 51080/137–8

Private   10, Downing Street

My dear Bob,

I have been very glad to get your letters.

You are having a most troublesome job and you seem to be getting through very well.

---

[11] Birkenhead was now Secretary of State for India.   [12] Joynson-Hicks, now Home Secretary.

You need not be anxious about the Protocol: I don't know what you may have seen in the papers, but I have only just got the result of Hankey's committee in print and shall study it over the week end. It is now to be circulated to members of the C.I.D.

Curzon is at Eze: writes in raptures about the sun and makes no mention of his return. A thousand men are on strike, liftmen, stokers and so on throughout the government offices. Winston is fighting the whole British Navy, Austen recovering from 'flu, Edward Wood is back after his, your brother has fled to the Continent, and the P.M. attended a 'social' of the L.N.U. [League of Nations Union] last night when all the refreshment he could get was a drop of lemonade about as lively as the few remarks he had just uttered. It was an audience after your own heart . . .

And now I think I have posted you pretty fully.

Yours ever/S.B.

30 JANUARY 1925: TO JOAN DAVIDSON

Lady Davidson papers; partly in M&B, p. 332

10, Downing Street

Little Maid,

I cannot manage to-morrow – it is a weekend of work:

A. I am taking down the Navy Estimates and shall have the 1st Lord[13] with me.

B. I have the C of Es scheme for Allied Debts to study and digest.

C. I must be near the telephone tomorrow as there is a conference between Peel & Steel-Maitland[14] on the one side and the Executive of the T.U. on the other with reference to the strike. I am not staying here for it but I have undertaken to be on the wire . . .

After winning over a reluctant Cabinet in late February, Baldwin created a great public impression on 6 March with a House of Commons speech persuading his own backbenchers to drop a private member's bill intended to cripple trade-union and Labour party finances. Churchill commented: 'I had no idea he could show such power . . . The whole Conservative Party turned round and obeyed without a single mutineer . . . I cease to be astonished at anything.'[15]

---

[13] Bridgeman, who with his wife spent the weekend with the Baldwins at Chequers.
[14] Respectively First Commissioner of Works, and Minister of Labour.
[15] *WSC V/1*, p. 425, also p. 426; and see *Amery Diaries*, I, pp. 398, 400; *NC Letters*, II, pp. 273–5.

Figure 5 A self-portrait, undated

10 MARCH 1925 KATHLEEN HILTON YOUNG DIARY

Kennet papers; partly in Kennet, *Self-Portrait*, pp. 232–3

Fun day. The Prime Minister came to lunch. He came about 12 & stayed till about 3. He was most especially confiding. Said he was a very silent man & needed <u>very</u> sympathetic company to make him talk. As he hadn't ceased talking for 2 or 3 hours I thought I could safely curtsey! I did. He told me he told nobody his political ambitions & trend, but he knew them well enough. He said when nobody could think of any fault to apply to him they said he had 'no character' . . . he drank nothing at lunch, but had a glass of cold water at 3. Said it was good for 'senile kidneys' whereat I retorted 'silly ass' & found a domestic standing by . . . Said Wheatley & Cook[16] were the things

---

[16] John Wheatley, Minister of Health in the 1924 Labour government, and Arthur Cook, general secretary of the Miners' Federation, could be regarded as left-wing 'extremists'.

he was afraid of. Said if they could get thro' this year without troubles he thought they'd be all right...

1 MAY 1925: TO JOAN DAVIDSON

Lady Davidson papers; *Davidson Memoirs*, p. 197

10, Downing Street

Little Maid,

...I feel most ungracious, especially when I think of that unvarying and thoughtful love and kindness you both gave me, to fail you when you have made such a happy plan for Saturday. But I feel worried – I rarely do – with so many little speeches, and about the business of the House, and I know I should be a poor companion if I tried to come. I just want a quiet morning to think. I have had no time all the week and though you may laugh, it is just that getting two or three hours undisturbed, walking about the room and sitting in an armchair, that restores my equilibrium. It is by turning over things in my mind that the precipitate is formed out of which the speeches come, and if I don't go through that curious preparatory cud-chewing, then the work suffers...

Baldwin's mother died on 16 May. Later that day he wrote from London to his aunt, Edith Macdonald: 'One half of me has been waiting at Wilden these latter days while the other half has been in the turmoil of the world, but now I have a quiet afternoon in which to thank God for so peaceful a release and to picture the passing of her soul on this day of exquisite beauty to a happiness beyond her dreams./ The tranquillity and the fragrance of this spring day are so symbolical of her life.'

4 JUNE 1925: TO JOAN DAVIDSON

Lady Davidson papers; partly in *Davidson Memoirs*, p. 197

[Blair Atholl]

Little Maid

...Saturday to Welbeck. There was a large party, but I gradually found it all different from what I had expected. There is a most kindly simple atmosphere under all the state of the great house, and the kindness and real consideration with which they all treated me was delightful. I mean, that they realized the poor devil was tired and had a speech on his mind and behaved accordingly. The meeting was wonderful. It was a fine day and the folk streamed in from about noon and were allowed everywhere. And as usual when trusted and not shoved about, they behaved admirably. I don't know how many listened to my effort. I never spoke to so many except possibly at Bellevue at Manchester, but the extraordinary feature was the enthusiasm after it. We drove in an open car, perhaps $\frac{1}{4}$ mile, from the ground to the house. The people were a solid crowd on each side, rushing up as they saw us, and my arms were nearly pulled out! It shewed that they were all behind the gov^{nt} as much as at the election. Very remarkable. And crowds of miners too . . .

Yesterday, Dundee. I can't make it out. We had a wonderful reception. Every child in the place turned out and yelled its little self hoarse. The Freedom was given in a very fine public hall seating 3000. The lunch was tedious. We started at one, and speeches began at 3.35. Two hours and a half at the meal!

We then drove off on a tour. We first visited some slum houses. I never saw such a sight. Oddly enough I have never been in real slum houses, and I as near as two pins sat down and howled: the whole thing came to me with such force. Five and six in one room. Think of the children!

We went on to see various housing schemes. They have unlimited room in which to build but they have hardly started on the real problem.

The people were very friendly which touched me very much. They seemed to know one would give one's life to help: they can't know how impotent one is.

To-morrow, to Worcestershire. It is all very tiring: these things take it out of me . . .

On 19 May Baldwin had unveiled the Hyde Park memorial to the naturalist and writer, W. H. Hudson. Epstein's modernist sculpture, a nude representation of 'Rima', caused a sensation. Kathleen Hilton Young recorded that as the curtain fell, the 'shocked crowd' initially made 'not a sound', followed by 'an intake of breath which finally exhaled with a horrified "Oh God"'.

22 JUNE 1925 KATHLEEN HILTON YOUNG DIARY

Kennet papers

. . . Stanley was very funny about the Epstein. He said if he'd known what it was like he would have made 'Oh such a different speech'. 'Of course I know what I should have done when the curtain went down. I should have brought up my breakfast'. Said he'd taken Balfour to see it & said to Balfour it looks like something conceived under drugs & executed in a brothel, & Balfour replied 'Aren't you a little hard on drugs?' . . .

In July the disagreement over the Navy estimates, the 'cruiser crisis', reached a climax. The Admiralty ministers and naval chiefs threatened resignation, which on such a sensitive issue as seapower would have been damaging within the Conservative party; also, Bridgeman was an old friend and Davidson was now his parliamentary secretary.

17 JULY 1925: TO DAVIDSON

Lady Davidson papers; M&B, p. 337

10, Downing Street

My dear old David,

I shall treasure your letter as long as I live, and it brought comfort to a very unhappy man.

I go down tonight to Chequers to think, and I have done nothing else for two or three days. All my heart pulls in one direction: my head is divided.

So little divides us from a settlement by agreement. 2 this year 2 next, and I think I could get the full 3 next year by agreement.

But if your people can't take this little step it will be disastrous for the gov^{nt} as whatever happens it means a split.

Politics is a cursed game, as Lord Salisbury[17] said.

I cannot see what is Right. The moment I do I shall feel better.

Burn this and bless you always, the best friend man ever had.

Yours ever/ S.B.

On 22 July Baldwin made his decision, which secured general acquiescence: to begin construction of four cruisers in the current financial year, and three the following year. There were now threats of a lockout in the coal industry and a sympathetic strike by transport and railway workers, bringing ministers into talks with miners', mine-owners' and TUC leaders. Cunliffe-Lister, as President of the Board of Trade the minister responsible for the coal industry, thought that as his wife had shares in a colliery company he ought to resign to avoid a clash of interest. Baldwin asked him to delay a decision, while he, Steel-Maitland and Bridgeman

---

[17] The 3rd Marquess, the Victorian Prime Minister.

conducted the negotiations. A statement which the Labour *Daily Herald* claimed Baldwin had made on 30 July became instantly notorious. On 31 July he took the considerable political risk of offering a government subsidy to the coal industry, to enable a royal commission to consider means of improving its condition.[18]

31 JULY 1925 HORACE WILSON MEMORANDUM[19]

SB papers 13/89

Reports appeared during the negotiations about the recent miners' dispute to the effect that the Prime Minister had stated that 'all the workers of this country have got to face a reduction of wages to help put industry on its feet'. It should be pointed out that the meetings between the Prime Minister and the Miners were confidential, the Miners agreeing that the proceedings should be regarded as private so that (in order to reach a settlement) the conversations might be perfectly frank and open. So far as regards the alleged statement by the Prime Minister about wages, the report is a misrepresentation of what in fact was said. What was under discussion at the time was the admittedly serious condition of the coal trade, where there is intense foreign competition and where at the present time there is no question of profits; on the contrary, over the greater part of the industry heavy losses are being incurred.

In so far as this is illustrative of the position of British trade in general what the Prime Minister clearly had in mind was that if a continuance of heavy unemployment is to be avoided it is essential that all parties should join in taking whatever steps are open to them, each in their several ways, to put their respective trades on a better footing by lowering the cost of production. In the absence of profits beyond what are requisite to provide the capital required by an industry, the ways open to bring about reduced costs of production are either improvements in management and equipment, greater effort on all sides to give more output, or longer hours, or lower wages.

The Prime Minister expressed no view as to how far wages generally or wages in particular trades are higher or lower than they ought to be or than he would like them to be; the point dealt with was merely what part adjustments in wages might have to play (together with changes that can be

[18] Jones *WD*, I, pp. 322–9, has material on Baldwin during this episode.
[19] Wilson (permanent secretary, Ministry of Labour) to Gower, 31 July 1925, Baldwin papers 13/87, states: 'The P.M. decided it was better not to issue any denial of the report . . . but he would like the enclosed note to go to the Central Office for use by them.'

made in the other factors in the cost of production) to help to meet foreign competition.

15 AUGUST 1925: TO CUNLIFFE-LISTER

typescript copy, SB papers 18/95, 97

10, Downing Street

My dear Philip,

I have received your letter asking me to accept your resignation.

Before I accept it, I feel bound to make one or two observations. I feel a special responsibility towards you, for we have worked so closely and so harmoniously through three shifting years.

The desire of your colleagues to keep you is strong and genuine: Derby wrote to me on the strength of rumours which had reached him, begging me not to let you go.

Tom Richards yesterday said that it was absurd that you should go and that none of them saw the least reason why you should, and the others present, Herbert Smith, Cook and Richardson[20] appeared to assent.

I ask you, if you can, to put the matter out of your mind for two or three weeks.

Review it after you have had a complete rest. We are all tired men. If you then are in the same mind, I will say no more. You know I understand your position.

And – though I dislike mentioning my difficulties – there could not be a more awkward moment for me to publish a resignation when I am leaving for my holiday to-morrow. It would be practically impossible to make the readjustments in office by correspondence: we are all scattered, yet to leave a vacancy in such an important place for a month would lead to much unpleasant comment (as well as press lobbying) as would do the government real harm.

I have of course advised the King and told him of the course I am pursuing.

The above is from a Prime Minister to a colleague: below is from an older man to – shall we say, a younger brother?

Think again after a rest. I am, I believe, the only one who understands and sympathises with your point of view. Yet I cannot feel that you would

---

[20] These were all miners' leaders.

be doing wrong in subordinating your feelings to the unanimous desire of your colleagues. If you stay with us, I shall rejoice.

But whatever you decide, you will have my full support wherever and whenever it is wanted.

Bless you, and a right judgment to you!

Yours ever/ Stanley Baldwin[21]

As usual the Baldwins spent several weeks in Aix-les-Bains, and several days in Paris. Baldwin lunched with French ministers at their war office and dined with the British ambassador. He returned on 17 September, and later in the month was the King's guest at Balmoral. Baldwin had taken the precaution of warning him that he 'did not play golf or shoot or fish, but he likes rambling over the hills'. He climbed Lochnagar, getting soaked in the mist.[22]

17 SEPTEMBER 1925: TO MACKENZIE KING

Mackenzie King papers 216/94742

Private   10, Downing Street

My dear Mr Mackenzie King,

Your most kind letter reached me when I was in the throes of my troubles with the miners, and I got off, tired out, for my holiday.

I had the best rest I have had for years – a whole month! and I am just back feeling in first rate condition.

I had to give up my idea of visiting Canada before I went away . . . it is impossible to be away till the industrial situation is cleared.

I have little doubt that Moscow is directing all the efforts at causing trouble in this country and she is undoubtedly a past mistress in that evil act. We shall beat her but at the moment she has captured a considerable section of the labour movement and money for the so-called minority movement is being spent very freely.

I see your election is now upon you, and you will be having a strenuous time. Whatever your fate may be, I hope it will not be too long before we

---

[21] Cunliffe-Lister accepted Baldwin's advice to reflect further, then withdrew his resignation. The Mines Department was removed from his ministerial responsibility, until his wife's shares were sold in 1927.

[22] Wigram memo., 13 Aug. 1925, RA PS/GV/K.2024/1; to Joan Davidson, 3 Oct. 1925.

meet for it would be a great pleasure to renew the acquaintance – or may I say friendship which we formed two years ago?

With kindest regards in which my wife joins.

Believe me to remain/ Very sincerely yours/ Stanley Baldwin

3 OCTOBER 1925: TO STAMFORDHAM

RA PS/GV/K.2025/1–2

10, Downing Street

My dear Stamfordham,

I have delayed writing to you because I thought His Majesty might like to have my impressions of my visit to Glasgow.

But first I beg you will convey to His Majesty my grateful thanks for such kindness and hospitality as made my visit to Balmoral a real pleasure.

I enjoyed every moment of my stay and left with regret.

As to Glasgow. I succeeded in evading all publicity on Wednesday afternoon and spent two or three hours with the late medical officer of health, Dr Chalmers, in exploring the slums. They are terrible and gave me the opportunity of saying something in public and more in private to stimulate the people of the city to fight the difficult problem with unusual energy.

But the curious thing was that, contrary to expectation, I had an amazingly popular welcome throughout the town. The reception we had in the poorer quarters was remarkable. The booing was completely drowned out by the cheering and red flags numbered under a dozen, compared with hundreds of Union Jacks.

And nowhere was the enthusiasm more marked than among the women and children. I don't lay too much stress on this but I feel that the visit did good and was certainly a stimulus to the decent elements.

Yours very sincerely/ Stanley Baldwin

Speaking on the coal inquiry at the Conservative conference at Brighton on 8 October, Baldwin said that the government 'must go to the fifty-ninth minute, the eleventh hour, in our effort to secure industrial peace', but that its primary duties were to maintain law and order and the essential public services. The Irish boundary commission reported in November, again raising the prospect of Irish violence and Conservative divisions. Baldwin brought Craig and Irish Free State ministers to Chequers on 28–9 November to negotiate an agreement.[23] On 8 January he delivered his acclaimed address on 'The Classics' to the Classical Association.

16 JANUARY 1926: TO REVD FREDERICK MACDONALD

in family possession

10, Downing Street

My dear Uncle Fred,

I am indifferent to most press criticism, good bad or indifferent, but I am sensitive to that of individuals who know what they are talking about, and it is an immense pleasure to me to know that you liked my Address. I wrote it in my brief Christmas holiday and it was sheer joy to live in such an atmosphere for four or five days.

I was in a blue funk when I read it: that wonderful hall in Middle Temple and the hundreds of 'first class brains' were rather overpowering and I didn't know whether I could get at them and hold them: but everyone was very kind and I feel I have made a host of unknown friends of the right sort which is a warm and comforting thought. Thank you so much for writing.

Your affectionate nephew/ Stanley Baldwin

23 JANUARY 1926: TO STRACHEY

Strachey papers 2/3/24

10, Downing Street

My dear Strachey,

Your kind and most generous letter gave me great pleasure, and though I am 'paucus cultor & infrequens'[24] of the daily press I need not tell you I read your article with pleasure.

I haven't enjoyed anything so much for a long time as writing that address: for four happy days I shed all thought of politics and lived in another world from which I emerged infinitely refreshed!

The Scriptores Augustus (is that right? it looks odd) are, I am ashamed to own, unknown to me but not for long: more power to the elbow of the immortal Loeb. How few of our millionaires have any imagination.

Yours always sincerely/ Stanley Baldwin

---

[23] See Jones *WD*, I, pp. 330–1, III, pp. 236–46 (30 Oct. – 17 Dec. 1925).
[24] 'A cursory and infrequent reader'.

A common Baldwin letter to his ministers was a brief note of support: 'I have been following the events of the week with infinite sympathy: you have been having a horrible time and the attacks directed against you by the anonymous inkslingers make me boil with fury. All good fortune attend you.'[25] Another was the encouraging reply to apologies for absence from Cabinet meetings or departmental work due to illness.

26 JANUARY 1926: TO LORD CECIL

Cecil of Chelwood papers 51080/157–8

10, Downing Street

My dear Bob,

... I rejoice that you are going on well: don't overdo it and don't worry. You have only to eat and drink and have beautiful thoughts so that you can plunge once more into your beloved arena like a giant refreshed.

I am just off on a devil's tour: 3 meetings and probably 'a few words' at overflows, nearly 24 hours in trains, conversations with strangers and my work all hung up for three precious and irrevocable days. So do we govern ...

Yours ever/ S.B.

Cecil had hesitated before joining the Cabinet because he wanted assurances of definite influence in the Foreign Office, which Austen Chamberlain refused. They frequently differed over League of Nations issues and Cecil periodically threatened resignation, for example in March over the persistence of what he called 'old diplomacy' at Geneva and what he considered to be the poor publicity the Foreign Office gave to League activities. Baldwin's technique was to listen to his complaints and to be conciliatory without weakening the authority of his Foreign Secretary. Cecil stayed.

30 MARCH 1926 CECIL MEMORANDUM

Cecil of Chelwood papers 51080/170–1 (extract)

... The Prime Minister said very little except that he hoped I should be able to go to Geneva on the Commission for the Re-organisation of the Council and on the Disarmament Committee; that he was quite sure I could be of more assistance to the League inside the Government than outside;

---

[25] To A. Chamberlain, 15 March 1926, AC 35/1/16a, on discussions at the League of Nations in Geneva.

and that he had some expectation that as time went on Chamberlain would be more and more inclined to transfer League duties to myself. I pressed him as to what his attitude was as to the necessity for publicity, but got no satisfaction. I also urged on him in the strongest terms that it was the duty and privilege of a Prime Minister to take a considerable share in foreign affairs. He recognised that that was so; but expressed the grave apprehension lest he should imitate the proceedings of Lloyd George in interfering too much. I entirely agreed that this was to be avoided and thought there was no danger of that happening with him. In the end I said that I thought he ought to consider very carefully whether it was any use patching the thing up now, if it was to begin again. I was conscious such controversies added greatly to his labours and that he ought to consider carefully whether he wanted them to be renewed. He expressed strongly his view that it would be much better for me to remain at present: that if the thing must come up again, it must, but that he hoped a modus vivendi might be arrived at. I told him that I would let him know before I left the country on Thursday what my final decision was.

From mid March, Baldwin was again engaged in negotiations with leaders of the Miners' Federation, mineowners' association, and the TUC. These discussions and those during the General Strike from 3 to 12 May and the lingering coal lockout over the summer can be followed in Tom Jones' published diaries. Baldwin's views also emerge from the report of his interview with a group of churchmen in July, printed below, pp. 184–8. The King wrote to congratulate him on the end of the General Strike.

13 MAY 1926: TO KING GEORGE V

typescript draft, SB papers 177/7

Sir,

It is my privilege to thank Your Majesty for the gracious letter which I have had the honour to receive at your hand.

If there was one mission more than another which as Your Majesty's first Servant it has been my dearest wish to fulfil, it was to lessen the misunderstandings which threaten industrial strife and to prevent the possibility of such conflicts as the one from which we are emerging.

At the moment when it might have seemed that these hopes had been in vain and that, amid great national damage and personal disappointment it was necessary to start again at the beginning, I am touched, Sir, beyond measure by the kind message of sympathy and trust which Your Majesty sends me, and am inspired with renewed confidence and strength to face the immediate problems which must arise in connection with the return of our industries to normal conditions, and the restoration of peace in the coal industry.

Your Majesty's words of encouragement, supported as they are by the spirit of fair play and the inborn common-sense of your people, reassure my faith in a brighter and a better future leading to that final and lasting settlement which can alone secure the prosperity of Your Majesty's Kingdom, Dominions and Empire.

I beg leave, Sir, to thank Your Majesty again most humbly and have the honour to be, with the greatest respect.

Your Majesty's dutiful and devoted Servant

15 MAY 1926: TO DERBY

Derby papers 920 DER(17)33

[Chequers]

My dear Derby

... The intellectuals and the clergy have as usual shewn a perfect ignorance of the big questions at issue. They have been in a complete fog as to what was going on, the motive forces, the issues at stake. And they have in consequence talked ROT, and rot that might have caused serious difficulties if the struggle had been protracted.

However thank God we are getting through in spite of 'em.

I am resting at Chequers: the first smell of fresh air I have had for three weeks.

Come and see me when you are in town.

Ever yrs/ S.B.

18 MAY 1926: KATHLEEN HILTON YOUNG DIARY

partly in Kennet, *Self-Portrait*, pp. 244–5

Stanley Baldwin came to breakfast & stayed a long while ... He said he thought his broadcast speech played some part in ending the Strike. He amusingly described conferences with Herb[ert]. Smith & Thomas. How Smith when asked to agree to something would say a blank '<u>no</u>' & Thomas would lean forward & say 'Of course really what H.Smith means is that we would consider etc. etc.'. Till at last Stanley would say to Smith 'Well now is that approximately what you mean', & Smith would reply 'Mr Thomas is speaking for himself. What I say is not a penny off wages not a minute on to time'. He . . . was an obstinate pigheaded Yorkshireman. Said Ramsay Mac[Donald] came to him at 10pm on the Monday night when the Strike began & wanted to get out of it. Baldwin . . . said 'First & before I can discuss, call off the Strike'. Said he was going to Chequers for Whitsun to do some hard thinking; thought a new state of affairs was coming. Said this had been threatening for 16 years & altogether he was very hopeful. I asked him if the O.M.S.[26] had been useful, he said he didn't know. I asked him why Winston had been in such a hurry to announce no taxation; he said he hadn't talked to him about it, but thought it was quite likely they would have to put on added taxation in the autumn ('It would be quite a possible thing to do', he said). Said 'Hasn't Ll. G. been rather bad'. I said that I thought Ll. G. was better handling situations than observing them. Galling to him perhaps to watch other people. Baldwin said 'I don't think I should feel like that'.

Lloyd George had already adopted radical positions, widening Liberal divisions and causing the notable loss of Mond to the Conservatives in January. He had now taken an independent line during the General Strike. His defiance of Asquith's leadership and criticism of the government precipitated a new Liberal crisis and further defections.

27 MAY 1926: TO HILTON YOUNG

Kennet papers 4/2

10, Downing Street

My dear Hilton Young,

I will send you a good stodgy letter, suitable for publication if you so desire, but this is just a note for your own eyes to tell with what pride and pleasure I received the news that you are joining us.

I always wished we might work together and now my dream has come true.

It is the most cheering thing that has happened to me for many a day.

Yours ever sincerely/ Stanley Baldwin

---

[26] The volunteer, but government-sponsored, Organisation for the Maintenance of Supplies, formed in 1925.

21 JUNE 1926: TO MOND

handwritten copy, SB papers 161/171–2

Secret   10, Downing Street

My dear Mond,

I am putting my reply to you in writing that it may be on record if I die or am deposed in the near future. When you told me that you wished to join our Party and accept my leadership, you said you would like to go to the House of Lords, a promotion to which you thought your services in the Coalition Gov^{nt} entitled you. I concurred and after some discussion consented to submit your name in June if you so desired, though as I told you I thought it would be wise to defer it in your own interests. However, you elected for June and I concurred.

Then came the Strike, & when I saw you the other day I told you that I regarded the loss of a seat at the present time as a matter of grave consequence to the party. I don't want a Conservative beaten by a Liberal or Labour while the coal strike is on, nor do I want an election. In these circumstances I asked you not to press me now and you very properly agreed.

I say 'properly' because I asked you as your leader not to put me in a position which I regarded as a serious one today, and you gave way to my judgement.

So much for that.

That being so, you want an assurance that as soon as these present troubles are over, my promise to you will be honoured. I am perfectly willing to recommend you in the New Years List, and would only ask you, whatever you say to your constituents, that you hold the seat until the coal strike is settled and the pits are working.[27]

Yours very sincerely/ Stanley Baldwin

In July members of the 'Standing Conference of the Christian Churches on the Coal Dispute', including Bishops Temple and Kempthorne and various Free Church leaders, published proposals for settling the coal dispute. Ministers believed

---

[27] In November Mond reminded Baldwin of his promise and asked for a viscountcy, but the Political Honours Scrutiny Committee raised an objection, relating to one of his recent business deals. After a lapse of time to allow the difficulty to subside, he was created Baron Melchett in June 1928: details in SB papers 161/167–9, 174, 178–81, and Jones unpublished diary, 18–19 May 1927.

that this intervention delayed a settlement, by giving undue encouragement to the miners' leaders. Baldwin spoke publicly of the churchmen's efforts as being as inappropriate as 'the Federation of British Industries . . . trying to bring about a reunion of the Particular Baptists with the Anglo-Catholics'. He responded more patiently when he met their deputation, but later commented that he 'wished they would go back to their flocks': 'What the Bishops do not seem to realise is that what they will do is to keep in power the latent atheist bolshevists, like Cook, and of whose leadership no good will come to the miners.'[28]

19 JULY 1926: REPLY TO A DEPUTATION

OF CHURCHMEN

SB papers 15/151–88 (extracts)

. . . I have been in industry the whole of my life, and I do know the working men . . . I am not unfamiliar with industrial disputes . . . I and my colleagues have lived with this subject for twelve months; we have seen it brewing for a long time. We have spent days and nights with Mr Cook and Mr Herbert Smith, and we spent long times with the owners, and I think we have a fairly intimate knowledge of both sides. Whatever may be said, we have no prejudice to either side . . . [A]s these remarks are not to be published, I may say that we think they are equally stupid and equally bigoted; but let us look for a moment at one of the troubles underlying the whole situation . . . [–] the view held by the miners' leaders about governments . . . This difficulty is caused by the unhappy way in which the Governments of the last dozen years have been drawn into all these disputes. There is nothing more unfitted to be embroiled in a dispute than a Government, and you can directly trace a good deal of the trouble we are in to-day to the action of former Governments. I am not saying that to blame former Governments and excuse myself, but they made mistakes which we cannot make owing to the changed circumstances . . .[29] [In 1925] there were signs of further trouble; the industry went from bad to worse . . . and we were threatened last summer with a general strike . . . It was then that I had my first negotiations with Mr Cook. Ultimately we avoided trouble . . . by that huge subsidy which amounted to

---

[28] Jones *WD*, ii, p. 63. Further details are in F. A. Iremonger, *William Temple* (1948), pp. 337–43.
[29] He commented here on the concession of the Seven Hours Act in 1919, and an increased minimum wage in 1924.

something like 22 or 23 millions, not given in panic or out of fear of what might be the result, but given in order that both the country might have time to learn something about the situation, and that the owners and the men might have an opportunity in the nine months that succeeded of composing their differences together, and a Royal Commission was set up to investigate the whole circumstances and to make recommendations... [W]e all know that in the interval neither the miners nor the owners succeeded in getting together at all, and they waited until the Commission made its Report. The Commission found the economic position of the industry deplorable, and they had to recommend – very much against their will – a reduction in wages, and they put a number of things in the Report... that they hoped might enable this reduction to be considered and taken without trouble, to tide over the time when they hoped it might be possible that their recommendations would lead to improved working of the pits. We got to work the moment that that Report was issued, and in the seven weeks from the 9th March to the end of April there was no progress made at all. We did offer... in March to carry on a subsidy while the pits were at work – a very different situation to what obtains to-day. The General Strike and the 12 weeks stoppage have of course impoverished the finances very considerably... [O]ne of our difficulties has been the tendency... I think more on the part of the men than of the masters, to look to the Government to get the mining industry out of the trouble caused by its disputes. The Government having got them out twice, although by only making what proved to be a temporary settlement, they got it firmly fixed in their heads that Government can always do it, and in a position such as we were in March or April, when it was impossible either to raise the wages or to shorten the hours, the only way in which the Government could have kept the pits at work would have been to have subsidised them. Well, of course, that was impossible... because it was not fair to the other industries in the country. There are industries which have suffered much more than the mining industry. I will mention but two instances – Iron & Steel and Shipbuilding, because where the mining industry has suffered for a year, they have suffered for four. The proportion out of work has been very great, the cuts in wages that have been made have been most severe, and it would be absolutely unfair and impossible to subsidise for any protracted period any industry, however important, when that subsidy must be borne at the expense of the other industries.

... Mr Cook has never given up the idea of getting a fresh subsidy; he has wanted a much longer one than he is asking at this moment. I have tried all I can since last March to make them believe that there will be no more subsidy . . . The reason I think why that idea is so firmly rooted in Mr Cook's mind is that when he looks back at the concessions the Government have made, either to avoid or bring an end to stoppages . . . it still rests in his mind that he scared me into doing it, and he thinks, having scared me once, he can do it again.

You must excuse me dwelling on the miners' side. If you came to talk to me about the owners, I can talk about them with equal freedom and equal vigour, but it is the miners' position at the moment we are looking at . . .

Now on the question of hours . . . When the Commission came to examine it, they found that owing to the peculiar conditions of the trade it would be necessary . . . for far greater sacrifices to be made in certain areas, Northumberland, Durham and South Wales, than in any of the others, and it was because of that that they put in the report what the miners have never accepted yet . . . that while they have a national settlement, they shall have varying terms in the districts . . . [T]he difficulty is that . . . there is in my view no reduction of wages which the men could take, or which any of us would like to see the men take, which would enable the exporting districts to carry on.[30] That is the whole difficulty, and the way Mr Cook faced up to it was this: he said he wanted the existing wages; and he did not care two-pence if those districts went out of work, and he would rather see half a million out of work than see the wages reduced, and it was on that difficulty that he had a great deal of trouble with his fellow trade unionists. And of course you must remember the efforts made by the Trades Union Council day after day, meeting sometimes the owners and sometimes the miners to get them to consider that question of wages . . . [T]he Government put before them in April . . . our complete agreement to push ahead . . . with everything in the report. We had discussions with them . . . on the various things that were contained in the report with regard to re-organisation. We could not get them to discuss them very clearly, or apparently with

---

[30] I.e., because the north-east England and south Wales coalfields faced the difficulties of selling in overseas markets, they could only remain competitive by accepting longer working hours as well as reduced wages.

very much interest. It was a purely negative attitude they took up at that time, and then, as now, it would be perfectly possible in my view, for an agreement to be come to even on the lines of the Report in a very short time . . .

. . . I do not want to say anything unkind. I know Mr Cook . . . I know his history and his mentality, and the difficulty with Mr Cook has been that he is an extraordinarily difficult man to deal with. His own people have had no success with him. His own people have been trying to move Mr Cook and trying to get definite things out of him; they have all given him up in despair, and where a man's co-equals and co-eternals fail, I doubt very much the success of any one else[31] in dealing with him . . .

. . . I think the economic difficulty . . . is . . . that to avoid a wholesale closing of the pits in certain parts of the country, it will be absolutely essential for a time to extend the length of the hours. The only alternative is to shut down completely. They are both of them disagreeable alternatives, but I have always felt that it must come to the men ultimately. You see when you pass an Eight Hours Act,[32] it does not mean that everybody has to work that time; you can work inside it. There are definitely restricted parts of the country where they can work on seven hours. There are other parts where it may be 7½, others at 8 . . .

[I]f you gave [miners or owners] one month, six months or 12 [in which to negotiate], they will never get to business until five minutes to 12 on the last night. That is a fact. I wish you had had a month or two with them. It is really a marvellous experience. I have dealt with every kind of industry, and there is nothing like this mining industry . . . It is one of the things we are going to straighten out . . .

[Bishop Kempthorne]: There seems to be a possibility of settlement on the lines of these propositions, but if this is turned down, what is going to happen? Are they to be starved into submission?

[Baldwin]: There is no starvation in this country; it is a historical phrase.

[A committee member]: As to the proposed scheme of re-organisation, the uncertainty as to the time when that scheme will be introduced is one of the things complicating the situation.

---

[31] I.e. this committee of churchmen.
[32] Extending the statutory limit of the miners' working day from seven hours, passed on 8 July. The government had also obtained an act to stimulate re-organisation of the industry.

[Baldwin]: The longer a word is the more misleading it is. We none of us know what is meant by re-organisation. One side has clung to it knowing nothing of what it means. Re-organisation, whether it is going to mean threepence a ton or two shillings cannot be achieved in weeks or months; it will be a matter of years before the whole of it can be seen, and that is the difficulty...

May I say this in perfect frankness – the frightfully difficult task I have to do is to wean this great industry from the breasts of the State, where it has been for ten years, and until that industry is on its own feet, we shall have this recurring over and over again, and it is a thunderingly difficult job...

...There is nothing that cannot be settled, if they make up their minds to it, in a week.

[A committee member]: In practice what will happen is that they will not settle, and they will go back because they are beaten.

[Baldwin]: I do not think that is the position. I cannot of course prophesy what will happen, but I do not want to see the miners beaten to their knees...

[A committee member]:... it is not a question of dealing with Cook, but of dealing with the extraordinary solidarity of the miners.

[Baldwin]: I would remind you that in 1921 the solidarity never looked so great as it did in the 12th week, and it all ended in a week from then...I think they will negotiate when they are done. Negotiations can always take place. They have seen figures on which they can go back, and it is open to them to go and negotiate...and say what they like and what they do not like. They have never tried: they will try before the end comes....[33]

7 AUGUST 1926 BISHOP H. H. HENSON[34] JOURNAL

Henson papers

...we had tea with the Prime Minister and Mrs Baldwin in their very attractive home [Astley Hall]...I had more than an hour's talk with the

---

[33] Despite continuing government efforts, the Miners' Federation rejected all proposals. In November the position of their members was so bad that resistance was abandoned, and from 20 November miners returned to work at the reduced wages imposed by owners at district levels, as well as the longer hours.

[34] Henson, Bishop of Durham 1920–39, was a critic of trade unions and of clerical intervention in industrial disputes. He and his wife were on a motoring tour on the Welsh marches and West Midlands.

P.M., who spoke with frankness & apparent sincerity. He told me much that was interesting and some things that were rather startling, but these were confidential, & had best, therefore, be omitted even from this journal. He evidently feels strongly about the intervention of the Bishops in the Miners' dispute, & thinks that it has done much harm. We discussed some ecclesiastical matters . . .

Mr Baldwin's observations on Lloyd George were very impressive, for he spoke with an earnestness and detachment which seemed to compel belief in his sincerity. He said that L.G. had a thoroughly bad influence on everybody with whom he came into contact: that he had spoiled Charles Masterman, and made Eric Geddes worse than he was: that he had done much injury to Austen Chamberlain & Sir Robert Horne. Auckland Geddes said of him that he looked over a man's character, detected its weak point, & worked on that. He spoke with severity of Ramsay MacDonald as a thoroughly untrustworthy man, and said that he had come to the conclusion that Lansbury was an arrant humbug. These severe judgements contrasted with the general kindness of his judgements on his opponents.

I took occasion to urge the importance of revising Trade Union law, and he agreed, but did not seem very clear as to the nature and extent of the revision. He is, I think, genuinely anxious to pursue the line of sympathetic goodwill towards the aspirations of artisans, which he has hitherto claimed for himself: & he shrinks naturally from any course which would obscure his true purpose in the eyes of the artisans themselves. An attempt to restrain the excessive powers of the Trade Unions, & to bring them under the control of the law, might easily be misrepresented and misunderstood . . .

Despite spending two weeks at Astley, on returning to London Baldwin was still tired and his secretaries obtained a medical opinion to overcome the King's doubts about his going abroad on holiday during the coal dispute. The Baldwins were again joined by the Davidsons. He left Churchill in overall charge of the coal negotiations. 'I shall have the code books at Aix for wires, and can always return at short notice. I haven't had any real holiday yet and must have a rest to shake off some gouty troubles and accumulate energy!'[35]

---

[35] Jones 'diary', 21, 23 Aug. 1926, partly in Jones *WD*, ɪɪ, pp. 63–4; to Joynson-Hicks, 21 Aug. 1925, Brentford papers J3/C-1d. Many of the telegrams and letters are in Jones *WD*, ɪɪ, pp. 70–80; *WSC* V/1, pp. 759–822; and *Davidson Memoirs*, pp. 255–9.

RA PS/GV/K. 2066/S

Hotel Bernascon, Aix-les-Bains

Sir,

On arrival here I take the earliest opportunity of conveying my respectful appreciation to Your Majesty for so graciously approving my departure from England.

I devoted the last three days to the Coal question and saw separately the Chancellor of the Exchequer and Lord Birkenhead. Both are within easy reach of London and will be accessible to the Ministers of Labour and Mines, who have the advantage of being advised by two most experienced Civil Servants.

I had a sudden and acute attack of lumbago on Saturday and though I am exceedingly strong and quite sound, I had got to the point when I needed, if possible, a complete rest for a short time, before facing the work of the autumn and winter.

Your Majesty will be amused to hear that I crossed yesterday with a number of members of the Council of the T.U.C. We had a most friendly conversation and parted with mutual protestations of affection, and on their side I hope respect as well.

I trust, Sir, that you enjoyed your visit to Bolton and that you will find at Balmoral the quiet rest which is so necessary for you.

I have the honour to be, Sir, with the greatest respect and devotion

Your Majesty's servant/ Stanley Baldwin

5 SEPTEMBER 1926: TO CHURCHILL

Churchill papers CHAR 22/112/78; *WSC V/1*, pp. 773–4

Regina Hotel Bernascon/Aix-les-Bains

My dear Winston,

I am grateful for your telegrams which with sundry précis I have received keep me posted as well as is possible at this distance.

Your speech in the House I thought admirable and I think that you have probably followed the only course available and followed it with skill and success. But it is just at the moment that one seems in a fair way to pass through a difficult channel that one has to look out for sunken rocks. I wish it had been possible to see a separate Notts agreement[36] drawn up before we came in but I dare say it was really impossible to wait. I am a great believer in paying out rope to the last but I recognise as I said in my telegram, that only the man on the spot can judge when the moment is come to jerk it in.

No doubt the immediate apprehension of a break in the Federation caused the swing round of the vote.

Now where I am anxious is just here at the point where the tripartite Conference begins.

My desire and I think the desire of all of us is to wean the Coal Industry from the Government, and that any agreement must be between owners and men. The men will be eager to have the government a party to any agreement because (A) if anything goes wrong, they can curse 'em and (B) so long as government can be indicated as a partner so long is there a peg for nationalization and all that the dreams of the wild men stand for.

If any declaration of gov$^{\underline{nt}}$ policy is involved, e.g. help for displaced men, it should be a separate undertaking.

And unless we are clear that a settlement contains – as far as human foresight can tell – no seeds of future trouble in it, it is far better not to pursue it: for any momentary kudos will be soon lost and failure in twelve months time would fall on us like a load of bricks within a measurable distance of the general election.

I am sure these points are as clear to your mind as they are to mine but being 800 miles away and ignorant of the shifting of the sands which are very quick just now, I cannot refrain from writing.[37] I intend in any case to be in London on the 15th. inst. which will have given me three clear weeks and a day, and if I can adhere to that date I shall of course be very happy. But I need not say I am ready to return any day that I am really wanted.

It is a great relief to me to feel what a strong committee I have left in charge to handle this most difficult situation.

Yours ever/ Stanley Baldwin

Asquith, made Earl of Oxford and Asquith in 1925, retired as Liberal leader, leaving Lloyd George in effective, but contested, control of the party.

---

[36] A model of a wages and hours settlement specific to conditions in a particular coalfield, contrasted with the national settlements demanded by the National Union of Mineworkers.
[37] Nor could he refrain from making an independent check, telegraphing to Jones on the same day: 'Are we right to assume that Government intend only to bring parties together if possible and that actual negotiations on terms of settlement will be between miners and owners alone': *WSC V/1*, p. 774.

23 OCTOBER 1926: TO LORD OXFORD

Asquith papers 18/127–8; Lord Oxford and Asquith, *Memories and Reflections* (1928), II, pp. 243–4

10, Downing Street

My dear Oxford,

I have wanted to write to you for several days but I have been more than usually busy and it is not easy to express what I feel.

I don't think that anyone who has not been a Prime Minister can realize the essential and ultimate loneliness of that position: there is no veil between him and the human heart (or rather no veil through which he cannot see) and in his less happy moments he may feel himself to be the repository of the sins and follies of the whole world. You can understand then how my heart has often gone out to you during these last years. I have admired without reserve your courage, your dignity, your self-restraint: you have set an example in circumstances of cruel difficulty that I hope we younger men may have the strength to follow when such trials come to us.

And I shall never forget the kindly courtesy which you shewed to me in the House of Commons.

The position of leader came to me when I was inexperienced, before I was really fitted for it, by a succession of curious chances that could not have been foreseen.

I had never expected it: I was in no way trained for it. You forbore to take advantage of these things and you gave me a lesson by which I hope I shall profit in the years to come.

I hope you will not feel that I have broken unduly through our English reserve in saying so much. But if I cannot speak now, the opportunity will never come, and so I have taken my courage in both hands.

Secure in the respect and affection of your friends, indeed of all Englishmen whose respect and affection are worth having, may you have as many years of peace and happy rest as you desire and not one more!

Believe me to remain/ Very sincerely yours/ Stanley Baldwin

3 NOVEMBER 1926 KATHLEEN HILTON YOUNG DIARY

Kennet papers; partly in Kennet, *Self-Portrait*, p. 251

Altho' breakfast was scheduled for 9, the P.M. turned up at $\frac{1}{4}$ to . . . He was awfully full of beans. He said when he wanted to go to Aix, the King didn't want him to go ('very nervous'). So he had to get a Dr to say he must. All the Drs out of town, so he got a friend of his, an <u>accoucheur</u>. I asked him of what he had delivered him, & he said 'No, not even you could I tell that!'. Then he was infinitely amusing about the Miners' leader, Herbert Smith, a Yorkshireman weighing about 16 ton . . . Then the P.M. recounted the dossier of Cook. It appears he was a Baptist preacher & when he gave up he became an atheist. Said he was much more truculent & cock a hoop July of last year than he is now.

He had been reading proofs of Winston's new book.[38] A good deal of self defence & a good deal of anti-L.G.

Then he consulted Bill about the chairman of the Conservative party. Said it was unpaid. I said how absurd, why? – he said he would have to alter that. Said Jackson wasn't quite good enough. Suggested Davidson, but said he knew that would not be popular as he was blamed for some aspects of the 1923 election. Bill suggested King & P.M. said he had thought of him, then we suggested David Margesson but P.M. said he wanted to keep him to train on for Chief Whip. Bill advised him against Linlithgow or any other Scotsman.[39] He was . . . cheery, amusing, confiding & excited. He wanted to know if Austen was happy in the Cabinet. I said I thought very, now.

Davidson was made party chairman a few days later. In December, Baldwin read 'one of the very best country novels I have ever read. <u>Precious Bane</u> by a Mrs Webb'. On asking John Buchan and J. M. Barrie about Mary Webb, he was told that she was among 'the three best living writers of English to-day, but nobody buys her books'. His praise of her when addressing the Royal Literary Fund in April 1928 produced such a demand for her novels and poems that a collected edition was published, with prefaces by distinguished figures (although Baldwin's preface to *Precious Bane* was actually drafted by Tom Jones).[40] A later comment on her books was: 'I am not sure that the "Golden Arrow" [1916] isn't my favourite. But I read "Precious Bane" first and got so excited at having discovered a new vein of pure ore that I cackled over it like a hen with her first egg.'[41]

[38] *The World Crisis, vol. 3, 1916–18*, published March 1927.
[39] Jackson had become Governor of Bengal; Douglas King was financial secretary, War Office 1924–8; Margesson, a whip since 1924, became chief whip 1931–40; Linlithgow had already refused the party chairmanship.
[40] To Joan Davidson, 24 Dec. 1926; *The Times*, 26 April 1928; M. S. Howard, *Jonathan Cape* (1971), pp. 98–102; Jones papers A7/17–39.
[41] To Bridgeman, 5 Sept. 1928, Bridgeman papers 4629/1/1928/126.

14 JANUARY 1927: TO MARY WEBB

facsimile in *Armour Wherein He Trusted*, in *The Collected Works of Mary Webb* (1929)

10, Downing Street

Dear Mrs Webb,

I hope you will not think it an impertinence on my part if I tell you with what keen delight I have read 'Precious Bane'.

My people lived in Shropshire for centuries before they migrated to Worcestershire and I spent my earliest years in Bewdley which is on the border. In your book I seem to hear again the speech and turns of phrase which surrounded me in the nursery. I think it is a really first class piece of work and I have not enjoyed a book so much for years.

It was given to me by one of my secretaries and I read it at Christmas within sight of the Clee Hills, at home.

Thank you a thousand times for it.

Believe me to remain/ Sincerely yours/ Stanley Baldwin

27 JANUARY 1927 KATHLEEN HILTON YOUNG DIARY

Kennet papers; partly in Kennet, *Self-Portrait*, p. 253

At 8.55 am Stanley Baldwin came to breakfast. He walked & arrived very fresh, gay and happy. He stayed till 10.15. He was very diverting. His Cabinet – ! What a lot! There was Freddy Birkenhead winning diving competitions in Madeira, Leo Amery leaping like a chamois over the Swiss snows on skis, Sam Hoare flying to & over India. 'Upon my word', said he, 'I feel like a keeper of performing fleas'. As always he gave a tremendous eulogy for Neville Chamberlain, so capable, so reliable so etc . . . He said nothing detrimental about Austen, but I felt an underlying criticism . . . When he wants to go to the theatre, he sends for Eddie Marsh as a sort of official adviser . . . & on Monday he is going to Nigel Playfair's play . . . I wonder why S.B. comes to breakfast with us . . . When he left he said 'Thank you so much, it is so refreshing'. I wonder whether it is Bill he likes or me & why he likes us, because it is always he who talks, we never do. Perhaps people are sufficiently rare in his life who ask nothing from him & have apparently no grinding axe. I wonder. Certain it is that I ask him to breakfast about once in six weeks & that he never has refused.

On 5 April Baldwin was suddenly taken ill, apparently an effect of strain and tiredness. Although he soon resumed work, he remained weakened until the early summer.

23 APRIL 1927: TO FRANCIS BRETT YOUNG

Brett Young papers 1953

10, Downing Street

Dear Mr Young,

I had the great good fortune to be ordered a rest at Easter and I was put to bed for three days for the first time in my life. This gave me the opportunity of reading your book[42] which I did with the greatest pleasure and appreciation. I valued it much as coming from you and more on account of the delightful letter which accompanied it.

East and West Worcestershire are very different: I always feel that Severn marks a real boundary, but I know enough of the east and of that part of the country where the Black Country persistently obtrudes to revel in your descriptions of it and your characterisation of its people.

More power to your elbow and I hope you will write much more of our own folk and particularly if the spirit moves you of our own working folk. I shall make myself acquainted with your other books without delay. Since I have been in office my reading has been desultory and intermittent, the greatest sacrifice I have to make.

I thank you most warmly for thinking of me and for the real pleasure you have given me.

Yours sincerely/ Stanley Baldwin

21 JUNE 1927 BISHOP HENSON JOURNAL

Henson papers

... interview with the P.M ... I began by enquiring about his health, and he replied, 'I'm quite fit: the doctors tell me that I have been suffering from a tired heart, but that I have the arteries of a child'. He then said that he was designing to speak frankly about Russia in the North of England.[43]

... We talked of the ominous signs of an approaching dark age in which civilization would again perish. 'I dare not let myself think on those lines, for, if I did, I could not go on in my place'. Well, I said, we can only go on

---

[42] *Portrait of Clare*, just published, and set in Worcestershire. Young became a friend: see David Cannadine, *In Churchill's Shadow* (2002), ch. 7.
[43] The 'Arcos raid' and rupture of diplomatic relations with Russia, arising from criticism of communist propaganda, had occurred in May.

by knowing that the courses of the World are in the Hand of God, & that so long as we are serving righteousness, we are doing his Will. Yes, I believe that, he said[44] . . .

The following letter to the Viceroy of India (the former Edward Wood and future Lord Halifax) contains one of Baldwin's most well-known phrases, quoted in his first biography. However, the letter remained unfinished and was not received by its intended recipient until much later, as Baldwin explained in a covering note when finally forwarding it to Halifax in 1938: 'The enclosed [this 1927 letter] may interest you. I am going through old boxes of my Downing Street papers and found it yesterday./ I evidently began it and was interrupted: it got lost in a pile of papers and was put in a miscellaneous box by a faithful secretary!'[45]

26 JUNE 1927: TO LORD IRWIN [INCOMPLETE AND UNSENT]

Halifax papers A.4.410.14.2

10, Downing Street

My dear Edward,

Profound reflection has convinced me that the one unselfish action of my life was persuading you to go to India.

I have missed you every day and you must attribute my long silence to the fact that I have had so much to say that I never knew where to begin!

Last year broke up the great deeps and you would hardly recognise the situation to-day.

I do not see how anything we could have done could have avoided the trouble. I still think we were right in buying off the strikes of 1925 though it proved once more the cost of teaching democracy.

Democracy has arrived at a gallop in England, and I feel all the time that it is a race for life: can we educate them before the crash comes? I think you would have been pretty depressed

On 4 May Baldwin had been shouted down by Labour MPs when speaking on the Trades Disputes Bill, which banned general and sympathetic strikes and reversed

---

[44] Another indication of Baldwin's religious sensibilities is his friendship with Father William Sirr, who in 1918 established a small monastery at Glasshampton, close to Astley Hall: see G. Curtis, *William of Glasshampton* (1947), pp. 144, 165; Jones *DL*, pp. 523–4.
[45] To Halifax, 14 Jan. 1938, Halifax papers A.4.410.14.8.

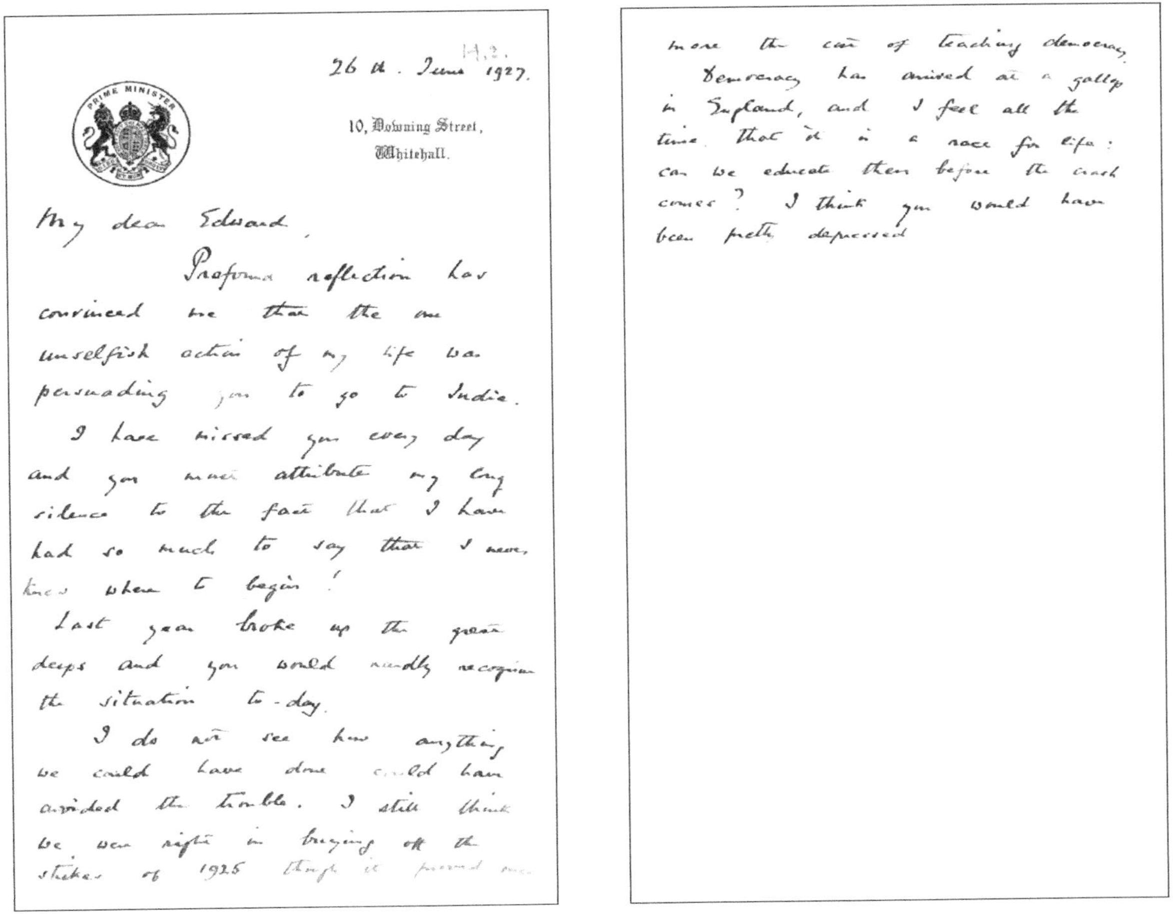

26 th. June 1927.

10, Downing Street,
Whitehall.

My dear Edward,

Profound reflection has convinced me that the one unselfish action of my life was persuading you to go to India.

I have missed you every day and you must attribute my long silence to the fact that I have had so much to say that I never knew where to begin!

Last year broke up the great deeps and you would hardly recognise the situation to-day.

I do not see how anything we could have done could have avoided the trouble. I still think we were right in buying off the strikes of 1925 though it proved more the cost of teaching democracy.

Democracy has arrived at a gallop in England, and I feel all the time that it is a race for life: can we educate them before the crash comes? I think you would have been pretty depressed

Figure 6 To Irwin, 26 June 1927 (unfinished)

his March 1925 position on trade union political funds. He reluctantly allowed his Cabinet to prepare legislation to strengthen the House of Lords by altering its composition, and was relieved when a Conservative backbench rebellion wrecked the bill on 20 June: 'We have had a worrying time over the Lords. It is small consolation to me to feel "I told you so" but the H. of C. has pretty well blown reform out of the water.'[46] During the Geneva naval disarmament conference from June to early August, Churchill caused the Cabinet to be apprehensive about the willingness of Bridgeman and Cecil to limit British naval building. Baldwin sent reassuring letters to Bridgeman: 'I couldn't stop Winston sending you a message which I thought a work of supererogation, but he has whacked himself up into a panic about the whole thing'; and, on Bridgeman being temporarily recalled, 'Don't worry about being asked to come home for consultation . . . The Cabinet want to be perfectly clear as to the lines on which a settlement may be reached./ I regard it as of great importance to have the discussion while I am here.'[47] In early August the conference ended without agreement, and Cecil resigned. From 23 July to 24 August, Baldwin fulfilled his promise to Mackenzie King and visited Canada, accompanying the Prince of Wales for part of the time. In April the King had been 'very anxious' to talk with Baldwin, travelling specially to Chequers with the Queen. This probably concerned the Prince of Wales' behaviour, on which Baldwin heard more criticism from the Prince's assistant secretary while in Ottawa.[48]

30 JULY 1927 MACKENZIE KING DIARY

. . . We spoke of his Govt. I sd I wd not have introduced the legislation re. H. of Lords or Trade Union Bill if I had been in his place. He told me it was not in accordance with his judgement but pressure from his party. He feels he is in better shape politically than a year ago – better to be in the trough early than later. He doubts if Ramsay MacDonald will be able to take hold again . . .

. . . walked over the Plains of Abraham . . . Baldwin told me that he had twice submitted to the King the 3 names suggested for P.C.s, that the King

---

[46] To Bridgeman, 7 July 1927, Bridgeman papers 4629/1/1927/71.
[47] To Bridgeman, 7, 12, 14 July 1927, Bridgeman papers 4629/1/1927/71, 81, 88.
[48] Lucy Baldwin to her daughter Margot, 17 July 1927, and see Baldwin's guarded recollection of the subject, 'a private matter of domestic concern', in John Gore, *King George V* (1941), p. 373n; *In Royal Service. The Letters and Journals of Sir Alan Lascelles 1920–1936*, ed. D. Hart-Davis (1989), pp. 50–1.

took the position if Canada wd not permit titles, he wd not consent to give the highest of all – membership of the Imperial Privy Council. Baldwin said Amery was favourable . . . & that he himself was favourable; he supposed a Prime Minister could override the King, but he hardly felt this particular matter was of sufficient importance for that . . .

In going over the battlefields we spoke of how the beginnings of the present Br. Empire were there & how the whole of British and world history had changed because of 1756 . . . In speaking of Amery he said that A. lacked judgement (I wd understand this, he was not speaking against a colleague), the best of men in some respects but no judgement at times. I told him I regarded the Dominions Office as a 5th wheel to a coach[49] – he agreed & indicated it might be done away with & some one appointed as under secretary in his the P.M.'s office for the purpose of direct communication with P.M. of Dominions. I tried to lessen B's bitterness against the U.S. . . .

4 AUGUST 1927 MACKENZIE KING DIARY

. . . At Kingsmere[50] Baldwin & I took off our coats . . . & went for a walk. . . . On our ramble Baldwin & I talked over many matters. He said to me the problem that was concerning him was what shld be done if the Royal family were to 'throw up' a sort of George IV, seeing that the Empire now rested so largely on a common allegiance to the Crown. He said 'let your fertile mind work on that'. He evidently does not feel too secure with the present heir to the Throne. He expressed strongly the wish that H.R.H. wd get married, & hinted at this being possible after his return. I told Baldwin I thought the way to meet the situation was to make so clear the power of the P.M. & the Cabinet that the public wd see it did not matter who was the figure head, that Const'l govt meant Govt by the people thro' their elected representatives & that the rest was framework.

He spoke very strongly & bitterly of the American press starting & circulating lies which could not be overtaken. He could not have felt more indignant at the press than I do myself. We both agreed that the

---

[49] On Amery's initiative, Dominions affairs had been separated from the Colonial Office.
[50] Mackenzie King's country house.

Govt had to be carried on in spite of the press, that it was a great menace . . .

RA PS/GV/J.2123/12

Canadian Pacific, S.S. Empress of Scotland

Sir,

Before arriving at Southampton I should like to express my most grateful thanks to Your Majesty for allowing me to leave England to spend nineteen wonderful days in Canada. I believe this visit has done good. I had the honour of travelling with the Prince of Wales as far as Calgary: the warmth of his welcome everywhere was a revelation to me. Popular enthusiasm was extraordinary, and I think that Prince George's appearance in an official capacity gave immense pleasure. He was naturally rather shy at first but I think the spontaneity of the welcome he got for himself pleased and encouraged him and he did his part well.

The Prince of Wales was at his best and it was a real pleasure as well as an honour to be with him.

The work has been hard. In the last six days I travelled nearly 3000 miles and spoke at Calgary, Regina, Winnipeg, St John, Monckton, Charlottetown, Halifax and North Sydney.

I am particularly anxious to counteract the effect of much loose talking in and out of England, and of the stuff that Mr Lloyd George puts into the yellow Yankee press. There has been too long an idea, uncontradicted, that we are played out, idle, hopeless and so on, and I went for that with all the energy I could command. The reception I got in consequence was amazing. I broadcast all over the west and northwest and at Winnipeg there must have been 15000 people present. There can be no question of the strength and depth of feeling of the unity of the race wherever it may be and of its' unity under the Crown.

It was a wonderful experience which I hope will be of the greatest service in my work.

I want to sort out my impressions quietly, and be in a position to speak later in the year on some of the problems ahead.

I took the opportunity of telling Mackenzie King that his present High Commissioner is no good. I did it delicately but clearly.

The Willingdons[51] are undoubtedly very popular everywhere. I do not think your Majesty could have a better representative than he is.

I hope Sir you will forgive a short and rather disconnected note of this kind, but I was anxious to do three things without delay: to express my gratitude, to assure you of the complete success of the Prince of Wales' visit and of the admirable way in which he has played his difficult part, and to express my conviction that my own visit will be of service to the Empire.

I am/ Your Majesty's most obedient, faithful servant/ Stanley Baldwin

15 SEPTEMBER 1927: TO IRWIN

Halifax Indian papers Eur c152/17/253f

[Aix-les-Bains]

My dear Edward,

Your letters always give me great pleasure and make me realise how badly I have treated you. You are quite right in the inadequacy of the medium – I miss you more than I can say, indeed I regard my sending you to India as the one unselfish act of my life! I would give worlds for a talk.

The Canadian tour was a wonderful experience. I made up my mind to go because something had to be done to counteract the poisonous stream of propaganda emanating from America and from all that hate us, making out that England is decadent, played out, and not to be considered in a new world of he-men. And let us not forget to pay our tribute to the little Goat for his articles in the Hearst Press. I think I've beaten it for the time. I was lucky enough to 'get across' – a vulgar but expressive idiom – and I know it has done good.

I came out here a few days after returning and I go back in about ten days.

I have lost Bob. He resigned a year ago, but I got him to withdraw. I knew I would not hold him for the natural life of a government, but I am sorry he has gone. I did my best. Austen has made an admirable Foreign Secretary. Read his speech of the 10th September at Geneva. First class. Our word goes once more and our prestige abroad stands where it ought to.

Labour is not progressing at present, nor, I think, the liberals!

---

[51] Governor-General of Canada 1926–31 and his wife, long-standing friends of the Baldwins.

There is a good deal of discontent among the farmers and an election to-day would mean the loss of a lot of agricultural seats. It has been fomented by a persistent campaign on the part of Rothermere in league with the Goat, but like these clever men they can't wait, and in my view they started firing a year too soon and they will be out of ammunition when the fight begins. The Goat of course wants to weaken us in our strongest part and hopes to detach enough seats to put him in a commanding position – say 250 Labour, 250–300 Tories, and 50–100 Liberals.

I will not prophesy; too early yet. But the Goat is a tactician, not a strategist, and my brief experience has led me to this profound belief: that these 'brilliant' men generally have not only an Achilles heel but an Achilles bottom which can be well kicked at the right moment.

I think it not unlikely that I shall have to find a new Archbishop before I go out. I should value your views very much. The Court will probably press for York. Of course it would be the line of least resistance. York to Canterbury, Oxford to York. Oxford might do for Canterbury.[52]

I should rule out every Bishop who appeared with the Industrial Christian fellowship during the Coal Strike,[53] because not to see what Cook was denotes a lack of that wisdom essential for the position. There is no obvious man.

Winston's position is curious. Our people like him. They love listening to him in the House; look on him as a star turn and settle down in the stalls with anticipatory grins. But for the leadership, they would turn him down every time. If anything happened to me, the best men are Neville and Hogg, and I think on the whole the second would be chosen. He needs more political experience, but he is first-rate and stuffed with character.

You, my dear Edward, will have to be Foreign Secretary in years to come; you have every qualification for it. Turn it over.

Bless you my friend. You are doing magnificently. Never mind whether apparent success or failure is yours. You won't.

It warms my old heart to hear what is said of you.

[52] See J. G. Lockhart, *Cosmo Lang* (1949), pp. 310–11, for Baldwin personally informing Archbishop Lang of York in July 1928 that he would succeed Archbishop Davidson at Canterbury. Thomas Strong remained Bishop of Oxford.
[53] He relented, and Temple replaced Lang as Archbishop of York.

My respectful duty to your lady. Tell Anne I thought of her when Austen and I lunched at Talloires.[54]

Yours ever/ Stanley Baldwin

The 2nd Earl of Lytton, Governor of Bengal 1922–7, had asked Baldwin's advice in July on whether he had any political prospects, or should go into business. He now reminded him of this discussion, and asked if he could be appointed to the post made vacant by Cecil's resignation. The post went to McNeill, financial secretary at the Treasury since 1925, now made Lord Cushendun. Lytton went into business.

26 OCTOBER 1927: TO LORD LYTTON

2nd Earl of Lytton papers

10, Downing Street

My dear Lytton,

You will I am sure understand that it was difficult to reply to your letter of Oct. 2nd., nor indeed did you desire me to do so.

But I cannot allow it to remain unanswered any longer.

I have had others in similar strain from men qualified as you are yourself to have undertaken further important work.[55]

The task of a Prime Minister is at all times difficult: but in no case is it more difficult or more unenviable than when he has to select a successor to a vacant office. He pleases one: he cannot please more than one: he may hurt some. He has, with due regard to the best interest of the country, to make such a selection as will accommodate itself best to the health and well-being of the large party of which he is for the time being leader. And in that he must rely largely – certainly finally – on his own judgement by which ultimately he must stand or fall.

To you, as to others, the government owes a deep debt of gratitude for services rendered to the empire, and it is constantly a source of unhappiness to me that I have not sufficient spheres of work available to retain continuously the help of those so well qualified to join us.

I cannot say more, nor could I well say less in answer to a letter as courteous and full of understanding as yours.

Believe me to remain/ Sincerely yours/ Stanley Baldwin

---

[54] On 12 September, to continue consultations on League of Nations affairs earlier conducted by telegram and letter.

[55] The 5th Earl of Onslow, under-secretary, War Office, also asked for the post, and received a shorter but equally sympathetic version of this letter: copy, 21 Oct. 1927, SB papers 115/250.

In May 1926 Baldwin commented that he had not seen his elder son for two years. Oliver was living with Boyle in Oxfordshire, working on their farm, writing books and newspaper articles, and speaking as a prospective Labour candidate. The surviving letters from father to son resume in 1927.

27 OCTOBER 1927: TO OLIVER BALDWIN

CUL MS Add. 8795/4

10, Downing Street

Dearest Son,

Your Sherlock Holmes of a father quickly guessed that a beautiful picture which arrived at Chequers came from you, and as one good turn deserves another I am sending you a picture in exchange, less beautiful but not less truthful.[56]

I seem to be overwhelmed this week with a number of small speeches – occasions in which I had promised months ago to be present: each occasion has led subsequently to a request for 'a few words' and one lot of devils with whom I had arranged for five minutes have billed me for half an hour!

'as that 'appened to you? as Mr Johnson of Kidderminster observed to me during the 1906 election when he was kissed in the street by a bevy of mill girls.

Well, well, I must get on and frame something for 1000 young ladies who will hang on my lips in another sense at three o'clock.[57]

Your garrulous/ but loving/ Father

28 DECEMBER 1927: TO BRIDGEMAN

Bridgeman papers 4629/1/1927/176

10, Downing Street

My dear Willie

... Get a good rest while you can: it will be a tough year and we have got to see this job through. We little thought what we had set our hands to when we broke loose from the Goat.

---

[56] Evidently an exchange of photographs of themselves.
[57] Baldwin was to speak at a meeting of the Union of Girls' Schools.

I think that will be our chief claim to fame. Talk of Pride's purge! not in it with ours, if you compare the muck that had to be shifted.

Isn't it jolly how these country similes come to mind? It would take a good deal of urbanization to destroy our simplicity.

. . . you've been a tower of strength always, bless you,

Ever yours/ S.B.

15 JANUARY 1928: TO JOYNSON-HICKS

Brentford papers J3/C-1f

10, Downing Street

My dear Jix,

I had a talk with Anderson[58] yesterday about Factories & Police and other things. Those don't matter. The only thing that did matter was that he told me you were thinking of coming back at the end of the month.

Now do be sensible. We shall have practically settled our programme then: I have your explicit letter about business and (unless the Revolution breaks out) there can be nothing for which you are needed (I say 'needed' because you are always wanted by your friends) until the House meets.

Take the other week. You will have a heavy year in any circumstances. And now that you have taken the Protestants of England under your wing[59] as well as the police, the publicans, the prisoners, the prostitutes, factories, flappers and children, you MUST learn to take [care] of yourself, or all the above will be ORPHANED.

Now just think this over. I don't want to see you till the sixth of February. All good be yours in 1928.

Yrs ever/ S.B.

Baldwin also excused Balfour: 'There is nothing to worry about at the moment except the selection of [parliamentary] business which is always tiresome, for no one knows better than you the difficulty of confining a quart of potable liquor into a pint pot and seeing that none of the ingredients are calculated to destroy the flavour of the beverage.'[60] In early 1928 Baldwin's principal problem

---

[58] Sir John Anderson, permanent secretary, Home Office 1922–32.
[59] On 15 December, in a debate conducted on non-party lines, Joynson-Hicks was a leader of the evangelical Protestant opposition to the revised Prayer Book, which Baldwin had supported.
[60] 30 Jan. 1928, Balfour Whittingehame papers GD 433/2/19/12.

was reconciling Churchill's plans to relieve industry of local rates ('de-rating') with Neville Chamberlain's delayed proposals for poor law reform. The published documents on the episode show that Baldwin managed both ministers very well, particularly in persuading Chamberlain, who had threatened resignation, that his acquiescence in Churchill's scheme had strengthened his personal position in the Cabinet.[61] On 15 February Lord Oxford died.

15 FEBRUARY 1928: TO LADY OXFORD

Margot Asquith papers MS. Eng *c.* 6669/98

10, Downing Street

My dear Lady,

You have been constantly in my thoughts these last days as you have in the thoughts of millions of his fellow-countrymen.

He has left his country a great legacy, a character of unassailable integrity, of high honour, of quiet dignity sustained through years of difficulty, and he was a great Englishman in times of unparalleled political prosperity and a greater in times of political confusion and disaster. For all of which things you may thank God (who has not forgotten you as you said hastily in your letter to me) and take courage for the days to come.

I shall ask the Dean that his ashes may lie in the Abbey, if it be your desire.

Be brave, as I know you will: your friends are many and their hands are outstretched.

With profound sympathy and true affection

As always/ Stanley Baldwin

15 MAY 1928: TO CHURCHILL

Churchill papers CHAR 18/90/33; *WSC V/1*, pp. 1286–7

10, Downing Street

My dear Winston,

Figure to yourself my feelings! Having still a vivid recollection of that frail invalid in bed and of the enthusiasm with which he welcomed the prospect of a call at Chartwell (somewhere about lunchtime). I telephone yesterday morning that I would farm out my questions and come down right away.

And then to be told that you had gone to Scotland!

I had not recovered from the shock before your letter was brought to me.

---

[61] *WSC V/1*, pp. 1128–266; *NC Letters*, II, pp. 434–6, III, pp. 73–83.

Well, I am delighted that you are better, but I beg you won't hurry back.

I am glad you are very contented with the Budget situation. Keep on with the cud.

And don't worry about Rothermere. He has done you all the service he can for the present, and I think you are a little disposed to overrate his influence in the country.[62]

It is suburban mainly, in a wide sense, but the provincial press is very strong and it is working well for us.

And I want you to consider two points when you think it desirable to bring in some of the benefits at an early date.[63]

A. The carrot side of it. If the carrot is to be served after the election it will be hanging up in sight during the contest and our opponents will have to promise not to interfere with our programme.

If swallowed before, it may be more in their stomach than in their minds.

B. By giving the carrot in instalments, may you not tend to dissipate the effect of the whole? I know this is Stamp's[64] view and I need not enlarge on it. It also adds to the difficulties on the financial side.

Enough for one day. I go to Manchester tomorrow to address the cotton people in words of one syllable at lunch.

Yours ever/ S.B.

What a fool R is allowing his boy to make of himself in Hungary![65] They haven't a ray of humour between them.

During the early summer protectionist backbench MPs, supported in Cabinet by Amery, had pressed for more industrial tariffs, and in late July Churchill and Joynson-Hicks gave speeches on opposite sides of the debate. Baldwin had been 'dictatorial' in Cabinet when insisting that he did not want protection revived before the election,[66] and against opposition taunts in the Commons he buried the ministerial agreement in laughter, by commenting on the 'many-sidedness of truth'. The Cabinet compromise was embodied in an open

---

[62] With a general election due within a year, Churchill was keen to overcome Rothermere's hostility towards the government. He proposed a knighthood for one of his associates (which was awarded): *WSC V/1*, p. 1285.

[63] The issue was the best time to include the railway companies in the de-rating scheme.

[64] Josiah Stamp, industrialist, railway director, taxation expert and government advisor.

[65] Rothermere had publicised the Hungarian government's grievances against the 1920 Treaty of Trianon. His son, Esmond Harmsworth, had been feted on a visit to the country.

[66] *Amery Diaries*, I, p. 560.

letter from Baldwin to the Chief Whip, stating that applications for safeguarding duties would be simplified after the general election, but ruling out general protection.

During his holidays in Aix-les-Bains, Baldwin normally left Austen Chamberlain in charge of the government. But as Chamberlain was now ill, Baldwin asked Hailsham (Hogg, made a peer and Lord Chancellor in March to replace the dying Cave) to cancel a planned visit to Canada in order to deputise for him.[67] Before Baldwin left for France, he travelled to Treorchy in the Rhondda valley, to speak at the National Eisteddfod.

11 AUGUST 1928: TO HAILSHAM

Hailsham papers 1/1/2

10, Downing Street

My dear Lord Chancellor,

Thank you for your letter. It was just like you. I am just off.

I saw Hankey yesterday: also my Lord Lloyd: had an hour with Ronnie at the F.O.[68] I think things are fairly straight and I hope nothing will occur to cause you anxiety while I am away.

I had a wonderful time in Wales. I drove through twenty miles of mining valleys: the whole population turned out to look at me and see if I had horns and a tail and I think they were agreeably disappointed.

Here and there quite a friendly reception. Infinitely better than I had expected: I was looking for half bricks!

The children appeared clean, well cared for and no open signs of distress.

Yours ever/ S.B.

Baldwin made further notable comments on this encounter with a mining population: 'No hostility and an unexpected amount of friendly greeting. It would have been impossible a year ago. I don't understand it'; and again 'the reception was remarkable. It shows there is little bitterness or resentment against the government.' He later made similar comments on a visit to Sheffield: 'we had a most friendly welcome from a lot of women who had assembled to look at us. The building is in quite a poor street and I shouldn't have been surprised if there had been some unpleasantness, for the unemployment is still pretty bad.'[69]

---

[67] 4 Aug. 1928, published in Heuston, *Lives of the Lord Chancellors*, p. 472.
[68] Sir Ronald Lindsay, permanent secretary, Foreign Office 1926–30.
[69] To Joan Davidson, 9 Aug. 1928; to Joynson-Hicks, 10 Aug., 13 Oct. 1928, Brentford papers J3/C-1g.

During Baldwin's holiday Cushendun, the acting Foreign Secretary, travelled from League of Nations meetings in Geneva to lunch with him at Annecy. Mackenzie King, also attending the League, was invited to visit too.

8–9 SEPTEMBER 1928 MACKENZIE KING DIARY

[8th] ... At 3 o'clock left by motor for Aix les Bains to spend the week end with Mr Baldwin ... Mr B. met me at the hotel door. He was looking very well, was most cordial in his welcome. We went down town together with Mrs Baldwin, had a talk in the public square seated at a little table each having a glass of water ...

After dinner we talked till about 8.30 in sitting room, Baldwin speaking very freely to me of his colleagues & problems. He believes he will come back at the next election & that Labour will do better than Liberals ... Birkenhead is going to resign at end of present parlt ... He feels he will be as well without B – never sure what may come out or what may happen at critical time. Thinks highly of Churchill, says his 'scouts' tell him Joynson-Hicks believes he will be able to lead if he, B[aldwin], drops out; in that regard he told a story of someone's remark that his manners were only on the surface, to which the reply was '& all else'. He is not considered a heavy weight. He said [Austen] Chamberlain had narrow escape for his life. Dr said it was touch & go two days with pneumonia ... Baldwin said he did not intend to let the party get divided on fiscal issues; he knew what he wanted & intended to hold on to it; any who wanted to bolt could bolt. I sd. that was his greatest danger – Amery etc. forcing tariff reform; he is determined not to permit that ... He agrees newspapers are a menace ... thinks the democracy will rise some day & hang a journalist or two ... Then when a Rothermere or Hearst is strung to a lamp post we will get decent journalism. He said they played terrible havoc with the naval issue[70] ... He is getting in good shape for election next year, intends taking complete holiday 8 weeks; has no private secretary with him at present. Davidsons were here for a time ...

[9th] ... at 8.30 Mr Baldwin and I were off for a walk together through the mountain sides, the valleys, the vineyards & villages in the near vicinity

---

[70] Hearst's American newspapers had helped poison Anglo-American relations during the 1927 Geneva naval conference. For a similar comment see Jones *WD*, II, p. 153.

getting back at 11.15 when we each had a bath and went to the 'source' to meet Mrs Baldwin. We had shirts, but not collars or ties or hats on our walk . . .

Baldwin talked <u>very</u> freely to me of his problems etc. Showed me a letter re. Austen Chamberlain from one of his secretaries which spoke of him looking exceedingly poorly, very weak, etc. He said he was too ill to think of going to Washington for a visit. Baldwin himself has a visit in mind two years hence, if he is returned to power. Churchill he speaks of as most companionable, coming to his room in 10 Downing Street each day walking up & down with cigar & water . . . He told me Cushenden was a 'stop gap' in office of Frgn. Minister. He has in mind the present Viceroy of India . . . He thinks Salisbury will not last long, nor Balfour. He feels very indignant at L.G. & use he made of honours to get party funds. Told me a very private thing – of a pearl necklace valued at 4,000[71] coming thro' the mail to L.G.'s secretary who 'did the work' re. honours . . . They came from [an Indian] & were part of the price of a knighthood or rather a G.C.B . . . What must L.G. have got himself for the honour bestowed[?]

B. continues to feel strongly on the U.S. press & trouble they make. I talked of immigration;[72] he approves of not too much being said & natural flow being right method – thinks there is a sort of industrial revolution at present in which labour must get transferred . . . He said there was no describing indignation in Eng. at large naval prog. of U.S. . . . .

He says his party is in better shape for campaign. Literature well prepared by younger men & organization in good hands. Speaking of speech at Carlton Club he sd. it was like a sort of David with a sling . . .

The Baldwins returned to Paris by means of an eight-day tour in a Rolls-Royce lent by Lord Derby (with their retinue of servants and policemen in another car), staying overnight in Avignon, Arles, Le Puy, Vichy and Fontainebleau. A motor tour either after or before their stay in Aix-les-Bains now became part of their holiday routine. As usual they spent a few days in Paris, where Baldwin had lunch with Poincaré on one day and Briand the next, and talked with Cushendun and his officials on their return from Geneva.

[71] £4,000 is about £160,000 in modern prices.
[72] A proposal for reducing British unemployment was government-assisted emigration to the Dominions.

[24 SEPTEMBER 1928] DAWSON MEMORANDUM,
WRITTEN 26 SEPTEMBER

Dawson papers 73/97–100 (extract); partly in Wrench, *Dawson*, pp. 265–6

. . . I had a talk in Downing Street with the Prime Minister, who had just returned from Aix and Paris, and was looking extraordinarily well. I had various definite questions to put to him, and he answered them with rather unusual adhesion to the point.

The General Election, so far as he could see, must be in June or July, probably early in June. It could not well be sooner because of the register and the Budget.

He was not going to say very much of interest at Yarmouth[73] on Thursday. The Conference was composed of delegates and agents, and he should try to hearten these up and make what is called a fighting speech. In the matter of safeguarding he was determined to stand firm by his letter of August to the Chief Whip. Iron and Steel would be treated like any other industry – that is, an application should be made to the proper tribunal with the proofs required in every case. He himself was in favour of a strong <u>permanent</u> tribunal to take the place of the <u>ad hoc</u> bodies which had been in operation hitherto.

We discussed the members of his Cabinet and their state of health. I told him that he was going to the country with a set of crocks and had better take the initiative by announcing this fact and saying that his colleagues had worn themselves out in the public service. But I thought it probably too late now to introduce new blood to any great extent. His experiments might prove failures at the eleventh hour and some of the people who were left out might be disgruntled. Having let things slide so long I thought that he had better content himself with saying clearly that if and when he was returned to power there would be very large changes in his team.

This brought us to F.E., about whose impending resignation a number of rumours had appeared in the press. I told him that . . . I had always assumed for months past that F.E. was going to be a partner of the Berrys. Baldwin said he knew nothing definite. F.E. had told him on various occasions that he had received a tempting offer from the City and felt that he ought to

---

[73] The venue for the annual party conference.

accept it. He had asked the Prime Minister for his advice on this point and the latter had told him that, if he cared to produce the offer in concrete form, he (Baldwin) would endeavour to advise him as to whether the people with whom he was going to associate were honest men or crooks. So far no such offer had been forthcoming, and there could be no meeting for another week . . .

We touched on House of Lords Reform . . . I asked him whether he had seriously considered the plan which I had several times put forward in The Times – namely a gradual reform based on fresh power to nominate life peers. I had always thought it the right line of approach, and the one which was most likely to commend itself to the Labour Party. Baldwin said he had given a good deal of thought to this idea and had gone so far as to broach it to MacDonald before he went away. But he does not seem to have had very much response. No doubt MacDonald was not likely to commit himself to anything which he might possibly be able to oppose with profit later on . . .

Birkenhead had perpetual financial worries, and had told Baldwin he would retire from the government in order to make more money. In the autumn he asked to leave early, rather than wait until the election. Baldwin agreed on 10 October, adding 'You will not misunderstand me when I tell you that we shall part on my side at least with a feeling of personal regret that I could not have believed possible four years ago!'[74]

On 16 October Baldwin and Oliver Baldwin appeared together at a public, but non-political, occasion. Baldwin had accepted his son's invitation to open the new town hall at Dudley: 'I shall like to feel we have shared a platform once.'[75]

Baldwin was drawn back into royal affairs in November, when the King became seriously ill. Halsey, head of the Prince of Wales' staff, decided to recall him and his brother, the Duke of Gloucester, from a safari in East Africa. Correctly judging that the Prince would be reluctant to return – he dismissed the recall as 'an election dodge' – the Palace asked Baldwin to reinforce their telegram. The Prince did return, and was met from the Channel ferry by Baldwin. For a time it seemed that the King might die, and Baldwin decided that if this happened he should broadcast to the nation in the belief that 'this would have a very steadying

---

[74] John Campbell, *F. E. Smith* (1983), p. 805. In 1926 Baldwin had agreed to Central Office payments of £10,000 (about £350,000 in modern prices) to him: see ibid., pp. 717–20, 804–6; *Davidson Memoirs*, pp. 276–7.
[75] 3 Sept. 1928, CUL MS Add. 9569/2.

and comforting effect'.[76] If the King had died, the general election might have been delayed. Baldwin was confident that whenever it was held the government would win, and he again used Dawson and Jones as sounding-boards for his ideas about reconstruction of the government.[77]

27 NOVEMBER 1928: TO THE PRINCE OF WALES

copy of cypher telegram, SB papers 177/36

Personal

Have seen Halsey's telegram with which I concur, but I approach question from another angle.

On my own responsibility, I suggest that you should both return at once.

We hope that all may go well, but if not, and you have made no attempt to return, it will profoundly shock public opinion.

Most important that it should be on your own initiative, and not in reply to anyone.

If you agree, suggest some such words as these, addressed to me which I can publish

'My brother and I are abandoning our tour and leaving for England immediately. We feel our duty lies at home'.

If rapid communication with the Duke of [Gloucester] impossible, you should not delay, as it is your return that is vital.

Stanley Baldwin

11 FEBRUARY 1929: TO BETTY BALDWIN

in private possession

10, Downing Street

Darling Betty,

I was delighted to get your letter and to hear you are enjoying the beauty of it all. It is a wonderful coast[78] and if it wasn't that I should meet all the people I spend my life in avoiding in London, I could wish I were with you . . .

---

[76] C. P. Duff to Jones, 13 Dec. 1928, in Jones 'diary', asking for a half-sheet of ideas on what Baldwin might say.

[77] See Jones *WD*, II, pp. 153–4, 172–3, 174, 179–80. Jones' unpublished text for 5 March 1929 has a Baldwin statement that 'Jix has just become a buffoon.'

[78] Betty was holidaying on the French Riviera.

Battersea was bad. The two comforting things were the heavy drop in the labour poll, following that of Midlothian and the absurd liberal vote. Half the bookies in England descended on Battersea and worked against us, and they brought such a fleet of cars for polling day as had never been seen before. But the lower middle classes went to the City and didn't trouble to vote. They were grumbling against the government on various counts and just abstained.[79]

However that has got to be remedied. And now two more elections in bad spots. Lincolnshire where the farmers are queer and N. Lanark which we won unexpectedly from labour in '24[80] . . .

Much love darling from your own/ F.

25 FEBRUARY 1929: TO IRWIN

Halifax papers A4.410.14.3

Secret   10, Downing Street

My dear Edward,

We shall probably get the election over by the beginning of June and we ought to come back, though the intervention of the Liberals may affect the result more than we think.

But I have to look ahead and decide how the new gov[nt]. is to [be] built up, for if we win events move quickly and the necessary changes must be made at once.

I have had an idea (amongst many!) of putting Winston at the India Office. He was very good all through the Irish trouble: he has imagination, courage: he is an imperialist; he is a liberal. BUT – we all know the risk. Should it be taken?

I should value a reasoned reply from you. I am quite content to go on with Peel but the boat would travel better with Neville at the Treasury.

The Indian question will be the biggest thing for the new parliament.

---

[79] At two recent by-elections, previously Conservative seats had been lost to Labour: Midlothian and Peeblesshire, 29 January, with a large increase in the Liberal poll, and Battersea, 7 February. There was an agitation to end the betting tax, introduced by Churchill in 1926.
[80] These seats, both Conservative, had just fallen vacant: on 21 March the Liberals won Holland with Boston, and Labour won North Lanarkshire.

Yours ever/S.B.

How about Ronaldshay? Yet he might be better to follow you.[81]

In anticipation of a long-promised review of the 1919 Montagu-Chelmsford reforms, which had extended representative government in the India provinces, the
Cabinet had in 1928 prompted the appointment of a three-party statutory commission, chaired by the Liberal, Sir John Simon, to review the prospects for further
Indian constitutional reform. Baldwin feared that this might cause party difficulties in Britain, and was determined to minimise these by maintaining the existing
agreement to settle Indian issues on an all-party basis. The appointment of the
Simon Commission had aroused Indian nationalist agitation, and Irwin suspected
that its eventual report would not go as far as he and his officials thought desirable. His idea for circumventing both difficulties was to propose a 'round table
conference' of all significant Indian and British parties to discuss (and revise)
the forthcoming Simon report. He asked Dawson, while touring India, to put his
proposals before Baldwin.

8–9 APRIL 1929 DAWSON TO IRWIN

Halifax Indian papers Mss Eur C152/18/243

. . . I went down to Chequers yesterday. . . . I found him extraordinarily receptive on the subject of India – far more than I had dared to expect at
this crisis in his domestic fortunes. So I was altogether indiscreet, told him
of all your general ideas, and only pledged him to lock them in his bosom
till they reached him through some more appropriate channel. He was extremely sympathetic, and seemed to think that he would have no difficulty
about coming to an agreement with MacDonald, with whom he has always
maintained friendly personal relations. I doubt whether there will be any
difficulty with the other Opposition leader, though S.B.'s feelings about him
are far less amiable! . . .

April 9th . . . Like everyone else he [the P.M.] has <u>immense</u> confidence in
you, and I think you can easily persuade him of anything you think right.
But whether he will be in power when you arrive seems to be a matter of

---

[81] Irwin preferred Ronaldshay, Governor of Bengal 1917–22, who succeeded as 2nd Marquess of
Zetland later in 1929. Zetland was denied the Viceroyalty in 1930–1 when the recommendation
lay with MacDonald, and again in 1935 when Baldwin had both the viceroyalty and the Indian
secretaryship to offer to his two leading Indian experts. Linlithgow, given first choice, took the
Viceroyalty, leaving Zetland with the India Office.

some doubt. He himself seemed fairly optimistic, thought that he would retain more <u>industrial</u> seats than were generally conceded to him, and was only nervous of sporadic Liberal successes in the <u>rural</u> constituencies where the farmers are thoroughly disgruntled and Lloyd George is concentrating his energies . . .

However, Baldwin is already very properly composing his reconstructed Government in his head. There is a certain amount of clamour for reconstruction <u>before</u> the Election and he asked me for my opinion on this point. I told him that, as he knew, I thought he ought to have done it long ago, but that it now seemed to me far too late to begin. He would merely antagonise the colleagues whom he turned out and run the risk of some new men proving failures at the eleventh hour. Moreover, it is quite uncertain how many of them will retain their seats . . .

Incidentally Baldwin asked me whether, in the event of his Government being returned, I thought that Peel should go on at the India Office; and I told him that I was quite clear that the new Secretary of State should be in the House of Commons.

He suggested <u>Winston</u> and I reserved judgement! He <u>might</u> be very good; but his love of a stunt, and his inevitable intoxication with the idea of using force! Anyhow, it is an interesting idea . . .

The general election was not announced until 24 April, but electioneering – including broadcasts, on which Baldwin had since 1924 made a habit of consulting John Reith, the BBC managing director – began earlier. The Conservative election campaign became associated with the slogan 'Safety First', which some critics later identified with Baldwin, presenting it as emblematic of his whole politics and even of interwar government in general. Its origin was a Conservative Central Office poster campaign to exploit 'Baldwin's intense popularity and the belief in his honesty', consisting of a photograph of him and the words 'The Man You Can Trust'. But Bensons, the Central Office's advertising agents, instead suggested the phrase 'Safety First' as more succinct and chiming with the first major road safety campaign. Neither foresaw that it would be attributed to the party as their election slogan. Baldwin only became aware of it when the poster appeared on the hoardings.[82]

---

[82] Gower (now the party's publicity officer) in Jones' unpublished diary, 20 June 1929; Gower notes, June 1953, Jones papers AA1/38.

13 APRIL 1929: TO REITH

Reith papers; *The Reith Diaries*, ed. Charles Stuart (1975), p. 102

10, Downing Street

My dear Reith,

I should be very glad of some information before I broadcast on the 22nd, though I am doubtful if you can give it to me.

I want to classify my potential listeners, e.g. what proportion may be working class?

Does wireless go to the workman, or is the workman listener an exception, or would he be likely to listen at a club or a pub?

Yours sincerely/ Stanley Baldwin

7 MAY 1929 J.R. MACDONALD DIARY

MacDonald papers 30/69/1753

Discussed meeting of new Parlt. &*c.* with P.M. Determined in his lack of confidence in LlG. Expects to come back with a majority. Said Winston would be a better leader of opposition than he. Not his piece. As PM he could do things (whatever my view of that might be) but he could not fuss windily and wordily (not his words). I said that between Winston & LlG we should have a renewal of the old noisy political sham fights. He said he would find it difficult to live as leader of the Opposition as he was poor & had lost so much & would consider whether he should not have to go into business & try & pull things round ...

Churchill telegraphed to say that after much negotiation, Rothermere had offered him space for a pre-poll article in the *Daily Mail*, and one for Baldwin the following day. Churchill 'earnestly' appealed to Baldwin to accept, arguing that these articles would be of 'very great' advantage to Conservative candidates around London. Baldwin replied: 'All power to your pen in your article. I will not write in any circumstances for that particular press. Believe me it would be the greatest mistake possible.'[83]

Balfour had replaced Curzon as Lord President of the Council in April 1925, and Baldwin had established a jocular friendship with the elder statesman. Among

---

[83] Telegram, 18 May 1929, Churchill papers CHAR 7/106/A/68.

notes which Baldwin passed to him during meetings were: 'I read with profound admiration your eloquent appeal to your peers to abstain, on the loftiest grounds, from making asses of themselves'; and 'I read your reply to Parmoor; it is a perpetual delight to me to see what beautiful tapestry you weave with such a meagre supply of thread.' A letter of May 1927 reads: 'As Prime Minister (who is grateful to you for serving in his Cabinet) I desire that you go to Epsom to-morrow to attend the Derby, and that you report to the Cabinet at its next subsequent meeting your impressions.'[84]

25 MAY 1929: TO BALFOUR

Balfour British Library papers 49694/12–13

Chequers

My dear Balfour,

During the last fortnight my thoughts often turned to you in your retirement at Fisher's Hill and I felt I must write to you before this tyranny is overpast.

I know it is not your intention or desire to continue in office if we should be returned again but I hope that you would not be averse from continuing your membership of the Committee of Imperial Defence which is your own child and would indeed feel an orphan without you.

But now that this government has only a few days to live, I want to thank you from a grateful heart for all that you have done both for it and for me.

I have always been conscious of the honour you did me in accepting office under my leadership. For a generation in a comparatively humble position I had been an admirer and loyal follower of you as a leader, and it was with no light heart that I found myself unable to see eye to eye with you in 1922.

No one could have foreseen the course events have taken and I was deeply touched by the magnanimity and desire for further service that led you to accept my offer in 1925. It has always been a pleasure to work with you and I know that these four years of close association with you in counsel have taught me much.

---

[84] 25 Nov. 1926, 5, 31 May 1927, Balfour Whittingehame papers GD 433/2/19/17, 20, 14.

Few things are more awkward than an Englishman trying to uncover his feelings but I hope you will recognise under these bare words something of the gratitude I feel to you and of the affection in which I hold you.

I am/ Always most sincerely yours/ Stanley Baldwin

At the election on 30 May Conservatives obtained the largest popular vote but fell to 260 MPs, less than Labour's 287. The Liberals, with 59 MPs, again held the parliamentary balance of power. At Chequers over the weekend of 31 May–3 June, in similar circumstances to those following the 1923 election, Baldwin considered how to proceed. Some colleagues advised him, as on the earlier occasion, to await the meeting of Parliament.[85]

31 MAY 1929 STAMFORDHAM MEMORANDUM

RA PS/GV/K.2223/24

I went to London to see the Prime Minister, who, naturally, is much disappointed at the result of the General Election, which is contrary to the forecasts of all their best experts: and he had been especially pleased with the enthusiastic reception given to him only two days before the Election in Lancashire, more enthusiastic than before the last Election. Mr Baldwin regrets the loss of some of his best young members of the House of Commons: but it is the result of the action of the Liberal Party, who have put up representatives to contest almost every constituency, with no chance of winning but taking away votes which would have been given to the Conservatives: and all this done with money subscribed to the Liberal Party with the specific object of keeping the Socialists out of power.

As to the Prime Minister's action, if the Labour Party have an over-all majority he would, he thought, at once tender his resignation. Mr Baldwin asked me what I thought; I replied that I was not sure but I fancied there were precedents for Governments beaten at the polls waiting to meet Parliament, but on the whole I should consider that constitutionally he would be right at once to resign. If there was no over-all majority, he would meet Parliament and if the two parties chose to pass a vote of Want of Confidence they could do so and then of course the Government would resign . . .

---

[85] See Jones *WD*, ii, pp. 185–7, 190–3.

2 JUNE 1929 STAMFORDHAM MEMORANDUM

RA PS/GV/K.2223/30

This afternoon I went to Chequers where I saw the Prime Minister.

He began by saying that never in his life had he been placed in such a difficult position. The following is a resume of what he gave me as his present views as to his course of action:-

In all his addresses during the past few weeks he has appealed to the Democracy to trust him as they did in 1924 and these were his final words in his broadcasted message on the eve of the General Election. The votes of the people, enormously increased by he himself having given the Women's Franchise, shows that the country has refused again to place its confidence in him and that the new electorate did not want him. He has been beaten and in the true English spirit he accepts his defeat and, if he resigns, the Democracy in an equally British spirit will take off their hats to him as a good sportsman, who has had his run, been beaten and takes his beating like a man. And, what is important, this will count in his favour whenever the next General Election takes place, when the electorate will say that he 'played the game' when they rejected him in May 1929.

If on the contrary the Prime Minister holds on and says he will meet Parliament, the voice of the Democracy will say: 'Here is this man clinging to office, he won't take his defeat, he is trying to prevent the Labour party from enjoying their victory'. There will also be an idea that he is trying to make terms with the Liberal Party to keep him in office and, moreover, if he should hold on and meet Parliament, the Government would be bound to be defeated very shortly.

The Prime Minister realises that there are strong arguments in favour of his meeting Parliament and these opinions are held especially by those of his colleagues who may fairly be called 'Professional Parliamentarians'. He mentioned in confidence that Winston Churchill, who two days ago was in favour of meeting Parliament, had telephoned this morning to say that he had changed his mind to some extent, but the Prime Minister considered it inadvisable to hold any conversation on the telephone, but he will see Churchill tomorrow in London at noon and probably afterwards meet most of his colleagues. He openly says that his mind is not made up. The above gives a fair exposition of his present view: his colleagues who disagree with him may induce him not to resign: but on the other hand he may refuse to adopt their views.

I impressed upon the Prime Minister that there was nothing in the condition of the King's health which should be regarded as a reason for any alteration in what otherwise would be the normal course of action to be followed in dealing with this somewhat exceptionally difficult political situation . . .

Baldwin resigned on 4 June.

*

The second opposition period

JUNE 1929 – AUGUST 1931

Oliver Baldwin, now elected as Labour MP for Dudley, sent his father a moving letter commiserating on the Conservative defeat: 'victory or defeat are both flatterers & as such are of no serious consequence./ You may be judged by History [for] your political actions, but you will be judged by God for the Spirit that is in your heart.'[1]

Baldwin's financial worries continued. As he explained eighteen months later: 'For years, my expenditure has largely exceeded my income and I fear must do till I revert to private life. I owe the Bank a large sum which increases year by year. I have during the last ten years parted with a good deal of capital.'[2] Dividends from his industrial shares had largely ceased, and when in 1928 Baldwins Ltd shares were written-down in value he lost some £140,000 of his capital. For some time he had been worried that if he lost his ministerial salary and the Downing Street accommodation he might not be able to afford a London house as well as Astley Hall. After the election the Baldwins had difficulty finding a suitable house, until the Duke of Westminster provided 10, Upper Brook Street in Mayfair at a 'peppercorn rent'.[3]

8 JUNE 1929: TO OLIVER BALDWIN

CUL MS Add. 8795/6

Chequers

Dearest Son,

Your letter gave me real pleasure.

---

[1] 3 June 1929, full text in M&B, p. 528, and see Walker, *Oliver Baldwin*, pp. 143–4.
[2] To Revd W. H. Cory (rector of All Saints Church, Wilden), 21 Feb. 1932, Wilden Church papers, WCRO 9410/5/(ii)5.
[3] Jones *WD*, II, pp. 138, 192; Jones' unpublished diary, 21 Jan. 1937; Williamson, *Baldwin*, pp. 140–1; M&B, p. 529. £140,000 is over £5 million in modern prices.

I shall not be sorry for a rest: I am tired, for I have had twelve and a half consecutive years in office, except for the nine months in '24 when I was leading a not very happy party in opposition.

I just want a period of reflection which you can't get in office. Physically I am fit as ever: it is the mind that is tired.

I shall take a long holiday this autumn, and I have some pleasant work to occupy the time, a rectorial address for Glasgow and an inaugural for St. Andrews.

I have had the choice to make of having help from friends to carry on for a time or going out of public life. I can't leave my party in the hour of defeat so I am going on on those terms. But I am fortunately so constituted that party triumphs or disasters do not unduly affect me, and my soul is quietly content.

Again, I was glad in my heart to get your letter.

Your loving/ F

Following the election defeat, dissatisfaction within the party and the shadow cabinet over policy, expressed chiefly in revived protectionist agitation, developed into persistent criticism of Baldwin's leadership over the next two years. Beaverbrook's newspapers contributed to the discontent with a campaign for 'Empire free trade'. Differences also developed over Indian policy. During the Baldwins' motor tour while returning from Aix-les-Bains, MacDonald sent a message asking for Conservative support for the Labour government's endorsement of the Viceroy's plans not just for a round table conference but now also a statement, the 'Irwin declaration', that the ultimate objective of British policy in India was to grant it 'Dominion status'. Baldwin replied that as he was deep in France he was 'unable to communicate with any of my colleagues'; but that as he had earlier discussed the new proposal with Irwin (then on leave in Britain), 'in the circumstances I am prepared to concur in what is proposed and you may rely on my doing all that is in my power to secure the unanimous support of my party'.[4] Baldwin's agreement surprised his shadow cabinet colleagues, and was criticised by some, including Churchill – the more so when it emerged that Simon and the Indian statutory commission disapproved of the declaration. Lloyd George joined in the criticism of the proposed declaration, evoking a jocular Baldwin comment when declining an invitation to join a weekend shooting party: 'I haven't had a gun in my hand for years and I should be reluctant to start shooting again at my age in your company./ I would rather go rabbit shooting on Hindhead with L.G.

---

[4] To MacDonald, 21 Sept. 1929, J. R. MacDonald papers 30/69/344.

and then if there were an accident — !'[5] The Rothermere press also seized on the opportunity to attack Baldwin's leadership, and he was placed under considerable pressure. He was able to defend himself by stating that he had not been informed of the Simon Commission's disapproval, by showing that the Rothermere papers had misrepresented his actions, and by a masterly House of Commons speech on 7 November upholding a tradition of liberal reform in India. Balfour wrote to praise the speech as giving him 'for all time an unchallenged position among the orators of the English-speaking race'.

[9–10 NOVEMBER 1929] LYTTON TO IRWIN, 20 NOVEMBER

Halifax Indian papers Mss Eur *c.* 152/18/309

Knebworth

... Baldwin came here for the weekend and he said he had been very depressed since the debate as it made him feel the hopelessness of trying to liberalise the Tory Party. While he had been speaking there had been no word of approval from his own colleagues and as soon as Lloyd George got up Winston and Worthington-Evans on each side of him leant forward and punctuated every sentence with emphatic 'hear hears'! If the matter had gone to a division half his colleagues would have voted against him. This would have meant a Party meeting and Baldwin's resignation ...

11 NOVEMBER 1929: TO BALFOUR

Balfour Whittingehame papers GD 433/2/19/7

House of Commons

My dear Balfour,

I found your letter awaiting me last night on my return from Knebworth ...

You can never know how welcome it was in the moment of its arrival, for its all too warm terms of appreciation touched my heart at a moment when I was feeling in despair about my party and in doubt as to whether my leadership 'served any useful purpose'.

But every leader has his black moments and they pass.

[5] To Ashley (Minister of Transport 1924–9), 31 Oct. 1929, Ashley papers BR 74/21. Lloyd George had a house at Churt, near Hindhead.

Your sympathy, your generosity, your approval of my attitude, and your appreciation have sent me on my way rejoicing and I thank you from my heart.

Yours gratefully and most sincerely/ Stanley Baldwin

Discontent among Conservatives was so severe that Neville Chamberlain, other shadow cabinet colleagues and Davidson as party chairman advised Baldwin to conciliate Beaverbrook, by listening to his proposals before speaking at the annual party conference at the Albert Hall. Baldwin acquiesced, very much against his personal instincts. This gives a special quality to a series of letters he wrote to Beaverbrook over the next few months, even those just arranging meetings; the variations in his style of address are notable.

11 NOVEMBER 1929: TO BEAVERBROOK

photocopy, Beaverbrook papers C/19

House of Commons

<u>Private</u>
Dear Beaverbrook,

I should be very glad if you could come and have a private talk with me to-morrow morning at as early an hour as is convenient to yourself.

Ten o'clock would suit me well and I suggest my library at 10 Upper Brook St.

I will ask Neville Chamberlain to join us (not as a witness!) because he is a colleague whom I trust implicitly, whose judgement I value, and who knows my mind.

It seems not inappropriate that this letter should be written on Armistice Day.

Yours sincerely/ Stanley Baldwin

Afterwards Baldwin commented 'I have seen Beaverbrook and heard him for an hour and a half on his scheme! Two things he is a devout believer in: the Empire and Hell, which latter clings to him as the last (but a very important) shred of his calvinistic upbringing.'[6] But such attentions encouraged Beaverbrook still more. He now formed an 'Empire Crusade' organisation, and on 1 January

---

[6] To Derby, 23 Nov. 1929, Derby papers 920 DER(17) 33. A fuller report is in *NC Letters*, III, pp. 161–2.

Rothermere moved towards him by declaring for tariffs on manufactures and for agricultural subsidies. Baldwin's comment was: 'It is comical, Ld.R. coming down to our '23 position, but it appears to my simple mind that we may yet drive the unbridled stallions of Fleet St. in a pair.' He asked another correspondent: 'What is your reading of the Beaverbrook-Rothermere game? and under which thimble is the pea, or in other words Ll.G.?'[7] But Neville Chamberlain, Amery and Davidson wanted Baldwin to try and keep Beaverbrook and Rothermere apart, by taking the initiative in proposing an extension of import duties. Salisbury, Conservative leader in the House of Lords, shared Baldwin's sensitivity towards free-trade opinion in marginal constituencies and his dislike of negotiating policy with any 'press lord'.[8] Nevertheless Baldwin again met Beaverbrook before making his policy announcement at a party meeting at the Coliseum on 5 February 1930.

28 JANUARY 1930 SALISBURY, 'NOTE OF A CONVERSATION WITH BALDWIN'

Hatfield House archives 4M/133/67

Neville Chamberlain would like in any declaration of policy that we should reserve to ourselves in return for great Empire concessions the power to tax food. Amery would like to propose to tax food right away as part of our fiscal policy. S.B. is however concerned that any suggestion that we will or that we might tax food would be fatal.

Nevertheless the press agitation has made a definite fiscal policy necessary. He is inclined to an immediate development of safeguarding – meaning thereby safeguarding steel and perhaps wool. Even free-traders admit that safeguarding is a fillip, and even from their point of view, if we are to go in for rationalising, industries which are being rationalised will require securing whilst the process is being put through; so a fillip is just what is required. But agriculture will stipulate for some quid pro quo, and indeed whilst rationalisation is being consummated under safeguarding, S.B. did not deny (though he did not admit) that prices would be raised, even if afterwards they would respond to the economies of rationalisation. In deference to this feeling of agriculture – real or imaginary – he would out of the safeguarding revenue subsidise it in some way or other, probably by guaranteeing the price of wheat.

---

[7] To Davidson, 3 Jan. 1930, Lady Davidson papers; to John Buchan, 11 Jan. 1930, Buchan papers Acc 7214 mss mf 306.
[8] *Amery Diaries*, II, pp. 59–60 (30 Jan. 1930) has an account of the shadow cabinet discussion.

But he does not look to safeguarding merely as a national policy. The prospect of its development on Imperial lines should be held out. He hopes that industries themselves would in the future negotiate with their opposite numbers in the Dominions, preferably through a non-political Imperial Council of (say) industrialists and Civil Servants, who if satisfied there was agreement and opportunity would allocate particular branches of an industry or a proportion of them to several parts of the Empire, and for this purpose the several Governments ought to be prepared to protect the industry by safeguarding.

I pointed out that a countervailing benefit to agriculture was not the only necessary consequence of safeguarding steel or wool. All industries would be affected by a rise in the price of these commodities and all would demand protection. I pointed out further that the eventual development of Imperial safeguarding would not satisfy the immediate aspiration of the Imperial feeling in the Party. I then called his attention to the weight of direct taxation and to the effect of it upon industry which will be intensified almost to breaking point by the additions foreshadowed by the Govt. There is no alternative to direct taxation except indirect taxation which is very difficult to impose. It could however perhaps be effected under cover of the Imperial feeling just mentioned, in the shape of a uniform revenue tariff on all commodities except food (? & raw material)[9] with preference. This would at once provide revenue and could be an immediate step forward towards the fiscal consolidation of the Empire. S.B. was much struck with this proposal. He asked how it would be regarded by Conservative Free Traders. I could only say that in so far as it was for revenue it violated no free trade doctrine and in so far as it was uniform it eliminated at any rate many free trade objections to a tariff. In these respects it was much safer than a development of safeguarding. He said the one did not exclude the other.

29 JANUARY 1930: TO BEAVERBROOK

copy, Beaverbrook papers C/19

House of Commons

My dear Beaverbrook,

You were good enough to come and see me before I spoke at the Albert Hall.

---

[9] The query is in the original text.

If you are agreeable I should be glad to see you when I am in a position to tell you my line for next Wednesday's meeting. It is only fair to you, after our conversations, that you should have an early acquaintance with my views . . .

Yours sincerely/ Stanley Baldwin

5 FEBRUARY 1930: TO BEAVERBROOK

copy, Beaverbrook papers C/19

Travellers' Club

Dear Beaverbrook,

After a good deal of deliberation, I decided not to make any allusion to you this morning in my speech.

I am quite sure it will make it easier for both of us if you decide to support my policy. And no harm is done, if you don't!

Yours sincerely/ Stanley Baldwin

Baldwin had evidently not been as conciliatory as his closest advisors wished. On 18 February Beaverbrook announced that the 'Empire Crusade' had entered into alliance with Rothermere to form a new party. Baldwin regarded the resumed conflict against the press lords with relish: 'I am fighting with beasts at Ephesus and I hope to see their teeth drawn and their claws broken before the battle is over!'[10]

19 FEBRUARY 1930: BEAVERBROOK TO GWYNNE

copies in Beaverbrook papers C/149, and SB papers 57/18–19

. . . The position is as follows:-

I went to see Stanley Baldwin. You know I like him. Further I come under the influence of his charm every time I talk to him.

Following along our conversations I asked him, respectfully and with discretion, three questions.

First. I said would he object if we put up Empire Free Trade Conservative candidates in constituencies. He replied that of course would be disastrous. I expected no other reply.

Second. Would he object if we tried to get Empire Free Trade candidates before the Selection Committees. Would the Conservative Central Office

---

[10] To Sir John Simon, 19 Feb. 1930, Simon papers 62/228.

accept such a situation. Would the candidates receive the Conservative leaders approval. He showed plainly that he would not countenance such a course.

Third. Would we be entitled to push over the brink into a declaration for Empire Free Trade members of the House of Commons sitting on the Front Bench, and others. He made it quite clear that he could not tolerate an Empire Free Trade declaration from his colleagues in the last Government.

I then said that as the movement depended upon a fighting policy on account of all the opposition from every quarter, I believed the only course would be to form the United Empire Party.

He indicated that he considered it the least damaging course from the Conservative Party's standpoint[11] . . .

25 FEBRUARY 1930: TO MACKENZIE KING

Mackenzie King papers 206/145544–5

10, Upper Brook Street, W.1

My dear Prime Minister,

. . . I find little relaxation in being out of office.

You may have seen Beaverbrook & Cos' campaign reported in your Press.

It is very dishonest and won't help matters, either at home or in the empire. But I am ready to 'take the bump' from the Press as I was with the General Strike, and they have equally to be beaten for the sake of democracy.

I wish we were near enough to have a talk occasionally. My visit to Canada is now a delightful memory: I can't tell you what good it did me in every way.

I hope very much we shan't have an election this year but the government is not happy.

Disillusionment has begun and will spread apace.

I dined last night with the Naval delegates at the Foreign Office. The conference is in the gluepot, and it is difficult to see how they will get out of it. And until the U.S.A. can get away from this in-and-out game in foreign policy it will be hard to settle anything.

All best wishes to you.

Very sincerely yours/ Stanley Baldwin

---

[11] Baldwin's version was that only a 'league' (a pressure group) had been mentioned, not a 'party': *Amery Diaries*, II, p. 63.

28 FEBRUARY 1930 2ND VISCOUNT ELIBANK
MEMORANDUM[12]

Elibank papers GD32/25/74; copy in Beaverbrook papers C/19

I went to see Mr Stanley Baldwin at his house at 10, Upper Brook Street, at his invitation, and spent three-quarters of an hour with him discussing the political position.

1. I informed him that Max Beaverbrook would be prepared to come to an agreement on the lines of Sir Robert Horne's speech at the Constitutional Club, viz. on the policy of a free hand to impose import duties on food-stuffs after negotiation, where commensurate consideration was given by the Dominions and Colonies.[13] I said that by his action yesterday in stating that he would impose counter-vailing duties on dumped oats he had already infringed the principles of no taxes on food-stuffs, and I suggested to him that I thought he could make quite a good case for himself on the policy of the free hand, because after all, he had always stated that he was in favour of the general policy and he could say now that he had discovered, since the Coliseum speech, that there was much more evidence in the Unionist Party of a desire for a wider programme and also in the country, as evidenced by the many recruits flocking to the United Empire Party than he had thought when he made the Coliseum speech.

2. I also suggested to him that Beaverbrook would not object to changing the name of the Crusade from 'Empire Free Trade' to 'Imperial Economic Unity'.

3. I suggested that Lord Beaverbrook should be included in his Councils until after the General Election so as to keep up the end of the United Empire Party.

4. I asked him whether he would agree to make, in consultation with Lord Beaverbrook, as leader of the United Empire Party, after the General Election, the appointments to the office of Chancellor of the Exchequer, Secretary of State for the Dominions and Colonies and the President of the Board of Trade. This he said he could not possibly accede to, as it would

[12] Unionist MP 1918–22, now a businessman and member of the Empire Crusade committee. Beaverbrook later denied that he had been authorised to negotiate offers of ministerial posts.

[13] Horne, while retaining his directorships, had become politically active again as a leading figure among protectionists, and was close to Beaverbrook. For the next twelve months he was regarded as a potential successor to Baldwin.

be relinquishing the prerogative of the Prime Minister to appoint his own colleagues. I informed him that I should like to find a formula in some way, because if the United Empire Party was sure that these offices would be filled by men who understood and were inspired by the policy of the Party which they represent, the Party would not feel that they had been sold. He agreed with this, but said that the Party would have to trust him in that matter.

I emphasised the matter by pointing out what might happen if Mr Winston Churchill were reappointed to the office of Chancellor of the Exchequer; he having Free Trade views could not possibly carry out the policy to be enunciated.

At the end of the discussion Mr Baldwin stated that he would think over what I had said, during the weekend, and that he would take the earliest opportunity to make a pronouncement in the form of a speech. I urged him to do this as soon as possible, as I pointed out that Lord Rothermere was getting out of hand with his Press, and that from the point of view of unity, the sooner such statement, whatever it was, was made the better so as to enable the two Parties, if that statement were a conciliatory one, to get together. He stated that he would take the earliest opportunity. I expressed the hope that this might be at Tuesday's meeting of the Council of the Unionist and Conservative Association.

I asked Mr Baldwin if, after he had made his speech, he would send for me, or whether I could come again to see him, and he said that he preferred to leave it thus: that he was always glad to see any of his friends who wished to come to see him.

Mr Baldwin throughout the interview took up the attitude that he would in any event only be prepared to come to an agreement with Lord Beaverbrook, and that he would have nothing to do with Lord Rothermere whom he thoroughly distrusted. I informed him that I had arranged with Lord Beaverbrook that any arrangement would be only between him and Lord Beaverbrook, and Lord Beaverbrook would have to make himself responsible for Lord Rothermere.

Mr Baldwin indicated that he did not mind if Lord Rothermere was left out of any arrangement altogether, but I think he overlooked that there might be some difficulty in this owing to the fact that Lord Rothermere had been collecting recruits for the United Empire Party as well as Lord Beaverbrook. I however emphasised several times that the question of Lord Rothermere was one for Lord Beaverbrook to deal with.

Baldwin had hoped that the formation of the United Empire party would produce a Conservative revulsion against Beaverbrook and Rothermere. He wanted 'to arrange a suitable by-election which should expose the real weakness of the "Press Lords"', but Davidson advised that discontent in Conservative constituency associations was so severe that this 'would be disastrous to the Party, and might break it up altogether'.[14] Accordingly, Baldwin accepted a conciliatory gesture from Beaverbrook and met him again on 3 March. After some negotiation he accepted Beaverbrook's proposal that the issue of food taxes should be referred to a public referendum. For Baldwin this was attractive because it postponed the electorally most delicate aspect of protection until after the next election: 'It is very simple and very clear: a free hand in safeguarding; no food taxes at the General Election./ After we get in, call an Imperial Conference and if we find we can obtain substantial advantages in Dominion markets for our manufactures and a British tax on foreign food stuffs is part of the bargain, then the deal is to be put before the country and they will be asked to say yes or no by means of a referendum.'[15] Baldwin announced this policy at a National Union Central Council meeting at the Hotel Cecil on 3 March, and Beaverbrook gave public support the next day. Rothermere initially concurred in the agreement but shortly afterwards declared that the UEP would continue as an independent party, chiefly to oppose Indian reform. The Empire Crusade reverted to being a pressure group, and campaigned vigorously on behalf of the Conservative candidate at the West Fulham by-election, won from Labour on 6 May.

5 MARCH 1930: TO BEAVERBROOK

photocopy, Beaverbrook papers C/19

House of Commons

My dear Max,

You have indeed played the game, and believe me I am grateful.

R. has done more than I could have expected, for I know and can fully appreciate his difficulties.

I hope to see you before long.

Yours/ S.B.

---

[14] *Amery Diaries*, II, p. 64; Davidson to Baldwin, 26 Feb. 1930, Davidson papers 190.
[15] To Derby, 18 April 1930, Derby papers 920 DER(17) 33. *Amery Diaries*, II, pp. 65–6 has material on Baldwin during this episode.

7 MAY 1930: TO BEAVERBOOK

photocopy, Beaverbrook papers C/19

House of Commons

My dear Max,

You must be nearly dead and I congratulate you on your gallant conduct in the arena once more: it must have brought back happy days at Ashton once again.

I am off to the stubborn north in the evening.[16]

Yours sincerely/ Stanley Baldwin

During May Baldwin accepted nomination as the Chancellor of the University of Cambridge: 'The honour is far beyond any merit of mine: I accept it with wonder and gratitude.' In reply to congratulations, he wrote 'Yes, Cambridge makes up for much that is unpleasing in the foul welter of politics./ That is a world in which the crooks play no part.'[17]

18 MAY 1930: TO JOHN MASEFIELD

John Masefield papers

10, Upper Brook Street

Dear Mr Masefield,

We are only known to each other by name but we come from the same blessed part of England and I want you to do something for me.

I want you to accept the honorary LL.D at my hands on the occasion of my installation at Cambridge on June 5th. Come and bring a breath of our west country into the chill east.[18]

Yours sincerely/ Stanley Baldwin

[16] Beaverbrook had been Unionist MP for Ashton-under-Lyne before becoming a peer; Baldwin was particularly concerned with the difficulties of winning marginal seats in northern Britain.
[17] To Allen Ramsay (Vice-Chancellor 1929–31), 14 May 1930, SB add. papers; to Lady Salisbury, 30 May 1930, Hatfield House archives 4MCH/5/1.
[18] Masefield declined; he had received an Oxford Hon. D. Litt. in 1922, and became poet laureate during 1930. A similar offer is printed in H. V. Marrot, *The Life and Letters of John Galsworthy* (1935), p. 628: 'You have a chance of giving me pleasure.' Galsworthy accepted. Baldwin's nominees for honorary degrees included a member of each political party: Bridgeman, Lord Beauchamp (a Worcestershire peer, Liberal leader in the Lords), and Arthur Henderson, now Foreign Secretary. Among those to whom he also conferred degrees, presumably on the University's nomination, were Einstein and Max Planck.

Criticism of the party leadership's presentation of trade policy focused on Davidson as party chairman and, without any breach in their friendship, Baldwin under great pressure had to accept his resignation. As his replacement Baldwin reluctantly accepted Neville Chamberlain, who had engineered Davidson's resignation and was a possible challenger for his own position.[19] With many Conservative protectionists becoming critical of the referendum proposal, on 17 June Beaverbrook re-joined Rothermere in attacking the leadership's policy. Another Conservative party meeting was called, with a carefully calculated composition. Baldwin had heard of a letter from Rothermere, stating that he would only support the Conservative party if he received guarantees on policy and on the membership of the next Conservative Cabinet.

[21 JUNE 1930]: PATRICK HANNON[20] NOTE

Hannon papers 17/1

Secret

   SB sent for me on Saturday morning June 21st and after a general preliminary chat on various things including cricket and the weather, he asked me to give him the letter which Rothermere addressed to me following upon an appeal which I made in a speech at Birmingham for joint action between Lord Rothermere and Baldwin. As Rothermere stated in the letter that I could make any use I pleased of it and that there was no conditions imposed on me whatever, I at once complied with SB's request. I gathered generally from his conversation that he is determined to have the whole situation brought up to touch on Tuesday next at the Caxton Hall. He said he has lain low for three months and has borne much personal attack and abuse and the time had come to put matters in their correct perspective. I anticipate a lively time on Tuesday.

23 JUNE 1930: TO SALISBURY

typescript, with handwritten p.s., Hatfield House archives 4M/135/184

24, Old Queen Street, Westminster, S.W.1[21]

My dear Salisbury,

   I feel a line is due to you about tomorrow's meeting.

---

[19] Details in *NC Letters*, III, pp. 178–9, 184–92. As Baldwin met the Davidsons almost daily, his private words on Davidson's resignation are not recorded, but his formal letter of gratitude, 29 May 1930, is in SB papers 165/88–9.

[20] Birmingham businessman and MP, prominent in protectionist groups, and an associate of Beaverbrook.

[21] Party offices containing the leader's office 1930–1, and the Conservative Research Department.

My idea has been to call together those who are actively engaged in the constituencies as members or candidates, and not to summon a party meeting in the accepted sense of the term, which would, of course, include the Peers.

Yours ever/ S.B.

The question of leadership, according to ancient practice, is as I understand a matter for Lords & Commons alone./ S.B.

At the Caxton Hall on 24 June, Baldwin successfully defended his leadership by attacking the political claims of Beaverbrook and Rothermere. After reading out Rothermere's letter, he ended by saying: 'A more preposterous and insolent demand was never made on the leaders of any political party. I repudiate it with contempt and I will fight that attempt at domination to the end.'

Neville Chamberlain again tried to make peace with Beaverbrook, in the hope that this would help pull the party together. But Beaverbrook persisted with a threat to run Empire Crusade candidates against official Conservatives at by-elections, as did Rothermere with UEP candidates. There were new troubles over India, as it had now become clear that Irwin wanted the Round Table Conference, starting in October, to set aside the Simon report, which had rejected an early advance towards representative central government. Baldwin and Kipling had now diverged politically; but when Baldwin stayed with him in late July 'after hearing that it was all up with the Empire, that India was gone and we were all ruined financially, we got quite jolly'.[22]

25 JULY 1930 BISHOP HENSON JOURNAL

Henson papers

... Athenaeum. Baldwin came in, and talked to me in the friendliest fashion. I congratulated him on his appointment to the Chancellorship of Cambridge, and he confessed to great satisfaction on that appointment. We spoke of Lord Beaverbrook. He said that B. was the son of a Canadian Presbyterian minister, and still retains much of the obsolete theology in which he was reared. Thus, although far from being personally a good man, he had an absolute fanatical assurance of his success in the course of which he supposed himself to be Divinely led. This accords with what Geoffrey Dawson said at Grillions about Beaverbrook. He belongs to the queer class

---

[22] To Gwynne, 28 July 1930, Gwynne papers 15.

of dissolute Calvinists, who find no difficulty in combining a firm belief in Divine Favour with an insolent contempt for the Divine Laws. Baldwin spoke with much anxiety about the situation in India, where he thought there was some ground for fearing that Lord Irwin was too incredulous of human baseness, & too sanguine of success, to be wholly adequate to the situation.

9 AUGUST 1930: TO BRIDGEMAN

Bridgeman papers 4629/1/1930/72

10, Upper Brook Street

My dear Willie,

I am off in an hour for my holiday and I send you a line to welcome you home as I depart.

Since you left, Neville after untold efforts, has failed to hold the lunatics and I rejoice to feel that that disgusting one sided alliance is now dead. Forget 'em all, and enjoy your glorious country, and if I get a few days at home early October and if you are at Leigh, I will try and come and see you.

Blessings on your feisty paw.

Yours ever/ S.B.

8 SEPTEMBER 1930: TO WINDHAM BALDWIN

SB add. papers

Regina Hotel Bernascon, Aix-les-Bains

Dearest Little,

A month has gone since we landed on this pleasant soil and the weary crotchety old man who left Astley is now quite a pleasant person. I don't mean to say I am looking forward eagerly to entering the arena once more but I am ready for the fray with my inner eye on our eternal hills and a deep longing to see them once more.

Our tour was a great success.[23] Mother and I were so tired we kept dropping off to sleep in the car but the heavenly peace of getting away from

---

[23] The Baldwins had reversed their earlier practice, and took their French motor tour before reaching Aix-les-Bains, where the Davidsons joined them for part of their holiday. For Baldwin thanking the Davidsons, especially Joan for accompanying him on his walks, see 23 Sept. in *Davidson Memoirs*, p. 353.

everything and everybody just for ten days passed all belief. Reims is a sight. It is of course wonderful how a great new city has been rebuilt with only a gaping wound here and there, but the cathedral stands up stark and gaunt to remind you of what happened so few years ago. They have done a lot of work by way of repair but it will take a generation to complete and nothing can ever replace the glass which was one of the glories of the world.

We liked Troyes, a quaint old town with three very interesting churches in one of which Henry V was married.

Evian was a gilded sty, most comfortable but expensive . . .

Here much is as usual. I walk every morning and then to the Lake to bathe. The water is beautifully warm and I sip a citronade afterwards in a condition of ecstasy.

In the afternoon I keep quiet for it has been very hot and early bed is the rule.

I am sure I have lost pounds and I feel as fit as a fiddle.

I have been so interested in the family genealogies which that Shropshire society has been working on . . .

We hope to be back on the 28th and I go for a night or so to the Bridgemans at Minsterley . . .

Someday we must try our hands at a run abroad together: I always dream of an Indian summer when politics will be a thing of the past.

Bless you. Much love from/ your old/ Father

On his return, Baldwin stayed with the Bridgemans in Shropshire. After consultation with Neville Chamberlain, Bridgeman warned him that his leadership remained under threat.[24] A few days later, the financial member of Irwin's council, calling to discuss the Round Table Conference, found him preoccupied with the party problem. The immediate prospect of a party rebellion was checked when statements by Dominion Prime Ministers, meeting at the Imperial Conference in London, enabled Neville Chamberlain to persuade Baldwin to drop the referendum and accept a 'free hand' to introduce food taxes, depending on negotiation with Dominion governments. It was expected that Churchill, who remained a free trader, would feel he had to resign from the party leadership's inner 'business committee' on the issue.

---

[24] *Bridgeman Diaries*, pp. 239–40.

9 OCTOBER 1930 SIR GEORGE SCHUSTER TO IRWIN

Halifax Indian papers Mss Eur C152/19/143a (extracts)

. . . On Monday (6th) I started with Mr Baldwin at 10. He said he was going to write to you fully after he had seen me. I found him very fit after his holiday, but much more occupied with his own troubles and the conflicts within his party than with India. In fact he did most of the talking and it was mainly on that subject. He says he would be very glad to be out of it all himself, but is obviously not contemplating any course of affairs which includes his own withdrawal, or any arrangement of forces at the next election which will not find him still leader of the Conservative party. He said he had kept himself out of the Conservative delegation to the Round Table Conference partly because he had to keep free to defend himself against personal attacks coming from any quarter and partly to prevent L.G. putting himself on to the Liberal delegation – which he thought would be disastrous.[25] He contemplates an election early in the New Year – not before . . . He says the whole country is 'tobogganing' now to protection, but his own conversation indicates that the Conservative party have not yet any very clear scheme. As regards wheat, and foodstuffs generally, he talked in terms not of protection but of 'preferential quotas' and when I questioned him agreed that these implied some national agency for the control of imports . . . I said I hoped to get in touch with [the Conservative delegation] so as to thrash out some of the practical issues in advance, and particularly financial and commercial issues. He said he would welcome this, would help me in every way himself, and would at all times be ready to see me again if I had particular points to discuss. He could not have been more helpful . . . I gave Baldwin a general sketch of the position; and of course he is very interested in the possibility of 'doing a deal' with India on Imperial Preference lines, but recognises that they must be free agents for this purpose. As to the boycott and the treatment of our last Cotton Tariff Bill he said 'we are now merely reaping the fruits of Lancashire's policy for the last 50 years' – which of course is true.[26] . . .

[25] To Lloyd George, 2 Aug. 1930, Lloyd George papers G/1/15/1: 'My dear Lloyd George,/ I have definitely decided not to serve on the Indian Conference. I let you know at once because my decision will affect your representation as you told me you had not thought of serving yourself and would not do so unless I did./ Yours sincerely/ Stanley Baldwin.'
[26] Lancashire cotton exports to India had undercut rather than competed fairly with native Indian manufacture; and a backlash was now being felt in the form of Indian boycotts of Lancashire goods and nationalist pressures for tariffs.

Churchill papers CHAR 2/572/75; *WSC V/2*, 193

10, Upper Brook Street

My dear Winston,

I cannot go to bed to-night without sending you a line, to assure you that if you adhere to what you said this morning there will be no feeling on my part that you have in any way let me down, nothing but profound regret that there is a real parting of the ways and a friendship towards you which has grown up through six years of loyal and strenuous work together. Six years ago, we knew little of each other. We have had good times and bad times and have come through them side by side and the memory of them will abide.

To what your further reflections may lead you, I cannot tell.

But for to-night I still cherish the hope that you may yet see your way to stay with us. Bob Cecil is the only colleague I have lost in seven and a half years: I cannot have many more years before me, and it would be a joy to feel that I had kept the leaders of our party together until the end.

But whatever happens,

I am your sincere friend/ Stanley Baldwin

Halifax Indian papers Mss Eur C152/19/147

10, Upper Brook Street

My dear Edward

I am fixing up your protégés and start with Haig[27] on Tuesday. Schuster I saw within two days of his arrival. My team[28] is a good one: I sent it to the P.M. six weeks ago but he only announced it the other day. I kept off, partly to keep Ll.G. off and partly because the political situation is far too tricky to allow me to be immersed in a Conference when every crook in the country is out for my scalp.

Salisbury objected to Austen going on because of his Irish chapter: he thought he would give everything away.[29] It is a curious psychological error on his part: Austen's rigidity would have been the danger.

---

[27] H. G. Haig, of the Indian government home department.
[28] The Conservative delegation for the Round Table Conference.
[29] Austen Chamberlain had signed the Irish Treaty in 1921.

I am taking a risk with Oliver Stanley,[30] but it will try him out. I don't really know him yet, but he is thought highly of by his generation.

You will see our programme; I think it probable Winston will resign on it. Salisbury on the other hand doesn't like the quota and has come to support what he calls a <u>Tareef</u> on agriculture!

I cannot begin to describe to you the sort of time I have had; but yours is pretty bad too, and, if and when (as old Squiff used to say) we emerge from our respective soups, we will foregather at Garrowby and fight our battles once more.

Bless you/ Ever yours/ S.B.

Wickham Steed sent an early copy of his book, *The Real Stanley Baldwin*. Baldwin very unusually commented on a particular sentence about himself, because it bore on his current relations with Churchill and criticisms of his leadership. Referring to a policy issue during the 1924–9 government, Steed reported Baldwin as saying to a friend 'with a gesture of resignation: "I thought we should have taken another line; but then Winston came along with his hundred-horsepower brain, and what was I to do?"' After G. M. Young's biography used a garbled version of the sentence as evidence that Baldwin tended to be politically inert, it became a saying commonly identified with him and is even found in dictionaries of quotations. It certainly misrepresents both Baldwin's political style, and the extent to which Churchill could exert his will within Baldwin's Cabinet.

16 OCTOBER 1930: TO WICKHAM STEED

Steed papers, Add. Mss 74120/222

10, Upper Brook Street

Dear Mr Steed,

I am much obliged to you for sending me a copy of your book which I have but this moment received: but it has given me a shock to open by chance on a story which will not do me much good and in which there is not one single word of truth. It occurs at the top of page 19.

---

[30] Second son of the Earl of Derby, an MP since 1924.

I not only never said it, or anything like it, but never thought it, sober or drunk, or dreamed it even in a nightmare.

Yours sincerely/ Stanley Baldwin[31]

Churchill decided not to resign.[32] Both Beaverbrook's Empire Crusade and the UEP ran candidates against the Conservative candidate at the South Paddington by-election. As the Davidsons were on a visit to Argentina, Baldwin's letters to them have reports on these and further episodes.[33]

23 OCTOBER 1930: TO JOAN DAVIDSON

Lady Davidson papers; Davidson *Memoirs*, pp. 353–4; M&B, pp. 577–8

10, Upper Brook Street

Little Maid,

... As for myself, the troops of Midian are gathering for the fray.

Paddington election has become the wildest farce. R[othermere]. has thrown over Mrs Stewart Richardson and the U.E. party in the borough are wild with him and are all backing Mrs S-R. Lord R. advised the Paddington electors to vote for the Crusader! I have written Ld.B. in answer to a challenge from him and also to make explicit to my fools what was implicit in the manifesto, and I think the publication has cleared the air. Derby spoke in Lancs. yesterday in favour of a free hand and a tax on wheat if necessary for a bargain!

Gretton and his friends have formally asked for a meeting of members of the Commons 'to discuss the situation' and Bobby[34] is due in half-an-hour to talk it over.

Winston has not yet given tongue on our manifesto. He told Freddy Guest[35] that he was in doubt whether to 'lay an egg' or not. To which Freddy replied, 'when in doubt whether to lay an egg or not, don't lay it !'

---

[31] Steed replied the next day that since the story was unfounded he would 'suppress it if the book goes into a second edition' (there was none). The exchange is in Steed papers, Add. Mss 74120/221–3. *Cf.* G. M. Young, *Baldwin*, p. 106.

[32] Churchill's unsent letter of resignation and further exhanges are in *WSC V/2*, pp. 191–3, 194, 204.

[33] See *Davidson Memoirs*, pp. 350–6, which includes further letters. In some cases it mistakenly gives Davidson rather than his wife as the addressee.

[34] Eyres-Monsell, still chief whip.

[35] Churchill's cousin; former Liberal MP and Coalition Cabinet minister, became Conservative 1930.

The press lords like the devil knowing his time is short are raving. They are really behaving like lunatics. I have rubbed the seat of my breeches with cobbler's wax as a precaution.

... I miss you both, badly. But I like to think what a wonderful time you are having. You both needed it and you have both deserved it, and just enjoy it with all your might.

Your loving/ S.B.

25 OCTOBER 1930: TO BUCKMASTER

Heuston, *Lives of the Lord Chancellors*, p. 305

I have seldom had a letter that has given me more pleasure than yours. It was just like your chivalrous spirit to rush to my side at this moment! I shall always treasure it.

You and I will never be in the same political camp, but please God whenever white men have to stand together we shall be found shoulder to shoulder, wearing our gas-masks and armed with clubs and heavy boots.

Baldwin agreed to call a party meeting for 30 October, again at the Caxton Hall but this time including Conservative peers, as he now wished to put his leadership to a vote. This was won by 462 to 116 votes, which Baldwin considered 'far better than I had hoped'.[36]

1 NOVEMBER 1930: TO HOARE

Templewood papers XVIII: 3c (36)

10, Upper Brook Street

My dear Sam,

The crowded hour of the last few days left me no time to look at your book[37] or even to acknowledge it.

My word, but it is good and I am reading it with the liveliest interest. Immersed as I was in my spy committee and then in the unromantic Treasury, I knew little of what others were doing.

---

[36] To Arthur Mann (editor, *The Yorkshire Post*), 1 Nov. 1930, Mann papers, MS Eng. *c*. 3279/ 107.
[37] *The Fourth Seal* (1930), about Hoare's wartime intelligence work in Russia.

Few can have had a time more thrilling than you, and few Englishmen in years to come will be able to say they saw Russia in labour, pregnant with the monstrosity of the bottomless pit.

Thank you again and again./ Yours ever/ S.B.

2 NOVEMBER 1930: TO JOAN DAVIDSON

Lady Davidson papers; partly in Davidson *Memoirs*, p. 354; M&B, pp. 578–9

10, Upper Brook Street

Little Maid

... This has been a hectic week. How David would have loved it! Events followed each other like lightning.

I gave the enemy all they wanted: choose their resolution, speak first and last, and have a secret ballot. Winston was under no illusions. At a meeting we had to discuss the procedure, he was all for coloured and numbered cards, for, said he, 'They will stick at nothing and they are quite capable of slipping in a dozen votes apiece'.

They staggered me by their reception, standing and cheering for two minutes by the clock. I assumed the air of a headmaster and spoke, though I say it, very well. Gretton said to Hogg when I finished, 'That's the best speech he has ever made!' I retired at 11.20 with hauteur. I went to Old Queen St and got the result at two o'clock. The Beaver would not have spoken but Francis Curzon[38] challenged him to speak. He was booed and made a poor speech. He talked about the quota which was out of order, and said he didn't care twopence who was leader as long as his policy was adopted!

The Paddington election has been a foolish and a dirty business. The fate of Mrs Stewart Richardson shews what a freak candidate is worth when the yellow press give her up. She made one memorable speech: 'I have no words bad enough to describe the conduct of Admiral Taylor. He has pinched my party, he has pinched my colours, and he has pinched my seat.'[39]

Pretty near an indecent assault I call it.

---

[38] Conservative MP 1919–29, when succeeded as 5th Earl Howe; no relative of the former foreign secretary.
[39] On the day of the party meeting, Admiral E. A. Taylor, the Empire Crusader won the by-election, defeating the official Conservative. The UEP candidate came bottom of the poll.

By the way, I wonder if David remembers what The Pink 'Un[40] said to Edmund Talbot when Balfour's stock was at its' lowest? 'Edmund, if we could only get Arthur into the Divorce Court, our fellows would be all right'. Did you ever hear of A.J.B.'s visit to the Derby? Jack Sanders[41] told me about it last week . . . They went down in time for the first race which he watched carefully. After the second, he observed 'And are all the races like this?' On hearing the answer in the affirmative, he returned to London without having seen the Derby at all. What he expected to see will ever remain a mystery.

I have had some hundreds of letters since the party meeting; as Geoffrey [Fry] said it is just like the spate of letters after a general election . . .

Don't give politics a thought. Think of me kindly and sympathetically . . . I have often thought of you this last week for it has been the atmosphere David loves.

Your loving/ S.B.

6 NOVEMBER 1930: TO DAVIDSON

Lady Davidson papers; *Davidson Memoirs*, pp. 354–5; M&B, p. 579

10, Upper Brook Street
. . . In my last letter I forgot to tell you about Derby. I saw him two or three days before the meeting and had a long talk. 'Tell me', said I, 'as an old friend: do you think I ought to resign?'

'Well, old man', he observed, 'I hate to say it but I think you ought'. Then he repeated all the old stuff about apathy and the impossibility of my keeping a united party. He wasn't going to the meeting at all: he was never going to take any further part in politics.[42]

On Thursday he attended the meeting after which he told Salisbury and subsequently put it in a letter that the meeting had completely changed his view and that he would do all he could to support me and the party!

The Beaver is now trying to climb back! He is beat, fair and square. The general movement is all away from him at the moment and the MPs who are known to have been rebels are having a jolly time in their constituencies! . . .

---

[40] Nickname, derived from obsession with hunting and horse-racing, of an Edwardian aristocrat.
[41] Balfour's private secretary 1892–1911; Balfour had died in March.
[42] This conversation took place on 27 October; Derby's grounds for his verdict are in an unsent letter to Baldwin, 28 Oct. 1930, 920 DER (17) 33, printed in Churchill, *Lord Derby*, pp. 583–5.

The Liberal Party is cracking badly and Labour is running about with its' tail between its' legs. Ramsay is tired and rattled. An election may come any day but I still feel they will see the New Year in . . .

Under the pressures of economic depression, disagreements over India and divisions within all three parties, some public figures began to argue that a 'national crisis' required the creation of some cross-party or non-party 'national government'. These included Gwynne of the *Morning Post* and Greig, a stockbroker and friend of both Prince Albert (the future King George VI) and MacDonald ('R.M.'). From Baldwin's perspective there were obvious advantages in encouraging discussions which might weaken the resolve of a Labour Prime Minister.

11 NOVEMBER 1930 GWYNNE TO LOUIS GREIG

typescript copy, Gwynne papers 20

. . . I had a long talk with S.B. yesterday and told him about my letter to you and R.M.'s answer to you. One thing was quite clear and that is S.B.'s real sympathy for the P.M. and his understanding of the difficulties which confront him. There was no bitterness such as R.M. indicates but rather a desire to give a helping hand to a good man and true, fighting for his life against strong and unscrupulous enemies. As for co-operation with L.G. you can dismiss that thought. There are two men in English politics who will never work with him and they are S.B. and R.M.

I gathered from S.B. that the P.M. does not realise quite the strength and the malignity of the forces working against him. He admitted that the suggestion[43] I made to you was a good one – a 'grandiose plan' he called it – but doubted its practicability, not from any feeling of hostility to R.M. but because, as he said, 'it is a terrible thing to break away from the party one has created'.

Hearing him speak with such sympathetic understanding of R.M.'s position, it occurred to me that the only thing I could suggest was that he and the P.M. should meet soon. My sole idea in making the suggestion was to disabuse R.M. of the idea that S.B. & L.G. were waiting for an opportunity of knifing him . . .

---

[43] For the formation of a 'national' government, with MacDonald entering into alliance with Baldwin.

13 NOVEMBER 1930: TO DAVIDSON

Lady Davidson papers; partly in *Davidson Memoirs*, p. 355

10, Upper Brook Street

. . . I attended the Royal opening of the Indian Conference yesterday and dined at the government dinner. I quite enjoyed that: I was separated from the P.M. by Baroda, and on my right was a pleasant young prince from the wilds of Kathiawar. But it was all very funny. Opposite to me was that prim old methodist Arthur Henderson . . . and at the next table the pale face of the Marquis of Salisbury next to a Burman with an immoveable countenance the size of a ham and with an unintelligible name like Burr-Fa, or words to that effect. Our delegation is starting well, but Winston is in the depths of gloom. He wants the Conference to bust up quickly and the Tory party to go back to pre-war and govern with a strong hand. He has become once more the subaltern of Hussars of '96 . . .

N.C. saw the Beaver at Abe Bailey's the other night and described him as down and out. He is trying to crawl back now. I don't think he is at all well . . .

My ex-colleagues have had a private meeting at Salisbury's instigation and have conveyed to me through him their view that no one has any claim to office if we come in again.

Leo suggested at the meeting that they should all sign the following letter 'Dear S.B.

All your old colleagues conscious of each other's senility desire to tell you that not one of them has any objection to any of the others being bumped off'[44] . . .

27 NOVEMBER 1930: TO DAVIDSON AND JOAN DAVIDSON

Lady Davidson papers; *Davidson Memoirs*, pp. 355–6

10, Upper Brook Street

. . . I am having a busy week and haven't had a minute to write. I had to speak in the House on Monday: on Tuesday I spoke to the National Union: yesterday I dined with Gretton and spoke to the 1900 Club! and to-day I lead off on a Vote of Censure. Saturday I do <u>two</u> speeches on the talkie film at Elstree.

---

[44] One of the complaints of the critics had been that Baldwin remained too attached to the 'old gang' of ex-Cabinet ministers: see *Amery Diaries*, II, p. 87.

For the moment the party is fairly happy: the agents at the N[ational].U[nion]. were all on their toes and certainly the change from six weeks ago is miraculous.

The Beaver is trying to crawl back, and the foul press is lying back very quiet . . .

I don't think now that there is a chance of an election before Xmas: I never did.

The Goat has finally failed to get any real arrangements with Labour and rumour has it he is going to make another attempt on us. But I doubt it.

The government is decaying daily and I can't see how in any way they can hold on much longer . . .

3 DECEMBER 1930 MACDONALD DIARY

D. Marquand, *Ramsay MacDonald* (1977), p. 578

. . . On Monday Baldwin came to 10 to tell me what he thought of India &c and made it plain that they would never accept G.[45] He casually & gingerly mentioned myself but evidently regarded it as forbidden though he made it clear they would welcome it. I raised the possibility of a change of government without an election. He thought I meant putting him in office & was favourable but I corrected him & explained that I meant a national Govt. He said protection made that impossible & I agreed. I further said that if such a step were taken the parties would go into the melting pot & the present grouping would not be maintained.

Baldwin publicly repudiated the idea of a 'national' coalition government in speeches on 12 and 17 December 1930, as did MacDonald on the 12th.

15 DECEMBER 1930: TO JOAN DAVIDSON

Lady Davidson papers; *Davidson Memoirs*, p. 356

House of Commons

Little Maid

. . . I am just back from Glasgow where I had a great day beginning at nine a.m. with a Students' breakfast party and ending at ten p.m. with an overflow from Andrew's Hall!

---

[45] Lord Gorell, proposed as the successor to Irwin as Viceroy of India, but opposed by Conservative and Liberal leaders and by the King and Stamfordham.

It has been a busy time since I last wrote, and a good deal of worry over the Indian Conference but I won't bore you with all that.

My Lord Salisbury is laid up for a month: I fancy he had a heart attack: he is overtired and strained.[46] ...

Winston is very well and has gone quite mad about India and has engaged the Free Trade Hall at Manchester in which to expound his views.

Some say that Ll.G will keep the gov[nt.] in for two years but I don't believe it. I still think the early spring.

The miners are at work at the moment by utilizing the spread-over put in by the Lords: but as the Federation have refused their consent, the pits are only working in defiance of the existing law passed a few months ago by the Socialist government![47]

Everything is very mad.

I shall be so glad to have you both back again: it's worth going away to be missed isn't it? ...

Your loving/ S.B.

16 JANUARY 1931: TO BRIDGEMAN

Bridgeman papers 4629/1/1931/3

Astley Hall

My dear Willie,

I am just leaving this enchanted country for my prison yard. I have had a peaceful time, broken by visits to London, Haresfield Beacon[48] and Birmingham, and I have pondered much and without much pleasure. I see nothing but trouble and anxiety ahead. I should like a long talk with you

---

[46] To Lady Salisbury, 4 Dec. 1930, Hatfield House archives 4MCH/5/1: 'Beg him from me not to worry. To read no papers, To forget the House of Lords. To forget British Dyes. To forget India./ And above all to forget ME because I am closely associated with everything great and small which may cause him trouble./ It will be sufficient for me if you will bear me in kindly remembrance.'

[47] The Labour government's Coal Mines Act, 1930, had reversed the 1926 Wages Act by restoring the seven-hour day. But it had been passed only after a compromise with Conservative peers which allowed longer shift patterns (the 'spread-over'), subject to approval of the Miners' Federation.

[48] A ceremony for handing the land to the National Trust.

as soon as you come up. There may be an election any day and I must be ready with a government.[49]

I have had two good talks with Neville and I want to check them with you: I can't talk to anyone else.

It is courageous of Freeman[50] to go to India and his appointment has been a great relief to me. He cabled me that he was old but would do his best. That is true of me too and we enter on our last lap together.

I feel like a sugar beet being dragged out of the soil and I go to London with the earth still sticking to all my nether regions but it will wear off.

My love to you and the Dame/ Ever yours/ S.B.

Baldwin wrote to commiserate with Hoare, whose mother had just died, and Salisbury, who remained too ill to work. Hailsham became acting Conservative leader in the House of Lords.

16 JANUARY 1931: TO HOARE

Templewood papers VI/1 (43)

10, Upper Brook Street

My dear Sam,

You have the true sympathy of one who has trodden the same path.

However long one has expected the end, it is never the less a shock when it comes and the link on earth that has lasted all one's life is broken. What a flood of memories engulf one at such a moment!

You will be torn between the great work you are engaged in and the recollections of your earliest childhood. But you have been fortunate in keeping her so long with you. The very feeling that the old are at rest is comforting but there will be moments until your last day when you will suddenly feel you must tell something to her, something that would amuse or interest her. Life is never quite the same when the last parent is

---

[49] To Evelyn Gynn Brown, 16 Jan. 1931, CUL MS Add. 8770: 'I think we shall have an election soon and it is quite possible that I may have to form another government. I dread it for the situation is pretty hopeless but it will be my last effort and I shall try to make a job of it.'

[50] Lord Willingdon, the compromise nominee as Viceroy of India.

gone: one is left in the front of the battle. But you will feel her near you, always.

Ever yours/ Stanley Baldwin

19 JANUARY 1931: TO SALISBURY

Hatfield House archives 4M/139/45

<u>Private</u>   10, Upper Brook Street

My dear Salisbury,

Your letter causes me more sorrow than surprise. You were very run down and you must take all the time necessary to build yourself up.

I have seen Hailsham and there is nothing at present to worry about.

It only shews as I have always maintained that no constitution can stand public life to-day when you get near seventy, unless you are made like Ll.G. with no bowels, no principles, no heart and no friends.

Ever yours/ Stanley Baldwin

On glancing at the concluding paragraph, I feel this letter should be marked 'Private'.

Baldwin and the Conservative 'business committee' agreed to accept the Round Table Conference recommendation that a representative federal central government should be established in India. This became the occasion for Churchill's delayed breach with the party leadership.

28 JANUARY 1931: TO CHURCHILL

Churchill papers CHAR 2/572/78; *WSC V/2*, p. 251

10, Upper Brook Street

My dear Winston,

I am grateful to you for your kind letter of yesterday and much as I regret your decision not to attend the meetings of your old colleagues, I am convinced that your decision is correct in the circumstances.

But I agree with you, gladly and wholeheartedly, that there is nothing in a difference of opinion on a single policy, however important, to prevent our close and loyal co-operation in doing our utmost to turn out the present government.

And with the latter part of your letter I am in complete agreement.[51]

Our friendship is now too deeply rooted to be affected by differences of opinion whether temporary or permanent. We have fought together through testing times: we have learnt to appreciate each other's good qualities and to be kindly indulgent to qualities less good, if indeed they exist, though in many but diverse quarters we are endowed with a double dose of original sin.

With my warm regards/ I am as ever/ Yours sincerely/ Stanley Baldwin

There were now two policies – imperial protectionism and India – on which Baldwin suffered considerable criticism within the party and from Beaverbrook and Rothermere newspapers. In late February Topping, the party's chief agent, produced a memorandum reporting widespread Conservative rank-and-file disillusionment with Baldwin's leadership. Neville Chamberlain as party chairman consulted other business committee members, most of whom thought Baldwin would now have to resign, and sent the memorandum to Baldwin on Sunday morning, 1 March. Tom Jones' diary for 11 March (see below) gives Baldwin's account of these events, and his decision the following day to stay and fight against the two 'press lords', now sponsoring an explicitly anti-Baldwin candidate at the St George's, Westminster by-election.[52]

1 MARCH 1931 NEVILLE CHAMBERLAIN DIARY

... During lunch I received a telephone message asking if I could see S.B. within an hour ... I found S.B. and Mrs Baldwin together, and she remained in the room for a few minutes while S. said that their reactions to the paper, which was not altogether a surprise, were identical. They both felt that he should go, since it was clear that he no longer commanded the support of the party and that his continued presence would be harmful to it. I did

[51] Churchill's letter, 27 Jan. 1931, *WSC* V/2, pp. 250–1, offered his continued support in defeating the 'Socialist' government.
[52] Further accounts are in *Bridgeman Diaries*, pp. 243–5, and *NC Letters*, III, pp. 240–5. The Topping memo. is published in Macleod, *Neville Chamberlain*, pp. 139–41 (the 'recollections' in *Davidson Memoirs*, pp. 357–60, actually draw heavily from the Jones and Bridgeman accounts).

not seek in any way to combat this resolution and after Mrs B. had left we continued to converse on the lines that it was settled. S.B. said he would not ask his colleagues for their opinion but would inform them of his decision. He & his wife had been discussing their financial position & the changes that they would make. They wd. move into a smaller house etc. He would not write a line for any paper but might join a Board or two. Probably he would not stand again. He sincerely hoped I shd be his successor & would gladly help to that end if he could. He thought it would be disastrous for Winston to have the leadership but did not for a moment think he would get it.

3 MARCH 1931 NEVILLE CHAMBERLAIN DIARY

Yesterday morning I received a note from S.B. saying a rumour had reached him which had given him an idea and asking me to go & see him. I had already heard the rumour & knew what it must be viz. that he was going to stand himself for St. Georges. When I got to the house I found Mrs B. in a state of great excitement and three secretaries in the room. The story they had to tell was that up to 10 p.m. on Sunday night they had resolved to go when Willie Bridgeman came in & made this suggestion urging that resignation would be a base surrender & desertion in the face of the enemy. Mrs B. & the secretaries were enthusiastically in favour. S.B. asked my opinion. I was very cold & asked what wd happen if he lost to wh. S.B. said he wd then go. I suggested that in that event his successor would find himself in the position of having to treat with 2 victorious generals. I said however that I must think it over. I got Austen to come round after lunch & found he was dead against the proposition. Topping was also against but Gower (a past p[rivate].s[ecretary]. to S.B.) strongly against resignation & rather favouring the challenge. I saw S.B. again in the afternoon & put it to him that he had no right to submit the leadership of the party to a single constituency. Luckily during the afternoon G. Dawson came in & as S.B. told me afterwards expressed his strong agreement with me. Later on I heard that Camrose had intimated that if S.B. stood the Daily Telegraph would not support him. I believe this has finally decided the matter. Today I had to go to Leicester. When I came back I saw S.B. who told me that Duff Cooper would stand for St. Georges, but he said nothing about resignation.

3 MARCH 1931 WIGRAM[53] MEMORANDUM

RA PS/GV/K.2324/1

I saw Mr Baldwin this morning and asked him what he thought of the political situation. He said he thought it was distinctly rocky and, with a wink, added that his own situation was not too bright.

I asked him if he thought that the Government were likely to take a cropper within the near future, and he replied that he considered that the next few days would be critical.

Then I asked him if, supposing the Prime Minister resigned and the King sent for him (Mr Baldwin), would he be able to form a Government? He unhesitatingly said 'No, certainly not, as Lloyd George would have me out in a week on a vote of confidence on tariffs. If the King sent for me, I could only recommend a dissolution'.

The present situation is, therefore, very similar to that of October 1924, when Baldwin and Asquith said they could not form a Government if Ramsay MacDonald resigned . . .

The situation was further complicated by news that Irwin was in negotiation with Gandhi, seeking to draw the Indian Congress party into the constitutional discussions. Lord Lloyd had joined Churchill in mobilising criticism of the leadership's support for the proposed reforms, acting through the party's backbench India committee.

4 MARCH 1931 LORD LLOYD MEMORANDUM

Lloyd papers 19/5

I went to see S.B. in connection with the India Committee's Meeting of yesterday, when S.B. informed us, through the Chairman, that he had acceded to the Committee's request urgently to place our views before the Prime Minister in regard to the present Indian situation but definitely refusing the request to make public a statement of Conservative policy in regard to India by means of a letter to the Prime Minister, or otherwise, before the statement he was going to make at Newton Abbott on Friday. He assured the Committee that he had every reason to believe that nothing would happen between now and the Newton Abbott meeting and that, in any case, he was

---

[53] Sir Clive Wigram was assistant private secretary to the King, and became principal private secretary on Stamfordham's death in April.

unprepared to do what we wished in this matter. I had got up at that meeting and said that I thought that S.B. was assuming a very grave responsibility in refusing to meet the Committee's request and in delaying the emission of the statement on Conservative policy. I felt by no means sure that things would not move very rapidly. At the same time, if the Leader flatly refused the request, it seemed impossible to press the matter any further.

I reminded S.B. of all this and pointed out that my apprehensions had only too rapidly materialised, for the statement in the House that afternoon, coupled with Reuters telegram in the newspapers this morning, showed that an agreement had been come to between the Viceroy and Gandhi; that we had, in fact, been overtaken by the very circumstances which we had all feared. I told S.B. that I had come to tell him that, in these circumstances, he must not be surprised if there was a grave split in the party in the next two or three days. He said that he had, for all the year past, viewed the possibility of a split on the Indian question and he shared my opinion as to the risk that I had warned him of. At the same time, he hoped I would remember that if there were no inconsiderable number who shared my views on India in the party, that there was also a very important section of people who did not. He candidly admitted that he was much more to the Left in his opinion on the matter than I was, and that in these circumstances he could not see his way to doing anything different to what he was doing. He had exerted all the influence he could with Ramsay and could now only await events.

I said that I thought that his Left-hand position had, in general affairs, been useful four or five years ago, and had conduced to an easier settlement of industrial troubles than an extreme Right attitude would have done but that I thought that the grave difficulties in which his Leadership found itself to-day was largely due to the fact that he entirely failed to discern a strong Rightwards current which had been flowing for the last year and a half and with very increasing intensity in the last three or four months, and I could assure him that if there was a large body of opinion in the House of Commons who were opposed to my views on India – a fact which I must accept his word for – all I could say was that these Members were rapidly getting out of touch with their constituents and there would shortly be an avalanche of opinion to the Right which would sweep the Members with it. S.B. then begged me to understand that he thoroughly appreciated my position and had no quarrel with it, though he could scarcely say that of Winston, who had been a member of the Cabinet who had been responsible for the very Reforms which he now criticised. He proposed to ask me a plain question, in confidence. He had asked it only of two others. Ought he to go or ought he not? He did not deny the gravity of the position in the Party but he could see no one to whom he could hand over the task who would not be in an even more difficult position than himself. Besides, there was always the capitulation to the Press. Would I give him my opinion frankly.

I replied that I could only answer his question if he could reply to the one I was about to put to him. Did he, in his heart of hearts, really believe or not that the proper cure for the country's ills lay in the application of Conservative principles? A large number of people who had a great regard for his character and his intentions were profoundly convinced that he did not believe that the application of Conservative principles was the right cure in present conditions. S.B. replied:-

'I do not think I can honestly answer that question. I have told you that I know I am much more to the Left than you and I have, all along, felt convinced that no election could be won on the kind of platform that you, for instance, would adopt.'

I replied:-

'I am so profoundly convinced, not necessarily that an election can be won on my platform – though I am confident it can – but that no election is worth winning on any other platform; and if you really feel that, I do think you ought to go. But, if you like to give me until tomorrow morning to give you a considered answer I will be very glad to do it, though I cannot pretend that it will be an agreeable occupation.'[54]

Baldwin's fight-back nearly collapsed when under further pressure from the backbench India committee, including Lloyd, he made a statement which was interpreted as withdrawing his party's support for the round-table process.

11 MARCH 1931 JONES DIARY

full text of an abridged version in Jones *DL*, pp. 3–5

10 am. Called at St. James Square [the London house of the Astors] on the way to the office. We got to India very quickly and to S.B.'s blunder. In Nancy

---

[54] Lloyd to Baldwin, 5 March 1931, Baldwin papers 104/226–7, re-stated his opposition on Indian policy, but did not comment on Baldwin's leadership.

burst: 'What did I think of my precious leader now? . . . I hear Winterton[55] is to open the debate on Thursday on India, and that S.B. is not going to speak. He ought to speak, and he ought to be made to speak.' I agreed that he ought to speak, and she urged me to go and see him right away. So I got on the telephone and asked if S.B. could see me for ten minutes. I got to Upper Brook Street at 11 o'clock, and found him not only alone, but, to use his phrase, 'very lonely'. With his unfailing courtesy he began by thanking me for some notes on Pepys which I sent him the other day for a speech. He got three or four pointers. I could see that he was excited from the frequent twitching of his facial muscles, and from his voluble talk. I pushed in my own point at once. 'You ought to speak on Thursday: you ought to open for your side.' 'I am going to speak,' he replied, 'I think I will speak immediately after Winston, which will be about six o'clock. Are you in a hurry? Can you stay and talk? I am free till lunch time. There is no one I could possibly be more glad to see. One is very lonely. The staff is not worth anything. Sit down and I will tell you all that has been happening'. So he fidgeted away as usual with his pipe and I smoked cigarettes. Frequently he got up and paced the room, tapped the floor with his feet excitedly. 'Last Sunday week David was here, and while he was here a letter marked "Secret" arrived from Neville Chamberlain. It announced a memorandum written by Topping, one of the Central Office. The substance of the memorandum was that I ought to resign the Leadership of the Party. Bobby Monsell, the Chief Whip, had been shown the memorandum and he had collected the views of my chief colleagues upon it. They were agreed that I ought to go. I saw Neville, the Chairman of the Party, and asked him did he also agree, and he said "Yes". I said, very well, the sooner the better. Let's have a meeting of my colleagues tomorrow, Monday, when I can say Goodbye. It so happened that David was dining that evening with Willy Bridgeman, and after dinner Bridgeman rolled in like an old Admiral and protested against my going out in so ignominious a fashion. Could I not make some stand, and go out on some first-class issue? Meanwhile my wife and I began to discuss our future plans, and especially what we could sell of our belongings in order to reduce our way of living. That was the position on Sunday night. On Monday these same colleagues had changed their minds, and were in favour of my

---

[55] Under-secretary, India Office 1922–4, and 1924–9: as no recent Conservative Indian Secretary sat in the House of Commons, he was technically the senior Conservative Indian expert there.

remaining on. I offered to fight St. George's, Westminster, and make that a test. On Monday I learnt through David, who got his information from Pat Gower of the Central Office, that Topping was not only in his memorandum officially interpreting what he thought to be the preponderant view of the Party, but giving vent to his own personal hostility to me – a pretty state of affairs. I must say I am very disappointed in Neville as head of the Office. David, at any rate, whatever his other defects, did know what was going on. Neville does not. He is, I am sure, perfectly loyal, which is what can be said of very few.' I butted in and said that there were a number quite ready to step into his shoes and that for some days it had been current talk that Hailsham would lead in the Lords, and Neville in the Commons, but that Horne hoped to slip into the top place between them. I told him that he was in a much weaker position than six months ago. Last autumn had there been a National or Coalition Government he would probably have been put at the head of it, but that was no longer true. I brought the talk back to India, and to Tuesday's bombshell. He confirmed Astor's account: 'It was brought to me just as I was leaving. The staff said nothing. Milne[56] told me that while it was secret it would be certain to leak out, so I agreed to publication. I made an error of judgement, I regret it infinitely.' I then told him how strange it seemed that he had paid no tribute to Irwin's work, either in the House or in his speech at Newton Abbot. He replied, 'I will do so on Thursday'. I let him realise how very strong and general the opposition to him is, and how much I hoped he could go out on a big issue like India. 'That is what I propose to do,' he replied 'No Party is so divided as mine. I have done my utmost to keep it together, but it ranges from Imperialists of the Second Jubilee to young advanced Democrats who are all for Irwin's policy. I am for that policy myself, and mean to say so. What is the best line I can take on Thursday? Would I just talk?' I proceeded to outline the speech for Thursday on the lines of Conciliation with safeguards which would be gradually dropped as experience of self-government developed. I talked very badly, though he made notes as I went along. I begged him to be absolutely frank, and show the country clearly the fissure in his party, and take his stand firmly with Irwin. He might lose his Party and his place, but he would go down with the great mass of the country on his side.

---

[56] Wardlaw-Milne MP, former businessman in Bombay; chairman of the Conservative India committee.

He told me how Sam Hoare was a timid rabbit, Oliver Stanley had cold feet; the Die-hards who for the last six years had loathed Winston were now running round him, the silly Burnham[57] had joined them – it was a Party of fools. I remarked that Winston had been canvassing for the support of the 'Daily Telegraph' and the 'Sunday Times'. S.B. knew of this, and went on: 'David has seen Camrose, and he is prepared to start at once a London evening paper to counter the "News" and "Standard". He can't put all the money into it at present, so David has gone down today to Bristol to ask the Wills' to put in £400,000'.[58] This news rather made me feel that S.B. was still counting on holding the leadership. He is convinced that he has the majority of the rank and file of the Party with him. I left him about 12.15.

I cancelled a promise to lunch with the Astors. I dined at the Athenaeum, and wrote an outline of a speech for S.B., posting it at 11.30, and so home.

Baldwin regained his position by a series of impressive speeches. At Newton Abbot on 6 March he emphasised that Conservative support for Indian constitutional reform was designed to preserve British influence in the sub-continent. In the Commons on the 12th he overcame Churchill and the Indian 'diehards' with a declaration of faith in Irwin's policy of conservative reform. Then on 17 March, supporting Duff Cooper at St. George's, Baldwin made one of his most famous speeches, execrating Beaverbrook and Rothermere, including the sentence: 'What the proprietorship of these papers is aiming at is power, and power without responsibility – the prerogative of the harlot throughout the ages.'[59]

Baldwin's suspicions about his close colleagues generated mutual ill-feeling. The two Chamberlains pointedly asked for Neville's release from the party chairmanship, plainly to improve his chances of replacing Baldwin. After a

---

[57] Viscount Burnham, former owner of *The Daily Telegraph*; member of the Simon Commission.
[58] The Wills family owned the Imperial Tobacco Co.; the sum was about £20 million in modern prices. This idea of challenging Beaverbrook and Rothermere on their own ground was abandoned once their political campaigns were defeated later in the month.
[59] The rebuke was supplied by Kipling, though it was perhaps an echo from a well-known published attack on Northcliffe: Williamson, *Baldwin*, p. 234 n.151. Kipling and Beaverbrook had once been friends. In one version of their parting Kipling, annoyed at some of Beaverbrook's actions, asked what his object really was, and received the reply 'I like to feel . . . that I can kiss a man to-day and kick him to-morrow. I want power without responsibility.' Kipling replied, 'The prerogative of the harlot throughout the ages': unpublished paragraph in proofs of G. M. Young's *Baldwin*, CUL MS Add. 7799, p. 159.

misunderstanding on 24 March produced the following placatory letter, the air was cleared with a frank exchange between business committee members of their various grievances.[60] At the end of the month Neville Chamberlain reached an agreement with Beaverbrook over the presentation of policy, which ended the press campaign against Baldwin's leadership. Stonehaven became the new party chairman.

24 MARCH 1931: TO NEVILLE CHAMBERLAIN

NC 8/10/31

Private   10 Upper Brook Street

My dear Neville,

I am distressed that you should think for a moment that I should intentionally keep anything from you. Such is not the case, nor could be the case.

I felt that after St. George's it was essential that I should get out into the country and that a preliminary intimation should be given at once and I embodied that in my message to Duff Cooper.

I was very occupied most of yesterday and hoped to talk to you to-day or to-morrow.

Of course I could not make any plans (nor have I yet begun to) until I had talked it over with the Chairman. Do let me assure you that <u>nothing</u> that has occurred during these last trying weeks has affected in any way my affections in regard to <u>you</u>. It has not been an easy time for either of us.

Very few things in politics have the power to hurt me: it would hurt me if I felt a shadow of misunderstanding between us.

If my manner has shown you that I have been worried, well, worried I have been: and God only knows whether history will write me down as a limpet or a patriot!

Yours ever/ S.B.

If you can give me an hour this afternoon or evening I should be grateful: perhaps I have been chary of asking you often when I know so well what the calls of the office are.

---

[60] See *AC Letters*, pp. 365–8; *NC Letters*, III, pp. 246–51; *Amery Diaries*, II, pp. 157–9.

26 MARCH 1931: TO EDITH MACDONALD

SB add. papers

House of Commons

Dearest Edith,

. . . I thoroughly enjoyed hitting those two rascals[61] and it has done a lot of good.

I am counting the days till Easter when I hope to get a quiet week . . . It has been a very difficult and trying time these last two or three months, and I have a heavy programme ahead throughout the summer.

However, if there isn't an election, one hopes for a good holiday in August.

I don't think the gov$^{\underline{nt}}$ can last beyond October and they will have at least two critical periods during the summer . . .

Much love . . . / Ever your loving/ Stan

In June Salisbury finally decided that he had to retire as Conservative leader in the House of Lords. Hailsham was confirmed as his successor.

17 JUNE 1931: TO SALISBURY

Hatfield House archives 4M/140/121–2

House of Commons

My dear Salisbury,

It would be almost an impertinence on my part to speak to you of the admirable patience, skill and devotion with which you have led their Lordships during so many difficult years: the country is in your debt far more than it knows or can ever realise.

But at the moment I think with profound gratitude of the loyal colleague and kind and long-suffering friend you have been to me, from the days when you watched (with what qualms I know not for you concealed them) my tottering steps as I slowly learned to walk unafraid in the high places of the world.

I have indeed been fortunate in such support: I always knew it but have never been more conscious of it than when the inevitable day came for us

---

[61] Beaverbrook and Rothermere.

to part. It so happens that the enforced rest has come to you first: my turn must come before long. If I can then feel that I have done my duty with as single a mind and as clear a heart as my co-leader, then I shall sing my Nunc Dimittis in peace.

But though we are no longer side by side in the forefront of the battle, our friendship will endure to the end.

> I am, with grateful affection/ Yours/ Stanley Baldwin

From June, a European banking crisis created a sterling crisis and then a budget crisis. With severe political difficulties expected in the autumn, discussion about the desirability of a 'national' government revived, but Baldwin again publicly rejected the notion on 1 August. His view was that the responsibility for dealing with the crises lay with the Labour government. If suitable measures were proposed Conservative leaders would help secure their passage through Parliament, but the Labour government must not be allowed to spread the odium for spending cuts and tax increases to the Conservative party. On 8 August the Baldwins began a motor tour from Cherbourg *en route* to Aix-les-Bains. On the 11th senior Bank of England directors, having already alerted Labour ministers to increased outflows of funds from London, asked to speak with Conservative and Liberal leaders. Following a telephone call and telegram from his office, Baldwin travelled back the next day. After meetings in London during 13 August he left that evening to rejoin his wife in France, on the understanding that the Cabinet would take effective action and in the belief that his physical distance would hinder any efforts to draw the Conservative leadership into compromising negotiations. He left Neville Chamberlain, now in effect shadow Chancellor of the Exchequer, to attend further consultations with ministers and Liberal leaders.

14 AUGUST 1931 SIR EDWARD GRENFELL TO J.P. MORGAN[62]

Morgan Grenfell papers

Private and Confidential

... S.B. was caught on the road near Poitiers and turned round and left his spouse and his clothes and motored to Havre, catching the night boat. He

---

[62] Chief partners in Morgan Grenfell, the Anglo-American merchant bank and British government financial agents in the USA. Grenfell was also a Bank of England director and Conservative MP for the City of London.

was not recognised till he got to Waterloo at nine in the morning. He sent for me at once and said he was in the humour to kick the first person he saw. After working off a little of his feelings he asked me to explain the situation as far as was proper. He had already known a good deal of what was going on from his talks with you and Monty on Friday last.[63] I also told him that we, i.e. the Bank, had told the Chancellor that we wished to explain matters to all the three leaders of the parties in the House of Commons, also that if he, S.B., were willing to see the Deputy and Peacock[64] it would be better than getting all details from me. He was ready to support any reasonable and solid proposals for balancing the budget but was not going to have the baby landed on his party and that he proposed, if asked by the P.M., to call upon him after which he would return to France, retrieve his wife and take her to Aix as originally intended.

The P.M. rang him up about 10am, asking him to call. Neville Chamberlain, his No.2, also arrived from Scotland yesterday morning and they together visited the P.M. The Deputy had visited the P.M. in the morning and still further rubbed things into him.

In the afternoon the Deputy and Peacock explained the situation at length to S.B. who satisfied them that he was ready to help the P.M. if he took resolute steps.[65]

All the Ministers, S.B. and Chamberlain left London last night for their respective holidays.[66] I understand that the chief Inland Revenue-taxing Authorities and the Treasury officials will consider fresh taxes at once and the five Principal Ministers will return to London in four or five days to receive the expert officials' report. Chamberlain and S.B. if necessary would return next week . . .

---

[63] 7 August. Montagu Norman was already ill, and shortly afterwards left London to convalesce.

[64] Sir Ernest Harvey and Sir Edward Peacock, respectively deputy governor and a senior director of the Bank of England, who in Norman's absence took charge of discussions with political leaders during the crisis. After Grenfell had left, Horne visited Baldwin on his own initiative to give another 'City' view.

[65] Chamberlain, who did not know that Baldwin had been briefed earlier by Grenfell, was also present: *NC Letters*, III, pp. 274–5.

[66] Geoffrey Lloyd (Baldwin's chief secretary at this point) to Cunliffe-Lister, 14 Aug. 1931, Swinton papers 174/2/1/26-8: 'The sudden departure of S. B., Neville etc. was largely for effect, it being calculated that if they all stayed in London, too much of an atmosphere of real crisis would be created.'

15 AUGUST 1931: TO NEVILLE CHAMBERLAIN

NC 7/11/24/1

Hotel Anjou, Angers

My dear Neville,

I never take a kindness as a matter of course and I am truly grateful to you for undertaking that work next week.

I should suggest a tariff to them, quoting Peacock.

David comes out to Aix on Thursday morning and you will be able to send latest particulars through him.

I think in the long view it is all to the good that the government have to look after their own chickens as they come home to roost, and get a lot of the dirt cleared before we come in.

To have the consequences of their finance exposed – and acknowledged before the world – within four months of their budget will be a wonderful lesson.

I had a good journey back, and last night I went to bed at nine and slept and slept and slept!

Ever yours/ S.B.

We must not forget on the platform that the liberals are just as responsible as the gov^{nt} for this crisis: indeed, more so, for their assistance was voluntary.

They have deliberately supported the gov^{nt} (which they were not obliged to) as being the less of two evils.

The Baldwins reached Aix-les-Bains on 18 August. During the 20th Chamberlain and Hoare, with Samuel and Maclean for the Liberals,[67] met MacDonald and Snowden to hear the Cabinet's proposals for balancing the budget. They considered these inadequate, and that evening Baldwin received a telephone call recalling him again. He left the next morning, leaving his wife behind but writing to her each day. As extracts from these letters are all that survive of Baldwin's letters to his wife, they are printed in full.[68] By the time Baldwin arrived in London, on the evening of Saturday 22 August, it had become clear both that the Labour Cabinet was split and that the exchange value of sterling (the 'gold standard') was close to

---

[67] Lloyd George was convalescing after a serious operation; Samuel became the acting Liberal leader.
[68] When transcribing the extracts, Windham Baldwin omitted 'the affectionate expressions at the beginning and the end'. The extracts are included in a typed note in SB add. papers.

collapse. The situation was now so serious that the participants in the three-party talks had discussed the possibility of an emergency 'national' government being formed under MacDonald's leadership.

21 AUGUST 1931: TO LUCY BALDWIN

Running into Bourg

... So far, so good. The ticket was only two pounds and the guard was so surprised and delighted with his tip that he got off at Amberjeu and sent a friend to finish the journey to Paris so the new comer informed me, beaming, and in anticipation of a handsome gift at Paris!

I followed the road we travelled so light heartedly only on Tuesday, but it was raining and water everywhere. It is not actually raining now and the platform is drying but there are big clouds ahead.

This is only a line, my love, and I shall try and prevail on some kind employee to stamp and post it somewhere, so that you can get a line to-morrow.

I have finished the Times puzzle and have read two or three chapters of the Shiny Night. It is just starting to rain again! ...

22 AUGUST 1931 (7.45 A.M.): TO LUCY BALDWIN

Ritz Hotel, 15 Place Vendome, Paris

... I had a very comfy journey but found it difficult to get the view both sides because as fast as I pulled up the blinds, the guard came along and pulled 'em down.

No one is allowed evidently to gaze at the occupant of a réservé.

I found the car, and the very agreeable manager whose name I forget was at the door to greet me.

I have a charming apartment, like the one we had years ago.

The good David turned up at half past eleven, having left Victoria at four. We talked till one, by which time Geoffrey Lloyd rang up with the latest news. The whole story is too long to tell but in short the government are rattled and divided. J.R.M. was for resigning at once yesterday afternoon and for 'making a statement' for the week end after he had dined!

But it is clear that I shall be in London for a few days and by Monday I may be in a position to write with more certainty.

I might be summoned to form a government any moment: again I might not! So there it is.

When I feel inclined to fret and grumble, I think of soldiers. One ought to be proud that some people think one can be of some use to the country.

You take care of yourself, and attend to your cure. Your health is everything. You might ask Francon what English waters he would recommend as equivalent to Aix in case you did cut your visit short.

There won't be an Election yet. The urgency of economy is so great that it has to be forced through this House. More from London.

David has offered me Gt. College St. for the weekend, so I shall stay with him till the kitchenmaid gets up and move in to U.B.S. on Monday...

23 AUGUST 1931: TO LUCY BALDWIN

Travellers' Club

... You know these times of 'crisis'! We had a most comfy journey and got in half an hour late in Victoria.

The pressmen were all over the place, in Paris and London, and batteries of cameras. There was an enthusiastic crowd of three or four hundred people to meet me at the station and a beery gentleman shouting 'You'll save the country!'

The two Geoffreys dined with us and I went to see Neville after dinner,[69] at half-past ten I left him and so to bed.

After breakfast, telephone calls for half-an-hour, Mimi operating. I spoke to Lorna, all well there, then to Brook St. where I changed into my new dark blue which is just right for the weather. It is like a crisp October day. I called on Geoffrey Dawson, and we came down here together where Sam lunches with me. I see the King at three o'clock.

Dawson gives me glowing accounts of the Stanhopes[70] who are happy as the day is long.

---

[69] N. Chamberlain to his wife, 23 Aug. 1931, NC 1/26/447: 'I gave him a full account of what had happened. He approved everything but hoped and prayed that he might not have to join a National Government.'
[70] The 7th Earl Stanhope and his wife had become friends of Baldwins. He was junior minister at the Admiralty 1924–9, 1931 and at the War Office 1931–4.

The crisis now will be a short one. We shall know to-morrow whether the P.M. will carry on to meet the House. If he can, I shall probably be able to come out in two or three days.

If he throws his hand in I don't know what will happen.

But you will probably know before you get this letter.

It's no good trying to explain the situation for it is kaleidoscopic and anything I say is out-of-date in an hour.

I saw Hilda[71] and told her that if I have to stay I will get the kitchen-maid up and that I should know in a day or two . . .

23 AUGUST 1931 DAWSON MEMORANDUM

Dawson papers 76/24–5; Wrench, *Dawson*, pp. 291–2

Clive Wigram rang me up soon after his arrival from Balmoral with the King[72] and we had some preliminary conversation on the telephone. H.M. was going to see the P.M. directly and was considering the line to take with him. He proposed to see Baldwin and Samuel later in the day, as to have the news of all parties at first hand. I suggested respectfully that H.M. should impress upon Ramsay that it was his business to get the country out of the mess and to dwell, with any flattery that he liked, upon the opportunity and the responsibility. The example of Scullin, who had become almost a popular hero by facing his problem in Australia,[73] was one that might profitably be pointed out to him. I repeated the arguments that we had been using in The Times and said that I thought it was everything to get a plan of national economy put out in public by a Labour Government, since it was the only course that would have a permanent effect in reversing a policy of extravagance.

C.W. said he quite agreed and would talk to the King on these lines at once.

Baldwin rang me soon afterwards, came round to my house in the middle of the morning, and stayed there talking to lunchtime, when we drove down together to the Travellers. He also agreed entirely with the views expressed above and was in hopes that the crisis would be temporarily settled on these

---

[71] Evidently a servant at 10 Upper Brook Street.
[72] The King and Wigram had been recalled from Balmoral by the Prime Minister's office.
[73] J. H. Scullin, the Labour Prime Minister of Australia, had faced a prolonged financial crisis from 1930, and imposed expenditure cuts against opposition within his own party.

lines by tomorrow. At the same time he felt it necessary to be prepared for any emergency, had summoned Stonehaven to London, and told Bobby Monsell in my presence that he must give up going to Scotland tonight.

He then fell to discussing what should be the <u>personnel</u> of a new Government if by any misfortune he was to be called upon to form one at once, saying that it was easier for him to talk these matters over with me than with any of his political colleagues.

[23 AUGUST 1931] WIGRAM MEMORANDUM ON THE EVENTS
OF 22–4 AUGUST

RA PS/GV/K.2330(2)/1 (extracts)

The King arrived at Buckingham Palace about 8.15 this morning.

On arrival I rang up to discover where Mr Baldwin was, and found that he was staying with Mr Davidson, his former Private Secretary. I said that I hoped that I could see Mr Baldwin some time later in the day.[74] . . .

At 3pm the King saw Mr Baldwin, and told him of the difficulties which the Prime Minister is having with his party and that it is possible that he might resign. Should this be the case, the King asked Mr Baldwin if he would be prepared to serve under Mr Ramsay MacDonald, as Prime Minister, in a National Government. Mr Baldwin said that of course he is prepared to do anything to save the country in the present crisis. Even if Mr MacDonald resigned Mr Baldwin would be prepared to carry on the Government if he could be assured of the support of the Liberal Party to effect the necessary retrenchment and save the financial crisis – after which he would ask the King for a dissolution. To this His Majesty said that of course he would agree.

The King was greatly pleased with Mr Baldwin's readiness to meet the crisis which had arisen; and to sink Party interests for the sake of the country.

Meeting the available business committee members immediately after speaking with the King, Baldwin was urged by Neville Chamberlain to persuade MacDonald, Snowden and a few other Labour ministers to join a new government.

---

[74] The memo. then records Wigram's conversation with Dawson, and the King's meetings with MacDonald at 10.30 a.m. and Samuel at 12.30 p.m.

Baldwin 'agreed'. Late that evening, MacDonald informed Baldwin, Chamberlain and Samuel that his Cabinet was irrevocably split and that he had recommended the King to see all three party leaders the next morning. Chamberlain, supported by Samuel, urged MacDonald to join a national government. Baldwin 'maintained silence', but later told Chamberlain that he 'entirely' approved and 'had only said nothing himself because he felt it was so hopeless to expect R.M. to join'.[75]

[24 AUGUST 1931]: TO LUCY BALDWIN

[10, Downing Street]

. . . I was rejoiced to get your dear letter.

London is like a madhouse: the telephones have been going until far into the night and Hilda can't get on with her work.

Last night it looked as if I should have to form a gov^{nt}. The P.M. said he couldn't form one. But this morning the King, the P.M., Samuel & I met, and Ramsay, with real courage, deserted by some of his leading colleagues and by his party, offered to form an ad hoc gov^{nt} to put through the financial legislation necessary and then to dissolve, for a general election, which will come probably in October.

I am going to be Lord President of the Council!

Politically I think it is the best thing for us.

My word! what a mess! The exchanges are nearly bust to-day and if we save the situation, it'll only be by the skin of our teeth.

There is no reason why you should return. I mean on public ground. Of course I hate our separation as you do, and if you feel you want to come back I shall welcome you with open arms. But your health is so important: it is very cold here and I wouldn't have you laid up with sciatica or rheumatism for anything. I move in to U.B.S. in a day or two and hope to get to Lorna's this weekend.

I can't write more (I am writing in the Cabinet Room) as I am at conference all day . . .

---

[75] N. Chamberlain diary, 23 Aug. 1931.

1 Lucy and Stanley Baldwin, in the 1920s

2 Baldwin's homes
  (a) Lower Park House, Bewdley, 1867–1870
  (b) Wilden House, 1870–1892, with the works across the road: a drawing by Lockwood Kipling, 1871
  (c) Dunley Hall, 1892–1902

(d)

(d) Astley Hall, 1902–1947: rear view, with Baldwin's 1912–1913 enlargement from centre to the right
(e) 27 Queen's Gate, South Kensington, 1908–1913
(f) 93 Eaton Square, Belgravia, 1913–1925 (in the 1990s)
(g) 69 Eaton Square, Belgravia, 1937–1947 (in the 1990s)

(e)

(f)

(g)

3 Wilden works, *c.* 1933 but substantially as they were in 1914

4 Baldwin the father, on holiday at Veules-les-Roses, Normandy, 1906:
Lorna, a governess, Margot, Oliver and Diana

5 Oliver Baldwin, *c.* 1929

6 Windham Baldwin, probably while
writing *My Father, c.* 1954

7 Baldwin's study at Astley Hall

8 Baldwin's library at 10 Downing Street, *c.* 1937

9 The Baldwins and the Davidsons, at Chequers in 1923:
back row: Davidson, Arthur Howard (the Baldwins' son-in-law),
Edward Robinson (a Baldwin cousin), Joan Davidson;
front row: the Baldwins and their second daughter, Lorna Howard.

(a)

(b)

10 Baldwin and his letters
(a) reading, at Chequers in 1923
(b) writing, at the Cabinet table, 10 Downing Street, *c.* 1935

EIGHT

*

The National government

AUGUST 1931 – JUNE 1935

On 26 August Baldwin wrote of the Conservative position that 'Politically we are on velvet.'[1] He had been converted to the idea of a 'national government' because it was expected to restore financial confidence, and because Conservatives alone would not be responsible for tax increases and more particularly spending cuts, especially in unemployment benefit payments. A combination of leading members of all three parties could more easily present these as necessary sacrifices for the 'national interest' than a Conservative or Conservative-led government, vulnerable to the charge that a 'party of the rich' was cutting the incomes of 'the poor'. The pressure of the financial crises meant that even diehard and protectionist groups supported the formation of a new coalition, assisted by assurances that it would be a short-term arrangement limited to balancing the budget and defending sterling. Under MacDonald, Baldwin and Samuel (Home Secretary), a small emergency Cabinet of ten members (four Labour, four Conservative, two Liberal) was appointed.

25 AUGUST 1931: TO LUCY BALDWIN

24, Old Queen Street

... It is cold and blustery to-day and I am lost as to the season and the day of the week. I spent most of yesterday at Downing St. trying to fit the jig-saw together and was pretty tired by bed-time. To-night I move in to Brook St.

---

[1] To Page Croft, Croft papers 1/3/6.

269

where I hope Little will be staying. He was at Wappingthorne last night.[2] Mimi spent two hours trying to get through to you on the telephone after dinner last night, because I had meant to telephone myself, but instead of the quiet evening I had anticipated I was at Downing St. from 8.30 till nearly 11.

I wanted to ask you if you could make all the necessary reservations or if we should do it here. But I shall try and get through to-day on a government call.

10, Downing Street.

Some hours have elapsed.

Another longish day at gov^{nt} buildings. We shall have the list in to-morrow's papers.

They tell me that with gov^{nt} priority I can get Aix in a quarter of an hour so I shall test them and hope we shall be audible. We swear in to-morrow morning and have our first Cabinet in the afternoon. There is something familiar about this paper! I am writing in the Cabinet Room. I have just seen my room. It is a beauty looking out west over the Parade and getting all the afternoon sun. Take great care of yourself. If I can't get a clear talk I shall telegraph at length to-morrow about the journey . . .

26 AUGUST 1931 (7.45 P.M.): TO LUCY BALDWIN

Oxford and Cambridge Club, Pall Mall, S.W.1.

. . . It was like the Angers telephone! I heard your first sentence dimly but could make it out, but after that confusion, and it was so difficult to try and put a conversation in a telegram. However, I got yours this morning and I will check all your reservations from Calais on, see about the Customs, and D.V. meet you.

I have been at it all day and this is the first lull I have had.

I like my room enormously. I saw Willie Tyrrell this evening for a minute and if there is a lucid interval he will drink tea with me to-morrow.

The Old University are billeted here and I am dining in a quarter of an hour with Neville and Philip C-Lister.

Little turned up on Monday and went back by the 12.45 to-day.

---

[2] The home of Baldwin's daughter Lorna Howard, near Steyning, Sussex.

I shall indeed be glad to see you and what a lot we shall have to talk about. I am trying to get to Wappingthorne on Friday night and shall come up again Saturday night . . .

As the Labour party and nearly all its MPs repudiated the 'MacDonaldites' and now opposed all social service cuts, the National government was not wholly secure. Unusually, a handwritten Baldwin letter was sent in fascimile to Conservative MPs. After success on a confidence motion on 8 September made it clear that emergency finance and economy bills would be passed, the question of the duration of the government became pressing. On 12 September Baldwin wrote that 'the last three weeks has been as heavy and as difficult a time as I have ever had./ This week in Parliament has gone off better than I expected and I am well satisfied with it. The future, politically, is very obscure and must be for some days or even weeks yet.'[3] Baldwin had told a party meeting on 28 August that after the National government had settled the difficult issue of expenditure cuts, Conservatives would fight an election independently on the issue of protection. But wide support for the 'non-party' government became evident, while none of the government partners – not even the Conservative leaders – was now confident of doing well if they fought the election separately against a Labour party repudiating reductions in public service incomes and unemployment benefits. Conservative opinion was divided over whether to end the existing government, and over the timing of the election. Arthur Mann, as editor of the *Yorkshire Post* an important authority on provincial opinion, wrote to Baldwin arguing that an election should be delayed, with the National government remaining in office to deal with protection.[4]

28 AUGUST 1931: TO CONSERVATIVE MPS

facsimile, Gilmour papers GD383/36

10, Upper Brook Street

My dear Sir,

The forthcoming Session will be one of the most critical in our history.

I beg you, at whatever personal sacrifice, to be present on the appointed day and to give your consistent support to the Government to enable them to pass the necessary financial legislation.

---

[3] To Edith Macdonald, SB add. papers.   [4] Mann to Baldwin, 7 Sept. 1931, SB papers 44/93.

Failure to do our duty throughout this crisis would be dishonourable to us as a party and disastrous to the national interest.

Yours very faithfully/ Stanley Baldwin

10 SEPTEMBER 1931 DAVIDSON [FOR BALDWIN] TO MANN

typescript copy, SB papers 44/94–5

Private and Personal

My dear Mann,

Baldwin has been trying to find time to answer your letter of September 7th for which he is most grateful. He has, however, not had a moment to do so, and he has, therefore, asked me to say that he would like very much to see you to talk matters over.

If by any chance you are coming to London, as I think you often do, on Monday would it be possible for you to come and see him in his room at the House of Commons at 2.30 pm that day?

It is very important that the Leader should know – if it is possible to ascertain the facts – how far the position of the Socialist party has been consolidated by the fact that the rank and file feel that they are being attacked. In some Socialist quarters the belief is widely held that the definite decline in the popularity of the late Government, which made its defence almost impossible even in the strongest Socialist seats, has been converted into a revival due to the fact that the Socialist Party is once again on the attack. That is one of the questions which is at the root of the difficult decision as to when the Election should come. The Party as a whole in its present temper in the House of Commons is saying 'The sooner the better'.

I hope to see you myself, and, for your private information, I am acting quietly as Parliamentary Private Secretary to the Leader during the next few difficult weeks.

Yours sincerely/ J.C.C.D.

A renewed sterling crisis culminated on 21 September with formal abandonment of the gold standard. The National government's failure in one of its prime purposes seemed to increase the vulnerability of each of its partners if the alliance was dissolved, and jeopardised a budget which they all thought it vital to preserve. The principal difficulty was the election programme, because Snowden and the 'Samuelite' Liberals refused to accept the Conservative programme of protection; and if they left the government, MacDonald might feel obliged to resign too. Baldwin's answers were to allow those ministers to leave, but to replace them with a dissident Liberal group, the 'Simonite' Liberals, who were now prepared to accept tariffs; and to renounce the Conservative – his own – claim to the premiership, in order to help persuade MacDonald to remain.

24 SEPTEMBER 1931 NEVILLE CHAMBERLAIN DIARY

(extract)

This afternoon at 6 there was a meeting of the business committee in S.B.'s room at which were present besides S.B. and myself, Austen, Hailsham, Philip C-L, Londonderry, Peel, Eyres-Monsell, Gilmour, Ormsby-Gore, W. Elliot, Kingsley Wood, Bridgeman and Amery.[5] S.B. made a statement of the conclusions at which he had arrived namely: (1) that an election should take place as soon as possible, (2) that the appeal should be on a national not a party programme which should ask for a free hand but include tariffs on the widest scale (3) that this appeal should come from a National Govt. reconstructed after the resignation of any who could not accept the programme. Of this Govt he felt MacDonald should be the head but he then came to what he called the 'fork' at which he had not made up his mind. Who should be P.M. in the Govt. formed after victory. Discussion then took place over the whole field. Everyone expressed their views in turn and the conclusion was quite unanimous. All were in favour of the National appeal by a National Govt. under MacDonald provided the programme embodied the full tariff. All agreed that the election should be at the earliest possible moment. All agreed that if we went to the election with R.M. as P.M. we must accept him as P.M. when we came back though we might well have an understanding as to the filling of posts in a new Govt . . .[6]

On 5 October the Conservative leaders agreed to a Cabinet compromise, by which each of the partners would issue separate election programmes, under the umbrella of a MacDonald statement asking the electorate for a 'free hand' to undertake whatever measures seemed necessary, the so-called 'doctor's mandate'. This allowed Conservatives to campaign for protection and Samuelite Liberals for free trade, but also for all ministers – and the 'Simonite' Liberals – to combine in a fierce attack on the Labour party. Baldwin was again helped with his election speeches by drafts from Tom Jones, who had retired from the Cabinet secretariat in autumn 1930 to become secretary of the Pilgrim Trust under Baldwin's chairmanship.

[5] *Amery Diaries*, ii, pp. 203–4, also has an account of this meeting.
[6] See also *NC Letters*, iii, pp. 280–1.

23 OCTOBER 1931: TO JONES

Jones papers A6/51

Royal Station Hotel, Newcastle upon Tyne

My dear T.J.,

All your stuff has been invaluable: I have worked nearly all of it off at one place or another. It has been the greatest help.

You wouldn't care for the broadcast: it was mainly Pat Gower, but a gentleman in a pub in Bradford observed after a deep sigh 'And 'oo the 'ell says 'e ain't an orator?'

A difficult question to answer!

Ever yours/ S.B.

At the general election on 27 October, the National government supporters – including 470 Conservative MPs – won a majority of 500 over the Labour party, reduced to just 52 MPs. (Oliver Baldwin, after a brief involvement with Mosley's 'New party', was among the defeated Labour candidates.) Reconstructing the government was difficult, particularly because Baldwin and MacDonald now wished to include the Simonite 'Liberal National' leaders. Austen Chamberlain, recognising that he would not be offered a major government post, wrote to Baldwin on 28 October withdrawing his claim to ministerial office in favour of younger men. The economic depression had further depleted Baldwin's income from industrial dividends, and in becoming Lord President he took a lower salary than that of Prime Minister and the chief departmental ministers, in accordance with reductions agreed as part of the national sacrifices.[7] So his return to office did not end his financial worries: in January 1932 he wrote 'I wonder if I can hold on to Astley.'[8]

28 OCTOBER 1931: TO MACDONALD

J. R. MacDonald papers 30/69/1441/58

Carlton Club, Pall Mall, S.W.1

My dear Prime Minister

I hold out both hands to welcome you back, not in the flesh, for you ought not to be bothered by anyone tonight, but in the spirit of warmest congratulations and sympathy. No man can have had a more searching trial

---

[7] Although his responsibilities might have entitled him to ask for the £5,000 salary for major Cabinet posts, he took only the normal Lord President's salary of £2,000.
[8] To Davidson, 7 Jan. 1932 [1931 written], Lady Davidson papers.

than you have had during these past weeks, nor have any body of men had graver responsibilities than those laid upon us by this amazing popular mandate.

It makes me feel mighty humble in the presence of such forces.

I pray we be not found wanting: we will do our best.

Yours most sincerely/ Stanley Baldwin

1 NOVEMBER 1931: TO AUSTEN CHAMBERLAIN

AC 39/4/4

Trent, New Barnet[9]

My dear Austen,

At last I have a lucid interval in which I can sit down and attend to my letters.

Your letter made me proud of having been your colleague and friend for so long. I admire the spirit of it, and I hope that same spirit may be mine in due time.

We do owe something to the many younger men who are crowding on our heels. You and I know the necessary hardship that these combinations of parties impose on them. And it is worth something when we say, freely and gladly, 'Come along and help: we have held the front line through times good and bad: it is now your turn'.

But wherever you may be I know you will always be available for counsel [, and if we can keep this national government going, we may be able to do what I have long maintained no party alone can do, reform the Lords.

Then there may be a Chamber in which you will feel able to sit not only for the benefit of the State but perhaps even to your own pleasure].[10] I hope you are too good a student of history to worry yourself about the judgement of your own generation.

I felt very strongly at the '29 election that the country completely failed to appreciate what you had done for them in their foreign relationships and at the League of Nations.

---

[9] The lavish country mansion of Sir Philip Sassoon, first lent to the Baldwins as a retreat after the 1929 election defeat.

[10] At Chamberlain's request this letter was published in the leading newspapers, with the omission of these bracketed references to the House of Lords.

But when the history of these years comes to be written with the fuller knowledge time brings, justice will be done and a place will be secured for you which your father would deem not unworthy for his son.

I shall take good care that our younger men know of your thought for them,

I am, my dear Austen,

As always/ Very sincerely yours/ Stanley Baldwin

2 NOVEMBER 1931 WIGRAM MEMORANDUM

RA PS/GV/K.2331(1)/48

The King saw Mr Baldwin who said that he was very tired.

Mr Baldwin told His Majesty that the Prime Minister was inclined to be wobbly and unable to make up his mind over the new Cabinet and had not advanced very far in its composition. Every new comer was inclined to sway him. The King told Mr Baldwin that he thought the Old Gang should be cleared out – Amulree, who did not fly,[11] Austen Chamberlain (who, Mr Baldwin said, had written that he was quite prepared not to be offered office), Reading, Crewe and Peel.[12]

The King thought that Neville Chamberlain was so good as Minister of Health that it would be a pity to make him Chancellor of the Exchequer, where he would be suspected of ultra-protectionist views. His Majesty said that he thought Mr Baldwin should go as Chancellor of the Exchequer but the latter said that he had asked for no Portfolio. He intimated that there would be plenty for him to do, as the Prime Minister knew nothing of his new Party, especially the Conservatives, many of them young, impetuous and ambitious men, with no chance of making reputations with no Opposition to speak against.

The Prime Minister has offered Mr Baldwin No.11 Downing Street, for which the latter was very grateful as he was very badly off now and a house with no rent and taxes would be a god-send.

[11] The Labour Secretary of State for Air since October 1930, at the age of seventy-one he had not taken to any kind of flying. He was replaced by Londonderry.
[12] Since August the Liberal Lords Reading (aged seventy-one) and Crewe (seventy-three) had been respectively Foreign Secretary and War Secretary, and the Conservative Lord Peel (sixty-four) Lord Privy Seal. None was re-appointed.

Mr Baldwin thought that perhaps Simon would be a good Chancellor of the Exchequer, as he had been investigating statistics of trade for some time. But Mr Baldwin was afraid that his Party might kick if they did not have some of the key positions, such as the Chancellor of the Exchequer, Home Office, Foreign Office, Dominions Office. Mr Baldwin advocated Neville Chamberlain being at the Foreign Office.

4 NOVEMBER 1931 WIGRAM MEMORANDUM

RA PS/GV/K.2331(1)/50 (extracts)

The King saw Mr Duff, Private Secretary to the Prime Minister, this morning . . . Mr Duff said that last night he had been talking to Mr Baldwin and had suggested Lord Irwin for the F. O. Baldwin was much taken with this idea and was seeing Lord Irwin this morning. I told the King that Warren Fisher had already suggested his name to me. The King thought that Lord Irwin would be very suitable for the Foreign Office.

. . . Later Mr Duff rang me . . . and said that the situation had become more critical and that I had better go and see Mr Baldwin.

I went off to see Mr Baldwin who said that he had seen Lord Irwin, whose first instinct was to decline the offer of Foreign Secretary. Mr Baldwin had just seen Mr Neville Chamberlain and Sir Bolton Eyres-Monsell, and I expect they told Mr Baldwin that Lord Irwin's appointment would be not too well received by the Conservative Party.

Mr Baldwin then asked what I thought the King's opinion would be of Simon for the Foreign Office, and I said I thought His Majesty would approve. Then Mr Baldwin said that perhaps it might be best if he led the House of Commons and the P.M. took over the Foreign Office for a certain time, after which perhaps Lord Irwin could come in. I did not express any opinion, but afterwards I gathered from Duff that such an arrangement would lead people to think that the Conservatives were beginning to try and get rid of Ramsay MacDonald as Prime Minister.[13]

Mr Baldwin said he hoped that the Prime Minister would make up his mind about the Cabinet as soon as possible.

---

[13] Irwin was not appointed. Simon became Foreign Secretary, and Neville Chamberlain Chancellor of the Exchequer.

I afterwards . . . went into the room of Sir Geoffrey Fry, Mr Baldwin's Private Secretary, where I again saw Mr Baldwin, and also Mr Geoffrey Lloyd, another of his secretaries . . . Mr Baldwin spoke to Mr Lloyd about the young Conservatives and how necessary it was to prevent their going off at a tangent and forming cliques and societies. Mr Baldwin said that he proposed to address the young Conservative Members and to try and steady them on the Tariff question. The Government must work by steady instalments and if some sort of tariff policy is necessary they must begin gradually and educate public opinion for stronger measures. Mr Lloyd thought this an excellent idea and hoped that Mr Baldwin would carry it out as soon as possible.

6 NOVEMBER 1931: TO LADY LONDONDERRY

Londonderry papers D3099/3/15/17

Chevening

My dear Lady Londonderry,

You say 'For God's sake don't answer this' but I cannot obey you for I am not accustomed to getting such letters so full of generous kindness, and I must tell you how I appreciate 'em and how cheered I feel.

I am undoubtedly up against the job of my life, to keep our huge majority happy and to make Ramsay's curiously composite government function. However I shall do my best, and honestly if I can't do it, I don't know who can!

I have at the moment a good deal of prestige to sacrifice in the effort and we may pull through.

At any rate we shall soon know what the chances are.

I will certainly come and drink your health at an early date. I shall need stimulating for I shall have a jolly time with those who have been left out of the Cabinet. It is a real testing time for men and there are a few who rise to it.[14]

I am really grateful for your letter as I am for the friendship and support I have always had from you and Charlie.

Ever most sincerely yours/ Stanley Baldwin

---

[14] *Sic*: Baldwin presumably meant to write either 'there are few who rise to it' or 'there are only a few who rise to it'.

11 NOVEMBER 1931: TO WINTERTON

Winterton papers 66

Privy Council Office

My dear Eddy,

Nothing has caused me more difficulty – and more personal pain – than the position of old friends who have emerged or ought to emerge from the Under Secretary stage. I fear they have inevitably suffered most from the kind of government the Prime Minister felt it his duty to form.

I wondered whether you would consider it an advantage at any time to take an English peerage and with it your chance in the Upper House? But I hope you won't feel that because the P.M. was unable to include you this time that I shall not endeavour to secure worthy work for you should opportunity arise.[15]

Yours always sincerely/ Stanley Baldwin

20 DECEMBER 1931 JONES TO FLEXNER

Jones papers S1/22

. . . I did see S.B. on Friday for a leisurely half hour and he said the National Government was 'welding' much better than he had imagined possible, that the average ability was higher than in a party government, & that a Free Trader who turns Protectionist in middle life is like a teetotaller who takes to brandy after a life of abstinence (I suppose he was hinting at John Simon). Ramsay & S.B., as you know, like each other personally but Ramsay as P.M. is very ill to live with because of his indecision & shall we call it mobility. S.B. is doing his utmost to play the national game & his stock just now is high in the country for that reason. . . .

21 DECEMBER 1931: TO FRY

Fry papers

[Astley Hall]

My dear Geoffrey,

. . . I want you to realise that irritable as I fear I get at times, I am extraordinarily grateful to you for all you do for me. I don't take such generous

---

[15] Winterton stayed in the Commons, but did not regain office until 1937, after Baldwin's retirement.

service for granted. There is nothing so unselfish as the work that men like you and David and Duff[16] have given and give to the poor devils whom God for His own inscrutable purposes has planted in the front row of His puppets.

Yours ever/ S.B.

In November Davidson had returned to the Chancellorship of the Duchy of Lancaster, which he combined during early 1932 with the chairmanship of the Indian States Committee, one of the inquiries created to prepare for the establishments of a federal Indian government. In mid January he and his wife left for a four-month investigative tour of India. Baldwin sent weekly letters to them both.[17] His long letters to Joan Davidson continued to consist largely of small personal or social matters and amusing stories. A complete letter is given as a sample, then the only significant political extract from the others. Baldwin marked the letters with two sets of numerals: arabic to indicate days since their departure and those to their return, and roman to number the letter. However, Joan became ill during February and returned to England early.

The Cabinet was soon divided, with Snowden and the Samuelite Liberal ministers threatening to resign if the Conservatives, supported by the Simonite Liberal ministers, insisted on imposing a general tariff. On 23 January, however, the split was circumvented by an 'agreement to differ', by which the free-trade ministers stayed in the Cabinet but were given licence to oppose the Import Duties Bill during its parliamentary passage.

24–5 JANUARY 1932: TO JOAN DAVIDSON

Davidson papers 195

10–112 LETTER no.11   11, Downing Street
Little Maid,

It is just six o'clock of a Sunday evening: it has gone colder and I am alone in the library and it seems a suitable moment to tell you something of the last week. Of course I shan't labour the point but I was wondering yesterday afternoon whether your conscience – if indeed you have one – was pricking you ever so slightly? You have mothered me now for more years than I like

---

[16] Sir Patrick Duff, although a civil servant, had become as much a personal assistant as Fry and Davidson: see Appendix D.
[17] The 1932 letters to Joan Davidson became separated from the main series and were deposited with her husband's political papers in the House of Lords Record Office.

to think of and taken me for walks and seen me safe over the crossings, and then – suddenly, all in a moment, with no reason, you rush to the other side of the world and expect me to step out into the London traffic, see myself over the roads and bring myself safe back. I dragged myself out yesterday, ALONE, and tramped through mean streets all the way to Battersea Park and back, what time you were riding in howdahs, dangling jewelled fingers over the elephants' flanks, and David is puffing at his hookah under a punkah! Well I say no more. We all have our feelings.

It was a joy to get your letter. Not wholly and altogether unexpected, I admit, but it was a joy. And I pictured you rolling through that golden landscape, passing towns with golden names, and indeed I have felt in close touch with you as long as you were this side [of] the Canal. But through that is another world though indeed I woke up this morning thinking I heard your voice, and when I was fully awake I found it was two pigeons talking outside my window!

Monday last I made a moving little speech at the Mansion House for the Winter Distress League. Tuesday I walked with Gordon[18] and had him to breakfast. We lunched at the Danish Legation. I don't think I like luncheon parties but I like Countess Ahlefeldt.[19] Then being my lady's birthday, to the play. We went to the Whitehall theatre which was new to me to see a play recommended by Eddie Marsh called the Gay Adventure. It was quite amusing. My entrance was the signal for enthusiastic applause from the pit which startled me and I tried to look un-self-conscious! Patrick Hastings sat behind us, and in our row were Christabel McLaren and three of her children.[20] We walked home across the Parade.

Then two days of cabinets, the result of which you will have heard long before you get this letter.

Thursday morning walked with Gordon and took him to breakfast with the Pollocks. It seemed so odd going there without you.[21] Willie Bridgeman came to lunch. They come up in a week and will be fixed in London for some time.

[18] His son-in-law, Gordon Munro, a member of the merchant bank Helbert, Wagg & Co.
[19] Wife of the Danish minister in London.
[20] Sir Patrick Hastings, barrister and former Labour MP and Attorney-General 1924; and the wife of Henry McLaren, iron- and coal-master, former Liberal MP (2nd Lord Aberconway 1934).
[21] A reference to Baldwin's and Joan Davidson's frequent pre-breakfast walks with Ernest Pollock, a Unionist MP 1910–23, law officer in the Coalition government, and Master of the Rolls from 1923, created 1st Viscount Hanworth 1926.

Yesterday I had the Stanhopes to breakfast and went to see a film produced by Puffin Asquith's company.[22]

And that brings me to my long and lonely walk to Battersea.

By the way I am going to order a suit of plus fours for week-end wear in London. It seems to be the fashionable kit for those who can't get out of town, and a rain coat to match, shewing about eight inches of plus fours under it.

11–111

25th January. Here is a still, cold, foggy morning. I read in my Times that you cleared Aden yesterday. I never enjoy a new week, and I have just had a tiresome letter from my lady Oxford wanting me to see Elizabeth Bibesco[23] which I suppose means lunch. Her argument for my seeing her is that life is short: I should have thought that an argument for not wasting it. I like Margot but I don't like Elizabeth and there you are.

I have just heard from Peter Sanders[24] that the Beaver is not coming to the Constitutional when I unveil Bonar's portrait so that nightmare is past.

I had a very friendly letter from Hamar[25] (in answer to mine which was in answer to a Christmas telegram) vowing himself to my service and offering to shew me round Gray's Inn. That I accept!

I wonder where this will catch you: I shan't finish it until to-morrow.

I am afraid this is boring but I am trying to keep you both in touch. I am just going to dress for dinner at the French Embassy. We had an hour this morning on parliamentary business, the P.M., the Chief Whip and I. We are in the gluepot already for we have the tariff and the Quota to get through by Easter. I hate going into this scramble without David: it takes so much of the fun out of it and makes it a grey business. The dissentients have swallowed the Wheat Quota whole which has surprised me.[26] I hear Ll.G. is out for the blood of Samuel and Sinclair[27] who will be in a very vulnerable position. I was chairman of the Cabinet Committee on the quota and had two sittings

---

[22] Lord Oxford's youngest (and Lady Oxford's only) son Anthony, better known as a film director.
[23] Lady Oxford's daughter, married to the Rumanian diplomat Prince Antoine Bibesco.
[24] Conservative Minister of Agriculture 1922–4, created Lord Bayford 1929.
[25] Greenwood, who with Churchill defected from Liberal to Conservative via the 'Constitutionalist' group in 1924, created Lord Greenwood 1929.
[26] To Davidson, 26 Jan. 1932, Davidson papers 195: 'There is a fearful programme of work for Parliament, but I am fairly satisfied. As Neville said to me last night, "We have got everything we wanted & all we could have got had we come in ourselves."'
[27] Sir Archibald Sinclair, the Samuelite Liberal Secretary of State for Scotland 1931–2, and leader of the parliamentary party 1935–45.

to get it through with a unanimous recommendation to the Cabinet. Two hours last Wednesday and rather less to-day.

Good-night, Little Maid, and good angels guard you. You are both constantly in my thoughts and I like to picture you enraptured with everything.

What a lot you will have to tell us!

I go to Himley on Friday to speak at the Birmingham Jewellers' dinner on Saturday evening: back here Sunday.

Your loving/ S.B.

31 JANUARY [−1 FEBRUARY] 1932: TO JOAN DAVIDSON

Davidson papers 195

17–105 no.III   Himley Hall, Dudley, Worcs.

Little Maid,

. . . We have had a busy week and I had to take Friday's cabinet as the PM had gone north. We spent two hours on the Import Duties Bill and the dissentients played the game and took no part in the discussions. The PM is going away for about a month as soon as we have got the House going and as soon as he can give a couple of days to Geneva.[28] Very very privately his eyes are giving him trouble, the result of fatigue and worry over a long time, and that is why he is going away for a complete rest . . .

18–104   11, Downing Street

Just back from the Londonderry party. It was all wrong without you. I stood behind the P.M. and shook hands from 4.30 to 6. I should think nearly a couple of thousand! . . .

I had a talk with Horder[29] and he told me the P.M. ought to be operated on at once; that he will be laid up a fortnight and that he ought to make a sound recovery. But the eye trouble is very real . . .

If you don't burn my letters, I hope you will keep them in one of David's boxes!

Enough for this week

Much love to you both/ Ever your loving/ S.B.

The reality of party strengths meant that Baldwin was effective leader of the House of Commons. In addition, MacDonald's prolonged eye problems and then

---

[28] For the Disarmament Conference.   [29] Sir Thomas Horder, senior medical consultant.

his absence at international conferences meant that for large parts of the next six months Baldwin was acting prime minister. On 4 February Neville Chamberlain introduced the Import Duties Bill in the House of Commons, at last implementing a version of his father's tariff reform of 1903 and Baldwin's protection of 1923.

5 FEBRUARY 1932: TO ANNE CHAMBERLAIN

NC 11/1/32

Privy Council Office

Dear Mrs Chamberlain,

... It isn't only that Neville made a great speech yesterday, but for all time these great changes – only beginning yet – will be associated with his name: whatever may result throughout the empire will be reckoned from yesterday. You must be a proud woman.

As an old friend through many vicissitudes I rejoice in his success and I delight in thinking of father and son secure in a niche of our national history for generations to come.

Yours very sincerely/ Stanley Baldwin

28 FEBRUARY 1932: TO MACDONALD

J. R. MacDonald papers 30/69/678/162–4

Privy Council Office

My dear P.M.

If I may borrow from the extensive and peculiar vocabulary of the Wing Commander,[30] to-day is 'devilish bracing' and all our colleagues arrived at No. 10 with blue noses. We had Neville, Sam, Jim Thomas and Charley Londonderry, with Van[31] and Hankey. We considered the telegrams which you will get with this letter, and told Van to telephone Simon to go ahead in accordance with the concluding paragraph of the 'en clair' message.[32] ...

We all feel that the move is a good one and may really lead to something.

---

[30] Louis Greig, who had served in the RAF.

[31] 'Sam' was Hoare, and 'Van' Sir Robert Vansittart, permanent secretary, Foreign Office 1930–8. The issue related to the Manchurian crisis; Baldwin was chairman of the Cabinet Far Eastern Committee.

[32] To Simon, 2 March 1932, Simon papers 71/101: 'My dear Simon,/ Don't worry. We shall support you whatever you do provided you don't do some damned fool thing of which I hope and believe you are incapable! / Yours ever/ S.B.' Simon was in Geneva for the Disarmament Conference.

The House is running smoothly. The Judge question went down quite quietly. I took the precaution of seeing Tom Williams[33] who had been asking questions as to the probability of our restoring their cut, and I explained the situation to him. I explained it so lucidly and so sympathetically that he said as he left my room 'I don't know that I don't feel a good deal of sympathy with the old gentlemen in the line they've taken!' So that little trouble is buried with no mourners.

We ran through nine estimates on report, two excess votes in committee, and two bills on Friday between 11 and 12.30! Monday is the first allotted day when Sam starts with a statement on India.

The comic relief has been provided by the Maxton group and Charles Buxton's private room.[34] They seized it by force and having captured it they arranged their forces night and day in this wise. One to sit in the room: one on guard outside, and two in their places in the House. They work in shifts, but of what length I don't know. The root of the trouble is that while, as I understand, old Lansbury is quite willing to give them a room, Maxton won't ask him for it, because (among other reasons) he says Lansbury would boast of it on the platform. You may follow this but it is too subtle for me. He further added, but this is still more cryptic, 'You can do these things in the Tory party but we can't!'

I hope you are beginning to feel the effect of a rest.

Take every care of yourself. You will be very welcome when you return, but <u>not</u> if you come back before you are really ready for it.

Yours always/ S.B.

1 MARCH 1932 LORD HINCHINGBROOKE[35] DIARY

Lord Sandwich papers

S.B. on King George V – 'The more I study the man the more convinced I am he is a very fine King . . . it is easy to laugh at him and some of his

---

[33] Front-bench Labour MP. The senior judges had protested against the application of the general cut in public service incomes to themselves, on the grounds of judicial independence.
[34] The six ILP MPs had formed a separate group, defying Lansbury, the new Labour party leader, and demanded a House of Commons room of their own. Buxton, though no longer an MP, was as an adviser occupying a room allocated to the Labour opposition. In July the ILP disaffiliated from the Labour party.
[35] Heir to the 9th Earl of Sandwich; Baldwin's assistant private secretary 1932–4.

little ways but we are fortunate indeed to have as our King a man with such a sense of duty'.[36]

S.B. after the second reading of the Import Duties Bill. 'I don't want to be a Pharisee but thank God I wasn't born a Liberal'.

2 MARCH 1932: TO MACDONALD

J. R. MacDonald papers 30/69/678/165–6

Privy Council Office

My dear P.M.

Much as I enjoyed getting your letter you must not really write yourself as we sent you away to rest your eyes.

I have only time to scribble a note as I have to dress and go to a dinner at the Constitutional Club where I am unveiling a portrait of Bonar and making a speech about him – no easy matter.

You will see from the Cabinet minutes that you had overlooked (as indeed we all had except the Chancellor and Hilton Young) the fact that the '29 Act gave the local authorities money which was to be expended partly on maternity services. So this year we propose to ginger up the backward authorities precedent to getting a move on all along the line.

I summed up and said I sincerely trusted that this gov^{nt}. before it went out would have succeeded in getting proper maternity services established throughout the country.

This wild talk in the Press about the Budget is wholly mischievous. The Tory papers are talking of big reductions of income tax, the others accusing us of that being our intention.

Snowden & Co. have intimated that if there is 'a class budget' out they go!

It is cooking your hare before you've caught it, for I believe next year's accounts will be very very lean.[37]

But it makes it difficult for Chamberlain.

---

[36] To Joan Davidson, 6–7 March 1932: 'I do admire him as a King: he does his duty as he sees it up to 100 per cent.' Baldwin had been to the Palace for 'a most interesting and confidential talk with the King, on family matters'.

[37] Chamberlain and Baldwin were also agreed that income tax should not be reduced until the other half of the 1931 measures, the spending cuts, could be reversed: this was achieved in 1934–5.

You may take it from me that if there is a substantial surplus, which we don't know yet and which I consider doubtful, he will be extremely prudent in his recommendations.

I only say this lest you should be worrying yourself: and there is certainly nothing to worry about now, nor I believe . . . there will be.

Yours always/ S.B.

De Valera's Fianna Fáil party, committed to revising the 1921 Irish Treaty, won the Irish Free State general election in February, to the alarm of some old Unionists.

3 MARCH 1932: TO SALISBURY

Hatfield House archives 4M/143/81a–b

Private Privy Council Office

My dear Salisbury,

The one good thing about Ireland is that it brings me from time to time letters from you, which afford me the happy opportunity of writing to you.

I don't know that that is a very good sentence, but I like the sentiment!

Now what can I say to allay your anxiety?

De Valera is not yet president. If he is elected, he will have to let out the gunmen.

They will be short of practice and may practise on him.

In which case he will (α) be shot or (β) will have to re-enact the provision he will have repealed.

That dilemma does not affect us.

So, if he is elected President and is <u>not</u> shot, he may abolish the oath. But the Senate will not. Therefore there will be at least a year's delay before anything effective can be done.

And in a year the chances of (α) or (β) happening are pretty good.

If (α) cadit quaestio.[38]

if (β) he is done politically.

And I think that is as far ahead as I can look in Ireland.

---

[38] 'The matter admits of no further argument.'

But you may take it that we have a very effective Cabinet C^tee^ appointed to watch the Irish situation from now on and to meet whenever events in Ireland necessitate counsel and to make recommendations to the Cabinet.

If this enables you to sleep o' nights let me know.

And in any case I am with affection and regard.

S.B./ Lord President of the Council

Let us meet when you return.

Salisbury replied that 'You have sent me a splendid answer . . . Who would have dreamed that your kindly appearance carried the highly tempered metal of a political tactician who shrinks from no speculative chance and even boldly hints at assassination?'[39]

An imperial economic conference was to meet in Ottawa during the summer, with the intention of negotiating trade agreements between Britain, the Dominions and India.

6 MARCH 1932: TO MACDONALD

J. R. MacDonald papers 30/69/678

Secret   Privy Council Office

My dear P.M.

Perhaps during the week you would turn over in your mind the question of personnel for the Ottawa delegation.

I gather that Lausanne will be over before it will be necessary for them to leave England, so the Chancellor will be free to go.

Runciman[40] obviously must go, but he feels strongly that much of the work must be cut and dried before the Conference, or there may be weeks of talk and nothing done.

But this is what worries me. The Chancellor is very anxious that I should go and head the deputation. I needn't point out to you the reactions if that were done. Personally I am not keen on going, but of course I would if it were thought desirable, if the House had risen, and if you could spare me.

[39] Salisbury to Baldwin, 7 March 1932, SB papers 101/249, and see Jones DL, pp. 33–4.
[40] President of the Board of Trade; now a 'Liberal National', allied with Simon.

There are certain obvious drawbacks to the Secretary of State for the Dominions leading the team with which you are familiar.[41] Unfortunately, after the dinner to John Anderson last Monday, Thomas stayed on with Ferguson[42] and two or three others, and there was a bit of a row: Ferguson threatened to report Thomas' behaviour and remarks to him to the Canadian government, and Austen intervened as the heavy father to restore peace. My informant was Camrose who was present. As I said, it was an unfortunate incident.

If I went out, I don't know what Thomas would say, but no one can reasonably object to being second string to an ex P.M. And it might make for peace. But I only want you to have all these things in your mind.

Go or stay, I will do what you, after reflection, wish me to do. And don't trouble to put anything in writing. We can talk it over when you return.

I was thankful to hear (via Duff) a good report from Horder of the eye.

I am lunching at the Inner Temple to-day so the legal profession bear me no malice!

I had nearly an hour on Friday with Norman and was glad to see him looking well. He says he has plenty of troubles but no worries now that the gold standard is gone!

Yours ever/ S.B.

Lloyd George had been seriously ill since July 1931, and Churchill had been injured in a traffic accident in New York in December. Baldwin commented on 23 March: 'The party is holding together and there hasn't been any trouble to speak of. Winston has just returned and Ll.G. is coming back, so we shall have to keep our eyes skinned.'[43]

APRIL 1932 HINCHINGBROOKE DIARY

Lord Sandwich papers

S.B. after the publication of Lloyd George's book 'The Truth about War Reparations and War Debts'[44] – 'I shall regret all my life allowing Bonar to

---

[41] J. H. Thomas, a former trade-union leader and one of MacDonald's Labour allies, was liked for his joviality but (even aside from his drinking and gambling) was not noted for official dignity.
[42] Howard Ferguson, Canadian High Commissioner in London. This incident is also described in *NC Letters*, III, p. 315, and *AC Letters*, p. 408.
[43] To Davidson, Davidson papers 195.
[44] To Joan Davidson, 20–2 March 1932, ibid: 'Ll. G.'s book about debts and reparations is an amazing production. He says among other things that he drafted the Balfour note! His effrontery is beyond words. Of course he had a good go at me. Poincaré and I are his bêtes noirs.'

die without getting out of him what he meant when he said that he had only to speak for ten minutes and Lloyd George would retire for ever from public life'.

2 MAY 1932: TO CHURCHILL

Churchill papers CHAR 1/231/9; *WSC V/2*, p. 424

10, Downing Street

My dear Winston,

I am profoundly touched by your generous appreciation of my work as expressed in your speech at the Academy on Saturday night.[45]

There is so much jealousy in the art world that a kind word to the genre painter from so distinguished an exponent of a far different style shows a breadth of mind as rare as it is delightful.

And I am glad to think that although my own preference is for still life and half-tone, I do enjoy the brighter and sometimes fierce light in which you revel, and no one will be more interested than I when you come to exhibit the work which is still on your easel.

Yours always/ S.B.

In May Baldwin wrote that 'nothing has worried me more than the whole Disarmament question'.[46] He made a considerable effort to produce a basis for effective international disarmament. In Cabinet he proposed that the British government submission to the Geneva Conference should be based on first principles, not the limited suggestions of the defence departments, and it was agreed that his proposals should be discussed informally with representatives of other powers. He himself raised them – and his concerns about the League of Nations doctrine of sanctions against an aggressor nation – with the United States delegates to the Conference. However, his idea of prohibiting military aircraft was resisted by the Air ministry, and that for abolition of battleships by the US State Department. The American 'Hoover Plan' of 22 June diverted discussion into arms *limitation* rather than abolition, though the 'British Plan' announced by Baldwin on 7 July retained a proposed prohibition of aerial attacks on civilians.

---

[45] Churchill had humorously represented Baldwin's politics in a painter's terms: a 'little lacking in colour', but 'very reposeful' in 'his twilight studies in half-tone': Gilbert, *Churchill*, v, pp. 229–30.
[46] To Eden (under-secretary, Foreign Office), 11 May 1932, SB papers 118/177–8.

4 MAY 1932 BALDWIN STATEMENT IN CABINET

Cabinet 26(32)

. . . He felt that all talk of achieving serious results by mere reduction and limitation of air armaments, and more especially by trying to civilize war in the air, was really a waste of time. He had been impressed with the appalling consequences of a future war conducted from the air. If the nations were serious on the question of Disarmament they ought to agree to scrap all military and naval aviation. Civil aviation also would have to be dealt with, perhaps by abolishing the costly subsidies devoted to this purpose. He was quite aware that his proposal was not likely to be accepted by foreign nations, and perhaps not by his colleagues. He emphasised, however, the impossibility of stopping the horrors of war once war had begun, as proved by our own experience. If his proposal should prove feasible it would remove one of the main elements of that <u>fear</u> that was such a disturbing feature in the international situation today. He realised that his proposal would evoke much opposition, especially from the young men, to whom air forces were attractive. If they rejected it they must not complain that the next war was an 'old man's war'. He had been forced to the present conclusion as he saw no other way out of the difficulty . . .

11 MAY 1932 BALDWIN STATEMENT IN CABINET

Cabinet 27(32)

. . . The Lord President of the Council pointed out the extent to which the various forms of disarmament were linked together. For example, the size of Capital ships depended to a great extent on the necessity of protecting them against Submarines and air bombers. The Italians refused to abolish Submarines unless Capital Ships were also abolished. If, therefore, it was possible, by abolishing military and naval aircraft, to make an offer greatly to reduce the size of Capital Ships in return for the abolition of Submarines, great results might be achieved. A reduction in the size of the Capital Ship would affect coastal defences and the size of new docks, and if Submarines were abolished, he gathered that the abolition of the laying of contact mines in the open sea would also be acceptable to the Navy. His proposal opened up the prospects of great economies at a time when the world could not afford their existing expenditure, and he thought the time was not far distant when the nations might be willing to listen to such proposals . . .

13 MAY 1932 HUGH GIBSON NOTE

telegram from Mellon to the Acting Secretary of State, in *Foreign Relations of the United States (FRUS), 1932* (Washington, 1948), I, pp. 121–5 (extract)

At half-past five yesterday afternoon Davis and I[47] called upon Mr Baldwin and Sir John Simon at the former's room in the House of Commons . . .

Mr Baldwin . . . said very definitely that Great Britain was not going to take on fresh commitments of any character and he and Sir John developed this idea along the lines . . . that in honoring its signature England had paid heavily in coming to the help of Belgium and that this made British governments extremely careful about any further undertakings; that in the Locarno agreements there had been a precise and limited liability, and that this had been recognized by the French as the liquidation of the security problem; that now the French were talking about a 'Mediterranean Locarno' as they did at the London Naval Conference but the British Government considered this a totally different matter as the obligations would be much broader in scope and more difficult to specify and that they were both convinced that nothing along the line of a 'Mediterranean Locarno' or other European agreement could be undertaken by Great Britain; whereas they would have the greatest sympathy toward any efforts among the various groups of powers on the Continent to organize peace among themselves.

Mr Baldwin then said that one question which would always come up in connection with any security agreement would be the possible course of the American Government as regards trade with an aggressor. He felt that provisions for economic sanctions and blockade were the greatest defect in the League Covenant and that agitation for recourse to these measures made him impatient; that he felt that sanctions of this sort were practically equivalent to war, and in talking of blockade we were not talking of realities, as blockade was really a thing of the past. However in conversation the question came up as to whether the fundamental purpose might not

---

[47] Mellon was the US Ambassador in London; Gibson and Norman Davis were the US representatives at the Disarmament Conference.

be achieved by prohibition of imports which coupled with prohibition of export of arms and munitions, would have the tendency to shut off trade entirely without need for the navy to enforce it. Mr Baldwin said it was a matter of indifference how our cooperation was achieved but that American cooperation was essential to any general movement for the long term peace.

Mr Baldwin then said that he was going to be thoroughly indiscreet in confidence; that he had given a great deal of thought to the whole subject of disarmament, as he felt the course we were now following was straight toward the destruction of our civilization and that something radical had to be done about it unless we were all going down together; that he did not believe there was anything to be accomplished by 'pecking at the problem' as the Conference was doing, and that we ought at least to try to agree upon some comprehensive and drastic measures fair to everybody, and then make a definite united drive to secure their adoption. He said that the plan he had in mind after hearing all the arguments for and against, was:

(1) the total abolition of military aviation including pursuit and observa-
    tions planes;
(2) some agreement to put a stop to subsidies for civil aviation enterprises;
(3) abolition of the capital ship;
(4) abolition of the aircraft carrier, which would follow automatically from
    item 1;
[(5) abolition of submarines]
(6) drastic reduction of land effectives;
(7) abolition of aggressive weapons such as heavy mobile guns and tanks.

He said that he realized that this was a revolutionary proposal but that whenever these items were attacked separately they were either opposed *in toto* or their acceptance made contingent on drastic dealing with some other item and that under this method we might go on for years without getting anywhere; whereas the world situation called for action now. He said that he realized the abolition of the capital ship would be shocking to us as it was to many people in this country, but he felt the continued possession of these vessels by the great naval powers was an insurmountable obstacle to securing action in regard to other categories which we all desired, and he put it forward in his own name but with a real belief that it contained the only method by which we could hope to rise to the situation. He said that he hoped we would consider this plan bearing in mind that while some of the features were very distasteful to us they constituted the price we should have to pay for any real relief. He felt the prohibitive cost of replacing these vessels doomed them to early disappearance and that as all our governments were under tremendous pressure to reduce expenditures it would be the part of wisdom to secure the strategic advantage which would come from their present abolition in order to force a general reduction. He repeated that he felt the only hope lay in a united and determined front on the part of our two countries to put over a comprehensive program. If we were successful it would be a long step toward world recovery and if we failed we should have to go back 'to scratching at the surface of the problem' as we were now doing, but at least we should have demonstrated our honesty. He spoke with great emphasis and obvious sincerity. He said he quite realized that we could not express an opinion on a proposal of this sort but hoped that we would send it [home] and bespeak consideration of it.[48]

19 JUNE 1932: TO MACDONALD

J. R. MacDonald papers 30/69/678/177–8

11, Downing Street

My dear P.M.

I am grateful for your letter which gave me just what I wanted, the atmosphere in which you had to start your work. I am following, as well as I am able, all that is going on both at Lausanne and Geneva.[49]

We have had a very busy week here and got through well. The Ottawa and Irish days were quite good days for us. Thomas did well on Ireland: he had taken great pains and after the inevitable funereal start he made the case clearly and dispassionately.

L.G. began by saying how odd it was that though elected to oppose the government, his first action in the new Parliament was to bless it. At

---

[48] The US State Department was much disturbed by these suggestions, and only gradually realised that these were not formal proposals: see the acrimonious Stimson–Gibson exchanges in *FRUS 1932*, I, pp. 163–8.

[49] The Lausanne conference negotiated the end of German reparations. For much of June and early July MacDonald, Simon, Chamberlain and the service ministers were at one or other of these conferences, leaving Baldwin to supervise much of their London work. On 1 July he acted for Chamberlain in making the broadcast announcement of the momentous war loan conversion.

that point I ejaculated with deep feeling 'Hard luck!' and the little sinner collapsed with mirth.

He looks the picture of health, is the colour of a coconut and will have to bury us all.

We have a vote of Censure on Thursday when I shall do my best to hold the fort and on Saturday I have an open air meeting at Sheffield.

And I am attending a luncheon of the lobby journalists and addressing a group of young members at dinner, so I may fairly be said to be warming both hands before the fire of life.

I forgot to say that Winston had prepared a powerful speech on Ireland but found his thunder stolen by L.G. whereupon he decided not to speak.

But when Lansbury sat down, he found a quarter of an hour left and he couldn't resist it. So he just had time to describe Cripps's speech as 'loathsome' and to tell Lansbury he had been most offensive the other day and to slobber over L.G. before the umpire called over and stumps were drawn.

I shall be glad when you are all back: the Cabinet is a sad sight these days and so is the front bench. And a Cabinet without Hankey seems unreal.

Donald Maclean's death was unexpected. I saw his son on Friday morning and he told me that the doctors did not anticipate death: they thought a couple of months of complete rest would put him right. He didn't suffer at all . . .[50]

I hope you will keep an open mind as to his successor till you return. No one expects you to act till then and you have Samuel, Simon and Neville at your elbow so no interest is unrepresented! Anyway I beg you won't commit yourself until you have seen me.

Of course I shall be quite satisfied with whatever you decide to do in communicating with the Americans. You have a microcosm of the Cabinet with you and you can judge where you are better than we can in London.

As to disarmament, I expected that the response would be as you reported. But I am not at all sure that the shock that such proposals coming

[50] Maclean had been President of the Board of Education since August 1931. He was replaced by Irwin, increasing the Conservative representation in Cabinet. Jones *DL*, pp. 44–5, has Baldwin's thoughts on the re-shuffle.

from us would make wouldn't be a good thing for the statesmen of Europe!

I am just off to Maclean's memorial service at St Margarets'

Greetings to you all/ Ever yours/ S.B.

From mid July to late August Baldwin was in Ottawa as leader of the British delegation to the Imperial Economic Conference. The Dominion governments were tougher in the negotiation of adjustments in their tariffs than the British delegates had expected. Mackenzie King had been replaced as Canadian prime minister by R. B. Bennett, who incurred the anger of some British newspapers (and, privately, the British delegates) by his fierce defence of Canadian commercial interests.

1 AUGUST 1932 MACKENZIE KING DIARY

. . . Baldwin agreed with me that he might be called upon to take office again [as prime minister], he was not sure tho' that at his age 67 he had not reached the time he should leave the task to younger men. He spoke of not having the energy to get about, he would like to have some opportunity for reading & reflection before the end came. He had been twice P.M. which was 'pretty good'. He told me of feeling he should agree to accept office in a national govt. when the King asked him to do so on the Monday morning at Buckingham Palace. He said without doubt England wd. have had a panic & a crisis if she had gone off the gold standard, as she certainly would have in the course of a general election. He spoke of Ramsay MacDonald leaving ministers a free hand, except foreign minister, that he feared strained relations might come between Simon and Ramsay, their minds were so completely different on many things. Ramsay liked the European side of things and handled them very well . . . He agreed that France had been ungrateful and was difficult . . . He thought Amery had made a mistake in coming out, that it was most undignified for him to have done so. He Baldwin had not found it possible to talk with him, save for half an hour on the ship.[51]

---

[51] Amery had received no post in the National government. Baldwin told him that MacDonald had objected to the inclusion of such a doctrinaire protectionist; but see NC Letters, III, p. 288, for 'no one' having any belief in his judgement. Amery travelled to the Ottawa Conference as a representative for various business groups, including the Central Chamber of Agriculture.

Re the Conference matters, I spoke about not liking bargaining – that attitude was more important. I gathered from Baldwin tho' he was most guarded that the most he was expecting was a declaration for gradual lowering of tariffs within Empire. That their problem was 'unemployment', that if in a year or two employment bettered the Conference wd. have been a success; if it became no better, it was hard to say what might result. The Nat'l Govt. would perhaps then go to pieces & old controversy of free trade vs. protection reassert itself.

1 AUGUST 1932: TO DAVIDSON

Davidson papers 195

Imperial Economic Conference 1932, United Kingdom
Delegation, Parliament Buildings, Ottawa

My dear old David,

Thank you so much for your letters. Geoffrey Dawson who is due in London on Sunday or Monday can give you a good account of everything here if you happen to be in London for a day and can catch him.

I think the most serious work should be finished by about the 11th or 12th when most of the hangers-on can be despatched home. I don't think we shall do more than lay foundations but I hope that may be done effectively. It is the first time we have all been able to talk over everything with complete freedom, tariffs always having been banned before. As a result everyone has learned a lot, not least the Dominions. All that will be to the good in the future.

I have just had an hour with Bennett: he is drafting a letter to me in which he proposes to define the Canadian offer and it is to be ready by Wednesday. By then we shall know where we are vis-à-vis all the dominions and India, and in the next few days we shall have to decide what we do. After that, the sooner we wind up the better.

I shall have a lot of funny things to tell you. Our Civil Service is wonderful and they are the admiration of all. I hope that is true of the delegates too!

We are still a happy family and pulling well together.

You would revel in the country round here. Bless you.

Ever yours/ S.B.[52]

---

[52] Further extracts from these letters to Davidson are in M&B, pp. 677–82.

5 AUGUST 1932: TO R. B. BENNETT

Bennett papers, 944/596327

<u>Personal & Confidential</u>   United Kingdom Delegation

My dear Prime Minister,

Neither I nor any of my colleagues had seen the blackguardly article about you in the London 'Star' when we met yesterday.

I speak for myself and for each of us when I tell you that we are ashamed that such stuff should appear in an English paper and my personal hope is that it will affect you as little as I am affected by my Lord Beaverbrook.

I think the latter's sponsorship of you has stirred the bile of the liberal press in London and a storm in the inkpot has been the result.

I am, with much regard,/ Very sincerely yours/ Stanley Baldwin

[AUGUST 1932] BRUCE MEMORANDUM

Cecil Edwards, *Bruce of Melbourne* (1965), pp. 209–10 (extract)

... Baldwin, who was leading the United Kingdom delegation, asked me to see him alone and, although all our preliminary discussions and those at Ottawa had been based on the assumption that Britain would agree to a duty on meat, he then told me that the U.K. Government could not do so.

I said: 'Well, I'm frightfully sorry, but this was absolutely fundamental to our coming to Ottawa. There is nothing for it but for me to take my delegation home forthwith'.

Baldwin then began to talk to me as one ex-Prime Minister to another. He pointed out the extreme delicacy in which the Empire stood at the moment. We had got the Irish there, and India, which had just achieved financial autonomy. If one of the old Dominions like Australia suddenly got up and went away, it would wreck the entire conference – if not the Empire, he said. We talked for a long time. I condemned the treachery of the U.K. Government in having misled us. Baldwin's only defence was that the British Government was a composite one, with Liberal and Labour representation, and that it was impossible to get agreement on a duty. I said they had known that all along. To have misled us into believing that they would put a duty on meat was an absolute outrage.

Finally, however, I agreed not to withdraw the Australian delegation and to try to vamp up some scheme to overcome the difficulty. There was a big party on that night. I didn't go, but stayed up most of the night working on a quota plan.

Two days after my interview with Baldwin, Neville Chamberlain sent for me, said that Runciman, the Liberal leader, would not permit a duty on meat, and used the same arguments as Baldwin had about breaking up the Empire.

By this time, I had had about enough of it. I told him of my interview with Baldwin (at which he expressed surprise) and said that I had worked out a compromise quota scheme. I said: 'I saved the bloody Empire on Monday. It's your turn to save it now' . . .

15 AUGUST 1932: TO DAVIDSON

Davidson papers 195

United Kingdom Delegation

My dear David,

. . . The last few days have been days of constant anxiety, fresh and unexpected demands appearing and difficulties cropping up.

Amery has done his best to stiffen some of the dominions delegates in their attitude and has generally been a first class impediment to progress.

Neville is perhaps carrying the burden and very well he does it. It is a sacred task to him and I am sure he feels he is labouring in his father's presence.

All however are working in unison and well.

I can't say how it may turn out: it looks better than on Saturday and that's all. But Saturday was a black day.

We don't expect to leave here except just to catch the boat.

The heat has some back and last night we worked for $2\frac{1}{2}$ hours after dinner and the sweat ran down! But all that is nothing to your time in India which would have killed me!

Ever yours/ S.B.

The 'Ottawa Agreements' consisted of bilateral trade arrangements among the various imperial governments, not a common imperial tariff as had once been proposed. Baldwin's conclusion was that 'Ottawa was just in time and only just' for keeping the Empire together.[53] While the Baldwins were on their French holiday,[54] the Samuelite Liberals and Snowden told MacDonald that they could not accept the Ottawa Agreements, and had to consider resignation. The Baldwins again motored back by stages, reaching London on 25 September.

12 SEPTEMBER 1932: TO MACDONALD

copy, SB papers 167/189–90; G. M. Young, *Baldwin*, pp. 171–2

Aix-les-Bains

My dear P.M.

First, my sympathy is with you: I will not express my feelings in a letter, but I shall have plenty to say. First, don't worry. You are bound to carry on. The many questions arising can be discussed during the autumn, but your duty is straight & clear. You must stick to the ship till we are in calmer waters. Secondly, something is due to your loyal supporters. You must hold up the resignations for a fortnight. I have never bothered you about the House, but it doesn't run itself & you need plenty of vitality to face it day in & day out. I have had 10 days here, my first clear holidays for two years, & if you can't give me till the end of next week, I can't guarantee the necessary steam for the job nor the calmer judgement that only comes with an untired mind. Neville, on whom the brunt of Ottawa debates must fall, was done in when we returned: & if he can't have a decent rest you will only have him laid up with gout at some critical moment. Half the mistakes from 1918 on have been the work of tired men. Run no risks for the sake of a few days. I was going to have returned on Oct. 2. I will be with you on Sunday week the 25th. A sudden return makes everyone yell 'crisis'.

I see all the difficulties, but though the boat may rock when our allies jump off, it may well sail henceforward on a more even keel.

I will write in a few days when I have thought a bit.

Yours always/ S.B.

---

[53] To Lord Lothian, 4 Sept. 1932, Lothian papers GD 40/17/261/39. See also Jones *DL*, pp. 49–51.

[54] Jones, as well as the Davidsons, joined them for part of the time: see ibid., pp. 52–63, for his holiday conversations with Baldwin.

25 SEPTEMBER 1932: TO NEVILLE CHAMBERLAIN

NC 7/11/25/4

11, Downing Street

My dear Neville

Here I am again, robbed of my last week by those – – –.[55]

Don't dream of coming up until you are obliged. It will be time enough for our talk later in the week.

I have had a wonderful holiday and I hope you have. We could both of us have done with a bit more.

I am grateful for your letter: the names you mention I should certainly suggest.

But enough till we meet. Enjoy another 48 hours of freedom.

Yours ever/ S.B.

At the Cabinet on 28 September the free trade ministers resigned. The readiness of the Simonite Liberals to stay in office and Baldwin's firm support persuaded MacDonald that the National government should continue under his premiership. While remaining Lord President, Baldwin replaced Snowden as Lord Privy Seal (without salary). He was asked to speak to a movement within the Church of England.

24 OCTOBER 1932: TO LADY BRIDGEMAN

Bridgeman papers 4929/1/1932/69

House of Commons

My dear Lady,

You gave me one of the most difficult questions to answer that I have had for a long time and the fact that you asked me made it far more difficult to decide because I would strain my conscience a good way to do what you want.

But I cannot speak for you at Queen's Hall.

You say I have addressed Nonconformists and so I have, two or three times, on general subjects. I would address in like manner a Church Assembly, or even more specifically if I were asked: I wouldn't mind talking on any

---

[55] *Sic*: expletive omitted.

individual life and its influence or any religious movement and its influence or anything of that sort.

But here I should be speaking at a gathering of Church people in support of a present day movement in the Church itself.

Now the movement may be a good one and I think it is, but I am not in it nor of it, nor am I likely to be. I fear I am a Churchman in little more than name and I should not feel I should be honest either to myself or to the audience if I stood up and addressed them on such an occasion as this would be, and on such a topic.

These reasons are for your eye and I shall tell Underhill[56] that I cannot undertake it with all the work I have on hand. But I think I owe it to you to tell you frankly how I regard it.

I may be wrong – I always admit that! – but I can only act according to my lights even if they seem dim to others.

All my hesitation has come from these uncomfortable feelings and my only distress is that they lead me to do something that will disappoint you and that you may not understand.

But there it is. And I will still sign myself, if I may, with affection and true regard

S.B.

26 OCTOBER 1932: TO SIR JOHN SIMON

amended draft, SB papers 167/252–3

My dear Simon,

At Blackpool on the 7th October[57] I ventured to make some observations upon the part which you and those who act with you have played in recent events, ~~in contrast to the partisan adherence to obsolete dogma by Samuel and his friends.~~

The assurance that I gave that none of those who supported the Ottawa Bill right through should suffer was received with enthusiastic cheers by the great audience – a large proportion of which were accredited representatives of the Conservative Party drawn from practically every constituency. While I can give no guarantee that will bind individual constituencies, for

[56] Perhaps the Very Revd Francis Underhill, Dean of Rochester, an Anglo-Catholic.
[57] Conservative party annual conference.

democracy is a reality in the Conservative Party and each constituency is a law unto itself, I believe that I am entitled to assume that support will be forthcoming for those Liberal members of parliament who are prepared to give consistent support to the Government. On that basis I can assure you that I, as Leader of the Party, and the Chairman, who directs the Conservative Party headquarters, will exercise all the influence and authority we possess to see that those who play a patriotic part ~~are not thrown to the wolves~~ receive the full support of our party in the constituencies which they now represent.

Yours very sincerely/ S.B.

Discussions at the Disarmament Conference had become stuck in the details of arms limitation, and in October were overtaken by the German government claim for 'equality' in armaments (i.e. its own rearmament). In the House of Commons on 10 November Baldwin attempted to revive one of his basic principles, using the striking phrase 'the bomber will always get through' to try and shock domestic and international opinion – especially among the idealistic young – into seriously addressing the problems of aerial disarmament. Ponsonby, Labour leader in the House of Lords and a leading peace campaigner, wrote to thank him for his 'remarkable speech' because 'people will listen to you and your appeal to youth is badly wanted', the more so because there seemed to be no really promising leaders among them.[58] Baldwin continued to argue in Cabinet for a 'convention prohibiting bombing' during the first half of 1933.

17 NOVEMBER 1932: TO LORD PONSONBY

Ponsonby papers, Ms Eng.Hist. c674/86

11, Downing Street

Dear Ponsonby

Thank you so much for your letter: it was kind of you to write. We have to wait a bit yet for leaders: they were killed off in the war.

I began to find it when I was P.M. in all the appointments I had to make. It is the men in the forties that are missing.

Yours sincerely/ Stanley Baldwin

[58] 11 Nov. 1932, SB papers 167/225.

27 DECEMBER 1932: TO CUNLIFFE-LISTER

Swinton papers 270/3/3

Astley Hall

Dear Philip,

Thank you so much for the cheese which arrived on Christmas Eve and received a warm welcome into the family circle.

I received four beautiful letters on Christmas Day:

1. Pages from Waldorf Astor on America with an offer to drive over from Cliveden with Salter to spend the holy season in talking about America.[59]
2. A long letter from a journalist who is writing a life of Jix and asking to come and see me to spend this holy season in discussing Jix's responsibility for the flapper vote.
3. An invitation to take a big meeting in the Eye division.
4. Do. do. to speak at a trade dinner at the Connaught Rooms because it would be a great help (in some unknown way) to the gentleman who will preside.

Every d— fool in the country seems to be employing his leisure in writing to me!

Blessings on you . . . / Yours ever/ S.B.

14 JANUARY 1933: TO SIR EDWARD ELGAR

Elgar papers 5447/12(iv)4232

11, Downing Street

My dear Sir Edward,

I want you to do something which will give pleasure to a number of people though it may not to you!

Come and dine with the Worcestershire Association on February 22nd and you shall NOT have to speak. We just want to see you among us.

With kindest regards/ Yours sincerely/ Stanley Baldwin

---

[59] Arthur Salter was an economic expert, and former League of Nations official. To Jones, 27 Dec. 1932, in Jones diary: 'Dear Waldorf wants to bring Salter to talk to me about America! The thought of America turns my stomach and the thought of Salter makes me sick . . . On second thoughts I think you ought to burn this!'

15 JANUARY 1933: TO AN AMERICAN AUTOGRAPH HUNTER

typescript copy, SB papers 168/230

11, Downing Street

Dear Sir,

You tell me you have a unique and interesting hobby, that of collecting autographs. Interesting it may be: unique I fear it is not.

I wish it were.

I am, dear Sir/ Faithfully yours/ Stanley Baldwin

Austen Chamberlain forwarded an invitation to address a League of Nations Union meeting in Birmingham, commenting that he would not be offended if Baldwin excused himself.

17 FEBRUARY 1933: TO AUSTEN CHAMBERLAIN

A. Chamberlain papers 40/5/13

11, Downing Street

My dear Austen,

I had hoped to have a word with you in the House about your letter. I am grateful to you for the way you put it.

I should be reluctant to add to my work by an extra speech on Saturday night: but further than that, I have always avoided these meetings of the League, except one which I addressed at the Albert Hall – or maybe two. There is so much I dislike in the Union propaganda and I should have to steer between the Scylla of cursing them and the Charybdis of mush and poppycock, and I might be wrecked on either!

So I will beg you to say how I recognise the honour due me in asking but in view of heavy commitments . . . Thank you.

Yours sincerely/ S.B.

In anticipation of a government white paper on Indian policy, Conservative opponents of a federal constitution were organising themselves. These included the Duchess of Atholl, an MP and former junior minister, who had acted as hostess to Baldwin during several of his Scottish speaking tours. Hoare was now Secretary of State for India.

23 FEBRUARY 1933: TO THE DUCHESS OF ATHOLL

Duchess of Atholl papers, bundle 72; Hetherington, *Katharine Atholl*, p. 143

Private
My dear Kitty,

I am sorry that you are perturbed but I am not surprised. The whole Indian question is the gravest and most difficult with which the government has to grapple.

I hear that the deputation of which you spoke had a couple of hours with Sam Hoare, but I fear that you were unable to accompany them.

I have always felt that it was inevitable that there would be a real honest difference of opinion in our party and that that difference would be expressed ultimately in the lobby.

It cannot from the nature of the case be otherwise.

I write frankly to you as an old friend for whom I have a true affection and a high regard.

You will not expect me to write a long letter of an argumentative nature: you will I know act as you believe to be right and honest and whatever you do, I shall take no exception to it.

There will be several days of debate before the Joint Committee is set up, and the final votes on the resulting Bill will not be required for many months.

For myself, I view the future with some apprehension and doubt: but my doubts and apprehension would be increased many times if the course advocated by Mr Churchill or any of his friends was taken.

I am with affection and much regard.

Your friend/ Stanley Baldwin

P. S. I was so sorry not to accept your invitation for to-night but though we are unexpectedly on the adjournment, I have a heap of arrears both of letters to write and papers to read. The past month has been a ceaseless round of Cabinet committees.

S.B.

10 MARCH 1933 BALDWIN STATEMENT IN CABINET

Cabinet 16 (33)

. . . As a Conservative his fundamental creed was the preservation of the Empire and some curious things had been done in relation to the white parts of the Empire by such Imperialists as the late Lord Balfour and

Mr Amery.[60] The present proposals for India might save India to the Empire, but if they were not introduced we should certainly lose it. The situation was full of dangers and difficulties, but these were greater if action were not taken.

Cecil wrote on the increasing difficulties at the Geneva Conference. In January Hitler had been elected Chancellor of Germany.

12 MARCH 1933: TO LORD CECIL

Cecil of Chelwood papers Add. Mss 51080/246

Private   11, Downing Street

My dear Bob,

Thanks for your letter. I don't think an Archangel could do much at Geneva at the moment. The European atmosphere since the German elections has deteriorated rapidly.

The French are in a panic: the Germans won't go to Geneva, and my unhappy colleagues are faced with an almost impossible situation.

The Americans are so immersed in their own trouble as to be completely useless in international matters.

Ever yours/ S.B.

During 1933 and 1934 Baldwin and Hankey were responsible for Cabinet Office vetting of the drafts of Lloyd George's *War Memoirs*. This, and the gift of inscribed copies of the published volumes, produced a series of friendly letters from Baldwin which much pleased Lloyd George. He had already received an impression that Baldwin 'would like to work with him'.[61]

19 APRIL 1933: TO LLOYD GEORGE

Lloyd George papers G/1/15/2

Trent, New Barnet

My dear Lloyd George,

I took your typescript up to London yesterday and left it with the secretary at No.10 with instructions to deliver safely to wherever Sylvester wished it to go.

[60] These had been chiefly responsible for the formula which at the 1926 Imperial Conference defined the Dominions as autonomous and equal in status to Britain within a British Commonwealth.
[61] *Life with Lloyd George. The Diary of A. J. Sylvester 1931–45*, ed. Colin Cross (1975), pp. 93, 95 (30 March, 22 April 1933).

I read every word – carefully, and with the greatest interest.

I think compared with some of our contemporary historians, you have published little in the way of documents, and I agree with Hankey that there is no publication to which exception could be taken.

I thought the Bonar chapter admirable and very fair.[62]

Perhaps you could come to my room one day when you are at the House; I should enjoy a talk about it and I'd rather talk than write.

But it'll sell, and on its merits, and we shall see 'counter-demonstrations'.

Thank you for letting me see it.

Sincerely yours/ Stanley Baldwin

The Baldwins were now so well established as visitors to Aix-les-Bains that their wedding anniversary had become 'a recognized Aix fête', with bouquets of flowers from the mayor and hotel owner, and at dinner a cake with candles and the band playing the wedding march. On the day he left Baldwin wrote that 'Savoy has become a kind of second home. I welcome it with enthusiasm and I always leave it with regret. I leave a little bit of me behind, walking, walking, in the hills.'[63] Irwin wrote to ask if he would speak at a meeting of a religious group.

8 SEPTEMBER 1933: TO IRWIN

Halifax papers A4.410.14.4

Regina Hotel Bernascon, Aix-les-Bains

My dear Edward,

I couldn't do it. I have rashly filled up the time before Parliament meets: I have two broadcasts, and they mean a lot of work; speech at Birmingham to the National Union: visit to Belfast to open a Students' Union at the University, and an address to some association of first division Civil Servants.

I can't think how I let myself in for so much: I always do it.

I am having a wonderful holiday and have seen many beautiful things on my way here.

---

[62] But see Jones *DL*, p. 105 (20 April 1933), for Baldwin commenting that 'there are plenty of backhanders in it' against Grey, McKenna, Samuel and the military chiefs.
[63] To Joan Davidson, 15 Aug., 14, 18 Sept. 1933.

I wish I had more energy. I thought once I might accomplish something: I have accomplished nothing.

One can't expect to see any result of one's work. I always preached to Winston that you couldn't.

But there are queer questioning moments as you grow older when you are apt to flag.

There is so much I hate in this age, but there is a lot of good and one must hold to it and have faith,

It ain't easy!

Bless you. I shall be glad to see you again.

Yours ever/ S.B.[64]

14 SEPTEMBER 1933: TO JONES

Jones papers A6/2; Jones *DL*, pp. 114–5

Regina Hotel Bernascon, Aix-les-Bains

My dear T. J.

. . . What a holiday I have had! The best and longest ever.

And what beautiful things this world has to show! You must come and see me as soon as I get back which I hope will be the 23rd. I have that wretched broadcast on the 27th. and I can't for the life of me get started on it. I wish you were here to talk it over.

Walking alone among these hills I have come to the conclusion the world is stark mad. I have no idea what is the matter with it but it's all wrong and at times I am sick to death of being an asylum attendant.

I think we are the sanest but the disease is catching.

I always dreaded Roosevelt's experiments and I think there will be an appalling mess up in America in a few months.

I hope to have three nights with Tyrrell on the way home to get myself familiar with the latest European developments.

I have walked hard and bathed nearly every day and am, so far as I know, as fit physically as I ever was.

---

[64] Irwin replied that 'I wish more people had your background of faith' to resist the 'temptation to flag': 21 Sept. [1933], SB papers 168/111.

My word! I have to get some money. I forgot all about it and I must fly before the Bank closes. Farewell, dear man.

Yours ever/ S.B.

In Paris Baldwin 'had long talks with Tyrrell . . . all very depressing. He agrees with me that the world is mad.'[65] He also joined Simon, Eden, and Tyrrell at a meeting with the French ministers Daladier, Paul-Boncour, Léger and Massigli to discuss a proposed security convention to help advance disarmament.[66] Baldwin's broadcast (actually on the 25th, for which Reith sent him a small fee) was to open a series by the historian Arthur Bryant on 'national character'. He used the opportunity to evoke democratic values as against those of dictatorship: ordered freedom, mutual service, respect for law and the individual. At the annual Conservative party conference in Birmingham on 6 October he spoke of the possible breakdown of the Disarmament Conference, and in a political broadcast on the 12th declared that one-sided disarmament could not continue. Germany left the Disarmament Conference and the League of Nations two days later. In November the Cabinet established the Defence Requirements Committee, to prepare for rearmament. Later in the month, Baldwin twice met Hitler's representative, Ribbentrop, who invited him to meet Hitler in Berlin. But Baldwin preferred that any discussions should be conducted through the Foreign Office; the visit to Berlin was made by Eden.[67]

28 SEPTEMBER 1933: TO REITH

Reith papers

11, Downing Street

My dear Reith,

How can I fail to acknowledge – and with gratitude – the first money I have earned since December '16, save only the beggarly pittance I receive quarterly from a grudging taxpayer?

I am as proud as Punch and wondering how I can best lay out my windfall!

Yours always sincerely/ Stanley Baldwin

---

[65] To Joan Davidson, 21 Sept. 1933. Tyrrell was now ambassador in Paris.
[66] See report in *DBFP* (2s.), v, pp. 618–19.
[67] See the record by the intermediary, E. W. D. Tennant, *True Account* (1957), pp. 164–72. In December Eden succeeded Baldwin in his second post of Lord Privy Seal.

13 OCTOBER 1933: TO JONES

Jones papers A6/73

11, Downing Street

My dear T.J.

I have been expecting daily to hear of you in London but I was wrong, and now learn that you never were coming up this week.

So a most grateful line for your delightful address for Belfast.[68] It is A1. I shall lift the bulk of it bodily! I really am the champion plagiarist: but it will puzzle posterity (if it is interested at all!) to say what is T.J. and what S.B.[69]

Come and see me as soon as you are up.

I hope the P.M. won't have a second Cabinet on Wednesday afternoon.

I do hope the B'ham speech pleased you. It was my very own idea and honestly I don't think it was bad.

Yours ever/ S.B.

The Coopers invited Baldwin to a dinner. Duff Cooper had been the successful candidate at the St George's, Westminster by-election that had been vital in helping Baldwin recover his authority in March 1931.

16 OCTOBER 1933: TO LADY DIANA COOPER

Duff Cooper papers 2/1

11, Downing Street

Dear my Lady,

Duff is right in this that I never dine out when the House is sitting.

And normally the contemplation of many plates of food palls quickly.

And it is noisy and I get all the noise I need in Parliament.

And it is exhausting for I try to play the social game not deeming it right to accept hospitality and give nothing back.

But all this – and much more – is by the way.

---

[68] Baldwin had opened an extension of the Queen's University students' union building, paid for by the Pilgrim Trust.

[69] See, similarly, to Jones, 31 March 1935, Jones papers A6/86, thanking him for a draft for a speech to the National Free Church Council: 'One of your best! The only thing that worries me is that it is too good for me and I don't know how to reduce it to my level.'

And if you say 'come' and mean it, of course I come with pleasure. I owe Duff and you much.

Yours sincerely/ Stanley Baldwin

1 NOVEMBER 1933: TO LLOYD GEORGE

Lloyd George papers G/1/15/3

11, Downing Street

Dear Lloyd George,

I am now the proud possessor of your two first volumes [*sic*] and I am very pleased to have received them from your hands.

I thank you.

Let me congratulate you warmly on your apples. My wife was shewn your Coxes at Harrods by Woodman Burbridge.[70] I expect your soil suits them either naturally or by art. They like a light sandy loam and fellows who stick 'em in a heavy soil which suits many trees find they can't grow the apples.

I wonder in what soil Winston would produce his rarest fruit?

Yours sincerely/ Stanley Baldwin

Hinchingbrooke failed to obtain the nomination as Conservative candidate for the Cambridge by-election.

17 JANUARY 1934: TO HINCHINGBROOKE

Lord Sandwich papers

<u>Private</u>   11, Downing Street

My dear Hinch,

I am very disappointed and I know how you are feeling. Over and above the keen disappointment there is a nasty jar to your pride, a feeling that somehow you have been let down, and a sneaking sympathy with Achilles for retiring to his tent. You know I have been through something not dissimilar.

---

[70] The chairman of Harrods. Lloyd George was developing commercial orchards and horticulture at his small estate at Churt.

When I was beaten at Kidderminster in 1906, I was disappointed not only for myself but for my father who wanted me to be in the House with him so much.

Then Worcester City became vacant, the member being unseated. I thought I was certain to be chosen at once, when a venomous radical moved the suspension of the new writ for a year and it was carried.

I was 39 and felt if I didn't get in quickly it would be too late. The year passed and I went before the selection committee holding my head high.

And they chose an Irishman whom I then thought – and think still – to be vastly my inferior.[71] So I was turned down in my own county town in favour of a stranger and bang went all my hopes.

As you may know my father died suddenly a few months later and the Bewdley division fell into my lap. But at a price I did not contemplate.

I remember vividly how I felt.

But these things are very personal. One's friends know, understand and sympathize.

The world don't care a damn. And one has to bite on it and go about one's job with a cheerful face.

I have been as distressed about this as if it had happened to me: I can't say more.

When you feel ready for it we must try and find a good seat for the general election.

Bless you./ Yours ever/ Stanley Baldwin

Elgar died on 23 February, and Baldwin wrote to his daughter.

25 FEBRUARY 1934: TO MRS BLAKE

Elgar papers 5447/3/(v)890

11, Downing Street

Dear Mrs Blake,

May I offer you my heartfelt sympathy? my thoughts have been much with your father these last weeks.

---

[71] Edward Goulding, Lord Wargrave 1922.

We knew each other but slightly but it was a great happiness to me to get him to the Worcestershire dinner last year where we sat next to each other and had much free and friendly talk. I was always shy about intruding on his privacy – I know what great artists are – but I held him in the greatest regard not only as one of our really great men but for his whole attitude and manner of life.

It was always a pleasure to see him and I valued much the warm handshake and welcoming smile I always had from him.

It would be an impertinence on my part to speak of your own loss, but my father meant much to me and the consciousness of the beloved presence and influence will be with you to the end as the day draws nearer when you will be together again.

Believe me to remain/ Sincerely yours/ Stanley Baldwin

27 FEBRUARY 1934 JONES DIARY

partly in Jones *DL*, pp. 122–4

. . . . T.J.: 'Have you thought lately of taking L.G. into the Government?'

S.B.: 'I have thought of everything.'

T.J.: 'Your talk on Saturday made me very solemn. We are heading for a grave situation when it will be important to have a genuine National government. If we are to re-arm and to avoid trouble in India it might be worth bringing L.G. in.'

SB: 'Do you really think he would work under anybody?'

T.J.: 'He is over 70; he has mellowed; Dawson tells me he has still lots of vitality. He wakes at 5 a.m. and works at his Memoirs. He likes you and will work under you; he won't work with Ramsay.'

S.B.: 'Anthony Eden is doing quite well in his talks in Paris, Berlin and Rome. He has seen Hitler and had a frank talk with him. You know I think Hitler wants peace, but Tyrrell and Vansittart are obsessed with Germany's determination to do us in. That may be true of von Bulow and Neurath, but there are other elements in Germany. There is a bare chance we may get a limitation of armaments, but even so that must mean for us a degree of rearmament as we have ourselves, as we did after the Napoleonic Wars, [become][72] defenceless. Then you have got Russia, Japan, U.S.A. Japan won't

---

[72] Word missing in original.

be bound by any London agreement. She can knock us out in the Pacific and land in Australia. That bletherer, Norman Davis, I see is due here in a day or two, bringing a message from Roosevelt to the P.M., no doubt to justify their Navy and Air building programme. I cannot stand these unctuous Americans, but we have got to reckon with them.'

T.J.: 'Another suggestion is that Bob Cecil should go to the F.O.'

S.B.: 'That would never do; as his uncle said of him, "Bob Cecil is impossible".'

T.J.: 'Well, why not send L.G. to the F. O. It is essential that if he came into the Cabinet he should be fully occupied and the F.O. or Agriculture would satisfy that condition.'

S.B.: 'It would certainly never do for him to be like me, without an office.'

T.J.: 'Elliot's policy is bound to lead to all kinds of difficulties presently, specially with the consumers, and if he is wise he will move from Agriculture. L.G. has long fancied himself as fitted for that office. But there is much to be said for putting him at the F.O. to deal with the scoundrels of Europe. You either want that type at the F.O. or the more saintly type like Grey or Edward Wood.'

S.B.: 'Someone said that the ideal Foreign Secretary is the simple English gentleman, so long as you have got a Tyrrell behind him. Now L.G. is neither simple, nor English, nor a gentleman.'

T.J.: 'Well, I think the opposite ought to be tried at the F.O. You are now in a different position vis-à-vis L.G. from 20 years ago; you are on top and the fires of his ambition have died down; as he is always saying, "I have had my day".'

S.B.: 'Yes, it is an extraordinary situation. In those days I had developed a protective barrage of innocence in the midst of wickedness. I gradually covered myself with stripes in the jungle until I got into a position where I could hurl my pebble and bring him down. Has he any following in the country?'

T.J.: 'I think not, and he would be very unpopular with many in the House.'

S.B.: 'And Labour still distrusts him. I should like to see in any reconstructed Government a strong Labour leader like Bevin.'

T.J.: 'I think bringing in L.G. and Bevin would impress the country with the gravity of the situation and make them realize that we seem to be shaping for another war.'

S.B.: 'I would not put it that way. I would say that we are the only defenders left in a world of Fascists.' . . .

'I have got a good idea for a speech on freedom. I was reading Lecky's *History of Rationalism* on Sunday, and it struck me that a parallel could be drawn between the wars of religion and the wars of politics; that these fascists and communists are the successors today of the wars of the sects. I think it is a parallel that I can work out for the House of Commons if by and by we have a debate on these Hunger Marchers and the coloured shirts . . .'

Baldwin renewed contact with a younger relative, the daughter of a cousin, for whom he had been legal trustee before she became a Roman Catholic nun. She now lived in the English Convent in Bruges as 'Sister Mary Cuthbert'.

26 MAY 1934: TO MONICA BALDWIN[73]

SB add. papers

Albury Park, Guildford

Dearest Monica,

. . . I do remember well a garden at your convent in which we walked long years ago, and if you will walk with me there again, I will if I live, come and see you this very August as ever is!

I have as usual had a very heavy spell of work since my holiday last year, and am spending a few days at Whitsuntide in this most beautiful spot with the Duchess of Northumberland.

Part of the garden was laid out by John Evelyn whose old home of Wootton is quite near, and the soil seems to suit every tree that ever was born. I don't know a more peaceful spot in which to lay up strength for the next two months when we hope to get our holiday.

Those genealogists . . . have been through over a hundred parish registers in Shropshire and still have a number to do.[74] It is tedious waiting so long when the work appears complete but there it is, and you shall hear as soon as I do, I promise you.

---

[73] She later renounced her vows, an experience recorded by her in *I Leap Over the Wall. A Return to the World After Twenty-Eight Years in a Convent* (1949, 1994).

[74] Letters to his cousin Constance Marshall, Baldwin WCRO collection 8229/12(ii), show that in 1930 Baldwin had asked the College of Arms to investigate the Baldwin family pedigree.

I am quite serious about coming to see you. It is too long since we met and there is much I should like to talk about with you.

You know I am 67 this August, though it is hard to realise and I begin to wonder how much longer I can carry the double burden of leading a party and helping to govern the country in a mad, mad world as it is to-day. And I find as the years go by, I feel more drawn to those who are associated with the old days: and of those days your father and Harold are often in my mind . . .

You must forgive a scrawl: I have a good deal to write in these few quiet days, but I have always told you I often think of you and my affection is unchanging. And I love your letters – at any and every time.

Always your loving old/ Uncle Stan

12 JUNE 1934 W. P. CROZIER[75] INTERVIEW NOTES

Crozier papers; partly printed in W. P. Crozier, *Off the Record. Political Interviews 1933–1943*, ed. A. J. P. Taylor (1973), pp. 24–7

Baldwin was in his private room [at the House of Commons]. It communicates with Palace Yard by a narrow little back staircase and a side door, so that it is rather like something out of Dumas. Baldwin's face, seen close to, was most interesting. I had never seen him before, and in his photographs his face had always seemed to be chiefly amiable and a little whimsical, just as his speeches sound simple, honest and ingenuous. Actually he is not like that at all. His face is rugged and nobbly; his right eye is either going wrong or has some sort of a cast in it and was mostly half-shut. But the characteristic of his face is its determination and shrewdness – or rather, because it is much more than shrewdness, a sort of deep rustic craftiness. More than any other politician he reminded me of Lloyd George in this, but while L.G. is gleefully and maliciously cunning, Baldwin seemed to me to look shrewd and crafty in a rather grim and hard way. I got quite a new idea of him and for the first time understood how he had come to be leader of the Tory party and Prime Minister. The good-natured mellow look of the photographs was only there when he greeted me and when he said good-bye, saying that I was to come again whenever I would like a talk. During most of the conversation he tried vainly to light his pipe.

---

[75] Editor of the *Manchester Guardian*, 1932–44.

I had no sooner begun to ask about the Privilege Report[76] than Baldwin turned the conversation on to Lancashire, and began to question me as to what could and should be done with regard to helping the cotton industry. He said he knew about steel but not about cotton. So far as he could see, nothing substantial could be done to assist the cotton industry until it could be got on the lowest practicable competitive basis and of that he gathered there was no prospect. You could do a lot in a case like Japan's, when you were building up an industry from the start, because you then organised it on the best economic basis. But what were you to do in a case like Lancashire with about five different processes all in different hands and all of them, he thought, probably accompanied by their middlemen, he did not know. A reference was made to the anti-Japanese quotas, and he said in a rather slighting tone that anyway quotas were no more than a temporary expedient.

Then we came to the Privilege Report. He said it was a great pity Churchill had not decided simply to accept it. He would have got a cheer from all sides of the House and the matter would have been finished. But, said Baldwin with much energy, Churchill was going to do nothing of the kind. He laughed and said it was reported that Churchill had sometime ago prepared two speeches – one in case the report went in his favour and the other in case it went against him, and that the latter was much the more bitter of the two. As to the publication of evidence, the truth was that the Manchester people themselves did not want the evidence to be printed, with its exposure of their original views and bickerings and changes of front; in fact they wanted the whole thing buried as soon as possible. Churchill would make as much capital as possible out of the thing as part of his general campaign against the Government. He could tell me something about Churchill. In 1929, after the Conservative defeat, the Tory leaders had been in the habit of meeting in committee to frame a policy with a view to the next election. They decided that they would advocate duties on meat – or it might have been wheat, he was not sure which – Churchill had refused to agree to this and had walked out from among them. That was all right, but what he actually did was to go to Rothermere and Beaverbrook and see what

---

[76] Churchill had caused a House of Commons Privileges Committee to investigate charges that Hoare and Derby, members of the joint select committee on Indian reform, had placed improper pressure on witnesses representing Lancashire cotton interests.

support he could get for his position. Of course on such a point he could not get support from them. He could not very well go back to the Liberals and he did not want to join Labour, so after a week he came back to the Tories in a chastened mood. When, however, the India business came up he thought he saw a great chance and leaped at it, and on this he had at any rate got the support of Rothermere. Incidentally Rothermere and also Lady Houston had provided large sums for Churchill's anti-Government campaign on India.

Baldwin added that Churchill's judgment was always wrong. He said that when Churchill was in the Cabinet with one this was not so disastrous if there was a week or so in which it was possible to delay action and persuade him to change his mind, but if it was a case where action had to be taken at once, then 'eight times out of ten' Churchill's judgment as to what ought to be done was a bad one. Of course it was the fact that the White Paper policy aroused some deep-seated opposition in the Tory mind. I suggested that it was the same as had been the case with Ireland: he replied that he could not admit any analogy with Ireland. He then proceeded to summarise the history of the Irish question; declared that it had been a great misfortune that it had become a purely party question so that each side was absolutely rigid, and the result in Ireland ultimately was revolt and civil war. He had all that in mind with regard to India and it had been his object throughout to put the Indian question on a non-party national plane. It had been a disappointment to him that Labour split over the National Government so that now he had on the side of the National Government 'only about half a dozen of these fellows'. I suggested to him that anyway Labour supported and would support the White Paper policy, and he said yes, of course, only it did not go far enough for them. Nevertheless he would like to have had Labour co-operating in the whole thing.

I inquired about the coming struggle in the Tory party about India, and whether the moderate centre Tories like Derby and Austen would carry the day. He said they were very important and without being positive he gave the impression that things would come out all right. He said he really did not know what Derby thought about the White Paper policy. He had never asked him and did not know. His impression was that when Derby joined the Select Committee he had no particular views at all about India – except that his job was to look after Lancashire's interests. Churchill, he thought, had no great following outside London and the Home Counties.

He did not cut much ice in the North of England: he was thinking particularly, he said, of Northumberland and the North East coast. He thought it was very important that Churchill in recent times had acquired no big recruits at all for his agitation; least of all from the ranks of people who had been in India and knew it. He was himself much impressed, he said, by the fact that every experienced person coming from India, including even soldiers (who were in the ordinary way of a Tory and no-surrender disposition) told him that we must persevere with the White Paper policy. Even Sir Philip Chetwode, the Commander-in-Chief, told him the same story. Chetwode had said to him that today he could hold India with the present British Army, but that if the White Paper policy was scrapped he would have to ask for twice the present strength. When one told the Die-Hards that the Indian soldiers took this view, the Die-Hards rejoined that the soldiers had to or they would lose their jobs. When you asked them if they meant to apply this to Chetwode they merely shook their shoulders and could not answer.

He then went on to say that he thought a good deal of the bitterness of the Die-Hard agitation was due to Lord Sumner,[77] who died a few weeks ago. He had been a Liberal and, having been converted to Toryism, had become thoroughly narrow and bigoted. I asked him about Lord Lloyd and he said 'A much over-rated person'. I said at any rate Lloyd had held some high offices; and he replied 'Not in this country. He was five years Governor of Bombay and two or three years in Egypt; Austen Chamberlain nearly recalled him, and Arthur Henderson did'. He then went on to say, what Hoare had said to me, that Lloyd had been intending to exploit the Privilege bomb himself, 'and now Churchill has anticipated him, they will scarcely speak to each other'.

In this connection I asked him where Lloyd George stood, and he said he did not exactly know: 'He keeps a free hand. He is very busy with his books, getting up early and working hard at them. He has made a lot of money out of them. They are well-written too, the last two not quite as well as the first two (a curious slip, as L.G. has only published two altogether).[78] Of course he makes out that no one thought of anything or did anything right except

---

[77] A Lord of Appeal 1913–30, thereafter active in Conservative politics in the House of Lords.
[78] Baldwin was, however, reading volumes in proof, sent by Lloyd George in advance of the publication of the third and fourth volumes in September and October 1934.

himself. I like the little man, but I cannot work with him. I got Hankey, by the way . . . to 'vet' those two volumes to see what Cabinet memoranda L.G. had used, but it was pretty well all right. About India L.G. is on the wrong track. He says that we ought to deal with Gandhi because it is no use dealing with anyone who cannot deliver the goods. He says this because he thinks that with regard to Ireland he himself dealt with the people – Michael Collins, etc. – who could deliver the goods. There are two objections to this policy in India. First of all that Gandhi is an impossible person to deal with and, secondly, that he cannot deliver the goods anyway. There are three people, you know, who are impossible to deal with – De Valera, Gandhi and Beaverbrook.' (To these he afterwards added Poincaré.) Baldwin added also with regard to L.G. 'He does not, of course, count for much in this present House of Commons'.

Then, speaking of the White Paper policy in general, he said that the Government meant to go on with it and would put it through. Of course there was a great risk and it was quite possible that it might fail. It was possible that instead of the Federal Constitution which we were going to give to India, India might develop a quite different form of Government eventually which was better suited to her character. Everything said to him by people who knew India indicated that it was changing at a tremendous pace. To give only one illustration, the way in which women had been coming out of their seclusion and plunging more and more openly into political life was amazing. People here – I think he had his Tory dissidents in mind – did not at all realise what sort of India it was with which we had now to deal. 'But how was it to be expected of them when they did not even realise the changes that had come and were coming over their own country?'

I asked him about the reports that the recommendations of the Select Committee and the Bill would be postponed. He said that he thought we should get the recommendations in October. He was very thankful himself that they were not going to come out in July. If they had, he would have been unable to call the meeting of the National Union of Conservative Associations, which he had promised to consult, until the autumn, and all the Churchill critics would have been free to carry on a raging campaign of attack during the summer months, nor would it have been possible to have a big debate in the House in July in order to steady opinion in the Tory party. If, on the other hand, the Select Committee reported in October, there would then be a discussion in the House and he would be able without delay to summon the National Union and to discuss the matter with them. This, he thought, offered a very much more satisfactory prospect.

Finally I asked him about foreign politics and air armaments. Was no sort of air convention now practicable and was there no chance of this country agreeing to a scheme of either internationalisation or international control of civilian aircraft as being the only thing that would make the abolition of air forces possible? He said that so far as he knew no scheme for controlling civilian aircraft was practicable, and no country so far as he knew had put forward any practicable scheme. He mentioned that it was he personally who had introduced into the Cabinet the question of disarmament in the air, but he was obviously disappointed about the prospects. He said the up-shot was that we could simply not avoid increasing our own air force. It ought to be realised that the whole situation had been altered for the worse by the rise of the new Germany. 'No one', he said and repeated more than once, 'knows what the new Germany means' – whether she means peace or war. He said that he himself was no alarmist. He did not believe in war in the near future and he did not think about it, though he was bound to say that most of the people who talked to him on this subject took a gloomy view about Germany's ultimate intentions. At all events he held that the Government could not take risks. It was the trustee for the people of the country and it had got to have adequate means of defence so far as those could be provided.

In March Baldwin had promised 'parity' in air power with any force within striking distance of Britain. Following Cabinet consideration of the first report of the Defence Requirements Committee, on 19 July he announced that the Royal Air Force would by 1939 be increased by forty-one squadrons. On 30 July the Labour party moved a vote of censure, rejecting any rearmament. In his reply, Baldwin criticised supporters of peace who failed to acknowledge that other nations were not animated by the same ideals as Britain, and declared that 'since the day of the air, the old frontiers are gone': for British defence, the frontier was now the Rhine.[79] MacDonald's eyes had again deteriorated, and on medical advice he took a long rest and holiday in Canada from mid July to late September.

[79] To Simon, 8 Aug. 1934, Simon papers 79/56: 'I had a call from the German Ambassador who wanted to know what I meant by the Rhine frontier! I gave Van a record of our harmless talk so I won't bother you with it.'

1 AUGUST 1934: TO MACDONALD

MacDonald papers 680/1/65–6

[Astley Hall]

My dear P.M.

It was a great pleasure to receive your letter and to get good news of you. It arrived just in time for me to pass on your message of greetings to our final Cabinet yesterday morning.

The adjournment was yesterday afternoon. I think we have finished up in a good position.

We put in a lot of time on the Defence Requirements committee and were able to bring up a Report yesterday which the Cabinet approved.

That will enable Hankey to go away with a clear mind.

The air debate went off well. The Opposition had no bite in it. Samuel only took a dozen of his liberals in support of the opposition: the rest abstained. Over thirty of Simon's voted with us.

All members of the gov^{nt} have worked well. Duff Cooper made an admirable speech on the Codex.

I performed the Asquith unveiling for you and I hope did not disgrace you.

I came down this morning and have a few odds & ends to see to in the country: I go to London next Tuesday and hope to get away on the 8th.

I have asked all the Cabinet to be at work by Oct. 1st and that if you weren't back I should probably have a Cabinet in the last week of September.

I intend taking the Distressed Area reports with me to study on my holiday.

Rushcliffe election is good and all our speakers said it was a pleasure to help the candidate. Very different from London constituencies![80]

Go on with your rest and I look forward to seeing you rejuvenated.

Yours ever/ S.B.

Following another motor tour, now taking in Belgium as well as France, the Baldwins as usual spent several weeks in Aix-les-Bains. They were joined by Jones and the Davidsons, and briefly by Churchill, his son Randolph and daughter Diana, and his scientific friend Lindemann, en route to Chamonix. As Baldwin put it, Churchill 'had never seen Mt. Blanc, so he was going there . . . letting

---

[80] Conservatives had lost to Labour at East Fulham in October 1933, North Hammersmith in April 1934 and Upton in May, but were retaining seats at by-elections elsewhere.

the mountain have a peep at him, and back to England'. Churchill and Lindemann discussed with Baldwin the issue of air defence research, which led to Lindemann being invited to submit his ideas to the government's defence advisers.[81]

24 AUGUST 1934: TO OLIVER BALDWIN

CUL Ms Add. 8795/17

Regina Hotel Bernascon, Aix-les-Bains

Dearest Son,

I never guessed the cheese came from you! it was a noble present and we managed half before we left and half for Little. I ate hard, and we took chunks with us for the journey. Thank you!

We saw Monica: very happy and childlike, and looking ridiculously young. I love Bruges: I don't know such a change in a few hours. You plunge into the middle ages.

Nancy was interesting. We stayed in a perfect square, built in the XVIIIth century and entered by beautiful wrought iron gates from every approach. Tyrrell came over from Vittal for lunch. Strasbourg was far more beautiful than I had expected. I had only walked round it thirty-six years ago in the dark, waiting for the midnight train to Paris. The glass in the cathedral is worthy of Bourges.

The town itself is so jolly: full of lovely houses and very clean. But no storks. So I lunched at Colmar where I felt certain I should see them and they had all gone the day before.

We drove down the Doubs valley to Besançon, on to Bourg, and so here.

I don't know whether I shall fight another election. I have a pretty hard year ahead and it will be time to decide when we have got our India Bill through.

It's more difficult to get out than to get in. Perhaps my finances will be a bit better in a year's time.

Come and see us before you go. We shall be back between the 20th and 23rd of September if no cataclysm intervenes.

Your loving/ Father

---

[81] To Joan Davidson, 2 Sept. 1934; M&B, pp. 781–2, 1083–91.

24 AUGUST 1934: TO THE DUCHESS OF ATHOLL

Duchess of Atholl papers, bundle 72

Regina Hotel Bernascon, Aix-les-Bains

My dear Kitty,

I hope you have got away from your constituency and have for the time being banished from your too active mind all these insoluble problems which oppress us for eleven months out of the twelve.

I was so beat to the world that I just couldn't take up my pen but my conscience couldn't be clear till I had done it!

I can't undertake to see anybody when I get back. I shall be immersed in work and as for India I shall wait and see what the Committee's Report says.

I have all the reports from the distressed areas with me and we shall have to decide in the all too short month before Parliament meets what we might do and can do.

We shall be running near to the election when next session ends and that brings with it a heap of difficult questions.

And none more difficult, and I may say this to you in confidence as an old friend, than my own position.

Sixty-seven this month is getting on and how much longer?

You may imagine this is ever present in my thoughts. I try and put myself outside and look at the whole question dispassionately. The defeat of the Socialists at the next election is vital for the country.

And after all it is the country alone we must think of.

However the light is clearer here for such meditations than in London.

Do take care of yourself. You look very tired sometimes and life isn't always easy.

My love to you both.

Always affectionately/ S.B.

30 SEPTEMBER 1934: TO LLOYD GEORGE

Lloyd George papers G/1/15/4

11, Downing Street

My dear Lloyd George,

I am the only Englishman who has got the better of you in a deal! I read, with keen pleasure, the proofs of your last book in the Easter holidays, and in the autumn there arrives the finished volume with the author's compliments. If that isn't getting ninepence for fourpence I don't know what is . . .

But you must do a Versailles volume.

I am really grateful for the gift,

Yours sincerely/ Stanley Baldwin

17 NOVEMBER 1934 JONES DIARY

partly in Jones *DL*, pp. 138–9

At 10.30 a.m. to 11 Downing Street where I found S.B. fit and voluble because he had spent yesterday at Cambridge where he enjoyed himself opening the Polar Institute and talking to the boys at the Perse School. He dug out the crumpled notes of his speech from his pocket in order to show me some happy phrases . . . I mentioned another recent speech of his, the one on the private manufacture of armaments, following Sir John Simon in the House about ten days ago. He told me all about that unfortunate debate. Simon had consulted the Cabinet on the line he should take. He prepared several drafts but was worried about them and on the morning of the debate he had a further consultation with a group of ministers – Ramsay, S.B., Hailsham, Hoare and Neville Chamberlain – and a line was agreed. The speech took an hour and a quarter and was a failure. The House quickly revealed this and Simon knew it and was so angry that he passed a note to the P.M. to the effect that the speech was a failure and that the P.M. was responsible for the failure. Simon snatched the note back from the P.M. who reported the incident to S.B.

S.B: 'I've made many bad speeches but I've never thought of blaming the Cabinet or the P.M. for them . . .

Dick Law[82] spoke in the debate. He is very diffident and not a good speaker, but he has influence with a group of younger Conservatives. I said he had an hereditary right to be heard. That phrase came back to me as it was applied to me by Balfour after my maiden speech. I don't think he remembered me for more than five minutes and doubt if he spoke to me again for five years. You won't easily guess what Simon's ambition is.'

T.J.: 'I know it is not the Woolsack.'

S.B.: 'He would like to lead the House of Commons if I go to the Lords.'

---

[82] Bonar Law's youngest son, an MP since 1931, Lord Coleraine 1954.

T.J.: 'How little we know ourselves.'

S.B.: 'Why is it that so many first-class brains are such bloody fools? He comes to the P.M. or to me for instructions on one thing after another. The other day, when Ribbentrop, an emissary from Hitler, came over to see him, he must first go to Ramsay and then independently to me to ask whether he should see the man.'

T.J.: 'I wish you could get rid of him.'

S.B.: 'But if I took on L.G. in his place I should have the resignations of half the Cabinet in my hands. I've often told you that L.G. has never really led a Party. He is not a cohesive but a disintegrating force . . .'

In early 1935 the government faced a series of difficulties, and Salisbury wrote in February that he was 'horrified to find the degree to which the disintegration of the Party in Parlt. and in the Country has proceeded'.[83] A 'Peace Ballot', a national referendum by an alliance of organisations to assess public opinion on the League of Nations and disarmament, seemed certain to complicate the Cabinet's rearmament plans. Randolph Churchill aggravated divisions over the India Bill by standing against the official Conservative candidate at the Liverpool, Wavertree by-election. His intervention enabled the Labour candidate to win the seat in early February. New, lower, benefit rates for the long-term unemployed created widespread protests, taken up by Conservative MPs in vulnerable industrial seats. Lloyd George launched an independent political campaign, offering a 'new deal' on unemployment. He had, however, already made it clear that he wished to negotiate with the Cabinet and in late December Baldwin agreed to do so. There were delays because MacDonald, Neville Chamberlain and other ministers and Conservative MPs opposed Lloyd George's inclusion in the Cabinet, but Baldwin's own attitude was that 'he had not the same objection to Lloyd George that he used to have, and . . . in fact he rather liked him'.[84] Eventually, in March, Lloyd George was asked to submit his policy proposals to a Cabinet committee.

26 JANUARY 1935 JONES TO LADY GRIGG

Jones 'diary'

. . . We had our 23rd meeting of the [Pilgrim] Trust on Thursday afternoon . . . Macmillan[85] and S.B. came early and gossiped. S.B. wound up about India and the folly of old men, white men too, like Fitzalan, who had signed some

---

[83] Salisbury to Baldwin, 10 Feb. 1935, SB papers 107/12–13.
[84] *Reith Diaries*, p. 120 (5 Feb. 1935).   [85] Lord Macmillan (no relation of Harold Macmillan).

protest or petition to Patiala, and the mischief of pig-headed men like Lord Lloyd who wanted Federation dropped 'and then all would be well'. And here was L.G. at 72 threatening to bring out 400 candidates and split the vote – all because he can't keep away from the 'game' and has plenty of money to squander. 'It's nothing but a game to him and to Winston'. Winston's son has gone off to fight Wavertree – never saying a word to his father. 'When I retire I'll have a farewell meeting at the Albert Hall and I'll deliver my soul on three topics and three only: the Press, the Americans, and the Tory Party. And then I promise you'll hear no more from me. I declare this now while I am in full possession of all my faculties.'

29 JANUARY 1935: TO JOAN DAVIDSON

Lady Davidson papers; partly in *Davidson Memoirs*, p. 406

House of Commons

Little Maid,

Alas! I fear I <u>must</u> stay in the House to-night. It was in a curious and rather ugly mood all yesterday: the debate[86] is being continued, and the division will take place after dinner time.

The whole debate, and the succeeding one, will want watching closely. The P.M. is no use on these occasions: and if anything happened and I were absent I should be in queer street.

It is awfully disappointing but one of the penalties of the holder of my job.

If we had got the division last night, it would have been all right. But we couldn't, without real trouble.

Your loving/ S.B.

12 FEBRUARY 1935: TO SALISBURY

Hatfield House archives 4M/153/58

House of Commons

My dear Salisbury,

Thank you for your letter. The situation you have come back to is indeed a difficult and complex one.

---

[86] On the unemployment regulations.

At the moment the government have to extricate themselves as best they can from the appalling mess we have got into over unemployment benefit. It is the worst mess I have ever been associated with.

As to the party, I don't think you exaggerate: unless it can be pulled together there will be a disaster. I have my own ideas as to how these troubles should be met but beyond that I can't say more yet.

Anyway, shine or storm, you will be welcome to-morrow as flowers in May.

Ever yours/ S.B.

25 FEBRUARY 1935: TO OLIVER BALDWIN

CUL Ms Add. 8795/19

11, Downing Street

Dearest Son,

It is four o'clock and nearly dark with the rain coming down in buckets, and I have a long committee ahead. So for five minutes I will try and conjure up an imaginary picture of your villa[87] and write you this line to say Many Happy Returns of Friday.

When I was thirty-six I was just starting on that long and dreary campaign in Kidderminster: not that I thought it dreary then, nor could I foresee into what strange paths it would lead me. But I begin to long for a lightening of the load and when I see a decent opportunity of getting out I shall seize it: I don't want to be kicked out at my age: it is undignified!

I don't know when you will consider England to be sufficiently aired but I suppose by May and it will be good to think of you in this country again. Blessings from

Your loving/ Father

In March the Cabinet published a White Paper on Defence, making the case for general rearmament. In response the German government made its own rearmament public. On the 11th Baldwin defended the White Paper against Labour party opposition to any rearmament; on the other hand Churchill criticised the Cabinet for insufficient rearmament, particularly attacking estimates given by Baldwin for the rate of German air-force construction.

---

[87] Oliver was at his Ridsdale uncle Arthur's villa in Algiers.

19 MARCH 1935: TO JOAN DAVIDSON

Lady Davidson papers

House of Commons Library

Little Maid,

This is real bad luck. I can't leave the House: Winston has been attacking my figures of last November & Philip [Sassoon] is answering for the Air Ministry about nine. There are several atttacking the Ministry in a not very nice temper and I daren't be away. I <u>am</u> sorry.

One can seldom be certain.

Yr loving/ S.B.

With MacDonald in obvious decline, Baldwin had to decide whether or not to resume the premiership. Most Conservatives understood the advantages of the National government, and its continuation was not in doubt. The alternative leader was Neville Chamberlain, who in February thought that Baldwin meant to retire; but by the end of March he had decided to become Prime Minister again. After the passage of the India Act, the Conservative party needed to be re-united while retaining its coalition partners, and at the next election rearmament would have to be justified in the face of considerable peace opinion. Baldwin believed that he could best achieve these tasks.

4 MAY 1935 DAWSON MEMORANDUM

Dawson papers 78/101–2; Wrench, *Dawson*, pp. 321–2

I found S.B. alone in Downing Street on the pre-Jubilee Saturday afternoon and quite glad to unburden himself about his troubles. Tom Jones, whom I'd just met in the Athenaeum, suggested that I should have a talk with him and I called, without warning, on the chance.

He opened up at once on the subject of 4 problems in connection with the impending and long expected reconstruction of the Government.

1. SHOULD WINSTON BE INCLUDED?

To this, contrary to some statements that had been made, he felt no personal objection, but Winston would be a disruptive force especially since foreign relations and defence would be uppermost. Moreover there was great feeling in the party about some of his recent activities against the Government's Indian policy. I suggested that the continuance of the Indian problem even when the Bill was through, was sufficient argument for keeping him out for the present.

2. SHOULD L.G. BE INCLUDED?

On this problem also S.B. has a perfectly open mind. He doubts L.G.'s effective support though he admits his nuisance value in opposition. He thinks that L.G. and Winston <u>together</u> would be impossible.

3. SHOULD AN EFFORT BE MADE TO ATTRACT SAMUELITE LIBERALS?

S.B. is not prepared to make any effort after Samuel himself, who was never, he says, a really loyal colleague and was always looking over his shoulder. I suggested that some of his followers, e.g. Foot, would be valuable and he agreed. He was less convinced about Philip, whom he likes but whose judgment he distrusts.[88]

4. IS ANYTHING TO BE DONE WITH REASONABLE LABOUR?

I thought it hopeless; but S.B. said (and I agreed) that some Labour leaders were no longer anxious to win the next election and that in these circumstances might conceivably be ready to come across.

He thought that under our democratic conditions the next Administration must be prepared to spend money, though not to the extent that L.G. wanted. Monty Norman had been over to see him at Trent and was prepared to look into the prospects of a big loan, which, said S.B., should cover not only roads, settlement, etc., but defence, particularly aircraft, destroyers, and small cruisers, if no limitation in this direction proved possible and other nations went on building. He thought that such expenditure would be highly popular, that it would provide a great deal of employment next winter, and that it would serve the essential purpose of keeping our skilled artificers in being.

Incidentally he told me that Ramsay would like to stay on, though not as P.M. and that he was determined to fight Seaham again, a very courageous ambition. In this connexion we discussed some of the misfits in the present Government.

20 MAY 1935 WIGRAM MEMORANDUM

RA PS/GV/K.2473/2; Hyde, *Baldwin*, pp. 383–4

The King saw Mr Baldwin this morning and talked to him about the probable reconstruction of the Government.

---

[88] Isaac Foot, Secretary for Mines Aug. 1931–Sept. 1932; the 'Philip' here was Lord Lothian.

Mr Baldwin said that he had lately been examined by Lord Dawson,[89] who said that organically he was quite sound, but required rest. If he would go away for two months there was no reason why he should not stand the strain for another 2 or 3 years. Mr Baldwin said that he had not yet seen the Prime Minister but understood that the latter wished to resign. The King asked what position Mr Ramsay MacDonald was likely to hold in the new Government: Mr Baldwin replied that Mr Ramsay MacDonald had offered him any position he liked in 1931 and that he should do the same now to him. The King suggested that probably Mr Ramsay MacDonald would like to be President of the Council and Chairman of the Committee of Imperial Defence, to which Mr Baldwin said he would be delighted for him to occupy these positions.

The King then said to Mr Baldwin that he, His Majesty, was a great Cabinet maker and made various suggestions regarding the Offices. With regard to the Foreign Office, Mr Baldwin was inclined to think that we ought to have a permanent Minister at Geneva and for wandering around the various capitals, while the Foreign Secretary stayed at home and did the work of a Foreign Secretary. Mr Baldwin said that Anthony Eden would probably fill the post of Wandering Minister, but was not sure who to put into the Foreign Office, as Sir John Simon would vacate this post.

Mr Baldwin told the King that Sir Samuel Hoare was very keen to go to India as Viceroy. The King deprecated this, as a Secretary of State for India had never been Viceroy. His Majesty said he would prefer Lord Linlithgow, with which Mr Baldwin was inclined to agree.[90]

Other Cabinet appointments and resignations were discussed. Mr Baldwin said that it was imperative that he should go away for two months rest and the King asked who would be Prime Minister in the interim. Mr Baldwin replied that Mr Ramsay MacDonald would probably take it on.

The King told Mr Baldwin that he hoped the reconstruction could be done before the 1st July meeting at Newmarket, and Mr Baldwin replied that he hoped everything would be finished by then.

---

[89] The doctor to royalty and many public figures; no relative of Dawson of *The Times*.
[90] Hoare became Foreign Secretary; Eden joined the Cabinet as minister without portfolio responsible for League of Nations affairs; Simon became Home Secretary, and Linlithgow the Viceroy.

❧

Prime Minister again

JUNE 1935 – NOVEMBER 1936

Baldwin resumed the premiership on 7 June. From 10 Downing Street he wrote to his aunt: 'It is a curious feeling coming here for the third time. If my health lasts, I hope to do a couple of years but I don't want a longer time. I think by then I shall have given out all that I have to give, and I should like to retire while still in possession of such faculties as I have!/ So I shall do my best for the time that is left.'[1] Lloyd George, conscious that his talks with the Cabinet committee were going nowhere and that the results of the 'Peace Ballot' were soon to be announced, on 12 June started a new movement – the 'Council of Action for Peace and Reconstruction' – supported by Free Church leaders and public figures in all parties and none. A week later, Baldwin formally ended the Cabinet's discussions with him.

12 JUNE 1935: TO BRIDGEMAN

Bridgeman papers 4629/1/1935/73

10, Downing Street

My dear Willie,

Thank you so much for your letter. I hope we shall meet soon and I will reply to all your criticisms. Don't think I don't know 'em!

The making of a party gov$\underline{^{nt}}$ is child's play compared with reconstructing a coalition.[2]

Yes. Ll.G. is out for mischief – dirty and unholy.

Yours ever/ S.B.

Winston is rapidly transferring his interest from India to Air!

---

[1] To Edith Macdonald, 22 June 1935, SB add. papers.
[2] For Baldwin's comments on reconstruction of the government see Jones *DL*, pp. 149–53.

Jones's wife was seriously ill; she died on 18 July.

1 JULY 1935: TO JONES

Jones papers A6/90

10, Downing Street

My dear T.J.

You are never out of my mind these days and this is just a line of unchanging affection – and I am only one of many.

As I grow older, I always feel that unless by the infinite mercy of God husband and wife are called together, one of them has to pass through the real Valley of the Shadow. You are being called even now to enter that Valley and watch over all that is so much to you, to see her suffering and to pray that the cup may yet be taken from your lips.

But, dear Tom, the heavy load is on _you_ and _you_ are bearing what it might have been hers to bear, to have seen her loved one suffer, perchance to finish her pilgrimage alone – and it is on you that the inscrutable will of God has laid the burden. I have thought much of these things of late.

Should she be spared a while to you, with what infinite tenderness and love you will care for her; but whatever comes to you, no man has a greater wealth of human love than you have, waiting for you whenever and wherever you need it.

With affectionate devotion/ S.B.

In early July Churchill accepted an invitation to join the Air Defence Research sub-committee of the Committee of Imperial Defence. He thereby became an unpublicised participant in a policy process which he publicly criticised.

8 JULY 1935: TO CHURCHILL

Churchill papers CHAR 2/236/106; _WSC V/2_, pp. 1207–8

10, Downing Street

My dear Winston,

I am glad you have seen Hankey and I take your letter as an expression of your willingness to serve on that Committee.

I am glad and I think you may be of real help in a most important investigation.

Of course you are free as air (the correct expression in this case!) to debate the general issues of Policy, Programmes and all else connected with the Air Services.

My invitation was not intended as a muzzle but as a gesture of friendliness to an old colleague.[3]

Yours very sincerely/ Stanley Baldwin

The Baldwins spent a weekend with Butler, under-secretary at the India Office 1932–7, at his country house, Stanstead Hall, Halstead, Essex, so that Baldwin could speak on 20 July at a 'demonstration' – a combined social event and political meeting – for East Anglian and Essex supporters of the National government.

[19–21] JULY 1935 R.A. BUTLER MEMORANDUM

R. A. Butler papers G6/57

I met the Baldwins at Mark's Tey soon after six on Friday evening. I had made several suggestions that fast trains should be stopped, but S.B. evidently had looked up the trains himself and had decided that this particular one suited his fancy. He likes travelling by train and dislikes motoring. He was much impressed by the country. He said that very soon after leaving the East end he had come into the most bucolic country unspoiled by ribbon development and had greatly enjoyed the journey. I had also made a suggestion that we should organise a big public reception at Colchester in order to give him a welcome and to advertise the Fete next day. He said to me that at any rate he was glad I had not done this, and he could arrive quite quietly at a country station amid the crops, which was what he liked to do. The station master and inspector of police were inclined to be surprised that the arrival was so quiet. He had a short word with them, and from being slightly supercilious they came under his personal spell. I asked him and Mrs Baldwin to travel in the Austin . . . together with the fatter of the two detectives. I followed immediately behind in the Wolseley with Geoffrey Fry, and the maid, other detective and luggage came in a Halstead car of immense size and capacity.

---

[3] See Churchill to Baldwin, 9 July 1935, *WSC V/2*, p. 1210: 'You have gathered to yourself a fund of personal goodwill & public confidence which is indispensable to our safety at the present time.'

On arrival we walked round the garden; he was very pleased with the roses, and said how quiet he wished to be before the meeting. He asked me to take him over the house. We stopped at all the book shelves while he took out and smelt different volumes before putting them back. He was very pleased with the view from Sydney's[4] room. He said 'This is like Cambridgeshire, where you get large expanses of sky'. I said that we could not compete with great views from Stanstead. He said, 'This view is perfect: the roses in the foreground, the corn under the trees and the woods in the distance'. He said 'I suppose this is near Constable's country', but when I offered to take him for a drive he said that he must remain quietly at home. He thought Sydney's book shelves contained a good mixed bag, and was pleased that we had a first edition of Mary Webb. He then fastened on one of my favourite books, 'Cicero et ses amis' by Boissier. I asked him if he read much French; so he rattled off all the other books by Boissier, 'La fin du paganisme' and others, all of which he appeared to know well.[5] You can imagine that this caused me to tread with care.

We had staying at the house Sam Courtauld, the Malcolm Sargents and Geoffrey Fry, who had come with him. The Trittons[6] came in to dinner. Otherwise we had no one from the district. He was High Sheriff and therefore there was no difficulty about the choice. They are a nice pair with whom S.B. enjoyed talking. Malcolm Sargent arrived very late for dinner which did not seem to disturb the atmosphere. S.B. at once spotted him as having a very clever mongrel face, and, as is his wont, when talking to anybody, he screwed himself right round, had a good look at him under his eyebrows and then talked to him intently on music while sucking his pipe. We sat for some time after dinner with the windows open on to the rose garden; he remarked how calm was the country air and how reposeful. Before going to bed, he talked intently to Sam about industry and hours of work.

Next morning both he and Mrs Baldwin wandered round the garden after breakfast without hats in the strong thundery sun. He talked to me about his speech and said that he was not worthy of a dog kennel before addressing a mass meeting. He always felt like this before his holiday at the end of July. Indeed, he seemed full of health but tired and did not sleep

---

[4] Butler's first wife, the daughter of the industrialist Samuel Courtauld.
[5] Gaston Boissier, 1823–1908, had been a leading French scholar of Latin antiquity.
[6] Herbert Tritton, president of Equitable Life Assurance and a leading figure in Essex society.

well through thinking of various problems of the week before in London. She was definitely tired, but nevertheless before lunch rose and went down the stalls with Sydney and talked to the women who were decorating them. She gave great pleasure, has considerable presence and made one or two very thoughtful little purchases. S.B. told me that he was not going to talk on foreign policy because there was nothing to say. I said 'Are you going to answer Lloyd George?' He raised his eyebrows and looked at me for a moment. 'Of course not, that is exactly what he wants me to do'. He said 'They tell me I should not mention tithe'.[7] I said 'I should naturally like you to do so, since feelings are very strong and I should like them to realise that you understand their difficulties, but I think it would be very dangerous to discuss tithe before the Commission has reported'. He said he was quite certain it would be, and was sorry he could not make any reference to it. Nor did he think any further reference to sugar beet was necessary in view of the recent decision to extend the subsidy. He told me that the Ministry of Agriculture had given him a great deal of material on which he would work. I said I hoped he would make some reference to East Anglia, where there was an independent feeling and which was a part of the world he had not previously visited very much. He told me he was going to strike the difference between Roundhead and Cavalier which he did, as you will have seen in the report of his speech. He retired very soon to my room where I promised he would not be disturbed.

At about noon he emerged and sat under the mulberry tree, where he continued calmly till lunch, while various others came up or left, according to our avocations, and preparations for the afternoon. He enjoyed the mulberry tree and said that Mr Speaker had recommended to him 'The Cherry Tree' by Adrian Bell as being a 'really good country book'. He agreed with me that Adrian Bell might get precious. He had read 'Joseph and his Brethren' by Freeman which is I think our best East Anglian country novel, but did not remember finishing it. He very often picked up books but was not able to finish them. He was very sympathetic with Kurd, the Irish wolfhound, who was restless owing to the crowds who had already come in to prepare for the afternoon, and who kept on raising and lowering his majestic frame.

---

[7] Falling prices had increased the burden of agricultural tithe payments. The Cabinet wished to offer relief to small farmers, but found the issue so complex and controversial that it had been referred to a royal commission in 1934.

He approached Robin sympathetically, but horror to relate, Robin turned on him and just caught the edge of his finger! He said quite calmly 'I quite understand how you feel', adding, 'I want to do that to every supplementary question in the House at this time of year.' He took an iodine pencil out of his pocket and painted the scratch. I led Robin away in disgrace and he had to remain shut up for the rest of the day – the only dog we have ever had who bit a Prime Minister.

Uncle Willy[8] and Aunt Cecily came into lunch. S.B. has always been friendly toward Uncle Willy since he gave that money for the Botanical Gardens at Cambridge. He said it was done in a manner which won his heart – by return of post and without conditions or amplifications. He discussed cream cheeses with Aunt Cecily in the same intent way as he had done other subjects the previous evening. After lunch he asked if he could have Sydney's room, since he agreed warmly that the public should be allowed through the gardens. He said they would flatten their noses against the window.

Sharp at two the tap proceeded to pour into the garden, and I could see early on that we were going to have large numbers. Mrs Baldwin asked if I could give her Morant's History of Essex and any other books on Essex, and she would like to sit with him during the afternoon in Sydney's room. So we left them, and went off to the Pageant.[9] Thanks to the stand and the arrangements, and the genius of Heaven Fitzgerald, this was an unqualified success, and really most entertaining. Its value to the fete was that it had spread the news over many villages and that it brought in many of the Essex families to represent their ancestors. I was able to stay for a short part of it, and afterwards went round watching the progress of the Fete. Just before tea, and after a great deal of the usual putting off, we had a group taken of all staying in the house, including De la Warr,[10] who had just arrived. The period from tea to the meeting was rather long, particularly as the louring sky, to which I have not yet made reference, came lower than it had previously been and we had a little rain. It seemed a very long day from the start, and the anxiety about the rain and the sultriness of the atmosphere made it seem

[8] William Courtauld (actually a cousin of Sydney), an Essex county councillor and chairman of quarter sessions.
[9] Historical pageants were common events in both rural and urban areas during the early twentieth century.
[10] A National Labour peer and parliamentary secretary, Ministry of Agriculture. The 'group' refers to a group photograph.

longer. 6.30 had been chosen as a suitable time for the meeting in order to get the maximum number of people, especially the poorer people from our immediate neighbourhood. But it means a long day of waiting for the speaker and the organisers particularly in our uncertain climate. Soon after 5.30 the officers of the local Associations trooped into the hall; just before their arrival, coming down from the top floor I had been horrified to see, on peering into the hall below, that the whole bottom of the house was quite full of people. I found that one door had been left ajar, again I expect by one of the wicked dogs: one inquisitive person had poked their head in at the back garden door and had been followed by at least three hundred people in a trice. I locked the door behind them and showed them out slowly through the billiard room, locking the door upon the last one and trying to remain very polite. Having the garden full to overflowing was enough: we could not have had these many thousands into the house as well. The hall being very full of the legitimate entrants, and S.B. upstairs beginning to get definitely anxious to proceed with the meeting, I brought him down at six and asked each Member to introduce their officers and show them out to the platform. This minute, Colvin, the Lord Lieutenant arrived: I had reserved seats in the front row for him but the crowd was so big that they had overflowed, so that I had to go out and place them and then hurry back. . . .

S.B. asked me to get his macintosh which I found hanging, as a typical English macintosh should, on a peg in a crumpled condition with a very faded and oily 'Stanley Baldwin' label in it. By 6.15 I saw that he would not stand waiting much longer, so I organised the police, got a way cleared to the platform through really quite a dense throng, and the meeting must have started ten minutes or quarter of an hour early. The crowds had been waiting for long. All 2,500 chairs had long since gone and they were standing on every side of the platform to a depth of about 50 yards. I reckon that there were 8,000 people at the meeting, considering that there were well over twice the number of chairs in standing room.

The Chairman got well started, and then S.B. rose, with great determination, jumping up to the microphone. This has been commented on by many observers. He is putting a great deal of force into his public speeches at present, and speaks with great determination and clarity. That is perhaps why he spends the whole day so very quietly before the big mass meeting.

The more one reads his speech the better it seems. At the time it was rather devoted to one subject, agriculture, and seemed a little technical. But he had in it several political allusions, notably one to the next election and one too of his most typical perorations on ordered liberty. Altogether it was a good speech which complimented our neighbourhood because it addressed itself to all our local problems. De La Warr spoke well and modestly, and Pybus, the National Liberal,[11] was commendably short, with the result that including two presentations, the meeting was over in an hour and twenty minutes. Old Mr Ruggles Brise, who has been fifty years President of the Maldon Conservative Association, said that the last time a Prime Minister visited our areas was when Disraeli came to Hedingham Castle.

I was glad to get the P.M. off the platform again, with the invaluable aid of the police, and back into the front door, which I shut. After his speech, Mrs B. had made him put on his macintosh, and had given him some resin pastilles, and she now plied him with a whisky and soda. He was much cheered as a result of the end of the meeting, and was pleased with the number of men present, the crowd which was presumably from a long distance, in a scattered area, its orderly attention and its size.

He was very glad to meet the Colvins at dinner, together with various of the visiting M.P.s such as Victor Raikes, and Henry Channon, the prospective candidate for Southend,[12] and Regina Evans, ex-National [Union] Chairman. He had been very abstemious before, but was glad to have his champagne after the meeting. He was pleased with the Shakespearean sight of dancing on the lawn outside the front door, but did not stay up for the rockets and fireworks and his own rugged picture spread down the drive. I wandered out, feeling tired but contented about 10.30, and mixed with the home goers. The atmosphere was very good; the Dodgems and mechanical boats were plying their last fares: a trickly 'good night' had been hoisted on the fireworks board and the last phalanx of local villagers were marching boldly past the front door on the way back to our own village, the distant visitors having left before.

Next morning he sat and talked after breakfast and then drifted, as I thought he might, towards the large book-case in the billiard room. He

[11] MP for Harwich, Minister of Transport 1931–3.
[12] See *Chips. The Diaries of Sir Henry Channon*, ed. R. R. James (1967), pp. 38–9, for his account of this day.

settled first on the India shelf, and said he thought Walter Lawrence's 'The India We Served' was the great classic about the country.[13] I said I thought 'Kim' deserved first place, though Lawrence's biography ran it close. He then started to talk about his uncle, Rudyard Kipling's father, and said that Rudyard had owed a great deal to John Kipling. It was extraordinary how the author of 'Kim' had sucked in the Indian atmosphere like a spoon in five or six years. After fingering and sniffing various other books, he said that he hoped young men would go out to India and make a career there, perhaps ending up in the highest places, as happened in the days of the Company. This led him to talk about the younger men in Parliament, and he spoke with particular affection of W. S. Morrison, Anthony Muirhead[14] and Geoffrey Lloyd. He said he thought the last would gradually step into the Chamberlain shoes in Birmingham, and would gain a territorial influence which would stand him in good stead in politics. He was clearly distressed that there had been a change over Geoffrey's appointment to be Civil Lord of the Admiralty. Both Sydney and I at different times assured him that Geoffrey was very happy looking after S.B. and that there was no feeling. He was immensely gratified to hear this, since I think he finds Geoffrey's efficiency very useful. He thought that J[ohn] Llewellin would make an excellent Whip, and mused that a whip was most important.[15]

He spent some little time looking over Basil William's 'Life of Peel'. He said that Balfour had discussed Peel with him and said that the reason why he, Balfour, never plumped either for protection or free trade was that he did not intend, like Peel, to split the party. This accounted for his apparently indeterminate attitude before 1906. I said that I had expected the India debates to be as bitter as the Corn Law debates had been. S.B. said fortunately the party had survived India. He agreed with me that controversy had not been so severe as he had anticipated. He said 'I thought I was done in 1929,

---

[13] After retirement from a distinguished military and government career in India, Lawrence lived next door to the Baldwins in Eaton Square. Baldwin used him as a source on Indian matters: Jones *DL*, pp. 28–9.

[14] Respectively financial secretary to the Treasury from November 1935, and parliamentary secretary at the Ministry of Labour since June 1935.

[15] Baldwin had offered Lloyd, now MP for Birmingham, Ladywood, an Admiralty post, but then withdrawn it in favour of Kenneth Lindsay, 'Independent National' MP for Kilmarnock, probably for Scottish political reasons. Lloyd remained Baldwin's PPS until appointed parliamentary secretary at the Home Office in November 1935. Llewellin had become assistant government whip in June 1935.

when Lloyd George spoke'. (I am going to look up exactly what speech he meant, but obviously that period was very uncertain.)[16]

S.B. went on to speak of Churchill. He said that like John Churchill, he was a military adventurer and would sell his sword to anyone. When he worked with him as Chancellor of the Exchequer he was the loyalest colleague: on leaving the ranks of commanders, he always felt himself completely at liberty to pursue what tactics he thought best. S.B. was interested that Churchill had written me a long letter,[17] part of which was read out on the platform at the meeting. He said 'So many of them wish to get back. Garvin suggested that I should take Ll.G. and Churchill into a great National Government. But I told him when I met him at Cliveden that that would make a very good Press Government, but that to rule the country a homogenous team with as much uniformity of ideas as possible was essential'. He asked to read Garvin in the Observer that morning, and I gave it to him to take with him on the train. But he deprecated the reading of Sunday papers, and said it was no pleasure to him that our man had delivered them at breakfast time on Sunday instead of at 11, in his honour and for the first time in local history.

In the garden he talked openly to Buck De La Warr about the Labour Party. He said he was going to make a speech about them when opportunity offered in the near future. The early Labour leaders he knew were like the Covenantors who would preach on the moors for hours on end. Now that old fire was leaving them and they were being led by economic dons such as Laski, and Dalton, who were using the working man as a tool for trying their intellectual experiments on England. Some of their leaders were intellectuals and others were frankly materialistic, and the fire which originally burnt in them was no longer there. De La Warr asked him if he had read Citrine's recent speech in which he hinted that the Labour Party was not the only one which could achieve improvement of conditions of trades unionists.[18] He said he had noticed it, and was following with great interest the developments which might occur.

---

[16] The reference was to the House of Commons debate on 7 November 1929.
[17] *WSC* V/2, p. 1213, including: 'Mr Baldwin commands a wider measure of public confidence and good-will throughout this island than any other statesman. Whatever our differences we must all support him in his effort to secure a sane and stable Parliament for the anxious, fateful years that lie ahead.'
[18] As the TUC general secretary, Walter Citrine was also urging the Labour movement to abandon its opposition to rearmament.

Our last conversation was held wandering up and down Kelvedon station, looking at the flowers in a market garden below. He liked the notice board proclaiming that Kelvedon was the junction for the Tollesbury Light Railway, and said 'What English names!' He said 'I am so glad to have seen you at home in the country. You must go on coming down every week end. Life in the country makes you see things whole and will enable you to steer, as I have done, between Harold Macmillan and John Gretton.'

The Chief Constable arrived to see them off: Richard[19] who came with me had a hasty view of the signal box prior to a blushing hand shake bestowed by the P.M. on the Kelvedon Station Master. Mrs Baldwin did not like the two expresses which rushed the other way. Nor did she like the slow train coming in. She had never liked trains. He held her arm and led her away, in the same careful and thoughtful manner that he invariably uses. Then they got into a brand new carriage on the front of the train. Richard refused an invitation to look inside, but waved merrily to them as the train steamed away.

4 AUGUST 1935: TO MONICA BALDWIN

SB add. papers

Astley Hall

My dearest Monica,

I am at Astley for the weekend, the first quiet moment since I took over from Mr MacDonald two months ago . . .

We leave for our holiday on Tuesday, spending the night in London, and going to Beauvais on Wednesday. Thence by slow degrees to Aix, returning about September 20th. But there is always the possibility of being brought home for some crisis, and I shall have work to do while I am away, for never have things in Europe been so difficult.

I often think of that beautiful Bruges and wish we were passing that way again. Perhaps next year – who knows?

It has been a heavy year, and I would have refused again to become Prime Minister, but my colleagues wouldn't hear of it and I fear I must see another General Election through and (if we get in again) form another government. But if I live and keep my faculties I cannot imagine that I can go on after 70, and I was 68 yesterday!

---

[19] Butler's eldest son, aged six.

I have had the Pedigree all nicely written out, and photostats taken of all relevant documents existing in the College of Arms dealing with our family. I am having the whole lot bound and it should be finished when I get back.[20]

When I have time which will probably be some Sunday afternoon in the autumn, I will transcribe for you as much as will give you the complete picture. I can only find one priest in the family and he was parish priest of Diddlebury in the middle of the XVth century. There was another who had a parish near Ludlow in Henry VIIIth's reign but whether pre- or post-reformation I can't remember. Both these were cousins by direct descent

I wish I could take you round the garden now: the northerly wind of the last days has shifted to north west and the distant views have sprung once more into clear light and the beauty of it is indescribable.

Well, bless you for your letter and your prayers. Never did we so-called statesmen need prayers more.

Ever your loving/ Uncle Stan

Bridgeman died on 14 August.

15 AUGUST 1935: TO LADY BRIDGEMAN

Bridgeman papers 4629/2/1935/27

Grand Hotel De La Poste, Beaune

My dear,

We got the news by telephone from the Embassy in Paris last night. You are both constantly in my mind. For Willie, I thank God for our friendship.

It was the most intimate and affectionate one through many long and difficult years. We looked at life from the same angle and there was nothing in my innermost thoughts that I could not tell him, with the sure knowledge that I should always be met with complete sympathy and understanding. I often looked forward to the day when I should be free, and pictured us talking over many things together, perhaps at Leigh, perhaps at Astley. I am so thankful that you came that day and that he looked out on our hills. You have my heartfelt gratitude for the effort you made. That drawing of him will hang in my bedroom and I shall write a little note on it for those who come after to read that they may know.

---

[20] The completed volume is in Baldwin WCRO collection 8229/15.

But it is just because I loved Willie that I know what you are passing through. It has fallen to you, instead of to him, to finish the pilgrimage alone and the cross you are bearing is indeed for him. That lies before one or other in all such marriages as ours unless God in His infinite mercy calls both together. No woman can have more sympathy and love than you are having at this time. That knowledge <u>does</u> help. The hands of friends are all round you when the time comes that you need them. I think the boys will know that something very fine and rare has gone with their father. No one can take his place.

I can't say more and I can't find the words I want. But you must let me come and see you from time to time when you feel that you care to see me.

And don't write unless you feel that in any way it helps you.

We go to Aix on Sunday to our old hotel, Bernascon. But I shall have to come back to London within the next fortnight for a Cabinet. Then – I hope – back to Aix, for I am very tired and need a rest.

Always in truest sympathy and affection/ Stanley Baldwin

On 29 June Baldwin had declared the League of Nations Covenant to be 'the sheet anchor of British policy', and when the Peace Ballot results were submitted to him on 23 July he welcomed them as demonstrating public support for the government's efforts to maintain the League's authority. The Cabinet thereby neatly appropriated the Ballot movement and deflated Lloyd George's Council of Action. One specific Ballot finding, that a majority of respondents supported military measures by the League against aggressor nations, helped Baldwin to present British rearmament more palatably as support for collective security, rather than purely national purposes. However, this approach was soon afterwards complicated by the Abyssinian crisis. Upholding collective security against Italy strengthened the case for British rearmament, but also created a risk that Britain might become a principal, and perhaps sole, opponent to Italy in a North African and Mediterranean war – itself undesirable, but also previously unforeseen and so not catered for in existing rearmament preparations. Baldwin was recalled from his holiday for ministerial and Cabinet meetings on 21–2 August, which authorised the sending of naval reinforcements to the Mediterranean. He went back to Aix-les-Bains for a few days, but then returned to London and Chequers in order to be available if further decisions were needed. Although Baldwin feared that in Mussolini they were dealing with a 'madman',[21] he agreed with Hoare's

---

[21] To Dawson, 22 Aug. 1935, Dawson papers 78/124.

policy of trying to warn him off. Accordingly, at the League of Nations Hoare committed the British government to 'collective resistance to acts of unprovoked aggression'.

At the TUC conference in early September Citrine recommended a Labour joint council resolution supporting firm League of Nations action against Italy, and expressed his own support for 'military sanctions'. A week later Baldwin invited him to Chequers, for a meeting which became the subject of controversy between Baldwin's early biographers. He evidently sounded Citrine on the extent of the Labour movement's readiness to abandon opposition to the government's rearmament programme. Citrine's suggestion that he might discuss the issue further with other TUC leaders came to nothing because of Bevin's dislike of such negotiations. Nevertheless, the discussion with Citrine had strengthened Baldwin's sense that at a general election Labour criticism of rearmament could be deflected.[22] Jones spent the weekend of 17–19 September at Chequers.

18 SEPTEMBER 1935: JONES TO LADY GRIGG

Jones 'diary'

... S.B. lit his pipe and talked world politics for half an hour, plugging and puffing his pipe, and marching nervously up and down. I had observed in the train coming down a slight return of the flicking of the fingers. 'I've had no real holiday. I could not keep this Italian business out of my mind.' The afternoon Committee [on defence policy] had plainly excited him and he talked now at great speed and with pounding emphasis. 'I've got a deputation coming from the Men of God. I told you I don't like that Dr Norwood.[23] He speaks for the L.G. Council of Action . . . They are the people who were all for disarmament . . . Yes, I know, we were all in it; for the last 16 years we've underspent a hundred millions on the Navy and Air. If only we had our 1914 naval preponderance neither Japan nor Italy would have shown their ugly faces. Now we have not the cruisers which can convoy our merchant ships through the Mediterranean. We've got the wrong sort of Navy now. Anyone who knew anything at the naval review the other day could see they

---

[22] Compare G. M. Young, *Baldwin*, pp. 204–5, with *My Father*, pp. 344–5, based on discussions and correspondence with Citrine (see Citrine papers 10/1), and W. Citrine, *Men and Work* (1964), pp. 353–4. See also Baldwin's comment below, p. 378 (July 1936)
[23] Free Church leaders wished to express their views on the Abyssinian crisis; Norwood was chairman of the National Free Church Council.

were all old junk. Italy was quite right to go for destroyers and submarines. We are stripped bare. Only 96,000 sailors instead of 150,000 and no stores ready, no reserves for either the sea or the air. Of course we shall get them but it will take time. Dictators act at once and Mussolini and Hitler have been at it for months. We are told that Germany is spending a thousand millions on rearmament. No wonder they have no unemployed. I can't use that argument but if we give orders for twenty cruisers and spread them over Barrow, the Tyne and the Clyde that will stir up some work. That leaves out S. Wales, I know, and we'll have to do something there'. I broke in with 'Woolwich?' 'Yes, that enquiry is going on. I don't know where they've got to'. I could have told him but didn't as I wanted him to go on. 'Our policy has been to put our finance right in the last few years. No doubt that was right. First line of defence. But now I'll have to tell the public the truth – that if we are to count at Geneva or anywhere else in a world which harbours Germany, Italy and Japan we must be strong. As for Russia, like ourselves, she does not want more possessions. Didn't you think Sam Hoare's speech good? I think he was right. Yes – that is the right policy'.

T.J.: Agreed, but how came we to let Mussolini go ahead without protesting much earlier and making clear our attitude, e.g. at Stresa or earlier.

S.B.: Easy to be wise after the event. Ask Simon or Ramsay. I wasn't P.M. I don't know whether Laval and Mussolini squared Abyssinia in the talk before Stresa. Could quite understand Laval doing so when it meant his being able to move 200,000 men from the Italian border of France. It is of Germany [that] France is always thinking. We do not know what Germany will do . . .

20 SEPTEMBER 1935: TO HAILSHAM

Heuston, *Lives of the Lord Chancellors 1885–1940*, p. 484

[Chequers]

My dear Douglas,

. . . I go to London on Sunday for good but unfortunately it is my turn at Balmoral next week and that falls awkwardly.

I have been very worried and shall be glad to have a talk.

Ll.G's speech in to-day's Times is so typical!

He is a wicked little fellow.

'If you want to get into a government' as he observed the other day to a friend of mine 'you must make a nuisance of yourself till they take you in'. He is not an Englishman and underrates the quiet resistance of the English, however stupid.

Yours ever/ S.B.

On 3 October Italian forces invaded Abyssinia, and shortly afterwards the League Council urged other powers to impose economic sanctions against Italy. At the Conservative party annual conference at Bournemouth Baldwin reiterated government support for collective security, while stating that Britain would take no 'isolated action'. He also praised the trade unions as a bulwark against fascism and communism, and welcomed the Labour party conference's decision to accept that collective security implied the possibility of military action, and therefore a need for rearmament. This conference decision precipitated the resignation of Lansbury and other pacifist parliamentary Labour leaders. Although a general election was not due until October 1936, Baldwin decided that political circumstances and the desirability of demonstrating public support for greater rearmament favoured an earlier election.

12 OCTOBER 1935: JONES TO LADY GRIGG

Jones 'diary'

. . . I was summoned to No.10 last Monday morning for a gossip. S.B. just back from a weekend with Fitzalan, where he had read the first vol. of the *Life of Lord Halifax*.[24] He was more 'cheerful and confident' than at any time during the last two months – the most anxious months of his life as Prime Minister. He was now satisfied there was no risk of a naval incident in the Mediterranean. He was sure of widespread support for rearmament. There had been a deputation of 'Six Men of God' – Berry, Aubrey, Scott Lidgett[25] and other 'religious' leaders. He had spoken with great plainness to them of the position of our defences and they had not resented the inference, though they hoped he would not forget the other half of the paradoxical policy – disarmament. He went on to talk to me of Germany. Germans were another 'cup of tea' as you would say. Italians we certainly

---

[24] J. G. Lockhart's biography of the 2nd Viscount, a leading Anglo-Catholic lay churchman and father of Edward Wood/Lord Irwin/3rd Viscount Halifax.
[25] Respectively the secretary of the Congregational Union, secretary of the Baptist Union, and the most eminent Methodist minister of the time.

could overcome in time, but Germans were thorough. Hitler's accumulation of war material is now well ahead of his training in personnel. He like Mussolini is up against vast unemployment if he calls a halt. During the next three years we ought to do all possible to cultivate German friendship. This was a rare and refreshing note from S.B. and I welcomed it warmly, adding that Phipps[26] is not the right instrument, as he is anti-German anyway. But, as he observed at Chequers, the F.O. and the diplomatic crowd are a mediocre lot just now, partly I suppose because of the lost war generation.

... And then came the real business. He has promised to speak at the Annual Meeting of the Peace Society and could I possibly put up something for him to say as he would be very busy round about the 31st. of the month.[27] His Bournemouth speech he proudly proclaimed was 'his own' especially the passage about Trade Unions. There was nevertheless a chunk in it which Leeper of the F.O. put in (I've been reading with curiosity a chapter in Austen's book 'Down the Years' on how the great men prepare their speeches ...).

18 OCTOBER 1935: TO KING GEORGE V

RA PS/GV/K.2497 A/2

10, Downing Street

Sir,

Your Majesty will have seen the rapid turn of public opinion in recent weeks towards an early General Election and the state of uncertainty which is produced by continuous comments and forecasts of the date in the public press. At the time of my last audience with Your Majesty it had seemed to me that the Election might be held back until the New Year, although in view of the requirements of public finance it could not then have been delayed beyond the first few weeks. The ground for this anticipation has, however, been altered by the developments in the international situation, and in looking into the possibilities of future policy the public mind works on the

[26] British ambassador in Germany.
[27] An allusion to his still secret plans for a general election.

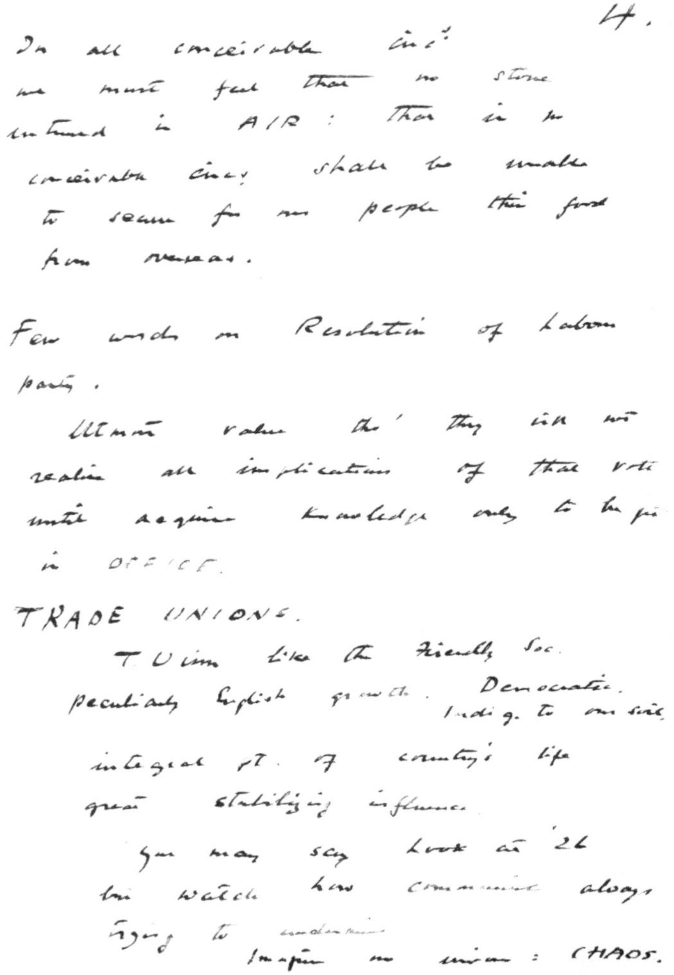
4.

In all conceivable circs
we must feel that no stone
unturned in AIR: that in no
conceivable circs shall we be unable
to secure for our people their food
from overseas.

Few words on Resolution of Labour
party.

Ultimate value tho' they will not
realise all implications of that vote
until acquire knowledge only to be got
in OFFICE.

TRADE UNIONS.

T. Uism like the Friendly Soc.
peculiarly English growth. Democratic.
Indig. to our soil
integral pt. of country's life
great stabilising influence.

You may say look at '26
but watch how communists always
trying to undermine
Imagine no unions: CHAOS.

Figure 7 A page from Baldwin's notes for his party conference speech, 4 October 1935. The section praising trade unions reads:

'T. Uism like the Friendly Soc[ieties]./ peculiarly English growth. Democratic. Indig[enous] to our soil./ integral p[art]t of country's life/ great stabilising influence./ You may say look at '26 but watch how communists always trying to undermine/ Imagine no unions: CHAOS' (cf. the spoken text in *The Times*, 5 October 1935) background that the present Government has entered upon the last year of its maximum life. With opinion now running so strongly the alternative of an autumn Election seems to me inevitable, and if Your Majesty concurs in my conclusion I would represent that to obviate uncertainty and particularly interference with Christmas trading, it would be advantageous if it were held on as early a date as possible.

I venture, therefore, to ask that Your Majesty may dissolve Parliament after the debate on the international situation next week. The debate will begin on Tuesday and can be expected to continue in both Houses until the rising on Thursday. There is no other business which it is essential to complete at once, so that if Your Majesty approves, dissolution could follow on Friday. The Election would then be held on the 14th November and Your Majesty could open the new Parliament on the 3rd December.

I have naturally hesitated and given much anxious thought to the situation before tendering this advice to Your Majesty. But it is manifest that the difficulties of foreign policy may be no less, and the prospect no clearer in the New Year. It would be my intention during the Election to make London my headquarters and to restrict my Election engagements to those which would not take me away for more than one night.

The subject of my letter is one which, had Your Majesty been in London, I should have asked to lay before You personally, and I shall look forward now to the honour of an audience with Your Majesty next week. But Lord Wigram will have told You of what has been in my mind, and I do not feel that my advice will be altogether unexpected. I sincerely trust that I am not making a request which will cause Your Majesty any inconvenience. For my part I am fortified by the recollection that Mr Bonar Law's Election was held on a 15th of November.

I have the honour to be, Sir

Your Majesty's humble, obedient servant/ Stanley Baldwin

Baldwin announced the general election in the House of Commons on 23 October. During this speech and again in his first election broadcast he declared that 'I will not be responsible for the conduct of any Government in this country at this present time, if I am not given power to remedy the deficiencies which have accrued in our defensive services since the War.' His address to the Peace Society on 31 October was concerned to show that rearmament was compatible with support for the League of Nations, and to refute the Opposition equation of 'great armaments' with a desire for war: 'I give you my word there will be no great armaments.'[28]

30 OCTOBER 1935: TO MARGESSON

Margesson papers 1/3/11

10, Downing Street

My dear David,

Your letter touched me very much. There is no relationship between men so close as that of a Prime Minister and his Chief Whip. For my part, it has been a joy to work with you: you have never failed me, and few can realise what difficult times we have been through.

The knowledge that you on your part feel as I do has given me a very real pleasure and satisfaction.

Englishmen may appear to take these mutual loyalties for granted: we don't talk about them. But it is good once and again to break the silence of our instinctive reserve, and say to each other what we might regret never having said if death came to one of us unexpectedly.

Our work is not yet done and I take fresh courage and inspiration from what you have said to me.

God bless you, my dear David/ Yours ever/ S.B.

31 OCTOBER 1935: TO JONES

Jones papers A6/91

10, Downing Street

My dear T.J.

My debt to you is piling up! We made a few excisions and a few trimmings and I delivered the speech with conviction and delight. I almost felt it was my own![29]

Thank you a thousandfold: you are indeed a present help in trouble.

---

[28] The allusion was to Grey's conclusion that an arms race was a major cause of the Great War – 'great armaments lead inevitably to war' – a phrase commonly used as a peace slogan.
[29] Unbeknown to Baldwin, Jones, who was ill, had asked his friend Wilfred Eady, assistant secretary at the Ministry of Labour, to prepare the main draft: Eady to Jones, 1 Nov. 1935, Jones 'diary'; Jones memo., 1 Feb. 1941, Jones papers AA4/58.

You will have a royal welcome when you return.

Ever yours/ S.B.

I am only just back from Guildhall and I must run up and change. I sweated like a pig!

At the election on 14 November, the National government won 429 seats (387 of them Conservative) to Labour's 154. The government majority was halved, but at 242 remained huge – far exceeding its leaders' expectations. The result was widely attributed to personal confidence in Baldwin. Among the defeated government candidates were MacDonald and his son.

15 NOVEMBER 1935: TO MACDONALD

J. R. MacDonald papers 757/10

10, Downing Street

My dear Friend,

You have shared the fate of the prophets and my heart is heavy for you.

I know your own defeat will not cause you the sharp, piercing disappointment that Malcolm's will. But it is something to have a son who stands by his father's side at all times, good and bad. And, if I know him, he would rather fall in battle with his father than win a score on the other side.

We will both have a day or two of rest and quiet before we have a talk. I shall be at Chequers Saturday and Sunday (I go down at five to-day) but at your service any time after lunch Monday, or indeed if you want to see me before – when you like.

But I do know much of what you are feeling, if not all. And I give you my hand in enduring friendship.

Yours ever/ S.B.

16 NOVEMBER 1935: JONES TO LADY GRIGG

Jones 'diary'

... Yesterday, Friday, soon after tea I had about forty minutes with [Baldwin] in the Cabinet room alone. He was not a bit tired and was no doubt buoyed up by the results. I'll sum up his talk for you.

'It's been a heavy week. I've had some speeches but I've had also time to think. You and I have often talked about the difference between my party and Labour. You remember before Ashridge[30] was founded we hoped we could get young men of the rank and file trained into becoming Conservative candidates. We have young men who are as keen on helping the working classes as Labour itself. The Labour Movement began with a number of men who were trade union leaders and local preachers – a good moral type. Ramsay tells me Labour is now a Tammany party, all out for jobs. I think it may be possible to detach the Co-operative Movement from it. They are small investors and proprietors and don't easily swallow Marxism. I don't think they have given Labour much financial help at this election. Labour is being drugged by its intellectuals – Laski, Cole & Co. – so far as their policy goes. I want to get together a group of our own men to answer these. You are not a Marxian? (T.J. No). I am thinking of Pickthorn of Cambridge[31] and men of that ability (T.J. described the procedure followed by the Fabian essayists and the Tracts.) We could get our ideas ventilated in the provincial press. The London Press is bad: <u>Daily Mail</u>, <u>Express</u>, <u>News Chronicle</u>, <u>Herald</u>, hard to say which is worse. Steward (No.10 Press Officer) suggested to me that the man who issued a morning paper at 5 p.m. would make a fortune (T.J. recalled Spender and the Westminster).[32] It was wise to take the Election now. We should not have done so well had we waited six months. I got two messages from Arthur Henderson, on his death bed: "Take the Election quickly", said each of them.'

T.J. Your attitude to Winston will be your first test. Tories and Liberals will be disgusted if you give him office.

S.B. If I consulted the Cabinet he would not get a single vote in his support. Besides there's no vacancy . . .

T.J. How are things going to pan out in Abyssinia?

S.B. No idea. I ought, I suppose, to see the Foreign Secretary. . .

Baldwin again found that government reconstruction had distressing aspects: 'This week now ending has been hell. I am temperamentally unfitted for cabinet making. A P.M. has to sacrifice his soul at times for his people. Who else has to say

---

[30] The Bonar Law Memorial College.
[31] Kenneth Pickthorn, history fellow at Corpus Christi College, Cambridge, just elected as Conservative MP for Cambridge University.
[32] J. A. Spender, editor of the quality Liberal newspaper, *The Westminster Gazette*, 1896–1922.

to an old and loyal friend "Get out?" To do the dirty, in short.'[33] The allusion was to Londonderry, moved under protest in June from the Air Ministry to become Lord Privy Seal and Leader of the House of Lords, and now dropped altogether from the government. Baldwin also had to deal with unwanted requests for office passed on by close colleagues.

21 NOVEMBER 1935: TO LONDONDERRY

Londonderry papers D3099/2/17/11; Hyde, *Baldwin*, pp. 400–1

Secret   10, Downing Street

My dear Charley,

I have been working for three days on one of the most difficult problems with which I have ever had to contend, and I am profoundly distressed that I find myself unable to offer you a place in the new government.

The refusal of Ramsay to serve unless accompanied by Malcolm and Thomas, and the desire of Halifax to continue,[34] have upset my calculations and I have more men than places.

You remember our talk in the House: you know what I feel. You have ever been a loyal and trusted friend: I think I know what you will feel.

Yet I have faith to believe that our friendship is too firmly based to be broken by a cruel political necessity that obliges a Prime Minister – and none have escaped it – to inflict pain on those they hold not only in regard but in affection.

I am yours very sincerely/ Stanley Baldwin[35]

22 NOVEMBER 1935: TO WINTERTON

Winterton papers 66

10, Downing Street

My dear Eddie,

I received a message from Sam [Hoare] that you would like to be considered in any changes that might result from the formation of the gov^{nt}

---

[33] To Lord Lytton, 23 Nov. 1935, 2nd Earl of Lytton papers.
[34] Irwin had succeeded his father as 3rd Viscount Halifax in 1934; he replaced Londonderry as both Lord Privy Seal and Leader of the House of Lords.
[35] See Hyde, *Baldwin*, p. 401, for Baldwin also writing to Lady Londonderry, to alert her to her husband's probable distress: 'I have never before written on such matters to the wife of a colleague.' For Londonderry's shock and his strained relationship with Baldwin, see below pp. 367–72.

after the general election. You have every right to make that request and I am always prepared to consider such requests.

But the General Election has been unique in this that every member of the gov^nt has come back with the exception of two of our labour colleagues. Now it is obvious that having appealed as a National gov^nt and been returned as such by an overwhelming majority, it is my duty to try and secure election for my defeated colleagues. I am therefore much in the position of the President of a University Boat Crew who finds his crew all coming into residence for a second year!

As a matter of fact, I have only one move I can make and by no juggling can I make more.

The disappointment I fear will be general amongst junior ministers who see for the time being chances of promotion blocked at a time when they might reasonably have expected a change.

I have written rather fully [to you] as a friend whom I can trust.[36]

I have had a far more difficult time for the last few days than any man can guess except those skilled to read between the lines.

Yours ever sincerely/ Stanley Baldwin

Although the Cabinet wished to halt Mussolini's aggression, it wanted still more to avoid a war against Italy – especially one in which Britain fought without allies, and the French government's attitude wavered alarmingly. Its caution was all the stronger because the German threat remained its priority, and it feared that Hitler might take advantage of an Italian war. Some of Baldwin's fundamental views were recorded by one of his private secretaries: 'Even a little war would upset Europe now'; 'French not really prepared to play', but it was necessary to keep in 'step w[ith] them'; 'What it amounts to is this. We must play out the L. of N. hand to the very end, and try not to be left holding the baby.'[37] Despite newspaper criticism of the Hoare-Laval pact – a proposed partition of Abyssinia, leaked from Paris on 9 December, which seemed to contradict the government's election commitment to uphold collective League action – the Cabinet was at first prepared to accept it, with Baldwin trying to deflect the criticism by hinting at their doubts about Laval's trustworthiness: 'my lips are as

---

[36] Baldwin's more candid view emerged in an outdoor conversation reported in Jones diary, 23 May 1936: 'Winterton [is] no more use in a Cabinet than that daisy.'
[37] Neville Butler notes, 2 Aug., Nov. 1935, FO 800/423/10, 13–14.

yet unsealed'.[38] On 13 December Baldwin received a League of Nations Union deputation.

13 DECEMBER 1935 HORACE WILSON NOTE[39]

PREM 1/195/15–19 (extracts)

... The Prime Minister said that the League policy is of course still the policy of the Government. We were all in agreement in desiring that the League policy would be effective. Translating desire into action is, however, another matter, raising extremely difficult questions for those responsible for the government of the country. He then reminded the deputation what we ... had done from the very beginning of the trouble – the fleet, reinforcements, etc. etc. No other member of the League had done anything at all and there was no evidence that any of them intended to do so or that, in so far as they might express their intention of doing so, that they were in a position to carry out their intentions.

We had therefore to consider the risks of a unilateral war – risks from the air, submarines, etc. Dealing with the unpreparedness of other nations, he referred particularly to France. Considerable time had been occupied in trying to secure from France a clear declaration of support on her part in the event of an attack upon us. A declaration had, indeed, been secured in the end; we were bound, however, to feel doubt about the reality of the intention expressed in this declaration, partly because of the anticipated action of the French people and partly because of our doubt as to France's ability to come to our aid at any rate in the near and vital future. The talks, which after much effort had eventually begun between our military representatives and the French representatives, had disclosed a state of military unpreparedness which we could not ignore.

Looking at the matter from the point of view of the League of Nations, the position which faced the Foreign Secretary on Sunday was, in fact, that

---

[38] For Baldwin's account of the crisis see Jones *DL*, pp. 158–60; and for his later explanations of 'lips unsealed', below pp. 468, 479.

[39] Although Wilson's official title was 'chief industrial adviser' to the government, as a highly experienced civil servant he had been seconded to the Prime Minister's office in order to supervise its work and advise Baldwin on a wide range of its business. Gilbert Murray's draft of the deputation's own record of the meeting is in Murray papers 223/203–4.

France was not ready and not willing to go on with more pressure but was insistent that proposals should at any rate be at first tried. Should we have broken with France then – giving her an opportunity, or in fact almost forcing her, to run away even from the obligations to which she has become a party? What would have been the effect upon the League then? Since action by France would necessitate mobilization,[40] and since a mobilization order would, the French felt, lead to riots, etc., should we have gone on, not only refusing to try out the proposals but at the same time pressing the oil sanctions, attempting to hold a reluctant France to her promise to give military aid – aid which we knew she could not in fact give?

Speaking again from the point of view of the League, should we have gone on and risked a unilateral war? Such a war, though of course ultimately resulting in the defeat of Italy (always provided that it did not lead to a general conflagration in Europe) would be almost certain to involve us in heavy losses, resulting in a domestic situation which would most seriously affect public opinion here in the support which hitherto they had been inclined to give to the League.

... The Prime Minister said that the experience of the last few months had disclosed a situation which would require the gravest possible attention on the part of all the States Members of the League. It was all very well to talk about dealing with the aggressor, but in the end the course of events seemed likely to require effective action upon the territory of the aggressor. With the exception of ourselves none of the members of the League were in a position to take action of that kind. Indeed, at the present moment the only countries that are in a position to take effective action are the Dictator countries...

Over the following days criticism of the Hoare–Laval pact increased, even among such normal supporters as Dawson of *The Times* and Conservative backbench MPs. Faced with a Labour vote of censure on 19 December and what Baldwin described as 'a worse situation in the House of Commons than he had ever known', the Cabinet decided that the pact had to be repudiated and Hoare asked to resign.[41] Lucy Baldwin noted in her diary that 'The H.of C. demands its [pound] of flesh & Stan is going to try in a speech to take the blame & try & help Sam

---

[40] I.e. the French government would have to call up soldiers for armies to defend its land frontier with Italy, whereas the British would use its standing naval forces.
[41] The minutes of the relevant Cabinet meetings are published in *DBFP* (2s.) 35, pp. 748–61.

Hoare.' Baldwin's speech of retraction and apology was the lowest point in his House of Commons career.[42]

The best speech in defence of the Cabinet was by Austen Chamberlain. It has become a historical commonplace that before the debate Baldwin secured Chamberlain's assistance by hinting that he would succeed Hoare as Foreign Secretary, but then withdrew the offer once the government had survived the vote. This is certainly inaccurate. The suggestion that an offer was made *before* the 19 December debate is not supported by Chamberlain's written and reported accounts at the time; indeed, these show that Baldwin and Chamberlain did not meet until the day *after* the debate. The story's sole source is a second-hand 'recollection' thirty years after the event, which seems actually to derive from a transposition of the well-documented 20 December meeting.[43] Amid widespread rumours that Chamberlain might become foreign secretary, Baldwin evidently intended to explain to him why he would not be appointed. However, the conversation descended into misunderstanding, with Chamberlain hurt by the references to his age yet still thinking he might be offered the post[44] and Baldwin left thinking that Chamberlain should be consoled and conciliated with a different post. The unravelling of this misunderstanding on the following day made Chamberlain very bitter. The real significance of the episode, like that of Baldwin's discussion with Chamberlain in May 1923, lies in what it reveals about the difficulties Prime Ministers can have in dealings with very senior politicians. Chamberlain took what he probably regarded as suitable revenge in the House of Commons on 14 February, with a damaging personal attack on Baldwin's conduct of defence policies.

21–2 DECEMBER 1935 SIR AUSTEN CHAMBERLAIN MEMORANDUM

AC 41/1/68

21 December
The Prime Minister asked me to call upon him yesterday morning...

---

[42] Baldwin and other ministers felt under an obligation to Hoare for sacrificing himself, and tacitly promised him a later return to government. He became First Lord of the Admiralty in June 1936.

[43] The source was Lady Waverley, formerly Ava Wigram: I. Colvin, *Vansittart in Office* (1965), pp. 83–4, also p. 8. It seems certain that she had muddled the dates and details given in a paraphrase of the following memo. in Petrie, *Austen Chamberlain*, II, p. 406. A. Chamberlain to N. Chamberlain, 20 Dec. 1935, NC 1/27/124, reported the essentials of the first conversation immediately afterwards: it confirms his fuller memorandum account.

[44] As is clear from Austen's observations recorded in N. Chamberlain to Baldwin, 22 Dec. 1935, SB papers 47/181.

He began by saying that he wished to speak with me about the Foreign Office, and that he wanted to talk with the same frankness that had always prevailed between us.

Without further preliminary he said that he would have 'loved' to have offered me the post, but that at my age and with my health he was afraid that I should break down. The Office required iron nerves. The strain of it had broken down Hoare and Vansittart as previously Crowe and Tyrrell. No-one would believe that my appointment could be more than temporary, or that I should last out the Parliament. He then expatiated at some length on the danger of a man becoming unfit for his work without himself being aware of it and illustrated his argument by reference to one of his colleagues in the Government. I could only infer that he thought I should 'crack' (his own word) under the strain, and should persist in continuing the work without realising my mental condition.

Having thus made it plain that he thought me unfit by reason of age and health for the post, he asked me what I thought about it! I replied: 'If that is your opinion, it is conclusive'. He again repeated that he would have 'loved' to have me, but he feared that I should break down. He said that his only comforting reflection as regards Sam Hoare's resignation was that he might now entirely recover his health and give many more years of service to the country, whereas if he had continued in office he would have had a permanent breakdown. He began again to expatiate on the way in which men continued to think themselves fit after it was clear to everybody else that they were past their work. I told him that it was unnecessary to say more on this subject, and asked him to come to the business for which he had summoned me, since I was due elsewhere at 1.30.

He then asked whether I thought Anthony Eden fit for the post. I told him that I had always thought that Eden had the making of a future Foreign Secretary, that he had certainly done his work well in the House of Commons, and I believed that he had done it well and won the confidence of his colleagues at Geneva, but the answer really depended upon two questions to which I could not give the answers.

In the first place, was he in good health and could he stand the strain? I had hardly seen him of late, but someone had told me that he was not looking well (it was in fact the Prime Minister himself, who, a few days before, had told me that Eden was in urgent need of a holiday) and I had heard that he was living on a diet of milk and eggs only. Did this mean merely that his digestion was momentarily upset, or did it in fact indicate something more serious? Even a disordered digestion was not good for the nerves.

Secondly, had he in those difficult times shown any sign of getting rattled? Had he, in fact, the 'iron nerves' which Baldwin himself had said were needed for the position? This question could only be answered by those who had seen Eden in the Cabinet, and without knowing the answer to it I could not reply with confidence to the question he had put to me.

Baldwin said that he should have a very frank talk about the health question with Eden. He spoke of the narrow circle of his possible choice, of the difficulties of having the Secretary of State at such a time in the House of Lords, and of the disappointment that some of his younger colleagues had been to him. He spoke, as he so often does, of his wish to retire, and fixed a new day (the third he has given me in recent years) for that event. I rose to leave and he thanked me for going to see him and said that he should take time to consider the position. After what had just happened, he was not going to hurry again.

22 December
The Prime Minister again asked me to call upon him yesterday and I went to 10 Downing Street at 3 p.m.

Repeating a phrase he had used the previous day he said that he had 'done much hard thinking' in the last twenty-four hours. He had seen Eden who had in turn seen his doctor and brought a most satisfactory report from him. He had practically decided to make Eden Foreign Secretary and to abolish the post of Minister for League of Nations Affairs, but he had not yet informed Eden. He wished now to ask me to help him and to render 'another great public service'. Would I join the Cabinet as 'Minister of State'? He believed that was the right term but must make sure. Anyway he did not like the term 'Minister without Portfolio', but what he meant was that I should be a member of the Cabinet without a Department. I could be of great help in two ways; it would be useful to have my advice in discussions on foreign affairs: and then there were defence questions on which my experience would be of great value. Later, if Ramsay MacDonald did not find a seat and had to retire, I could, if I wished, have the Lord Presidency. In such a position I could do just as much as I liked or as little. If at any time I needed a holiday I could go away 'for a fortnight' and he believed that in such conditions there was no reason why I 'should not last out this Parliament'.

He again spoke of the sad case of men whose powers failed without their realising it and dwelt on the unhappy case of a colleague who was in this position. Similarly, he repeated his disappointment in some of his younger colleagues and of their lack of experience.

This proposal was entirely his own idea: he had not discussed it or spoken of it to anyone, though he had asked Eden whether, if he became Foreign Secretary, he would be embarrassed if I should join the Cabinet. Eden had replied that on the contrary there was no one whom he would sooner see in the Cabinet than me.

Baldwin dwelt upon the gravity and importance of the defence questions – the extent and character of rearmament – which had been under consideration during the last twelve months and which must be decided in January. If I accepted, he should send me the papers to read at Christmas. He thought me qualified for this work and my experience would be of use in it, and it would not impose too great a strain on me. If I was not prepared to accept at once, he would at least beg me to think it over.

I told him that I certainly could not accept at once, if for no other reason because I had promised my wife that, if he made me any proposal, I would neither accept nor refuse until I had consulted with her.

I then said that I was sorry to have to raise the question of salary, but I was now living on what I earned by other work, that if I gave that up, I could not hope to resume it or to build up a new income four or five years hence and that I was therefore obliged to ask what salary would be attached to the position which he offered me. On his replying £3,000, I told him that, if I accepted, I could not afford to take less than the salary of a Secretary of State and asked if that would make any difficulty for him. He at once said that for a man of my experience who had held the positions I had filled, he thought that was quite reasonable and it would create no trouble.

I asked whether if my decision reached him by the first post on Monday that would be time enough. He replied that he would like to be able to publish both appointments in Monday morning's papers and I promised to let him know any decision on Sunday afternoon at the latest.

I then left him.

I had no doubt in my own mind that the position would be thoroughly unsatisfactory and that I ought to refuse, but I put the proposal to my wife without any indication of my own feeling, and asked her opinion. She had no hesitation in saying that I ought to refuse, and I accordingly sent the following reply to the Prime Minister by hand at 7 p.m. last evening.

> The Goring Hotel, S.W.1./ 21st December, 1935, 7 p.m.
>
> My dear Prime Minister
>
> After careful consideration of the proposal which you made to me this afternoon and after discussing it with my wife, I have decided that it is not one which I can accept.
>
> As we both reached this conclusion without hesitation, I feel that I ought to communicate it to you at once, so that you may complete your arrangements without loss of time.
>
> You laid so much emphasis on my age and health both when I saw you yesterday morning and again this afternoon that I am compelled to add that anxiety about my health has played no part in my decision.
>
> If you should feel at any time that I could be of any use in the Committee of Imperial Defence as a Privy Councillor without ministerial position or salary, I am at your service.
>
> Yours sincerely, / Austen Chamberlain[45]

I have no doubt that my situation if I had accepted would have been most unsatisfactory. Neither in foreign affairs nor in defence should I have had any defined position or authority. He himself said when speaking of the term 'Minister without portfolio' that he had made a mistake in appointing Eustace Percy who had not enough to do and was 'restless and unhappy' in consequence. His repeated references to Ramsay MacDonald's condition and to the danger of men becoming senile without being aware of it were offensive in their iterations. I could perceive no prospect of public usefulness in the acceptance of such an offer so conveyed and I came to the conclusion that what he wanted was not my advice or experience, but the use of my name to help patch up the damaged prestige of his Government.

After MacDonald's defeat at the general election he was nominated, against some opposition, as candidate for the vacant Scottish Universities seat. He won the by-election in February.

---

[45] Baldwin replied next day, AC 58/98: 'My dear Austen,/ I am very, very sorry.'

22 DECEMBER 1935: TO MACDONALD

J. R. MacDonald papers 30/69/683/40–1

10, Downing Street

My dear Lord President,

I was sorry not to have the opportunity of seeing you again but I have been very busy and hope to get home in the morning.

After looking at it all round I have decided to put Eden at the F.O. and to abolish the post of Minister for L. of N. affairs. I offered Austen a seat in the Cabinet to help in Defence problems where he would have been most useful: but after consideration he declined. I expect financial reasons.

These things are not easy to talk about, but I have felt profound sympathy with you this last month. Seaham, and then all this worry about the Universities. I shall wait anxiously to hear how the past week has affected them. And it worries me that you can't yet get away for that rest you so badly need.

I do hope you will do so the first moment you can even though, with your marvellous recuperative power, you may feel the need of it less for the moment.

Last week will have one good result: for the first time our democracy will think seriously about sanctions: what they mean and imply. That they have never done before.

A good New Year to you: it has been and is a pleasure to work with you and I shall rejoice when your worries and all this uncertainty is over.

Ever yours/ S.B.

22 DECEMBER 1935: TO MONICA BALDWIN

SB add. papers

10, Downing Street

My dearest Monica,

Your letter gave me keen pleasure, but I have been so immersed in my work since the election that I haven't had a moment in which to draw breath. I hope to get home to-morrow but I fear only for a few days.

I am sending you a book I have just had published and there are some good things in it which I hope you will like.[46] You see my job is to try and educate a new democracy in a new world and to try and make them realise their responsibilities in their possession of power, and to keep the eternal verities before them.

I have written a note to your reverend mother to apologise in case I am breaking any of your regulations.

We have a sharp frost all over the country and I am writing in my cosy library overlooking Downing Street and the Foreign Office. Aunt Cissie and I are alone with such of the servants as have not gone to Astley but Betty went down yesterday.

Don't worry about me. If I am spared in health I think another three years will see me through. A Prime Minister's job is not one for men over seventy.

I have just had a week fit to kill most people, and though I feel a bit battered I have emerged all right, and my spirit unabated!

But it is a different world from the one you knew and one you wouldn't like. Pray for it.

Much love my child this Christmas and always.

Your loving/ Uncle Stan

Kipling died on 18 January, and King George V two days later. Following the procedure planned during the King's serious illness in 1928, Baldwin gave a broadcast on his death – relayed across the Empire and North America – on the evening of the 21st,[47] which did much towards restoring his own moral authority. Amid the pageantry of the King's lying-in-state and funeral, Baldwin was a pallbearer at his cousin's funeral in Westminster Abbey on the 23rd. He wrote of Kipling that he was 'the last of my men contemporaries who remembered me in the nursery and we became boys together again whenever we met. I have always felt convinced that in another century when our great men are sifted out, he will be on a peak, alone, in his generation, while many, now so loudly acclaimed, will find worthy and respectable places on the lower slopes of the mountain.'[48]

Following a weekend visit shortly afterwards, Baldwin wrote to thank the absent host and his sister.

[46] *This Torch of Freedom.*
[47] For help in its preparation, see Jones *DL*, pp, 163–5, and *Reith Diaries*, p. 185.
[48] To Lady Bathurst, 1 Feb. 1936, Bathurst papers 1990/1/2647.

[LATE JANUARY 1936]: TO SIR PHILIP SASSOON

Sassoon papers

Trent

My dear Philip,

Shod in your shoes, warmed by your wine, expanding under the influence of Sybil's Stilton, I can just rise to call you blessed. Without your bounty, I should be shoeless, chill, and empty.

And then where would the country be? Answer: exactly where it is now!

With grateful affection (or should it be affectionate gratitude?)

S.B.

[EARLY 1936] SIR DONALD SOMERVELL NOTE, 1950S

note on front-paper of Somervell's copy of D. C. Somervell, *Stanley Baldwin* (1953)

Harold Nicolson told me of a conversation he had with Baldwin soon after entering the House. Baldwin gave him three pieces of advice. First grow an extra skin against attribution of motives. Second, never criticise the opposition. Third, 'If you belong to a press cutting agency, cancel your subscription'.

During February Baldwin began to speak seriously about the time of his retirement.

8 FEBRUARY 1936 NEVILLE CHAMBERLAIN DIARY

S.B. . . . told me he had just been overhauled by Ld. Dawson who had found him quite sound but tired as evidenced by his circulation and I suppose low blood pressure. He had been thinking about his future. He wanted to see the new King well started and he wd. like to see some agreement with Germany. But his prestige was now probably at its zenith and it would be bad for the country and for his successor if it declined. He therefore thought of getting out in about 2 years, say in 1938 if he could stick it so long. Dawson approved of this and his 'Missus' was in full agreement. This is the most definite statement he has yet made to me. I said I was grateful to him for letting me know his plans for although no one could foresee the future in politics in which the unexpected was always happening at present it looked as though I were the most likely successor. SB: 'I should think there is not much doubt of that. I don't want in the circ[umstance]s to make any drastic changes but I should recommend you if you form a Cabinet to go in for a good deal of reconstruction' NC: 'Well, if I should ever be in that position I should like to consult you. Do you mean to go on . . . ?' S.B.: 'Oh I think I should go out. I don't <u>want</u> to go to the Lords. If there were Life Peerages I should take one like a shot. But I don't know what I shall do. I should like three months to rest & turn things over . . . '

Another personal dimension of managing a government and a party is shown by an after-effect of Baldwin's dropping of Londonderry from the Cabinet. It is also a further example of his directness in certain types of private discussion.

[*c.* FEBRUARY 1936 CONVERSATION] VISCOUNT
CASTLEREAGH[49] MEMORANDUM, WRITTEN AUGUST 1936

W. Baldwin papers

Shortly after the General Election was over Romaine and I travelled over to London. That evening we paid a visit to Maureen's house and heard from Oliver[50] the names of the members of the new Cabinet. As we expected my Father's name was not included.

The next morning we went round to Londonderry House to see my Father. He was a tragic sight: I never really knew before the meaning of the phrase – 'A broken man'. He was sitting sideways in his chair with his legs dangling over the arm. Holding a letter in his hand and with tears running down his cheeks he kept muttering: 'I've been sacked – kicked out.' The letter was from Baldwin giving a number of reasons for not including him in the Cabinet. We could do nothing except say how sorry we were and we left as soon as possible.

From abject despair my Father's mood turned to extreme bitterness. Baldwin became his bête-noir and he pursued him with undying hatred. His attitude was very puzzling. He must have been aware that all was not well with his political career. During the early part of the election he was in Northern Ireland and he must surely have thought it strange not to say significant that there was no demand for his services – a Cabinet Minister – as

---

[49] Unionist MP, County Down since 1931, succeeded as 8th Marquess of Londonderry 1949. His letter to A. W. Baldwin, 5 Dec.1951, W. Baldwin papers, gives the date of the discussion.
[50] Respectively Castlereagh's wife, his sister, and her husband, Oliver Stanley.

a speaker. It was unheard of, but my Father was very like an ostrich and like many a weak character he was apt to skirt around an unpleasant situation. Moreover he and my Mother had been living in a little world of their own, surrounded by hangers on and flatterers and it is possible that they just did not know what was happening. Some two years previously Maureen and I had warned him of the grave harm the alliance with Ramsay MacDonald was doing to him and he certainly seemed to be impressed.

My Father instead of getting over his disappointment grew more and more embittered. Eventually I told Maureen that I was going to seek an interview with S.B. and tell him straight out that he had not behaved at all well to my Father and that I wanted an explanation. Maureen was against it: like Oliver she had no use for S.B. but I liked him. He had always been very good to me and had shown his confidence in me before I became a M.P. Accordingly when the House reassembled after the Christmas Recess I wrote a letter marked 'strictly private' asking him if I could see him on an urgent personal matter. In reply I had a short note in his own hand telling me to wait for him behind the Speaker's chair after questions on Wednesday being private members day. I duly met him and he led me to his room. We sat down and he told me to go ahead and take my time.

I told S.B. that he had not treated my Father at all fairly and that I spoke not merely as a son but as a member of the party. This was a poor reward for a man who had worked hard and rendered such services to the Conservative cause. My Father was asked by you, I went on, to give up his job as Air Minister because you felt that such a post should be held by a M.P. rather than a peer. Accordingly he made way for Cunliffe-Lister, who was actually created a peer a few months later. My Father was offered the post of Leader of the House of Lords and told he could hold it as long as he liked. However after the election he was asked to resign, one of the reasons given being that the defeats of the two MacDonalds had added unforeseen complications to the making up of the new Cabinet. I ended by saying that in my opinion my Father had had a raw deal.

S.B. sat in silence for a long time puffing at his pipe which was continually going out. Then he began to speak. Naturally I cannot recall his exact words after the lapse of some months. I made very copious notes directly I left him from which I quoted to Maureen and it is from these that I am now writing a full account of the interview. The following represents fairly accurately what he said.

'I have always liked your Father very much. I have a great admiration for him. He certainly looked and acted the part of the old aristocrat. I was vastly impressed by his courage in learning to fly at his age – even more so by the boyish enthusiasm he took in it. It used to scare me to death. Any day I expected to hear of a fatal accident and of course he very nearly killed himself a year or two ago. I could always count on your Father's complete loyalty as a colleague. Loyalty is the rarest virtue in politics.

I always tried to be friends with your Father but he was aloof and stand-offish. As you know I gave your Father his first Cabinet appointment: it was not an altogether popular choice and I was largely influenced by Winston. In offering him the job I paid him a little compliment which I hoped would show that I was seeking his friendship as well as his services. Instead of writing him a note or summoning him to Downing Street I paid him a visit at his house and asked him to join my Cabinet. After all, I had done four years in my second term as Prime Minister and he had never been in the Cabinet before; it was too the junior post of all.[51] However he seemed not to notice my gesture. I always had the impression that your Mother looked down on my wife and myself.

As an individual your Father was popular enough but as a politician it was different. He owed a great deal to privilege and naturally this made for jealousies. He had travelled the easy road in the House of Lords whereas his colleagues had gone the hard way – back bencher, under-secretary and eventually Cabinet Minister in the Commons. He had escaped the searching test of a young minister at question time. This of course was not his fault but he had served several years in the Commons without making an impression. He became a M.P. at a time when the Conservative opposition consisted of a small handful. Making a speech then was simple. The Whips urged you to speak, instead of dissuading you as you found in the last Parliament. It was a heaven sent opportunity for an able young man to make his mark. Later on in the 1910 Parliament Home Rule was the main topic and here your Father was batting on a really good wicket. But he made no impression in the rough school of the Commons. Bonar Law, a great admirer of your Grandfather, was never impressed by his son and used to tell him so openly.

---

[51] I.e. the appointment, as First Commissioner of Works, was to the lowest-ranking Cabinet office at that time (1928).

After the war everything was changed. Your Father found himself still a young man in the House of Lords, where his chances of promotion were infinitely greater. By style and appearance he was more at home there than in the Commons. In addition he succeeded to the wonderful position and goodwill created by his parents and of course he was enormously rich. This latter was all important. I have always called that Coalition period "The Golden Age of Corruption". Money and titles were paramount. Much as I admired Lloyd George as an unsurpassed war leader I regarded him as a mass corrupter in peacetime and I was determined to oust him. But when it was done, it was not enough. As I told you before I fought an election on protection to rally the party: to enable it to find its soul again and cleanse itself from the corruption of Lloyd George's contact.

Your parents started off to play politics in the old style. They proceeded to entertain politically on a vast scale with of course the set purpose of political advancement. "F.E." with that caustic wit of his used to describe your Father as "catering his way to the Cabinet". It was very magnificent and beautifully done but to me it was out of date and at times in dubious taste. It did not fit in with my idea of true Tory democracy. Central Office of course loved it. These methods were not calculated to make your Father popular with his colleagues.

I have never professed to be an expert in foreign affairs. I prefer to be advised by those who really know. Your Father appeared to his colleagues to be donning the mantle of Castlereagh a little too often. Frankly I do not think he had a flair in that direction; he was not a success at Geneva. I have always thought that his knowledge of history was too scanty to support the role to which he aspired.

I have been candid. I shall be more so. I do not think your Mother has been a very happy influence on your Father in politics. She is a very remarkable person. She was a creative genius in the war. It was she who first set the women at work. There was a mass of feminine energy warped and wasted in the suffragette movement. She diverted it into the war effort. She has great charm, vitality and courage – priceless assets. But if allied to faulty judgement they became even greater liabilities. I believe your Mother's judgement to be unsound and she is much too stubborn ever to admit a mistake. She makes no attempt to conceal her likes and dislikes. She was always rude to John Simon – as a consequence he and your Father never hit it off. All my life I have always liked to keep people contented. Our old family business used to be a model.

The happy relations between masters and men were unique. You know how hard I worked for peace in industry and indeed peace in Parliament. It is a difficult task keeping a party Cabinet together but a Coalition Cabinet is a desperate problem. She used to make slighting remarks: "That common little man, I forget his name" was the way she referred to Kingsley Wood in the presence of a number of people. It does not help matters, least of all your Father, especially when it is common knowledge that she rules him completely.

But the worst thing of all was the alliance with Ramsay MacDonald. I have Highland blood in me and I understand the bond which unites highlanders, but 90% of people do not. To them your Mother's friendship with Ramsay is purely an act of political expediency to help your Father's political career. All his life Ramsay has fought against everything your Father stands for. The abrupt change is too good to be true in their eyes. I know that your Mother is genuinely fond of Ramsay and that she has greatly helped a very lonely man, but I also know that it has driven a very wide cleft between your Father and all his old friends in the Conservative Party, while the mention of Londonderry House produces broad smiles in the House. Poor old Ramsay was a doughty fighter in his early days; it was tragic to see him in his closing days as P.M., losing the thread of his speech and turning to ask a colleague why people were laughing – detested by his old friends, despised by the Conservatives. Your Mother certainly provided a refuge for Ramsay for which your Father paid a high price.

I have said enough to show that though the Prime Minister was a close personal friend, your Father's position was the reverse of secure. Unfortunately he proceeded to make a speech which had the most unfortunate consequences.[52] I have never understood why he made it. I believe he used to read all his speeches and I imagine he read over a brief without checking it over. I know nothing about the air, but admirals always want more and bigger battleships and I suppose the Air Ministry is the same. But the Air Minister is the mediator between the Air Marshals and his Cabinet colleagues. As an

---

[52] On 21 May 1935 Londonderry had said that during 1932 he experienced 'the utmost difficulty ... in preserving the use of the bombing aeroplane'. This was accurate – the Air ministry had resisted the proposed ban on military aircraft – but politically inept: it referred to past conditions of disarmament at a time when the Cabinet was trying to justify rearmament, and it encouraged both an opposition outcry against the horrors of bombing and criticism from Conservatives wanting still greater rearmament.

island people the only things we need fear are submarines and bombs from the air. Your Father's speech was contrary to the policy of his colleagues and the views of the country. Peace talk was in the air: we were still badly shaken by [East] Fulham and a General Election was in the offing. It was all very unfortunate. I feel now that your Father should have offered his resignation at once. As you know there was an outcry. The opposition seized the opportunity and made it the spearhead of their election and pre-election campaign, but a far bigger outcry came from the Conservative party.

Members were beginning to look to their seats and here was a Cabinet Minister giving the enemy ammunition free and for nothing. The Air Minister must go. Naturally this came up to Cabinet level. Neville, as an ex-Chairman of the party, gave it as his opinion that your Father's continued presence in the Cabinet would not assist our chances in the election. My first duty when I became P.M. last June was to groom the party for an election and any Minister who had erred would have to be asked to go. I know my many weaknesses as a P.M.: not the least of them is my inability to be a good butcher. It is not in my nature. An F.E. or a Winston would not hesitate: to them public service comes before sentiment and your Father would have been dismissed at once. I could not do that. To me it is all wrong. Your Father had given years of devoted service to his country and you cannot summarily fire a man with such a record. We had already decided to make a change at the Air Ministry. With the increase in air strength we felt that we required a Minister with more experience of business and industry in general, such a man too should be in the House of Commons, but no one can foretell the results of an election and the ensuing complications. I found it more convenient to make Cunliffe-Lister a peer. But the reason he was chosen to replace your Father was that with his wider experience he would be better qualified to deal with expansion.

I do not understand what you mean when you say I promised your Father he could remain leader of the House of Lords as long as he liked. No P.M. is in a position possibly to make such a promise. No Minister could ever take such a promise as valid. It does not make sense. He must have misunderstood something I said. I know that I never wittingly said anything of the sort and that in his disappointment he must have got hold of the wrong end of the stick. Instead of asking him to resign as I was advised to do, I actually promoted him to leadership of the House of Lords, thinking this would be a very appropriate wind up to an honourable career.'

On 7 March German armies breached the treaties of Versailles and Locarno by occupying the demilitarised Rhineland, but at the same time Hitler held out offers of non-aggression pacts, airforce limitation and re-entry into the League of Nations. The French and Belgian governments asked for British support for an escalating series of sanctions against Germany but the Cabinet, supported by much British public opinion, was not prepared to risk war when offered a chance of a general European settlement.

11 MARCH 1936: STATEMENT IN CABINET

Cabinet 18(36)

The Prime Minister thought at some stage it would be necessary to point out to the French that the action they proposed would not result only in letting loose another great war in Europe. They might succeed in crushing Germany with the aid of Russia, but it would probably only result in Germany going Bolshevik . . .

The Prime Minister pointed out that at the time when Locarno was signed the Government had felt that the commitments could be accepted without undue risk owing to the strength of the French forces and the fact that Germany was totally disarmed. When the Disarmament Conference failed and Germany started to rearm, the Government here started to do the same. In a democratic country, however, a good deal of time was taken to educate public opinion and get a plan accepted and consequently we were now caught at a disadvantage. All that was perfectly well known to the French Government, and it seemed very unfriendly of them to put us in the present dilemma. People would take a long time to forget it. He himself had said at the Election that he was never going into sanctions again until our armaments were sufficient. He felt that the French ought to welcome our coming rearmament, rather than expose us to the present embarrassments.

On 9 March Baldwin had announced a new Defence White Paper, containing accelerated rearmament programmes for all the armed services. The scale of these programmes and pressure from Churchill, Austen Chamberlain and other Conservative critics persuaded the Cabinet to appoint a minister to co-ordinate defence preparations. Churchill considered himself a candidate, but after considering various other alternatives Baldwin made the much-criticised appointment of Inskip, previously the Attorney-General. In July Churchill, Austen Chamberlain and Salisbury organised a deputation of Conservative MPs and peers to raise their concerns about the implementation of rearmament with Baldwin, Inskip, and Halifax. Baldwin's statement in reply included, in more cogent form, the essence of his notorious 'appalling frankness' passages in the House of Commons on 12 November.[53]

28 JULY 1936: REPLY TO A DEPUTATION OF CONSERVATIVE PEERS AND MPs

PREM 1/193/102–93; *WSC V/3*, pp 277–95 (extracts)

... I should like to begin by pointing out some of the earlier difficulties of the situation, with no desire to dwell on old history, but just to see how we have got into the present position. You may feel, many of you, that we might have gone on faster than we have ... Lord Salisbury ... hoped we felt as deeply as you do about these things. There is not an anxiety mentioned that is not weighing on me ... and has done night and day for the last three or four years. This country, of course, when the war stopped suffered from the usual relapse she usually has had after wars. We know the temper of our people. The moment war is over they think there will never be another one and undoubtedly we have suffered from what all of us who have held office is concerned with, that is the ten years' rule.[54]

I do not want to say anything about what took place in Cabinets, but the ten years' rule existed until we abolished it in 1932 and you will remember at one time – I do not think I am saying anything I should not here – at one time the ten years' rule was more narrowly defined as ten years from any given date, and of course, at that time in the state of the world it did look safe, but of course, it did have this effect. It had the effect, an effect aided by the economies we have had to practise since the war and very much by the economies we had to practise in 1931, 1932 and 1933, at the time of the financial crisis, the result was every Service was skinned. It was done before we went out in 1929 and I do not think there is any secret about this. I think

---

[53] *HC Debs* 317, cc. 1143–5. The phrase 'appalling frankness' was one Baldwin occasionally also used in private, meaning with 'complete candour' – not something shocking or dreadful: see above p. 118. For explanation of this November 1936 passage see Williamson, *Baldwin*, pp. 306–7, 312–13.

[54] A 1919 Cabinet instruction to the defence departments and military chiefs that their plans should assume that no great war would occur for ten years. As Chancellor of the Exchequer in 1928 Churchill had been responsible for a Cabinet decision that this 'ten year rule' should be not just renewed, but assumed to roll forward automatically each year.

we should all agree.[55] Partly owing to the admirable management of the then Secretary of State,[56] I think probably the War Office was skinned more than any of them. I think we should all agree the Army paid a larger price at that time than the Navy or the Air Force. They all paid a price and a big price it was.

Then another bad effect it had was when orders were curtailed to the minimum, gradually, and . . . it was a very serious thing, with the depression in trade in certain lines that came owing to the interruptions in international trade and so forth, the skilled men in so many of the most important trades of the country got broken up, particularly in ship-building and in munition making. A good many emigrated at one time, but they did get broken up. One of the great difficulties today is in the re-assembling of such skilled men as you have got and the teaching of the younger generation to do that work. That was a very great loss.

Then it was I think in 1933 when the Nazi government came into power and very soon after that although it was extremely difficult to get absolutely accurate and reliable information, we, and the world, knew re-armament on some scale was beginning in Germany. This was the great difficulty we were up against, and I do beg you to realise what an awful responsibility this was. I was not Prime Minister at the time, but as somebody who had some influence in the country I have said in many speeches and it is a tragic fact, but it is a true statement and I want to drive it into the heads of other people, a democracy is about two years behind an autocracy and it has proved so in this case.

It would have been an extremely difficult thing in a free country to have started arming freely in 1934. This was a thing which was in my mind tremendously, and during the winter of 1933 we began to study this question and what the requirements of the country would be to bring it up to a perfectly equipped force, to the extent of such forces as we thought this country would require for her defence, and we began to consider the speeding up of the existing air programmes. When that was done, of course, starting from scratch

[55] In the November defence debate these years in the 1920s were described by Inskip as 'the years the locust hath eaten' (from Joel 2: 25), and Baldwin in reiterating the phrase explicitly mentioned Churchill's role at the Treasury in cutting the armed services and tightening the ten years' rule. Churchill, however, immediately and with lasting historical effect re-defined 'the locust years' as applying to the later, post-1931, MacDonald-Baldwin years of responsibility for armaments policy.

[56] Worthington-Evans.

took a long time to do. It was done extremely thoroughly. Then we had a ministerial examination upon which the Chancellor and I, among others, were on, and we went through everything ourselves. It took a long time; it was a very careful examination and, if I remember rightly, we got it finished in about July 1934. The only outcome of that practically was ... we proposed an increase in the air, not as much as you wanted, but an increase, but not in anything else.

This was the problem in my mind. Most of you sit for safe seats. You do not represent industrial constituencies; at least, not many of you. There was a very strong, I do not know about pacifist, but pacific feeling in the country after the war. They all wanted to have nothing more to do with it, and the League of Nations Union have done a great deal of their propaganda in making people believe they could rely upon collective security, and it was a question in 1934 whether if you tried to do much you might not have imperilled and more than imperilled, you might have lost the General Election when it came. I personally felt that very strongly, and the one thing in my mind was the necessity of winning an election as soon as you could and getting a perfectly free hand with arms. That was the first thing to do in a democracy, the first thing to do, and I think we took it at the first moment possible. For some time a great many powerful influences were against me on that. They wanted to postpone the election until 1936, and I think the Central Office was against me, as we are all Tories here together, but it was wrong. We took it at the first moment we could and we had two elements with us, and I think we used them to the full. The first was people had begun to realise what Hitler meant, and, secondly, that time coincided with a great wave of feeling for what they called collective security. The position was complicated by Lloyd George and his Council of Action, which was meant to rally in the pacifists and appeal to the Non-Conformists in the country, but, fortunately for us, there was some delay in bringing it into action. There was a good deal of examination needed of the programme which he submitted to us, and we fought the election immediately after the holidays before he had a chance of getting to work, so it did not function at the election though it looked at one time as though it might be a dangerous element. We fought the election, and we won it and won it more handsomely than anyone in this room, I think, would have expected before the election. That was a great thing done. It was done and you had the support of the democracy for your armaments. I think we were perfectly honest about it because we did try out, both before the election and into this year, we did try out at the first opportunity we had of trying out, collective security. We tried it out short of war. We tried it out and showed the people – people will only learn, unfortunately, in a democracy by putting their heads against a brick wall; they would never believe or realise what sanctions meant unless they tried them. They tried them and they saw what they meant. I was able to take the line at the election broadcast that I would never be responsible for sanctions again until the country had re-armed. That made them think a bit, and you all know what the history of that has been.

We started, of course, as I said, from scratch. I do not know, looking back, I do not know whether starting in peace conditions we could have done much better or got on much faster. The spade work to be done in beginning . . . is very heavy and very difficult, and it is being gone on with every day . . . we have had in our minds, very present to our minds . . . could we do better if we were to turn over, Mr Churchill did not say definitely to war conditions, but to some kind of half-way house[?] This is a question which I have thought about a good deal and mainly discussed with the Chancellor of the Exchequer; it touches him so closely, and we have always felt up to now, we have felt to do that might throw back the ordinary trade of the country perhaps for many years. It has never been done in peace time, throw it back for many years and damage very seriously at a time when we might want all our credit, the credit of the country. If the emergency were such as obviously demanded it, of course, it would have to be done, and I am not afraid of emergency powers. I am not afraid of anything if it has to be done.

Then you come to the peril itself. Some observations were made . . . by one of the speakers that seemed to me to envisage – I may have misunderstood them – a possibility of a war between ourselves and Germany alone. I do not know if anybody does envisage that, but unless Germany goes mad and attacks us and France refuses to come in, which she is bound to do, I do not think that can happen. I mean, if there is going to be a war it will be with France and Belgium and possibly Holland and ourselves on the one side, and Germany on the other . . . I would like to ask one or two questions about it . . . in no captious spirit because we want to help each other, that is as to how you would propose to warn people; what would you tell them? Germany is arming to fight us? It is not easy when you get on a platform to tell people what the dangers are. I have not dotted the i's and crossed the t's, but I have often spoken of the danger to democracy from dictators which I think is the one line whereby you can get people to sit up in this country, if they think dictators are likely to attack them. I think that is so, but I have always found it, but I have never quite seen the clear line by which you can approach people to scare them but not scare them into fits . . .

Again speaking in confidence in this room, there is one very important man in the Labour Party with whom I am on very good terms, that is Sir Walter Citrine of the TUC. He has just come back from Russia. I have had some interesting talks with him. I had a talk with him before bringing out the programme. I told Sir Walter Citrine about the situation in Europe and about organised labour and how we should all have to play up . . . When he heard all I had to say he thanked me for what I had said, and he said 'take your courage in both hands and go to the country with it', and intimated he for one would not complain. Of course, that is in the minds of a good many of them, though they do not come out and say so. I wish you could go to a body like that and tell them the same thing. You could talk to the Privy Councillors. I believe most of those fellows of the George Hicks[57] type would come in and you would have Labour with you, and it would arm them against the Communistic influence which at the moment is causing a great deal of anxiety both to them and to us.

. . . is it in the mind of most of you that a war with Germany is inevitable?

Sir Austen Chamberlain: I never call a war inevitable.

Prime Minister: . . . I hope you do not feel that . . . Because I do not frankly. I am not sanguine, and I think the times are most anxious.

Sir Austen Chamberlain: . . . all the omens are, in my opinion, worse to-day than they were in the years which preceded the Great War.

Prime Minister: The worst of it is we none of us know what goes on in that strange man's mind; I am referring to Hitler. We all know the German desire, and he has come out with it in his book,[58] to move East, and if he should move East I should not break my heart, but that is another thing. I do not believe she [Germany] wants to move West because West would be a difficult programme for her, and if she does it before we are ready I quite

---

[57] General secretary of the Amalgamated Union of Building Workers since 1921, a member of the TUC General Council, and Labour MP for East Woolwich since 1931. Baldwin had been on cordial terms with him since the 1920s, and regarded him as a model 'moderate' and 'patriotic' Labour leader.

[58] I.e. *Mein Kampf.*

agree the picture is perfectly awful and will be perfectly awful. I do quite agree with you, and every effort of our work and diplomacy must keep us out of it if it can be done. If the man goes stark mad and is determined to fight, as in a small way Mussolini did with the Abyssinians, we must try and get everybody against them and have the whole of Europe in the war again, which is too ghastly for anything. We may know more about it if we get talking, but, as you said the other day, you would not believe a word they say. That is one of the tragedies. No engagements, no treaties, no promises, no anything, seem to be worth while with anybody. That is one of the terrible features of it. If they come to talk we may find out what the value of all the speeches he has made about peace, and peace in the West, is, and what his undertaking not to effect changes except by peaceful means may be. I do not know.

I am not going to get this country into a war with anybody for the League of Nations or anybody else or for anything else. There is one danger, of course, which has probably been in all your minds – supposing the Russians and Germans got fighting and the French went in as allies of Russia owing to that appalling pact they made, you would not feel you were obliged to go and help France, would you? If there is any fighting in Europe to be done, I should like to see the Bolshies and the Nazis doing it. You are dealing more with specific points and I have made general observations, but I do not want you to believe that everything you have said is not most powerfully present to our minds and most of it has been for some time.

. . . Mr Churchill: . . . I certainly do not consider war with Germany inevitable, but I am sure the way to make it much less likely is to afford concrete evidence of our determination in setting about re-armament.

Prime Minister: I am with you on that.

Mr Churchill: I am sure that is a Bull point.

Prime Minister: I am with you there whole-heartedly.

In mid June Baldwin felt ill and tired, and suffered from insomnia. He consulted his doctor, Dawson, who gave him sleeping pills, and took a week's rest at Chequers – prompting rumours of his imminent retirement. He did alert Neville Chamberlain to this possibility, but expected to recuperate during his summer holiday. During July worry, depression and lack of sleep brought a relapse, and

Dawson advised him to take a long rest. Because of the international troubles, now including the Spanish civil war, the Foreign Office advised Baldwin not to go to Aix-les-Bains, apparently because of a danger of demonstrations – 'undesirable characters about'. Instead, Jones arranged that the Baldwins should borrow a house in Wales for a month, and then after a week at Chequers spend a further period in Norfolk.[59] While in Wales he asked Eden to visit and brief him before a Cabinet Foreign Affairs committee meeting: 'Dawson won't let me go to any meetings, Cabinet or otherwise, but I must be clear what is in your mind and see that you and I, in any case, are in complete accord./ . . . If you feel impatient you may remember that in Ll.G's spacious days we all were summoned to a Cabinet in Inverness!'[60]

3 AUGUST 1936: TO JOAN DAVIDSON

Lady Davidson papers; *Davidson Memoirs*, p. 412

Chequers

Little Maid

. . . We came down here on Thursday . . . and go to Gregynog, Newtown, Montgomeryshire, on Friday for a month.

Dawson spent an hour here on Saturday and took a 'cardiograph' (heart record). It was a funny performance. I sat as if I were going to be electrocuted, in a chair with wires attached to both arms and one leg. Anyway my heart is sound and it doesn't shew any signs of one of the sixty-five ailments which may be revealed by the instrument.

But I am to go easy and try and lose sense of time, and he forbids me to go to any cabinet committees this month or to cabinets in September.

He says three months is the least time I ought to have and if I go to any meetings of that kind it will undo all the good of the rest. Forgive all this but I know you want to know.

I'm quite all right, but tired right out, with no desire to move. But he looks for all the good to come in the third month . . .

I am being deluged with volumes of verse since I spoke at Cambridge: some are too comic for words.

---

[59] N. Chamberlain diary, 17, 22 June, 5, 26 July 1936; Jones *DL*, p. 230, supplemented by the fuller unpublished diary, 24 July 1936. King Edward was also advised to change his plans to holiday in southern France; hence his notorious cruise on the *Nahlin* in the eastern Mediterranean.
[60] To Eden, 8 Aug. 1936, Avon papers 14/1/557.

I hope you liked my address to the Canadians: it was the most moving spectacle I ever saw[61]. . .

Your loving/ S.B.

31 AUGUST 1936: TO BRETT YOUNG

Brett Young papers 1962

Private   [Gregynog Hall]

My dear Brett Young,

. . . we are really grateful when you send us your books. If I may say so without impertinence there are two things about your books that give me complete satisfaction. Your craftsmanship: how I respect the good workman! and your capacity to give the smell and the spirit of the choicest country in the world.

You get it both ways, physical and spiritual.

I have had one of the happiest months of my life. I was more done up when I left London than I have ever been, and Ld. Dawson said I must have three months as complete rest as possible. Kind friends of a friend lent us their house in Montgomeryshire and I have been exploring Shropshire and tracing old tombs of long vanished forebears, and visiting old houses and meeting with thoughtful kindness everywhere.

I go to Chequers on Wednesday for a few days to get in touch again, and then I am to have three weeks at Blickling which Lothian is lending me. What luck! But I have given out through the last fifteen years pretty well all that is in me.

Yours very sincerely/ Stanley Baldwin

Of course I would be proud to have a book dedicated to me.[62]

In Norfolk he was visited and briefed by his secretaries and by Horace Wilson, Jones and Hankey. After a further week at Holker Hall in north Lancashire and a

---

[61] On 14 July he had as President of the 5th Congress of the Universities of the British Empire unfavourably compared scientists to poets, and on the 29th he had addressed the Canadian pilgrimage, commemorating their war dead, in Westminster Hall.

[62] *They Seek a Country* (1937) is dedicated 'To The Earl of Baldwin, K.G., with the homage and gratitude of a friend and neighbour'.

weekend at Longleat House in Wiltshire, the Baldwins returned to London and Chequers on 12 October. Lloyd George, who had visited Hitler during September, was publishing the last two volumes of his *War Memoirs*.

11 OCTOBER 1936: TO LLOYD GEORGE

Lloyd George papers G/1/15/10

Longleat, Warminster

My dear Lloyd George,

I hear that you most kindly expressed a wish that I should come to a dinner which is being given to you at the Reform Club.

I had to tell my secretary to refuse your publisher but I feel I owe you a line of apology. I have had to cut out everything until Parliament meets – Margate a week ago, my own Worcestershire Association dinner a fortnight hence, and so on. And I cannot make an exception.

When the House meets, I never go out, and week ends I go to Chequers.

I am quite fit but am cutting out all 'extras' for whatever time I may have left. Any reports you may have seen of my brain going are greatly exaggerated!

I was just tired out for the time being, and I think the last thirteen years would have told even on your amazing vitality.

By the way, I hear that vitality of yours was never more amazing than in Germany! Dawson and T.J. are lyrical about it.

I have to thank you for your last volume and I look forward to the completion of the series which <u>must</u> include the Peace.

Yours very sincerely/ Stanley Baldwin

From mid October he consulted a wide range of individuals about the problem of King Edward's relationship with Mrs Simpson. Two of these reported conversations contain material of wider interest.

23 OCTOBER 1936 MACKENZIE KING DIARY

... As we drove up to the front door at Chequers, the maid opened the door and Mr Baldwin came himself to greet me. His son, who was with him in Canada, joined us a few minutes after. Baldwin was most hearty in his welcome. He looked to me much heavier both in face and body than I had hoped to find him, like a man greatly fatigued. He told me he had come as near to a breakdown a little while ago as possible but was feeling more rested now . . . He began to tell me of some of the problems he was having and of which he said he had spoken to only three or four of his principal Ministers. He also let me know of his own intentions as he walked up and down the floor. He said he would be glad to get away out of these Isles altogether for a time. He has felt the strain terribly and the newspapers' criticism. He felt very deeply having to part with [J. H.] Thomas who, he said, had been very loyal in his helping him to form a national government and his support of it. He did not think Thomas could have been found guilty in a court of law, that the judgement against him was pretty harsh, that Thomas had said to him in parting that he was a real nobleman[63] . . . He told me he had been down to see Lord Snowden who has been far from well; is very lonely and poor. He had enjoyed his talk with him . . . Baldwin seemed greatly pleased that he had gone to see him. Speaking about the European situation, Baldwin said it was a return to the religious wars of the old days when men were prepared to slaughter each other because of the different views they held. It was a most difficult kind of situation to deal with. He felt the League of Nations had become an embarrassment. He said that he was very much alarmed in the early Summer at the situation that, as a matter of fact, England was quite unprepared in the Mediterranean, that they had not a single aircraft gun over Malta, that he felt Mussolini might have taken action if military sanctions had been applied and no one can say where conflagration, once started, would end. He was doing the best he could to keep England out of war, and was being damned by those who did want war . . . for being a pacifist. He was prepared to go any length to save war . . .

. . . After dinner, we all sat in front of the fire in the library until after half past ten, went over incidents connected with the Imperial Conference, had a good many hearty laughs. Baldwin told me at the time of the King's death, his own cousin (Kipling) had passed away at the same time, that the strain of the service in the Abbey was always great, that the speech he delivered on the King was spoken in an address to the people practically without notes. The King, he said, for months before his death was quite clearly expecting

---

[63] Thomas had resigned as Colonial Secretary on 28 May, after an enquiry into a leak of budget information had revealed that he was the source, more by careless talk than by deliberation. Baldwin had done his best to ease his departure, with a generous speech in the House of Commons.

the end to be near. He had become singularly thoughtful and gentle, he was very home loving; very fond of Sandringham . . . During the evening, he talked about the pernicious influence of the press, of the danger of some of the American press reports making trouble between the two countries and also influencing Canadian opinion. He said the King knew I was spending a night with him at Chequers and the King might bring up himself some of the subjects on which we had been talking. He felt that he had some fine qualities and was really anxious to measure up to his obligations. He was, however, a very difficult person to deal with. He wanted his own way, did not like to be interfered with. It was hard to get him to see that he had public life which was separate from his private life, that he must recognise what was due to the former. Speaking of defence, Baldwin said England was now getting in shape where she would have double the air force of the other countries, would be able to take care of herself in that respect. He did not think she need to be concerned about her navy, that Britain was safe enough on the seas. He said nothing about the army. He said if a war should come, they would like to get munitions and war equipment made in Canada rather than in America. He thought what we should give attention to was mostly air force; while Canada might be the last country to be attacked, the air force would be the most helpful of any in case of attack, and training of men for the air and plenty of air equipment was the essential of modern warfare . . . He would like me to see Inskip, spoke well of Swinton.[64] I spoke to him about Cooper, said I thought Cooper was likely to get them all into trouble and advised him very strongly at least to change him from the portfolio he has.[65] At the table he said very little about him but later told me that he had been a disappointment. That he was not a good administrator, was getting behind in his work, had felt he ought to have his chance. I told him he was too indiscreet in his remarks. Both he and his son said Cooper was the same in private conversation, apt to be explosive and argumentative. He had been good in fighting a by-election and shown great courage, and deserved a chance. I advised Baldwin again in the morning not to delay in changing him, if possible. I spoke to him highly

---

[64] The former Cunliffe-Lister, now Secretary of State for Air.
[65] As Secretary of State for War, Duff Cooper had spoken in July of Britain and France being bound together against a common danger. This provoked Labour accusations of a planned military alliance and renewed Dominion government fears of their being dragged into a continental commitment.

of Malcolm MacDonald[66] and the way in which he had managed affairs, the judgement he had shown, et cetera. I asked him if he did not think it would be well for him to see Hitler personally. He said he was not adverse to do that and might go to Germany for the purpose. The trouble with these dictators was that they could not leave their own countries.[67] I mentioned I thought the people had confidence in him (Baldwin). He said he believed that was so and it was very touching. He felt, however, that the job of Prime Minister had become an almost impossible one for a man in the Commons. It would be different if he were in the Lords where he could be freer and have some time to himself. He was not a debater, felt having to stay in the House of Commons was a great restraint and trial. Thought this session he would do less of it. Also he was refusing to go anywhere to any dinners or to speak anywhere. He dreaded the Coronation period. I was surprised to discover he had not considered particularly the Conference following the Coronation[68] and what it too might involve. He spoke several times of the frightful congestion there was likely to be in the streets of London at the time of the Coronation. That people would be coming in their cars from all parts of the Isles, with travellers coming from other countries. The condition would be well nigh impossible. Every one seems to be at a loss to know how the traffic is to be managed. It was bad enough at the time of the King's funeral but this was nothing as to what it will be at the time of the Coronation . . .

7 NOVEMBER 1936 CITRINE MEMORANDUM

Citrine papers 10/1

. . . Baldwin said, 'Probably you think I am not a quick thinker. But that is not right, I am a very quick thinker but I do not like people knowing it. I always remember my own father down at our works when I was a lad. The men used to say that there is one thing about old Baldwin, he may not agree with you but he always listens to your case'.

---

[66] Dominions Secretary.
[67] During May and June Baldwin had seriously considered an invitation to meet Hitler, brought privately by Jones. The proposal eventually lapsed after consultation with Eden, who was furious that such irregular approaches had been encouraged and argued that unofficial unilateral talks would jeopardise the chances of a general European settlement: Jones *DL*, pp. 194–202, 205–24, and Jones unpublished diary, 16 June 1936.
[68] A planned Imperial Conference, timed to coincide with the coronation in May 1937.

I said that was exactly what I had told many of our people. Baldwin went on to say that his father always smoked a pipe and spoke slowly when talking to his own workmen. He was never sarcastic at the expense of any of them. Nothing offended people so much as sarcasm at their expense. I said I had noticed that in the House of Commons Baldwin never took advantage of his opponents in that respect, with the consequence that he usually left a very deep impression of fairness in their minds. He was the most dangerous orator the Tory Party had. He nearly succeeded in convincing his opponents.

'Workmen probably haven't had the advantages in education of some of our people', he replied. 'It is not only unfair but it is unmannerly to be sarcastic to them. Furthermore, I always try to speak slowly for the reason that people can't take it in when you speak quickly. When I broadcast I always go along at a crawling pace so that people can not only hear plainly but can take it in as I go along'.

TEN

The Abdication crisis

Since at least 1927 Baldwin had known that the Prince of Wales might become a public problem, with his mistresses and lapses in performance of duties. After King George V's death Baldwin commented that he 'had rather hoped to escape the responsibility of having to take charge of the Prince as King. But perhaps Providence has kept me here for that purpose.' He already knew about Mrs Simpson: 'When I was a little boy in Worcestershire reading history books I never thought I should have to interfere between a King and his Mistress.'[1] He did suggest to Duff Cooper, a friend of King Edward and Mrs Simpson, that she might be persuaded to go abroad for a time, saying that he 'wouldn't mind' if she were 'a respectable whore', kept out of the public view.[2] But Baldwin declined suggestions from Buckingham Palace officials and senior civil servants that he should speak with the King himself.[3]

Mrs Simpson remained married, most of Baldwin's advisors did not believe that the King seriously considered marriage with her, and Baldwin probably hoped the experience of kingship would teach him greater responsibility and prudence. Meanwhile, so long as no public scandal arose advising the King remained a problem for Palace officials, not government ministers. There is no evidence that Baldwin was concerned about two matters later claimed to have been significant: the King's attitudes on policy (including his opinions on Nazi Germany) and, in November, his statements about unemployment in South Wales ('something must be done').

Baldwin was almost certainly alerted during September 1936 to North American newspaper stories about the King's relationship with Mrs Simpson, and her public

---

[1] Jones *DL*, pp. 164–5 (24 Jan. 1936).
[2] Cooper diary, Jan. 1936, in Philip Ziegler, *King Edward VIII* (1990), p. 248.
[3] Ibid., pp. 273–4, 277–9; M&B, p. 980.

presence with the King at Balmoral. But what prompted him to act was news of Mrs Simpson's impending divorce case, strengthening the gossip about a marriage with the King and perhaps actually preparing the way for it. On 20 October he had an interview with the King. 'I spoke plainly and he listened and we had such a talk as I hoped we should. At any rate the ice is broken but whether I made a real impression I don't know.'[4]

Baldwin gave reports of this first discussion to his wife, recorded in a memorandum of 17 November, and in a statement to the Cabinet on 27 November: these are printed below. A number of other reports survive, because he now began to consult senior ministerial colleagues, legal officers, Dominions' representatives and trusted friends, seeking advice and wishing to assess wider opinion.[5] A conversation with Tom Jones includes a passage not printed in the published diaries.

5 NOVEMBER 1936 JONES DIARY

passage following from Jones DL, pp. 284–5

[Baldwin, speaking of Mrs Simpson, said:] 'I have grown to hate that woman. She has done more in nine months to damage the monarchy than Victoria and George the Fifth did to repair it in half a century. A lot of money must have passed to her from the King. Walter Monckton[6] sat next to her recently and came to the conclusion that she was a hard-bitten bitch. I have turned on the lawyers and ascertained what our powers are. If he marries her she is automatically Queen of England. I would then hand in my resignation and I think my colleagues would agree to do so. Of course he may offer to abdicate. The best thing that could happen just now would be that he should be received in silence in the streets, but outside London the facts are not widely known. He excused himself to Sam Hoare by comparing himself to George the Fourth, but Sam knew too much history for him. I told Megan

---

[4] To Tweedsmuir (John Buchan, Governor-General of Canada), 26 Oct. 1936, Buchan papers Acc 7214 mf mss 307.

[5] E.g. Mackenzie King diary, 23 Oct. 1936, and Citrine, *Men and Work*, pp. 323–8, an important account taken almost verbatim from his memo., 7 Nov. 1936, Citrine papers 10/1. The reports of meetings with Baldwin in the Duke of Windsor, *A King's Story* (1951), are based not on his own records, but on Baldwin's House of Commons speech on 10 December. *Reith Diaries*, p. 196, and J. Reith, *Into the Wind* (1949), p. 277, record Baldwin saying he would write, or had written, an account of the crisis. He did not do so. Baldwin may have been referring to his wife's memoranda; or perhaps he decided that Horace Wilson's Abdication memorandum (copies in PREM 1/466, CAB 127/57, and SB add. papers), reporting the crisis from the perspective of his private office and using Cabinet records, was adequate.

[6] As leading barrister and friend of the King, who became his principal adviser and liaised between him and ministers.

[Lloyd George's daughter] yesterday that L.G. could do us a great service by taking Mrs Simpson with him on his holiday next week[7]. . .

On 13 November Baldwin discussed the problem with his senior ministers, MacDonald, Simon, Neville Chamberlain, Halifax and Runciman. It was agreed that the King should be asked to declare his intentions, not least because the self-censorship of almost all British newspapers about the King's relationship could not last much longer, and once it became public the Cabinet would have to make some statement. Baldwin declined Chamberlain's proposal to confront the King with the prospect of formal constitutional advice which, if rejected, would lead to the Cabinet's resignation. This, Baldwin thought, risked the political embarrassment of a breach with the King. Instead, he preferred to speak with him informally again.[8] This second discussion took place on 16 November.

17 NOVEMBER 1936 LUCY BALDWIN MEMORANDUM

SB add. papers

For some time there have been rumours & more than rumours about the King & a certain Mrs Simpson – an American woman who was enjoying (?)[9] her second marriage with Mr Ernest Simpson. This we knew had been going on before King George's death & as a matter of fact I had met this Mr & Mrs Simpson at a luncheon party at Lady Cunard's at which the then P. of Wales was present. I believe that rumours had already been busy but it had not come my way. And when the party was breaking up & many of my friends were discussing the Prince & his escorts (the Simpsons left with him) I electrified the remaining company by saying 'Who is Mrs Simpson'. After the laughter had subsided I was given to understand that she was a great friend of the Prince of Wales. Since King George's death her name has been more & more coupled with that of the new King & on May 27th last he gave a private dinner party to which we were bidden as well as the Wigrams, Chatfields, Louis Mountbattens, Col & Mrs Lindbergh of America, Lady Cunard, Mr & Mrs Simpson, Duff Coopers & some others. On our return

---

[7] Lloyd George was going to Jamaica for most of the winter, partly to continue writing his memoirs.
[8] Baldwin also received advice from Bruce, the Australian High Commissioner in London: see Bruce memo., 15 Nov. 1936, in Edwards, *Bruce of Melbourne*, pp. 251–4, and his 16 Nov. letter in M&B, pp. 991–2.
[9] Question mark and brackets in the original.

to the world after Stanley's 3 months rest, we found that the one topic of conversation was the King & Mrs Simpson in practically all walks of life. Stanley was feeling more & more that he ought to make a move, for on his return to office work he was shown the piles of letters from all over the world denouncing the King & his liaison with Mrs Simpson – my letter bag also was not immune. Then came the news that Mrs Simpson was divorcing Mr Simpson & the ultimate anticipation was that she would then make the King marry her. At Cumberland Lodge where we were staying for the week-end of Oct. 16th were the Salisburys & Stanley told him that he had made up his mind to see the King about this very unpleasant situation. Poor Stan how he hated the idea. However he had written & asked for an interview & asked if he might come over & see him. The answer came back that His Majesty had flown to Sandringham, however telephones were got to work & an appointment fixed for Tuesday Oct. 20th when the King would fly over from Sandringham for the (secret) interview. S. told me afterwards that the King was most charming & that he (S.) laid the case before him & begged him to use his influence to prevent the divorce going through – this the King said was not his affair & he couldn't interfere. Anyway S. warned him that if it went through things might be more difficult still. S. also left him some of the letters he had received & newspaper articles from America to glance at at his leisure. Poor S. asked for a whisky & soda in the middle of the confab for he felt the strain of it all intensely. All the time the King was most courteous & at his nicest, but would not commit himself only begged S. to control the Press.[10] Since that interview which S. kept secret except for 3 or 4 of his elder colleagues things have been getting to boiling point. The King has been told that there has been practically a Cabinet meeting to consider his case & so last night before he went to S. Wales he sent for S. S. told him that he couldn't control the British Press (who have behaved admirably in not mentioning the subject) & they are clamouring to air the subject but out of respect for the throne had refrained. And then the King said to him these words 'I want you to be the first to know that I have made up my mind & nothing will alter it. I have looked at it from all sides. I mean to abdicate & to marry Mrs Simpson.' S. replied 'Sir, this is a very grave decision & I

---

[10] Given the existing restraint of British newspapers Baldwin had not needed to take action except, on 13 November, to ask Gwynne to continue advising other editors to wait for an official announcement.

am deeply grieved' & then went on to tell him that according to some legal opinion the divorce ought not to have been granted, that there were certain aspects of it that in any ordinary case would not have gone through. His Majesty I gather did not quite like that. Stan put to him the feelings in the Empire, how he had seen Mackenzie King of Canada & Bruce of Australia (who came down to Chequers on Sunday) both agreeing that it would break up the Empire – the throne was the one thing that held the Empire together. Again the King said 'I have made up my mind & I shall abdicate in favour of my brother the Duke of York & I mean to go & acquaint my mother this evening & my family. Please don't mention my decision except to 2 or 3 trusted privy councillors until I give you permission'. All the time the King was most charming, but S. said he felt a streak of almost madness.[11] The King simply could not understand & S. couldn't make him. The King was obsessed by a woman & that was the long & short of it – he said he couldn't do his work without her & that she was the best friend he had ever had & he couldn't live without her. S. was so impressed by the want of sanity & clear vision in it all that he feared that really he might completely go 'off it' if at the moment he was more directly opposed & Mrs Simpson disappeared. On leaving, the King held Stanley's hand for a long time & there were almost tears in his eyes when he said good-bye.

This is a faithful record as Stanley told to me on his return from his interview with His Majesty King Edward VIII at 6.30 pm. in the early evening of November 16th 1936.

Lucy Baldwin

Speaking with Duff Cooper that evening, Baldwin commented that 'he was not at all sure that the Yorks would not prove the best solution. The King had many good qualities, but not those which best fitted him for the post, whereas the Duke of York would be just like his father.'[12] On 23 November the law officers submitted an outline of an abdication bill and associated procedures. However, during that day Baldwin learned that the King was likely to propose a 'morganatic marriage': that he should marry Mrs Simpson without her becoming Queen. Baldwin's reaction was: 'he could not carry the Commons on that and did I see him attempting to

---

[11] After the first interview, Baldwin had spoken 'of the King's mind not being fully developed on some sides. It was as if certain cells had not developed, while others had. He was a man in some particulars, in some others he was not yet grown up': Mackenzie King diary, 23 Oct. 1936.
[12] 'Abdication diary', p. 1, Duff Cooper papers 2/16 (the diary was written after the crisis had ended).

do so. "Is this the sort of thing I've stood for in public life? If I have to go out, as go out I must, then I'd be quite ready to go out on this."' He suspected that the proposal would form the basis of a campaign against him and the government by the Rothermere and Beaverbrook newspapers, joined by Churchill.[13]

On 17 November Baldwin had received a deputation of Conservative and Liberal 'elder statesmen' led by Salisbury who wished to 'strengthen your hands', and on the 25th he held separate meetings with Attlee, the Labour leader, Sinclair, the Independent Liberal leader, and Churchill to assess their reactions to a possible government resignation. He had continued to consult the group of senior ministers, but now that the King had asked for an opinion on the morganatic proposal, which would require legislation, he referred the matter to the full Cabinet. He instructed Hankey not to produce the usual minutes, copies of which were circulated to the King as well as Cabinet members. Instead he asked for a single note for his own use and for the record, to be retained in the Cabinet Secretary's 'personal care'. Unusually, Baldwin made handwritten amendments to this typed report, indicated below by square brackets. For subsequent Cabinet meetings Hankey resumed the circulation of brief formal minutes, with references to the King carefully worded for his eyes. But for each discussion of the royal problem he continued to preserve a unique verbatim record, which Baldwin checked. Baldwin's main statements in these secret reports are printed here,[14] omitting only a few redundant comments.

27 NOVEMBER 1936 (FRIDAY, 11.30 A.M.): STATEMENT AT CABINET MEETING

Cabinet 68(36), in Baldwin's room, the House of Commons

The Prime Minister said that the time had come when the Cabinet ought to know of certain discussions he had had with the King in regard to His Majesty's relations with Mrs Simpson. This had not been necessary earlier, and it had been a matter in which the less that was said the better. He emphasised the great importance of secrecy . . . He himself had for a long time been worried about the situation, and had known that some time or another he would have to approach the King on the matter. He had delayed, not from any apprehension, but in order to find a satisfactory opportunity. When the time of Mrs Simpson's divorce was seen to be approaching, the

---

[13] Jones *DL*, pp. 287–9, an important report of Baldwin's views at this point.
[14] Baldwin's notes for his Cabinet statement on the 27th survive, in SB papers 176/23–6.

opportunity had arisen[15] . . . his first interview on the subject had taken place at Fort Belvedere on Tuesday, October 20th, at 10.30 a.m.

The Prime Minister . . . had begun by letting the King know that his relations with Mrs Simpson were attracting a good deal of notice . . . at the time when he left London for his rest cure there had been no criticism of the King. On his return he had found in his letter-bag a good deal of correspondence on the subject, which had resulted from statements in the American Press. He had recalled how, some nine years ago, at the time of the late King's illness, the then Prince of Wales had told him that he could say anything he liked to him at any time. The King said that this still held good, and had himself recalled that at the time of the late King's death he had told him how glad he was to have him as Prime Minister. Mr Baldwin had wondered at that time whether the King would allow him, if necessity arose, to speak about a woman . . . the Prime Minister . . . had then told the King that a continuance of the present state of affairs would sap the public respect for the Throne. If that respect went, nothing could restore the position of the Throne, and on the Throne depended the solidity of the whole Empire, including India. He himself could never forget that he was addressing his King, but he also had to think of him as a man. He had entertained great hopes from the pre-eminent gifts of popularity which the King possessed, but these would be counter-balanced by imprudent conduct and His Majesty's moral influence throughout the Empire might be dissipated. He had asked the King if he could stop the divorce, but the King had replied that this was impossible, it was the affair of Mrs Simpson over which he had no control. The Prime Minister had replied that after this case everybody would be saying 'What is to happen at the end of six months, when the decree is due to be made absolute?' When that time was reached the Press would no longer keep silence, and when that moment came a Press storm would arise. That would be just before the Coronation. [He said that a dangerous situation would arise for King and Gov^nt.] This he had repeated. He had added that the King might think perhaps that with his great popularity he might 'get away with it'. 'You can't do that', the Prime Minister had said: 'You may think that I am an old man dating from the Victorian <u>régime</u>, but I do know public opinion

---

[15] Seven sentences follow on the difficulty of arranging the meeting. Although he did not say this to the Cabinet, Baldwin suspected that the King was secretly visiting Mrs Simpson in Essex: Jones *DL*, p. 284.

in this country. Since the War there has been a lowering of the public standards and of public morals, but people expect even more of the Monarchy and they won't tolerate what they did tolerate in the early part of the last Century'. He had then begged the King to think the matter over. That was the first warning he had given. When the conversation was over he felt glad that he had broken the ice, but he wondered if he had made much impression.

Coming to the next interview with the King, the Prime Minister said that it had been his intention to see the King after his visit to Wales. As a matter of fact, however, the King had summoned him before that visit, on November 16th, and he was glad of this renewed opportunity to discuss the matter. On this occasion he had begun by pointing out the impossibility of the marriage so long as His Majesty remained King. Public opinion, neither in the United Kingdom nor in the Dominions, would stand for it, for the reason that the Wife of the King automatically became Queen. They had talked on this matter for a quarter of an hour. The King said that he would now say something that had long been in his mind to say to the Prime Minister: 'I am going to marry Mrs Simpson. You are right about opinion in the country, so I shall go'. The Prime Minister then said that in that event it should be done in such a manner as to avoid any Constitutional struggle, so as to make matters easy for his successor. The King had said, rather plaintively, that people did not seem to mind if he had a mistress, but what they objected to was his having a wife, and that this was hypocrisy. The Prime Minister replied that public opinion did not refuse to recognise that the King had a private life, but appreciated that the Wife of the King must become Queen. He had told the King of an interview he had had with Mr Bruce, the Australian High Commissioner, who had asked to see him in order to represent the Australian point of view. Mr Bruce thought that if the King married Mrs Simpson the Crown would not last long in Australia. He had added that the stories in the American Press were not sufficient to break up the position of the Crown in Australia, but marriage was a different matter. The High Commissioner had described a talk he had had with an old Anzac soldier – a New Zealander, as a matter of fact. The soldier had said that it was 'a bit thick, his taking that woman with him to Gallipoli!' Mr Baldwin had told the King that there was a nasty feeling about the circumstances of the divorce, more especially as the King was not liable in his own Courts. He had again asked the King for no reply, but that His Majesty should think the matter over.

After this interview the King had told the Queen and his three brothers that he was going to marry Mrs Simpson and abdicate. He had thought it over, and it would be an act of volition.

On the following Sunday apparently a change had come over the King's mind. On Monday, November 9th, the 'New York American' had published articles to the effect that the King intended to marry Mrs Simpson in the Chapel at Buckingham Palace. Other American papers had published similar paragraphs, describing how Mrs Simpson was to become a Duchess at the time of the marriage.[16]

On Friday, November 20th, the Prime Minister had asked Mr Esmond Harmsworth to see him. He had thought it useful to ask him, as Chairman of the Newspaper Proprietors' Association, how long the newspapers would hold off on this matter. When he had asked to see him the reply from the 'Daily Mail' was that they did not know where Mr Harmsworth was – which he believed was not correct.[17] He had not been able to see Mr Harmsworth until Monday, November 23rd. During the conversation he had noticed that Mr Harmsworth was bursting with a desire to talk freely, and though Mr Baldwin had not invited him to do so in so many words he had asked for permission for this. He had said that he knew a great deal, that it was a terrible situation, that all courses appeared to lead to disastrous consequences. Was there, he asked, no compromise? He had then proceeded to describe what was being said in the American papers. He had asked why the King should not marry Mrs Simpson in a private capacity, on the condition that she was not to become Queen. The Prime Minister had asked if this would not mean legislation. Mr Harmsworth agreed that it would. He thought of seeing Mr Elias, the proprietor of the 'Daily Herald', whom he thought would agree in such a course. Sir Walter Layton had told Mr Harmsworth that his readers, who were Liberals and nonconformists, only wanted marriage. Mr Baldwin had replied that [that was exactly like an intellectual.][18]

---

[16] Baldwin read selections from several of these articles at the meeting, the implication being that they derived from inside information about the couple's intentions. Baldwin had been advised that Mrs Simpson was telegraphing information to Hearst, even that she was 'a paid agent of the Hearst Press': Nancy Dugdale diary, 26, 27 Nov. 1936, Crathorne papers; Baldwin reported in O. Sitwell, *Rat Week* (1986), p. 36.
[17] Baldwin probably suspected that Harmsworth was meeting Mrs Simpson and the King.
[18] Amended from Hankey's original text, 'he did not think Parliament would accept that'. Baldwin held that intellectuals rarely understood popular feelings.

The Prime Minister had again seen the King on November 25th. He knew that in the interval Mr Esmond Harmsworth had seen the King. He saw that the King had changed his mind, and His Majesty had a bad cold and was not looking as fit as usual. He had said 'I gather that Esmond Harmsworth has been to see you', and had sketched out the same ideas as Mr Harmsworth. Mr Baldwin had made a preliminary comment that he did not think the House of Commons would agree to that arrangement, but had offered to think it over, to consult the Cabinet and to try and find out, discreetly and informally, the views held by Party Leaders here and in the Dominions. He had asked if the King proposed to marry before the Coronation.[19] This, he said, would be very awkward. He had then told the King one or two things which he thought it would be useful for His Majesty to know. First, he said that the 'Daily Mail' [was the worst judge in England of what the people were thinking].[20] Whatever view was expressed by the 'Daily Mail' would only mean the opposition of Labour. The King had said 'I believe many people would be sorry to see me go'. The Prime Minister had agreed that everyone wanted to avoid the King's abdication but that there were things that public opinion would not stand and that they attached most tremendous importance to the integrity and position of the Crown, which were the only things that held the Empire together. He had agreed that if the King abdicated there might be a wave of reaction in his favour, but also there might be a wave of fury against Mrs Simpson. All the women would put the blame on to her. The King had said 'I agree, but it is most unfair'. The Prime Minister agreed that it was unfair, but it was the way of the world. He had asked the King if he would put on half a sheet of notepaper the proposal that he wanted examined. The King had promised to do so, but he had not received it yet. If he did not receive it after the week-end he would again ask for it. The King had expressed regret that certain articles had appeared in the Press suggesting that there was a divergence [between himself and his ministers].[21] The Prime Minister had replied that it was very important to avoid that. He had then told the King of the words of a Clydeside[22] Member of Parliament 'I see we are going to have a Fascist King, are we?' He himself

[19] Deletion by Baldwin, who added a marginal note: 'I have no recollection of saying this. The King in fact told one of his brothers that he hoped to be married on April 27th.'
[20] Original text: 'the views expounded by the "Daily Mail" were of no importance'.
[21] Hankey's original words – 'divergence of view in the Ministry' – appear to have been a simple drafting error. The Daily Mail, 23 November, had presented some of the King's comments in South Wales as implied criticisms of government policy.
[22] Baldwin amended this word from Hankey's original 'Communist'.

had added that he did not like the word 'Fascism' for at once it was echoed by the word 'Communism'. He had added that whatever happened delay in a decision was bad. The King agreed. The Prime Minister had then promised to look into the whole matter and to consult the Cabinet on the subject.

The Prime Minister informed the Cabinet that of one thing he had no doubt, and that was that at any rate for the time[23] the King was passionately in love. His Majesty believed that his happiness was to be found in a union with Mrs Simpson. In all human experience, however, he himself doubted whether this would be the case. A man he knew had urged Mrs Simpson to leave the country. She had replied 'If I do, the King will follow me'.[24] He did not want the matter to end that way. It would be an indelible disgrace for the whole country. He repeated a strong appeal to the Cabinet for secrecy.

The Prime Minister then said he had forgotten to mention that on the previous day he had had a talk with Mr Attlee. The latter's first impression of the suggestion the King had asked him to examine was that Labour would not touch it 'with the end of a bargepole', but had promised to make discreet enquiries. The Prime Minister had then asked what would be the reaction of Labour to abdication. Mr Attlee had replied that he thought on the whole that they would be sympathetic to the King and would say that he had done the right thing and that there would be a sigh of relief.

It still remained for him to see Sir Archibald Sinclair, Lord Salisbury, who had brought a small deputation to him on the subject, and Mr Attlee more formally. He also proposed to make some very discreet enquiries as to feeling in the House of Commons. Finally, it was necessary now to consult the Dominion Prime Ministers. He did not ask the Cabinet for a decision that day . . .

According to one minister the subsequent short discussion, not reported by Hankey, touched upon the possibilities of government resignation and a constitutional crisis; and it was suggested that the King might look to Churchill to form an alternative government, creating a 'grave risk' of deep divisions in the country.[25] Afterwards a group of ministers chaired by Baldwin prepared the messages to Dominion Prime Ministers, which were sent in Baldwin's name but drafted by Malcolm MacDonald, Hankey and Simon, now Home Secretary.[26] The

---

[23] *Sic*: presumably meaning 'for the time being'.
[24] The 'man' was almost certainly Cooper: see his 'Abdication diary', p. 8 (19 Nov. 1936).
[25] Zetland to Linlithgow, 27 Nov. 1936, in *WSC V/3*, pp. 439–40.
[26] Reinforced by Somervell and further officials, this ministerial group continued to meet during the next two weeks, normally without Baldwin, to supervise continuing telegraphic exchanges

Prime Ministers were asked for their opinions on three possibilities: Mrs Simpson becoming Queen; legislation for a morganatic marriage; and the King's voluntary abdication. They were informed that the British Cabinet considered that 'neither Parliament nor the great majority of the public in all parties' would accept the first two alternatives, and additionally that it seemed 'very probable' that any morganatic arrangement 'would prove to be temporary', because pressure would develop to have the King's wife made Queen. On 2 December leading provincial newspapers broke the silence of most of the press, by treating an address by Bishop Blunt of Bradford as criticism of the King's relationship with Mrs Simpson.

2 DECEMBER 1936 (WEDNESDAY, 11.00 AM): STATEMENT AT CABINET MEETING

'Most Secret' addendum, Cabinet 69(36)[27]

The Prime Minister said that he was to see the King at 6 p.m. that evening, at His Majesty's request. All he wanted to be in a position to say was that the Cabinet did not consider that legislation in respect of a marriage under which Mrs Simpson would not become Queen was practicable. He had again seen the Leader of the Labour Opposition, who had told him that not a single member of the Labour Party would vote for such a Bill. The Leader of the Opposition Liberals was still considering the matter and he hoped to see him that afternoon. His enquiries did not indicate that the Government's supporters would vote for legislation of this kind. The Prime Ministers of the Dominions were against the proposal, with the sole exception of New Zealand, whose Prime Minister thought [some such arrangement might be possible but had added that, if legislation on these lines should prove impossible, he would be guided by the decision of His Majesty's Government in the United Kingdom].[28] He then read a telegram from the Prime Minister of South Africa, two telegrams from the Prime Minister of Australia, and a telegram from the Prime Minister of Canada. Sir Harry Batterbee, of the

with Dominion governments, and preparation of the legislation and procedures for an abdication. Simon and Neville Chamberlain took the largest parts, and were now Baldwin's closest advisers.
[27] Hankey added a handwritten minute: 'Seen and approved by the Prime Minister at the House of Commons. He instructed me to correct as below, 2.xii.36, 5.30 p.m.' These corrections are indicated by brackets.
[28] Hankey's original text read: 'thought it possible, owing to the King's personal popularity, to pass such legislation'. The amended phrases were not only more accurate, but important in showing effective agreement among the Dominion Prime Ministers. Further explanations soon brought Savage, the New Zealand Prime Minister, into full agreement.

Dominions Office, had seen Mr de Valera, who had found himself placed in a very awkward position. At first he had been inclined to say that this was a Protestant business and that in a Roman Catholic country divorce had no place, but he had been rather staggered when he discovered that if the King were to abdicate and this was rendered possible by legislation in every other part of the Empire, he would be left with King Edward VIII still as King.

The Prime Minister then informed the Cabinet that articles had begun that day to appear in certain provincial newspapers. He feared that it would be the beginning of a serious newspaper storm.

... The Secretary of State for War[29] suggested the possibility that Mrs Simpson might go abroad ostentatiously for twelve months, on the under-standing that the whole matter was to be adjourned during her absence. He suggested this because he felt that the Cabinet ought not to accept a possible decision by the King to abdicate without trying to find some way out of the difficulty.

The Prime Minister felt sure that the feeling in the country would not diminish but would get greater with the lapse of time. He doubted if the King, in his present mood, would be willing to stay away from Mrs Simpson for twelve months.

The Prime Minister's view met with strong support.

The Cabinet agreed –

That the Prime Minister should be authorised to tell the King their view that [, in view of the result of the Prime Minister's enquiries as to the state of opinion in the House of Commons and in the Dominions,] it would be useless to proceed with any legislation designed to enable him to marry Mrs Simpson [without her becoming Queen].

4 DECEMBER 1936 (FRIDAY, 10.30 A.M.): STATEMENT
AT CABINET MEETING

secretary's note, Cabinet 70(36), in Baldwin's room, the House of Commons (extracts)

The Prime Minister said that it was now obvious, the Press having got loose, that the situation with regard to the King's marriage could not be held. Some

---

[29] Duff Cooper.

statement was essential, at the latest after the week-end.[30] He had asked the Leader of the Labour Opposition not to put a Question that day, but to be available in case some statement could be made.

The Prime Minister said that he had seen the King on Wednesday, December 2nd, and had reported the result of his enquiries as to the proposed Bill to sanction what was sometimes called a 'morganatic' marriage. He had said that it was impossible of acceptance by the present House of Commons; that Mr Attlee had told him the whole of the Labour Party would vote against it, and that the Parliamentary Secretary to the Treasury[31] had informed him that the supporters of the Government would be almost unanimous against it. As to the Dominions, he had not shown the King the text of all the telegrams but had given him a very complete summary, showing him, in addition, the important second telegram received from Mr Lyons.[32] The King had not appeared much impressed by all this. He himself had then repeated that there were only the following alternatives:-

(1) For the King to give up Mrs Simpson.
    The King replied that this was impossible, and the Prime Minister said he knew it.
(2) For the King to marry Mrs Simpson and that she should become Queen.
    This was also admittedly impossible.
(3) For the King to marry 'morganatically'.
    But that, as he had just said, was impossible.
(4) For the King to marry and abdicate.
    The King said he knew that before long he would have to abdicate if he married.

Continuing, the Prime Minister said that at that moment the King had, for the first time, been subjected to hostile criticism by the Press and was rather feeling it – as he himself had felt it on the first occasion when he was subjected to it. It was obvious that His Majesty was under a strain. He had said that he had decided not to go to the Black Country; not that he was

---

[30] In the Commons on the previous day, the 3rd, by arrangement with Attlee and in reply to a question from Churchill, Baldwin had acknowledged that there was a possible constitutional crisis but declared it 'inexpedient' for him to make a statement at that time.
[31] I.e. the chief whip, Margesson.
[32] Lyons of Australia (in telegraphic shorthand) had expressed 'his strong view that situation now passed possibility of compromise, i.e. that even should H. M. now drop proposal of marriage nevertheless abdication should take place since in [his] view public confidence in Australia is so shaken that no other course is possible': 2 Dec., CAB 127/156.

afraid, but because it was clear that these people did not want him, and he had picked up the 'Birmingham Post' as he said this. There had been a little more talk, but nothing of importance had transpired.

On the previous day, December 3rd, he was to have seen the King at 6 p.m., but he received a message from the King's Valet asking him to come to Buckingham Palace secretly at 9p.m. He had driven there and had been taken in by the back entrance: but all the same he had been photographed. Then he had been introduced through a window. Sir Godfrey Thomas had awaited him, looking twenty years older. On this occasion the King came back to his idea of a broadcast[33] which he wanted to make this very evening (December 4th). His Majesty had read to the Prime Minister a draft and had said he thought it right, before he abdicated, that on behalf of Mrs Simpson and himself he should say what they wanted to do. He had been frantically keen to do this and had said that he felt sure the Prime Minister knew at heart that he was right in this. The Prime Minister had replied that it was a matter of the Constitution and that he would have to consult the Cabinet. Making clear that he was speaking informally, he had reminded the King of what he had told him as to the attitude of his Cabinet colleagues, the Party Leaders in Parliament and the Prime Ministers of the Dominions; adding that now the King proposed to go over the heads of his Ministers and talk direct to the people. He had gone on to say that he felt certain that when the matter was examined it would be found to be a thoroughly unconstitutional procedure. The King had been somewhat impressed by the Constitutional point. His Majesty then said 'You want me to go, don't you?' The Prime Minister had agreed. The King had told him that he wanted to go with dignity, in the best possible manner for Mrs Simpson and himself and his successor, and without dividing the country.

Referring to the proposed broadcast, he had continued that the King would be telling millions of people throughout the world, including a vast number of women, that he wanted to marry a married woman. He would have to mention her name. Everyone would want to know who she was and all about her, and the newspapers would be full of gossip. This would bring the very result that the King did not want. To some extent it might divide opinion in the Empire, but undoubtedly it would harden the strongly predominant opinion against the marriage if the King was to stay in

---

[33] The words 'came back' are obscure, as this appears to have been the first time Baldwin heard the proposal.

his present position. This, the Prime Minister remarked to the Cabinet, was another instance of a certain lack of comprehension which he had observed in the King. He had then recalled to the King how, as he had previously said, everyone up to now had adopted great restraint in this matter, yet he knew that the religious denominations were straining at the leash. The King did not in the least seem to appreciate the importance of this. The Prime Minister then pointed out that only three papers were taking the King's view, and they were perhaps the worst papers in London – the News Chronicle, the Daily Mail, and the Daily Express.

In reply to the Chancellor of the Exchequer he said he had mentioned the probable effect of the broadcast on Mrs Simpson's divorce, namely, that if the King became a private individual there was less prospect of affidavits being lodged. If there was a broadcast this was much more likely, as extremists would certainly try to stop the divorce.[34] Summing up, he had said that the ultimate result of the broadcast, in his view, would be that he would have to go, with opinion in the country divided; that his exit would be an undesirable one; that it would be worse for Mrs Simpson, and worse for his brother. The King had used every argument to urge the broadcast, and asked him to consider it. He had promised to do so.

As Attlee now felt he could not postpone a further parliamentary question, the Cabinet adjourned for twelve minutes while Baldwin, replying both to him and to Churchill, said he could add nothing to his previous answers.

At the resumed Cabinet meeting, Simon read the draft of the King's proposed broadcast and all ministers agreed that they could not permit it to be made because its clear implication was that the King sought public support for a morganatic marriage, despite ministerial advice to the contrary. Prolonged discussion followed on the constitutional and political delicacies, for themselves and the Dominion governments, of a formal letter of advice against the proposed broadcast from Baldwin to the King and a supporting memorandum on the constitutional principles, both drafted by Simon. During this discussion Baldwin said that 'speaking

---

[34] A decree nisi allowed a period of six months during which objections (affidavits) might be raised. A divorce would only be made absolute if the court were satisfied that there was no proof either of collusion between the wife and husband, or of an offence (such as adultery) by the 'innocent' applicant. It was believed that the Simpson divorce might be open to challenge on both counts; and discussion in the public courts on whether Mrs Simpson's relations with the King were adulterous would have been embarrassing for the monarchy and the government.

for himself, he had told the King informally that . . . he thought his best course was to go', and later that he

> was anxious not to be constantly running to and fro between the King and the Cabinet as this gave a bad public impression. He, therefore, wanted to send a document in which the Cabinet would be based on the rock bottom of constitutional principle. He thought that he ought also to consult the Leaders of the Opposition, both Labour and Liberal. If he himself were in Opposition he would think he had a right to be consulted. In reply to a question as to whether the Leader of the Opposition Liberals supported the attitude of the News Chronicle he replied that the Leader was not a person who made very definite statements and he did not know his exact position. He had seemed to agree with the Prime Minister when he talked.

After Neville Chamberlain reported Margesson, the chief whip, as saying that Churchill was working with Beaverbrook to support the King and prevent abdication, there was much discussion of Chamberlain's proposal that Baldwin should insist on the King deciding 'that very day' either to abandon marriage or to abdicate, 'otherwise the matter might blow up very seriously and split the Empire in two'. There was also some anxiety that the King might leave the country, as his draft broadcast suggested (and he had now sent Mrs Simpson to France). It was even suggested that if the King did not immediately make a decision, the Cabinet should resign that evening. But Baldwin 'did not want to put the pistol at the head of the King in this matter'. Instead there was agreement on two actions. First, in order to limit public discussion over the weekend to the two alternatives of renunciation or abdication, Baldwin would make a statement that afternoon in the House of Commons. Drafted by Chamberlain, Simon and Inskip, this referred to 'widely circulated suggestions' relating to a possible marriage by the King; declared that morganatic arrangements were not recognised in English law and so would require special legislation; and announced that the Cabinet was 'not prepared to introduce such legislation'. Second, Baldwin would ask the King to make his decision as soon as possible, and preferably in time for it to be announced when Parliament resumed on Monday. He reported the outcome to the Cabinet next morning.

5 DECEMBER 1936 (SATURDAY, 10.00 A.M.): STATEMENT
AT CABINET MEETING

Cabinet 71(36), extract

The Prime Minister said he wished the present Meeting to be as short as possible, partly because he had to see Mr Monckton during the morning and he had certain matters to discuss with some of his colleagues who had been helping him: also because he wished to avoid any appearance of a crisis which did not exist at the moment. He did not anticipate it would be necessary to hold another Meeting that day, nor, probably, tomorrow.

Continuing, the Prime Minister said that he had seen the King on the previous evening. At the King's request Mr Monckton had been present. Mr Monckton and Mr Allen, the King's Solicitor, had convinced His Majesty as to the constitutional impropriety of a broadcast address. The Prime Minister had given the King the pertinent parts of the memorandum drawn up on the previous day. The King had been calmer than at his previous interview, and he had himself felt that possibly he had made up his mind. He had then told the King of the reasons for urgency in this matter, and had begged him to reach a decision at the earliest possible moment, though he had not in any way put a pistol to his head. He had rather put the King on his honour to let him know his decision as soon as possible. The King had agreed, and promised to do this. He was to see the King again the same afternoon.

The King had expressed a wish that the Prime Minister should make a statement in Parliament on Monday afternoon in the course of which he wanted him to say, first, that the King had decided to marry Mrs Simpson, and, second, that he had wanted to announce it on the broadcast himself. There were difficulties in the way of this, but the Prime Minister had promised to consider it, and Mr Monckton was coming to discuss the matter with him that morning.

The King had then asked if the Prime Minister would object to his seeing Mr Winston Churchill, and he had agreed – though he now felt some misgivings on the subject.[35] He himself felt a very great sympathy for the King in his difficult predicament. He had explained that he had no friends to discuss the matter with. The only people he had wanted to see were Mr Winston Churchill and Lord Derby. He had not sent for Lord Derby, but had explained to the Prime Minister that Mr Winston Churchill had known him from his boyhood and had always been most friendly. He himself had

---

[35] According to Cooper, 'Abdication diary', p. 21a, his actual words were more colloquial: 'I made a bloomer.' But on 10 December, ibid., p. 32, he said privately that 'I never doubted that I was right for a minute. I am only a simple lad, you know . . . but there were reasons why I thought it best to put it to the Cabinet in the way I did.' He presumably meant the probability of objections from some ministers.

felt that he must bear in mind the difficult position of the King, faced with the serried ranks of the Cabinet and Parliament and without anyone with whom to discuss the matter. The Prime Minister's visit the same afternoon was being made at the King's request, and it would give him an opportunity to correct any undesirable advice which Mr Winston Churchill might offer. The King had said that he had no opinion of Mr Churchill's judgment. He was seeing another politician. His Majesty had added that from the first he had wanted the whole business to be conducted between the Prime Minister and himself. He had gone on to say 'I have never let you down, have I?' The Prime Minister might have to remind him of that, especially if he agreed to something which did not meet the approval of the Cabinet. Mr Monckton had afterwards expressed the view that the Prime Minister had been wise in agreeing to Mr Churchill's visit.

Commenting further on his assent to the King consulting Churchill, Baldwin said that 'if he had been trying to put pressure on the King to leave the Throne it would be a different matter, but that all his efforts were being directed towards an act of free will by the King'. In reply to some ministers' concern about the advice Churchill might give, Baldwin said that in his view 'the present position was that the King was considering the right moment for him to renounce the Throne'. There was agreement that public reference to the King's wish to broadcast fell under the same objections as those to the broadcast itself. At this point, Baldwin received and read out a letter from Churchill stating that he had found the King under great strain and had asked for a doctor to be called, and urging that Baldwin should allow the King more time and not 'extort a decision from him'.[36] This led to an inconclusive discussion on how to prevent further delay, but also how to make it public that abdication was the King's choice, not a Cabinet demand.

One continuing difficulty was the possibility that Mrs Simpson's decree nisi might face successful legal challenge. After Baldwin spoke with the King that evening, he had consultations with Simon, Neville Chamberlain and officials which continued late into the night. Shortly after midnight a ministerial meeting was arranged for the morning, to hold a preliminary discussion while the rest of the Cabinet was assembled. Only ministers thought to be specially relevant or easily available were summoned to the preliminary meeting: under half were present, and given the legal issues Somervell also attended.

---

[36] Printed in M&B, pp. 1009–10, and *WSC V/3*, p. 455.

6 DECEMBER 1936 (SUNDAY, 10.00 A.M.): STATEMENT
AT A MEETING OF MINISTERS

filed with the Cabinet minutes, in CAB 23/86

The Prime Minister said that the present Meeting was one of the greatest importance. On the previous evening he had seen the King. He had confirmed that there was no truth in Mr Winston Churchill's suggestion that His Majesty's health was seriously impaired. The King had been annoyed at what Mr Churchill had said. The Prime Minister himself had never known the King more cool, clear minded, understanding every point and arguing the different issues better. No man could have done this better.

The King, said the Prime Minister, had sent for him on the previous day and said he was prepared to sign his abdication, which would enable the necessary legislation to go through the House of Commons on Tuesday, but –....[37] There was a 'but'. It arose in a case which the Prime Minister thought could be got through the House of Commons. In putting that case he would propose to begin by saying that this was no Constitutional struggle between the King and the Prime Minister, or the King and his Ministers. There was nothing of the kind. It was a struggle in a human heart, a struggle in which he himself was trying to find a solution. He would then propose to tell the story of his relations with the King in this matter. He would tell how the King had always insisted on his intention to marry Mrs Simpson and had said that in order to carry this out he would go. On this he had never wavered for an instant.

The Prime Minister said that the King believed that his own honour was involved in this marriage and that nothing would turn him from it. At the same time His Majesty's wish was to avoid dividing the country into two parts. He hated the suggestions that were being made in the Press of divisions in the country and in the Empire. He would go of his own free will.

The Prime Minister himself had explained to the King that it was a point of honour in the interests of the nation and the Empire to take his decision soon. But what had troubled the Prime Minister himself was as to the next five months. Supposing the King renounced the Throne, a King who had abdicated could not live in his own country, and there seemed no alternative but for His Majesty to drift around Europe. At the present moment even,

---

[37] Ellipsis in the original.

he did not care to be in London and would probably stay at Fort Belvedere until the whole matter was settled. What troubled him, therefore, was that if the divorce decree was not made absolute he would have abandoned the Throne and might well be unable to marry – a very terrible position. Only on the previous day a solution to this problem had been suggested. It had appeared to him a possible way out, and he hoped that on examination it might be possible to accept it. It was the only solution that he himself could see, or for which it might be possible for him to be responsible. He asked the Home Secretary to explain the suggestion.

This suggestion was that the abdication bill should be accompanied by a second bill to make the Simpson divorce absolute, with immediate effect. Baldwin justified the proposal by saying that 'the King was making a tremendous sacrifice in the interests of the country. Ever since he had become Prince of Wales he had been doing his duty to the people with great assiduity, and he thought he was entitled to ask that the people should free him in the present case.' If he abdicated but then had to wait six months to marry, 'the eyes of the whole world would be focussed upon him' and this 'would tend to degrade kingship itself'. Simon and Chamberlain were the chief advocates, evidently regarding the bill as a means to expedite the King's departure. However, during an extraordinarily tortured discussion the proposal was criticised as likely to create an appearance of condoning the divorce, of being a bargain with the King to secure his abdication, and of giving the King and Mrs Simpson special treatment denied to ordinary people. It would, it was argued, face church and nonconformist hostility, and damage the moral standing of the government, monarchy and nation.

Discussion then returned to Baldwin's proposed parliamentary statement for Monday, drafted by Chamberlain and to be agreed with the King. Chamberlain and other ministers were now reversing their attitude on Friday, accepting that it was publicly important for the King to be allowed more time to make his decision, as this would help ensure that his abdication was seen to be voluntary (although other ministers still evidently believed that he might renounce the marriage).[38] The statement aimed to deflate criticisms that the King had been placed under pressure: the government desired to give him 'the fullest opportunity' to weigh his decision and, except on the morganatic proposal, as already announced (and overlooking the still secret question of his proposed broadcast), it had tendered no advice.

---

[38] Further considerations were that more time was needed for the King to settle his private financial arrangements, and the government and Dominion governments to finalise the legislation.

6 DECEMBER 1936 (SUNDAY, 5.30 P.M.): STATEMENT
AT CABINET MEETING

secretary's notes, Cabinet 72(36)

The Prime Minister gave the Cabinet some account of his talk with the King on the previous evening. Contrary to Mr Churchill's report, he had found the King in excellent health, and he had learned that, after he himself left, the King had been talking with his Staff until 1 a.m. and had been the life and soul of the party. The only thing was that he was not sleeping very well, but that was not peculiar to the King. With the Prime Minister the King had been in very good form, talking rationally, quietly and calmly. What had been worrying the Prime Minister himself was the thought of the King drifting about for four months or so with the possibility of matters going wrong for him at the end. This had been troubling the King, too. His Majesty now made a suggestion which he thought would make him happy and at the same time enable him to abdicate at once. It was important that the matter should not be represented as a bargain. He himself had replied that anything that could be done to end the present crisis would be very desirable. He had promised to put the proposal to the Cabinet and try to get it accepted. The idea was that Parliament should pass a Simpson Divorce Bill, which would do away with the remainder of the period before the decree was made absolute. It would be passed together with the Abdication Bill. The divorce would become absolute from the moment of the passing of the Act. He did not want to say any more, nor to prejudice the discussion by those present. He would prefer to hear their views first. They must bear in mind the danger of any break between the King and his Ministers. He had discussed the matter with some of his colleagues that morning, and Mr Monckton had been asked to tell the King the first weight of opinion of those who had discussed the matter. Mr Monckton was expected back the same evening, and he would know the King's first reaction to those opinions. Mr Monckton had been going to and fro between the King and himself, which saved him the Prime Minister from continually running up and down between Fort Belvedere and London. As it was, he had found it necessary to visit the King several times in the last three days. Mr Monckton had come up early that morning and had returned to the King at midday to show him a draft of the Statement which it was proposed to make in Parliament. The opinion of those present that morning had been rather strongly against the new proposal. Mr Monckton had reported this to the King and was coming back to report the first impression of His Majesty to the attitude of Ministers. He himself was anxious not to press the King too hard for a decision at the moment. If they did this the Cabinet would be getting near the position where they might have to give advice to the King, and that was what he wanted to avoid. The King himself was most anxious to avoid the creation of anything in the nature of a 'King's Party'. He gathered that Mr Churchill had not made much impression on the King. His Majesty was deliberately staying away from London as he did not want to court demonstrations, cheering, and the like. In reply to a question the Prime Minister said that under the present proposal the King's abdication would be voluntary. The matter would be proceeded with rapidly. He himself would have to make an announcement and state that the Bill of Abdication would be introduced on the following day. He would then point out the appalling difficulties of the King's wandering about while waiting for the decree to be made absolute, pestered everywhere by the Press. He would recall how the King had always done his duty from his boyhood; for example, in the War and after; and would suggest that, for reasons of State, the Government ought to do something to help him in his difficulty so as to get the whole question settled.

The effect of another long discussion was final rejection of the proposed divorce bill, and agreement, after further revisions, on Baldwin's parliamentary statement. Made on 7 December, this was received 'with cheers from all quarters of the House ... An intervention by Mr Churchill aroused general hostility.'[39] During that same day Mrs Simpson issued from Cannes a press statement saying she was willing to withdraw from her relationship with the King, 'if such action would solve the problem'. The statement was conditional, and Baldwin later told the Cabinet that 'he did not think that Mrs Simpson would throw the King over'.[40] Nevertheless on 8 December Baldwin decided to 'make one last appeal to him to reconsider his position': 'He must wrestle with himself now in a way he has never done before and if he will let me I will help him. We may even have to see the night through together.'[41] During this discussion the King stated his final decision to abdicate.[42]

[39] Telegram to Dominion Prime Ministers, 7 Dec. 1936, PREM 1/454.
[40] Secretary's notes, Cabinet 73(36). A telegram to Dominion Prime Ministers, 7.15 p.m., 8 Dec. 1935, PREM 1/454 stated: 'Have every reason for doubting bona fides of Mrs Simpson's statement'; it was an attempt to placate public opinion and reduce fears about 'her personal safety'.
[41] Wilson memo., and Dugdale note, 8 Dec. 1936, PREM 1/450.
[42] Lord Birkenhead, *Walter Monckton* (1969), pp. 147–9, contains a first-hand account of the evening's events.

9 DECEMBER 1936 LUCY BALDWIN MEMORANDUM

SB add. papers

Stanley was summoned again to Fort Belvedere last evening, he paid 3 visits there last week with Mr Monckton & all the time has to calm an impatient Empire and H. of C. until the King is able finally to make up his mind. He went back upon the idea of Abdication after the Harmsworth Press in the shape of Esmond H. had been at him suggesting a morganatic marriage which having been turned down by the Gov. as impracticable except through legislation, a lull descended upon the negotiations. All was made more difficult through this & the interventions of Mr Churchill who is apparently trying to form a King's Party from gossip one has heard. Anyway Stanley made a statement in the H. of C. on Monday to the effect that His Majesty was still asking for time & couldn't make up his mind. Stanley received an ovation & W. Churchill who tried to make a speech in question time was shouted down.

Last evening at 5.15 pm. Stanley left for Fort Belvedere he took with him a bag with his night things in case he should have been obliged to stay the night as he thought the King might have been in an excited state owing to the fact that there is some difficulty about the divorce with Mr Simpson going through. (Incidentally Mr S. has called here twice asking if he can help in any way. How? I wonder.[43])

The King did get excited but calmed down after a conversation with Mrs S. on the telephone to Cannes & the Royal Dukes of York & Kent arriving eased the tension for Stanley. After the King's telephone talk he entered the room gesticulating with his arms above his head. 'She is the most wonderful woman, I have the most wonderful woman in the world behind me in this, she does not mind, it will simply draw us nearer together. I mean to go & leave the way clear for my brother'. He seemed transported with joy & transfigured. Here I should say that Mrs S. issued a manifesto on her own account yesterday from Cannes, saying that she gave the King up & would set him free. (Of course a farce as she is not yet free from her 2nd. husband!) On receipt of this news on Mon. night her solicitor flew off to Cannes early on Tues. accompanied by his doctor & secretary. The poor man had never been in an aeroplane before & as he was a bad sailor on the sea he took the precaution of taking his doctor to revive him on arrival &

---

[43] Ministers were advised not to meet Ernest Simpson, to avoid any risk of legal embarrassments: Gwyer to Wilson, 7 Dec. 1936, PREM 1/449.

fortify him to interview Mrs Simpson as to what she was doing without consulting him. All very like an Edgar Wallace tale or penny dreadful.

Stanley had talks last night with both the Dukes of York & Kent. Both furious against the lady. Then when Stanley & Mr Monckton were in conclave with the King & the Duke of York, the Duke of Kent had a heart to heart outpouring with Tommy Dugdale Stanley's parl: secretary & I believe was very like King George V in his outspoken language. At dinner the King was in the highest spirits, laughing & making jokes, as though there was no Empire & no distracted country to consider. Stanley described it to me that the King behaved just as a happy man might the night before his wedding & honeymoon. There were present the gentlemen in waiting, solicitors & secretaries, Stanley at dinner sat between the King & the Duke of York. He left about 10.15 p.m. as he evidently wasn't wanted for anything serious & got back home shortly before 11.30 p.m. His first words to me were 'Well I feel as though I have been in Bedlam, the King doesn't seem in the least put out, he just wants Mrs Simpson & doesn't seem to grasp the gravity of the whole affair'. Later Stanley told me the King said to him 'I quite understand the reason you & Mrs Baldwin don't approve of my action. It is the view of another generation, my generation don't feel like that about it'.

Poor dear loveable man – impossible as a King, & how one regrets & prays for him, & his happiness.

Dec 9th/36 Lucy Baldwin

9 DECEMBER 1936 (WEDNESDAY, 11.00 A.M.): STATEMENT AT CABINET MEETING

secretary's notes, Cabinet 73(36)

The Prime Minister told the Cabinet of his Audience with the King on the previous day and of the present position. He referred once more to the importance of great secrecy at the present stage.

He had found the King in excellent health, lucid in his conversation, and well controlled, except on the one subject with which they were concerned today. The King had been talking on the telephone to Mrs Simpson when he arrived, and came into the room with high encomiums of the lady.

On the general position all he could say was that everything had happened exactly as he had apprehended in the development of public opinion.

His talks with the King had been sometimes alone, sometimes in the presence of one or both of the brothers, sometimes Mr Monckton and

Mr Allen had been present. He had stayed to dinner with the King. Throughout the King had been bright and cheerful. He had tried his utmost to reason with the King, and his efforts were recognised by Sir Edward Peacock,[44]
Mr Allen and the brothers of the King, all of whom had also tried to reason
with him, but with the same negative results. On leaving he had said to the
King 'I suppose if an Archangel asked you to give up Mrs Simpson it would
have no effect?' 'Not in the least' replied the King. The King was longing to
abdicate and to sign and send a Message to Parliament. There was only one
thing left to be done.

Meanwhile Mr Goddard, Mrs Simpson's Solicitor, had gone to Cannes
to see his client. If that meeting should by any chance result in a decision
on her part to give the King up, there was every risk that the King would at
once proceed to Cannes by air if he could obtain an aeroplane.[45] The cir-
cumstance made it difficult to take a decision at the moment. He might get
further news in the course of the day. The King had been in communication
by telephone with the lady at Cannes and had probably told her about the
Cabinet's advice on broadcasting. The American Press had reported that the
King had abdicated. The British Press was still keeping silent, but wanted
to know where this news originated. The Dominions were beginning to get
restive. He was quite convinced that nothing could alter the King's mind
and that his wishes would have to be met. Mr Monckton and Sir Edward
Peacock said the same. The King's brothers knew that this affair could end
in nothing but misery and disaster, but had not been able to persuade the
King. He thought, therefore, that nothing could be done to stop the King
sending his Message to Parliament, but whether it would be on Thursday or
Friday was a matter for consideration. A great deal remained to be done and
to be thought out. He himself, after his last interview, had now the gravest
doubts as to whether in any circumstances, even if the King threw the lady
over and whatever steps were taken, such as an interval for a rest-cure to
restore his perspective on this matter, the King could recover his position or
whether his own successor as Prime Minister would not be later confronted
with equally difficult situations. He deeply regretted this. He knew and admired the King's fine qualities, but doubted if, even so, he could recover his

---

[44] As Receiver-General of the Duchy of Cornwall and a director of Baring Bros. as well as the
Bank of England, the King's financial adviser.
[45] This possibility had caused a scare four days earlier, when ministers discovered that the King
had a royal aircraft on standby: Nancy Dugdale diary, 5 Dec. 1936.

position. In reply to a question he expressed serious apprehensions as to the effect on the King if it turned out that the divorce would not be completed.

The time and manner of announcing the abdication were then discussed. It was agreed that Baldwin should send the King a formal statement, drafted by Simon, expressing the Cabinet's regret and asking him to reconsider, with the effect of prompting the King to submit a formal re-iteration of his decision. Baldwin's House of Commons speech on 10 December, immediately after the King's declaration of abdication had been read out, was a triumph.

In conversation immediately after the speech, Baldwin commented that its success was a fitting end for his career – 'Now is the time to go.'[46] He was 'deluged' with letters of gratitude for his handling of the crisis, including some from members of the royal family. Several comments from his letters of reply are notable. 'It has been a strange time and the end of it was inevitable, but there were possibilities of real trouble in the situation, trouble beyond the comprehension of the silly people who fluttered round Mrs Simpson.' 'There is a profound sense of relief throughout the country and indeed the Empire and I shall go now with no fears for the future as far as the Crown is concerned. But for King Edward it is [a] tragedy, though he doesn't know it yet.' 'I think I have nearly finished my job now and if I live I shall be an ex-Prime Minister in a few months. But I must see the new King well in the saddle. He is going to be his father over again.'[47] After King Edward had declared his final decision on the evening of 8 December, Dugdale commented to Baldwin on the Duke of York's 'dullness'. Baldwin replied that 'he is very like King George V as a young man. George V was most uninspired and dull; only by perseverance, reliability, example to his people, and a sense of duty did he gain himself the much loved position he held when he died.'[48]

13 DECEMBER 1936: TO QUEEN MARY

typescript copy, RA PS/GVI/C 019/359

Madam,

Your most kind and generous words have indeed brought me comfort and strength.[49] That Your Majesty, his mother, feels that I have not failed

---

[46] *Harold Nicolson. Diaries and Letters*, ed. N. Nicolson, 3 vols. (1966–8), I, p. 286 (10 Dec. 1936).
[47] Respectively to Lady Londonderry, 19 Dec. 1936, Londonderry papers D3099/3/15/22; to N. Butler, 29 Dec. 1936, FO 800/423/18–19; and to Phyllis Broome, 29 Dec. 1936, Lorna Howard papers.
[48] Nancy Dugdale diary, 8 Dec. 1936.
[49] 11 Dec. 1936, SB papers 176/17–18, thanking him for his kindness towards the former King, and towards herself 'in my grief at the failure of my son in not carrying on the duties & responsibilities of the Sovereign of our great Empire'.

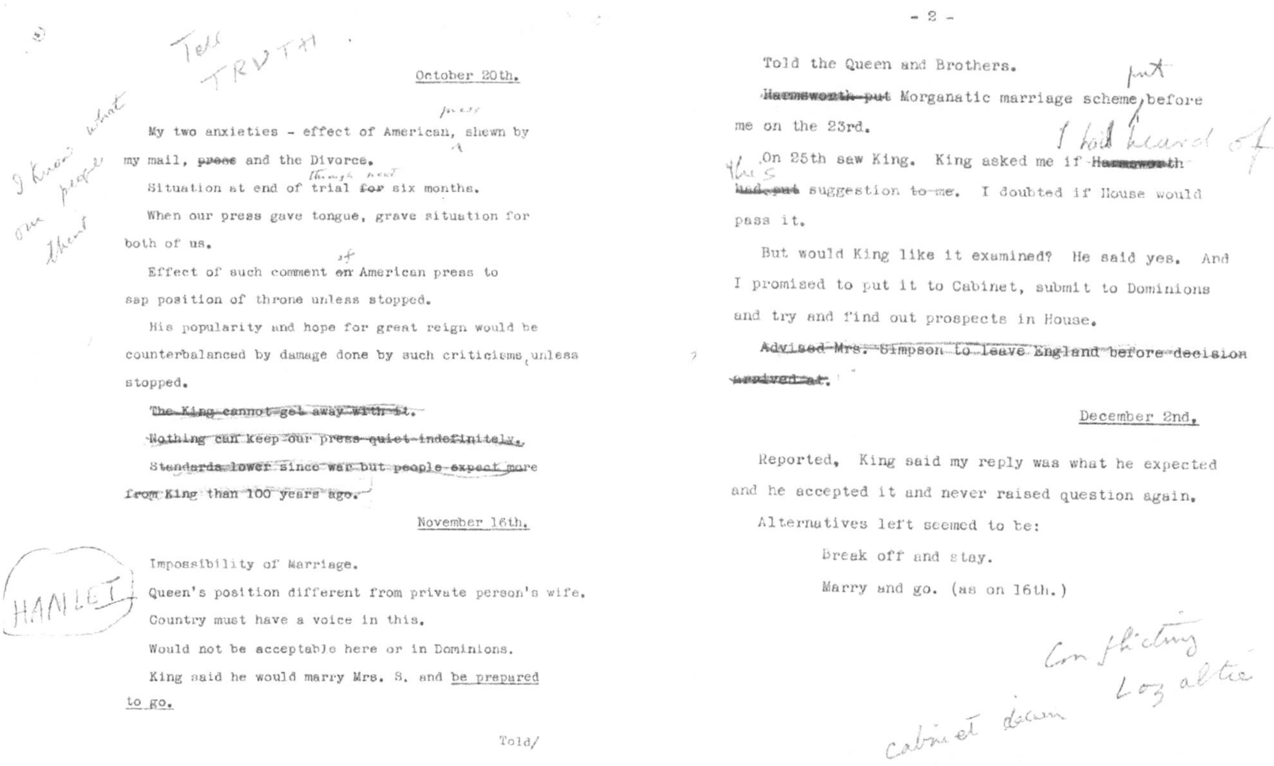

Tell TRUTH

October 20th.

My two anxieties - effect of American, shewn by my mail, press and the Divorce.

Situation at end of trial for six months.

When our press gave tongue, grave situation for both of us.

Effect of such comment on American press to sap position of throne unless stopped.

His popularity and hope for great reign would be counterbalanced by damage done by such criticisms, unless stopped.

The King cannot get away with it.

Nothing can keep our press quiet indefinitely.

Standards lower since war but people expect more from King than 100 years ago.

November 16th.

HAMLET

Impossibility of Marriage.

Queen's position different from private person's wife.

Country must have a voice in this.

Would not be acceptable here or in Dominions.

King said he would marry Mrs. S. and be prepared to go.

Told/

- 2 -

Told the Queen and Brothers.

Harmsworth put Morganatic marriage scheme, before me on the 23rd.

On 25th saw King. King asked me if Harmsworth had put suggestion to me. I doubted if House would pass it.

But would King like it examined? He said yes. And I promised to put it to Cabinet, submit to Dominions and try and find out prospects in House.

Advised Mrs. Simpson to leave England before decision arrived at.

December 2nd.

Reported, King said my reply was what he expected and he accepted it and never raised question again.

Alternatives left seemed to be:

Break off and stay.

Marry and go. (as on 16th.)

Conflicting Loyalties

Cabinet down

Figure 8 The first two pages (of three that survive) from Baldwin's notes for his abdication speech in the House of Commons, 10 December 1936. The dates refer to his successive discussions with the King.

you at this time, that I have done all that was possible, has removed a burden from my mind.

I feel now after calm reflection – I feel it in my soul – that we have been guided aright. I believe we shall emerge stronger from this cruel time of strain and that strength will be given to our new King to tread the path his Father trod, and I am confident that long after our work is done his people will recognise his life for them as they recognised his Father's.

But Your Majesty may have seen what I have written to the Princess Royal.[50] I believe that to be profoundly true. And you may rely on my helping King Edward in any way I can if the need should arise and my help be of any service to him.

I am/ Your Majesty's loyal and devoted servant,/ Stanley Baldwin

In a controversial broadcast on Sunday, 13 December, the Archbishop of Canterbury spoke of King Edward's abandonment of a 'high and sacred trust', seeking happiness in a manner inconsistent with Christian principles of marriage and 'within a social circle whose standards and ways of life are alien to all the best instincts and traditions of his people'.

14 DECEMBER 1936: TO ARCHBISHOP LANG

Lang papers 192/379

10, Downing Street

My dear Archbishop,

I listened to you last night and I must send you a line of gratitude and admiration for your Address.

You said just what was wanted and, if I may say so, just what you ought to have said.

---

[50] Not found. On 11 Dec. 1936, SB papers 177/93–4, she thanked Baldwin 'from the bottom of my heart' for having helped the King: 'The action of my brother has distressed me more than I can say.'

I know how difficult a task you had, but you triumphed over all difficulties and you were indeed the voice of Christian England.[51]

Thank you.

Yours most sincerely/ Stanley Baldwin

At the end of the year the new King expressed his admiration for the 'dignified way' Baldwin had handled his 'very difficult & delicate task': 'I am new to the job, but I hope that time will be allowed me to make amends for what has happened.'[52]

2 JANUARY 1937: TO KING GEORGE VI

RA GVI/PRIV/3/B/01

Astley Hall

Sir,

You have honoured me with a most kind and generous letter which has given me sincere pleasure.

None of us who went through those two months will ever forget it, but it was a constant source of comfort and strength to me that I enjoyed the confidence of yourself, Sir, and of the Royal Family throughout, and that the friendship with which the late King honoured me, remained unimpaired to the end. We owe much to his determination not to force a constitutional issue, and to make things as easy for his successor as was possible in the circumstances.

I liked to think of you at Sandringham and I felt certain that the peace and quiet obtainable there would do you good.

I too needed a quiet time and we have had a very happy holiday.

I return to London next Thursday, but I have anything of importance sent down by bag.

I rejoice that the Queen and Queen Mary are better and trust that they may be able to stay in the country until their recovery is complete.

---

[51] Writing on 12 June 1937 to thank Lang for a letter on his retirement (Lang papers 191/253), Baldwin commented on 'the abdication when you faced a situation of extreme difficulty and delicacy as Archbishop and as the voice of a Christian country: a situation in which you were bound to face criticism of a bitter kind whatever you did or said or failed to do or say'.

[52] 31 Dec. 1936, SB papers 77/66–7.

Sir, if I may say so, you need have no fear for the future, so far as you are concerned. The whole country is behind you with a deep and understanding sympathy.[53]

I am with profound respect/ Your Majesty's/ loyal and devoted servant

Stanley Baldwin

As Baldwin liked to give his own account of the crisis to friends and acquaintances, various retrospective reports survive. The following are among the most interesting.[54]

26 FEBRUARY 1937 HINCHINGBROOKE NOTE

Lord Sandwich papers; Best and Sandwich, *Hinch*, pp. 50–3

S.B. desired that people should always remember two things about Edward VIII.

1) That the King did not drink at all during the crisis and that his decision to abdicate was in no way affected by drink.

2) Except for one lie, which in the circumstances could be forgiven, he had played straight with S.B. throughout. The occasion was when he had told S.B. that he had had nothing to do with Mrs Simpson's divorce case.

S.B. said that throughout all the talks he was always conscious that one part of the King's mind had not grown up. He seemed to have no spiritual belief or religion to guide him in times of crisis. He said that George V had foretold that his son would bring ruin on himself within twelve months of his accession. S.B. said that Edward VIII had not the vital gifts which make a King – patience and devotion to duty. It was fortunate for the country that he went when he did; the downfall would have been more catastrophic in later years.

The most disgusting side of the business had been the attitude of his friends. Sutherland had been to S.B. fearful of losing his job and explaining

---

[53] To Monica Baldwin, 27 March 1937, SB add. papers: 'I am very happy about our new King and Queen. I stayed a week end at Sandringham soon after Christmas and had much talk with both of them./ They will make a great place for themselves in the country's life.'

[54] Published reports of Baldwin's reminiscences include: *Reith Diaries*, pp. 195–6; R. Rhodes James, *Victor Cazalet* (1976), pp. 189–91; Thelma Cazalet-Keir, *From the Wings* (1967), pp. 99–101; R. A. Jones, *Arthur Ponsonby* (1989), pp. 217–18.

that he didn't really know Mrs Simpson. Brownlow had been to see S.B. after returning from Cannes complaining 'that he was exhausted by it all' and deploring the Archbishop's speech and censure and the effect it would have on his, Brownlow's, reputation.[55]

The Dominions from the first had been adamant. Bruce had told S.B. that the King could not expect sympathy from the Australians who knew that he had taken Mrs Simpson to Gallipoli.

The night before the King left there was a pause in the talk with S.B. while the servant went out to get drinks. While out of the room S.B. said 'Well Sir to forget for the moment all that we have been saying – there are no two people in the country who have shared your anxiety of the last few weeks to a greater extent, nor wish for your future happiness more than the Missus and myself'. The King appeared moved and thanked him. Later S.B. heard from the secretary that the King had said – 'The Prime Minister is the only man who has said any kind word to me about the future and wished me good luck'.

7 OCTOBER 1937 MONICA BALDWIN DIARY

extract, W. Baldwin papers

This afternoon Uncle Stan and Aunt Cissie came to see me on their way back from Aix-les-Bains. He still looks frightfully tired and Aunt Cissie told me it might be years before he really recovered from the strain of the last 12 months.

It was growing dark when I went into the parlour but I could see them sitting there in the deep Rembrandt shadows, just two faces looking at me from the other side of the grilles . . . and later, just a voice out of complete darkness.

Naturally we started almost immediately to talk about the Abdication.

About Edward VIII, he said:

'He is an abnormal being, half-child, half-genius . . . It is almost as though two or three cells in his brain had remained entirely undeveloped while the rest of him is a mature man . . . He is not a <u>thinker</u>. He takes his ideas from

---

[55] The 5th Duke of Sutherland, Lord Steward of the King's Household, did lose his post, in 1937. The 6th Lord Brownlow, a lord-in-waiting to King Edward, had been asked by him to accompany Mrs Simpson to France.

the daily press instead of thinking things out for himself. He never reads –
except, of course, the papers. No serious reading: none at all . . .

He is <u>reasonable</u>: that is to say, when he really <u>sees</u> a thing he does it.
You might say he is amenable to reason . . . except, of course, on that one
subject.

I found it curiously difficult to approach the subject when for the first
time I went to see him about it at Fort Belvedere.

It was a divine day of gold and green with the first leaves fluttering to the
ground . . . All the way from No. 10 – I was praying and planning as I drove
along in the car. Reviewing my knowledge of him, I remembered how, when
we had to recall him from Africa at the time of the old King's first serious
illness, I had gone down to [Folkestone] to meet him with the delicate task
of explaining to him exactly how the land lay. We had dined together as we
travelled up by train to London and during the meal we had talked more or
less indifferently of this and that. At last he said to me:

"You know, Prime Minister, I should like you to remember that you can
always speak of <u>anything</u> to me."

I seized on this and I answered:

"Sir, I shall remind you of that".

And as I said it a most curious impression came over me – a feeling of
certainty that one day I most certainly <u>should</u> have to say something to him –
and that it would be about a woman. And then, as suddenly as it had come,
it was gone.

When he arrived at . . . Buckingham Palace – he was told that he might
not on any account go <u>near</u> his father, who was, we all thought, near death,
for at least 48 hours.

He simply took no notice, damned everybody, and marched in. The old
King who had for nearly a week been practically unconscious, just opened
half an eye, looked up at him and said:

"Damn you, what the devil are <u>you</u> doing here?" And from that moment
he turned the corner and began rapidly to get better.

It was exactly like the scene in "Henry IV" when Prince Henry tries on
the crown.

The old King knew all about the Simpson affair from the very start, and
he and Queen Mary were simply worried to death.

That of course was what the old King was thinking about when he said
these often quoted words, "What of the Empire?"

George V said to me only a few days before his death that "Edward would pull the whole throne and Empire about his ears before a year was out". And the Duke of Kent said exactly the same . . .

He can't endure any kind of cleric. One day at the Fort when the Duke of Kent and the Archbishop of Canterbury and I had all been at him during the entire morning, the Duke of Kent came into the room where I was waiting alone until the Archbishop's interview with the King was ended.

"He is", said the Duke, "damning the whole root and stock of the Episcopacy. He has just showed the Archbishop of Canterbury out of the house".

And even as he spoke the King came in, looking ruffled, and the Archbishop's car went snorting down the drive[56] . . .

Another time the Duke of Kent came in looking furiously angry. "He is besotted on the woman", he said, "One can't get a word of sense out of him".

Edward was quite certain that he could "get away with it".

. . . Esmond Harmsworth, son of Lord Rothermere the proprietor [of the Daily Mail] (which, my dear, with the Daily Express I always call the Devil's Press) – managed to get an interview with him at Fort Belvedere shortly before the end. It was he who suggested the morganatic marriage to the King. The King at once sent for me, and told me what Harmsworth had said. I assured him that the British people would never agree to it, and left him to digest that.

Harmsworth then called upon me – a disgustingly conceited fellow and yet curiously timid at heart.[57] And he told me what he had suggested to the King. I told him that he and his filthy paper did not really know the mind of the English people: whereas I did. And I explained to him that a morganatic marriage would mean a special Bill being passed in Parliament; and that Parliament would never pass it.

Harmsworth said: "Oh, I'm sure they would! The whole standard of morals is so much more broad-minded since the War."

---

[56] As noted in Frances Donaldson, *Edward VIII* (1974), p. 223, which used these notes, there are difficulties about this story. The Archbishop did not meet the King during the Abdication crisis, but it possibly refers to an earlier incident.

[57] Either Baldwin's recollection or Monica's record was at fault on the precise chronology. But both Dawson diary, 26 Nov. 1936, and Cooper, 'Abdication diary', p. 11, noted Baldwin's 'unmitigated dislike' and 'great hostility' towards Harmsworth.

I replied:

"Yes: you are right: the ideal of morality and duty and self-sacrifice and decency certainly <u>has</u> gone down since the War; but the idea of Kingship has gone <u>up</u> – in fact, never in history has it stood so high as now. And I tell you that the English people will never accept the thing that you suggest".

Harmsworth was frightfully funny, though he didn't realise it.

When I returned to the King, I went all over the ground again.

He said that he wished such a Bill as the morganatic marriage would involve to be drawn up.

I said: "Sir, do you realize that I shall have to assemble the Cabinet, make the whole thing public, and then sound the Dominions?".

He said: "Yes".

And then, Monica, I did a thing which I don't expect your Reverend Mother would have approved of. I said to him, was it absolutely necessary that he should <u>marry</u> her? In their peculiar circumstances, certain things are sometimes permitted to Royalty which are not allowed to the ordinary man.

To this he replied immediately:

"Oh, there's no question of that. I am going to marry her . . .".

After that began an unforgettable period.

I had nine secretaries <u>sleeping</u> in at Downing Street, working night and day; private cables whizzing backwards and forwards between the Dominions Prime Ministers and myself: private Cabinet meetings and so on, and all the time I had to be going back and forth between Fort Belvedere and Buckingham Place and Downing Street.

The King was in a curious state of mind. He kept on repeating over and over again:

"I can't do my job without her. I am going to marry her, and I will go."

What rather shocked me if I may say such a thing, was that there seemed to have been no <u>moral</u> struggle at all.

The last days before the Abdication were thrilling and terrible. He would <u>never</u> listen to reason about Mrs Simpson. From the very first he insisted that he would marry her. He had <u>no</u> spiritual conflict <u>at all</u>. There was no <u>battle</u> in his will. I tell you this, and it is true. He is extraordinary in the way he has no spiritual sense: no idea of sacrifice for duty. <u>That</u> point of view never came before his mind. I set it all before him. I appealed to one thing after another. Nothing made the least impression. It was almost uncanny: like talking to a child of 10 years old. He did not seem to grasp the issues at stake . . . He seemed <u>bewitched</u> . . .

He has no religious sense. I have never in my life met anyone so completely lacking in any sense of the – the – what is <u>beyond</u> . . . And he kept on repeating over and over again: "I can't do my job without her . . . I am going to marry her, and I will <u>go</u>."

There simply was no moral struggle, and it appalled me.'[58]

(Here Aunt Cissie interrupted. She said: 'Monica dear, do you know what he did on the night before the Abdication? He had been through the most awful day imaginable and at about 7.30 p.m. he looked in at No. 10 and said to me: "Have my bag packed quickly. The King will be going through hell tonight, and I am going with him." So I hurled his things into his bag and off he went'.)

Uncle Stan went on:

'Yes. And when I got there, he was in what I can only describe as a perfectly exalted condition. He would spend nearly the whole day telephoning to that woman and would come in from the telephone box with the most beautiful look I have ever seen on his face, like a young knight who has just seen the Holy Grail, and say:

"I've just been talking to Her: talking to the most wonderful woman in the world." It was hopeless to reason with him.

When dinner came we sat down, the three brothers and I, like graven images, all round the table: our hearts like lead at the thought of the impending Abdication; whereas he – the little man at the head of the table, was as lively as anything, and kept on saying that he would "soon be with the most wonderful woman in the world." Besotted. That was what the Duke of Kent called it over and over again.

All those days when we were discussing the matter together, we had to walk up and down, talking, in the garden at Fort Belvedere. And when I reasoned with him, arguing and trying to make him realize that he was risking the destruction of the Monarchy, it seemed to make no impression upon him whatever. He would keep on throwing his arms out with a curious gesture,

[58] Baldwin used similar words in the fuller original version of Nicolson diary, 10 Dec. 1936, printed in the 'condensed edition', ed. S. Olsen (1980), pp. 107–8.

repeating: "SHE is beside me . . . the most wonderful woman in the world". Whether he meant actually or symbolically, it would be hard to say . . .

Just before the Abdication I told him that when the whole affair was made public, there <u>might</u> be a wave of sympathy for her, but that it might equally be a wave of hatred. (You never know how people will take these things). And I advised him to get her out of the country that very night. I was afraid, myself, that some woman might shoot her. So he did.

And then began a series of comic episodes. For in all great tragedies, Monica, there are <u>always</u> comic episodes.

Mrs Simpson – who is a third-class kind of woman – began communicating with the Press. And this very much worried her lawyer, because she did <u>not</u> consult <u>him</u>. He, you see, was getting the divorce affairs wound up.

He was a fellow called Goddard – a man whom every crook in London employs by reason of his cleverness; everybody who gets into a mess applies immediately to Goddard, who gets them out at once. He is, I may say, a man of blameless reputation but extraordinary ingenuity.

Well Goddard did not like this, and he said he <u>must</u> see her, as it compromised him when she made statements to the Press unknown to him. So he wanted to follow her to France. But the King forbade him. So Goddard came to see me.

Well, he was shown up – a big, burly chap, with a large face, "plain and pale like a ham" . . . He told me his trouble. And I was very wiley indeed. I said:

"Mr Goddard, the relation between a lawyer and his client is the most sacred in English Law. Even the <u>King</u> cannot come between them. Do you consider it your duty to your client to follow Mrs Simpson to Cannes?"

He said: "I do."

I said: "Then don't ask <u>my</u> advice, Mr Goddard, but do your duty to your client, and take no notice of the King."

So this man, who had never set foot in an aeroplane in his life, got in at Croydon and flew across the sea . . .

Some of the European papers got hold of the story – or rather the fringe of it – and reported that an obstetrician of world repute had left England for the Rogers' villa at Cannes . . .

Well, the important thing was not to let the King know that Goddard had left, before Goddard had arrived. He was to let us know the instant he had reached Lyons. Well about 11 p.m. came a frantic message from some of my sources in Paris, saying that an English plane had just crashed a few miles from Cannes.

"Bang goes Goddard" said I, and began wondering what the King and I would say to one another.

I did not report that night. But early next morning who should walk in at No. 10 but Goddard.

"I feel just like a Crusader", said he. It had not been his machine but another that had crashed. He had seen Mrs Simpson, done his business, flown home, and nobody the wiser. And he looked more like a ham than anything that I have seen that was <u>not</u> a ham.

At the end of it all, when I was beginning to say Goodbye to him [the King], he held my hand and touched me profoundly by saying:

"Prime Minister, I know that you and Mrs Baldwin do not approve of what I am doing. But you belong to another generation, you know."

I said: "Sir, it is quite true that there are no two people among your subjects who are more grieved at what has happened than we are; but I beg that you will always remember that there are no two people who hope more truly and sincerely that you may find happiness where you believe it is to be found."

At that his eyes filled with tears, and he said:

"Of all the people I have had round me during these last months you are the only ones that have said anything that showed you cared about my happiness" . . . '

Later, I asked him what Queen Mary was like when one really knew her. He said:

'Queen Mary is one of the shyest women I have ever met in my life. This shyness puts a kind of barrier between her and you which it is well nigh impossible to get across. I had suffered from this, though she was always very nice to me. But I was always expected to keep the conversations going: and it sometimes flagged.

She had a way too of standing at the end of the room when one was shown in at Buckingham Palace; and she would remain there like a statue while you made your bow and walked over a sometimes very slippery floor to kiss her hand. But all that was one day changed quite suddenly, and I will tell you how.

The first time I was sent for to see her at the beginning of this Simpson story I had a tremendous shock. For, instead of standing immobile in the middle distance, silent and majestic, she came trotting across the room <u>exactly</u> like a puppy dog; and before I had time to bow, she took hold of my hand in both of hers and held it tight.

"Well, Prime Minister, she said, here's a pretty kettle of fish!"

After that I can assure you, my dear, the barriers were down.'

Do tell me, I asked him, what Mrs Simpson is really like.

He said: 'Mrs Simpson? A third-class woman; passably good-looking; very small, and very elegant; knows exactly what to say, and how to say it. But no heart. His family are all wondering what will become of him when at last he opens his eyes and sees the sort she really is. Or – will he remain besotted to the end?'

ELEVEN

✺

Towards retirement

DECEMBER 1936 – MAY 1937

Baldwin now began to make his decision to retire known among friends, and he became increasingly reflective about his own career and the historical past. Among those he spoke with were Clement Davies, the Liberal National MP and future Liberal party leader.

UNDATED [BUT RELATING TO DECEMBER 1936]
CLEMENT DAVIES MEMORANDUM

J. Graham Jones, 'The Reminiscences of Clement Davies, M.P.', *The National Library of Wales Journal*, 28 (1993–4), 411–13: extracts

I had seen a great deal of Mr. Stanley Baldwin from early in July until the matter regarding King Edward VIII had been finally settled... A few days later I had a message that he wanted to see me in his Room at the House of Commons. I went along and he kept me for well over an hour. The whole conversation is still vivid in my memory. He began by saying, '... I am about seventy years of age and I am going to resign'. I said, 'Why do you do that now that you have come through the greatest difficulty which has confronted any Prime Minister for well over a century and more? I should have thought you would now have said you could devote your whole attention to dealing with other mighty problems which are confronting us and which may very soon bring about disaster unless some reasonable solution can be found'.

He replied, 'No, it is not right that I should go on. No man ought to continue at the helm directing the course of the ship when he has reached the full span of three score years and ten.'

Then, he suddenly turned and said, 'Why is your Party sunk so low in the estimation of the people who have lost their confidence in you?' I replied, 'Oh, it is largely due to the war. The Liberals' main concern at all times is with liberty and its voice is heard in the protection of individual rights. That voice is silenced by thunder of the guns in war'. He said, 'There are other matters too'. I said, 'The personal quarrels which grew to such disastrous degrees around the personalities of Asquith and Lloyd George?' He said, 'No, I grant you that war would have affected the course of the Liberal position and undoubtedly a great deal of harm has been done by these quarrels which always affect the family much more than they do the outside strangers. But earlier than that'. 'Oh,' I said, 'the quarrels at the beginning of the century between Rosebery and the others, the formation of the Liberal Independent Group?' He said, 'No, earlier than that'. I replied, 'I do not know to what you are referring, for we had those tremendous victories of 1906 and 1910 after the quarrels during the Boer War'. So he said, 'No, I am referring to Gladstone'.

At once I bristled and said, 'Are you condemning the Old Man? He was the greatest of them all'. Whereupon he said, 'I quite agree with you. He was the greatest of them all, and it was Gladstone I had in mind and how right he was. You remember when he was approaching seventy he gave you all warning that he was now resigning and foolishly you insisted upon his remaining on. Gladstone was right and the rest of you Liberals were wrong'. 'Well', I said, 'what else could we do for undoubtedly he was the main cause of the great Liberal victory of 1880; his vigour was unimpaired; he carried out those wonderful whistle-stop speeches and went through the great Midlothian campaign – which is still remembered nearly sixty years later'. He said, 'Yes, that is true, but he realised, and the rest of you did not, that he had completed his great work in fighting for freedom everywhere and he realised that a new generation, with new ideas was coming forward and would soon be dominating thought and policy'. I said, 'Yes, I agree. Gladstone believed in the freedom of – but he was certainly not enthusiastic on that freedom from'.

Stanley Baldwin said, 'What on earth do you mean by those phrases?' I said, 'He believed in freedom of the individual, in the freedom of speech, in the freedom of conscience, in the freedom of association, in the freedom to choose and to criticise the Government of his country and the freedom to change his views regarding the Government; but he was not enthusiastic about freedom from suffering, the freedom from disease, the freedom from poverty, the freedom from social and economic injustices, the freedom from ignorance, and so on'. Baldwin said, 'Exactly. Those were the new ideas being put forward by Dilke and Chamberlain and the younger generation. The Grand Old Man could see it and knew that his time had come to hand over the duty of steering the ship of State to the newer generation. Do you realise what would have happened? Dilke, Chamberlain, and others would have quickly assumed command. They would have brought forward their policy and methods for dealing with those very matters you have mentioned. The political fight would have started then in the early '80s and I believe those great questions would have been settled by the beginning of the century and I doubt very much if we would ever have heard of a Socialist Party'.

'The Old Man was right and the others who insisted on his staying on were wrong'.

Then he said to me, 'With that in mind, I am going and it gives me added pleasure that I go in my own time, following my own decision and not giving those two noble Barons, Beaverbrook and Rothermere, any excuse for saying that they kicked me out. I go of my own free will'.

Then he suddenly switched and said, 'Clem, what period is like this?' I said, 'Obviously, all those periods that have followed a disastrous, destructive, war, much like the period after the Napoleonic War.' 'Yes', he said, 'I agree, but I think the period resembles much more the condition in which we found ourselves after the Marlborough Wars and the Treaty of Utrecht.' Then he turned to me with a twinkle in his eye and said. 'Who do I resemble?' I replied 'That [is] a damned silly question. I am surprised at you. Nobody resembles anyone else. Each of us has his own personality. Obviously you think that you do resemble somebody in the past. Who is it?'

To my astonishment he said, 'Halifax'. I said, 'What Sir, the Great Trimmer?' He said, 'Yes, only, Clem, I shall probably be known as "The Little Trimmer"'.[1]

---

[1] The closing tease is characteristically Baldwinian, but the comparison was intended seriously: cf. Young, *Baldwin*, p. 54, and below pp. 430. George Savile, Marquess of Halifax (1633–95) was author of the *Character of a Trimmer*, meaning 'trimming' in the sense of preserving stability, cohesion and thereby liberty.

21 DECEMBER 1936 EDEN DIARY

A talk with S.B. in the morning who was in excellent spirits . . . He . . . spoke in round terms of Sam [Hoare]'s lack of judgment. The latter had given Winston a question to ask about cruisers in order to get a bouquet or as schoolboys would say 'to suck up'.[2] David M[argesson] had reported the back benches furious & Attlee also. 'Really' said S.B., 'I am sometimes horrified to think of what will happen, I am amazed at the foolishness of some of my colleagues. Only the other day Sam was warning us in cabinet of Rothermere & Beaverbrook. He hasn't yet learned they don't matter'. I replied 'Sam's manoeuvres were clear. He was a born intriguer & wanted to be Prime Minister'. 'Well he must be mad. He hasn't the least chance of it & wouldn't get 50 votes in the party'. 'I am tempted to write to him & shall certainly speak to him', he wound up. I have never known S.B. so outspoken about Sam. He congratulated me warmly on my speech in the House on Friday.[3]

15 JANUARY 1937: TO QUEEN MARY

RA GV/CC 47/1591

10, Downing Street

Madam,

Your Majesty's most kind thought has touched me and I accept with sincere pleasure the book you have so graciously sent to me. Arthur Bryant is a friend of mine for whom and for whose work I have a high regard. He is a real scholar and a real historian.[4]

His selection of letters looks fascinating and the period has long been to me one of the most interesting in our history. It has a fundamental similarity

---

[2] In the Commons on 17 December Churchill had asked whether Hoare could comment on five elderly cruisers, due for scrapping under the 1930 naval treaty. After Hoare had confirmed that due to international conditions these would be retained, Churchill had proposed 'general congratulations on his considerable achievement'.

[3] On non-intervention in the Spanish civil war, on 18 December.

[4] The Queen had sent him Bryant's *Postman's Horn* (1936), a collection of seventeenth- and eighteenth-century letters. Baldwin had known and corresponded with Bryant since the late 1920s, as a lecturer and later governor of the Bonar Law College at Ashridge, and as a writer of historical books which he admired.

with our own and I spent a delightful evening here not long ago talking it over with George Trevelyan.

The statesmen of the latter part of the century had been young men at the time of the Civil War and their constant problem was the unity and stability of the nation, to build in so solid a fashion that the troubles of 1640–60 should never recur. Like true Englishmen, thank God they were not logicians. Their work was largely empirical: they faced, and overcame difficulties as they arose and by the mercy of heaven they helped – and those that followed them – to evolve the British Constitution that has seen us through two centuries, but which has never been understood or emulated by any continental country.

So after the War when we had packed half a century of political evolution into four years, we had to re-adjust for a new age.

Unity and stability again had to be sought, in the middle of a world falling to pieces. We don't know, any more than they knew, where we may go: but we know as they did the objective.

I have always been an admirer of Halifax, one of the wisest heads that ever took part in politics, much of whose writings might have been written to-day. Forgive me, Madam, for running on in this way. It all comes from dipping into these XVIIth century letters!

I am with profound respect/ Your Majesty's/ loyal and devoted servant/

Stanley Baldwin

28 FEBRUARY 1937: TO OLIVER BALDWIN

CUL MS. Add. 8795/24

10, Downing Street

Dearest Son,

Here is a small offering for to-morrow.[5]

It seems a long time ago that mother and I were walking in the Cloisters of the Abbey, when, inspired by the surroundings, you suddenly decided on an immediate appearance in the world. However, we got safely back to St Ermin's and it was a toss up whether it would be Feb. 28th or March 1st.

And you chose St David's day!

---

[5] Oliver's thirty-eighth birthday; he was born in his Baldwin grandparents' apartments in St Ermin's Mansions, central London.

Which reminds me. Ll.G. has returned from Jamaica with a brick red face which makes his eyes more wicked than ever. He would never have taken me in if I'd been Little Red Riding Hood.

God bless you/ Your loving F

By late January Baldwin had definitely fixed his retirement for the end of May, after the Coronation. Largely, it seems, on his wife's prompting, he had now decided to accept a peerage and to find a London house suitable for social entertainment. A difficulty was that he still had financial anxieties: although Baldwins Ltd had resumed dividend payments in 1934, he had a bank overdraft of over £10,000.[6] Although his son-in-law, Arthur Howard, bought him a house – 69 Eaton Square – he did not think he could afford the costs of maintaining this as well as Astley Hall. Wilson, Fry and Jones had the idea of a fund created by donations from his rich friends, from which he would receive an annuity. This, however, became unnecessary when in February the Cabinet decided on new financial arrangements for politicians. As well as increased ministerial salaries and the introduction of a salary for the Leader of the Opposition, these would provide a pension of £2,000 a year for former Prime Ministers. After some hesitation Baldwin decided to draw this pension himself.[7] Any serious parliamentary criticism of ministers making themselves beneficiaries of their own measures was removed when in May the Cabinet accepted the Opposition case for an increase in MPs' salaries. Shortly after his retirement Baldwin wrote: 'I have declined certain very tempting offers of Boards: I was very anxious not to be dependent on any aid of that kind and the P.M.'s new pension will just keep me going, I hope in quiet comfort.'[8]

15 MARCH 1937: TO JOAN DAVIDSON

Lady Davidson papers

Little Maid,

Two latest to cheer you.

1. Horne was telling Titchfield how Ll.G was enjoying some music at a party at which they were present together. To which Sonny[9] observed meditatively 'snakes like music.'

---

[6] About £400,000 in modern terms.
[7] Jones diary, 21 Jan., 18 Feb. 1937; Jones *DL*, pp. 316, 330.
[8] To Alan Dore (a former manager at the Wilden works), 16 June 1937, CUL MS Add. 8812/224.
[9] The nickname of the Marquess of Titchfield, MP for Newark from 1922, 7th Duke of Portland in 1943.

2. At the Speaker's last dinner on Friday were, amongst others, Ll.G, Winston, Horne, Gilmour & Amery. My Tommy [Dugdale] was next Winston who started the evening in a gloomy mood. 'A dismal spectacle! All the flotsam and jetsam of public life washed up on the same beach. A dismal spectacle!'

In March Baldwin received a deputation from the National Peace Council. A recollection by one member, the Dean of St Paul's, reveals how by this time Baldwin had become strikingly blunt in private discussion with peace campaigners.

[21 MARCH 1937]: REPLY TO A PEACE DEPUTATION

W. R. Matthews, *Memories and Meanings* (1969), p. 205

...We had presented a plan of economic appeasement...When Mr Baldwin ... had passed round copies of a considered reply to our memorandum, politely dismissing it, he talked freely and his words scared me so much that I remember some of them verbatim. He said, 'I know some of you think that I ought to speak more roughly to Hitler than I do, but have you reflected that the reply to a stiff letter might be not a stiff reply but a bomb on your breakfast tables? We are living in a time when there is no Christian public opinion in Europe to which we can appeal. The peace of the world lies in the hands of these dictators. For all I know they may be insane, and unlimited power drives men mad. Stalin is unapproachable, Hitler will talk, but who can rely on what he says?' ...

From April Baldwin spoke at a number of valedictory gatherings. Asked for advice at a farewell dinner given by ministerial parliamentary private secretaries he is reported to have replied: 'Never try to score off the Labour Party, or to be smart at their expense. Never do anything to increase the sense of bitterness between parties in Parliament. Never go out of your way to irritate or anger the Labour Party. Remember that one day we may need them.'[10] A further statement survives in the papers of his own parliamentary private secretary.[11]

---

[10] *The Political Diary of Hugh Dalton*, ed. Ben Pimlott (1986), p. 205.
[11] As no indication of authorship or the occasion is given, it is not clear whether Baldwin wrote the words or whether it is a report of his spoken words.

28 APRIL 1937 'MR BALDWIN'S TESTAMENT'

typescript note, Crathorne papers

When I had been eight years in the House, I said to my wife: 'I shall never be any good here. I would be of far greater use in Worcestershire doing local Government work'. My wife replied: 'Complete your ten years and then see'. I did, and have been here ever since.

To be Prime Minister is different from anything else, and it takes time to get into the saddle. Give my successor time to settle in before you start criticising.

I know my own failings: I never was any good in Opposition.

You can't understand events unless you know the immediately preceding history which led up to them. The real trouble with the times is that immediately after the war progress which would normally have taken forty or fifty years was made in two or three – in the way, for example, of granting universal suffrage to the masses. But the masses were not, of course, educated up for it; nor will they be for another twenty or thirty years. That lag is the danger.

I have always tried to educate the Labour Party. I know the English working man, and I know this: Liberals and Conservatives, Whigs and Tories, always used to abuse each other in the old days with the utmost freedom; but such freedom of abuse would never be understood by the Labour Party: you must treat them gentlemanly. So don't abuse them; treat them gently and never forget to widen the breach between the working man and the intellectual. They hate one another.

Never forget that the leaders of the Tory Party have always understood and been sympathetic to the working man.

The heart of the country is sound, but it wants watching. (1) It is a remarkable thing that ever since the war we have had a Right Government, although, with the extension of the Franchise and the influx of subversive ideas, one would have expected otherwise. (2) As soon as the 1926 strike was over, employers and employed settled down to work without resentment. (3) No less remarkable was the way in which the Labour Opposition worked the Parliamentary machine from 1931–1935, only a handful of them, instead of sulking, as they might well have done.

The German war minister was visiting London, and had interviews with various ministers and leading politicians. Baldwin assumed his best diplomatic manner for the occasion.

13 MAY 1937 FIELD MARSHAL VON BLOMBERG
MEMORANDUM

Documents on German Foreign Policy 1918–45, series C vol. VI (1983), pp. 759–60 (extract)

Baldwin emphasized at the beginning that even in his earliest youth he had been extremely fond of Germany and that even now he was still of the opinion that both countries must cooperate as friends. The difference between the forms of government ought not to be any obstacle to German-British cooperation. Every country had the form of State that seemed suitable to it. The British were very ready to cooperate with Germany. There was much sympathy for Germany among the broad masses of the people. It would be a terrible catastrophe if the two countries were some day to confront each other once again with weapons in their hands, for the two most manly peoples in the world would, from their very nature, carry through such a struggle to the point of complete exhaustion, so that the end could only be the collapse of both countries. This, however, would be equivalent to the destruction of European culture and the victory of Bolshevism in Europe.

Field Marshal von Blomberg replied that the Führer, too, was wholly of the same opinion as Mr Baldwin in these matters. The German people, the German Government, and particularly the German Wehrmacht ardently desired to be on friendly terms with Britain. But it was sometimes not altogether easy to put this desire into practice if the Germans gained the impression that Britain did not attach too great importance to German friendship, especially in connexion with certain utterances in the press. The Führer regretted such difficulties all the more because he, for his part, had always from the beginning of his political career onwards stood for good German-British relations, and had fully and absolutely adhered to his conviction.

Mr Baldwin admitted that a section of the British left-wing press was hostile to a German-British *rapprochement*. Otherwise, however, cooperation with Germany was extremely popular in every circle of the population and especially in the Army and among ex-Servicemen. He himself hoped to be able to devote his strength to the service of this cause, even after laying down the office of Prime Minister. He would undertake various journeys which he had not been able to manage during his period of office, owing to pressure of work, and now wanted to visit Germany, too,[12] which he already knew

---

[12] It is not easy to assess this statement. No other source indicates such a desire, and these may just have been placatory words; alternatively, it might have been a serious intention, which

from before the war. He had even spoken German himself once. The lady who had taught him at that time had, significantly, revered as one of her greatest treasures the medal won by her father at the Battle of Waterloo, and later, during the World War, had died from grief at the bloodshed between Britain and Germany. He, Baldwin, would in any case do everything possible to prevent the repetition of such a misfortune.

His knowledge of German had unfortunately faded so much that he could not converse direct with the Führer, whom he hoped to be able to visit during his intended journey to Germany. Nevertheless, despite this he would attach great importance to a conversation with the Führer.

Finally, Baldwin mentioned the Coronation celebrations, which, he said, having existed for a thousand years until the present day, were, together with the attitude of all classes of the population, the best proof that a Communist danger did not exist in Britain. Nevertheless, the British did not wish to deny that the Communist danger in other countries was greater and deserved more attention . . .

The most impressive of Baldwin's valedictory addresses was given at an Empire Rally of Youth on 18 May, broadcast in Britain and across the Empire. He intended this to be a major declaration of his political faith, though he worked around a draft volunteered by Reith and re-drafted by Jones.[13] It spoke of 'ordered freedom' as derived from the Christian truths of the 'essential dignity of the individual human soul', the 'brotherhood of man' and 'Fatherhood of God'. Leading figures from all the British Christian denominations wrote to express their gratitude.

20 MAY 1937 JONES DIARY

On arrival from Ruthin at six o'clock I found a message: 'The Prime Minister wonders, if you are not tired after your journey, if you could look in and see him some time. He will be free up to dinner time.' I went across at 6.45 to No. 10, stayed to dinner and left at 9.15, Mrs Baldwin joining us at dinner, both dressing. Miss Watson told me he was receiving a large 'fan mail' just now. I found him contented and cheerful though a trifle tired judged by the way he nervously swept his tongue rapidly to and fro across his lips. Asked

---

later came to seem unnecessary due to Halifax's visit and meetings with German leaders in November.
[13] *Reith Diaries*, p. 215; Jones unpublished diary, 18 May 1937.

after my welfare and what Ruthin Castle was like, and then said 'thank you' for my help with the Albert Hall speech. I said I only provided him with words for the faith which I knew was in him. 'I do believe them and that is why I spoke them so earnestly, but I often wonder what Mrs Jerome[14] thinks of me cribbing so much from you.' I told him he had gone very fast, 6,000 words per hour instead of his usual 5,000 or less. He had received letters of appreciation this morning from the Roman Catholic Archbishop (who was at the meeting) and from Dr Berry of the Evangelical Free Churches, which pleased him.

'I have had my talk with Eden. He goes off to Geneva. During the last month the tension has eased a bit, especially with Germany. I have had half an hour alone with Blomberg. Luckily he speaks English well, for I speak no German. Struck me as being a gentleman. Mussolini is madder than ever. The King of Italy wanted to be represented at the Coronation but it was forbidden. I sat next to the Brazilian Ambassador at the Guildhall yesterday and, deliberately indiscreet, told him that I was sorry to see a member of the Latin race behaving in so ungentlemanly a fashion. I never remembered France or Spain showing such discourtesy. I have a number of interesting letters to show you. Here is one with an extract from Crabb Robinson's Diary. He was travelling in the Lakes in a stage coach and met my grandfather, 97 years ago, and discovered he was a person of discriminating taste and a student of Shakespeare. Here is one from a Lancashire working man, anonymous, enclosing a pound note with which I am to buy a book for myself. Here is a letter from Lady Snowden; that was a good comradeship. I went twice to see him after his retirement. L.G. is arranging the memorial service.[15] Did you see that L.G. says he and Foch are Basques?' Then with pride and emotion he handed me a letter to read from his son, Oliver, full of delight in the reception which had been given to his father and mother in the coronation procession. 'It has been worth waiting years to have that'.[16] He has to say a few words next Monday at an Empire dinner. He liked Lyons and was counting on him to deal at the Imperial Conference with the constitutional

---

[14] Jones' secretary and typist.
[15] Lord Snowden had died on 15 May. He had supported Lloyd George's Council of Action in 1935.
[16] Oliver's letter (13 May) also commented on the 'glorious end to your rule', paid a tribute to his mother, and ended 'God bless you.' Baldwin replied (16 May): 'Dearest Son,/ You can never know what happiness your letter brought to your mother and me: it went straight to our hearts and will remain there always. And God bless you too.'

refinements which were troubling Hertzog and the South Africans. Then he must fix the hour with the Palace for giving up and for Neville's taking over. This week he would go to Arundel to see the gardens. The young Duke had done well as Earl Marshal. Then a farewell weekend at Chequers with the family. And after that Wordsworth's 'Prelude' and 'Excursion'. 'It was a pity', he went on, 'that Ramsay had decided to linger on in the Commons. He was probably too tired to decide otherwise. One of the things I am most grateful for to you, T.J., is that you got me away last year to Gregynog and Blickling. But for that I should never have got through with the Abdication' . . . Horace Wilson would stay on with Neville, 'but I don't know whether he will know how to use him. Later when Warren Fisher decides to go Horace should succeed him'.[17]

At dinner Mrs Baldwin told how during a recent audience which the P.M. had with the King, a scratching at the door was heard to which the P.M. called the King's attention. It was the two Princesses who had been dressed up in their Coronation robes and wished to show themselves to the Prime Minister. He made them march to and fro, the Queen joining them. Much talk of the Abbey ceremony, S.B. saying how his thoughts frequently turned to the Duke of Windsor and Mrs Simpson, and how as the Service proceeded he felt such a Service would have been blasphemous with them and impossible for him and the Archbishop. He and Mrs Baldwin have a profound feeling of Divine guidance. They had been given a remarkable reception by the crowds throughout the procession of two and a half hours. 'I felt quite humbled,' he said, 'and am glad to be going before my head is turned' . . . He has read the Halifax report on the gift by Strakosch[18] and there will be an announcement shortly.

We sat in the Library for a short spell after dinner. Outside on the pavement, on the Foreign Office side, people were waiting on the chance of a glimpse of him and earlier in the week there had been crowds shouting, 'We want Baldwin,' but he had not responded. He has ceased to be thought of as leader of the Tory Party and stands out as the national leader 'par excellence'.

[17] I.e. as permanent secretary of the Treasury.
[18] A City financier and government adviser of South African origin, who in thank-offering for Baldwin's handling of the Abdication crisis presented him with £250,000 to use for strengthening the relations between Britain, the Dominions and India. A committee chaired by Halifax and including Jones recommended the creation of an Imperial Relations Trust, to disburse the money for educational purposes: its papers are in DO121/40.

Hard to realise this sitting ever so quietly together, the three of us, in the deserted rambling house. Servants far away in the basement. One little man in the front hall to answer the door bell. Mrs Baldwin reminded me how right she and S.B. and Salisbury had been after the defeat in 1929 in not going (as Austen and I had advised) to meet the House of Commons and how consistently S.B. had throughout 'stood for certain things.' She meant integrity and the co-operation of all classes.

I left her and he said goodnight at the top of the staircase where hang all the portraits, in order, of the Prime Ministers with his at the foot of the stairs. All was very still, the Cabinet room empty and all the adjoining rooms of secretaries and typists empty. I walked along the passage past the large photographs of Imperial Conferences and a case of richly bound volumes in a show case presented by Sir Henry Fildes in memory of Vernon Hartshorn and Stephen Walsh – and the little man in the hall helped me on with my coat and I passed out from what I felt was likely to be my last evening at No. 10 with a Prime Minister.

Baldwin's last Cabinet meeting was on 26 May.

27 MAY 1937 SIR JOHN SIMON TO LORD TWEEDSMUIR

Buchan papers Acc 7214 mf mss 308

. . . Well, Baldwin is going and Neville will reign in his stead. Baldwin's last Cabinet was a memorable meeting; Chamberlain admirably expressed the feelings of us all and Baldwin made his exit with a characteristic reply. Tugging at his pipe he started by saying that it would be churlish to say nothing, but he didn't know what to say. He had looked forward for a long time to his release and was absolutely certain that he ought to go now (repeating this two or three times); he got tired more easily than of old, and his successor ought to have at least two years in the saddle before a General Election. But now that the moment had come he felt the wrench – felt it more than he had ever expected. He would not be seeing us every day as of old and this made him sad. But he thanked us and was happy to think how wonderfully well we had all pulled together.

All this was very characteristic of Baldwin – no palaver, no fulsomeness, but very affecting because it was unaffected. I could not help thinking of some other cases of Cabinet leave-taking – Mr Gladstone's for

instance, of which Rosebery said that 'William Harcourt burst out blub-
bering like a child, at the same time drawing from an inner pocket a <u>much
corrected</u> manuscript, <u>yellow</u> with age, from which he read a valedictory
address'.

Fortunately Neville starts without any unkind looks between his lieutenants, and though we shall miss Baldwin terribly we shall maintain the
fraternal spirit which he has done so much to establish...

In parliament, the press, and letters from many individuals, political opponents
as well as supporters, it was the same: 'No man has ever left in such a blaze
of affection.'[19] Baldwin's last House of Commons statement, on 27 May, was to
announce the increase in MPs' salaries. He formally tendered his resignation to
the King on the following day. For a brief period he bore the title of a knight
of the garter, before it was superseded by his earldom on his introduction to
the House of Lords on 10 June. In the same short honours list, Lucy Baldwin
received a Grand Cross of the British Empire order, and Davidson was made a
Viscount.

29 MAY 1937: SIR STANLEY BALDWIN TO JOAN DAVIDSON

Lady Davidson papers

Chequers

Little Maid,

For forty-eight hours I haven't known whether I was on my head or my
heels: times and seasons are remote to me.

The first contact with reality came at one o-clock this morning when,
lying awake, something said to me 'the twenty-ninth of May, oak apple day'
but what else? 'The twenty-ninth of May' – the Child's Birthday! And then it
flashed on me that the Child was a Viscountess! And how had that happened?
She must have married a Viscount! But she hadn't; I was sure of that.

And gradually things sorted themselves out. And I thought, well we members of the ARISTOCRACY must stick together and I'll write her a line. And
here goes!

You've got as lovely a day for it as you've ever had and that is delightful and we enter a new path of life with a very wonderful friendship only

---

[19] *Nicolson Diaries*, p. 301.

strengthened through many long and extraordinary years. Perhaps the predominant memory among so many is the way you and David have kept
through these years a little sanctuary to which I could always bolt from the
House, sure of finding peace and sympathy and understanding.

And when you regard my wild career and certain oddities, inescapable
from me, that is a marvellous tribute to what real friendship can do. And
for that I can never be too grateful and thankful.

And we will sit in our coronets and wag them at each other like old
oracles!

God bless you and both of you.

Your loving K.G.

no, no, and a thousand times no! Of course I meant/ S.B.

The King wrote to express the 'admiration and confidence, and . . . the affection
of the vast majority of your countryman', and his own 'deep gratitude for your
great services' to his father and himself.[20]

31 MAY 1937: TO KING GEORGE VI

RA PS/GVI/034/011

10, Downing Street

Sir,

The kindness and the generosity of Your Majesty's letter has touched me
profoundly.

To have served you these last months has not only been a great honour
but, if I may say so, the greatest pleasure.

I go with complete confidence in the future as far as the Throne is concerned. If I may speak with freedom, you and the Queen have more than
fulfilled my hopes. I expected much but my heart is full of thankfulness as I
watch the way in which you are facing the responsibilities of your tremendous position. It will be not my duty but my greatest pleasure if I can ever
be of service to you. May God bless you both.

I am, Sir, your loyal, grateful and obedient servant/Stanley Baldwin

[20] Printed in John Wheeler-Bennett, *King George VI* (1958), p. 318.

Baldwin also wrote a letter to be delivered 'by the hand of Sir Walter Monckton', who attended the Duke of Windsor's marriage to Mrs Simpson, in Austria on 3 June.

1 JUNE 1937: TO THE DUKE OF WINDSOR

RA DW/3290

10, Downing Street

Sir,

Do you remember that last evening at the Fort when I told you that my wife and I hoped from our hearts that you might find the happiness you desired in the course you were proposing to take?

I cannot at this moment refrain from saying again what I then said to you, and I hope you will accept my message in the spirit in which it is sent.

I do want also to say this. I realise that in your new life there must be difficulties inherent in the situation, not all of which could have been foreseen. I am convinced that you will triumph over them but I want to assure you of an understanding sympathy.

Through all that time in the early winter you ran dead straight with me, and you accomplished what you said you would do. You maintained your own dignity throughout: you did nothing to embarrass your successor, nor anything, as might so easily have happened, to shake the Monarchy more than was inevitable in the circumstances.

I am confident that your mind to-day is as it was then.

Sir, I beg you will regard this letter from a private English citizen as a renewal of confidence in one who was for so short a time his master, and affection for a Prince who honoured him with his friendship.

I am, Sir,/ Your Royal Highness's obedient servant/Stanley Baldwin

Halifax wrote to say that 'A good deal of the savour of political life so far as I am concerned goes out with you . . . you have taught me more about life than anybody except my father.'[21]

---

[21] 27 May 1937, SB papers 173/58.

8 JUNE 1937: TO HALIFAX

Halifax papers A4.410.14.5; The Earl of Halifax, *Fulness of Days* (1957), pp. 182–3

69, Eaton Square, S.W.

My dear Edward,

I shall value your letter as long as I live. Our friendship has been a very real thing to me and a real influence which I treasure.

This last ten days have been a strange time: a time that comes only once and cannot recur.

All hearts seem open for the moment: most will close again, some perhaps be kept ajar, but it is very wonderful. I feel tired, happy, and at peace: and mighty humble. I wish my dear Dickens hadn't destroyed what is really a very beautiful word: but you will know all I mean by it.

I still have that sense of wonder that the Blessed Damozel shewed in her face as she leaned over the gold bar of heaven. It wore off: so will mine. But it leaves something good, I hope, behind.

I hope indeed we may see something of each other: it will be a joy to me.

I won't say more: I am sitting among stacks of letters, but they are diminishing: but may all good be with you for long years.

Ever yours/ S.B.

❧

TWELVE

Elder statesman

JUNE 1937 – APRIL 1940

For the next three years Baldwin's reputation remained high, and senior politicians continued to seek his advice and approval. A collection of his recent speeches was published, his three previous volumes were re-published in popular editions,[1] and his new addresses continued to be well reported. He intended to have an active retirement. At his last Cabinet meeting he said that 'he felt . . . that he still had some good work in him and he hoped that his services to the State would not entirely cease'. This did not mean continued participation in party politics. 'He was not in future going to interfere in any way with the Government', and as he stated later 'to write or say anything about any of my old friends and associates still in active politics would be a breach of that resolve which I am not prepared to make'. Nor was he 'going to write for the press: no memoirs or nonsense of that kind'.[2]

Baldwin accepted positions on further philanthropic bodies, notably as president of Dr Barnardo's Homes. But his chief ambition was to promote 'political education': 'He intends to go after the Reds every chance he gets, and to create a public opinion in opposition to them.'[3] During a meeting of the Ashridge College governors in May 1936, he had suggested the desirability of creating a rival to the newly established Left Book Club, regarded as disseminating dangerous communist and 'fellow traveller' propaganda. Bryant had since organised a National Book Association (NBA), and for its launch in May 1937 one of the first books offered was Bryant's biographical 'tribute' to Baldwin. The Conservative Central Office

---

[1] *Service of our Lives* (1937). From 1938 to 1940 cheap hardback reissues of all four volumes sold around 50,000 copies: Hodder and Stoughton archives, Guildhall Library London, 16312/3. In addition *On England* (1926) had several impressions as a Penguin paperback from 1937; and there was a new selection, *This Torch I Would Hand to You*, ed. R. Bennett (1937).

[2] Cabinet 22 (37), 26 May 1937; to Pick, 2 April 1940, in Hyde, *Baldwin*, p. 550; to Robertson Scott, 4 Jan 1938, CUL MS Add. 8770.

[3] Mackenzie King diary, 9 May 1937.

gave the NBA unpublicised support, but Baldwin agreed to become its president only if its council was broad based: it should seek to 'embrace everyone . . . from the Right to the Left' prepared to 'come under the same umbrella to protect the country from the Red rain'. He was particularly concerned to have 'figures in the academic, literary and educational world (such as G. M. Trevelyan) whose names carry the hallmark of integrity and a distinction so great as to be above Party':

> Lord Baldwin is convinced that if we are to succeed . . . we have got to be wary of frightening away the moderate intelligentsia and the centre, who still are very chary of anything that savours of Conservatism and have got to be weaned from their 'pink' bias gradually. He feels that we have got to win the confidence of academic and educational circles, and if we can do that, we may be able to do a very great work and turn the whole tide of national education, which for many years past has been running towards the Left.[4]

During 1938 Baldwin similarly accepted presidencies of the Association for Education in Citizenship and the British Association for International Understanding, both organised on non-partisan lines. He also wanted to visit Canada again and then other Dominions, to help encourage the loyalty to Britain displayed during the Abdication crisis. However, during July 1937 he fell ill with exhaustion and arthritis, and on doctor's advice cancelled all his engagements. From August to October he had a prolonged holiday, taking in La Rochelle, Limoges, several weeks in Aix-les-Bains, a fortnight near Vevey in Switzerland, then Basle, Strasbourg, Luxembourg and a visit to Monica Baldwin in Bruges. On 5 November he ceremonially received the formal thanks of the City of London for his public services, and on the 29th spoke at a private dinner arranged in his honour by his friends.

1 DECEMBER 1937 EARL OF CRAWFORD TO TWEEDSMUIR

Buchan papers Acc 7214 mf mss 308

. . . I must tell you about the Athenaeum Dinner to Baldwin, a great success . . . Baldwin looked harassed and worn. He walked with the help of a stick. I fancy he is heavier, and certainly much less erect than twelve months ago, slower in movement and gesture – much older in fact. We were all curiosity, and some too were apprehensive, but after a few moments every fear was dispelled – for his voice, vivacity and vigour, his witty sallies,

---

[4] Davidson to Bryant, 7 May 1937, and Bryant to Hutchinson (the NBA publisher), 24 June 1937, Bryant papers C/41, C/40. The Association struggled to obtain sufficient subscribers and Bryant's increasingly right-wing book choices undermined Baldwin's conception of its purpose. He resigned his presidency in July 1939.

and his brooding aloofnesses were all what we used to know and admire – while the element of surprise was never absent from his speech, which lasted thirty-five minutes. Sometimes he spoke with great speed.

What can one say about it? – except that, oddly enough, it was political from beginning to end, being ostensibly addressed to an audience in which no Liberal, let alone any Socialist, was present. It was an apologia for the last fifteen years, beginning with 1922, during which the spirit of the country was nearer the danger point than ever before, while politics were envenomed and social differences more exacerbated than for a hundred years past; in short that Britain was in a parlous state, owing to internal and class strife which might have exploded at any moment. Violence, and indeed revolution, were in the air. Was there a note of exaggeration in all this? We wondered. And then he went on to explain that these circumstances caused him such alarm that he broke up the Coalition. His object was to disembarrass the Conservative Party from its allies, and thus to make a clear and clean-cut division of Parties. With Lloyd George out of the way, with his intrigues and combinations, it should be possible to make the Socialists think, to teach the Labour Members to believe in our English system rather than go hunting in Moscow or Rome. This he developed with a convincing candour, and perhaps with a certain resilience[5] about chronology, but it fairly arrested our attention.

Assume some years to have passed – Socialists in power and Socialists out of power, and a new National Government coming into office, everybody learning all the time, while the Socialists themselves formed the chief bulwark against Communism – and so we came to eighteen months ago when he himself, after a sick leave of two months, apparently worn-out and therefore about to retire – he then became suddenly conscious that with the death of King George V a new problem was on us – that which reached its crisis last Christmas. He settled to stay on, although it meant a year more of office than he had intended; but he had not immediately realised that it would involve another six months in order to see the young Sovereigns through the Coronation. He felt that he could give advice which nobody else could do. It was no doubt his only way of saying and seeing things which made him so invaluable to our gallant young Monarch. 'I told the King (he said) that the average working man likes to spend Sunday morning in bed reading the

---

[5] *Sic*: in the sense of 'elasticity'.

newspaper, if possible to the accompaniment of a pint of beer. But he says to himself all the time, "Well, anyhow, I am glad to know that the King and Queen are going to Church even if I am not doing it myself this morning"'.

Baldwin's speech did not sound in the least egotistical, though throughout it was a record of his own sentiment and philosophy. It was a desperately serious affair, but objective, at times very moving, and we all felt we were hearing a pronouncement of concern to every observer of public life. It was none the less light of touch and skilfully relieved from the duress of Parliamentary style or the impediment of press reporters. There was, for instance, a really wonderful narrative of his earliest election experience in the '80s, when the Liberal candidate was accused of pulling his own horse at a race meeting on the Riviera. The effect upon the electorate was curious, as the allegation was true. 'Years afterwards (said Baldwin, in a casual way) I made him a Knight'. There was also a conversation with Garter about the coat of arms Stanley B. had to assume on taking a Peerage. The heraldry itself did not interest him much, but he was very keen for the College of Arms to work into his supporters the effigies of Rothermere and Beaverbrook . . .

16 DECEMBER 1937: TO MONCKTON

Dep Monckton Trustees 15/326

69, Eaton Square

My dear Monckton,

We have sent a Christmas Card, signed, to the Duke of Windsor: I don't want an old friendship to die in my hands.

Of course, she will look over his shoulder and say "That old b——?" (or whatever may be the Baltimore equivalent!) "pitch it in the fire".

But I must take the risk of that.

Every good wish to you and yours./ Yours ever/ S.B.

28 JANUARY 1938 J. W. ROBERTSON SCOTT[6] MEMORANDUM

typescript, with pencil emendations, CUL MS Add. 8770 (extracts)

. . . Baldwin said that he had one hundred applications to make speeches, but he had made all the speeches he had wanted to make . . . His voice is a fine

---

[6] Journalist and writer on rural subjects, since 1927 editor of *The Countryman*.

one, pervaded by the Worcestershire accent. He was smoking an American corn cob pipe. He showed me some of his William Morris treasures . . .

His King's speech over the wireless[7] was made with only a few notes on a postcard, except at the end when he had something written down. He gave me several instances of men who had taken trouble with their speeches, and yet failed to get them over. Once he asked Winston Churchill to come down to Worcestershire to speak at a Worcestershire dinner, and he delivered a speech over which he had obviously taken a great deal of trouble. He told him he had given twelve hours to it. But able though the speech was, it did not get over. One wanted more than matter and more than brains – heart and feeling – to get over a speech.

Spoke of Ramsay's last years. He was worn out and quite unable to concentrate, yet wanted to write. He was afraid of the House of Commons and his nerves gave way. He had to do a great deal of his work for him. Said his death in mid-ocean was a merciful release[8] . . .

He thought very highly of Malcolm MacDonald. He got on famously with de Valera. Whether he would be able to do anything with him was another matter.

He spoke very highly and repeatedly of Morrison.[9] Elliot was a man of great ability, but Morrison was more remarkable, certainly to his mind a future Prime Minister. He said this twice. He was a great friend and he thought very highly of him. He was glad he had been able to get him into the Cabinet before handing over . . . He came from the Hebrides and the Celtic contribution was valuable.

I spoke of Cripps and his good work in Cotswold building, also about the £250 he gave me for local building.[10] He said he was very much struck by Cripps' first speech in the House of Commons. So much so, that he went up

[7] Presumably his broadcast on the death of George V, 21 Jan. 1936.
[8] Ramsay MacDonald died on 9 Nov. 1937, *en route* to a South American holiday.
[9] W. S. Morrison, Minister of Agriculture since October 1936.
[10] Sir Stafford Cripps, a supporter of various conservationist causes, but as leader of the Socialist League from 1933 a particular target of Baldwin's criticisms of the 'extreme' left. Nevertheless during June 1939 he called on Baldwin to ask him to support a campaign for a 'genuine National Government', to include Labour and Liberal leaders and Churchill, as a means of demonstrating the nation's determination to resist Hitler. Baldwin thought it would be possible under Halifax, but not Chamberlain; yet 'unless Neville could be carried along the result would be complete political chaos, as so many of the Tory Party would stand by Neville who had the machine'. He promised to speak with Halifax, who was presumably discouraging: Jones memo., 20 June 1939, Jones papers P4/54, and see E. Estorick, *Stafford Cripps* (1949), pp. 171–5.

to him afterwards and said he hoped he would excuse him speaking to him but he had been a member of the House for a long time, and he suggested Cripps would do well not to keep his hand in his pocket while addressing the House. That was what lawyers did in court, but the House of Commons would not like it. He was glad that Cripps took this very nicely.

His books were all on plain shelves marked A, B, C, D, and so on. As I ran my eye over them he said, 'A workman's library'.

What one was struck by all the time was there was no nonsense about him. His extraordinary friendliness, candour and liberality of mind. He is an admirable talker. In spite of his limp, for which Lord Dawson wanted him to get away into the sun – he had a stick standing beside his desk – he got up without using it. At the end of our talk, which lasted three-quarters of an hour, he insisted on coming down two flights of stairs with me. Just behind the door he spoke of Japan, and some other matters. He opened the front door himself, and once more said that he had greatly enjoyed our talk.

Upstairs, he had said that owing to House of Commons work he had not for many years seen Worcestershire in the spring, and whereas once he could speak to anybody in the lanes, he now felt somewhat of a stranger. He spoke generally of the great change in the villages, and of wireless. We agreed that it had completely revolutionised the rural situation. 'Give me the wireless a week before a General Election, and anybody can have the papers'. Wireless was a sad show up of the pretentious. Listeners got to the real man.

. . . He said his room was quite a confessional. People of all parties came to see him, particularly the Labour men, many of whom he liked.

I am sure that no one can know Baldwin without liking him, even getting fond of him.

. . . Said when he spoke on wireless thought of addressing 2 or 3 people round a fire.

9 FEBRUARY 1938 HINCHINGBROOKE NOTE

Lord Sandwich papers; Best and Sandwich, *Hinch*, pp. 53–4

Breakfasted with S.B. today. He is better and seems happy. He says his pension and income from Baldwins enable him to live without overspending.

He may do some writing later and is going to make a speech or two in the summer. He showed me a letter from Ramsay MacDonald offering him the Garter in the Autumn of 1932 which had touched him. He spoke warmly of MacDonald and said it was a mercy that he died when he did because he was always talking of returning to public life in some way when he came back from the cruise. He said that MacDonald's powers of control had entirely gone and that when he came to exert himself he would realise it and suffer very much.

S.B. also told me that Arthur Henderson had sent him a message from his death bed in September 1935 telling him that he, S.B. had made a mistake in holding up the 1929 election and that he was to be sure and not repeat it this time. S.B.'s comment to this was – 'You see where his heart really lay'.

S.B.'s conscience is clear about rearmament. He said that in 1934 when the Peace Ballot was held and the country was still wedded to disarmament he heard rumours of German rearmament but nothing more. He said 'we never had the <u>facts</u> for another year and then I determined to go ahead and the country gave me their mandate at the election.' He believes sincerely that we started rearming as soon as we could and the country could not have stood it a moment sooner, nor had the Government the information to acquaint the country with.

From mid February the Baldwins spent several weeks at Beaulieu and then Mougins. On 21 February Eden resigned as Foreign Secretary. When he and his ally J. P. L. Thomas also visited the French Riviera during March, they had long talks with Baldwin over three days. Thomas reported Baldwin as being furious with Chamberlain – 'all my work in keeping politics national instead of party undone' – and as planning Eden's 'movements and speeches for him: he considers Anthony the next P.M.'[11] For the next twelve months Eden looked to Baldwin as an adviser and a figure who could influence the future of Chamberlain's government and help restore him to office: some of Eden's friends even suggested that Baldwin himself might return to the Cabinet. Chamberlain also took care

[11] *The Diplomatic Diaries of Oliver Harvey 1937–1940*, ed. J. Harvey (1970), p. 115, and *passim* into early 1939 for further Edenite-Baldwin contacts; Thomas to unknown, 12 April 1938, Cilcennin papers 40. (A document cited in M&B, p. 1043, is actually a recollection about a letter, in Thomas to W. Baldwin, 13 Oct. 1959, W. Baldwin papers).

with him, inviting him to Downing Street in May to 'hear the latest developments from the inside'. During the spring and summer, Baldwin increased his speaking engagements.

11 APRIL 1938: TO DAVIDSON

Davidson papers 258; M&B, pp. 1043–4

Astley Hall

My dear old David,

Welcome home! You might like to hear my views on the political crisis. When I got back I had visits (all at their own request) from Halifax, Kingsley, Malcolm, the P.M., Horace, and at mine from Tommy,[12] T.J., and Jim Thomas.

The parting of Anthony & the P.M. was inevitable and in all the circumstances, the retiring minister was right to go. Whether A. could have been brought along with tact and understanding I don't know, nor is it of any use wondering now.

But the loss of any other colleague would have passed without a ripple on the surface, for A. was the only Minister who had got across in the country.

The net result in the Cabinet is shown below:

$$\left.\begin{array}{l} \text{S.B.} \\ \text{Anthony} \\ \text{Runciman} \end{array}\right\} = \left\{\begin{array}{l} \text{Belisha} \\ \text{Burgin} \\ \text{Winterton} \end{array}\right.$$

In these circs. it was of the first importance to be extra careful in promotions. What worries me is the wider strategy of politics over the whole country.

I fear the growth of an impression that the gov^{nt}. is swinging to extreme right.

> Lennox Boyd to Labour ministry
>
> Winterton in Cabinet
>
> Chips Channon P.P.S. to under-secretary at F.O.

Now that is as bad a set of appointments as you could conceive and the responsibility is the Chief Whip's.

In the House, the P.M. is supreme. He is [a] far better debater than I: he hits his opponents hard and our backbenches are enthusiastic. All good

---

[12] Dugdale, now a government whip.

as far as it goes. But the Labour fellows say 'We are back to the Party dog fight. The P.M.'s are A1 partisan speeches but if he talks as if he were on the hustings, so can we. And there never can be a national foreign policy as long as he is there'.

The manners of the House are getting worse: young Henderson said the Shinwell episode couldn't have happened in my time. I fear the loss of the shifting vote.

Now all this is very bald and I can fill in when we meet. I don't think it is the criticism of an old man who is jealous of his successor.

The P.M. has a heap of fine qualities and I hope devoutly for his success.

But general elections do matter and I am sure that there is an absence of thinking (indeed of knowledge) about working class psychology which will lessen our chances of success in the country.

As for Anthony, I have advised him not to go near the House for some time: to make no political speeches. To make two or three in the country such as I used to make on non-political subjects. He is making the speech on 'England' at the St George's day dinner[13] and he is addressing the Brotherhood Conference in June. Admirable, both of 'em. He must keep his prestige in the country for he is one of the few assets we have and one never knows when he may be wanted . . .

Much love/ Always/ S.B.

Oliver Baldwin was asked by a member of the Berry family of newspaper owners to persuade his father to speak at a function.

14 JULY 1938: TO OLIVER BALDWIN

CUL MS Add. 8795/33

69, Eaton Square

Dearest Son,

I knew Berry would be after me but I can't do it. I promised to go to the Wor[cestershire Association]. dinner which I couldn't go to last time: I have the Paris address in December.[14]

---

[13] *Harvey Diaries*, p. 132 (25–6 April 1938), records that Baldwin inserted a paragraph in Eden's address 'about the danger of democracy ending if allowed to deviate too much to Right or Left'.
[14] The French Academy had invited Baldwin to speak, and he had chosen Kipling as his subject; but in the event he withdrew due to ill-health.

I decided a month ago to make no engagements this autumn as I am going to go through all my papers, a daily task that may take months. There is at least 15 years of stuff in Downing St. and no one can do it but I.

The invitations are pouring in, as badly as last winter. Five yesterday for speeches, all of real importance: one calm request to write a book, another to write an address for the Society of Arts for a £20 fee! I have turned 'em all down. I hope you don't mind. The Berrys can never be out of my debt (that is a beastly way to talk!) but I gave 'em three peerages[15] and I always have an uneasy feeling that I oughtn't to have done that for any family, but I was awfully tired that last year or two and I let myself be squeezed in one or two matters of honours, though I could still keep firm on the big things.

It was such a pleasure having you at the Test match: I missed you very much at the Eton and Harrow, where we had a jolly family party down to Kiloran and John Miles.

I talked for 90 minutes to the Eton boys last night and stayed with the Master . . .

Off to Cheltenham early to-morrow, Swansea on Sat., Merthyr Monday and Batemans[16] Tuesday.

Your loving old/ F

For some time members of the Oxford Group, the evangelist Christian movement led by Frank Buchman, had sought Baldwin's support. Some of his friends – Davidson, Halifax, Salisbury and Lady Bridgeman – were sympathetic towards it, and his relatives, the Mackails, were enthusiasts. In October 1936 he had been 'profoundly' interested by Salisbury's report of a weekend party at Hatfield, where Buchman and his aides described their work to prominent politicians. Shortly after the Abdication he had invited Buchman to Chequers, and expressed agreement on the great contemporary importance of Christian principles.[17] Baldwin had, however, insisted on the meeting being strictly private; the Group was controversial, and he was wary of becoming publicly associated with it. As the international crisis intensified during summer 1938, the Group organised a series of open letters from groups of public figures – sportsmen, trade unionists, businessmen, MPs.

---

[15] Buckland (1926), Camrose (1929) and Kemsley (1936). Camrose and Kemsley had supported Baldwin's leadership even at the depths of the Beaverbrook and Rothermere attacks.

[16] To speak at Cheltenham Ladies College; to receive an honorary doctorate from University College, Swansea; to open an education centre financed by the Pilgrim Trust; and to visit Kipling's widow.

[17] To Salisbury, 22 Oct. 1936, Hatfield House archives 4M/OG1/198; Buchman note, 19 Dec. 1936, Buchman papers; Garth Lean, *Frank Buchman. A Life* (1985), pp. 249–55.

They particularly wished to have Baldwin heading a group of largely House of Lords signatories.

[LATE JULY 1938] JONES TO LADY GRIGG, 1 AUGUST

Jones papers WW1/34

...At breakfast alone with S.B. for two hours. 'I hope you don't want to hurry away' he began. Much of the talk was about the Oxford Group. Lord Salisbury & the Mackails of all people have for some time been laying siege to him. They want him to sign a manifesto to the World calling it to repentance. He asked me to read it there & then which I did. It was I suppose drafted by Mackail though I find it hard to think so. It was for the most part unexceptionable in its aspirations but there was a paragraph injected in the body of it which introduced Buchman & quoted some moral sentiments from Hitler & Roosevelt which jarred and screeched. I said <u>No</u> emphatically & not only because of the contents of the letter, but because to sign it would label him and diminish the influence he has with all sorts and conditions of men. He agreed, adding that if people responded to the appeal he would not know what to do. He was not St Francis. And he disliked as intensely as I do the Public Confession practised by the Groupists. 'We have all done things of which we were ashamed but I cannot imagine the Almighty wants us to add to the world's misery by confessing it to all & sundry. He'll be content if we repent to him'. And so say I. He was deeply 'concerned' about this request because of his friendship with the prime movers, and I tried to dissolve the solemnity by illustrating the trivial examples of Guidance which Groupists had produced to me as a reason for joining them. Anyway he has not been idle, & has preached a series of Lay Sermons recently at Cheltenham, Swansea, Merthyr & Eton.

We turned to politics & he expressed his anxiety about the way Neville was recreating the Opposition & dividing the country...

Did I tell you that after S.B.'s return from Merthyr I sent him an expenses form from the Pilgrim Trust & he returned it filled up to the following effect...

'To wear & tear of travel & speech making £105
By pleasure of seeing T.J. at Merthyr   £105
                                    Due – Nil'

No wonder I like him, is it? ...

[AUGUST 1938]: NOTE 'FOR COUSIN'
[MARGARET MACKAIL][18]

W. Baldwin papers; *My Father*, pp. 327–8

It was during the War that I found my soul. There came to me by degrees a changed sense of values, and I began to feel that I might be used for some special work. I didn't know what. I had been very restless as a Member of Parliament and felt I was no use to God or man. And I was becoming very well off, which rather frightened me and I saw myself 'tame in earth's paddock as her prize'. So I began by getting rid of about £200,000[19] which I gave away, mostly anonymously. I felt better, as though I had pulled my sweater off for a race, though I didn't see where the race would be or how long the course. And gradually after much thought it seemed to me that all this bloodshed would be wasted if the world couldn't be made a better place: I felt that the men who had made such sacrifices and in such a spirit were capable of rising to any heights, and I began to think out the kind of leadership the country would want when the peace came. The peace came, and by 1919 and 1920 the temper of this country was worse than it had ever been.

It was obvious that the first thing to be done was to pull the country together: to make them realise the brotherhood of the human family. It seemed simple and obvious, but how to do it? The bitterness in the country was of the devil: no one in the higher political world seemed to realise it or give it a thought. One thing was clear to me, that under the then government, which was Lloyd George, F. E. Smith and Winston, buttressed by the respectability of Balfour and Austen Chamberlain, things would get rapidly worse, until you might pass quickly into a condition little short of revolution. I felt that it was essential to break up that government but it looked impregnable.

Well in 1922 it was smashed to bits. Bonar Law won the election: we had a weak team of honest men, and in a few months he became mortally ill and I was Prime Minister. Quite unfitted for it, with little experience. I had never contemplated it, but I was never in doubt. I could see the hand of God in it, and I recognised that my peculiar life had been a preparation for

---

[18] A note by Baldwin's daughter Lorna reads: 'in reply to repeated letters asking him to become a Buchmanite'. On the original undated document a subsequent note offers October 1937 as the date, but internal evidence seems to confirm the date here, as suggested by Windham Baldwin on a typescript copy.
[19] About £4.8 million (*c.* 2000).

the very work that lay before me. The problem was to get at the soul of the working people. I found that those long, quiet years at Wilden had given me a knowledge of them that few men in politics had. The lines of my policy grew clear, and I <u>knew</u> that I had been chosen as God's instrument for the work of the healing of the nation. But you can understand how puzzled I was that He should choose such a specimen of His creatures to work through!

For sixteen years I worked, through difficulties and disappointments, with increasing faith and incessant search for God's will. In May of last year I was worn out. But I had got at last to the point when I could say with deep conviction 'Use me as Thou wilt or throw me away. Thy will be done.' But I took a long time to get to that point! I believe my work has not been in vain; I believe the feeling in industry is better than it has ever been, and I think I still have a good deal of influence on the ordinary folk in our country.

I needn't tell you that what work I may yet do has been and is the subject of constant prayer and thought: on prayer I have been increasingly dependent for many years. I emphasise this because of your dear letter to me on my birthday. I cannot change the direction of my life at any suggestion from others however deep my respect and love for them.

I believe that in my public life I have been increasingly led, and I mean to be led to the end.

The Baldwins were at Aix-les-Bains from late August to mid September, as the Czechoslovakian crisis developed. Oxford Group members and Salisbury had re-drafted the letter they wanted Baldwin to sign, and Mackail telephoned to Aix and obtained Baldwin's consent: 'I don't think it can do any good but it is a voice from England to like minded people in every country.'[20]

[SEPTEMBER 1938] BALDWIN AND OTHERS
TO THE EDITOR OF *THE TIMES*

The Times, 10 September 1938, p. 6e

Sir, In this letter there is no intention of questioning the convictions of those nations who are struggling for principles in which they believe. Nevertheless to-day all are anxiously asking, to what is the world heading? What is the future of civilization?

---

[20] To Joan Davidson, 9 Sept. 1938.

The world cannot for ever continue plunging from crisis to crisis. We must act, before crisis ends in catastrophe; we must use the present breathing space, which may be brief, to penetrate below symptoms into their causes, and initiate that fundamental change which alone will break a vicious circle. In the words of the leader of a great nation: 'It is an entirely new spirit which must be acquired and enthroned'.

In a striking letter in *The Times* last week a number of Members of Parliament, representing different political parties, emphasized the fact that in every country national security at home and abroad can only be gained through moral regeneration. The strength of a nation consists in the vitality of her principles. Policy, foreign as well as domestic, is for every nation ultimately determined by the character of her people and the inspiration of her leaders; by the acceptance in their lives and in their policy of honesty, faith and love as the foundations on which a new world may be built. Without these qualities, the strongest armaments, the most elaborate pacts, only postpone the hour of reckoning.

The real need of the day is therefore moral and spiritual rearmament. A growing body of people in this and other countries are making it their aim. It is a work in which all men and women, in all countries and of all races, are called to share and have power to help. Were we, together with our fellow men everywhere, to put the energy and resourcefulness into this task that we now find ourselves obliged to expend on national defence, the peace of the world would be assured.

God's Living Spirit calls each nation, like each individual, to its highest destiny, and breaks down the barriers of fear and greed, of suspicion and hatred. This same Spirit can transcend conflicting political systems, can reconcile order and freedom, can rekindle true patriotism, can unite all citizens in the service of the nation, and all nations in the service of mankind. 'Thy will be done on earth' is not only a prayer for guidance, but a call to action. For His Will is our Peace.

Yours faithfully,

Baldwin of Bewdley, Salisbury, Amulree, Birdwood, William Bragg, Clarendon, Cork and Orrery, Desborough, Kennet, Lytton, J. W. Mackail, Milne, W. D. Ross, Sankey, Stamp, Stanmore, Trenchard

During the crisis Baldwin wrote three letters to Chamberlain, and was invited to lunch with him on 21 September.

15 SEPTEMBER 1938: TO NEVILLE CHAMBERLAIN

NC 13/11/618

Regina Hotel Bernascon, Aix-les-Bains

My dear Neville,

I rejoiced when I heard of your decision to see Hitler. You are right, whatever the outcome, a thousand times over. You are shewing real courage and wisdom. Bless you!

Ever yours/ S.B.

26 SEPTEMBER 1938: TO NEVILLE CHAMBERLAIN

NC 13/11/620

69, Eaton Square

My dear Neville,

This wants no acknowledgment.

You are constantly in my thoughts. You are carrying on a magnificent fight and at times I wish I were with you to support you. I couldn't stand the strain now, alas. But I do pray your strength will hold. It is amazing how one does have strength for a crisis. If you can secure peace you may be cursed by a lot of hotheads but my word you will be blessed in Europe and by future generations.

This is only a line to shew you that an old friend is thinking of you.

Yours ever/ S.B.

30 SEPTEMBER 1938: TO NEVILLE CHAMBERLAIN

NC 13/11/619

69, Eaton Square

My dear Neville

There is no prouder and happier man in England to-day than I! To see my old friend and trusted colleague of long and difficult years acclaimed by the world for what he is and has done is pure joy for me. God bless you and give you strength to go on and accomplish those things of which we used to talk. You have everything in your own hands now – for a time – and you can do anything you like. Use that time well for it won't last.

Ever yours in admiration and true affection/ S.B.

No answer!

On 4 October Baldwin made his only House of Lords speech, in the debate on the Munich settlement. He praised Chamberlain's success in avoiding war and sought to reassure doubtful government followers, but also called for all-party co-operation in continued defence preparations. Eden invoked Baldwin's name when privately arguing the case for a reconstructed all-party government, while Baldwin himself tried without success to persuade Chamberlain to at least re-shuffle the existing Cabinet.[21]

14 OCTOBER 1938 HINCHINGBROOKE NOTE

Lord Sandwich papers

Saw S.B. again today. He was grave and anxious and said that democracy was entering a testing time. I asked him if he had given up hope of its coming through and he replied 'not by any means'. He said he did not relish the idea of Westminster Abbey and the records of a thousand years history being pulverized by German bombers. The fears of Germans for their own capital city could not be comparable. He said – 'can't we turn Hitler East? Napoleon broke himself against the Russians. Hitler might do the same'. He criticised Chamberlain for his emotional outburst in Downing Street. 'Peace with honour' was a most unfortunate phrase, it was only necessary to say a few words. 'I should have done it very differently' – and then, very significantly, 'I love a crisis'. I asked him about the current opinion that Chamberlain was conducting Foreign Affairs like a dictator without the Cabinet and he said 'you have to act quickly and alone on these occasions but when I was Prime Minister I always had Neville, as Ramsay had me, to interpret my views to the Cabinet and carry them along. The trouble is Neville has nobody'.

I was glad to hear him say that those in control of affairs from now on should be young enough to experience the results of their efforts. It was not right, he said, that some of those who had at the most a few years left to them should be responsible for the decisions taken today.

He seems to be in favour of the transfer of Colonies to Germany but only providing heavy disarmament is secured in return. His difficulty was to trust the Germans to carry it out.

I asked him about our secret service in Germany from 1933 to 1935. He said we could not get reliable information through the ordinary channels.

---

[21] *Harvey Diaries*, p. 213; Eden diary, 11 Oct. 1938; Jones to Lady Grigg, 19 Nov. 1938, Jones papers WW1/51.

No one would speak: they were afraid. He said 'Hitler is a much greater man than any of us dreamed of some years ago'.

25 OCTOBER 1938 DAVIDSON [ON BALDWIN'S BEHALF]
TO SIR WILLIAM COX[22]

copy, Davidson papers 258

... I have tried, and Baldwin has tried, during a life of public service, to enthuse others with a pride in British citizenship, and with the realisation that it carries duties and well as obligations; that to take advantage of the freedom and economic strength of England, and in that security to increase one's private fortune, without putting some of it back to help the people amongst whom one lives is wrong. We who have lived and worked at the centre know how difficult it is to keep democracy safe, and how little in terms of cash is needed to educate the people to be vigilant against the attacks on their liberty. This is no question of party politics. It is citizenship in the broadest sense – willingness to serve voluntarily in the thousands of jobs which constantly need refilling if the vitality of the country and its stability are to be maintained. We believe that education in citizenship and public service should be available to all who seek it . . .

Men like Baldwin, and I in my humble way, have sacrificed wealth and the opportunities for making it, to help to maintain the principles and character of the government of the country, and to improve the condition of the people . . .

. . . Baldwin has . . . so often said, 'I can spend my remaining days in guiding the nation through non-political channels towards the greater unity which, while I was Prime Minister, I gradually brought to pass after the purge of the General Strike' . . .

Baldwin is no dreamer of dreams that cannot come true. National unity and stability can be achieved, not by slogans or party propaganda, but by the education of the children and the young men and women to appreciate their traditions and their rights, and to take their full share of responsibility and service as citizens of a free country.

---

[22] Cousin and advisor of the shipping multi-millionaire Sir John Ellerman, who was prepared to make money available for Conservative causes: see Stephen Roskill, *Hankey*, 3 vols. (1970–4), III, ch. 9. Davidson and Baldwin were seeking an endowment of up to a million pounds for Ashridge College.

After *Kristallnacht*, the Nazi attacks on Jewish property on 9 November, representatives of the Church of England Assembly asked Baldwin to lead an appeal
in support of their refugee organisation. Baldwin agreed on condition that it
should be a 'national' appeal, on behalf of all the British religious denominations, including Free Church, Roman Catholic and Jewish. This was arranged,
and with advice from Tom Jones, the Archbishop's office and the Foreign Office Baldwin on 8 December made one of his most impressive and important
broadcasts. He appealed for donations to the 'Lord Baldwin Fund for Refugees';
all bank branches co-operated, many fund-raising events were organised, and
over the next two months *The Times* printed pages of donors' names. The broadcast also drew personal attacks on Baldwin in the German press, and protests
from German diplomats in London. By summer 1939 the Fund had received
£522,000,[23] with half disbursed directly to assist child refugees and the rest allocated to Jewish and Christian refugee organisations. The broadcast was also relayed
to North America and parts of the Empire, to support separate appeals in those
areas.

'CHRISTMAS DAY 1938': TO HALIFAX

Halifax papers A4.410.14.10

Astley Hall

My dear Edward,

I waited till this blessed day to send you a line: your greetings came a
couple of days ago.

I can't shake off a feeling of heaviness – I may be the less a Christian for
that.

Yet I feel millions will be thinking hard this season, all through Europe,
and one must have faith that the prayers of millions will prevail.

How little that phrase 'spiritual wickedness in high places' used to mean
to us and how it nearly knocks one down to-day!

It is not easy to drown these thoughts just now when we must be bright
for the young.

Perhaps I am an old fool! And I hold by some of my friendships of which
I value none more than yours. My love and blessings to you all.

Ever yours/ S.B.

---

[23] About £26.8 million (*c.* 2000).

29 DECEMBER 1938: TO LORD LINLITHGOW

Linlithgow papers Ms Eur F125/154

Astley Hall

My dear Hopie,

... Eden is all right. It is always difficult, when you are young and keen, to go on keeping your mouth shut. And of course every disgruntled man tries to use him: he is a natural focus. But he won't play and all attempts to use him by Ll.G. and Winston have come to nothing. I shall be glad to see him back after, say, a year. But even then that can only be when the P.M. wants him back.

The fact remains that his personality can draw big audiences and no Cabinet minister can compare with him in that respect, so for the party's sake it is important that this separation shouldn't last until the Election.

His American tour has been a success. I told him that if Kennedy[24] thought he ought to go and if the P.M. approved, then he should face the real risk of failure and go.

Kennedy was worried by a wave of anti-British feeling and he thought Anthony could render really valuable service by going at that moment. Of course the Jew baiting has done more to help, from our point of view, than a century of British propaganda.

I saw the P.M. after Berchtesgaden and after his holiday which succeeded the Munich meeting. He seemed very fit and refreshed.

You may have seen that I had the King to dinner before Christmas to meet Attlee and half-a-dozen or so of his merry men.

The interesting thing is that I left the choice to Attlee (subject to our discussion) and he never picked a single intellectual. They were all working men by origin![25] The party was a roaring success. H.M. stayed till 11 having ordered his car early. We dined at 8, dinner jackets: no champagne. White and red wine, lemonade, port and brandy after dinner, cigars, cigarettes and pipes. No decorations, except a waiter from Downing St. who had a jubilee medal! My labour friends behaved like the gentlemen they are, and were enthusiastic about the monarch after he had gone. I am sure it did real good.

---

[24] The United States ambassador in London.
[25] Those present were Attlee, Greenwood, Grenfell, Tom Williams, Marshall and Henderson (Herbert Morrison and Hallsworth, the TUC chairman, were also invited, but unable to attend).

I suggested it to the King before I left office and he liked the idea. He has no chance of getting to know the men who will be his ministers in case of change, and he could never get on terms with them in the Palace.[26] . . .

Yours ever/ S.B.

In January Baldwin was asked to deliver a series of addresses at the University of Toronto during April, to be broadcast across North America. He thought that 'such a visit might do much good. Canada in my view is suffering from want of leadership. There is no one to pull them together. There is a nasty undercurrent of neutrality: why should Canada be drawn into war in Europe? The British Government is Fascist and so on and so on. So I thought I ought to go.'[27] Drawing on his many earlier speeches on freedom and democracy, and recalling a long British tradition of resistance to continental tyrannies, the addresses were 'meant to get at the ordinary men in Canada to help to pull 'em together and in the U.S. to make 'em think and realise what is at stake'.[28] They were published verbatim in leading British newspapers and collected as *An Interpreter of England*.

17–18 APRIL 1939: MACKENZIE KING DIARY

. . . Baldwin said the pressure was getting terrible in England. They were getting to a nervous state of tension where they were preferring almost anything than the long continued uncertainty. . . Chamberlain had done the only thing possible at Munich. . . I could see that Baldwin believed war was coming though he did not seem to think that it would be immediate. On the other hand, he was by no means sure that it might not come suddenly any day. He said England was much better prepared than she had been, and will continue to advance rapidly. . .

He kept impressing on me as he did on those present at the dinner that Their Majesties were really two persons of exceptional character, with a high sense of public duty, and that the Throne would be back to where it was in King George's days, under their regime.[29]

When I talked with him of the Duke of Windsor, he told me that what the people really felt was that he had quit his job, and let them all down in so doing. He said he never had the reliability or character for a kingship. . .

[18 April] . . . I asked him about how he managed his days when Prime

---

[26] See Jones *DL*, pp. 303, 330 (11 Jan., 20 April 1937). Both Baldwin and Buckingham Palace staff had consulted Chamberlain, who thought it a 'favourable time' for such a meeting.
[27] To Davidson, 23 Jan. 1939, Lady Davidson papers.
[28] To Dawson, 8 April 1939, Dawson papers 80/155.
[29] There was to be a royal visit to Canada and the United States in May and June.

Minister. He said he had been particularly careful to cultivate the H. of C. Seldom went home for dinner. Stayed around the buildings all the time; not always in the House but continually in touch with members. When a man made a good speech, regardless of the side he was on, he would have a word of praise for him. He came to know the House so well, he could scent out what was coming – if there were a storm ahead. Did not try to make strong speeches. He said he was not given to that sort of thing. He kept in touch with members, gaining their confidence. He said he had been able, as a result of that, to hold it in times of emergency. That a much more brilliant man than either 'you or me' had not been able to hold the House, as he had not gained their confidence. He referred to Lloyd George who spent little time in the House. . .

. . . What impressed me most in talking with Baldwin was how clearly he foresaw the danger of democratic states becoming Fascist through developing a single political party, getting into extreme measures, etc. . .

In mid August the Baldwins again travelled to North America. Baldwin spoke at the British pavilion at the New York World's Fair, and gave two addresses – the main purpose of the visit – to the international Congress on Education in Democracy at Columbia University. His chief address, on the spiritual basis of political freedom, was broadcast across the United States and received considerable newspaper coverage. As the Baldwins returned, the international crisis and then the outbreak of war caused them to abandon their usual French holiday and return to Astley Hall, to receive evacuated schoolchildren and their teachers. After Reith was appointed Minister of Information, as a new MP he asked for Baldwin's advice.

31 JANUARY 1940: TO JOHN REITH

Reith papers; Reith, *Into the Wind*, pp. 363–4

PATIENCE

First   Last

    and   Astley Hall

All the Way

BE YOURSELF

ALWAYS.

My dear Reith,

    The present House is four and a half years old: it has had time to have taken on a character of its' own and its' atmosphere is familiar to each individual in it. Every House has its own distinctive character and every man of position has to make good (or not!) in a new House.

You come in like a new boy at a new school and you must learn its' ways. Time will soon show you what instinct you possess in understanding it.

But here is some of your A.B.C. They are of <u>general</u> application.

Don't lecture them.

Don't joke.

Don't try and be an orator.

Don't be sarcastic.

Just talk naturally.

You want to take them with you.

Your job is to see that there is no friction between Parliament and your Ministry.

A Minister is in the House to get the business of his Office through.

You will probably be asked to address the 1922 Committee. Go, and talk freely about your job; seek their co-operation.

I should address the other parties too: consult the Whips on this.

Make the acquaintance of the Smoking Room: your P.P.S. or a whip should arrange this for you. Look in and let them get a few of the right men to sit with you. A pipe and chat and get them to talk. You want it to get about that you are accessible: that you are ready to hear complaints and meet them when reasonable. You can often avoid questions in the House by personal contact in time and a debate in which you are the principal figure will often go much more smoothly if you can create the impression of yourself which I am sure you can.

As to Questions. It is worth while (for a time) sitting through questions to study both the questioner and the Minister.

In the original answer, always be short but don't evade anything. Neither in the original or supplementary answer, reply to something that has not been directly asked.

You will only start a fresh hare. Only an ass starts an unnecessary hare.

In answering supplementaries, only experience can teach you the best way.

Such phrases as: 'I will bear that in mind' 'I have nothing to add' (not with a snap but as if you wished you had, but it is impossible to do it!).

Wait for freedom in replying to supplementaries until you are familiar with the idiosyncrasies of the questioner and until you can sense the House. There is a lot of fun in answering when you have learnt the game and <u>the House knows you know it</u>.

So go quietly for some time.

Don't attempt to be funny or sarcastic in your early days, or you may prejudice your usefulness.

One thing the House will NEVER forgive and that is if a Minister misleads it. If you find you have given an answer that isn't true, acknowledge it at once and express your regret. The blame is always on <u>you</u> and <u>not</u> on the Civil Service.

That will do to go on with.

Good luck!

BE YOURSELF ALWAYS.

Ever yours/ S.B.

14 APRIL 1940: TO LINLITHGOW

Linlithgow papers F125/154

Astley Hall [but Trinity College, Cambridge notepaper]

My dear Hopie,

We are short of paper and I found this in a drawer, representing the last sheet of some lovely writing paper I used in the year of Queen Victoria's first jubilee!

Your letter delighted me: you seem full of vigour and cheer and I loved your reference to old man Stalin and your desire to welcome him while you are still Viceroy if he should be thinking of a visit to India! I don't think there's much chance of that. I have never been afraid of the Muscovite as an invading force.

I have made my headquarters in Worcestershire and go up to London every few weeks for the inside of a week. I am very well but very lame and hobble about the garden.

We have had Birmingham evacuees for five months but they have all gone home again now.

I make a little speech now and again but there is nothing I can do and for the first time in my life I find myself wishing I were ten years younger that I might lend an effective hand. I see Edward [Halifax] every time I go to London and I hope to see him again next week. He keeps well: doesn't look at all overdone and is calm. The P.M. I have seen two or three times and he too is wonderful in his physical condition and complete freedom from nerves. Old friends are good enough to find time to come and talk and I spend all day (when I am up) in delightful interviews.

Anthony is doing well at Dominions and is moving up again: I don't think he has ever lost his popular appeal but his stock fell in the House and Press for a time...

Winston is becoming a great popular figure. His expositions whether by wireless or in the House are admirable, and I think go on getting better. The flamboyance is less, he seems more sober and to my mind more convincing and impressive in consequence.

I haven't been so long continuously in the country since 1907! I am enjoying watching the spring coming more than I can say.

But we can't get rid of the oppression that war brings with it, an oppression that weighs more heavily if one feels oneself useless...

Bless you./Yours ever/ S.B.

24 APRIL 1940 MRS BURGES[30] NOTE

typescript, W. Baldwin papers

This morning I had a long talk to Lord Baldwin at 16, Great College Street. I told him that I was going to ask him a very impertinent question and that I hoped he would not mind. He told me to ask on, and I therefore enquired bluntly whether he would amplify some remarks he made in a speech in [November] 1936, when he told the House that he was speaking with 'appalling frankness'. I explained that I was always being told by people that his remarks on this occasion meant that he knew Germany was rearming, and deliberately hid this fact from the people in order to win the Election. This was so unjust a version that I hoped he would sometime set on record what he had really meant,

Lord Baldwin looked quite relieved when I blurted this out, almost as though he had thought I was going to ask something much more serious than a question affecting his own reputation. He said at once that history would have to sort it out, and he was confident that in years to come unbiased

---

[30] Davidson's secretary.

historians would say he could have done no more than he did. He added with a smile that it was perhaps a stupid speech to make, and he repeated this observation several times later in our talk, finally saying that it was perhaps the most indiscreet speech he had ever made – and that was saying a lot!

He explained that it was hard for people today to remember the circumstances of the time. In 1933 the Disarmament Conference was sitting, and Mr MacDonald was P.M. By 1934, the Government began to get worried by the reports of German re-armament which filtered through, although it was realised that they had to start from scratch, as Germany was completely disarmed. The news which came through was scrappy and unreliable. No-one knew how long it would take the Germans to rearm, none could foretell how long they would continue. Moreover, he thought history would confirm that Hitler hoped for an agreement with this country until some years after 1934 – perhaps until almost the end. The trouble was that he was mad – each success whetted his appetite for more, his ambitions became more and more grandiose – as Sir Nevile Henderson's book[31] clearly shows. But not until Hitler realised that to get an agreement with us meant he must forego some of his ambitions did he definitely give up hope of an agreement. The present Prime Minister went on hoping right up until the seizure of Bohemia and Moravia; and Lord Baldwin did not blame him for doing so, though he did feel that time had been wasted in not bringing our rearmament production up to wartime pitch some months earlier. He reminded me that he had only made one speech in the Lords since his retirement (which he said was, he thought, not a bad speech), and that was when after Munich he urged that our factories should be nationalised for armament production.

In 1933–4 it was easy for Winston to urge great rearmament Programmes. Lord Baldwin had made up his mind that, once he became P.M., he would get a mandate at the earliest possible moment, because he knew we must rearm. But how could he stump the country, calling for expenditure of £200 million, when the only reasons he could give were that we did not know much about Hitler, that we had reports that Germany was rearming, but we did not know how much or how long it would take her? There would have been a howl of indignation at this unjust attempt to 'keep Germany

---

[31] *Failure of a Mission* (1940), his account of his ambassadorship in Berlin, 1937–9.

down'. Moreover, it was easy to say now that we ought to have known more, to have got better information: the fact was that at the time the Government had not got it. How could he call for rearmament against Germany on such a flimsy basis?

He went on to say that he had never known the country in a rottener state than in 1933, with the Peace Ballot agitation.[32] That had to be recovered from, and it took some doing. He did have an election as soon as he could but he did not talk a great deal about rearmament: he only referred to the necessity for our rearming in order to fulfil our obligations under the covenant. Even so, many of his friends thought this might make difficulties; but in the event he won the Election with a very large majority and we did begin to [rearm] as fast as we could from 1935 onwards. He had always said that a democracy was 2 years behind a dictatorship, and it was true; but, as a statesman, he ought not to have made that speech. He was probably very tired when he did so, as he often was during his last years in office.

It was always difficult to realise how ignorant the people were. One made a speech with one's mind full of facts which one could not disclose. I said that no doubt in years to come what he had then stated with appalling frankness would be looked upon as a simple and obvious remark, to which he agreed. I added that though this might be criticised now, as it was at the time, he was also criticised for being too discreet when his lips were still not unsealed. This remark brought a quick smile; he remembered the context of that immediately, and said 'Ah yes, that was another stupid thing to say. I have said many stupid things! But what of course I meant was that I was morally sure that Laval had been bought by Mussolini, and I could not very well say that to the House. After all, we had to remain on good terms with the French'. We both laughed at this, and I said (thinking of Sir Sam) 'And another of your troubles was that you were always so loyal to your colleagues'. He nodded and said with a little grin, 'Yes, they did give me trouble sometimes'.

Lord Baldwin then talked of the Abyssinian crisis. He said he could have talked till he was black in the face, but the country would not have believed that the other countries in Europe were not ready for 'collective security' until it was proved to them in that unhappy period when sanctions were imposed on Italy. Then we found, as he had always expected, that no country wanted to go to war for collective security, not even the bellicose Frenchman.

[32] A chronological slip, as the Peace Ballot began in late 1934.

They all made excuses to run out. Our people for years had had dinned into them the notion that all that was needed to stop an aggressor was for all the other countries to say 'stop!'. It was not easy to prove to them, as he knew all along it had to be proved, that that was entirely wrong. It had to be learnt by experience and it was difficult to gain that experience without plunging the country into war. He often thought that it was only by the mercy of God that Englishmen, when gaining experience by running their heads into a stone wall, only stunned themselves and did not kill themselves outright.

He then reverted to my original question, and said it always seemed to him a pitiful thing when men tried to justify their actions and speeches after retirement. 'I did not learn much at school, but one thing I did learn, which one cannot learn too soon in life, and that was what my Headmaster continually stressed: "Never judge history in the light of after events." It would be wrong to criticise the actions of 1860 for example, in the knowledge of conditions in 1900. I mean that as a general rule; of course one could knock such a theory to bits, and I would never put it out in an essay. But generally it is well to remember that'. I said it was so easy to look at even the very recent past through the spectacles of today. I knew that I myself would have been miserable at the time had military action been proposed when Hitler marched into the Rhineland. Lord Baldwin said he had often thought over the past, and he always remembered how little then was known and how impossible it was to prophesy. Who in 1930 could have foreseen what Hitler would become? Was there not a big chance he might have been a very different man? Both the P.M. and Lord Halifax had told him last time he saw them that they had gone over the past again and again, and as the P.M. said, 'I could not see where we had done wrong, or what we could have done differently in the circumstances of the time'. Lord Baldwin thought that the fact that it was only at the very end that Hitler was singled out as The Enemy brought the country unitedly to war, as might not have happened earlier. The best among the Labour leaders had realised some years ago the truth about Russia; but it had taken the invasion of Finland to open the eyes of the rank and file, and they had now shed their old prejudices very thoroughly. Not that he had known beforehand that the Russians would strike where they did; but that they were the sort of blackguards to do that if it suited them.

Lord Baldwin, with a smile, acknowledged that one always received some abusive letters, but it was useless to worry about them. He would always be attacked too in the Beaverbrook Press; the Beaver knew he could sell his papers better by attacking one or two public men than by support of the Government of the day, and therefore he would always do so. It was odd that, whereas when he had been in power he had been accused of indolence, lack of grip and control of his colleagues, now (to judge from the tone of letters and articles) he was assumed to have been a sort of dictator who held all his Ministers in the palm of his hand and was solely responsible for all that had happened. 'People can't have it both ways', said he, 'I was very far from being a dictator!'

When Lord Baldwin was speaking of the error of looking at the past from the point of view of today, and the necessity for judging things to the best of one's ability at the time, I remarked that this was really the same point negatively as Mr Eden had made in his speech at the Constitutional Club ten days ago, when he spoke of the impossibility of trying to fetter the future by outlining what destiny was to be. Lord Baldwin agreed, saying that he had read every word of the speech with great appreciation, and he thought it the finest delivered since war began. Mr Eden had said what needed saying; the issue had never been clearer than in this struggle – no doubt the Americans would wake up to the fact in 1960. I laughed, and enquired whether this lag proved they were not a democracy, or that they were super-democrats, to which he smilingly answered that he would be sorry to see the U.S. left as the sole repository of the democratic spirit. They were a democracy of a sort, but they had a very great deal to learn.

❦

THIRTEEN

Last years

MAY 1940 – DECEMBER 1947

After the military and political crisis over the Norwegian campaign, Chamberlain resigned as Prime Minister on 10 May. With German armies advancing into France, on the 19th Churchill made his first broadcast as leader of a new all-party coalition government. Baldwin thought Churchill 'the right man at the moment and I always did feel that war would be his opportunity. He thrives in that environment.'[1]

11 MAY 1940: TO NEVILLE CHAMBERLAIN

NC 7/11/33/17

Astley Hall

My dear Neville,

You have passed through fire since we were talking together a fortnight ago and you have come out pure gold.

Last night as I heard you on the wireless I felt proud that I could call you my friend.

God bless you through these days of trial – and always.

With true affection and regard/ Always yours/ S.B.

20 MAY 1940: TO CHURCHILL

Churchill papers CHAR 20/1/20; *The Churchill War Papers*, II, ed. M. Gilbert (1994), p. 94

My dear P.M.,

I listened to your well known voice last night and I should have liked to have shaken your hand for a brief moment and to tell you that from the

---

[1] To Joan Davidson, 22 June 1940.

bottom of my heart I wish you all that is good – health and strength of mind and body – for the intolerable burden that now lies on you.

Yours always sincerely/S.B.

Baldwin participated in one further episode in high policy, when on Jones' suggestion the new Dominions Secretary, Lord Caldecote (formerly Inskip), asked him to help persuade the Northern Ireland Prime Minister to allow defence co-operation with the Irish Free State, considered vital for strengthening British security against German invasion. Craigavon, however, refused to meet de Valera, knowing that he would be placed under pressure to consider the issue of Irish unity.[2]

c. 23 MAY 1940: TO VISCOUNT CRAIGAVON

copy in Lady Craigavon diary, 24 May 1940, PRONI D/1415/C/236–433

My dear James,

You and I have been through many hard times together; today I am no longer capable of bearing such a burden as that which still rests on you. I never interfere in matters of State but I feel I must write you a line as I have been pressed to do so by Tom Inskip. He is profoundly anxious about Ireland and I beg you to be helpful to him at this time of national danger. If it is a question of meeting de V – well I know the difficulties in ordinary times. But the times are not ordinary and,

1. It seems to me possible that we may want to move troops into the Free State in certain contingencies and it seems to me that such action, instead of being acquiesced in, might be welcomed with enthusiasm if it were known that you and de V. had met and discussed matters relating to the common safety of Ireland as a whole.

2. And secondly; the repercussion through the Irish in America would be like a flash of lightning and the idea of all Irishmen joining hands to protect their common country might just cause that tilting of the scales that would bring America into the War.

Forgive me; but the times justify me as one of your oldest friends in giving you my considered views.

Yours ever/ S.B.

[2] Jones to Violet Markham, 24 May, 13 June 1940, Jones papers T7/20, 21, describes this incident, including his visit to Baldwin at Astley.

On 2 June Baldwin delivered his last public address, during the Thomas Hardy centenary celebrations at Dorchester. After the fall of France, Halifax as Foreign Secretary made a broadcast on 22 July describing Nazism as 'the challenge of anti-Christ', and invoking the comfort and power of trusting in God's will.

23 JULY 1940: TO HALIFAX

Halifax papers A4.410.14.11; Halifax, *Fulness of Days*, pp 225–6

Astley Hall

My dear Edward,

Thank you for your broadcast: it was what many were waiting for. It ran so closely along the lines my own thoughts have been travelling that I cannot resist writing to you what otherwise I should have hesitated about saying even to you: at least I should have said it more easily in conversation than in a letter.

With millions of others I had prayed hard at the time of Dunkirk and never did prayer seem to be more speedily answered to the full. And we prayed for France and the next day she surrendered. I thought much and when I went to bed I lay for a long time vividly awake. And I went over in my mind what had happened, concentrating on the thoughts that you dwelt on, that prayer to be effective must be in accordance with God's will, and that by far the hardest thing to say from the heart and indeed the last lesson we learn (if we ever do) is to say and mean it, 'Thy will be done'. And I thought what mites we all are and how we can never see God's plan, a plan on such a scale that it <u>must</u> be incomprehensible. And suddenly for what must have been a couple of minutes I seemed to see with extraordinary and vivid clarity and to hear some one speaking to me. The words at the time were clear but the recollection of them had passed when I seemed to come to, as it were, but the sense remained, and the sense was this. 'You cannot see the plan' then 'have you not thought there is a purpose in stripping you one by one of all the human props on which you depend, that you are being left alone in the world? You have now one upon whom to lean and I have chosen you as my instrument to work with my will. Why then are you afraid?'

And to prove ourselves worthy of that tremendous task is our job.

Bless you: I rejoice that you are where you are at this time. Don't feel that this needs an answer. I know what your load is.

Yours ever/ S.B.

During July Baldwin wrote that 'for three months, since the intensification of the War, I haven't been up [to London] for I couldn't ask overworked ministers in present circumstances to let me bother them'.[3] There is no corroboration for G. M. Young's claim that he was advised to keep away for fear of attracting popular hostility.[4] Nevertheless, Baldwin was aware of a collapse in his public reputation. The first surviving letter accusing him of having 'failed to rearm' Britain followed a hostile article by Peter Howard in *The Sunday Express* on the day the war began. In May 1940 Baldwin wrote that 'I don't get much of this sort, but about one abusive anonymous letter a week, and if the Beaver has anything particularly poisonous about me in the Sunday Express, I get perhaps a couple of such letters enclosing the cutting. It is only to be expected.'[5] When during 1945 he received more of the 'beastly letters' he wrote that 'I can understand his bitterness: he wants a scapegoat and the men[6] provided him with one.' These reactions were characteristic of 'a kind of humble magnanimity' which Hensley Henson noted in a 1944 letter from Baldwin: 'We have both ridden on the crest of the waves, each in his peculiar sea, but I am in the trough now where many a better man has been before me.'[7] He was most hurt by what seemed to be a vindictive targeting in early 1942 of his Astley Hall gates and railings for use as scrap metal, and an apparent obstruction to his second son's promotion in the RAF 'because he was his father's son'.[8]

When Chamberlain, who had become Lord President of the Council, was forced by a fatal illness to retire from the Cabinet in October, Baldwin wrote the following letter with the intention of helping him find a final peace. However, it provoked Chamberlain to write an irascible reply denying that office had tired him, rejecting any doubt about his past actions, and dismissing his critics as 'wilfully ignorant' – a response which Baldwin 'did not relish ... at all'.[9]

13 OCTOBER 1940: TO NEVILLE CHAMBERLAIN

NC 13/18/783

Astley Hall

My dear Neville,

I wish we were not so far apart just now. It is so easy to talk and so hard to write and try to express thoughts that come so much more clearly from

---

[3] To Cranborne, 31 July 1940, Hatfield House archives.   [4] Young, *Baldwin*, p. 250.
[5] To Davidson, 19 May 1940, Lady Davidson papers.
[6] Presumably a reference to 'Cato', *Guilty Men* (1940, republished 1945, 1998).
[7] *Letters of Herbert Hensley Henson*, ed. E. F. Braley (1950), pp. 150–1.
[8] M&B, pp. 1059–61; Jones *DL*, p. 515 (26 March 1944).
[9] Ibid., p. 482; Feiling, *Chamberlain*, pp. 455–6, has Chamberlain's reply.

the lips than from the pen. Again you have done the only thing you could do but it is cruelly hard at the present time and you leave a place that no one can fill. I have a dread of operations at our time of life and no man can be fit again for a much longer time than he can spare. For in our jobs there is no seconding for a matter of months which is really necessary to restore health. I knew in '36 when I had to knock off for ten weeks that I should have to give up and if it hadn't been for the King and the subsequent succession of his brother I should not have stayed as long as I did.

The moment I retired I felt an enormous relief, but I was so tired that I could do nothing and think of nothing for months and it was over a year before I felt normal and the jangled nerves began to tune themselves again to their respective duties. I am so glad your correspondence gives you pleasure. But I do hope your mind is keeping calm and that you are not worrying yourself about anything that is past.

Whether our work has been good or not will not appear until long after we have passed away, and no worrying on our part will affect the verdict.

We have both done the best we knew. In old days when Winston used to drop into the Cabinet room on his way from no. 11 to the Treasury, a glass of water in his hand and a long cigar in his mouth, I used sometimes to preach that doctrine to him and he hated it. He was all for instant recognition: he wanted the people to throw up their sweaty nightcaps and shout 'Vive Winston!'.

But tired out or not, the final resignation is a solemn moment. The chapter is closed and the end of the record is come. I haven't found the re-adjustment easy. But I know enough to wish you from my heart all that you need for this time. You have fought a good fight: you have kept the faith as you saw it. What can man do more? and you have suffered bitter disappointments with a spirit and in a temper that have filled your friends with admiration.

Perhaps you will be coming into this part of the world again and if you do I hope you will let me come and see you.

I fear I have expressed myself but ill and conveyed but little of the sympathy and affection I feel for you. I would give you a grasp of the hand that would give it so much better.

I feel a very special message is due to your Lady, for you have both been in my mind these last months almost continuously.

Don't trouble to answer: you have much to do.

Yours ever/ S.B.

Baldwin reflected a good deal on his own career, and continued to respond readily to questions about controversial incidents from sympathetic friends or acquaintances. Some of these reminiscences have historical value.[10] The first was a comment on a newspaper article which asserted that Baldwin had been pushed into the 1923 election by his protectionist colleagues.

25 NOVEMBER 1940: TO JONES

Jones papers A6/2

My dear T.J.

There is not one word of truth in the Guardian extract which you sent me. I spent a lot of my holiday of '23 walking in the hills round Aix and thought it all out by myself. I came to the decision by myself and how I drove that Cabinet to take the plunge I shall never know! I must have more push than people think. The old protectionists were delighted, e.g. Amery and Neville. Half the Cabinet very reluctant.

But consider the position: Bonar was returned because the country wanted a change from the Ll.G coalition. He had no programme. Unemployment was coming,[11] tho' no one could say for how long or to what extent. The Tory party had lost its' brains, so we were told, and were still dazed by Ll.G.

In the early years after the war it was clear that tariff reform had gone back as a battle cry: the free trade element was stronger in the party than in '14 and a large number, never perhaps keen or convinced protectionists would leave it alone.

I wanted it because I saw no other weapon then to use in the fight against unemployment. What would be the position of the gov^{nt} a year or two later if we had drifted on with no mandate for anything, unemployment rising, and the old coalition group hostile? A smash up of the party. Then, the temper of labour!

Very, very bad.

---

[10] Interesting published conversations are Jones *DL*, pp. 481–3; Arthur Baker, *The House is Sitting* (1958), pp. 42–3; Citrine, *Men and Work*, pp. 354–6; Hesketh Pearson and Hugh Kingsmill, *Talking of Dick Whittington* (1947), pp. 186–93; D. H. Barber, 'Tea with Lord Baldwin', *Tory Forum* (Jan. 1948), pp. 5–8.

[11] *Sic.* As unemployment had already been a problem since 1920, the meaning is presumably that it was again rising as winter approached.

There was only one thing to do. F.E., Horne and Austen, and Worthy, were all keen tariff men: if we could go into a fight together we should emerge a much more united party at any rate.

No, the idea was mine alone and why my course was not clearly seen by clever men outside, I have never understood. As the result of the Election, Ll.G lost the chance of his life of smashing me. If he had promised liberal support and kept me in office! But that is another story! Fortunately Asquith wouldn't play that game. I had an interesting talk with Winston about it: he saw the political opportunity right enough but said Ll.G saw red and wanted at all costs to get the Tories out...

Ever yours/ S.B.

Melbourne once said of a similar statement to that of the Guardian '– says it is a fact. But it is not correctly stated. Facts seldom are'.

15 FEBRUARY 1941: TO DEREK PEPYS-WHITELEY

CUL MS Add. 8770

Astley Hall

Dear Mr Whiteley,

It was kind of you to write and your letter gave me great pleasure.

I tried hard in those confused years immediately following the war to get a re-orientation as it were of the Tory party and in Disraeli's words to make it national, i.e. to give it a national rather than a party outlook. If such a spirit should animate those who undertake the great adventure of government after the war then I could feel that I had not worked in vain. So I thank you warmly for your letter...

I am/ most sincerely yours/ Baldwin of Bewdley

AUGUST 1941: TO SIR HORACE WILSON

extract, NC 11/15/133

Astley Hall

My dear Horace

...I will gladly talk with Feiling when he feels the need of it. Of course Neville was never in touch with the events that led up to the breaking of the coalition.

In the '24–29 government he was immersed in Health and not till '31 did he play his full part. His chief friends in these far off days I should say were Sam and Philip Lister.

It was not until the end of Ramsay's regime when it was obvious he would be P.M. if he lived that I talked with more or less freedom to him on all kinds of subjects. There were few of my colleagues who really knew me intimately or understood what I was driving at . . .

Yours ever/ S.B.

In August 1941 Baldwin was asked if he would meet Peter Howard, who had been one of Baldwin's harshest newspaper critics and also (though Baldwin may not have known this) a co-author of *Guilty Men*. Howard had now joined the Oxford Group and ceased to work for Beaverbrook, and 'felt he must make restitution . . . for all the harsh and unkind things he had written' about Baldwin. With some hesitation, Baldwin agreed to the visit: 'I can't get over a certain distrust of Group methods. Peter Howard is of course one of them now and whether it lasts or not it must have meant a great effort, and who am I to take a lofty position and refuse to see him?' During his visit to Astley Hall Baldwin accepted the apology, though he declined to help on Howard's other purpose – to seek support for a campaign to have Oxford Group evangelists exempted from conscription.[12]

During 1940 and 1941 Baldwin declined occasional suggestions that he might make BBC broadcasts, in order not to risk arousing controversy 'that would do no good and might do harm'.[13] Nevertheless he remained active and in touch with many people. His correspondence remained considerable, though now restricted to personal matters – still including many letters to Lady Davidson[14] – and to the business of organisations with which he was associated. In Worcestershire he made what public contributions he could, for example helping regional hospitals in their dealings with central officials. In February 1941 he stayed with the King and Queen at Windsor, and in June with the Davidsons in Hertfordshire, visiting the Salisburys and other neighbours. From autumn 1941 he and his wife resumed periodic visits to London, partly for Pilgrim Trust, Dr Barnardo's Homes or other

---

[12] Baker note, 2 Nov. 1956, W. Baldwin papers; Baldwin to Davidson, 20 Aug. 1941, Davidson papers 283. Baker, *The House is Sitting*, pp. 40–2, and Peter Howard, *Beaverbrook* (1964), pp. 77–8, 114–15, both follow Howard's contemporary note of the discussion, though the latter version – on which Beaverbrook commented – gives it a critical gloss: see Beaverbrook papers K/1/79. Baker, *The Times*' parliamentary correspondent, an Oxford Group member and a friend of Davidson's, had arranged both Buchman's 1936 visit and Howard's visit.

[13] To Ogilvie (BBC director-general), 15 May 1940, BBC Written Archives Centre; to Curtis, 30 Sept. 1941, in Jones *DL*, pp. 491–2.

[14] *Davidson Memoirs*, pp. 427–8, has a representative sample.

meetings, partly to meet friends in public life, and on occasion for audiences with the King. On three occasions Churchill entertained him in Downing Street. As 69 Eaton Square had been requisitioned for war purposes, during their visits the Baldwins took rooms in the Dorchester Hotel.

27 FEBRUARY 1943: TO DAVIDSON

Davidson papers 289

Astley Hall

My dear David,

... I never to my knowledge said that I withheld information for fear of losing an election. It sounds like a Daily Mirror quotation![15]

I never saw it in print but innumerable people believe that I went to America to hide!

'Sealed lips'. If I remember rightly that was said during the Sam Hoare crisis with Laval. I had to speak in the House before I knew the facts of the Paris meeting and by that rather foolish expression I meant that I couldn't say what I believed to be the truth because (A) I had no proof (B) because of the effect in France. I had become convinced that Laval was in Mussolini's pocket and that French help would not be forthcoming (in spite of what they said) in the event of Italy going to war over sanctions. I had thought Laval the biggest crook I had ever met! ...

Much love to you both/ Yours ever/ S.B.

7 APRIL 1943 JONES TO VIOLET MARKHAM

Jones papers T7/74

... S.B. told me something of his three hours with Winston ... They had not met for six years. S.B. found the P.M. calm, steadfast, conscious of great power but in no wise conceited, conscious that he was the instrument of the divine will to bring this grand old country through its troubles. 'We all knew' said S.B. 'that Winston had great stuff in him. The furnace of the war has burnt out the dross; the great stuff has come to the top. He told me that he had been wrong about the Abdication, & he was very glad that the

[15] This letter arose from an enquiry to Davidson from Bryant. From 1940 the *Daily Mirror* contained the most violent attacks on Baldwin, notably by 'Cassandra', William Connor.

present King is on the throne. He drank with moderation at lunch . . . It was he [who] asked to see me, & asked me to let him always know when I'm in town, so that, if he can manage it, we may meet'.[16]

The sudden death of his wife on 17 June 1945 left Baldwin 'stunned'. He received some 500 letters and telegrams of sympathy, and over the next few months personally replied to many of them. He remained based at Astley Hall after the war, cared for by his daughter Diana, whose Grenadier Guard husband had been killed by a bomb in London in June 1944. One of Baldwin's grandsons, 'Peter' Huntington-Whiteley, was also killed by enemy action, in France during September 1944.

Baldwin had been commissioned to write the *Dictionary of National Biography* article on Kipling. He collected a good deal of material, and began a draft. After Lucy's death, however, he handed the task over to the historian G. M. Young, whom he had come to know through their work as respectively president and chairman of the British Association for International Understanding.

Baldwin remained president of the West Worcestershire (Bewdley) Conservative Association, and from summer 1944 felt obliged, in the absence of most of its officers, to help revive its organisation in preparation for a post-war election. But he declined to make further political speeches or take any part in the June-July 1945 election campaign – during which the Conservative party nationally, trying to dissociate itself from its controversial recent past, made no reference to Baldwin. After the Conservative election defeat by Labour, Butler asked for his advice about seeking an alternative source of income to his ministerial salary.

12 AUGUST 1945: TO R.A. BUTLER

R. A. Butler papers G17/225

Astley Hall

My dear Rab,

Thank you for your letter. I wish you could just drop in for a talk! my pen is exhausted after having written some 300 letters in a month and I cannot express myself with the facility that I could in conversation. There is much to be said about the Election which will go down to History as the classic example of democratic ingratitude.

[16] A further Baldwin comment on this meeting is in *Nicolson Diaries*, ii, pp. 306–7, which adds him saying 'the only person he could never forgive was Beaverbrook'.

I don't think it is time for you to decide what you are going to do. The obvious place for you is the House and you may find you can travel in these days of flight. I should think twice before you engage in business. Of course you could get Boards and good ones. But I imagine you don't need them for financial reasons and there is much to be said for our leaders keeping outside the City. I know some who were really badly off e.g. Austen and Amery and perhaps more, but it doesn't look well if our people rush into these jobs which in practice are not open to our opponents. But I wouldn't lay down any rule. Circumstances differ and each man must judge for himself. I would only say 'don't be in a hurry'.

I don't expect to be in London in the near future. Railway travelling is quite impossible for the old and lame. But whenever I am able to get up I hope you will find time to come and see me . . .

Always, my dear Rab/ S.B.

Baldwin's few wartime duties as Chancellor of the University of Cambridge had been conducted by correspondence (including friendly exchanges with Keynes), but from 1945 his periodic ceremonial duties were resumed. Early that year he reluctantly yielded to the persuasions of Fry, Davidson and Jones and commissioned G. M. Young to write a book about his political career.

23 JUNE 1946: TO OLIVER BALDWIN

CUL MS Add. 9569/7

Astley Hall

Bless you, dearest Son, for your letter which I found on my return from Cambridge. Your thinking of me during these last days was in some mysterious way transformed into a support of real help.

You have your mother's gift of telling one just what one wants to know and the picture of how you fare made me very happy! . . . I am glad you liked G.M.Y. I can't tell you exactly what he is doing and I have to see Watt[17] when I am in London. I was anxious for him to do a history of the inter-war years which I thought would be an introduction to such biography as could be written after my death, and I thought it would be a good thing to get the material into shape – e.g. the Abdication history for use when the time came

---

[17] The literary agent for the Young book.

when that history could be written. Poor old Winston: I am glad he asked after me.

I always thought that when the end came it would be quick: he used to look awfully ill way back in the India Bill days which now seem so prehistoric. The happy Death should follow quickly on the completion of a man's job.

If Ll.G had died in 1918 what a reputation he would have left behind him!

We gave Louis Mountbatten a degree in Cambridge: our last meeting had been on Derby night in 1936 when we dined at York House with K. Edward VIII to meet Mrs Simpson. Pre-historic again . . .

Your loving old/ Father

OLIVER BALDWIN MEMOIRS

extract from unpublished typescript, Oliver Baldwin papers

. . . As a result of my mother's death my father was extremely lonely and I saw more of him in the last years of his life than ever before. He had been much hurt by the political attacks that had been made on him during the war and although he did not refer to them unless asked I could feel they had made him unhappy. He told me how he had travelled home by train from London one day during the war and had had to stand in a corridor most of the way, no one having the decency, soldier or civilian, to offer an old man a seat, and their ex-Prime Minister at that. He was particularly hurt at the ruthlessness shown in the taking away of his wrought iron gates for scrap. The main gates had been hand-made by a local blacksmith before the first war and as the craft is dying out, such English gates may never be seen again. Among the other gates taken was a really beautiful eighteenth century Florentine wicket. One can only hope the gates were of use to someone in their lethal state. We spoke much of the House of Commons and of old friends and he asked often of Anthony Eden whom I first brought to his notice in the '29 Parliament. We spoke of the abdication, and of King George VI and I well remember his remark on the latter: 'at any rate he knew where his duty lay'.

We spoke of the dearth of working-class candidates in the Tory party and he blamed Arthur Balfour for this, who, he said, had consistently refused to countenance their adoption at a time when the Labour party was not a socialist one. He thought had the Tories been broader minded in this respect much fire could have been taken from the Labour Party. He referred to his belief in the inevitability of socialism,[18] averring that he had long felt this and that he had conceived his part to be that of a brakesman to see the transition was not too headlong. He had tried, by example only, to train a new Party into a sense of responsibility and he was sure that under Attlee and Bevin that was being effected. He spoke affectionately of Ernest Bevin[19]... A charwoman at Downing Street pleased my parents when it was reported to them that she had said: 'Mrs Baldwin's bed is Mr Baldwin's bed and Mrs Baldwin's pillow is Mr Baldwin's pillow – and that's what I call proper and respectable'. He loved tales of that sort and especially those in Worcestershire or Black Country dialect.

Yes, he was a lonely man in those days, a bit absent-minded but ever full of humour and affection for the people. He could not walk much and he could not concentrate on reading. One day I noticed the books by his chair were all of a religious nature and I realised, true to his Macdonald blood, he was a little apprehensive of the future. He had taken to going to Holy Communion every Sunday morning, being motored down in a little baker's van type of car by the gardener. I commented on this because in the old days he had rarely taken Communion except on important Church festival days.

He talked much of religion and was interested to know I had written a life of Christ. He had not read it so I sent him a copy. When next I saw him I asked how he was getting on with it. He was not: he did not wish anything to disturb his faith which was most orthodox C. of E...

We discussed death and there is no doubt he was apprehensive and said his wife had never been and that he had envied her that. We spoke of his funeral and I suggested he might be wanted in the Abbey. He did not like that idea and anyhow, he said, it would be impossible because his ashes would be mixed with his wife's and she had never been baptised and therefore it would not be proper. Apparently he did not think that trouble would arise elsewhere. He would like to be buried in the garden, he said, but only if I were financially able to live on in the house.

. . . On one of my visits I found him wrapped in an overcoat sitting by a miserable fire, the only one in that large house, because he had heard

[18] This seems unlikely. It is probably Oliver's transposition of a lesser meaning, that his father had long anticipated the election of a majority Labour government.
[19] Bevin had also spoken at the Congress on Democracy in August 1939, travelling to New York on the same ship as Baldwin.

Mr Shinwell's appeal not to use too much coal. He refused to have the central heating on for the same reason.

...He died as he would have wished peacefully in bed. No bed-clothes were ruffled, no attempt made to ring a bell or turn on a light. His ashes are buried in Worcester Cathedral by the West door and when, in the summer, the great doors are open he will be able to look out over our lovely county cricket ground away to the Malvern Hills where all those years ago Edward Langland wrote 'Piers the Plowman'. Many letters and telegrams were received from all sorts and conditions but no letter came to me from either the leader or deputy leader of the Party he had done so much to lead into democratic channels...

Baldwin died on 14 December 1947. Both Houses of Parliament adjourned as a mark of respect. There were memorial services in Westminster Abbey, All Saints' Wilden, and the two universities of which he had been Chancellor, Cambridge and St Andrews. In his will he left £280,971 net.[20] Oliver did not feel able to maintain Astley Hall, which was sold to Birmingham Education Committee. During 1950 a plaque in Stanley Baldwin's memory was unveiled at Aix-les-Bains by his grandson, Edward; and a memorial erected on the road by Astley Hall was dedicated by Churchill, who spoke of the former Prime Minister as 'the most formidable politician I have ever known' and 'in domestic politics... one of the most capable leaders... for many generations'.

[20] About £6.3 million (*c.* 2000).

APPENDIX A

٭

Family trees

1. The Baldwins and the Ridsdales

The Baldwins of Stourport-on-Severn were a well-established industrial dynasty, whose male members (as marked) had in overlapping partnerships created several firms bearing the Baldwin name. The original family iron-founding firm, Baldwin, Son & Co., formed by Thomas Baldwin in about 1813, descended to Alfred and the second Enoch. In 1886 they merged it (while retaining its name) with Kenricks of West Bromwich, and Stanley Baldwin inherited a substantial block of Kenricks shares.

E.P. & W. Baldwin, tinplate and metal sheet manufacturers, formed by the first Enoch with his nephews Pearce and William at Wolverhampton in 1850, later established its main works at Wilden. In 1870 it came under the sole control of Alfred. In 1886 he also established Alfred Baldwin & Co. Ltd, in the same line of manufacturing, at Pontypool, Monmouthshire. Stanley became a partner in the first firm, and a director of the second. In 1902 the two companies joined with Alfred's South Wales allies in steel production and coal-mining to form Baldwins Ltd.

The Baldwins had long been involved in the town life and associational activities of Stourport and the surrounding area. The second Enoch was Liberal MP for Bewdley 1880–5, when the borough constituency was merged into the West (Bewdley) division of Worcestershire, of which Alfred became Conservative MP in 1892 and Stanley in 1908. Stanley's wife's family, the Ridsdales also had a tradition of public service. Her father had been a senior official at the Royal Mint, and her brother Aurelian was Liberal MP for Brighton, 1906–10, and chairman of the British Red Cross Society 1912–14.

2. The Macdonalds

The Macdonald sisters and their marriages are well-known. A point to emphasise is how many members of the extended family, over four generations, became published authors (as marked). Rudyard Kipling was only the most celebrated. Books were written at Wilden House by Baldwin's mother and maiden aunt, and his two sons also published books.

The Baldwin and Ridsdale families

* partners in Baldwin firms
† published authors

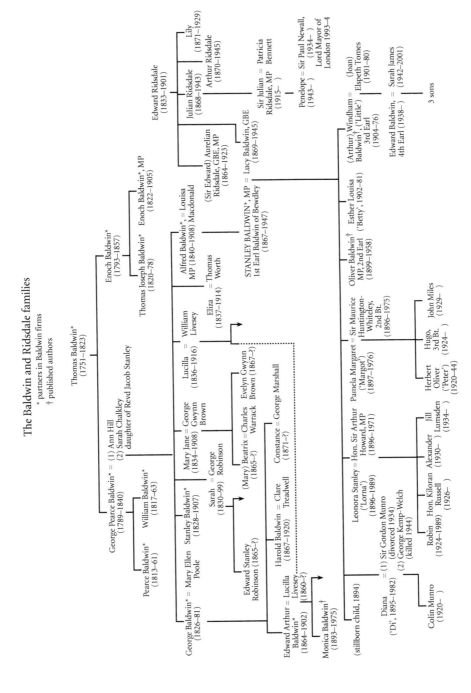

The Macdonald family

† published authors

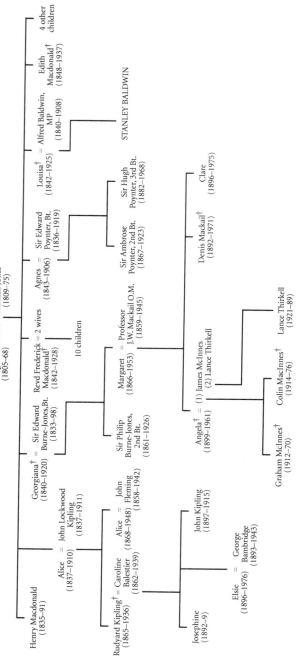

APPENDIX B

§

The People interview, 18 May 1924

The following front-page article caused a political sensation. For public reasons, and perhaps to pre-empt any action for slander, Baldwin felt obliged to deny that he had spoken the words attributed to him.[1] Those close to him, however, thought they did represent his personal views; as Jones noted, 'Anyone who knows S.B. intimately cannot but feel that the interview reflects substantially his general attitude to politics and to his colleagues.'[2]

Although party leaders often spoke confidentially with newspaper owners and editors, in this period interviews with journalists were uncommon and Baldwin was perhaps unfamiliar with the protocols. It appears that Blain, the Conservative party's new chief agent, persuaded him to talk with a journalist from the right-wing *People* in order to help explain the party leadership's new stance on social reform – and indeed the article has important evidence of Baldwin's conceptions about his party's future. But no party official was present at the interview, held at Baldwin's house in Eaton Square on 16 May; and none had checked on the reporter, F.W. Wilson, who was later discovered to have a 'bad record' of embarrassing politicians. Nor did anyone ask to see an advance copy of the article. After the interview, they had an informal conversation about personalities over tea, which Baldwin assumed was purely private. Wilson mentioned the conversation to his editor, Hannen Swaffer, who persuaded him to report it.

After hearing Baldwin's account of the episode, the experienced Lord Long thought 'his error was one of indiscretion and of trusting to the honour of the paper to treat him fairly'. But Long placed greater blame on the journalist and editor: it was a 'well-established and unbroken law of public life', that a journalist

---

[1] See above pp. 148–50.
[2] Jones *WD*, I, p. 280 (25 May 1924). Fry to W. Baldwin, 26 Feb. 1956, W. Baldwin papers, commented that 'some of the unflattering words were not unknown to S.B.'

should be 'scrupulously careful to send a full transcript' to the interviewee, and 'secure his approval before publication'. Apart from Baldwin's and the Central Office's denials, pressure was brought on the newspaper and its proprietor, the businessman and MP Grant Morden, to retract. Instead, on the following Sunday the paper published a much fuller Wilson account of the episode and similar conversations with party officials, which it was thought wise to ignore.[3]

BALDWIN TURNS AND RENDS HIS CRITICS
SENSATIONAL DISCLOSURE TO 'THE PEOPLE'
Why the Trust Press Attacks Him
PARTY'S GREAT SOCIAL PROGRAMME REVEALED
by our Political Correspondent

A dramatic situation, with far-reaching consequences for a great political party and the country, has been unfolded to me by Mr Stanley Baldwin, the leader of the Conservative Party and ex-Prime Minister.

I asked Mr. Baldwin what was the real significance of his new programme, expounded in his last three public speeches.

'I have attempted,' he said, 'to tell the country what I honestly believe. Every future Government must be socialistic, in the sense in which our grandfathers used the word. Personally I don't know what Socialism means, but I do know that if the Tory Party is to exist we must have a vital, democratic creed, and must be prepared to tackle the evils, social and economic, of our over-populated, over-industrialised country.

'The cost of living must be reduced, the producer must get more reward for his article, and it ought to cost the consumer and buyer less.

'I believe the Tory Party is the only party that can tackle such problems satisfactorily. In the past we have been accused, and often rightly, of being too closely identified with vested interests. In the future we must put our house in order, and remove many of the abuses, whose existence is food for Socialistic argument. If we are to live as a party we must live for the people in the widest sense.

'Another reason why we should do this is because our party contains,

---

[3] James Margach, *The Abuse of Power* (1978), p. 27; Long to Grant Morden, 22 May 1924, Long (Trowbridge) papers 947/849.

and can command, the best brains and the best business experience in the country, which may be used to break rings and trusts. For trusts exist under Free Trade, just as much as they might do under Protection. We have people trained in national war service, who could help us, and it might be necessary to mobilise them, in a great campaign for cheaper food.

'We alone can tackle these social problems. The Socialists fall into class warfare difficulties and the Liberals are too inelastic.

MR BALDWIN'S WAR ON PROFITEERING

'First and foremost, I attach tremendous importance to a speedy attack on food profiteering. Some facts which have come to my notice recently are very significant.

'An allotment-holder found it impossible to obtain more than a penny apiece for the cauliflowers she grew. These same cauliflowers she saw being sold at the local market next day for 6d. each. A Worcestershire farmer told me that he sold pigmeat to Birmingham for 8d. a pound; it was resold there for 1s. 8d. a pound. A Nottingham firm made a frock for 25s; it was sold at a Regent Street sale for £4 4s. These margins of profit and difference of price are, I am sure too great.

'We want a strong Royal Commission to investigate all the facts before we formulate legislation. I am certain the index cost of living could be reduced, as a result of action in these matters, by 25 points.

'This is but part of the programme I propose. It is part of the new spirit we have in industry. We must educate the workers in industrial matters. They should know all the details of management, all about the ratios of wages to sinking funds and depreciation, etc., and all about the competition with which their firm is faced. If trade unions had spent their money educating their members instead of fighting strikes, the workers would now be controlling industry everywhere.

'The Tory Party cannot go on on the old lines. I am certain that if we had not gone to the country and been defeated last year – though that, of course, is not why I went, I believed in something I wanted the country to adopt – we should have died of dry rot in two years, and Labour would have come in with a sweeping majority.

'We must recognise facts, and the new programme I have preached is an attempt to bring the Party up to date.

'But the lot of a leader in opposition is a difficult one. Read "C. B's" life and see the kind of time he had.[4] I know I am abused, and jeered at, and intrigued against. But why?

SECRET HISTORY OF THE CRISIS

'When I spoke at the Carlton Club meeting I never expected that we should win. I took my political life in my hands and I was prepared to retire from politics. I did not know that Bonar Law would lead us. In fact, the night before I spent two hours with him, and he had sealed a letter to the chairman of his Glasgow Association telling him that he would not stand for Parliament again. In that mood I left him.

'And then we won. I spoke because I was determined that never again should the sinister and cynical combination of the chief three of the Coalition – Mr Lloyd George, Mr Churchill and Lord Birkenhead – come together again. But to-day you can see the signs of the times.

'But I didn't expect the exiled Conservative ex-Ministers would take things as badly as they did. Before the election last year I welcomed Mr Austen Chamberlain back, and I accepted his friends, though I could easily have stopped their return to our councils.

'With Austen came Lord Birkenhead, who had attached himself to the strings of Austen's apron the year before very cleverly. And Austen is one of those loyal men who could not see disloyalty or intrigue even if it was at his elbow. But I am under no illusions as to Lord Birkenhead. If his health does not give way[5] he will be a liability to the Party. But can a leader in opposition shut the door to an ex-Minister?

'And at the same time I am attacked by the Trust Press, by Lord Beaverbrook and Lord Rothermere. For myself I do not mind. I care not what they say or think. They are both men that I would not have in my house. I do not respect them. Who are they? I was attacked, I am told, in the 'Evening Standard', over my arrangement for the Budget speakers. I did not read it. Why should I?

---

[4] J. A. Spender, *The Life of Sir Henry Campbell-Bannerman* (1924), revealed efforts by Asquith, Grey and Haldane before December 1905 to prevent the Liberal party leader from becoming Prime Minister.
[5] Generally interpreted as an allusion to his heavy drinking.

'This Trust Press is breaking up. The "Daily Mail" is dead; it has no soul. Northcliffe, with all his faults, was a great journalist, with a spark of genius. But this man! I get much correspondence about him. A post-card the other day said "If Lord Rothermere wants a halo in Heaven or a coronet on earth, why don't you get it for him?"

'The last time I spoke to Lord Beaverbrook was at Bonar's funeral. He had contracted a curious friendship with Bonar and had got his finger into the pie, where it had no business to be. He got hold of much information, which he used in ways in which it was not intended.[6]

'When I came in, that stopped. I know I could get his support if I were to send for him and talk things over with him. But I prefer not. That sort of thing does not appeal to me.

'As I said, I do not mind attacks on myself. I often wonder if my silent contempt irritates them more than if I were to speak out. I suppose it is my lot to suffer disloyalty. But there are limits.

'Take the article in the recent number of "English Life". That's a pretty dirty bit of work. It is written by "A Conservative ex-Minister", and I am pretty certain that if it is not written by the man I suspect, it was certainly inspired by him.[7] It was a stab in the back. Now, it attacks my officials – the heads of the Central Office – and that I won't stand. If anybody had attacked a Treasury official when I was at the Treasury I would have come down to the House and made a very furious speech. And I intend to do so now.

'Besides, all this intrigue – this Churchill plotting – is bad for the Party, for all the young men who are looking to Toryism for the salvation of the country.[8] What do these intriguers want? Simply to go back to the old dirty kinds of politics! Not while I'm leader of the Party.'

And Mr Baldwin yawned with disgust and weariness at discussing for so long so unpleasant a subject.

---

[6] Baldwin was particularly concerned to repudiate this phrase: Jones *WD*, I, p. 280.

[7] Wilson's article in *The People*, 25 May 1924, gives Birkenhead as the suspected man.

[8] Wilson's article stated that Baldwin had said more about Churchill: 'I do not think Churchill understands the post-war mind . . . if he got into the House he would only annoy Labour and there would be scenes. It is no use just denouncing Socialism as he does. You have got to have an alternative.'

APPENDIX C

*

Palmstierna's memoir

Baron Erik Palmstierna was Swedish minister in London, 1920–37. His volume of recollections includes a memoir of Baldwin based on contemporary notes, which has not previously been published in English. Some reflections clearly dating from the 1940s have been omitted. The first conversation was in 1925, the last in 1932.

From Erik Palmstierna, *Åtskilliga egenheter. Karaktärsstudier och silhuettklipp* (Stockholm, 1950), pp. 153–63; translation in Jones papers AA1/27 (extracts)

The sun blazed down upon the road. It was a still, summer Sunday when we drove through the gates to the ancient Chequers, the Prime Minister's country seat, to lunch with Mr and Mrs Baldwin. A single police constable was slowly pacing through the great park, with its trees widely spaced in English fashion.

The Prime Minister meets us on the steps, a typical squire in country clothes. Boots and a couple of dogs would complete the picture. Red-haired, somewhat awkward in his movements and with an outstretched hand. He appears uncertain how to open the conversation, although we know one another well and we are the only guests in the garden. Mrs Baldwin hastens forward and welcomes us as a hostess in the country usually does, simply and heartily, without any fuss, but one can see that she is more conscious of her duties than her husband is. We go to view the house, as is also usually done, to see the historical relics and curiosities: Queen Bess's ring with her rival's portrait which she always wore, Richard Cromwell's Bible and sword, portraits and rooms which bring to life the dramas of the past.

Baldwin tells us how Lloyd George enjoyed preening himself among the relics of bygone glories and how MacDonald had Lloyd George's portrait put out of sight when he came down to Chequers for the weekend. He could not bear to see it hanging on the walls of the study.

After lunch I find myself with a cigar alone with Baldwin on the terrace, and for a whole hour a conversation takes place which discloses his true characteristics in a remarkable manner. 'You are a puzzle to me', I say by way of introduction. 'How? What have I done?' he asks. 'Well, it has always been my custom to try and study the people I meet in life, but I find it difficult to get at the truth about you. I notice how rapidly you have changed under the influence of your governing position. New sides of your character assume form and surprise one. All this is extremely bewildering to observe. I am not the only one who has said so.' 'It is too bad that I should have bewildered you', he replies, smiling, 'but can I not help you out of your dilemma? Perhaps I can give you an explanation.' 'In what way?' I say. 'One cannot sit by the roadside and watch oneself pass by and say "that is what the man is like". No one can describe himself accurately.' 'Let me try, at all events', he replies, sinks into a reverie and begins to give an account of his life as if cogitating and talking to himself.

He begins, as if groping, among the memories of his childhood and traces his career up to the historic Carlton Club meeting and his present position in a way which seems to indicate that he himself wants to know how all these things hung together.

He was an only child, and that led to more intimate intercourse with his parents than is customary. The father had marked literary tastes and after business hours his conversation and intercourse were always in literary and artistic circles. On his mother's side he was closely related to Rudyard Kipling, who was his constant companion, and to Burne-Jones. Rossetti and William Morris, among others, were seen at his home. Another younger cousin was the author and dramatist [Dennis Mackail].[1] He absorbed the atmosphere of his home. His father's books were his property and he lived among them. His mother's artistic interests and literary friends, unconsciously, were his own. This world, together with business, was the real one for him and not till late, at 40 years of age, did he take any interest in politics. In his first year in the House of Commons he used to go around with one of R.L. Stevenson's

[1] The name is misunderstood in the original.

books under his arm and look for a secluded, out-of-the-way corner for reading. He felt uncertain and not at home in Parliamentary life, and this was enhanced by a natural shyness.

'I have never had any ambitious plans and I do not know how it has come about that I am the Prime Minister of England. To me it is very strange.' He had never elbowed himself into the front places or sought distinction, but when Lloyd George's lack of principle (the grey eyes flashed) appeared to be dangerous not only for the Conservative Party, which he was on the point of breaking up in 1922, but even for the maintenance of the integrity and morale without which the life of a State is ruined, he was driven to come to grips with him. He knew that it might cost him dear and before the Carlton Club meeting which broke up the Coalition he telegraphed to his wife in Switzerland: 'Tomorrow I am going to tackle Lloyd George. That means Goodbye to politics. Do you consent?' He made up his political accounts, prepared to take the consequences and aimed the 'death blow', as he called it, at the historic encounter.

The attack had for him very unexpected results. The following election soon carried him towards the top of the Conservative Party. He entered Bonar Law's Ministry and was his successor in the post which every Eton boy dreams of winning. Then followed the collapse of 1923 and his fate hung by a hair. He was raised again to power after the greatest swing to the Right that had taken place since Salisbury's days. 'That is altogether an extraordinary adventure', he said reflectively.

In his first period of government he felt his want of experience and had to go carefully, but in the second when the vote of the <u>nation</u> called upon him to lead . . . he was sure of himself and was able to express himself in an unconstrained manner. He was henceforth his complete self and knew that what had been instilled in his childhood had now come to life and found an outlet. He could understand that people who did not know of his secluded past must be surprised, but the explanation he gave was the natural and correct one and had nothing remarkable in it.

'You must not believe that I am particularly clever or specially intelligent, I am not.' – 'A Campbell-Bannerman type', I ventured to interpolate and mentioned a conversation at the Garrick Club where with the Lord Chancellor, Cave, we were discussing Baldwin's qualifications for leading a Government which was distinguished by the quick-witted Birkenhead and Winston Churchill, and in which I presumed to say that a man with a simple countryman's understanding and character was the best to hold together a Cabinet of such heterogeneous intellectual capacity. Baldwin looked at me with a smile and said 'Perhaps'. Was he uncertain whether I was criticizing or appreciative? 'One thing I know, however, and that is that I give expression, in some unaccountable way, to what the English people think. For some reason that appeals to me and gives me strength. The present Ministry I formed myself, without taking the advice of any other person, and the members of the Government know that if I were to go to the poll alone without their support I should nevertheless have the game in my hands.' And he discussed his colleagues openly with me.

I am certain that he was right in that utterance in May 1925. His personal position was extraordinary. It was affection rather than attachment, esteem rather than respect which met him on all sides, and even the Opposition treated him in a way which revealed liking. There was, moreover, a certain common trait in Baldwin and Ramsay MacDonald, an undertone of sensitivity for other values in life than political commercialism, and that brought them personally closer together.

That Sunday conversation at Chequers remained in my memory as something of human beauty, guileless and deep at the same time. It revealed a character of unusual measure. A detachment, a capacity for calm and free examination of his own life and a considered evaluation of its significance. Such a capacity for self-examination and for the judgment of one's actions from a definite standpoint must, however, emanate from a state of soul indicating life of a kind different from that of the average politician. It was some time before I tracked the secret.

It was at Lord Curzon's funeral in Westminster Abbey.[2] The sun's rays shone in through the tall glass windows under the dark blue vault, the choristers' voices rang through the old church, the dignitaries of the State bowed before the splendidly draped coffin in which one of the late Victorian statesmen was borne from time. Close to me sat Mrs Baldwin. She took part in the singing with an expression which showed that her heart was in it. We left the Abbey together.

'You are a believer, Mrs Baldwin', I whispered to her. 'I am indeed', she replied, 'and I must tell you that every morning when we rise we kneel

---

[2] The chronology has become confused here. Curzon had died before, not after, the discussion at Chequers.

together before God and commend our day to Him, praying that some good work may be done in it by us. It is not for ourselves that we are working but for the country and for God's sake. How else could we live?' She looked at me sincerely and naturally, and I realized the simple earnestness of their conception of life.

What an unusual and noble picture of a British statesman. Could anything like that be found anywhere but in an Anglo-Saxon country?

At the same time this attitude of soul implies a temperance in the man of action. The transcendental element which is contained in St Paul's saying that we should 'use this world, as not abusing it' [1 Cor. 7. 31] restrains and lifts the eyes upwards, instils caution.

... Once we sat talking together in the Travellers' Club, where they used to leave him alone to eat his lunch in peace and quiet with a book in his hand, and I observed: 'Two of your speeches have become a standing monument to your credit.' 'Which?' he asked. I referred to his speech at Edinburgh on 'classical education' and to that in the House of Commons on Asquith's departure. I said jokingly that it was fortunate for a Prime Minister to have good secretaries and relations (Kipling). 'What do you mean?' he asked, and turned in his chair, 'oh, I understand. No, the first speech I wrote alone on Boxing Day and the speech on Asquith I thought out while walking from Travellers' to Westminster. I was uneasy lest I had said too much, but the House approved.'

Both speeches were well built up and had an outlook which revealed that not only the Christian faith but also a classical discipline and idealism had given rise to his personality. A Christian platonism, paradoxical it may be, moved him inwardly. For a romantically inclined man like him that combination, illogical as it may appear, gives a satisfactory balance and an elevated outlook which Baldwin never lost however much his position may have changed.

One can well understand that a man like Lloyd George must have an extremely irritating effect on Baldwin and arouse feelings of indignation. I once saw him springing briskly downstairs at the Club, delighted to have discovered at the last minute before a debate an appropriate quotation from Carlyle which might be useful for giving 'L.G.' a rap on the knuckles.

But how can Baldwin be such an admirer of Disraeli? Is it the attraction of contrast, literary sympathy or merely party political form which causes this country squire to be constantly quoting the ostentatious Jew? I cannot understand it.

Do I over-simplify the picture of Baldwin by looking for the basic element of his nature? He is more complex than the simplicity of his appearance leads one to suppose. 'He is for ever giving one to understand how "simple" he is', Sir Ronald Waterhouse, Baldwin's principal secretary, said to me, 'and he employs a naiveté which to a certain degree is studied.' With a simple word he stills the unruly waves of the Lower House and moves calmly over its surface. He keeps himself under constant control and tells the truth in the plainest way without any pretensions, but he obtains his effect and upon that he has reckoned.

Baldwin is not lacking in intelligence, although he is accustomed to deny this. He approaches men by a way which runs deeper than thought and appeals to deep-seated motives through direct personal communication. He knows that himself, but he overrates the possibilities offered. His own personality gradually wears down the general consciousness, while new thoughts and actions fail to appear. Baldwin's extraordinary skill in manoeuvring his Party in the House of Commons has been underestimated. At times he appears shrewd and calculating. One after the other possible rivals are decently and unobtrusively set aside, while he himself remains at the centre.

His astonishment after the 1929 election was unfeigned. He was fully and firmly convinced that he was in such intimate touch with the British people that they would follow him in an overwhelming majority and this was apparent in his last radio speech. When people cheered him at meetings he was sure of victory. We met after the election at Gray's Inn, and I pointed to my black slouch hat. 'I won this at the election! The fact is that personally you are prevented from acting in this country', I said, 'but the working classes are relying rather upon themselves and want to go forward under their own leaders. This election indicates a new direction in British politics. It may happen that next time they will get a majority[3] and that the working class will govern.' 'But we are not classes, but men' interrupted Baldwin with an expression of sincere distress . . .

These notes on Baldwin were written in the autumn of 1929 before I forgot the occurrences and conversation and in a presentiment that Baldwin

[3] I.e. an overall parliamentary majority.

himself might quietly disappear behind the course of events. If that should happen – and he once whispered to me that he would not remain in politics for ever – there would nevertheless remain the picture of a statesman who, although better fitted for a dreamer's reign of peace than for the hard post-war world, through the strength of a lofty example had a purifying and ennobling influence.

Baldwin was never a Marcus Aurelius, but unconsciously he enabled me to ponder over the sources of these 'meditations'.

Events took, as so often in politics, an unexpected turn. The year 1931 was one of testing for Baldwin. His own party wanted to be rid of him, he told me later, and he was at first ready to retire, but just then the financial storm broke with unlooked-for fury over the world, party considerations and Parliamentary intrigues became secondary matters, and the nation's most able men were called together. It was now that Baldwin showed his real strength of character. He subordinated himself to MacDonald's leadership and took up a supporting position behind his political opponent. He might easily have demanded the Premiership, as many of his party required after the great swing to the Right of the autumn election, but higher considerations dictated a withdrawal, and that was made unpretentiously and in an admirable way. I could not refrain from writing him a line to say how greatly it aroused my esteem.

It was curious to see MacDonald standing beside the Marchioness of Londonderry to receive the thousands of Government supporters of all parties in the stately Londonderry House at Hyde Park the day before the opening of Parliament, with Baldwin a few steps behind him. A genuine victory over self was expressed therein.

Some months afterwards we were sitting in the gilt drawing room of the same house, for Lady Londonderry had called together 'Ye Arch Association on ye Island of Æaea', a social club she assembled about her, its Circe with an unusual pouter of enchantment. James Stephens, the Irish poet and author, a dwarfish gnome, was questioning Baldwin about everything possible in a bewildering fashion; about his view of life, his method of speaking, his habits and mode of existence. 'Are you chaffing me or do you mean it seriously?' asked Baldwin doubtfully (does one ever know with an Irishman?). 'I am absolutely serious', answered Stephens, and added a last question: 'Tell me, what do you yourself consider to be the secret of the success of your particularly changeful life?' After a moment's deliberation Baldwin replied: 'Yes,

I have been both out of things and also the foremost in them, at the top and a long way down, alternately, but cannot answer your question, for I hardly know myself.'

'Let me give an explanation', I heard myself say, 'the secret lies in your own characteristics and intuitive insight. Isn't that right?' I asked Baldwin. 'I hope so', he replied and was about to add something when Mrs Baldwin interrupted across the table: 'We must go home now, Stanley. It is one o'clock.'

I ought to have said that to a man like Baldwin service is the principal thing, not high office. As he goes on his way, unheeded, with a grey woollen pullover hanging from under his short coat, one is seized with the impression of human greatness, which moves quietly aside from all the commotion of the times.

The Prime Minister's staff
and daily routine

Few records exist about the private office and daily activities of any Prime Minister before 1940, so the following documents – presumably written by a 10 Downing Street private secretary – have general importance. For Baldwin their significance relates to criticisms, contemporary and historical, about his working methods – an alleged laziness, including excessive attendance in the House of Commons.[1]

The documents were among several produced as advice for Mackenzie King. He had created a post of executive-assistant to the Canadian Prime Minister, and sent his proposed appointee, the academic administrator J. Burgon Bickersteth, to collect information on the British Prime Minister's staff, which he had admired while attending the 1926 Imperial Conference. Even in the late nineteenth century private secretaries seem to have conducted much prime ministerial office work and correspondence, and during the First World War, when the Cabinet secretariat and the so-called 'garden suburb' of assistants grew up around Lloyd George, these 'permanent' civil-service office arrangements had become still more highly developed and specialised. During July and August 1927 Bickersteth, as well as obtaining these documents, interviewed Hankey and Jones as Cabinet secretaries, and Waterhouse from Baldwin's private office.[2] His notes of these interviews[3] contain useful further information.

The Prime Minister had five private secretaries (as well as his parliamentary private secretary, Sidney Herbert):

Sir Ronald Waterhouse dealt with non-ecclesiastical patronage (appointments), honours, and civil lists;

---

[1] For comment, see M&B, ch. 18; Williamson, *Baldwin*, ch. 2.
[2] See Jones *WD*, II, pp. 106–7, 108. Bickersteth's enquiries persuaded him to reject the post, presumably as too onerous for someone without civil-service experience.
[3] Copy in Jones papers B1/32.

Sir Patrick Gower in the Prime Minister's name wrote the traditional daily letters
  to the King on parliamentary proceedings, and public messages and letters to
  the press and Conservative by-election candidates;
Miss Edith Watson prepared answers to parliamentary questions, seeing the Prime
  Minister at 12.45 p.m. every day when the House of Commons was sitting,[4] and
  dealt with his personal affairs, including some of his personal correspondence;
Geoffrey Fry (unpaid) dealt with all ecclesiastical patronage;
C. P. Duff dealt with everything else, and was more properly the Prime Minister's
  'close private secretary'.[5]

Their work was evidently supplemented by Jones, who said that he saw Baldwin
every weekday morning. He considered that 'one of his chief contributions' was
to inform Baldwin of wider opinions on current questions, and he also helped
liaise between him and individual ministers. In dealing with Cabinet business, his
practice with Bonar Law had been to go through each agenda item by item, but
Baldwin's method was 'to allow the several government departments to run their
own affairs and not to interfere', so Jones only alerted him to possible difficulties.[6]

10 DOWNING STREET MEMORANDA, JULY–AUGUST 1927

Mackenzie King papers, C41776–80 and C108379–82[7]

Specimen Day of the Rt Hon. S. Baldwin

7.45 a.m.   Go for a walk.

9.0 a.m.   Breakfast. Read the daily papers.

9.45 a.m.   Read private letters and give Secretary any instructions about
             them.

10 a.m.   Interview with newly arrived Foreign Ambassador.

10.15 a.m.   Interview with distinguished person whose services the
             Government desire to secure on some important Committee of
             Enquiry.

10.30 a.m.   Interview with Cabinet colleague who desires to seek authority
             for taking a decision on policy in a matter not of sufficient

---

[4] This is inconsistent with the daily timetable given below.
[5] Duff usually accompanied Baldwin on his trips away from London. The staff also included
several 'lady typists'. During his periods as leader of the Opposition, Baldwin had a similar
number of private secretaries provided by the party.
[6] Jones also claimed that he prepared most of Baldwin's ministerial speeches (and to have written
many of Lloyd George's and Law's too), which is certainly an overstatement: see, before 1923,
Ellis, *Thomas Jones*, pp. 258–9, and thereafter, Williamson, *Baldwin*, pp. 158–65.
[7] Only the second copy, filed in the 1930s, has the additional 'Note'.

moment to warrant consideration by the whole Cabinet but which transcends the competence of an individual Minister.

10.45 a.m. Ditto. } or interviews with outside persons on

11 a.m.   Ditto. } some matter of importance.

11.15 a.m. Interview with Chief Whip to discuss course of Parliamentary business.

11.30–1.15 Preside over Cabinet Council or Committee of Imperial Defence, or some Committees of Cabinet investigating urgent problem, e.g. unemployment, Economy, China etc. Or Deputation from important bodies on matters of policy with which the departmental Minister concerned cannot authoritatively deal (there are not many of these).

1.15 p.m.   Go to lunch (to Club, 10 minutes walk away).

2.15 p.m.   Leave for House of Commons.

2.30 p.m.   Read through Questions to be asked that afternoon, and the Answers prepared.

3.00 p.m.   Answer Questions in the House of Commons.

3.45 p.m.– As Leader of the House of Commons it is politic for the

11.0 p.m.   Prime Minister to be in his place during debates as much as possible. When he is not sitting on the Treasury Bench he has at intervals through the evening further appointments with e.g. Members of Parliament, or with persons specially qualified to give valuable information about Imperial or domestic matters of current interest. Sometime during the evening the Prime Minister would read the memoranda prepared by different Ministers in regard to matters on which they desire a decision of the Cabinet at an early date; reports from our Ambassadors abroad; and his official correspondence generally.

11.0 p.m.   The House of Commons rises. The Prime Minister returns to Downing Street where, like the Kings in the 'Gondoliers'

> 'With a pleasure that's ecstatic,
> He retires to his attic
> With a gratifying feeling that his duty has been done'.

The above programme contains no room for a speech by the Prime Minister in the House of Commons or at any public function, and he would have to make a speech on average once a week.

Generally speaking, interviews in the morning are at 10 Downing Street and in the afternoon and night at the House of Commons when the House is sitting.

On ordinary week days there is no time earmarked for private life. Personal friends come to breakfast and to lunch occasionally. The only time which the Prime Minister has to himself is Saturdays and Sundays, when he goes to Chequers and every effort is made to keep him free. As a rule there is no house party beyond close personal friends so that the Prime Minister can have time to himself to catch up on his personal correspondence and think over any forthcoming speeches or the problems of the week ahead. A Private Secretary is nearly always there in case of any emergencies arising or to mop up work left over from the previous week.

You mention the Prime Minister's books. The only book in his name is a collection of the speeches he had delivered in the past and he took no personal part whatever at any stage either in the selection of the speeches or their production in book form.[8]

Mail Routine

Letters marked Personal and Private, unless they are obviously impostures, are placed on the Prime Minister's table in the morning unopened. But a Private Secretary is there ready to take away and deal with any that the Prime Minister does not feel that he has to answer himself.

Letters addressed to any Private Secretary by name are given to that Private Secretary unopened. The general post addressed formally to 'The Prime Minister' or 'The Private Secretary' is opened and sorted out first thing in the morning by the Staff, and the letters are dished out to each Private Secretary correspondingly to their contents and to the special subject that each Private Secretary deals with.

The Prime Minister lives at 10 Downing Street: therefore, there is no private house where letters can go elsewhere than to the office. But, if he lived elsewhere, it would be necessary to represent to the Prime Minister that he must let the office collect and deal with the post arriving at his house, as otherwise all continuity of correspondence would be liable to be incomplete and there would be risks of every sort of slip up. It is neither fair to the office, nor in the Prime Minister's own interest, that people should be encouraged

---

[8] *On England*, published in April 1926, was largely compiled by Jones, who also wrote the preface.

to think that by calling a thing 'Personal' and sending it to the private house they can get behind the backs of the Private Secretariat. Letters sent in this way to Chequers are always returned to 10 Downing Street.

Note

On Monday, Tuesday, Wednesday and Thursday, the Prime Minister works at 10 Downing Street in the morning. He goes to the House of Commons after luncheon and is at the House (either in his own room or on the Bench) from 2.45 p.m. It is not possible to generalise about the time that he spends on the bench, nor is it possible to give any average of the amount of time he spends there. It may, however, be said that he is normally on the bench from 2.50 p.m. to 4 p.m. for Questions, and that thereafter he would return to his room for meetings, interviews and work, going on the bench at intervals. It will, however, be appreciated that on days when there are Debates in which he is concerned (either as Prime Minister, as Leader of the House, or in his present capacity of dealing with important Foreign Office Questions in the House) he spends the greater portion of his time until the House rises, on the bench. In any case, his room is only a stone's throw from the Chamber and he is in a position to go into it in a minute if necessary.

Normally, the Prime Minister would leave the House between 11 and 11.30 p.m., but if an important Debate ran through the night he would, no doubt, be in attendance.

Friday is in rather a different category, since, for a large portion of the year, Private Members' business is taken on that day; Government business is normally taken on Fridays from March to July, and during that period the procedure would be on the above lines, though less important business is then taken and the Prime Minister's attendance is not so regularly required.

It may be added to the above

1. that it is not an invariable rule for the Prime Minister to stay at the House for a Division if business is being taken in which he is not directly concerned, though he would be available if required; and
2. that the amount of time spent on the bench itself necessarily varies according to the temperament of individual Prime Ministers.

✽

The Baldwin collections

Baldwin decided in October 1937 to bequeath 'all my political papers' to the University of Cambridge, and since the late 1960s a large collection – 233 volumes, including twenty-two volumes of newspaper cuttings – have been available to researchers in the University Library. As the handlist of the collection indicates, however, this is not a complete gathering of Baldwin's papers, even the incoming political material; and Baldwin's first biographer, G.M. Young complicated matters by mistakenly stating that 'a large collection of papers was destroyed after his death'.[1] Baldwin's papers have a history of their own, which may have affected interpretations of some aspects of his career.

Under Cabinet rules of 1934, 'a great quantity' of official papers was returned to the Cabinet Office and government departments soon after Baldwin's retirement. Two further batches followed in the early 1950s, including material on the Abdication, Irish policy, and defence, and seventy secret intelligence 'intercepts'. Some of this material (though certainly not the intercepts) has presumably reappeared in the PREM files in the Public Record Office.

During the war, Tom Jones had arranged for Baldwin's papers to be removed from London for safe-keeping, first in Coleg Harlech and then the National Library of Wales. During this period they were sorted by Baldwin's private secretary, Geoffrey Fry, who separated out material which, though relating to public life, was deemed not to fall within the classification of 'political'. Many would now be considered significant: files on Ashridge College, the Refugee Fund, the 1939 visits to Toronto and New York, 'interviews' and engagement diaries, and also Lady Baldwin's papers relating to the National Birthday Trust Fund and

---

[1] A.E.B. Owen, *Handlist of the Political Papers of Stanley Baldwin* (1973); Young, *Baldwin*, p. 11. The following account supplements Owen's introduction, pp. 3–5, with further evidence, particularly from CAB 106/665 and SB add. papers.

other organisations. In 1943 these files were sent into storage, and cannot now be found.

In 1945 the main political collection was brought to Fry's house in Oare, Wiltshire, for the use of G.M. Young, who lived close by. A further three boxes, discovered in 10 Downing Street, were added in 1951. Young was not a careful custodian, and some documents were transferred into drafts of his book and into his own papers, although many seem to have been recovered after his death in 1960. In addition, Baldwin and later Young gave one or two documents of historic interest on the Abdication crisis – one of King Edward's notes, Mrs Simpson's messages from Cannes – to the King or the Royal Archives.

Meanwhile, during the war Baldwin had destroyed some, perhaps much, of his personal correspondence, particularly current letters which came to him in Worcestershire, where he had no secretarial assistance. After his death some of the remaining papers at Astley Hall were sorted by Oliver Baldwin. The basis of Young's story of a large destruction is that Oliver burnt some letters of the 1940s from Baldwin's correspondents which he described as 'hair-raising': an example seems to be J.P.L. Thomas's critical comments on Churchill.[2] But he preserved most of the papers. He returned a few political letters to their authors. He retained some items in his own papers, which passed to his partner. These were cited by Middlemas and Barnes as the 'John Boyle papers', but are now again known as the 'Oliver Baldwin papers'; Baldwin's own letters from these papers have been passed to Cambridge University Library. Most of the Astley papers came to Windham Baldwin, fellow executor of their father's will. He added various post-1937 letters from public figures to the main collection of papers which Young passed to him in 1952, and which he sent to Cambridge later that year.

As Baldwin's gift to Cambridge specified only 'political papers', all other papers remained with Windham Baldwin. To these Windham gradually added further material (including political documents) written or received by his father which he collected from other family members and further sources, including, it seems, G.M. Young's and Oliver Baldwin's papers after their deaths. After his own death in 1976 these family papers were divided into three collections. A substantial amount of Baldwin company papers and the papers of Alfred and Louisa Baldwin, together with some Stanley Baldwin material associated with Worcestershire relatives, were deposited in Worcestershire County Record Office (which in the 1990s acquired further Baldwin company papers inherited from the steel companies nationalised in the late 1940s). Papers related to Kipling were sent to accompany the main collection of his papers in the University of Sussex Library.

---

[2] Oliver Baldwin to Margesson, 14 March 1951, Margesson papers 1/4/2; Thomas to W. Baldwin, 7 Feb. 1954, W. Baldwin papers.

The more strictly Stanley and Lucy Baldwin family papers – used by Windham himself and by Middlemas and Barnes for their biographies – have now been given to Cambridge University Library, and designated as 'Baldwin additional papers'. To these have been added the 'Windham Baldwin papers': an important collection of interviews, notes, correspondence and news-cuttings relating to his father.

SOURCES

A. ORIGINAL PAPERS

(The following lists indicate all the collections that have been searched; not all have yielded documents included in this volume.)

1. Baldwin and related family and business papers

(a) Cambridge University Library
Stanley Baldwin political papers
Stanley Baldwin additional papers
Stanley Baldwin letters to his son, Oliver, 2nd Lord Baldwin (MS Add. 8795)
further Stanley Baldwin letters to Oliver Baldwin, and letters to John Boyle (MS Add. 9569)
Lucy Baldwin papers
Windham Baldwin papers
Derek Pepys-Whiteley collection of Baldwin material (MS Add. 8770)
Certain other MS Add. documents

(b) Worcestershire County Record Office
Alfred and Louisa Baldwin papers, with some Stanley Baldwin family material (accession 8229)
Baldwin business papers, largely pre-1908 (accession 6385)
Baldwin Ltd papers, formerly in British Steel Archives, Irthlingborough (accession 12382)

(c) University of Sussex Library
Baldwin papers (material relating to Rudyard Kipling)

(d) in private possession
Oliver, 2nd Lord Baldwin papers, courtesy of Mr Christopher Walker
Lorna Howard papers, courtesy of Mrs P. Lumsden
Margot Huntington-Whiteley papers, courtesy of Mr Miles Huntington-Whiteley

Betty Baldwin papers, courtesy of Mr Charles Yorke
Revd Frederick Macdonald papers, courtesy of Mrs Macdonald Bendle

2. Other private papers

* indicates substantial quantities or significance of Baldwin letters
+ indicates very few or insignificant Baldwin letters
# indicates no Baldwin letters but useful reported material about him

1st Lord Altrincham (Sir Edward Grigg): microfilm in the Bodleian Library, Oxford[+]
L. S. Amery: seen by permission of Lord Amery; now in Churchill Archives Centre, Churchill College, Cambridge
Wilfrid Ashley (Lord Mount Temple): Broadlands Archives, University of Southampton Library[+]
W. J. Ashley: British Library[+]
H. H. Asquith (1st Earl of Oxford and Asquith): Bodleian Library, Oxford
Margot Asquith (Countess of Oxford and Asquith): Bodleian Library, Oxford
Lady Asquith of Yarnbury (Lady Violet Bonham Carter): copies courtesy of Mr Mark Pottle
Katharine, Duchess of Atholl: Blair Castle, Perthshire
1st Earl of Avon (Anthony Eden): University of Birmingham Library
1st Earl of Balfour:
   (a) British Library
   (b) Whittingehame papers, Scottish Record Office*
Sir Joseph Ball: Bodleian Library, Oxford[+]
Lilias, Lady Bathurst: University of Leeds Library[+]
1st Lord Beaverbrook: Parliamentary Archives (House of Lords Record Office)*
Viscount (R. B.) Bennett: Harriet Irving Library, University of New Brunswick
9th Earl of Bessborough: West Sussex Record Office
Robert Bingham: Library of Congress[+]
Sir Basil Blackett: Oriental and India Office Collections, British Library
5th Lord Brabourne: Oriental and India Office Collections, British Library#
1st Viscount Brentford (Sir William Joynson-Hicks): in the possession of the 4th Viscount Brentford
1st Viscount Bridgeman and Caroline, Lady Bridgeman: Shropshire Record Office*
6th Lord Brownlow: Lincolnshire Record Office#
Viscount Bruce of Melbourne: Australian Archives#
Sir Arthur Bryant: Liddell Hart Centre for Military Archives, King's College, London*
Frank Buchman: Oxford Group (MRA) archives#
Sir William Bull: Churchill Archives Centre, Churchill College, Cambridge#
R. A. Butler: Trinity College Library, Cambridge
Lord Carson: Public Record Office of Northern Ireland
Viscount Cave: British Library[+]
Victor Cazalet: by permission of Sir Edward Cazalet

Viscount Cecil of Chelwood:
  (a) British Library*
  (b) Hatfield House Archives+
Sir Austen Chamberlain: University of Birmingham Library*
Neville Chamberlain: University of Birmingham Library*
Sir Winston Churchill: Churchill Archives Centre, Churchill College, Cambridge*
Viscount Cilcennin (J. P. L. Thomas): Carmarthen Record Office*
Lord Citrine: British Library of Political and Economic Science#
Revd W. H. Cory: Worcestershire County Record Office
Lady Craigavon: Public Record Office of Northern Ireland#
Sir Henry Craik: National Library of Scotland+
1st Lord Crathorne (Thomas Dugdale): by permission of the 2nd Lord Crathorne*
27th Earl of Crawford: National Library of Scotland#
Marquess of Crewe: Cambridge University Library+
1st Lord Croft (Sir Henry Page-Croft): Churchill Archives Centre, Churchill College,
  Cambridge+
W. P. Crozier: John Rylands University Library of Manchester#
Lionel Curtis: Bodleian Library, Oxford+
Marquess of Curzon: Oriental and India Office Collections, British Library
1st Viscount Davidson: Parliamentary Archives (House of Lords Record Office)*
Joan, Viscountess Davidson: by permission of Mr Richard Oldfield*
Archbishop Randall Davidson: Lambeth Palace Library
Geoffrey Dawson: Bodleian Library, Oxford*
17th Earl of Derby: Liverpool Record Office*
Lord and Lady Desborough: Hertfordshire Record Office
9th Duke of Devonshire: Devonshire Collections, Chatsworth
10th Duke of Devonshire, and Mary, Duchess of Devonshire: Devonshire
  Collections, Chatsworth
Sir Willoughby Dickinson: Gloucestershire Record Office+
8th Lord Dynevor (Charles Rhys): National Library of Wales
2nd Viscount Elibank: Scottish Record Office
Sir Edward Elgar: the Elgar Birthplace Museum+
H. A. L. Fisher: Bodleian Library, Oxford
Sir Almeric Fitzroy: British Library#
Sir Geoffrey Fry: Cambridge University Library
Sir John Gilmour: Scottish Record Office
Viscount Gladstone: British Library#
Edmund Gosse: Brotherton Library, University of Leeds
Sir Arthur Griffith-Boscawen: Bodleian Library, Oxford#
H. A. Gwynne: Bodleian Library, Oxford
1st Viscount Hailsham: Churchill Archives Centre, Churchill College, Cambridge
Viscount Haldane: National Library of Scotland
1st Earl of Halifax (Edward Wood; Lord Irwin):
  (a) Borthwick Institute, York*
  (b) Oriental and India Office Collections, British Library*

1st Lord Hankey: Churchill Archives Centre, Churchill College, Cambridge
Sir Patrick Hannon: Parliamentary Archives (House of Lords Record Office)
1st Viscount Hanworth (Ernest Pollock): Bodleian Library, Oxford
Sir Cuthbert Headlam: Durham County Record Office+
Sybil Heeley: Devon Record Office
Bishop H. H. Henson: Dean and Chapter Library, Durham Cathedral#
W. A. S. Hewins: University of Sheffield Library
Viscount Hinchingbrooke: by permission of the 11th Earl of Sandwich
Lord Hore-Belisha: Churchill Archives Centre, Churchill College, Cambridge
Thomas Jones: National Library of Wales*
1st Lord and Lady Kennet: Cambridge University Library
Lord Keynes: King's College Library, Cambridge
William Lyons Mackenzie King: National Archives of Canada (the diaries in
    microfiche edition, Toronto 1973–80, and memoranda on microfilm are available
    in the Brotherton Library, University of Leeds)
Rudyard Kipling: University of Sussex Library
Archbishop Lang: Lambeth Palace Library
Andrew Bonar Law: Parliamentary Archives (House of Lords Record Office)
Lord (Jack) Lawson: University of Durham Library+
Viscount Lee of Fareham: Courtauld Institute
2nd Marquess of Linlithgow: Oriental and India Office Collections, British Library
1st Lord Lloyd: Churchill Archives Centre, Churchill College, Cambridge
1st Earl Lloyd George: Parliamentary Archives (House of Lords Record Office)*
7th Marquess of Londonderry, and Edith, Marchioness of Londonderry: Public
    Record Office of Northern Ireland*
1st Viscount Long:
    (a) British Library
    (b) Wiltshire Record Office, Trowbridge
11th Marquess of Lothian: Scottish Record Office
2nd Earl of Lytton: Knebworth House Archive
J. R. MacDonald: Public Record Office*
Malcolm MacDonald: University of Durham Library
Reginald and Pamela McKenna: in private possession
Sir Donald Maclean: Bodleian Library, Oxford
Harold Macmillan: Bodleian Library, Oxford
Arthur Mann: Bodleian Library, Oxford
1st Viscount Margesson: Churchill Archives Centre, Churchill College, Cambridge
John Masefield: Humanities Research Centre, University of Texas, Austin
Leo Maxse: West Sussex Record Office
1st Earl of Midleton: Public Record Office
1st Viscount Monckton: Bodleian Library, Oxford
Gilbert Murray: Bodleian Library, Oxford
1st Viscount Norwich (Alfred Duff Cooper): Churchill Archives Centre, Churchill
    College, Cambridge
1st Lord Ponsonby: Bodleian Library, Oxford

Lord Quickswood (Lord Hugh Cecil): Hatfield House Archives[+]
1st Marquess of Reading: Oriental and India Office Collections, British Library[+]
Lord Reith: BBC Written Archives Centre
1st Viscount Runciman: Robinson Library, University of Newcastle
4th Marquess of Salisbury, and Alice, Marchioness of Salisbury: Hatfield House
    Archives[*]
5th Marquess of Salisbury (Lord Cranborne): Hatfield House Archives
1st Viscount Samuel: Parliamentary Archives (House of Lords Record Office)
Sir Philip Sassoon: by permission of Lord Cholmondeley
C. P. Scott:
    (a) British Library[#]
    (b) *Manchester Guardian* Archives, John Rylands University Library of Manchester
Leslie Scott: Modern Records Centre, University of Warwick[+]
1st Viscount Simon: Bodleian Library, Oxford
Lord Somervell: Bodleian Library, Oxford[#]
J. A. Spender: British Library
Wickham Steed: British Library[+]
Sir Arthur Steel-Maitland: Scottish Record Office
1st Viscount Stonehaven: National Library of Australia
St Loe Strachey: Parliamentary Archives (House of Lords Record Office)
7th Earl Stanhope: Centre for Kentish Studies, Maidstone
1st Earl of Swinton (Sir Philip Lloyd-Greame, later Cunliffe-Lister): Churchill
    Archives Centre, Churchill College, Cambridge
A. J. Sylvester: National Library of Wales
Viscount Templewood (Sir Samuel Hoare): Cambridge University Library[*]
J. H. Thomas: Centre for Kentish Studies, Maidstone
Sir Charles Trevelyan: Robinson Library, University of Newcastle
1st Lord Tweedsmuir (John Buchan): National Library of Scotland, including
    microfilm of collection in Queen's University, Kingston, Ontario[*]
Helen Waddell: Stanbrook Abbey
1st Viscount Weir: Glasgow University Archives
6th Earl Winterton: Bodleian Library, Oxford
Sir Laming Worthington-Evans: Bodleian Library, Oxford[+]
Francis Brett Young: University of Birmingham Library
2nd Marquess of Zetland:
    (a) North Yorkshire County Record Office[+]
    (b) Oriental and India Office Collections, British Library[#]

3. The Royal Archives, Windsor Castle

King George V papers
Queen Mary papers
King George VI papers
Duke of Windsor papers

4. Official and organisational records

CAB (Cabinet) and PREM (Prime Minister's Private Office): National Archives (Public
    Record Office)
Conservative Research Department: Bodleian Library, Oxford
The Times archive: News International Record Office
Wilden Church: Worcestershire County Record Office (accession 9410)
Worcestershire and West Worcestershire Conservative and Unionist Associations:
    Worcestershire County Record Office (accession 956)

B. EDITIONS

These are organised by the subject's name. All contain observations on Baldwin.
† indicates inclusion of copies of his letters
~indicates substantial quantities of reported conversations

Amery: *The Leo Amery Diaries*, ed. John Barnes and David Nicholson, 2 vols. (1980,
    1988)~
Bayford: *Real Old Tory Politics. The Political Diaries of Sir Robert Sanders, Lord Bayford
    1910–1935*, ed. John Ramsden (1984)
Bernays: *The Diaries and Letters of Robert Bernays 1932–1939*, ed. Nick Smart (Lampeter,
    1996)
Bridgeman: *The Modernisation of Conservative Politics. The Diaries and Letters of
    William Bridgeman 1904–1935*, ed. Philip Williamson (1988)~
Austen Chamberlain: *The Austen Chamberlain Diary Letters 1916–1937*, ed. Robert Self
    (Cambridge, 1995)~
Neville Chamberlain: *The Neville Chamberlain Diary Letters 1915–40*, ed. Robert Self
    4 vols. (Aldershot, 2000–4)~
Churchill: *Winston S. Churchill, Companion Volumes IV–VI*, ed. Martin Gilbert, 7 parts
    (1976–94)†
Crawford, 27th Earl of: *The Crawford Papers*, ed. John Vincent (Manchester, 1984)~
Crozier: *W. P. Crozier, Off the Record. Political Interviews 1933–1943*, ed. A. J. P. Taylor
    (1973)
Davies: 'The reminiscences of Clement Davies', ed. J. Graham Jones, *The National
    Library of Wales Journal*, 18 (1993–4), 411–13 (see above, pp. 426–8)
Fitzroy: Sir Almeric Fitzroy, *Memoirs*, 2 vols. (1923)
Headlam: *Parliament and Politics in the Age of Baldwin and MacDonald. The Headlam
    Diaries 1923–1935*, ed. Stuart Ball (1992)
Hinchingbrooke: *Hinch. A Celebration of Viscount Hinchingbrooke, MP 1906–1995*, ed.
    Andrew Best and John Sandwich (privately published, 1997)
Jones: *Whitehall Diary* [1916–30], ed. Keith Middlemas, 3 vols. (Oxford, 1969, 1971)~†
    Thomas Jones, *Diary with Letters 1931–1950* (Oxford, 1954)~†
Kennet, Lady: *Self Portrait of an Artist. From the Diaries and Letters of Lady Kennet*,
    ed. Lord Kennet (1949)
Kipling: *The Letters of Rudyard Kipling*, ed. Thomas Pinney, 4 vols. and continuing
    (1990–)

Nicolson: *Harold Nicolson. Diaries and Letters*, ed. Nigel Nicolson, 3 vols. (1966–8), and
    further matter in *Harold Nicolson. Diaries and Letters 1930–1964*, ed. Stanley Olsen
    (1980)
Reith: *The Reith Diaries*, ed. Charles Stuart (1975)†

C. FURTHER PUBLISHED LETTERS AND CONVERSATIONS

Baker, Arthur, *The House is Sitting* (1958), pp. 41–3: visits to Astley Hall in the 1940s
Barber, D. H., 'Tea with Lord Baldwin', *Tory Forum* (Jan. 1948), 5–8: a 1943
    conversation
[Begbie, Harold] 'A Gentleman with a Duster', *The Conservative Mind* (1924): draws on
    conversations with Baldwin
Blackett, Monica, *The Mark of the Maker. A Portrait of Helen Waddell* (1973): several
    Baldwin letters and notes of meetings
Cazalet-Keir, Thelma, *From the Wings* (1967): ch. 6 has conversations and letters
Citrine, Lord, *Men and Work* (1964): important conversations in 1935, 1936 and
    1943
Edwards, Cecil, *Bruce of Melbourne* (1965), pp. 251–4: on the Abdication crisis
Herbert, Sir Alan, *A.P.H. His Life and Times* (1970), pp. 296–7, 300: includes a letter of
    advice on after-dinner speaking
Howard, Peter, *Beaverbrook* (1964), pp. 77–8, 114–15: a 1941 conversation
Kingsmill, Hugh and Hesketh Pearson, *Talking of Dick Whittington* (1947), pp. 186–93: a
    1946 conversation
Lees-Milne, James, *Another Self* (1970), pp. 146–9: a 1935 encounter
Rhodes James, R., *Victor Cazalet* (1976): various diary extracts and letters

D. BALDWIN'S FAMILY

Baber, Colin and Trevor Boyns, 'Alfred Baldwin', in *Dictionary of Business Biography*, ed.
    David Jeremy, 1 (1984), pp. 116–18
Baldwin, A. W., *The Macdonald Sisters* (1960)
Baldwin, A. W., *A Flying Start* (1967)
Baldwin, Monica, *I Leap Over the Wall* (1949, reprinted 1994)
Baldwin, Oliver, *The Questing Beast* (1932)
Flanders, Judith, *A Circle of Sisters. Alice Kipling, Georgiana Burne-Jones, Agnes Poynter
    and Louisa Baldwin* (2001)
Lycett, Andrew, *Rudyard Kipling* (1999)
Macdonald, Edith, *Annals of the Macdonald Family* (1923)
Macdonald, F. W., *A Tale That is Told* (1919)
Taylor, Ina, *Victorian Sisters* (1987)
Walker, Christopher, *Oliver Baldwin. A Life of Dissent* (2003)
Williams, A. Susan, *Ladies of Influence. Women of the Elite in Interwar Britain* (2000),
    ch. 2 (on Lucy Baldwin)

E. LITERATURE ON BALDWIN (select list)

1. Books and pamphlets

Baldwin, A. W., *My Father: The True Story* (1955)
Barber, D. H., *Stanley Baldwin. Patriot Statesman* (pamphlet, privately printed, 1959)
Hyde, H. Montgomery, *Baldwin. The Unexpected Prime Minister* (1973)
[Jones, Thomas] *Lord Baldwin. A Memoir* (*The Times*, 1947)
Middlemas, Keith, and John Barnes, *Baldwin. A Biography* (1969)
Williamson, Philip, *Stanley Baldwin. Conservative Leadership and National Values*
    (Cambridge, 1999)
Young, G. M., *Stanley Baldwin* (1952)
Young, Kenneth, *Stanley Baldwin* (1976)

2. Articles and essays

Ball, Stuart, 'Stanley Baldwin', *The Oxford Dictionary of National Biography* (2004)
Blake, Robert, 'Baldwin and the Right', in John Raymond (ed.), *The Baldwin Age*
    (1960), pp. 25–65
Cannadine, David, 'Politics, propaganda and art: the case of two "Worcestershire
    lads"', *Midland History* 4 (1977), 97–122, revised version in idem, *In Churchill's
    Shadow* (2002), ch. 7
Jones, Thomas, 'Stanley Baldwin', *The Dictionary of National Biography 1941–1950* (1959)
Nicholas, Siân, 'The construction of national identity: Stanley Baldwin, "Englishness"
    and the mass media in inter-war Britain', in M. Francis and I. Zweiniger-
    Bargielowska (eds.), *The Conservatives and British Society 1880–1990* (Cardiff,
    1996), pp. 127–46
Ramsden, John, 'Baldwin and film', in N. Pronay and D. W. Spring (eds.), *Propaganda,
    Politics and Film 1918–45* (1982), pp. 126–43
Schwarz, Bill, 'The language of constitutionalism: Baldwinite Conservatism', in B.
    Schwarz *et al.*, *Formations of Nations and People* (1984), pp. 1–18
Ward-Smith, Gabrielle, 'Baldwin and Scotland: more than Englishness', *Contemporary
    British History*, 15 (2001), 61–82
Williamson, Philip, 'The doctrinal politics of Stanley Baldwin', in Michael Bentley
    (ed.), *Public and Private Doctrine. Essays in British History Presented to Maurice
    Cowling* (Cambridge, 1993), pp. 181–208
    'Baldwin's reputation: politics and history 1937–1967', *Historical Journal* 47 (2004),
    127–68

F. LITERATURE CLOSELY RELATING TO BALDWIN (select list)

Ball, Stuart, *Baldwin and the Conservative Party. The Crisis of 1929–1931* (1988)
Cowling, Maurice, *The Impact of Labour 1920–1924. The Beginning of Modern British
    Politics* (Cambridge, 1971)
    The Impact of Hitler. British Politics and British Policy 1933–1940 (Cambridge, 1975)

Dilks, David, *Three Visitors to Canada: Baldwin, Chamberlain and Churchill* (pamphlet, Leeds, 1985)

Hazlehurst, Cameron, 'The Baldwinite conspiracy', *Historical Studies* (Melbourne), 16 (1974–75), 167–91

Matthews, Kevin, *Fatal Influence. The Impact of Ireland on British Politics, 1920–1925* (Dublin, 2004)

Ramsden, John, *The Age of Balfour and Baldwin* (1978)

Self, Robert, *Tories and Tariff. The Conservative Party and the Politics of Tariff Reform 1922-1932* (1986)

   'Conservative reunion and the general election of 1923: a reassessment', *Twentieth Century British History*, 3 (1992), 249–73

Williamson, Philip, ' "Safety First". Baldwin, the Conservative party and the 1929 general election', *Historical Journal*, 25 (1982), 385–409

   National Crisis and National Government. British Politics, the Economy and Empire 1926–1932 (Cambridge, 1992)

   'Christian Conservatives and the totalitarian challenge, 1933–40', *English Historical Review*, 115 (2000), 607–42

INDEX

Lightning Source UK Ltd.
Milton Keynes UK
UKHW010425071218
333549UK00001B/282/P